Cybersecurity in Poland

Katarzyna Chałubińska-Jentkiewicz •
Filip Radoniewicz • Tadeusz Zieliński
Editors

Cybersecurity in Poland

Legal Aspects

Springer

Editors
Katarzyna Chałubińska-Jentkiewicz
Akademickie Centrum Polityki Cyberbezpieczeństwa/Academic Center for Cybersecurity Policy
Akademia Sztuki Wojennej w Warszawie/War Studies University in Warsaw
Warsaw, Poland

Filip Radoniewicz
Akademickie Centrum Polityki Cyberbezpieczeństwa/Academic Center for Cybersecurity Policy
Akademia Sztuki Wojennej w Warszawie/War Studies University in Warsaw
Warsaw, Poland

Tadeusz Zieliński
Wydział Wojskowy/Faculty of Military Studies
Akademia Sztuki Wojennej w Warszawie/War Studies University in Warsaw
Warsaw, Poland

ISBN 978-3-030-78550-5 ISBN 978-3-030-78551-2 (eBook)
https://doi.org/10.1007/978-3-030-78551-2

This Springer imprint is published by the registered company Springer Nature Switzerland AG.
The registered company address is: Gewerbestrasse 11, 6330 Cham, Switzerland

Preface

The creation of a coherent system to ensure the cybersecurity of the Republic of Poland was the purpose of the Act of the National Cyber Security System adopted by the Sejm of the Republic of Poland on the 5th of July 2018. It was the first attempt to create a comprehensive legal regulation, which assigned specific tasks and competences to its constituent entities and defined their responsibilities in order to enable effective operation in order to detect, prevent and minimise the effects of network incidents (such as, e.g. network attacks or failures) violating cybersecurity of the state and its citizens.

In addition, the Act on the national cybersecurity system and the implementing regulations accompanying it have implemented the provisions of the Directive (EU) 2016/1148 of the European Parliament and the Council of the 6th July 2016 on measures for a high common level of security of network and information systems within the Union (the NIS Directive).

The first part of the book is an introduction to cybersecurity issues.

In the main part of the publication, the authors, guided by the systematics of the Act, discuss the role of individual entities included in the cybersecurity system, Part II presents tasks and competences of entities responsible for ensuring cybersecurity under the national cybersecurity system ("imperious entities", e.g. competent authorities, CSIRTS), Part III describes the obligations of other entities included in the national cybersecurity system ("participants" of the national cybersecurity system, especially operators of essential services and digital service providers).

The last part is dedicated to cybercrime and combating this phenomenon.

In addition, the problem of collision of state actions ensuring cybersecurity, which is often associated with the possibility of state interference in the rights of individuals, and the right to privacy and the protection of personal data were raised.

The monograph is an attempt to comprehensively discuss the issue of ensuring cybersecurity. Therefore, the authors are not limited to the framework created by the Act on the national cybersecurity system, but may discuss a number of other issues. First of all, it presents international and EU regulations in the field of cybersecurity, issues of combating cybercrime and cyberterrorism, which are the greatest threat to cybersecurity. Moreover, regulations concerning cybercrime in a few selected European countries are presented.

The monograph is an attempt to comprehensively discuss the issue of ensuring cybersecurity.

The authors are researchers at the War Studies University in Warsaw. A part of them also works at the Academic Centre for Cybersecurity Policy (the think-tank created by Ministry of National Defense).

Warsaw, Poland

Katarzyna Chałubińska-Jentkiewicz
Filip Radoniewicz
Tadeusz Zieliński

Contents

Introduction 1
Tadeusz Zieliński

Part I Providing Cybersecurity as a New Challenge for Governments

Cyberspace and Cybersecurity 9
Tomasz Zdzikot

Cyberspace as an Area of Legal Regulation 23
Katarzyna Chałubińska-Jentkiewicz

Cyberspace, Cybercrime, Cyberterrorism 33
Filip Radoniewicz

International Regulations of Cybersecurity 53
Filip Radoniewicz

Cybersecurity in the European Union Law 73
Filip Radoniewicz

National Cybersecurity System Act 93
Filip Radoniewicz

The New National Security Strategy of the Republic of Poland 111
Jacek Sobczak

The Cybersecurity Strategy of the Republic of Poland 137
Waldemar Kitler

The Functioning of State Power Structures and Cybersecurity 155
Marzena Toumi

Personal Data Protection in the Context of the Act on the National Cybersecurity System 171
Monika Nowikowska

Space Security and Cybersecurity in Poland 177
Małgorzata Polkowska

Part II Competences, Obligations and Tasks of Entities Responsible for Ensuring Cybersecurity Under the National Cybersecurity System ("Imperious Entities")

Cybersecurity as a Public Task in Administration 191
Katarzyna Chałubińska–Jentkiewicz

The Authorities Competent for Cybersecurity 209
Agnieszka Brzostek

The Main Tasks of the Network of Computer Security Incident Response Teams in the Light of the Act on the National Cybersecurity System in Poland 223
Monika Nowikowska

Tasks of the Minister of National Defence in the Field of Cybersecurity 243
Krzysztof Wąsowski

Role of the Minister Competent for Computerisation in the Cybersecurity System 253
Katarzyna Chałubińska-Jentkiewicz

The Duties and Legal Status of the Government Plenipotentiary for Cybersecurity and the College for Cybersecurity 277
Agnieszka Brzostek

Part III Obligations of Other Entities Included in the National Cybersecurity System ("Participants" of the National Cybersecurity System)

Tasks of Operators of Essential Services and Digital Service Providers 293
Katarzyna Chałubińska-Jentkiewicz

The Obligations of Public Entities 331
Krzysztof Wąsowski

The System of Control and Supervision of Operators of Essential Services, Digital Service Providers and Entities Providing Cybersecurity Services 347
Monika Nowikowska

Monetary Penalties in the National Cybersecurity System Act 365
Filip Radoniewicz

The Liability of Entities Providing Services by Electronic Means for Digital Content 383
Paweł Zając

Part IV Combating Cybercrime as a Special Task in the Area of Cybersecurity

Cybercrime and Cyberterrorism in Polish Law 405
Filip Radoniewicz

Cybercrime in Selected European Countries 419
Filip Radoniewicz

The Entities and Institutions in Charge of Combating Cybercrime in Poland 441
Jerzy Kosiński

Operational Activities in the Field of Cybersecurity 455
Justyna Kurek

Operational Activities and the Right to Privacy 465
Katarzyna Chałubińska-Jentkiewicz

Summary 481
Katarzyna Chałubińska-Jentkiewicz

References 485

About the Editors

Katarzyna Chałubińska-Jentkiewicz dr. hab. of legal sciences (University of Warsaw and the Jagiellonian University), legal advisor, associate professor and head of the Department of Cybersecurity Law and New Technologies at the Institute of Law in the Faculty of National Security at the War Studies University in Warsaw. She is also a lecturer at the SWPS University and director of the Academic Center for Cybersecurity Policy. In the years 1996–2010, she worked as a lawyer in the National Broadcasting Council and with the public broadcaster TVP S.A. Between 2011 and 2017, she was deputy director of the National Audiovisual Institute (her competence centred on the field of digitisation). As a scientist, she conducts research on cybersecurity, information security threats, the development of electronic media law, protection of intellectual property and the impact of new technologies on the development of the state and the legal situation of the individual. She is the author of monographs and numerous articles, which include topics such as new technologies law, cyber responsibility, information security law and audiovisual media: Regulatory conflict in the age of digitisation, audiovisual media services, regulation in the conditions of digital conversion, information and computerisation in public administration and cultural security law and reuse of public sector information. She is head of the Ministry of Science's research project "Polish Cybersecurity System—A Model of Legal Solutions".

Filip Radoniewicz PhD; legal advisor; adjunct in the Department of Cybersecurity Law and New Technologies at the Institute of Law, War Studies University, Warsaw; expert at the Academic Centre for Cybersecurity Policy, War Studies University and in the Ministry of Justice; he worked as an assistant judge (in the Fourth Criminal and Sixth Penitentiary Department of the Regional Court in Lublin); graduate of postgraduate studies: "European Union Law" at the Jagiellonian University, "Human Rights and Freedoms", co-organised by the Institute of Legal Sciences of the Polish Academy of Sciences and the Helsinki Foundation for Human Rights, and "Computer Network Administration" at the Lublin University of Technology; author or co-author of approximately fifty publications, mainly in the field of broadly understood criminal law, new technology law and human rights. His selected publications include: F. Radoniewicz (2016) Odpowiedzialność karna za hacking i inne przestępstwa przeciwko danym komputerowym i systemom informatycznym/criminal liability for hacking and other offences against computer data and information systems/Wolters Kluwer, Warszawa; Ustawa o krajowym systemie cyberbezpieczeństwa. Komentarz/ Act on the National Cybersecurity System. Commentary/(2019) ed. W. Kitler, J. Taczkowska-Olszewska, F. Radoniewicz, CH. Beck, Warszawa.

Tadeusz Zieliński dr. hab., associate professor at the War Studies University in Warsaw and vice-rector for Scientific Affairs at WSU. He is a lecturer in the field of air power, unmanned aircraft systems and global threats security. His scientific area of interest is defence and security, in particular the EU Common Security and Defense Policy and the theory and practice of the use of military aviation and unmanned (autonomous) air systems in conflicts and crisis response operations.

Abbreviations

Legal Acts

CMA	Computer Misuse Act 1990 (c. 18)
CMSA	Act of 29 July 2005 on Capital Market Supervision, consolidated text, Polish Journal of Laws of 2020, item 1400, as amended
Convention on Cybercrime	Convention on Cybercrime of the Council of Europe of 23 November 2001
CAP	Act of 14 June 1960—the Code of Administrative Procedure, consolidated text, Polish Journal of Laws of 2020, item 256, as amended
CC	Act of 23 April 1964—the Civil Code, consolidated text, Polish Journal of Laws of 2020, item 1740, as amended
Directive 2000/31/EC	Directive 2000/31/EC of the European Parliament and of the Council of 8 June 2000 on certain legal aspects of information society services, in particular electronic commerce, in the Internal Market, Official Journal EU L 178/1 [the e-Commerce Directive]
Directive 2013/40/EU	Directive 2013/40/EU of the European Parliament and of the Council of 12 August 2013 on attacks against information systems and replacing Council Framework Decision 2005/222/JHA, Official Journal EU L 218/8
NIS Directive	Directive (EU) 2016/1148 of the European Parliament and of the Council of 6 July 2016 concerning measures for a high common level of security of network and information systems across the Union, Official Journal EU 2016 L 194/1

Directive 2017/541	Directive 2017/541/EU of the European Parliament and of the Council, of 15 March 2017 on combating terrorism and replacing Council Framework Decision 2002/475/JHA and amending Council Decision 2005/671/JHA, Official Journal EU 2017 L 88/6
ECHR	The European Convention for the Protection of Human Rights and Fundamental Freedoms signed in Rome on 4 November 1950
Framework Decision 2002/475	Council Framework Decision 2002/475/JHA of 13 June 2002 on combating terrorism, Official Journal EC 2002 L 164/3
Framework Decision 2005/222	Council Framework Decision 2005/222/JHA of 24 February 2005 on attacks against information systems, Official Journal EU 2005 L 69/67
Framework Decision 2008/841	Council Framework Decision 2008/841/JHA of 24 October 2008 on the fight against organised crime, Official Journal EU 2008 L 300/42
GDPR	Regulation (EU) 2016/679 of the European Parliament and of the Council of 27 April 2016 on the protection of natural persons with regard to the processing of personal data and on the free movement of such data and repealing Directive 95/46/EC (General Data Protection Regulation), Official Journal EU 2016 L 119/1, as amended
LCEA	The Act of 28 October 2002 on Liability of Collective Entities for Prohibited Acts Punishable by Sanction, consolidated text, Polish Journal of Laws of 2020 item 358, as amended
LEA	Act of 6 March 2018—the Entrepreneurs Law, consolidated text, Polish Journal of Laws of 2019 item 1292, as amended
LPACA	Act of 30 August 2002—the Law on proceedings before administrative courts, consolidated text, Polish Journal of Laws of 2019, item 2325, as amended
NCSA	Act of 5 July 2018 on the National Cybersecurity System, consolidated text, Polish Journal of Laws of 2020, item 1369, as amended
PC	Act of 6 June 1997—the Penal Code, consolidated text, Polish Journal of Laws of 2020, item 1444, as amended

PCI	Act of 5 August 2010 on the Protection of Classified Information, consolidated text, Polish Journal of Laws of 2019, item 742, as amended
PFA	Act of 27 August 2009 on Public Finance consolidated text, Polish Journal of Laws of 2019, item 869, as amended
PSEMA	Act of 18 July 2002 on Providing Services by Electronic Means, Polish Journal of Laws of 2020, item 344, as amended
StGB	Strafgesetzbuch [German Penal Code of 15 May 1871 as published on 13 November 1998 (BGBl. I S. 3322)]
TFEU	Treaty on the Functioning of the European Union (consolidated version of the Treaty on the Functioning of the European Union: Official Journal EU C 326/47)
TL	Act of 16 July 2004—Telecommunications Law, consolidated text, Polish Journal of Laws of 2019, item 2460, as amended

Other Abbreviations

BGH	Bundesgerichtshof (German Federal Court of Justice)
BVerfG	Bundesverfassungsgericht (German Federal Constitutional Court)
CaaS	Communications as a Service
CCPCJ	(UN) Commission on Crime Prevention and Criminal Justice
CERT	Computer Emergency Response Team
Cf.	Confer
CSIRT	Computer Security Incident Response Team
ECHR	The European Court of Human Rights
e.g.	Exempli gratia
ENISA	European Union Agency for Cybersecurity (former European Network and Information Security Agency)
GCA	Global Cybersecurity Agenda
GPS	Global positioning system
IaaS	Infrastructure as a Service
ICT	Information and communication technologies
iPaaS	Integration Platform as a Service
ISA	Internal Security Agency
ITU	International Telecommunication Union
Polish Journal of Laws	Journal of Laws of the Republic of Poland
LAN	Local area network
Legalis	Legalis Legal Information System

Lex/el	Lex Legal Information System
MAN	Metropolitan area network
NATO	North Atlantic Treaty Organization
NGO	Non-government organisation
No.	Number
OECD	Organisation for Economic Co-operation and Development
op. cit.	Opus citatum
OJ EU	Official Journal of the European Union
OJ EC	Official Journal of the European Communities
OSCE	Organization for Security and Co-operation in Europe
p.	Page
PaaS	Platform as a Service
passim	Frequently
RAM	Random access memory
ROM	Read-only memory
SaaS	Software as a Service
SSA	Situational awareness system
SST	Space surveillance and tracking
TLP	Traffic light protocol
WTSA	World Telecommunication Standardization Assembly

Introduction

Tadeusz Zieliński

Historically, humans have been, and continue to be, active in environments that have accompanied our species since its beginnings. We needed some time to discover these environments and learn how to manage them effectively. Initially, our primary natural environments were land and sea, but over time we also learned to fly, and eventually started to explore the outer space. For decades no one would expect that in addition to these three, and then four, domains, which are currently considered traditional, there is also a fifth—cyberspace, which permeates all the other. The discoverers of the electromagnetic field may have had an inkling that the waves they explored could form part of a new environment. But at that time no one used the term *cyberspace*, let alone being able to define it. Leaving aside the term itself, which emerged only in the second half of the twentieth century, cyberspace has become another area of exploration that is commonly considered to be interdisciplinary, and which at the same time is generating many new challenges, including especially those related to broadly defined security.

The significance of this new domain in the context of the security of both individuals and nations has become evident as technology continued to advance, ushering in computerisation in all its forms, and widespread access to the Internet. This direct access to information, available thanks to the rapid development of computer systems, is now one of the primary determinants of social and economic growth, and often determines the success or failure of an undertaking. Access to network services has influenced social relations and can be a tool for encouraging or controlling specific behavioural patterns, such as political decisions. Actions taken by various actors in cyberspace can directly produce specific economic, social, or political outcomes. This makes cyberspace an area that affects the security of the public and private sectors, and also that of citizens, and, by extension, of nations as a

T. Zieliński (✉)
Wydział Wojskowy/Faculty of Military Studies, Akademia Sztuki Wojennej w Warszawie/War Studies University in Warsaw, Warsaw, Poland
e-mail: t-zielinski@akademia.mil.pl

K. Chałubińska-Jentkiewicz et al. (eds.), *Cybersecurity in Poland*,
https://doi.org/10.1007/978-3-030-78551-2_1

whole. Poland is no exception here, and it constantly articulates the importance of cyberspace for its national security in its National Security Strategy publications. The latest (2020) publication is no different, as its authors emphasise the role of cyberspace and information space in the social, economic, and military aspects. In this context, key postulates are to increase resilience to cyber risks and provide a better protection of public, military, and private information. Other worthwhile goals are to raise awareness and promote good practices so that citizens can protect their information better, and to create a safe information space for the state and society to function in. These objectives clearly show that cyberspace needs to be considered in terms of challenges and hazards, because these are what will constitute the blueprint for actions to ensure national security. This is also true for Poland, and it seems useful to see how the Polish national cybersecurity policy has developed in relation to these goals.

It is important to note that efforts to develop a comprehensive national strategy for counteracting security risks in cyberspace have been undertaken since 2008. By 2011, seven draft documents had been developed, but those were not adopted by the government, mainly because of poor content quality. The first strategic document on Poland's cybersecurity was Policy on Protecting the Cyberspace of the Republic of Poland (2013), as adopted by resolution of the Council of Ministers. While the document was designed to help achieve the appropriate level of security in cyberspace, it failed to identify any risks and only described them in general terms. As a result, the first systemic actions of government administration to identify the risks and challenges in cyberspace are those identified in *The Cybersecurity Doctrine of the Republic of Poland* (2015). That was the first document to describe the strategic directions and a shared vision for cybersecurity in relation to public administration units, security services, public order, and armed forces, but also the private sector and citizens. Of course, the question remains whether it was not too late for the state to address cyberspace security issues at the systemic level. Attacks in cyberspace, whether aimed at the public or private sectors, have happened virtually from the start of the computer revolution. But it was not until the cybernetic attack in 2007 on Estonia's critical infrastructure that many decision-makers realised that national security could be at risk and the components that are vital for state functioning could be paralysed. Therefore, the decision to adopt a systemic approach to cybersecurity by developing a consistent strategy, as found in *The Cybersecurity Doctrine of the Republic of Poland*, was certainly sensible but belated. Its authors divided challenges and risks into internal and external. When it comes to the former, these are considered similar to traditional risks and challenges, and differ only in terms of their environment and the tools that are used. This creates such categories as cybercrime, cyber violence, cyber protests, and destructive cyber demonstrations, which can disrupt some crucial functions within public administration and the private sector. The cyber risks that were considered particularly important were those related to state's critical infrastructure relying on computer systems. As regards internal challenges in cyberspace, special attention is given to legal loopholes and unregulated or poorly regulated relations between the individual members of the cybersecurity system. The authors of the Doctrine were right to note that this problem might be exacerbated as individual elements of national, public, or private infrastructure become more dependent on computer systems. What seems interesting are conclusions drawn from the analysis of external risks and challenges. It was clearly shown that cyber conflicts and cyber crises involving national and non-national parties, including cyberwars, are likely to happen. In other words, cyberspace was considered among the domains which can serve as yet another battlefield for military operations. National security can also be compromised by cyber espionage involving foreign services and non-state parties, including terrorist organisations. As regards to challenges, there was apparently no shared terminology and definitions for allied cyberspace operations, which seems natural but needed addressing, as the allied cybersecurity system was only developing.

The next step in developing our national cybersecurity policy were efforts by the government administration to work out a cybersecurity strategy. Its first draft was completed in 2016, and a year later we adopted *The Cybersecurity Strategy of the Republic of Poland for 2017–2022*, also referred to as The National Framework of Cybersecurity Policy. That document did not identify any specific risks or challenges for Poland's cyberspace security, but this was not the objective behind the Strategy. In the context of risks, those are collectively referred to as cyber risks. The challenges that were considered crucial were

> to ensure information safety across all members of the national cybersecurity system, i.e. businesses that provide their services using communication and information systems, as well as cyberspace users, public government authorities, and professional organisations dealing with ICT security in the operational domain.

The Cybersecurity Strategy identifies the primary goal, "to ensure a high level of security for the public and private sectors and for citizens in relation to providing or using essential services and digital services", and four sub-goals,

> (a) to achieve capability for nationally coordinated action to prevent, detect, fight, and mitigate the consequences of incidents that compromise the security of state's critical communication and information systems; (b) to enhance the capacity to prevent cyber risks; (c) to develop the national cyberspace security potential and expertise; (d) to position the Republic of Poland as a strong international player in cybersecurity.

Without going into details, it can be claimed that the Cybersecurity Strategy addresses some major issues, as found in similar documents prepared by other countries. Is it a complete document? Probably not, but at the time it was adopted (2017), it served as the basis for some more advanced work, including at the legal level, to make it a complete strategy in the future. Importantly, as the document was approved, experts argued that it needed to be quickly implemented, which was ultimately to translate into the development of the Act on Cybersecurity. Consequently, it was only natural that in 2018 the Minister of Digital Affairs presented an action plan referring to the National Framework of Cybersecurity Policy, a planning document to describe in detail how to achieve the sub-goals identified in the Cybersecurity Strategy. An important element of that document was also the division of responsibilities between the relevant government administration authorities.

Cybersecurity actions taken by government administration authorities ultimately made it possible for the Sejm, the Lower House of the Polish Parliament, to adopt in 2018 the Act on the National Cybersecurity System. This was the first legal Act in Poland to regulate this field. The goal of that regulation was to ensure cybersecurity in relation to the provision of essential services and digital services, and to define the rules for selecting the operators of essential services and defining their responsibilities in cybersecurity matters. The Act also defined the bodies in charge of cybersecurity, which are responsible for supervising the operators of essential services. In addition, the regulation describes the scope of the Cybersecurity Strategy of the Republic of Poland. Following the above, in 2019, Poland adopted *The Cybersecurity Strategy of the Republic of Poland for 2019–2024*.

The current Cybersecurity Strategy is similar to that adopted in 2017. What makes it different from its antecedent is the new vision which is to "continuously strengthen and develop the national cybersecurity system." The new strategy seems to be more mature and more specific, also in relation to its goal and implementation details, which are "to increase resilience to cyber risks and improve the level of information protection in the public, military, and private sectors, as well as to promote good practices to help citizens better protect their information." There is also a new, important sub-goal, namely to raise awareness and social expertise related to cybersecurity. Unfortunately, the government did not secure the funds to implement the tasks defined in the Cybersecurity Strategy. Its provisions are to be implemented from the budgets of individual units, and from the funds of the National Centre for Research and Development, and EU funds.

The presented overview of how Poland's national cybersecurity policy has developed, and lessons learned from this demonstrate that the issues related to cybersecurity in its broad sense can be reduced to three key areas—technology, law and organisation, and society. These are complementary to one another and equally important.

There is no doubt that technology is an important area in preventing cyber risks. This is clearly articulated in the current Cybersecurity Strategy. Access to new technologies is accelerating globalisation, which in turn is generating further technological advancements. Cyberspace is an environment in which new technologies are crucial and determine the success of any endeavour. The transformation of society, through the development of computer technologies, into information society with access to cyberspace resources has produced more risks for nations and citizens. On the one hand, modern technology has contributed to improved cybersecurity, but on the other hand it can compromise the security of citizens and nations. Research and development, and technological advancements in cybersecurity, should definitely be aimed at enhancing Poland's cyberspace security. These technologies should make it possible to detect, notify and protect us against the existing and future risks in cyberspace, and their consequences.

The second area, law and organisation, is directly associated with legal regulations on cybersecurity and with systemic solutions adopted in Poland. The national cybersecurity system has been functioning on the basis of the Act on the National Cybersecurity System, which also aligns Polish law with Directive 2016/1148 of the

European Parliament and of the Council concerning measures for a high common level of security of network and information systems across the Union, known as the NIS Directive. The main goal of this legislation is to ensure cybersecurity at the national level. The system relies on the operators of essential services, including from the energy, transport, health, and banking sectors, digital service providers, Computer Security Incident Response Teams (CSIRTs) at the national level, sectoral cybersecurity teams, cybersecurity service providers, responsible cybersecurity authorities, and single points of contact as part of the European Union cooperation on cybersecurity. Cybersecurity, understood as the resilience of computer systems to any action that compromises the confidentiality, integrity, availability or authenticity of processed data, or the related services offered by those systems, requires the appropriate organisation of the entities referred to in the Act. After the 2 years that the national cybersecurity system has been in operation (since 2018), it is possible to state that the undertaken actions have proven successful, and the development of a resilient system is a continuous process. Despite many difficulties and challenges along the way, the system has slowly become more and more methodical and informed, even though it still requires legislation adjustments to standardise the solutions used across the various sectors involved in its development. At the same time, an insufficient pool of well-qualified personnel and experts on cybersecurity requires further systemic solutions related to education and scientific research.

The social area of cybersecurity in Poland is directly associated with information society, often referred to as cybersociety. Similarly to other countries, in Poland society, meaning citizens, but also public organisations, is more and more dependent on technology and network services. By using the available network solutions, people, either consciously or unconsciously, share data about their lives, behaviour, and interests. As a result, they are increasingly vulnerable to risks which require "cyber awareness". This, in turn, generates educational needs in this area related to the fundamentals of personal safety online, safe shopping and payments, safety of parents and children online, safe use of social media, and many more issues on which various social groups need to be educated. This generates demand for various types of educational services, which are expected to contribute to raising knowledge and social awareness, and, by extension, to improving state security. Cyberspace is also an environment where educational services can, and are, provided. This also applies to the public sphere, which should foster appropriate values and behaviour in cyberspace through educational activities. In the future, knowledge of technologies that protect our life in cyberspace should be common, especially given that we are heading towards becoming a cybersociety.

To sum up, the national cybersecurity system built in Poland plays an important part in improving national security in general. In addition to the other four domains, cyberspace is starting to serve a crucial role in security, which is only natural as our society is becoming a cybersociety. Of course, many questions remain unanswered, and not all of the challenges and risks in the area of cybersecurity can be anticipated. Nevertheless, the actions taken by the government administration in Poland to improve its cybersecurity system can be assessed positively.

Tadeusz Zieliński dr. hab., associate professor at the War Studies University in Warsaw, and vice rector for Scientific Affairs at WSU. Tadeusz Zieliński is a lecturer in the field of air power, unmanned aircraft systems, and global threats security. His scientific area of interest is defense and security, in particular the EU Common Security and Defense Policy and the theory and practice of the use of military aviation and unmanned (autonomous) air systems in conflicts and crisis response operations.

Part I
Providing Cybersecurity as a New Challenge for Governments

Cyberspace and Cybersecurity

Tomasz Zdzikot

Abstract The purpose of this chapter is to discuss two basic concepts—cyberspace and cybersecurity. The author describes the genesis of both and attempts to define them. In the introduction, the author briefly addresses the issue of the progress of information technology in recent decades and the impact of this factor on security. Then, he indicates the source of the term "cyberspace" and presents the definitions in American documents, doctrine and Polish law. Defining the concept of "cybersecurity", the author starts from the definition of the term "security". Then he presents selected definitions of this term. He also emphasizes that cybersecurity should be viewed broadly and that a definition should be made taking into account both the attacks by hackers or foreign forces and the "plain" failures.

1 Introduction

In April 1998, during a widely commented lecture on information security in an increasingly digital world delivered at the Georgia Institute of Technology in Atlanta, CIA Director George J. Tenet warned: "We are staking our future on a resource that we have not yet learned to protect".[1] As the reality changed, the people responsible for the security of states and citizens accurately anticipated the threats they would soon face on an unprecedented scale. The increasing digitization and automation of every area of life would make more and more processes without digital support impossible with each day. An increasing part of human activity is also moving to the web, and access to information and keeping constantly "in touch" have become, in many spheres, the basic determinants of individual and organizational success. At the same time, the ease of access to information, as well as to the

[1]Tenet (1998).

T. Zdzikot (✉)
Warsaw Bar Association, Warsaw, Poland
e-mail: tomasz@zdzikot.pl

K. Chałubińska-Jentkiewicz et al. (eds.), *Cybersecurity in Poland*,
https://doi.org/10.1007/978-3-030-78551-2_2

technologies enabling its generation and dissemination, contributes to a constant increase in data supply.

In the past, a few centuries ago, the best university libraries had hundreds of volumes in their book collections. Thus, reading them all did not exceed the capabilities of a single reader. Today, hundreds of thousands of new books are published every year. In Poland alone, more than 36 thousand titles[2] were published in 2017, while the number of books published annually in other countries often exceeds 100 thousand. The global network aggregating knowledge, information and access to entertainment and communication platforms is also growing rapidly. It is estimated that every second the network grows by 30 GB of data, that is, as much as the entire Internet[3] covered 25 years ago, while the number of websites increased from just over 17 million to one billion from 2002 to 2014.[4] Every second, Internet users carry out hundreds of thousands of operations on various social networking, entertainment and transactional sites. According to data quoted by Edward Lucas, the number of Internet users has exceeded 3 billion, and in "richer countries almost all are Internet users – in the USA, 88% of Americans are online (...) In 2015, the number of e-mails sent exceeded 200 billion per day. This means that more e-mails are sent in two days than traditional letters for a year." According to J. Surma: "The daily average number of searches using the Google browser is around 3.5 billion. Assuming that each search is made by a different person, almost every second person on the planet makes one search a day! The number of Facebook users is 25% of the world's population. In the case of Poland, almost 70% of the population use Google and almost 60% are Facebook users".[5] Therefore, today we receive as much information every day as our grandparents did throughout their lives. At the same time, the concept of the Internet of Things (IoT), in which the devices of everyday use around us become part of a trans-boundary information exchange system, is developing extremely intensively. It is assumed that within a few years there will already be more than 50 billion devices permanently connected to the Internet in the world.

At the same time, it must not be forgotten that the digital world today cannot be regarded as an anchor of stability and security. It is also a space where organized crime groups actively and creatively use new tools, improving new methods of committing known crimes and creating completely new categories of crimes. At the same time, in geopolitical and institutional terms, it is an attractive place for many

---

[2] *BN: in 2017, the number of books published in Poland increased by 6%, http://www.pap.pl/aktualnosci/news,1436634,bn-w-2017-roku-liczba-wydanych-w-polsce-ksiazek-wzrosla-o-6-proc.html* Accessed on 7 July 2020.

[3] *Co może zdarzyć się w sekundę w Internecie? (2015). https://www.focus.pl/artykul/co-moze-zdarzyc-sie-w-sekunde-w-internecie* Accessed on 7 July 2020.

[4] *Ile waży praca? (2017) https://www.forbes.pl/technologie/jak-wiele-danych-produkujemy-kazdego-dnia/4mn4w69* Accessed on 7 July 2020.

[5] Surma (2017), p. 74; the author also states that: "Such a widespread use of Google, Facebook and other similar companies in the global economy is of great importance for the security of individual states and the whole world".

countries to pursue their political objectives, intelligence tasks or a manifestation of power. Actions in cyberspace can also be a preparation for military operations or an element of those already under way.

In view of the outlined changes in civilization and new challenges, the performance of the basic tasks of a state, which include ensuring internal and external security, requires an adequate response from the state administration today. It is necessary to adapt to a situation in which a new field of action is cyberspace, and the ability to ensure the digital security of citizens and to secure one's own networks and systems represent the fundamental elements of national security.

In the face of globalization, security in cyberspace has become one of the priority tasks in the internal affairs of each country, while at the same time affecting international security. Any serious disruption to the operation of cyberspace will affect citizens' sense of security, the security of business trading, the efficiency of public sector institutions and, consequently, security in general. Therefore, it has become necessary to implement legal solutions which will make it possible to organize an effective and efficient system for protecting the information resources of public entities, entrepreneurs and also citizens.

2 Definitions of Cyberspace

One of the areas which has been partially governed by law, and which can be distinguished in the legal system and in the duties of public administration, is cybersecurity, which is the subject of this monograph. Any consideration of this subject must be preceded by defining the meaning of the terms cyberspace and cybersecurity, taking into account the typology of possible threats.

Cyberspace is one of the many concepts discussed in this monograph, which must be considered to be highly underdefined, eluding a uniform approach. No uniform definition has yet been established at the national or international level that could be considered universally accepted, although numerous attempts have been made and are being made on the basis of legislation, programming, legal commentary and strategic and political documents, as well as in legal commentaries and literature (including popular literature). Even the etymology of the word cyberspace is ambiguous. According to the literature "it can only be said in general terms that it is a blend (hybrid) of two words – *kubernḗtēs*, which in Greek means a helmsman, a governor, to control, and the English word *space*".[6]

The term cyberspace was first used by the American science-fiction author William Gibson in his short story "Burning Chrome" published in the "Omni" magazine in July 1982. Cyberspace was also mentioned in his novel "Neuromancer", published 2 years later, as

[6]Banasiński (2018), p. 23.

> a consensual hallucination experienced daily by billions of legitimate operators, in every nation, by children being taught mathematical concepts (...). A graphic representation of data abstracted from the banks of every computer in the human system. Unthinkable complexity. Lines of light ranged in the nonspace of the mind, clusters and constellations of data.[7]

It is noteworthy that 37 years ago, several characteristic features of the digital reality that surrounds us today were captured in this way—its global nature, the aggregation of data from a huge number of sources, dispersed network architecture, graphical visualization of complex source codes, light as an information carrier.

According to the Dictionary of the Polish Language, "cybeprzestrzeń" (cyberspace) is "a virtual space in which communication between computers connected to the Internet takes place".[8] However, this approach focuses only on one of the dimensions of cyberspace. Many experts divide cyberspace into layers, distinguishing between the physical network (hardware—connections and computers), the logical network (software – network and service software, such as websites), and a kind of human network (people functioning in cyberspace).[9] Such a comprehensive approach may also serve to create a definition, such as that of Z. Trejnis and P. Trejnis, according to which "Cyberspace encompasses all information and communication means in a collection of networks, techniques, users and digital space, which in turn is assigned three layers: material, logical and informational".[10]

The US Department of Defense, while unifying military terminology, has also introduced a definition of cyberspace as

> a global domain within the information environment consisting of the interdependent network of information technology infrastructures and resident data, including the internet, telecommunications networks, computer systems, and embedded processors and controllers.[11]

Compared with the aforementioned division of cyberspace into three layers, it can be noted that this US military definition seems to ignore the human aspect—participants and users of cyberspace—and to focus solely on the infrastructural and logical aspects.

Interestingly, a uniform definition of cyberspace was not adopted by the North Atlantic Treaty Organization until 2019. According to the NATO Glossary of Terms and Definitions, cyberspace is "The global domain consisting of all interconnected communication, information technology and other electronic systems, networks and

[7]Gibson (2009), p. 59; New York: Berkley Publishing Group, 1989; after: https://techterms.com/definition/cyberspace, accessed on 3.10.2020.

[8]https://sjp.pwn.pl/szukaj/cyberprzestrze%C5%84.html Accessed on 3.10.2020.

[9]For example, Crowther Alexander (2018), pp. 83–84 https://www.heritage.org/sites/default/files/2017-09/2018_IndexOfUSMilitaryStrength_CROWTHER.pdf Accessed on 3.10.2020.

[10]Trejnis and Trejnis (2017), p. 27 http://bobolanum.pl/images/studia-bobolanum/2017/03/StBob_2017_3_Trejnis.pdf Accessed on 3.10.2020.

[11]Department of Defence Dictionary of Military and Associated Terms (2010) (Joint Publication 1-02), p. 58 https://fas.org/irp/doddir/dod/jp1_02.pdf Accessed on 10.10.2020.

their data, including those which are separated or independent, which process, store or transmit data."[12]

In Poland, threats associated with cyberspace have already been mentioned in the "National Security Strategy of the Republic of Poland" of 2007, but without precise terminological specification.[13]

The first official definition of cyberspace was contained in the assumptions for the "Government Cyberspace Protection Programme of the Republic of Poland for the years 2009-2011", for the purpose of which it is understood as "a communication space created by a system of Internet connections".[14] An attempt was also made to distinguish the category of state and, specifically, Polish cyberspace by stating that

> State cyberspace is understood to be the communication space created by the system of all Internet connections within the state. In the case of Poland, state cyberspace is also referred to as the cyberspace of the Republic of Poland. The cyberspace of the Republic of Poland comprises, among others, information and communication systems, networks and services of particular importance to the internal security of the state, the banking system, as well as systems ensuring the functioning in the country of transport, communications, energy, water and gas infrastructure and healthcare information systems, the destruction or damage of which may pose a threat to human life or health, the national heritage and the environment on a significant scale or cause serious material losses.[15]

In the "Government Cyberspace Protection Programme of the Republic of Poland for the years 2011-2016" prepared by the Ministry of the Interior and Administration in June 2010, the definition of cyberspace was developed. The document states that it is "digital space for the processing and exchange of information created by information and communication systems and networks, including the links between them and relations with the users".[16] The cyberspace of the Republic of Poland, on the other hand, was closely linked to the territory by indicating that it is "cyberspace within the territory of the Republic of Poland and in locations outside the territory

---

[12]NATO Glossary of Terms and Definitions AAP-06 Edition 2018 https://nso.nato.int/nso/ZPUBLIC/_BRANCHINFO/TERMINOLOGY_PUBLIC/NON-CLASSIFIED%20NATO%20GLOSSARIES/AAP-6.PDF Accessed on 3.10.2020.

[13]As part of the outlined challenges and threats to security, it was pointed out that one of them "may be the impact in cyberspace, directed at the information and communication systems and networks of critical infrastructure. Such actions may result in both material losses and the paralysis of important spheres of public life." *National Security Strategy of the Republic of Poland* p. 10. However, one of the objectives of economic security was to continue the development of "a modern, integrated electronic communication structure that would be resistant to failures and potential cybercrime attacks. This will require proper interaction between relevant ministries and agencies as well as private actors", p. 19, http://www.bbn.gov.pl/dokumenty/SBN_RP.pdf, Accessed on 3.10.2020.

[14]https://www.msz.gov.pl/resource/93e1e4c7-e129-41c7-8365-39dbad8b1c54:JCR, p. 4, accessed on 3.10.2020.

[15]Ibidem.

[16]Government Cyberspace Protection Programme of the Republic of Poland for the years 2011–2016.

where representatives of the Republic of Poland operate (diplomatic posts, military contingents)".[17]

The Act of 30 August 2011 amending the Act on Martial Law and the Powers of the Commander-in-Chief of the Armed Forces and the Rules for Their Subordination to the Constitutional Authorities of the Republic of Poland and certain other Acts[18] had a significant impact on the establishment of the concept of cyberspace in the Polish legal system. As stated in the justification of the Presidential bill, the basic aim of the regulation was

> to take into account threats resulting from activities and events in cyberspace as a circumstance complying with the normative content of the reasons for the introduction of one of the states of emergency referred to in Articles 229, 230 and 232 of the Constitution of the Republic of Poland.[19]

The legal definition established for the purposes of the amendment, setting out cyberspace as

> space for the processing and exchange of information created by information and communication systems, as defined in Article 3(3) of the Act of 17 February 2005 on the Computerization of the Operations of Entities Performing Public Tasks including the links between them and relations with the users,

by virtue of the amending act in question, was added to the provisions of:

1. the Act of 29 August 2002 on Martial Law and the Powers of the Commander-in-Chief of the Armed Forces and the Rules for Their Subordination to the Constitutional Authorities of the Republic of Poland—where actions in cyberspace were also included as one of the reasons for the introduction of martial law by the President of the Republic of Poland, at the request of the Council of Ministers, on part or all of the territory of the country;
2. the Act of 21 June 2002 on the State of Emergency—actions in cyberspace that pose a threat to the constitutional system of the state, security of citizens or public order may constitute a basis for the Council of Ministers to adopt a resolution to submit a request to the President of the Republic of Poland to introduce a state of emergency;
3. the Act of 18 April 2002 on Natural Disasters—indicating at the same time that a natural disaster or technical failure may also be caused by events in cyberspace.

---

[17] Government Cyberspace Protection Programme ...., p. 6

[18] Act of 30 August 2011 amending the Act on Martial Law and the Competences of the Commander-in-Chief of the Armed Forces and the Rules for Their Subordination to the Constitutional Authorities of the Republic of Poland and certain other Acts, Polish Journal of Laws of 2011, No. 222, item 1323.

[19] Parliamentary paper No. 4355. http://orka.sejm.gov.pl/Druki6ka.nsf/0/0C7D2B7644A7B3C5C12578BD00339405/$file/4355.pdf, accessed on 3.10.2020.

The definition developed for the purpose of introducing to the aforementioned acts on emergency states, referring directly to their content,[20] was transferred to the "Government Cyberspace Protection Policy of the Republic of Poland", prepared in June 2013 by the Ministry of Administration and Digitization and the Internal Security Agency. The definition of the cyberspace of the Republic of Poland is basically a repetition of the one established on the basis of the discussed "Government Cyberspace Protection Programme of the Republic of Poland for the years 2011-2016."

An extensive definition of cyberspace is included in the "Cybersecurity Doctrine of the Republic of Poland" of 2015, according to which it is

> a space for the processing and exchange of information created by information and communication systems (groups of cooperating IT equipment and software that ensure the processing, storage, as well as sending and receiving of data through telecommunications networks by means of telecommunications terminal equipment appropriate for a given type of network and intended to be connected directly or indirectly to network terminations), including the links between them and relations with the users.[21]

Despite the lack of a single common definition of cyberspace, a number of common features have been identified:

1. a seamless, flexible and non-material nature;
2. lack of clearly and unambiguously identifiable boundaries;
3. decentralization;
4. lack of a centre of control and supervision over it as a whole;
5. universal accessibility;
6. digital information processing and calculations in real time with high accuracy;
7. numerical, hypertext, interactive and virtual nature.[22]

A number of common features of cyberspace are also noticed by the Supreme Audit Office, which, in its information on the results of the audit on the "Implementation of tasks in the field of protection of the cyberspace of the Republic of Poland

[20]The full definition is as follows:

> space for the processing and exchange of information created by information and communication systems, as defined in Article 3(3) of the Act of 17th February 2005 on computerisation of the activities of entities performing public tasks (consolidated text Polish Journal of Laws of 2020, item 346, as amended), including the links between them and relations with the users; pursuant to Article 2(1b) of the Act of 29th of August 2002 on Martial Law and the Competences of the Commander-in-Chief of the Armed Forces and the rules for their subordination to the constitutional authorities of the Republic of Poland (consolidated text Polish Journal of Laws of 2017, item 1932, as amended), Article 2 (1a) of the Act of 21st of June 2002 on the state of emergency (consolidated text Polish Journal of Laws of 2019, item 1928, as amended) and Article 3(1)(4) of the Act of 18th April 2002 on the state of natural disaster (consolidated text Polish Journal of Laws of 2017, item 1897, as amended).

[21]Cybersecurity Doctrine of the Republic of Poland (2015) https://www.bbn.gov.pl/ftp/dok/01/DCB.pdf, accessed on 3.10.2020.

[22]Kasprzyk et al. (2015), p. 529.

by state entities", also attempted to formulate a specific definition, perceiving cyberspace as "a virtual area created inside and within the range of influence of IT and telecommunications equipment",[23] whose common features include global reach, easy access, efficiency, universality and relative "cheapness".

In its electronic glossary related to information society, the European Commission has proposed a definition of cyberspace that emphasizes the hardware and software layers, but excludes the user sphere. In this sense, cyberspace is the "virtual space in which the electronic data of worldwide PCs circulate".[24]

On the basis of legal commentaries and literature, an interesting definition of cyberspace has been provided by M. Lakomy, who, summing up his multi-faceted considerations on the understanding of the concept, finally concludes that, in practice, cyberspace is

> a domain for the processing, storage and transmission of information in digital form, based on the transmission of digital signals and electromagnetic radiation. It is an immaterial space in its essence, but one that functions through the ICT infrastructure that produces and transmits these signals.[25]

The author stresses that this domain is created by "every bit of data stored, processed and transmitted in computers and computer networks, and all other elements that make up the ICT infrastructure in the broad sense".[26] Importantly, M. Lakomy also emphasizes that computers and other devices that are not currently connected to the global network should not be overlooked in this context, because even though they are not connected, these devices

> can perform important functions from the perspective of the interests of individuals, businesses or entire societies and countries: they control machines, help with calculations, support education and development, and therefore have a significant impact on the functioning of various areas of human life.[27]

In addition, isolation from cyberspace can be temporary, impermanent and illusory, and computers can communicate with other devices even when they remain offline, for example using various types of physical data carriers.

C. Banasiński very rightly connects the individual layers (spheres) of cyberspace, noting that it consists of both tooling and the social component. Of course, this author also states that "The basic factor that makes up cyberspace is the material information and communication system, which is a set of cooperating ICT equipment and software ensuring the processing, storage, as well as sending and receiving of data by telecommunications networks by means of telecommunications terminal equipment appropriate for a given type of network.[28] C. Banasiński notes, however,

---

[23]https://www.nik.gov.pl/kontrole/P/14/043/, accessed on 3.10.2020.

[24]After Wasilewski (2013), p. 229.

[25]Lakomy (2015), p. 83.

[26]Lakomy (2015), p. 83.

[27]Lakomy (2015), p. 83.

[28]Banasiński (2018), p. 25.

that the focus on the infrastructural and logical sphere (which he collectively calls the instrumental sphere) leads to the omission or marginalization of the

> social component of cyberspace, which refers to cyber users, and which treats cyberspace as a complex environment resulting from the immaterial interaction between people, software and services on the Internet provided through technical devices and networks connected to it; an equally important, integral and interconnected element with the technical infrastructure is its relationship with people and the interaction between people related to its use.[29]

Other authors also draw attention to the need for a comprehensive approach to cyberspace, not only as an infrastructure domain. According to R. Tadeusiewicz, cyberspace is

> a set of hardware and software tools related to the techniques of collecting, processing, transmitting and sharing information, used by people to acquire knowledge and to communicate with other people. The most important, but not the only, component of cyberspace today is the Internet.[30]

Similar conclusions are also drawn by J. Rzucidło and J. Węgrzyn, who stated that the notion of cyberspace "certainly includes at least a specific type of infrastructure and processes that take place in it, or includes people and the relationships that exist between them through this infrastructure, as well as between them and this infrastructure".[31]

Legal commentators also draw attention to the legal difficulties, both international and national, associated with the nature and essence of cyberspace as a cross-border, immaterial creation, with an unlimited number of users.[32]

3 Definitions of Cybersecurity

In the theory of security studies, it is assumed that the concept of security (from the Latin *sine cura*—"without concern") is interpreted primarily as a state of peace, safety and no threat.[33] At the same time, however, "security" should also be understood as a process, thus emphasizing that security and its organization are constantly changing, and therefore cannot be considered to be permanently established and organized.[34] In this sense, security means "the continuous activity of individuals, local communities, states or international organizations in creating

[29]Banasiński (2018), p. 26.
[30]Tadeusiewicz (2010), p. 32.
[31]Rzucidło and Węgrzyn (2015), p. 144.
[32]Wrona (2015), p. 872.
[33]Ściborek et al. (2015), p. 26.
[34]Marczak (2011), p. 15.

the desired state of security".[35] Cybersecurity can also be defined both by reference to the desired state and as a continuous process leading to it.

Closer to the first interpretation is the legal definition introduced by the Act of 5 July 2018 on the National Cybersecurity System,[36] which gives priority to the term "resilience". According to Article 2(4) of this Act, cybersecurity is therefore "the ability of information systems to resist any action that compromises the confidentiality, integrity, availability and authenticity of processed data or the related services offered by those systems". This term is based on the definition of "security of network and information systems" in Directive 2016/1148,[37] taking into account the evolution of certain concepts (e.g. information system).

The strategic document adopted by the Council of Ministers in 2017, entitled the National Cybersecurity Policy Framework of the Republic of Poland for 2017–2022, associates cybersecurity with the security of network and information systems and ICT security, using them interchangeably and treating them as synonyms. However, the interpretation set out in the document is consistent with the definition mentioned above, introduced into the legal framework by the provisions of the Act on the National Cybersecurity System, and focusses on the ability of

> information and communication systems to resist, at a given level of confidence, any action that compromises the availability, authenticity, integrity or confidentiality of stored or transmitted or processed data or the related services offered by, or accessible via, those network and information systems.

The definition established at the Community level in the Digital Single Market Glossary leads to an emphasis on action and processes aimed at ensuring cybersecurity. According to it, cybersecurity

> commonly refers to the safeguards and actions available to protect the cyber domain, both in the civilian and military fields, from those threats that are associated with or that may harm its interdependent networks and information infrastructure. Cybersecurity strives to preserve the availability and integrity of the networks and infrastructure and the confidentiality of the information contained therein. The term cybersecurity also covers prevention and law enforcement measures to fight cybercrime.[38]

[35]Marczak (2011), p. 15.

[36]Act of 5 July 2018 on the National Cybersecurity System (Polish Journal of Laws of 2020, item 1369, as amended, hereinafter "NCSA").

[37]Directive (EU) 2016/1148 of the European Parliament and of the Council of 6 July 2016 concerning measures for a high common level of security of network and information systems across the Union (OJ EU 2016 L 194/1) For the purposes of the provisions of the Directive, "security of network and information systems" means the ability of network and information systems to resist, at a given level of confidence, any action that compromises the availability, authenticity, integrity or confidentiality of stored or transmitted or processed data or the related services offered by, or accessible via, those network and information systems.

[38]Digital Single market Glossary, https://ec.europa.eu/digital-single-market/glossary, accessed on 3.10.2020;

According to C. Banasiński, cybersecurity can be reduced to "an undisturbed way of collecting, processing and exchanging information recorded and processed digitally".[39]

The explicit process-oriented understanding of cybersecurity indicates that it is not about an existing or desired state, but "a process which consists of actions taken by technical and non-technical means to protect cyberspace, including hardware, software and information or data".[40] This dynamic approach to cybersecurity (specifically the cybersecurity of the Republic of Poland) was also adopted in the already mentioned Cybersecurity Doctrine of the Republic of Poland, stating that it is

> a process of ensuring the safe functioning in cyberspace of the state as a whole, its structures, natural persons and legal entities, including entrepreneurs and other entities without a legal personality, as well as the information and communication systems and information resources at their disposal in global cyberspace.[41]

The community-created definition in the Cybrary glossary is also process-oriented, according to which cybersecurity are "the processes employed to safeguard and secure assets used to carry information of an organization from being stolen or attacked".[42] At the same time, the definition also stresses that cybersecurity requires broad knowledge of the possible threats, such as viruses or other malicious objects, and that identity management, risk management and incident management are the crux of cybersecurity strategies of an organization.

A comprehensive understanding of the term cybersecurity is proposed in the dictionary of the US Department of Homeland Security, according to which it should be defined strictly as the activity or process, ability or capability, or state whereby information and communications systems and the information contained therein are protected from and/or defended against damage, unauthorized use or modification, or exploitation. An extended definition is also available, referring to strategy, policy, and standards regarding the security of and operations in cyberspace, and encompasses the full range of threat reduction, vulnerability reduction, deterrence,

---

[39]Banasiński (2018), p. 33.

[40]Wasiuta et al. (2018), p. 223.

[41]https://www.bbn.gov.pl/ftp/dok/01/DCB.pdf Interestingly, the document distinguishes between the cybersecurity of the Republic of Poland and the security of the cyberspace of the Republic of Poland as "a part of state cybersecurity comprising a set of organisational and legal, technical, physical and educational projects aimed at ensuring the undisturbed functioning of the cyberspace of the Republic of Poland with the public and private critical information and communication infrastructure that constitutes its component and the security of information resources processed therein." Accessed on 3.10.2020.

[42]Full quote:

> Cyber Security are the processes employed to safeguard and secure assets used to carry information of an organization from being stolen or attacked. It requires extensive knowledge of the possible threats such as Virus or such other malicious objects. Identity management, risk management and incident management form the crux of cyber security strategies of an organization.

https://www.cybrary.it/glossary/c-the-glossary/cyber-security/ accessed on 3.10.2020.

international engagement, incident response, resilience, and recovery policies and activities, including computer network operations, information assurance, law enforcement, diplomacy, military, and intelligence missions as they relate to the security and stability of the global information and communications infrastructure.[43]

Among the numerous typologies, the one proposed by M. Lakomy, who, from the point of view of national security, has divided threats into structured and unstructured ones, is particularly noteworthy. The former are characterized by a high degree of organization of their sources, technical sophistication and, from the point of view of the attacker, domination of political, military, religious and economic motivations, and these include cyberterrorism, cyber espionage and military operations in cyberspace. Unstructured threats, on the other hand, are characterized by a low level of organization, generally posing a lesser threat to national security, with the dominance of political, social and individual motivations. According to the author, they include hacking, hacktivism, "patriotic hacktivism", and cybercrime in the strict sense.[44]

The threats to cybersecurity can also be divided by:

- subject: criminals, terrorists, state entities,
- motivation: the intention to obtain profit, to exert political pressure, to obtain information, to gain military advantage, a form of a joke, the desire to become known in a particular environment, to gain popularity or publicity,
- *modus operandi*: immediate or long-term action, action with publicity or concealed action".[45]

In my opinion, it is appropriate to define cybersecurity also through the prism of threats that hinder the achievement of the desired state and are a challenge to ongoing processes.

It can be assumed that, in the broad sense, cybersecurity will be threatened by failures, accidents and, finally, attacks. Of course, failures and accidents will most often be strictly dependent on technical conditions, or, for example, an unintentional human error or, in general, random events. This is not the case for attacks which are deliberate in nature.

References

Banasiński C (2018) Podstawowe pojęcia i podstawy prawne bezpieczeństwa w cyberprzestrzeni. In: Banasiński C (ed) Cyberbezpieczeństwo. Zarys wykładu, Warsaw

Crowther AG (2018) National Defense and the Cyber Domain, pp. 83–84 https://www.heritage.org/sites/default/files/2017-09/2018_IndexOfUSMilitaryStrength_CROWTHER.pdf. Accessed 3 Oct 2020

[43]https://niccs.us-cert.gov/about-niccs/glossary#C accessed on 3.10.2020.

[44]Lakomy (2015), p. 137.

[45]Wasiuta et al. (2018), p. 223.

Gibson W (2009) Neuromancer. Katowice
Kasprzyk R, Maj M, Tarapata Z (2015) Przestępstwa w cyberprzestrzeni. Aspekty technologiczne i prawne. In: Przestępczość w XXI wieku. Zapobieganie i zwalczanie. Problemy technologiczno-informatyczne, Warsaw
Lakomy M (2015) Cyberprzestrzeń jako nowy wymiar rywalizacji i współpracy państw, Katowice
Marczak J (2011) Bezpieczeństwo narodowe. In: Jakubczak R, Marczak J (eds) Bezpieczeństwo narodowe Polski w XXI wieku, Warsaw
Rzucidło R, Węgrzyn J (2015) Stany nadzwyczajne w sytuacji szczególnego zagrożenia państwa w cyberprzestrzeni. Przegląd Prawa Konstytucyjnego 5(27)
Ściborek Z, Wiśniewski B, Kuc R, Dawidczyk A (2015) Bezpieczeństwo wewnętrzne. Podręcznik akademicki, Toruń
Surma J (2017) Cyfryzacja życia w erze Big Data. Warsaw
Tadeusiewicz R (2010) Zagrożenia w cyberprzestrzeni. Nauka 4
Tenet GJ (1998) Information Security Risks, Opportunities, and the Bottom Line. https://www.cia.gov/news-information/speeches-testimony/1998/dci_speech_040698.html. Accessed 3 Oct 2020
Trejnis Z, Trejnis PZ (2017) Polityka ochrony cyberprzestrzeni w państwie współczesnym. Studia Bobolanum 28(3)
Wasilewski J (2013) Zarys definicyjny cyberprzestrzeni. Przegląd Bezpieczeństwa Wewnętrznego 9
Wasiuta O, Klepka R, Kopeć R (2018) Vademecum bezpieczeństwa. Kraków
Wrona J (2015) Jurysdykcja państw a zwalczanie cyberprzestępczości. In: Pływaczewski EW, Filipkowski W, Rau Z (eds) Przestępczość w XXI wieku. Zapobieganie i zwalczanie. Problemy prawno-kryminologiczne, Warsaw

Tomasz Zdzikot attorney-at-law, a graduate of the Law Faculty at the Cardinal Stefan Wyszyński University in Warsaw. He also completed, among others, postgraduate cybersecurity studies at the Polish Naval Academy in Gdynia, the *Top Public Executive* program co-organized by IESE Business School in Barcelona and the Lech Kaczyński National School of Public Administration in Warsaw and the *Higher Defence Course* at the National Defence University in Warsaw. Former Deputy Minister of National Defence and Plenipotentiary of the Ministry of Defence for the security of cyberspace (2018–2020), creator of the program for developing the capabilities of the Polish Armed Forces to operate in cyberspace—"Cyber.mil.pl". Deputy Minister of Interior and Administration (2015–2018) and Government Plenipotentiary for the Preparation of State Administration Bodies for Cooperation with the Schengen Information System and the Visa Information System (2017–2018) Currently—CEO of the Polish Post. Author of numerous publications on cybersecurity issues as well as media law and new technologies. ORCID: 0000-0003-4369-7146.

Cyberspace as an Area of Legal Regulation

Katarzyna Chałubińska-Jentkiewicz

Abstract The rapid development of the Internet, which rose to prominence at the turn of the twenty-first century, is one of the most significant technological breakthroughs in human history. Cyberspace has now become the environment for the functioning of modern society, particularly the young generation. Under the influence of globalisation, computerisation and digitisation, human activity began to penetrate the virtual world. This shift has contributed to raising the standard and quality of life of citizens, increasing the productivity of entrepreneurs and the efficiency of the state. However, the changes have resulted in society's increasing dependence on cyberspace and created the need to protect the public against potential attacks. Specifying the definition of cyberspace security was required in the course of developing the Cybersecurity Doctrine of the Republic of Poland.

The dynamic civilisational changes which have been observed in the last few years have arisen from a rapid growth in information and supporting ICT technologies. The information revolution and the evolution of the information society, which affect every sphere of human activity, are undoubtedly two of the major trends shaping the contemporary information environment. Access to new technologies, and the fact that they are so commonly used by the public, have created a need for distinguishing another dimension of physical reality, namely cyberspace. The convergence of information and communications technologies and the media, which has been intensifying for at least a quarter of a century, and, in consequence, the convergence of the info-, socio- and techno-spheres, has contributed to the emergence of a global, timeless cyberspace, not defined by either geographical or political borders.

The development of the Internet, the worldwide computer network, towards the end of the twentieth Century, was one of the most significant technological

K. Chałubińska-Jentkiewicz (✉)
Akademickie Centrum Polityki Cyberbezpieczeństwa/Academic Center for Cybersecurity Policy, Akademia Sztuki Wojennej w Warszawie/War Studies University in Warsaw, Warsaw, Poland
e-mail: k.jentkiewicz@akademia.mil.pl

K. Chałubińska-Jentkiewicz et al. (eds.), *Cybersecurity in Poland*,
https://doi.org/10.1007/978-3-030-78551-2_3

breakthroughs in the history of humanity. At first it was used exclusively in scientific research; as time went by, and as the tools making it easier to use the Internet were developed, it became a key and fundamental element in the functioning of individuals in all spheres of life.[1] Falling in the Cold War period, the 1960s marked the beginning of the computer network. In that period, a communications system was created in the United States, which gave rise to the ARPANET network (Advanced Research Projects Agency Network), considered to be the first prototype of the Internet. The combination of information and telecommunications technologies ushered in a new era of global communication. By the end of the 1990s, the growth of the Internet had made many spheres of life which were based on computer technology dependent on the net. It became a tool whereby people could enrich their knowledge, a source of information, and an integration point.[2] The domain underwent rapid commercialisation and development. New services sprang into existence—websites, social networks, electronic mail, forums, blogs, search engines, instant messaging, multimedia streaming, to name a few. The expansion of the physical infrastructure of the global network has resulted in a steady growth in the number of Internet users. As the information society continues to develop rapidly commensurately with the expansion of the reach of the Internet, other areas of human activity extend into cyberspace. Instant access to the Internet from almost every place on Earth, and its worldwide reach, in connection with low usage fees, have made more and more entities (governments, institutions and businesses) and individuals move large parts of their daily activities to the virtual network.[3]

Cyberspace has become a domain which pertains to many areas of human life. Although still considered a "novum", the term was first used in the 1980s by W. Gibson, who described it as follows:

> A consensual hallucination experienced daily by billions of legitimate operators, in every nation, by children being taught mathematical concepts [. . .]. A graphical representation of data abstracted from the banks of every computer in the human system. Unthinkable complexity. . . Lines of light ranged in the non-space of the mind, clusters and constellations of data.[4]

Gibson pointed out some characteristic features of the environment: unlimited time and space, virtuality, complexity, and the collation of all resources in one huge database.[5] Visualisation, in Gibson's words "a graphical representation", has become characteristic of a trend called cyberpunk.[6]

---

[1]Ciekanowski and Wojciechowska-Filipek (2016), p. 91.

[2]Ciekanowski and Wojciechowska-Filipek (2016), p. 14.

[3]M. Grzelak, K. Liedel, *Bezpieczeństwo w cyberprzestrzeni. Zagrożenia i wyzwania dla Polski – zarys problemu*. https://www.bbn.gov.pl/download/1/11469/str125-139MichalGrzelakKrzysztofLiedel.pdf (accessed on 01.10.2020).

[4]Gibson (2009), Katowice, p. 59.

[5]Szczepaniuk (2016), p. 69.

[6]Cyberpunk is a subgenre of fantasy literature and cinematography which foregrounds the relationship between man and the advanced technology which surrounds him. The defining feature of

At the beginning of the last decade of the last century, during the Gulf War (1991), which was the first information war,[7] there appeared a thesis that cyberspace had become the fifth environment (besides land, sea, air, and the cosmos) in which combat and warfare were being conducted (Warden's model).[8]

P. Sienkiewicz set out to interpret the essence of the construct called cyberspace. He distinguished the following basic perspectives from which the topic can be approached.

- "Cyberspace is essentially a huge social network—a net of nets, the participants in which, either individuals or groups (societies), utilise global resources provided by the Internet (generally speaking, the net)
- Cyberspace is identified with the virtual reality generated by the computer, the network, and the Internet
- Cyberspace is simply the Internet, its resources, services, and users
- Cyberspace is merely an evolving, dynamic, complex, system (a system of systems), and it should be seen as such, no matter whether we foreground its technical, informational, or social aspects".[9]

"In physical terms, cyberspace may be characterised by Maxwell's four equations, which are

- Gauss's law for electric fields
- Faraday's law of induction
- Gauss's law for magnetism
- Ampère's law (further developed by Maxwell)".[10]

The capability of analysing, generating, receiving, and measuring fluctuating electric and magnetic fields was knowingly applied, for the first time, in a device called the telegraph.[11]

D. E. Denning defines cyberspace (its technical aspect) *as* "[...] the space of information created by all computer networks put together".[12] A similar definition is formulated by G. T. Rattray. "A physical domain which is the result of the creation of information systems and networks which enable mutual interactions through electronic communication".[13] *P. Sienkiewicz defines cyberspace in the technical dimension.* "[...] a global network made of a time-variable number of constituent

---

the genre is depiction of a vision of a future in which the environments of people, appliances, and computers start to permeate one another.

[7]Campen (1996), p. 11.

[8]Warden (1995).

[9]Sienkiewicz (2015), pp. 89–102.

[10]Słota-Bohosiewicz (2015), pp. 155–166.

[11]Ibidem.

[12]Denning (2002), p. 24.

[13]Rattray (2004), p. 30.

networks (TCP/IP), with unlimited and open resources and available services".[14] In the above definitions cyberspace is compared to computer systems operating within computer networks.

One of the definitions of cyberspace cited in literature is the one provided by the United States Department of Defence. According to this definition, cyberspace is

> A global domain within the information environment consisting of an interdependent network of information technology infrastructures and resident data, including the Internet, telecommunications networks, and embedded processors and controllers.

The above definition refers merely to the technological dimension of cyberspace. It does not make any references to the social sphere—to mankind, the user of cyberspace. In addition, the definition firmly ascribes the hardware aspect of infrastructure with the leading role of the Internet, whereas the software aspect is overlooked.[15]

In Europe one can refer to a series of definitions adopted in official documents released by various countries, and by the European Union. The European Commission defines it in the following way. "Virtual space in which electronic data circulate, and are processed by PC computers from all over the world.".[16] The basic element of this definition is virtual space's constituting a data system which is accessed through ICT systems. The interpretation by the European Commission *also* disregards the user sphere.

Another, more exhaustive definition, of cyberspace is proffered by the NATO Cooperative Cyber Defence Centre of Excellence in Tallinn, which says "Cyberspace is a time-dependent set of interconnected information systems and people/users who interact with those systems".[17] The need to regulate the matters related to cyberspace security has been reflected in a large number of strategic documents and legislation. NATO's new strategic concept[18] and updated cyber-defence policy identify cyber threats, in special cases, as potential reasons for exercising collective defence.[19]

In accordance with the Polish regulations, cyberspace is defined as "virtual space in which information is processed and exchanged by ICT systems, as set out in Article 3(3) of the Act of 17 February 2005 on the Computerisation of the Operations of the Entities Rendering Public Services,[20] and the interrelations between the

---

[14]Sienkiewicz (2012), p. 324.

[15]Szczepaniuk (2016), p. 71.

[16]Wasilewski (2013), p. 229.

[17]R. Otis, P. Lorents, *Cyberspace: Definition and Implications, the Cooperative Cyber Defence Centre of Excellence*, Tallinn. http://dumitrudumbrava.files.wordpress.com/2012/01/cyberspace-definition-and-impications.pdf (accessed on 01.10.2020).

[18]*A Strategic Concept for the Defence and Security of the Members of the North Atlantic Treaty Organisation*, Lisbon 2010. https://www.bbn.gov.pl/download/1/15758/KoncepcjastrategicznaNATO.pdf (accessed on 01.10.2020).

[19]Szczepaniuk (2016), p. 72.

[20]I.e. consolidated text Polish Journal of Laws of 2020, item 346, as amended, hereinafter **the Computerisation Act.**

entities and the relationships with users".[21] Cyberspace is therefore a generalisation of the concepts of "systems" and "ICT networks". An essential aspect of defining cyberspace is the relationships between its users.

In that respect, this definition converges with the one proposed by CCDCoE[22] since it includes both the human and the technical components of cyberspace. One of the essential aims of its amendments was to introduce the category of cyberspace as one of the constituents of national security. The introduction of the definition became especially important to the institutions and bodies which were in charge of broadly understood security, allowing one to create a power *instrumentarium*, necessary for those entities to perform tasks in accordance with the constitutional principle of legalism. The solutions adopted complied with NATO's Strategic Concept from 2010,[23] which was in effect at that time, and at the same time they complemented the Cyberspace Protection Policy of the Republic of Poland for 2011–2016[24] prepared by the Council of Ministers.

In accordance with this document, the following definition of cyberspace was adopted.

- "*Cyberspace*—a digital space for processing and exchanging information created by ICT systems and networks, together with the connections between one another and relationships with the users;
- *The cyberspace of the Republic of Poland* (hereinafter CRP)—cyberspace within the territory of the Polish State, and in locations outside that territory, in which representatives of the Republic of Poland (diplomatic posts, military contingents) operate".[25]

Cybersecurity had to be defined in view of the works which were meant to develop the Doctrine of the Cybersecurity of the Republic of Poland. The document contains the following definition.

> A part of the State's cybersecurity which covers a range of organisational, legal, technical, physical, and educational ventures aimed at ensuring the uninterrupted functioning of the

[21]The Act of 29 August 2002 on Martial War and the Powers of the Commander-in-Chief and the Rules of His Subordination to the Constitutional Bodies of the Republic of Poland, i.e. consolidated text The Polish Journal of Laws of 2017, item 1932.

[22]NATO CCDCoE, officially *the Cooperative Cyber Defence Centre of Excellence*, is one of NATO Centres, based in Tallinn, Estonia. The centre conducts research and training in cybernetic security.

[23]Translation by the National Security Bureau: Andrzej Juszczak, 17 January 2011. https://www.bbn.gov.pl/pl/wydarzenia/2694,dok.hml (accessed on 27.01.2020).

[24]Werner (2014), p. 36.

[25]*The Cyberspace Protection Policy of the Republic of Poland for 2011–2016*. http://bip.msw.gov.pl/bip/programy/19057,Rządowy-Program-Ochrony-Cyberprzestrzeni-RP-na-lata-2011-2016.html (accessed on 28.10.2020).

> cyberspace of the Republic of Poland, together with its critical public and private ICT infrastructure, and the security of the information processed within that infrastructure.[26]

This definition emphasises the functional aspect of cybersecurity, i.e. activities of which the aim is to protect that space and its users.

One of the defining features of cyberspace is its network character. It is very often associated with the information revolution, and is undoubtedly connected with the rapid growth of telecommunications and the popularisation of the Internet.[27] The network character is to be understood as a constitutive attribute of cyberspace, virtuality, a potential one, and as far as the communication advantages are concerned, one should not overlook hypertextuality, multimediality, and interactiveness. "The combination of constitutive features and their semantic interrelations is one of the ontological aspects of cyberspace".[28] Computer networks are a system of interrelated workstations, peripheral devices (such as printers, hard drives, scanners and workstations), and other devices. Computer networks, because of their functionality, constitute the core of all computer systems. By working within a computer network, one can share data, hardware and software, and manage all the devices connected with that network from one computer.[29]

These days, cyberspace has become an environment in which contemporary society, especially its young generation, lives and functions. Affected by globalisation, computerisation or digitalisation, human activity has begun to permeate the virtual world. This has contributed to the raising of the living standards and the quality of the lives of citizens, and has boosted the productiveness of entrepreneurs and the efficiency of the State. The consequence of those changes, which are becoming more and more evident, is society's dependence on cyberspace. This dependence requires the reliability of the ICT infrastructure, which in turn involves protection against potential attacks.[30] Cyberspace affords huge opportunities, such as e-learning, e-administration, and telecommuting, but has its "dark side" as well. In the field of cybersecurity one can observe an increase in the number of incidents of various kinds. Cyber attacks can also have a destructive influence on the State's critical infrastructure, the functioning of which is based, to a large extent, on ICT systems.[31]

Space associated with certain real places has been replaced with the space of flows, as wrote M. Castells. Formerly, space was defined geographically, whereas today it consists of various layers of unimaginable complexity.[32]

The table below sets out the development stages of cyberspace (Table 1).

---

[26] *The Doctrine of the Cybersecurity of the Republic of Poland.* https://www.bbn.gov.pl/pl/prace-biura/publikacje/6818,Doktryna-cyberbezpieczenstwa-RP.html (accessed on 27.01.2021).

[27] Szczepaniuk (2016), p. 69.

[28] Sienkiewicz (2015), p. 92.

[29] Szczepaniuk (2016), p. 70.

[30] Chałubińska-Jentkiewicz (2019), p. 18.

[31] Szczepaniuk (2016), p. 84.

[32] Ibidem, p. 71.

Table 1 An evolutionary stage model of cyberspace

Development stage	General description
Cyberspace—0	• "The Gutenberg Galaxy" (M. McLuhan) • The development of print and the beginnings of telegraphy, telecommunications; radio, television
Cyberspace—1	• "Galaktyka Wienera" (P. Sienkiewicz) [T.N. – in Polish "Wiener's Galaxy"] • "The information society" (Masuda) • Cybernetic concepts of the development of social systems, the evolution of digital electronics, computer systems, satellite communications (TELSTAR), the computer network (ARPANET), "PC boom" • Artificial intelligence
Cyberspace—2	• "The Internet Galaxy" (M. Castells) • The Internet (WWW), the knowledge-based economy, globalisation
Cyberspace—3	• "The Galaxy?" (we can't predict) • The Internet (Web 2.0), the globalisation of the social-communications network, new forms of social behaviour • "The knowledge society" (we can't predict)

Source: Sienkiewicz (2012) *op. 324*

The raising of awareness related to secure cyberspace goes hand in hand with rapid increases in the number of computer incidents, and new categories of threats. Poland is also a target for attacks on its cyberspace. Similarly to other countries, it is faced with the challenge of working out organisational and legal changes which will ensure an appropriate level of cybersecurity, and the security of the citizens who function within that space.[33]

In the field of cybersecurity, there are such new terms as information security, computer-network and computer-systems security, ICT security, and cybersecurity. According to P. Potejko,

> one can assume that information security consists of a set of activities, methods, and procedures employed by competent authorities which are aimed at ensuring the integrity of collected, stored and processed information resources by protecting them against undesirable, unauthorised disclosure, modification or destruction.[34]

The Cybersecurity Strategy of the Republic of Poland[35] defines IT security as

> [...] the resilience of ICT systems, with a given level of trust, to counter any actions or activities which violate the accessibility, authenticity, integrity, or confidentiality of the data which are stored, shared, or processed, or related services afforded or rendered via those computer networks and systems [. . .][36].

[33]Werner (2014), p. 31.

[34]Potejko (2015), p. 228.

[35]The Cybersecurity Strategy of the Republic of Poland for 2017–2022. https://mc.gov.pl/aktualnosci/strategia-cyberbezpieczenstwa-rzeczypospolitej-polskiej-na-lata-2017-2022 (accessed on 24.05.2020).

[36]Ibidem, p. 23.

By comparison, the Cybersecurity Strategy of the European Union[37] defines cybersecurity as

> the safeguards and actions which can be used to protect the cyber domain, in both the civilian and the military fields, from those threats associated with or which might harm its interdependent networks and information infrastructure. Cybersecurity strives to preserve the availability and integrity of these networks and infrastructure, and the confidentiality of the information contained therein.[38]

In the States which are involved in the development of the information society, cybersecurity is considered one of the most serious challenges in the realm of national security. It refers to both the security of the State and of its individual citizens. The appropriate functioning of public administration is highly important for the maintenance of cybersecurity. The last few years have also brought a revolution in the understanding of the concept of national security as regards the subject matter. One has begun to notice the significance of not only military or political aspects, but also economic, cultural, ecological and ideological facets, among others. Seeing those changes, the Polish State has started to develop the National Security System, the primary focus of which is to ensure broadly understood integrated national security, in which cybersecurity occupies a very important place, covering all other aspects of social life.[39]

The increased significance of cyberspace in the functioning of numerous aspects of the State and society has brought the development of national and international cybersecurity strategies, and the further development of cybersecurity management systems.

References

Campen S (ed) (1996) The first information. AFCEA, Washington

Ciekanowski Z, Wojciechowska-Filipek S (2016) Bezpieczeństwo funkcjonowania w cyberprzestrzeni Jednostki – Organizacji – Państwa, Warsaw

Chałubińska-Jentkiewicz K (2019) Cyberbezpieczeństwo – zagadnienia definicyjne. Cybersecurity and Law 2

Denning DE (2002) Wojna informacyjna i bezpieczeństwo informacji [T.N. – original title: Information Warfare and Security], Warsaw

Gibson W (2009) Neuromancer, Katowice

Grzelak M, Liedel K. Bezpieczeństwo w cyberprzestrzeni. Zagrożenia i wyzwania dla Polski – zarys problemu. https://www.bbn.gov.pl/download/1/11469/str125-139MichalGrzelakKrzysztofLiedel.pdf. Accessed 1 Oct 2020

[37] *The Cybersecurity Strategy of the European Union: An Open, Safe and Secure Cyberspace*, OJ EU C 2014.32.19., http://www.europarl.europa.eu/meetdocs/2009_2014/documents/join/com_join(2013)0001_/com_join(2013)0001_pl.pdf, hereinafter the Cybersecurity Strategy of the European Union (accessed on 12.10.2020).

[38] Ibidem, p. 3.

[39] Chałubińska-Jentkiewicz (2019), p. 20.

Otis R., Lorents P, Cyberspace: Definition and Implications, the Cooperative Cyber Defence Centre of Excellence, Tallinn. http://dumitrudumbrava.files.wordpress.com/2012/01/cyberspace-defini tion-and-impications.pdf. Accessed 1 Oct 2020
Potejko P (2015) Bezpieczeństwo informacyjne. In: Chałubińska-Jentkiewicz K, Karpiuk M (eds) Prawo nowych technologii - wybrane zagadnienia. Warsaw
Rattray GT (2004) Wojna strategiczna w cyberprzestrzeni [T.N. – original title: Strategic Warfare in Cyberspace], Warsaw
Sienkiewicz P (2012) Bezpieczeństwo cyberprzestrzeni. In: Sienkiewicz P (ed) Metodologia badań bezpieczeństwa narodowego, vol 3. Warsaw
Sienkiewicz P (2015) Ontologia cyberprzestrzeni. Zeszyty Naukowe Warszawskiej Wyższej Szkoły Informatyki 13(9)
Słota-Bohosiewicz A (2015) Zarzadzanie bezpieczeństwem w cyberprzestrzeni obywatela. In: Wybrane aspekty bezpieczeństwa cybernetycznego sił zbrojnych Rzeczypospolitej Polskiej. vol. 2, Warsaw
Szczepaniuk E (2016) Bezpieczeństwo struktur administracyjnych w warunkach zagrożeń cyberprzestrzeni państwa, Warsaw
Warden JA (1995) The enemy as a system. Airpower Journal 9(1)
Wasilewski J (2013) Zarys definicyjny cyberprzestrzeni. Przegląd Bezpieczeństwa Wewnętrznego 9
Werner J (2014) Zagrożenia bezpieczeństwa w cyberprzestrzeni. Warsaw

Katarzyna Chałubińska-Jentkiewicz dr. hab. of legal sciences (University of Warsaw and the Jagiellonian University), legal advisor, associate professor, and head of the Department of Cybersecurity Law and New Technologies at the Institute of Law in the Faculty of National Security at the War Studies University in Warsaw. She is also a lecturer at the SWPS University and director of the Academic Center for Cybersecurity Policy. In the years 1996–2010, she worked as a lawyer in the National Broadcasting Council and with the public broadcaster TVP S.A. Between 2011 and 2017, she was deputy director of the National Audiovisual Institute (her competence centered on the field of digitization). As a scientist, she conducts research on cybersecurity, information security threats, the development of electronic media law, protection of intellectual property, and the impact of new technologies on the development of the state and the legal situation of the individual. Katarzyna Chałubińska–Jentkiewicz is the author of monographs and numerous articles, which include topics such as new technologies law, cyber responsibility, information security law, and audiovisual media: Regulatory conflict in the age of digitization, Audio visual media services; Regulation in the conditions of digital conversion; Information and computerization in public administration; Cultural Security Law and Reuse of public sector information. She is head of the Ministry of Science's research project "Polish cybersecurity system – a model of legal solutions."

Cyberspace, Cybercrime, Cyberterrorism

Filip Radoniewicz

Abstract The purpose of this chapter is to synthetically characterize the phenomenon of cybercrime, cyberterrorism and cyberwar. It presents attempts to define computer crimes and their classification, history of criminalization of this phenomenon together with related difficulties. The author consistently distinguishes cybercrime from cyberterrorism and cyberwar.

1 Cyberspace

The term "cyberspace", the combination of the two words "cybernetics" and "space", meaning cybernetic space, was coined in the 1980s. It is thought that the originator of this term was William Gibson, a Canadian writer, who used it in his novel *Neuromancer* of 1984, to define computer-generated virtual realities, which the protagonists inhabit. The notion found its place in mass culture, and it is currently used to define virtual space, understood as space for communication via computer networks.[1] This term is sometimes (incorrectly) used as a synonym for the Internet.[2]

As regards Polish Law, cyberspace is defined, i.a., in Article 2(1a) of the State of Emergency Act of the 21st of June 2002,[3] Article 3(1)(4) of the Natural Disasters Act of the 18th of April 2002,[4] and Article 2(1b) of the Act of the 29th of August 2002 on Martial Law and the Competences of the Commander-in-Chief of the Army

[1] For more details, see Kosiński (2013), pp. 462–463.

[2] Cf. Liderman (2012), pp. 62–63; Wall (2013), pp. 10–11.

[3] Act of 21 June 2002 of the State of Emergency Act, consolidated text, Polish Journal of Laws of 2016, item 886, as amended.

[4] Act of 18 April 2002 on Natural Disasters, consolidated text, Polish Journal of Laws of 2017, item 1897, as amended.

F. Radoniewicz (✉)
Akademickie Centrum Polityki Cyberbezpieczeństwa/Academic Center for Cybersecurity Policy, Akademia Sztuki Wojennej w Warszawie/War Studies University in Warsaw, Warsaw, Poland
e-mail: filip.radoniewicz@radoniewicz.eu

K. Chałubińska-Jentkiewicz et al. (eds.), *Cybersecurity in Poland*,
https://doi.org/10.1007/978-3-030-78551-2_4

and the Rules of the Commander-in-Chief's Subordination to the Constitutional Authorities of the Republic of Poland,[5] according to which the term is understood as *"a space for the processing and exchange of information, created by information and communication systems, defined in Articles 3(3)* of the Act of the 17th of February 2005 on the Computerisation of the Operations of Entities Performing Public Tasks, *including the links between them and their relations with users."* Within the meaning of the said Act on Computerisation, a communication and information system is a set of interfacing IT hardware and software, providing the facility to process, store, send, and receive data via ICT networks, with the use of an end device suitable for a given network type. According to this relatively comprehensive definition developed by the legislator, cyberspace includes not only communication and information systems, comprising hardware and software facilitating the performance of system functions (processing, storage and sending computer data), but also computer data and interactions between devices and their users.[6]

2 Cybersecurity

The concept of cybersecurity is currently defined under Polish law in the National CyberSecurity System Act of the 5th of July 2018.[7] Given the significant role this legal Act plays in the field of "cybersecurity law", it may be assumed that the definition can be applied across the entire legal system. Pursuant to Article 2(4) of the NCSA, cybersecurity is

> the ability of information systems to resist actions, which compromise the availability, authenticity, integrity, and confidentiality of processed data, or the related services provided by those information systems.

Under Article 2(4) of the NCSA, the legislator referred to the notions of confidentiality, integrity, availability, and authenticity, i.e., the so-called information-security components (of computer data and communication and information systems). Traditionally, the list has been limited to three "main" components. In addition to confidentiality (covered by protection at the earliest point in time), the list comprised availability and integrity. Availability means the facility to use the

---

[5]Act of 29 August 2002 on Martial Law and the Competences of the Commander-in-Chief of the Army and the Rules of the Commander-in-Chief's Subordination to the Constitutional Authorities of the Republic of Poland (consolidated text, Polish Journal of Laws of 2016, item 851, as amended).

[6]For more details see Aleksandrowicz and Liedel (2014), pp. 23–27; Banasiński (2018), pp. 23–27; Kosiński (2013), pp. 462–463; Liderman (2017), pp. 62–63; Trąbiński (2018), pp. 70–74; D. Wall (2013), pp. 10–11.

[7]Act of 5 July 2018 on the National Cybersecurity System (consolidation text Polish Journal of Laws of 2020, item 1369, as amended, herein after "NCSA").

information by authorized persons whenever necessary. According to the guidelines included in the Recommendation of the OECD Council[8] concerning Guidelines for the Security of Information Systems C(92)188 of the 26th of October 1992, availability means that data is accessible and usable on a timely basis in the required manner. Under Article 4(d) of Regulation 460/2004, availability means that data is accessible and services are fully operational. According to the definition laid down in Recommendation C (92)188, integrity is understood as the characteristic of data and information being accurate and complete, and the preservation of accuracy and completeness. It refers to the integrity of both data and computer systems. As for information processed in an IT network, integrity means that the sent and received data are identical. This feature is defined in a similar way in Article 4(f) of Regulation (EC) No 460/2004 of the European Parliament and of the Council of the 10th of March 2004 establishing the European Network and Information Security Agency[9] (repealed, but the replacement regulations did not include the definition), as "the confirmation that data, which has been sent, received, or stored are complete and unchanged." It is worth mentioning that this is a theoretical scenario, which is impossible in practice. The vast majority of the currently existing ICT networks, including the Internet, are based on packet-switching technology (for more details, see further remarks in the discussion on the definition of information systems). This means that the data sent via such networks are divided into packets (millions of packets in the case of large data portions), which are then sent (often along various routes) and "compiled" together at the end point. It often happens that the some of the packets "get lost on the way" (it is easy to check, there are small differences between the sizes of the sent and the received file). Confidentiality means access to data only by authorized persons, excluding third parties. It involves the protection of data against the reading and copying of data by unauthorized individuals. The guidelines set out in recommendation C (92)188 define confidentiality as the characteristic of data and information being disclosed only to authorized persons, entities and processes at authorized times and in the authorized manner. In turn, under Article 4(g) of Regulation 460/2004, confidentiality is understood as the protection of communications or stored data against interception and reading by unauthorized persons.[10]

In addition to the ("core") attributes discussed above, one can currently speak of other properties of information. In line with the ISO 27001 standard (PL-EN IDO/IEC 27001, an international standard specifying the requirements for information-security management systems), information security is interpreted as the maintenance of the confidentiality, integrity, and availability of information. However, other components, such as authenticity, accountability, and reliability, may also be taken into consideration. Authenticity guarantees that the identity of a

[8]Recommendation of the Council concerning Guidelines for the Security of Information Systems of 26 November 1992, C(92)188/FINAL.

[9]OJ EU 2004 L 77/1.

[10]Radoniewicz (2016), pp. 143–144.

given entity or resource is as declared. Accountability means the assurance that the actions of such an entity can be assigned in a straightforward way only to this specific entity. Reliability is a property designating cohesive and intentional conduct and results.

These terms are defined in a similar way in the Regulation of the Council of Ministers of the 12th of April 2012 on the National Interoperability Framework, the minimum requirements for public records, the exchange of information in electronic form, and the minimum requirements for communication and information systems.[11]

- Authenticity: a property consisting of the fact that the origin or contents of data defining an object are as declared (§ 2(2))
- Availability: a property consisting of the fact that a given ICT-system resource can be used on demand, in a specified time, by an entity authorized to work in the communication and information system (§ 2 (4));
- Integrity: a property consisting of the fact that a given communication and information system resource has not been modified in an unauthorized manner (§ 2 (5));
- Confidentiality: a property consisting of the fact that information must not be provided or disclosed to unauthorized natural persons (§ 2 (14)).
- Accountability: a system property, which involves the attribution of a specified action to a natural person or process, and placing it within a specific time frame (§ 2 (18)).

The concept of "cybersecurity", as defined under Article 4(2) of the NCSA, was meant to constitute the equivalent of the expression "the security of network and information systems", as defined in NIS Directive[12] as the capacity of network and information systems to resist, at a given level of confidence, all actions, which compromise the availability, authenticity, integrity, or confidentiality of stored or transmitted or processed data, or the related services provided by, or accessible via, those network and information systems. It is clear that the two definitions differ in terms of defining elements. First, the term "information system" was used as the equivalent of "network and information system". Second, the legislator removed the phrase "at a given level of confidence", referring to "the ability to resist", with a view to 'relativising' the expression. It should be stressed that the phrase was present in the first draft of the Act, i.e. in the version referring to social consultations (prior to the work on the Bill in the Sejm, the lower house of the Polish Parliament, but was not included in the final version of the Bill,[13] due to the controversies, which had

[11]Regulation of the Council of Ministers of 12 April 2012 on the National Interoperability Framework, the minimum requirements for public records, the exchange of information in electronic form, and the minimum requirements for communication and information systems, Polish Journal of Laws of 2017, item 2247, as amended.

[12]OJ EU 12016 L 194/1.

[13]See: https://legislacja.rcl.gov.pl/projekt/12304650, accessed on 01/12/2020.

occurred during the consultations. First of all, the consultations indicated the need to define the phrase.[14] As shown above, the author of the Bill chose a simpler solution. Another difference is the narrowing down in the schedule of actions listed in the definition laid down in the Act by omitting the word “all” before “actions”, which stressed the broadest possible scope of such activities, at the same time replacing the conjunction “or” with “and” in the catalogue of such actions. Therefore, one is dealing with conjunctions here, not alternatives, which seems to imply that the actions referred to in the said provisions must be simultaneously directed against the confidentiality, integrity, availability, and authenticity of the processed data, or the related services provided by those network and information systems. The next difference also resulted in the narrowing down of the scope of the definition, as the services “accessible via” information systems were omitted, and only “provided” services were retained. The definition in the NIS Directive mentions stored or transmitted or processed data, whereas the Polish legislator limited the list to the concept of “processing”, which is a generic term in relation to storage and transmission.

To conclude the discussion on the differences between the definitions, it should be stressed that the definition in the NIS Directive was used in the National Framework of the Cybersecurity Policy of the Republic of Poland for 2017–2022 (Resolution of the Council of Ministers No. 52/2017 dated the 27th of April 2017 on the National Framework of Cybersecurity Policy of the Republic of Poland), as well as in the draft Cybersecurity Strategy.

3 The Notion of Cybercrime

To date, no legislator has decided to introduce the legal definition of a computer crime into the legal system. There have been attempts to define this term as part of penal-law studies. A comprehensive definition proposed by Ulrich Sieber during an OECD Expert Committee meeting in Paris in 1983, later included in the OECD report, according to which “computer crime is any illegal, unethical, or unauthorised behaviour involving the automatic data processing and/or transmission of data”[15] can be considered one of the first. A general definition of computer crime was developed several years later for Interpol. According to this definition, computer crime means “criminal activities in the scope of computer technologies”, which can be divided into the following groups.

(1) The breach of resource-access rights
(2) Fraud with the use of computers

[14]See, for example, Remarks expressed by the Business Centre Club, the Polish Chamber of Commerce for Electronics and Telecommunications, and the Polish Chamber of Digital Broadcasting—See https://legislacja.rcl.gov.pl/projekt/12304650, Accessed on 1 December 2020.

[15]Sieber (1998), pp. 20–21; cf. Czechowski and Sienkiewicz (1993), p. 52.

(3) The modification of computer resources
(4) The reproduction of software
(5) Hardware and software sabotage
(6) Offences committed with the use of BBS
(7) The storage of illegal resources
(8) Crime on the Internet.[16]

Along with technological advancements, the terms describing the phenomenon of computer crime are also evolving. The earliest ones are, of course, "computer crime", "computer-related crime", "crime by computer", and "digital crime", the last one having a broader scope than "computer crime." The development of the Internet in recent years has led to the creation of a strong, and practically inseparable, relationship between information and telecommunication technologies. For this reason, numerous suggestions for terms and definitions have been coined to describe the phenomenon of computer crime. These include "Internet crimes", "e-crimes", "net crimes", virtual crimes", and finally "cybercrimes", "IT crimes", and "data-processing crimes."[17]

Without doubt, the term, which has gained greatest popularity is "cybercrime", used both in the literature on the subject and in some international documents (in particular, in the Convention on Cybercrime).

During the Tenth United Nations Congress on the Prevention of Crime and the Treatment of Offenders,[18] held in Vienna in April 2000, it was found that cybercrime referred to any crime, which can be committed by means of a computer system or network, in a computer system or network, or against a computer system or network. At the same time, the following classification of cybercrime was proposed.

(1) In a narrow sense (computer crime), meaning any illegal behaviour directed by means of electronic operations, which targets the security of computer systems and the data processed by them, i.e.

    - unauthorized access
    - damage to computers, computer data, or computer programmes
    - computer sabotage
    - unauthorized interception, and
    - computer espionage

(2) Cybercrime in a broader sense ("computer-related crime"): any illegal behaviour committed by means of, or in relation to, a computer system or network, including such crimes as illegal possession, and offering or distributing information by means of a computer system or network.[19]

---

[16]Fischer (2000), pp. 27–28.

[17]Adamski (2000), pp. 32–33. Cf. Fischer (2000), pp. 23–31; Wójcik (1999), pp. 52–57; Clough (2013), p. 9.

[18]*The Tenth United Nation Congress on the Prevention of Crime and Treatment of Offenders.*

[19]Cf. Smarzewski (2014), p. 267; Shinder and Tittel (2004), pp. 35–36.

4 The Classification of Cybercrimes

First, it is necessary to point to the simplest possible dichotomous classification of computer crime, divided into "old" and "new" offences. This refers to the "novelty" of an offence as such (not as a computer crime). The first group includes conventional (common) offences, which had gained a new or modified form due to technological developments (e.g. fraud, harassment, dissemination of child pornography). "New" offences are those, which came with the development of computers and advancements in information technology, and its further convergence with telecommunications. Obtaining unauthorized access to, or unauthorized modification of, computer data can serve as a classic example here.[20]

Both in the literature on the subject and in the legislations of various countries, it is possible to find a similar "tripartite" division of cybercrime[21] into computer crimes, computer-facilitated crimes, and computer-supported crimes.[22]

The above classification was also adopted in the Convention on Cybercrime.[23] Offences amounting to illegal acts categorized in the first group was grouped together under the single title "Offences against the confidentiality, integrity, and availability of computer data and systems." Offences in the second group are to be found in the subsequent three Sections of the Convention, and they are referred to as "computer-related offences", "content-related offences", and "offences related to infringements of copyright and related rights."

The last group in the tripartite division does not fall within the ambit of substantive penal law, but rather procedural law, in particular the law of evidence. Therefore, they are usually not considered in discussions on computer crime.

The issue of defining and classifying computer crimes has been taken up in the Polish literature on the subject. Andrzej Adamski pointed out that under the penal

[20]Cf. Grabosky (2006), pp. 12–14.

[21]Clough (2013), p. 10. Cf. Dudka (1998), p. 105. For information on the classification of computer crimes, see also Chałubińska-Jentkiewicz (2019), pp. 251–261; Kosiński (2013), pp. 463–465; Siwicki (2012), pp. 241–252; Smarzewski (2014), pp. 264–267.

[22]At the Forensic Science Society Convention held in April 2001 in Huntingdon, a classification of computer crime was made based on the criteria of the techniques applied by offenders, and the nature of their acts. It is a detailed version of the tripartite division described above. The classification features six categories of computer crime (cybercrime): computer-assisted crime (in which the committing of such a crime is facilitated by using computers), computer-enabled crime (in which computers enable the committing of such a crime), computer-only crime (which cannot be committed without using computer technology), Internet-assisted crime (which can be committed both in a conventional (common) way and via the Internet), Internet-enabled crime (in which it is easier to commit a given crime with the use of the Internet), and Internet-only crime (crime possible only via the Internet), meaning those offences in which the data sets on servers or data packets sent between network nodes are used by the perpetrators in the course of their actions (Hołyst 2009, pp. 19–20).

[23]The Council of Europe Convention on Cybercrime of 23 November 2001, https://www.coe.int/en/web/conventions/full-list/-/conventions/treaty/185 accessed on 1 December 2020.

law, it is possible to differentiate between two meanings of the term "computer crime", from the substantive and procedural-law perspective,[24] and from the substantive-law perspective, in the latter of which two types of attacks can be identified.

(1) Attacks in which computer systems, applications, data, and information, are the subjects of crime, for example, hacking. The Polish legislator treats them (similarly to other penal-law legislations) as separate types of offence in which information is a generic object of protection. In the Polish Penal Code, such acts were addressed in Chapter XXXIII Offences Against Information Protection (offences in which computers, networks or computer data constitute the target of the perpetrator's actions), which corresponds to the first group of crimes, in which computers are the subject of illegal activities (the computer as a target).
(2) Attacks in which the targets include various legally protected rights, whereas a computer, computer network, data-processing systems and electronic devices serve as tools. They are used for committing both common offences, e.g. fraud, forgery, and unconventional crimes, such as money laundering (corresponding to the second group of offences included in the aforementioned tripartite division—"the computer as an instrument").

From the procedural perspective, computer crimes are offences in which computer systems can store evidence of criminal activities. Therefore, the group of computer crimes from the procedural perspective includes, in particular, any prohibited acts in which access to information processed in a computer system is required for prosecution purposes. This includes situations in which a computer system was an instrument used in an attack, and instances in which such a system was the target of the attack.[25]

In the Polish literature on the subject, some attention has been given to the issue of singling out Internet crime as a subcategory of computer crimes.

As B. Świątkiewicz noted, Internet crime cannot be treated as the equivalent of computer crime, since the Internet is a tool used for committing a wide range of offences, which are not necessarily reflected in the statutory criteria of a crime as laid down in the Penal Code.[26] First and foremost, it is certain that the term covers a narrower scope. Michał Sowa suggests that "Internet crime" can be defined as offences

> "for which the opportunities provided by the Internet" (web services) or services provided by people via the Internet allow the perpetrator to perform an intentional criminal act, or its individual stages, or at least facilitate the performance of such a criminal act.[27]

[24] Adamski (2000), p. 30.

[25] Adamski (2000), pp. 34–35.

[26] Świątkiewicz (2005), p. 111.

[27] Sowa (2001), p. 28.

Based on the above definition, it is possible to distinguish between Internet crime, in the strict sense of the term (types of prohibited acts, in which the main activities are conducted with the use of the Internet) and Internet crime in the broad sense (in which the committing of a given prohibited act is facilitated by the use of the Internet, including those offences in which the Internet is only a means to an end, or a tool to achieve the expected results outside the network).[28]

5 Challenges Related to the Emergence of Computer Crime

There are numerous characteristics of new technologies, which facilitate criminal activities, and, which at the same time hinder the prevention and prosecution of crime.

First of all, it is the sheer reach of the phenomenon. The Internet has provided communication opportunities on an unprecedented scale. It is estimated that approx. one and a half billion people have Internet access, which accounts for 24% of the world's population. It is an enormous number of potential perpetrators and victims.

The second feature is availability. The use of computers and the Internet has never been easier or cheaper. On the one hand, the prices of computer hardware and computer-network communications have fallen considerably, and, on the other hand, the use of technological advancements has become easier than in the past. The times when computers were enormous and expensive devices, requiring additional advanced knowledge to be operated are long gone. The Internet can currently be used on mobile phones. Computer programmes have a friendly graphical user interface, and the vast majority of users cannot imagine operating a computer in the so-called text mode (using command lines in MS Windows systems, or consoles in Unix/Linux systems).

Third is the ability to remain anonymous (often not as reliable as it might seem), which both Internet users and potential perpetrators of crimes committed via the Internet can enjoy. It creates an illusion of full confidentiality (or even secrecy) of all the activities performed by network users, and the related chance of avoiding potential penal liability.

Fourth is the possibility to collect a substantial quantity of information across a small space, from which the data can be easily retrieved, and in which it can be reproduced and disseminated without limitations.

The fifth feature is its global reach, which means that the offences committed by perpetrators in one country can have a negative effect in another country. This can create extremely complex situations. For instance, this is the case when a perpetrator based in country A carries out a DDoS attack (Distributed Denial of Service) against a server located in country B, using computers located in countries C and D, while residents of countries E and F can suffer the consequences of such activities.

---

[28]Sowa (2001), pp. 29–30.

The last, yet equally important, factor, indicated in the literature on the subject, which hinders counteracting computer crime, includes circumstances related to investigating crimes and conducting penal proceedings. The ephemeral nature of computer data is a source of problems related to collecting and securing evidence. There are also problems arising from the international reach of the network, and the private nature of many of them, which obstructs the access to, e.g., traffic data, which is stored on servers only for a specified period of time. The obvious consequence of the technical nature of computer crime is the fact that individuals dealing with the prosecution of perpetrators must have knowledge of state-of-the-art technology and the appropriate hardware.[29]

When discussing the issue of cybercrime definitions and classifications, it is worth mentioning those acts, which cannot be placed in the category of computer crime.

6 Cyberterrorism and Cyberwar

Susan W. Brenner makes a precise distinction between computer crime and the phenomena of cyberterrorism,[30] and cyberwarfare, treating them as notions separate from cybercrime. She assigns a very broad sense to the former term, making the assumption that it includes terrorist attacks which are planned, carried out, and coordinated, via computers and computer networks, while the latter is defined as actions taken by states using information technology with a view to achieving military or other strategic goals.[31]

The second most frequently cited definition of cyber-terrorism, provided by D. Denning, has a much narrower meaning. According to this author, cyber-terrorism is a combination of terrorism and cyberspace. In general, it is understood as unlawful attacks and threats of attacks against computers, networks, and information collected in networks to intimidate or coerce governments, or the residents, of a given state, to fulfil political or social objectives. Moreover, in order to be classified as cyberterrorism, a given attack should result in violence against people and property, or cause such a degree of harm that it could evoke fear. Attacks resulting in death or injuries, explosions, plane crashes, water pollution, or severe economic loss, might serve as examples here. Major attacks against critical infrastructures can be treated as cyber-terrorist attacks, depending on their outcomes. The category does not include attacks, which lead to the disruption of non-critical services, or mainly result in financial problems.[32]

[29]Clough (2013), pp. 5–8; Radoniewicz (2016), pp. 128–129.

[30]Unlike D.L. Shinder and E. Tittel, who classified cyberterrorism as cybercrimes involving the use of violence. See remarks above.

[31]Brenner (2010), p. 16.

[32]Verton (2004), p. 20.

7 Terrorism in EU Law

The first EU legal instrument aimed at counteracting terrorism was Council Framework Decision of the 13th of June 2002 2002/475/JHA on combating terrorism[33] (further referred to as "Framework Decision 2002/475"). The document was replaced by Directive (EU) 2017/541 of the European Parliament and of the Council of the 15th of March 2017 on combating terrorism and replacing Council Framework Decision 2002/475/JHA and amending Council Decision 2005/671/JHA, which is based on the Framework Decision, and substantially replicates its solutions (this refers to, e.g., the definition of a terrorist offence), at the same time clarifying some solutions and adding new ones.

Most of all, Directive 2017/541 established the minimum rules concerning the definition of criminal offences and sanctions in the field of terrorist offences,[34] offences related to a terrorist group, and offences related to terrorist activities, as well as measures for the protection of, support for, and assistance to, victims of terrorism. The definition of a terrorist offence laid down in Article 3 of Directive 2017/541 (similar to the one included in Framework Decision 2002/475) is composed of two elements, i.e. objective (*actus reus*) and subjective (*mens rea*) elements. For a prohibited act to be considered a terrorist offence, first of all, it must meet an objective criterion, i.e., it must be one of the acts listed in an exhaustive schedule included in Article 3(1)(a) to (i),[35] or the threat to commit any of the acts (Article 3(1)(j)). Second, a terrorist offence must meet at least one of the subjective premises listed in the second part of the definition, i.e. it must be committed with one of the aims listed in paragraph 2, including

---

[33]Council Framework Decision 2002/475/JHA of 13 June 2002 on combating terrorism, OJ EC 2002 L 164/3.

[34]Framework Decision 2002/475 and Directive 2017/541 refer to "terrorist offences", while the provisions of the Polish Penal Code of 6 June 1997 (consolidated text, Polish Journal of Laws of 2020, item 1444, as amended, hereinafter "PC") refer to "offences of a terrorist nature".

[35]The following acts were listed in Article 3(1): (a) attacks on a person's life which can cause death; (b) attacks on the physical integrity of a person; (c) kidnapping or hostage-taking; (d) causing extensive destruction to a government or public facility, a transport system, an infrastructure facility (including an information system), a fixed platform located on the continental shelf, a public place or private property, likely to endanger human life, or result in major economic loss; (e) seizing aircraft, ships, or other means of public or goods transport; (f) the manufacture, possession, acquisition, transporting, supply or use of explosives or weapons, including chemical, biological, and radiological or nuclear weapons, as well as research into, and development of, chemical, biological, radiological, or nuclear weapons; (g) releasing dangerous substances, or causing fires, floods or explosions, the effect of which is to endanger human life; (h) interfering with or disrupting the supply of water, power, or any other fundamental natural resource, the effect of which is to endanger human life; (i) illegal system interference, as referred to in Article 4 of Directive 2013/40/EU of the European Parliament and of the Council of 12 August 2013 on attacks against information systems and replacing Council Framework Decision 2005/222/JHA, in cases in which Article 9(3) or points (b) or (c) of Article 9(4) of that Directive apply, and illegal data interference, as referred to in Article 5 of that Directive in cases in which point (c) of Article 9(4) of that Directive applies (see further remarks).

(1) seriously intimidating a population
(2) unduly compelling a government or an international organisation to perform or abstain from performing any act
(3) seriously destabilising or destroying the fundamental political, constitutional, economic, or social structures of a country or an international organisation.[36]

Under Article 4 of Directive 2017/541, Member States are obliged to make sure that directing a terrorist group,[37] and participating in the activities of a terrorist group, are acts punishable as criminal offences. It was pointed out that the latter should also be understood as including supplying information or material resources, or by funding its activities in any way, in the knowledge of the fact that such participation will contribute to the criminal activities of the terrorist group.

Pursuant to the subsequent Articles of Directive 2017/541, Member States are obliged to criminalise "offences related to terrorist activities", involving certain activities, which are not terrorists acts per se, but might constitute the preparation to commit terrorist acts.[38]

Under Article 15(1) of Directive 2017/541, the offences referred to in the Directive should be punishable by effective, proportionate, and dissuasive, criminal penalties, which may entail surrender or extradition.

The terrorist offences referred to in Article 3 of Directive 2017/541, and in Article 14 of the said document (aiding and abetting, inciting and attempting offences laid down in the Directive),[39] should be punishable by custodial sentences heavier than

[36]The aforementioned Framework Decision 2002/475 was enacted into the Polish legal framework by way of the Act of the 16th of April 2004 on amending the Penal Code and certain other Acts (Journal of Laws of 2004, No. 93, item 889). For more details, see Chapter 23 of this monograph. See also Radoniewicz (2015), pp. 192–196.

[37]According to the definition laid down in Article 2(3) of Directive 2017/541, the terms should be understood as "a structured group of more than two persons, established for a period of time and acting in concert to commit terrorist offences." According to the definition included in the second part of the cited provision, "structured group" means a group which is not randomly formed for the immediate commission of an offence, and that does not need to have formally defined roles for its members, continuity of membership or a developed structure."

[38]They include the following offences: public provocation to commit a terrorist offence (Article 5); recruitment for terrorism (Article 6); providing training for terrorism (Article 7); receiving training for terrorism (Article 8); travelling for the purpose of terrorism (Article 9); organising or otherwise facilitating travelling for the purpose of terrorism (Article 10); terrorist financing (Article 11), and other offences related to terrorist activities, listed in Article 12: (a) aggravated theft with a view to committing one of the offences listed in Article 3; (b) extortion with a view to committing one of the offences listed in Article 3; (c) drawing up or using false administrative documents with a view to committing one of the offences listed in points (a) to (i) of Article 3(1), point (b) of Article 4, and Article 9.

[39]Aiding and abetting the offences referred to in Articles 3 to 8, 11 and 12 (and Article 14(1)), inciting the offences referred to in Articles 3 to 12 (and Article 14(2)), and attempting to commit the offences referred to in Articles 3, 6, 7, Article 9(1), point (a) of Article 9(2), and Articles 11 and 12, with the exception of possession as provided for in point (f) of Article 3(1), and the offences referred to in point (j) of Article 3(1) (and Article 14(3)), should be punishable by law.

those imposable under national law for such offences, which have no element of "terrorist intent" (Article 15(2).

The offences listed in Article 4 of Directive 2017/541 (offences relating to a terrorist group) should be punishable by custodial sentences, with a maximum sentence of not less than 15 years for the offence referred to in point (a) of Article 4 (directing a terrorist group), and a maximum sentence of not less than 8 years for the offences listed in point (b) of Article 4 (participating in the activities of a terrorist group) (Article 15(3)).

When a criminal offence referred to in Article 6 (recruitment for terrorism) or 7 (providing training for terrorism) is directed towards a child, this may, in accordance with national law, be taken into account when sentencing (Article 15(4) of Directive 2017/541).

8 Cyberterrorism: Terrorism in Cyberspace

The first binding European Union legal Act relating to attacks against security in cyberspace was Council Framework Decision 2005/222/JHA of the 24th of February 2005, on attacks against information systems[40] (Framework Decision 2005/222). Work on the draft began in 2001, as a result of the European Commission's announcement of the so-called Communication on Cybercrime,[41] containing certain proposals for substantive and procedural-law provisions, directed at combating computer crime, at both the national and Community levels. The outcome of those activities was, i.a., a proposal for the aforementioned framework decision.[42]

In citing Framework Decision 2005/222, it was indicated that its objective was to improve cooperation between the judicial authorities and law-enforcement services of Member States, through approximating the rules on criminal law in Member States in the field of attacks against information systems. The legislative activities at the EU level were substantiated by the need to counteract attacks against information systems, due to the possible relationship between this type of offence and organised crime, and terrorist attacks against information systems, which formed part of the critical infrastructure of the Member States.

First and foremost, under Framework Decision 2005/222, the most important terms were defined ("information system", "computer data", "legal person" and "without right"), and Member States were obliged to make sure that illegal access

---

[40]Council Framework Decision 2005/222/JHA of 24 February 2005, on attacks against information systems, OJ EU 2005 L 69/67.

[41]Communication from the Commission to the Council, the European Parliament, the Economic and Social Committee and the Committee of the Regions COM(2000)890 on Creating a Safer Information Society by Improving the Security of Information Infrastructures and Combating Computer-related Crime of 26 January 2001.

[42]Proposal for a Council Framework Decision on attacks against information systems, COM (2002) 0173.

to information systems, illegal system interference, and illegal data interference, were punishable as offences. The document also refers to the issues of the liability of legal persons, jurisdiction, and the use the network of operational points of contact available twenty four hours a day, seven days a week, for the purpose of exchanging information on attacks against information systems.

The limited number of offences referred to in Framework Decision 2005/222, the need to incorporate new threats, and the wish to adapt the existing legal regulations to new European Union initiatives in the field of cybersecurity, and to supplement them in order to regulate the matter comprehensively, led to a decision to commence work on a new legal instrument addressing the issue of cybercrime. The result was the enactment of Directive 2013/40/EU of the European Parliament and of the Council of the 12th of August 2013 on attacks against information systems and replacing Council Framework Decision 2005/222/JHA[43] (Directive 2013/40).

In citing the Directive, it was stressed that attacks against information systems, and, in particular, attacks linked to organised crime, and the potential for terrorist or politically motivated attacks against information systems, were a growing menace, and that they could pose a real threat to information systems forming part of critical infrastructures of Member States and the European Union.

The contents of Directive 2013/40 are largely based on the provisions of Framework Decision 2005/222/JHA, at the same time providing for certain new solutions (new types of prohibited acts: the illegal interception of computer data, and offences related to the use of "hacking tools", and the specification of additional aggravating circumstances to consider when sentencing offenders).

For the purpose of Directive 2013/40 (and previously for the purpose of Framework Decision 2005/222), an "information system" is defined as a device or group of inter-connected or related devices, one or more of which, pursuant to a programme, automatically processes computer data, as well as computer data stored, processed, retrieved or transmitted by that device or group of devices for the purposes of its or their operation, use, protection and maintenance (Article 2(a)).

The above definition can be characterised by a broad objective scope. Given the above, an information system should be understood as both a single data-processing device (e.g. a computer or a smart phone) and a computer network, including small networks (e.g. LAN[44]), covering several computers, and large-scale structures consisting of interconnected networks (e.g. MAN[45]).[46]

---

[43]Directive 2013/40/EU of the European Parliament and of the Council of 12 August 2013 on attacks against information systems and replacing Council Framework Decision 2005/222/JHA, OJ EU 2013 L 218/8.

[44]LAN—Local Area Network.

[45]MAN (Metropolitan Area Network)—covering numerous interconnected local area networks, networks of this type are developed by public institutions, universities (university networks) or private entities (enterprises).

[46]Due to the volume limits of this study, the issue will not be discussed in detail. For more details, see Radoniewicz (2016), pp. 244–249; Radoniewicz (2019a), pp. 42–47.

Under Article 2(b) of Directive 2013/40, the term "computer data" was defined as a representation of facts, information, or concepts in a form suitable for processing in an information system, including a program suitable for causing an information system to perform a function.

Under Article 2(d) of Directive 2013/40, "without right" means conduct referred to in this Directive, including access, interference, or interception, which is not authorized by the owner, or by another rights holder, of the system, or of part of it, or not permitted under national law.

Article 3 of the said Directive includes an obligation imposed on Member States to ensure that, when gained intentionally, access without right to the whole or to any part of an information system, is punishable as a criminal offence committed by infringing a security measure. Access to information systems is understood as the possibility of using their resources (i.e. using the data stored in the systems, and the use of hardware, which, in fact, results in access to data and software used for controlling such access).

Another offence defined in Directive 2013/40 is illegal system interference, which consists of seriously hindering or interrupting the functioning of an information system by inputting computer data, by transmitting, damaging, deleting, impairing, altering, or suppressing such data, or by rendering such data inaccessible, intentionally and without right (Article 4 of Directive 2013/40). This mostly includes activities involving logic operations directed against information systems, with a view to hindering or disrupting system functions by affecting the processing of the computer data of the software used for the purpose.

Under Article 5 of Directive 2013/40, Member States are obliged to criminalise logical attacks directed against computer data. The provision identifies illegal data interference as deleting, damaging, impairing, altering, or suppressing computer data in an information system, or rendering such data inaccessible. Such interference includes both deleting data and installing software on the compromised computer, facilitating further illegal activities (e.g. data theft), or carrying out a DDoS attack (Distributed Denial of Service) by using malware to connect a compromised computer to a botnet.

The first "new" prohibited act (in relation to Framework Decision 2005/222) was illegal interception, defined in Article 6 of Directive 2013/40 as intercepting, by technical means, non-public transmissions of computer data to, from, or within, an information system, including electromagnetic emissions from an information system carrying such computer data, intentionally and without right.

Another type of offence, which was not provided for in Framework Decision 2005/222, is referred to in Article 7 of Directive 2013/40. Under the said provision, Member States are required to criminalise the intentional production, sale, procurement, importing, possession, and distribution, or otherwise making available, of tools (colloquially referred to as "hacking tools") used, without right, to commit any of the offences referred to in Articles 3 to 6 of Directive 2013/40, in which such acts are performed with the intention to commit the said offences.

"Tools" means

(1) a computer programme, designed or adapted primarily for the purpose of committing any of the offences referred to in Articles 3 to 6
(2) a computer password, access code, or similar data, by which the whole or any part of an information system is capable of being accessed.

In line with Article 9(1) of Directive 2013/40, the offences referred to in the said Directive (including incitement, aiding and abetting, and attempting to commit offences under Articles 4 and 5—see Article 8(1) and (2)), should be punishable by effective, proportionate, and dissuasive, criminal penalties. At the same time, it is stipulated that the offences referred to in Articles 3 to 7 of Directive 2013/40 (which means that it does not apply to incitement, aiding and abetting, and attempting to commit offences) should be punishable by a maximum term of imprisonment of at least 2 years, at least for cases which do not involve a minor (Article 9(2)).

Furthermore, Article 9 of Directive 2013/40 provides for a number of aggravating circumstances. However, they only apply to offences listed in Articles 4 and 5 (i.-e. illegal system interference and illegal data interference). The first aggravating circumstance includes a situation in which a significant number of information systems have been affected through the use of a tool, referred to in Article 7 of Directive 2013/40, designed or adapted primarily for that purpose. In such an event, the perpetrator should be sentenced to a maximum term of imprisonment of at least 3 years (Article 9(3) of Directive 2013/40).

Under Article 9(4) of Directive 2013/40, aggravating circumstances, resulting in the possibility of the perpetrator's being sentenced for a maximum sentence of imprisonment of at least 5 years, include the commitment of offences within the framework of a criminal organisation, as defined in Framework Decision 2008/841/JHA of the 24th of October 2008 on the combating organised crime,[47] causing serious damage, and the committing of an offence against a critical-infrastructure information system.[48]

[47]Framework Decision 2008/841/JHA of 24 October 2008 on the fight against organised crime, OJ EU 2008 L 300/42. Pursuant to Article 1(1) of the said Decision, "criminal organisation" means a structured association, established over a period of time, of more than two persons acting in concert with a view to committing offences which are punishable by deprivation of liberty or a detention order of a maximum of at least four years, or a more serious penalty, to obtain, directly or indirectly, financial or other material benefit. "Structured Association" means an association which was not randomly formed for the immediate committing of an offence, nor does it need to have formally defined roles for its members, continuity of membership, or a developed structure (Article 1(2) of Framework Decision 2008/841). A solution similar to the one stipulated in Framework Decision 2005/222 was adopted in Directive 2013/40, under which the penalty provided in Framework Decision 2008/841 was not taken into consideration when establishing whether a given structured association can be considered a criminal organisation.

[48]Under Article 2(a) of Council Directive 2008/114/EC of 8 December 2008 on the identification and designation of European critical infrastructures, and the assessment of the need to improve their protection, OJ EU 2008 L 345/75, the term critical infrastructure means an asset, system, or part thereof, located in Member States, which is essential for the maintenance of vital societal functions, and the health, safety, security, economic, or social well-being of people, and the disruption or

The last aggravating circumstance affecting penal liability (Article 9(5)) is a situation in which the offences referred to in Articles 4 and 5 are committed by misusing the personal data of another person (identity theft).[49]

The Directive was criticised for the failure to provide severe sanctions, especially in relation to acts, which can be classified as terrorist attacks against IT systems. This reservation can currently be considered outdated. Discussing the issue of making more stringent the penal liability of a perpetrator accused of an offence of a terrorist nature, one should take into account the legal regulations laid down in Directive 2017/541. Pursuant to point (i) of Article 3(1), in conjunction with Article 3(2) of the said Directive (see remarks above), illegal system interference as referred to in Article 4 of the Directive in cases in which Article 9(3) or points (b) or (c) of Article 9(4) of that Directive applies, and illegal data interference as referred to in Article 5 of that Directive, in cases in which point (c) of Article 9(4) of that Directive applies, constitute a terrorist offence. This means that terrorist offences should include acts involving illegal system interference committed with one of the aims listed in Article 3(2) of Directive 2017/541, with the use of one of the tools referred to in Article 7 of Directive 2013/40, designed or adapted primarily for that purpose, in which a significant number of information systems have been intentionally affected, or in which substantial damage has been inflicted. In addition, an unlawful act under Article 5 should be considered a terrorist offence if it has been directed against a critical-infrastructure information system.[50]

References

Adamski A (2000) Prawo karne komputerowe, Warsaw

Aleksandrowicz TR, Liedel K (2014) Społeczeństwo informacyjne – sieć, cyberprzestrzeń. Nowe zagrożenia. In: Aleksandrowicz TR, Liedel K, Piasecka P (eds) Sieciocentryczne bezpieczeństwo. Wojna, pokój i terroryzm w epoce informacji, Warsaw

Banasiński C (2018) Podstawowe pojęcia i podstawy prawne bezpieczeństwa w cyberprzestrzeni. In: Banasiński C (ed) Cyberbezpieczeństwo. Zarys wykładu, Warsaw

Brenner SW (2010) Criminal threats from cyberspace crime, media, and popular culture. Preager

Chałubińska-Jentkiewicz K (2019) Cyberodpowiedzialność. Toruń

Clough J (2013) Principles of cybercrime. Cambridge University Press, New York

Czechowski R Sienkiewicz P (1993) Przestępcze oblicza komputerów, Warsaw

Dudka K (1998) Kontrola korespondencji i podsłuch w polskim procesie karnym, Lublin

Fischer B (2000) Przestępstwa komputerowe i ochrona informacji, Kraków

Grabosky P (2006) Electronic crime. Pearson Prentice Hall, Upper Saddle River

Hołyst B (2009) Internet jako miejsce popełnienia przestępstwa, Prokuratura i Prawo, 4

destruction of which would have a significant impact in a Member State as a result of the failure to maintain those functions.

[49]See more Radoniewicz (2018), pp. 111–121.

[50]Cf. Radoniewicz (2016), pp. 267–268. For more details about combating cyberterrorism in UE, see Radoniewicz (2019b), pp. 193–205.

Kosiński J (2013) Cyberprzestępczość. In: Jasiński W, Mądrzejowski W, Wiciak K (eds) Przestępczość zorganizowana. Fenomen. Współczesne zagrożenia. Zwalczanie. Ujęcie praktyczne, Szczytno
Liderman K (2012) Bezpieczeństwo informacyjne, Warsaw
Liderman K (2017) Bezpieczeństwo informacyjne, Warsaw
Radoniewicz F (2015) Techniki implementacji do polskiego porządku prawnego postanowień decyzji ramowych Rady Unii Europejskiej dotyczących prawa karnego materialnego, Przegląd Prawa Konstytucyjnego 3
Radoniewicz F (2016) Odpowiedzialność karna za hacking i inne przestępstwa przeciwko danym komputerowym i systemom informatycznym, Warsaw
Radoniewicz F (2018) Identity theft in the polish criminal code. In: red. Brzostek A, Nowikowska M, Taczkowska-Olszewska J (eds) Reform of protection of personal data system - purpose, tools. Poznań
Radoniewicz F (2019a) In: Kitler W, Taczkowska-Olszewska J, Radoniewicz F (eds) Ustawa o krajowym systemie cyberbezpieczeństwa. Komentarz, Warsaw
Radoniewicz F (2019b) Zwalczanie cybeterroryzmu w prawie UE – aspekty karnomaterialne. Cybersecurity and Law 2
Shinder DL Tittel E (2004) Cyberprzestępczość. Jak walczyć z łamaniem prawa w sieci [Original title: "Scene of the Cybercrime. Computer Forensics Handbook"], Polish Version: Gliwice
Sieber U (1998) Legal aspects of computer-related crime in the information society – Comcrime-study, Würzburg
Siwicki M (2012) Definicje i podział cyberprzestępstw. Prokuratura i Prawo 7–8
Smarzewski M (2014) Cyberprzestępczość a zmiany w polskim prawie. In: Sepioło-Jankowska I (ed) Reforma prawa karnego. Księga po Zjeździe Młodych Karnistów, Warsaw
Sowa M (2001) Ogólna charakterystyka przestępczości internetowej, Palestra 5–6
Świątkiewicz B (2005) Przestępstwa internetowe w praktyce policyjnej, Studia Prawnicze 4
Trąbiński P (2018) Podział kompetencji w zapewnianiu cyberbezpieczeństwa. In: Szpor G, Gryszczyńska A (eds) Internet. Strategie bezpieczeństwa. Warsaw
Verton D (2004) Black Ice. Niewidzialna groźba cyberterroryzmu [Original title: Black Ice: The Invisible Threat of Cyber-Terrorism], Polish edition: Gliwice
Wall D (2013) Cybercrime. The Transformation of Crime in the Information Age, Malden
Wójcik JW (1999) Przestępstwa komputerowe. Część I. Fenomen cywilizacji, Warsaw

Filip Radoniewicz PhD; legal advisor; adjunct in the Department of Cybersecurity Law and New Technologies at the Institute of Law, War Studies University, Warsaw; expert at the Academic Centre for Cybersecurity Policy, (War Studies University) and in the Ministry of Justice; he worked as an assistant judge (in the Fourth Criminal and Sixth Penitentiary Department of the Regional Court in Lublin); graduate of post-graduate studies: "European Union Law" at the Jagiellonian University, "Human Rights and Freedoms", co-organized by the Institute of Legal Sciences of the Polish Academy of Sciences and the Helsinki Foundation for Human Rights, and "Computer Network Administration" at the Lublin University of Technology; author or co-author of approximately fifty publications, mainly in the field of broadly understood criminal law, new technology law and human rights. Selected publications: F. Radoniewicz (2016) Odpowiedzialność karna za hacking i inne przestępstwa przeciwko danym komputerowym i systemom informatycznym/Criminal liability for hacking and other offences against computer data and information systems/, Wolters Kluwer, Warszawa; Ustawa o krajowym systemie cyberbezpieczeństwa. Komentarz /Act on the National Cybersecurity System. Commentary/ (2019) ed. W. Kitler, J. Taczkowska-Olszewska, F. Radoniewicz, CH. Beck, Warszawa.

International Regulations of Cybersecurity

Filip Radoniewicz

Abstract There is no doubt that, due to the global nature of modern ICT networks, international cooperation plays a key role in ensuring cybersecurity, including in the fight against cybercrime.

This chapter describes initiatives taken within international organizations to ensure cybersecurity and the prevention of cybercrime. The presentation will start with the initiatives of the OECD and the Council of Europe. This is due not only to some kind of "Eurocentrism" but above all to the fact that these two organisations were the first to address cybersecurity and cybercrime issues. In addition, the Council of Europe Convention 185 on CyberCrime of November the 23rd, 2001, an international agreement concluded in the Council of Europe, is a milestone in the prevention of computer crime, remaining the only binding act of international law to combat it. Its importance is best demonstrated by the constantly growing number of signatories (and countries that model without signatures after the provisions, e.g. Pakistan) and the fact that international organisations, or recommend that their members accept (UN, G7/G8, European Union) or "copy" provisions, creating their own model legal acts (e.g. Commonwealth).

1 General Remarks

Given the global character of modern tele-information systems, international cooperation undoubtedly plays an instrumental role in ensuring cybersecurity and combating cybercrime. Therefore, efforts to establish legal frameworks of the interstate cooperation aimed at ensuring computer data and information system security have been made on the international arena since tele-information became supranational. It should be stressed that, for any cybersecurity-oriented measures to be effective,

F. Radoniewicz (✉)
Akademickie Centrum Polityki Cyberbezpieczeństwa/Academic Center for Cybersecurity Policy, Akademia Sztuki Wojennej w Warszawie/War Studies University in Warsaw, Warsaw, Poland
e-mail: filip.radoniewicz@radoniewicz.eu

K. Chałubińska-Jentkiewicz et al. (eds.), *Cybersecurity in Poland*,
https://doi.org/10.1007/978-3-030-78551-2_5

international cooperation must be pursued not only at the national level, but it must also involve private entities, representatives of the IT industry, and including in particular Internet service providers.

Initiatives launched by international organisations to ensure cybersecurity and to combat cybercrime are outlined below, starting with those devised by OECD and the Council of Europe. This line of presentation was motivated not only by the Euro-centric approach, but also by the fact that these two organizations had been the first to deal with cybersecurity and cybercrime issues. Furthermore, Convention on Cybercrime No. 185 of the Council of Europe of the 23rd of November 2001,[1] being an international treaty drawn up within the Council of Europe, was a milestone in the field of combating computer crime. It has also served a binding international legal act adopted with this objective in mind. Its importance is best reflected in the still growing number of signatories (as well as non-signatories, which otherwise commit to follow its provisions, e.g. Pakistan) and in the fact that international organizations either recommend their members to adopt the Convention (the UN, G7/G8, the European Union) or "map" its content when drawing up their own governing agreements (e.g. The Commonwealth of Nations).[2]

2 Organisation for Economic-Cooperation and Development

Recommendation C (92)188[3] was the first document on cybercrime within the Organisation for Economic-Cooperation and Development (French: *Organisation de coopération et de développement economiques*, abbreviated as OECD), adopted on the 26th of November 1992 by the OECD Council. In 2000, following its revision, it was deemed indispensable to draw up entirely new guidelines.[4] Work that was launched to this end took on momentum after 9/11, and eventually resulted in the formulation of the Recommendation of the Council Concerning Guidelines for the Security of Information Systems and Networks—Towards a Culture of Security,[5] which replaced Recommendation C(92)188. For nearly 13 years, it was the landmark OECD legal act dealing with widely understood computer network security. It drew attention to the increasing role of, and the fact that national economies, international trade, as well as social, cultural and political life are becoming

[1]https://www.coe.int/en/web/conventions/full-list/-/conventions/treaty/185, Accessed on 1 September 2020.

[2]Cf. Chałubińska-Jentkiewicz (2019), pp. 261–262.

[3]Recommendation of the Council concerning Guidelines for the Security of Information Systems of 26 November 1992 (C(92)188/FINAL).

[4]Gercke (2011), Accessed on 1 September 2020.

[5]Recommendation of the Council Concerning Guidelines for the Security of Information Systems and Networks—Towards a Culture of Security of 25 July 2002, (C (2002) 131).

increasingly dependent on information systems and networks, which should prompt efforts to protect and foster confidence in such systems and networks. At the same time, as was also stressed in the Recommendation, information systems and networks, as well as data stored on, or transmitted over, such systems and networks, are subject to new and increasing threats (various types of unauthorized access, use or alteration, malicious code transmissions, and mass denial-of-service attacks affecting a significant number of computers and paralyzing tele-information systems). In consequence, governments of Member States were advised, in particular, to develop new or revise existing policies, practices, measures and procedures based on the Guidelines attached to Recommendation C(2002)131, and at the same time to promote a culture of security as set out in these Guidelines among all concerned parties (which are understood as including all entities which develop, own and use information systems and networks, and which provide related services, i.e. governments, enterprises, other organizations and individual users). Given the technological progress, work to revise the Guidelines commenced in 2012 and resulted in adopting, on the 17th of September 2015, the Recommendation of the Council on Digital Security Risk Management for Economic and Social Prosperity (C(2015)115).[6] It was stressed in the Recommendation that the global interconnectedness has created considerable opportunities, but the risks emerging throughout its development are becoming more common and refined, and may affect the functioning of both the public and private sectors. The problem should, therefore, be now approached from a bigger perspective, one that is not limited to technological aspects. For this reason, the terms "cybersecurity" and "cyberspace" were abandoned in the Recommendation, and broader terms, "digital security risk" and "digital environment", were used instead. The Recommendation clearly stated that governments and private enterprises should share responsibility for combating digital security risks. It laid down the principles of digital security risk management to be followed by all concerned parties (governments, public and private organizations, as well as natural persons whose social or economic activities are pursued, whether in whole or in part, in the digital environment), along with guidelines for national strategies to ensure digital security, the implementation of which should be advocated by governments. These strategies are expected to present a clear and 'whole-of-government' approach, which should be flexible, technology-neutral and coherent with other strategies fostering economic and social prosperity. It should also cover best practices for the public sector, large, medium-sized and small enterprises, and individual citizens.[7]

Among other OECD guidelines related to widely understood information technologies, the following are worth noting:

---

[6]Recommendation of the Council on Digital Security Risk Management for Economic and Social Prosperity of 17 September 2015 (C(2015)115).

[7]See more in Radoniewicz (2016), pp. 152–156.

1. Recommendation of the Council concerning Guidelines Governing the Protection of Privacy and Transborder Flows of Personal Data of the 23rd of September 1980 (C(80)58)[8] (still in force but revised in 2013), which was the first set of principles established at the international level, which countries should be guided by when developing regulations on the protection of privacy in connection with cross-border flows of personal data;
2. Recommendation of the Council on Cross-border Co-operation in the Enforcement of Laws Protecting Privacy of the 12th of December 2007 (C(2007)67)[9] (revised in 2013), including proposals of measures to be taken with a view to streamlining international co-operation in the field of privacy protection in connection with cross-border flows of personal data;
3. Recommendation of the Council on Cross-Border Co-operation in the Enforcement of Laws against Spam of the 13th of April 2006;[10]
4. Recommendation of the Council on Protection of Critical Information Infrastructures of the 30th of April 2008 (C(2008)35)[11] containing guidelines for countries on ensuring the protection of critical information infrastructures (CIIs) at the national and international level.[12]

To sum up OECD's activities in the field of regulations on new technologies, it should be stressed that, although the Organization was first to implement measures aimed at combating cybercrime, its major interest is now limited to cybersecurity.[13]

3 Council of Europe

A discussion on the Council of Europe activities in the field of cybersecurity and combating cybercrime should start with Recommendation No. R(89)9 on Computer-Related Crime, adopted by the Committee of Ministers of the Council of Europe on the 13th of September 1989.[14] The document required Member States to take into account, in the course of legislative work on regulations directed at eliminating computer crime, the proposed solutions included in the report attached to it.[15]

---

[8]Recommendation of the Council concerning Guidelines Governing the Protection of Privacy and Transborder Flows of Personal Data of 23 September 1980 (C(80)58(final).

[9]Recommendation of the Council on Cross-border Co-operation in the Enforcement of Laws Protecting Privacy of 12 December 2007 (C (2007) 67 (final).

[10]Recommendation of the Council on Cross-Border Co-operation in the Enforcement of Laws against Spam of 13 April 2006 (C(2006) 57).

[11]Recommendation of the Council on Protection of Critical Information Infrastructures of 30 April 2008 (C(2008)35).

[12]See more Radoniewicz (2019).

[13]S. Schjølberg, *The History of Global Harmonization on Cybercrime Legislation – The Road to Geneva*, http://www.cybercrimelaw.net, accessed on 10 October 2020, p. 17.

[14]Recommendation No. R(89)9 on Computer-Related Crime.

[15]See more in Radoniewicz (2016), pp. 158–160.

The aforementioned Convention on Cybercrime was the first, and only, international treaty on crimes committed via the Internet and other computer networks.

Work on the Convention, which took over 4 years to complete, was carried out with the participation of not only representatives of most Member States of the Council of Europe (including Poland) but also by U.S., Japanese and Canadian delegates (as observers), representatives of European institutions, and independent experts. Its main objective was to develop a legal framework to facilitate international crime prosecution. It proposed a range of solutions, which were innovative (at least at that time, given that the Convention was drawn up at the end of the previous century). Compared to some earlier documents adopted at the international level, it featured an extended list of criminal offences (including illegal access, illegal interception, system interference, acts involving hacking tools, computer-related forgery, computer-related fraud, offences related to child pornography,[16] and offences related to infringements of copyright and related rights). Furthermore, it contained provisions on recognizing criminal liability depending on the stage of commitment, as well as aiding and abetting, and provisions on corporate liability (including also the liability of organizations without a legal personality). Several procedural solutions were also envisaged, including the preservation of data, search and seizure of stored computer data, real-time collection of traffic data, and the like.[17]

The obvious advantages of the Convention on Cybercrime include its open character, with countries not belonging to the Council of Europe being allowed to accede, and the fact that it contains optional clauses. The latter enable the Convention to be adopted with the exclusion of certain provisions, as a result of which on implementing the Convention the signatory countries, within their national laws, can reconcile the solutions it envisages with their own legal culture and tradition, and with the regulations already in force within their respective jurisdictions.[18] Considering the above, by the first of January 2021, the Convention on Cybercrime had been signed by almost all Council of Europe Member States (more specifically, by 46 countries, with Russia being the only exception), and 44 of these had ratified it. Furthermore, the Convention was signed by 4 countries from outside Europe (Canada, Japan, the United States, and the Republic of South Africa, and the first three have already ratified it). Other 18 states (i.a., Australia, the Dominican Republic, Israel, Panama) acceded to it. It is also worth noting that several countries, including Egypt and Pakistan, while not signing the Convention on Cybercrime, used its provisions as a basis when developing their own domestic regulations.

---

[16]The Convention on Cybercrime only refers to one group in this category—offences related to child pornography. Initially, it was meant to additionally include offences driven by racism or xenophobia. Eventually, these were included in a separate Additional Protocol to the Convention on Cybercrime regarding the criminalisation of acts of a racist and xenophobic nature committed through computer systems of 28 January 2003. See further comments.

[17]Cf. Adamski (2001), pp. 9–11; Radoniewicz (2016), pp. 162–164; Tarnogórski (2009), pp. 207–210.

[18]Cf. Adamski (2001), pp. 9–17.

The Convention on Cybercrime entered into force on 1 July 2004 after it had already been ratified by five signatory countries. Although Poland was one of the first countries to sign the Convention (on 23 November 2001), it did not ratify its provisions until the 29th of January 2015. To date, two amendments have been made to the Criminal Code with a view to adjusting its content to the provisions of the Convention.[19]

The aforementioned Additional Protocol of 28 January 2003 to the Convention on Cybercrime[20] regarding the penalisation of offences motivated by racism or xenophobia, committed using computer systems (hereinafter the Protocol),[21] is the only binding international law act developed within the Council of Europe which deals with the issues of crimes motivated by racism or xenophobia.

The fact that the provisions on crimes motivated by racism and xenophobia were included in a separate protocol, and not in the Convention on Cybercrime, resulted from the dissenting views expressed by delegates of the countries involved in its creation. Differences in the constitutional standards of free speech in individual countries substantially hindered a common standpoint. As a result, in order not to delay work on the Convention, it was decided that the provisions regarding such matters be included in a separate act.[22]

1. Distributing, or otherwise making available, racist and xenophobic material to the public through a computer system (Article 3);
2. Threatening (persons or groups of persons) with the commission, through a computer system, of a serious criminal offence as defined under its domestic law, motivated by racism or xenophobia (Article 4);
3. Insulting publicly, through a computer system, persons or groups of persons, based on racist or xenophobic motives (Article 5);
4. Distributing or otherwise making available, through a computer system to the public, material which denies, grossly minimises, approves or justifies acts constituting genocide or crimes against humanity, as defined by international law and recognised as such by final and binding decisions of the International Military Court, established by the London Agreement of 8 August 1945, or of any other international court established by relevant international instruments and whose jurisdiction is recognised by that party (e.g. the International Criminal Tribunals for the former Yugoslavia or Rwanda, or the International Criminal Court in Hague)—Article 6.

[19]Act of 18 March 2004 on amending the Criminal Code, the Code of Criminal Proceedings and the Code of Offences, Polish Journal of Laws No. 69, item 626 and the Act of 24 October 2008 on amending the Criminal Code and certain other acts, Polish Journal of Laws No. 214, item 1344.

[20]Convention on Cybercrime of the Council of Europe of 23 November 2001 (https://www.coe.int/en/web/conventions/full-list/-/conventions/treaty/185 Accessed on 1 September 2020).

[21]Protocol of 28 January 2003 to the Convention on Cybercrime https://rm.coe.int/168008160f, accessed 1.12.2020.

[22]Adamski (2001), p. 49.

The Protocol entered into force on 1 March 2006. In accordance with its Article 9 (1), it is open for signature by the states which have signed the Convention, which implies that it is also open to countries which are not members of the Council of Europe, both from Europe and outside of it. Such countries can accede to the Convention on Cybercrime provided that they participated in work on its development (as did the United States, Canada and Japan), or once they are invited to the Committee of Ministers or have obtained the consent from all the signatories.

Among other documents adopted by the Council of Europe, the subject-matter in question was also indirectly discussed in the following:

1. Convention No. 108 for the Protection of Individuals with regard to Automatic Processing of Personal Data, done at Strasbourg on 28 January 1981;[23]
2. Convention No. 201 on the Protection of Children against Sexual Exploitation and Sexual Abuse, on 25 October 2007;[24]
3. Recommendation CM/R(99) 5 on the protection of privacy on the Internet of the 23rd of February 1999;[25]
4. Recommendation CM/R(2009)1 electronic democracy (e-democracy) of the 18th of February 2009;[26]
5. Recommendation CM/Rec(2018)2 of the Committee of Ministers to Member States on the roles and responsibilities of internet intermediaries.

4 Organisation for Security and co-Operation in Europe

Security of the data processed in computer systems has not formed the area of interest of the Organisation for Security and Co-operation in Europe (OSCE). However, this does not mean that cybersecurity issues are entirely neglected is OSCE activities. Examples testifying to the contrary include four decisions by the Committee of Ministers: two on combating the use of the Internet for terrorist purposes,[27] in which it was indicated that the use of the Internet by terrorist groups for such purposes as member recruitment, collection and transfer of funds, organisation of terrorist acts or propaganda, must be prevented. However, this must be

[23]Convention No. 108 for the Protection of Individuals with regard to Automatic Processing of Personal Data, done at Strasbourg on 28 January 1981 (https://www.coe.int/en/web/data-protection/convention108-and-protocol, accessed on 1.12.2020).

[24]Convention No. 201 on the Protection of Children against Sexual Exploitation and Sexual Abuse, done at Lanzarote on 25 October 2007 (https://rm.coe.int/1680084822 accessed on 1.12.2020).

[25]Recommendation CM/R(99)5 on the protection of privacy on the Internet of 23 February 1999 Recommendation Rec (99)5 on the Protection of Privacy on the Internet.

[26]Recommendation CM/R(2009)1 electronic democracy (e-democracy) of 18 February 2009 Recommendation CM/Rec(2009)1 on Electronic Democracy (e-Democracy).

[27]Ministerial Council Decision of 7 December 2004 No. 3/04 on combating the use of the Internet for terrorist purposes and Ministerial Council Decision of 7 December 2006 No. 7/06 on combating the use of the Internet for terrorist purposes.

done in observance of human rights, and in particular the right to privacy and the freedom of expression of opinions and views. This objective is to be facilitated by information exchange between the concerned parties and by establishing strategies for effectively combating this phenomenon. The other two decisions concern enhancing OSCE efforts to reduce the risks of conflict stemming from the use of information and communication technologies.[28]

5 United Nations

First and foremost, it is worth noting that the United Nations initially attached importance mainly to preventing computer crime by referring to theoretical considerations and empirical studies conducted by criminologists in this field. In recent years, this approach has been changing gradually, as reflected in the so-called Salvador Declaration (see further comments).

Special attention to cybersecurity issues on the UN forum was paid for the first time at the Eighth United Nations Congress on the Prevention of Crime and the Treatment of Offenders, held from 27 August to 7 September 1990 in Havana (such congresses regarding the prevention of crime are organised by the UN every 5 years, recently—i.e. since the Congress in Bangkok in 2005—as Congresses on Crime Prevention and Criminal Justice), and at the Symposium on the Prevention and Prosecution of Computer Crime, organised by the Foundation for Responsible Computing, which was an event accompanying the Congress. The discussions held at the Congress led to the General Assembly of the United Nations adopting, on the 14th of December 1990 at the initiative of Canadian representatives, Resolution 45/121 on Combating the Criminal misuse of Information Technologies.[29]

As proposed by Hubbard and S. Schjølberg,[30] the subsequent resolutions adopted by the General Assembly of the United Nations can be divided into the following groups:

1. Resolutions 53/70 of 3 December 1998, 54/49 of 1 December 1999, 55/28 of the 20th of November 2000, 56/19 of the 29th of November 2001, 57/53 of the 22nd of November 2002, 58/32 of the 18th of December 2003, 59/61 of the 3rd of December 2004, 60/45 of the 8th of December 2005, 61/54 of the 6th of December 2006, 62/17 of the 5th of December 2007, 63/37 of the 2nd of

[28]Decision No. 5/16 of 9 December 2016 on enhancing OSCE efforts to reduce the risks of conflict stemming from the use of information and communication technologies and Decision No. 5/17 of 8 December 2016 on enhancing OSCE efforts to reduce the risks of conflict stemming from the use of information and communication technologies.

[29]Cf. Adamski (2000), pp. 9–10; Sieber (1998), pp. 162–163.

[30]A.M. Hubbard, S. Schjølberg, *Harmonizing national legal approaches on cybercrime*, http://www.itu.int/osg/spu/cybersecurity//docs/Background_Paper_Harmonizing_National_and_Legal_Approaches_on_Cybercrime.pdf, p. 6; accessed on 10.10.2020.

December 2008, 64/25 of the 2nd of December 2009, 65/41 of the 8th of December 2010, 66/24 of the 2nd of December 2011, 67/27 of the 3rd of December 2012, 68/243 of the 27th of December 2013, 69/28 of the 2nd of December 2014, 70/237 of the 23rd of December 2015, 71/28 of the 5th of December 2016, 73/27 of the 5th of December 2018, of 73/266 of the 22nd of December 2018, 74/28 of the 12th of December 2019, and 74/29 of the 12th of December 2019—all referred to as *Developments in the Field of Information and Telecommunications in the Context of International Security*, which contain rather general provisions, indicating the threats which may be posed by advancing IT, and recommending that countries adopt the guidelines periodically formulated in the information security reports drawn up by the Group of Government Experts on Information Security;
2. Resolutions 55/63 of the 4th of December 2000 and 56/121 of the 19th of December 2001 (both referred to as *Combating the Criminal Misuse of Information Technology*), in which more specific measures were indicated which should be taken at the international level, and implemented in national legal systems, with the aim of effectively preventing cybercrime. According to their authors, it was seen as indispensable to establish such legal regulations that would guarantee the protection of all aspects of computer data and system security (i.e. confidentiality, integrity and accessibility) from unauthorised impairment, and to ensure that criminal abuse is penalized in all countries. The need to take measures facilitating the cooperation between law enforcement authorities in the prosecution and penalization of perpetrators of computer misuse acts was also highlighted.
3. Resolutions 57/239 of the 20th of December 2002 (*Creation of a global culture of cybersecurity*), 58/199 of the 23rd of December 2003 (*Creation of a global culture of cybersecurity and the protection of critical information infrastructures*) and 64/211 of the 21st of December 2009 (*Creation of a global culture of cybersecurity and taking stock of national efforts to protect critical information infrastructures*), which all focused on the need to guarantee an increased security of computer systems and data processed in such systems. Resolution 57/239 focused mainly on the consequences of the interdependence between computer infrastructure and other sectors of the global infrastructures critical for public administration, while Resolution 64/211 encouraged Member States and international organizations, when developing strategies related to cybersecurity and the protection of critical infrastructures, to share their experience with other countries. In addition, the annex to the resolution featured guidelines intended to facilitate the creation of an effective system to ensure cybersecurity.[31]

At the aforementioned Eighth United Nations Congress, taking place in Havana in 1990, Resolution 45/121 on Combating the Criminal Misuse of Information Technologies was developed, together with the United Nations Manual on the

[31]Radoniewicz (2016), pp. 196–200.

Prevention and Control of Computer-Related Crime, which was published in 1994. In the declaration issued at the Tenth United Nations Congress on the Prevention of Crime and Treatment of Offenders in Vienna,[32] which was annexed to Resolution 55/59 of the General Assembly of 4 December 2000, computer crime was referred to in a very general manner (in Point 18 which dealt, *inter alia*, with the planned policy for issuing guidelines on the prevention of this phenomenon). In the declaration entitled *Synergies and Responses: Strategic Alliances in Crime Prevention and Criminal Justice*, annexed to Resolution 60/177 of the General Assembly of 16 December 2005 "Follow-up to the Eleventh United Nations Congress on Crime Prevention and Criminal Justice",[33] ending the Eleventh Congress in Bangkok, attention was again paid to the significance of criminal law harmonisation, as a factor indispensable for the efficient fight with cybersecurity, and the instrumental roles of both by the UN and other international organisations were highlighted. In the so-called *Salvador Declaration on Comprehensive Strategies for Global Challenges: Crime Prevention and Criminal Justice Systems and Their Development in a Changing World*, adopted at the Twelfth United Nations Congress in Salvador (12–19 April 2010), as the document concluding the event (annexed to Resolution 65/230 of the General Assembly of 21 December 2010), a recommendation was made for the UN Commission on Crime Prevention and Criminal Justice (CCPCJ), in cooperation with Member States, representatives of international communities and private sector entities, to develop draft versions of new solutions, both at the national and international levels, in response to the threat posed by cybercrime. At the Thirteenth United Nations Congress, which took place on 11–19 April 2015 in Doha (Al-Dauha), Qatar, attention was focused on the issue of integrating crime prevention and criminal justice into the wider United Nations agenda to address social and economic challenges, and to promote the rule of law both at the national and international levels, also by involving society at large. As regards cybersecurity issues, the Congress participants once again stressed the need to take specific measures to establish a secure cyberspace. As regards preventing and combating Internet crime, emphasis was placed on such issues as identity theft, botnets, online recruitment for terrorist and human trafficking purposes, and the need to protect children. Furthermore, the significance of enhancing international cooperation as a condition precedent to ensuring cyberspace security was also stressed. The Doha Declaration on Integrating Crime Prevention and Criminal Justice into the Wider United Nations Agenda to Address Social and Economic Challenges and to Promote the Rule of Law at the National and International Levels, and Public Participation,[34]

[32]The Vienna Declaration on Crime and Justice: Meeting the Challenges of the Twenty-first century); http://daccess-dds-ny.un.org/doc/UNDOC/GEN/N00/562/93/PDF/N0056293.pdf?OpenElement, accessed on 1 December 2020).

[33]Follow-up to the Eleventh United Nations Congress on Crime Prevention and Criminal Justice; http://daccess-dds-ny.un.org/doc/UNDOC/GEN/N05/498/22/PDF/N0549822.pdf?OpenElement, Accessed on 1 December 2020).

[34]The Doha Declaration on Integrating Crime Prevention and Criminal Justice into the Wider United Nations Agenda to Address Social and Economic Challenges and to Promote the Rule of

the provisions of which were adopted by acclamation on the first day of the Congress, was the concluding document of the Thirteenth United Nations Congress. It summarised the 60-year achievements of the UN congresses and activities in the field of preventing crime. It also marked an attempt at responding to contemporary challenges emerging in this respect. With a view to implementing the objectives envisaged in the Doha Declaration, the United Nations Office on Drugs and Crime, using Qatar's financial support, launched an ambitious programme with global coverage, aimed at supporting countries in crime prevention efforts, developing criminal justice, preventing corruption and promoting the rule of law. Next congress was scheduled on 20–27 April 2020, and was to take place in Kyoto (a city which hosted the Fourth United Nations Congress in 1970). However, due to the COVID-19 pandemic, it had to be rescheduled.

It is common knowledge that the speed of action is of utmost important in conducting criminal proceedings on cybercrime, considering that digital evidence is non-permanent ("perishable"). To accelerate and facilitate information exchange, *inter alia*, by more intensive cooperation with the private sector, a joint initiative has been launched by the Counter-Terrorism Committee Executive Directorate (CTED), the United Nations Office on Drugs and Crime (UNODC), and the International Association of Prosecutors—Lawful Access to Digital Data Across Borders.

The UN Security Council also implements activities in the field of cybersecurity and fight against cybercrime. In Resolution 1373 (2001) of 27 September 2001, it called Member States to intensify the exchange of information on the ICT use by terrorist groups, and to block any terrorist recruitment attempts via the Internet. In Resolution 2129 (2013) of 17 September 2013, it stressed that the Internet and social media were increasingly used for facilitating various terrorist acts, including communication, abetting, recruitment, training, preparations, planning, financing, and information collection.

Recognising the need to engage the private sector in combating organised crime and terrorism, CTED has launched the Tech Against Terrorism initiative, its objective being to encourage private sector entities to take measures aimed at self-regulation and at counteracting the use of their platforms by terrorist groups.

In addition, Security Council Resolutions 2341 (2013) of 13 February 2017 imposed on CTED the obligation to verify Member States' efforts to protect critical infrastructures against terrorist attacks, and to identify threats and future challenges likely to emerge in this field.

Law at the National and International Levels, and Public Participation; http://www.unodc.org/documents/congress//Declaration/V1504151 English.pdf, accessed on 1 June 2020).

6 The International Telecommunication Union

The International Telecommunication Union (ITU), with its seat in Geneva, is a United Nations specialised agency which is currently the most dynamically operating body in the field of ensuring cyberspace security by harmonising the legal orders in various countries, and by establishing international regulations. The ITU duties include standardising and regulating the telecommunications market, promoting international cooperation in the field of telecommunication, providing technical assistance to developing countries, and taking measures aimed at establishing a global telecommunication network combining multiple technologies.[35] The Plenipotentiary Conference composed of representatives of the ITU Member States is the chief political body of the Union. The Conference gathers every 4 years and sets the principal directions of the ITU policy, as well as elects members of the Council and defines the organisation's financial plans. The Council is entrusted with supervising the ongoing policies, strategies and activities of the Union in the periods between the consecutive Plenipotentiary Conferences. The General Secretary elected for a four-year term of office manages the General Secretariat, which is an office dealing with ITU resource and activity administration. The General Secretary is a legal representative of the Union.

The ITU conducts its activities in three principal fields which are supervised by separated structures, i.e. the radiocommunication sector (ITU-R), the standardisation sector (ITU-T) and the telecommunication development sector (ITU-D). ITU-T is in charge of examining and adopting guidelines pertaining to technical, operational and pricing issues, aimed at telecommunication standardisation globally. These are divided into series (each assigned a different letter of the alphabet), and feature separate and more detailed categories. The X series is entitled *Data networks, open system communications and security*, and it contains guidelines on general security, information and network security, application and service security, cyberspace security, the exchange of information on cybersecurity, and cloud computing security.[36] The World Telecommunication Standardization Assembly (WTSA), which gathers every 4 years, is a non-ITU institution. However, it sets the general direction of the activities of the standardisation (ITU-T) and radio communication (ITU-R) sectors. It is in charge of approving the list of technical topics related to telecommunications (referred to as queries) which can form the subject-matter of research and are submitted to the research groups operating within those sectors, which are established on an as-needed basis and comprise experts from various countries. These groups are in charge of drawing up *responses* which, in principle, take the form of a draft recommendation or a partial recommendation on a given issue, which is then subject to WTSA's approval. In addition, WTSA can adopt resolutions. For instance, the most recent WTSA, which gathered between 25 October and

[35]See more in Kubicka (2007), pp. 127–128.

[36]https://www.itu.int/en/ITU-T/publications/Pages/structure.aspx#Z; accessed on 1 September 2020.

3 November 2016 in Hammamet, adopted Resolution 50 (Rev. Hammamet, 2016) on Cybersecurity, and Resolution 52 (Rev. Hammamet, 2016) on Countering and Combating Spam.[37]

The Plenipotentiary Conference is yet another body issuing resolutions on the subject-matter discussed in this article, including Resolution 179 (Rev. Busan, 2014) of the Plenipotentiary Conference on ITU's role in child online protection, and Resolution 181 (Guadalajara, 2010) of the Plenipotentiary Conference on definitions and terminology relating to building confidence and security in the use of ICT.

The executive body is the permanently operating secretariat with the Secretary General in the lead.

In 2001, the General Assembly of the United Nations passed Resolution 56/183 of 21 December 2001 on the World Summit on the Information Society (WSIS),[38] in which it approved the concept of conducting WSIS as proposed by ITU. The Summit was divided into two stages, the first of which took place on 10–12 December 2003 in Geneva, and the second on 16–18 November 2005 in Tunis.

The principal objectives of the first stage of WSIS included developing a shared viewpoint and adopting a statement expressing the political willingness to lay the foundations for "information society for all", taking into consideration the diversified interests of all participants while also heralding the implementation of initial measures to attain this objective. The first stage resulted in adopting, on the 2nd of December 2003, the Geneva Declaration of Principles (*Building the Information Society: a global challenge in the new Millennium*) and the Geneva Plan of Action. The second stage of WSIS was aimed, in particular, at initiating the implementation process of the provisions of the Geneva Plan of Action, and at searching for solutions in such fields as Internet management and financial mechanisms on the Internet. On 18 November 2005, the Tunis Agenda on Information Society was announced, in which the role of international cooperation in combating cybercrime was stressed, entailing both collaboration between law enforcement authorities, and the establishing of dedicated legal frameworks by governments jointly with parties concerned (representatives of the IT industry and NGOs).[39]

On 17 May 2007, the ITU Global Cybersecurity Agenda (GCA) was initiated. It acts as a framework for establishing international dialogue and cooperation to facilitate the coordination of global measures, serving as a response to the challenges related to combating cybercrime and building a secure information society. It is based on five strategic pillars (legal measures, technical and procedural measures, organisational structure, capacity-building, and international cooperation), its objective being to develop model cybercrime legislation that is interoperable with existing

[37]https://www.itu.int/en/publications/ITU-T/pages/publications.aspx?lang=e&parent=T-RES&version_date=2016; accessed on 1 September 2020.

[38]http://www.itu.int/wsis/docs/background/resolutions/56 183 unga 2002.pdf, accessed on 1 September 2020.

[39]Radoniewicz (2016), pp. 206–207.

national and regional legislative measures, and potentially applicable in the global context.[40]

7 Group of Eight

At the meeting of representatives of the Justice and Home Affairs Ministries of the countries belonging to the Group of Eight,[41] held on 10 December 1997 in Washington, a programme for combating computer crime, which was drawn up by the Subgroup on High-Tech Crime,[42] was adopted featuring ten principles of combating cybercrime, together with a ten-point action plan.[43] The primary objectives included eliminating "hacker havens", coordinating the prosecution of cybercrime regardless of where it was committed, as well as training and equipping law enforcement officers with adequate tools to combat high-tech crime.[44]

The Ministerial Conference on Combating Transnational Organized Crimes which took place on 9–20 October 1999 in Moscow was dominated by such issues as financing terrorist activities, human trafficking or cybercrime. The last two issues were further discussed in annexes to the document[45] summarising the event. The

[40] Radoniewicz (2016), pp. 207–208.

[41] The Group of Seven (G7)/the Group of Eight (G8) is not an international organisation but a sort of a "semi-institution"—a political and economic forum involving the most influential countries in the world, including France, Japan, Canada, Germany, USA, the United Kingdom, Italy, representatives of the European Union, and Russia. Their leaders gather at annual political and economic summits. The first such gathering took place in 1975. The G7/G8's main objectives include strengthening international cooperation, coordinating foreign policies of its Member States, and improving international commodity turnover. See Łoś-Nowak (2009), pp. 291–293.

[42] On 15–17 June 1995, at the G8's Summit in Halifax, a dedicated expert group was established, which was entrusted with designing solutions to improve the procedures related to combating organised crime. Its work resulted in formulating, in 1996, a set of Forty Recommendations which were adopted at the G8's Summit in Lyon on 27–29 June 1996. The group was, therefore, named the G8's Lyon Group for fighting international organised crime. Several subgroups were established within its framework, the activities of which involve diversified issues of combating crime, including the aforementioned Subgroup on High-Tech Crime established in 1997. Other subgroups focus on fighting human trafficking or on providing legal assistance. The principal duties of the G8's Lyon Group related to criminal procedures, international cooperation and effective prosecution of computer crime. At the G8's meeting held on 19 October 2001 in Rome, following the 11 September 2001 attacks, representatives of the Justice and Home Affairs Ministries decided that the G8's Lyon Group be merged with the G8's Rome Group dealing with fighting terrorism. Following that merger, the G8's Lyon/Rome Group was formed.

[43] Principles to combat against high-tech crime and Action Plan to combat against high-tech crime.

[44] See also The Information Economy Report drawn up in 2005 at the UN Conference on Trade and Development, http://www.unctad.org/en/docs/sdteecb20051ch6_en.pdf, accessed on 1. September 2020.

[45] Communiqué of the Ministerial Conference of the G8 Countries on Combating Transnational Organized Crime.

said document included basic principles to combat cybercrime, which were later restated in numerous international strategies dealing with this subject-matter.[46] The practical effect of the Conference was the expansion of the international network of 24/7 points of contact operating within the Group of Eight.[47] At the Conference in Paris, attention was once again drawn to the need to eliminate the so-called lawless digital heavens or Internet heavens, and to the role which the Convention on Cybercrime could play as an international agreement open also to those countries which are not members of the Council of Europe, thus potentially serving as a global regulation. At the G8 Government-Industry Workshop on Safety and Security in Cyberspace held in May 2001 in Tokyo, the issues of data retention and securing data for criminal proceedings were dealt with.

At the Washington meeting of representatives of the Justice and Home Affairs Ministries of the countries belonging to the Group of Eight, the continual development of (and amendments to) the national regulations on penalising computer misuse acts, in order to reflect the actual technological progress, was recognised as a condition precedent to effectively combating Internet misuse for terrorist and criminal purposes. Such an approach should accelerate international criminal proceedings on computer crime. With reference to the Convention on Cybercrime, it was pointed out that measures were taken to encourage countries to accede to that document.[48] At another meeting of representatives of the Justice and Home Affairs Ministries which was held in Sheffield (Great Britain) on 16–17 June 2005, Member States were recommended to develop regulations which would guarantee a prompt response to serious cyberthreats and network incidents.[49]

At a meeting held in Moscow in 2006,[50] representatives of G8's Justice and Home Affairs Ministries and Prosecutors focused on the issues of terrorism and cybercrime. They stressed that these phenomena are inter-related, and the establishing of effective measures against cybercrime was, therefore, recognised as the condition precedent to effectively combating terrorist acts in the domain of modern technologies.[51]

[46]Gercke (2011). p. 177.

[47]The network of points of contact serving the purpose of information exchange for conducting proceedings in cybercrime cases, operating on a permanent (24/7) basis, parallel to the 24/7 network operating under the Convention on Cybercrime. See Adamski (2011), p. 179.

[48]The statement by G8's Justice and Home Affairs Ministries of 11 May 2004, the Summit of G8's Justice and Home Affairs Ministries held in Washington on 10–11 May 2004, http://www.g8.utoronto.ca/justice/justice040511_comm.htm, accessed on 1 September 2020.

[49]See General objectives adopted at the Summit of G8's Justice and Home Affairs Ministries on 16–17 June 2005, http://www.g8.utoronto.ca/justice/justice_uk2005.htm, accessed on September 2020.

[50]The Summit of G8's Justice and Home Affairs Ministries and Prosecutors held in Moscow on 15–16 May 2006.

[51]See the press conference of representatives of G8's Justice and Home Affairs Ministries, http://www.g8.utoronto.ca/justice/justice2006.htm, Accessed on 1 September 2020.

At the conference of G8's Justice and Home Affairs Ministries held on 23–25 May 2007 in Munich, the attendees undertook to work on the penalisation, also through domestic measures, of computer misuse acts committed via the Internet for terrorist purposes.[52]

On 7–9 July 2008, at the summit of G8 Member States in Hokkaido Tokyako, Japan, a report drawn up by the Rome/Lyon Group was presented,[53] which once again outlined the various ways of exploiting new technologies by terrorist groups. A further extension of the network of 24/7 points of contact was also recommended, including in particular the extension of its coverage (at that time, the network covered around 50 countries).

At the 2009 meeting of G8's Justice and Home Affairs Ministries and Prosecutors, which was held on 29–30 May 2009 in Rome, the report prepared by the G8's Lyon/Rome Group for the UN Commission on Crime Prevention and Criminal Justice (CCPCJ) was discussed.[54] In the statement[55] containing a summary of the Summit, attention was drawn to the technological progress and new forms of Internet misuse, such as the criminal misuse of social networks, encryption services, VoIP services, the Domain Name System, and other new and evolving criminal attacks on information systems.

At the Summit in Muskoka, Canada, held on 25–26 June 2010, cybercrime was only mentioned in the context of Internet misuse by terrorists. Attention was drawn both to the problem of networks being put under terrorist threat, and their misuse by terrorists for communication purposes[56] (i.e. for disseminating ideologies, recruiting new members, training terrorists or coordinating terrorist activities).[57]

On 24–25 May 2011, Paris was home to the e-G8 Forum *The Internet: Accelerating Growth*, in which Internet-related issues were discussed in attendance of representatives of scientific circles and enterprises operating in the widely understood IT industry (e.g. Microsoft, HTC, Google, Facebook, Alcatel, France Telecom, Eutelsat).[58] The Conference immediately preceded the G8 Summit scheduled on 26–27 May 2011 in Deauville (France). It was attended by representatives of the e-G8 Forum participants who brought a special message to governments (*Message to Deauville*), which stressed the significance of the Internet as a major drive of both

[52]Gercke (2011)p. 180.

[53]http://www.g8.utoronto.ca/summit/2008hokkaido/2008-crimereport.pdf, accessed on 1 September 2020.

[54]Cf. http://www.cybercrimelaw.net/G8.html, Accessed on 1 September 2020.

[55]http://www.g8italia2009.it/static/G8_Allegato/declaration1giu2009,0.pdf, accessed on 1 September 2020.

[56]See *Muskoka Declaration: Recovery and New Beginnings*, Point 42, http://www.g7.utoronto.ca/summit/2010muskoka/communique.html#peace, accessed on 1 September 2020.

[57]Cf. The statement from the G8 Summit held in Heiligendamm on 8 June 2007 on combating terrorism, http://www.g8.utoronto.ca/summit/2007heiligendamm/g8-2007-ct.html, Accessed on 10 October 2020.

[58]http://www.g8.utoronto.ca/summit/2011deauville/eg8/index.html, Accessed on 1 September 2020.

social and economic development and recognised it as an "engine for change" (with the Arab Spring as an example). Governments of the G8 Member States were called to provide an unconstrained, fast and secure Internet. Although the Message met with a full understanding, and even approval, of the addressees, it did not translate into any specific recommendations.[59] At the subsequent G8/G7 summits[60] (the 2012 Summit in Camp David, the 2013 Summit in Lough Erne, the 2014 Summit in Brussels, and the 2015 Summit in Schloss Elmau), the issues of cybercrime were not dealt with, while at the 2016 Summit in Ise-Shima (Japan, the 26th–27th of May 2016), cyberspace security was again one of the most important subjects of the debate. In the declaration[61] adopted at that Summit, it was stressed that a secure cyberspace was one of the main contributors to economic growth and prosperity. An undertaking was, therefore, made to establish close cooperation against the malicious use of cyberspace both by state and non-state parties, including terrorist units. The existing international law was again recognised as applicable to states' operations in cyberspace. An undertaking was made to protect and promote human rights on the Internet, and to support a multilateral approach to Internet management entailing a full and active involvement, *inter alia*, of governments, private sector entities, civic societies, technological communities and international organisations. The specific duties and roles of countries in the tele-information environment aimed at ensuring security, stability and prosperity were stressed. Finally, a promise was made to establish a new G7 working group for cyberspace, with a view to facilitating concerted measures to ensure security and stability in cyberspace.

At the 2017 Summit in Taormina (Italy, 27 May 2017), attention was drawn to the fact that cyber attacks targeted at critical infrastructures worldwide highlighted the need to strengthen international cooperation aimed at ensuring cyberspace security as a condition precedent to economic growth and prosperity.[62]

At the subsequent summits, taking place on 8–9 June 2018 in Charlevoix, Canada,[63] and on 24–26 August 2019 in Biarritz, France,[64] the issues of cybercrime and cybersecurity were barely touched upon. The 2020 Summit was planned to be held in March in Camp David. However, due to the COVID-19 pandemic, it was cancelled and a series of videoconferences were organised instead.

---

[59] Gercke (2011), p 181.

[60] In consequence of the events taking place in Ukraine in 2014, the G7 formula was restored, with Russia's membership being "on suspension". Thus, the 2014 Summit which was initially planned to be organised in Sochi was eventually held in Brussels (without Russia's attendance).

[61] G7 Ise-Shima Leaders' Declaration, http://www.g8.utoronto.ca/summit/2016shima/ise-shima-declaration-en.html, Accessed on 1 December 2020.

[62] Taormina Leaders' Communiqué; http://www.g8.utoronto.ca/summit/2017taormina/communique.html, accessed on 1 December 2020.

[63] The Charlevoix G7 Summit Communiqué, http://www.g8.utoronto.ca/summit/2018charlevoix/index.html, accessed on 1 December 2020.

[64] G7 Biarritz Leaders' Declaration; http://www.g8.utoronto.ca/summit/2019biarritz/declaration-of-leaders.html; accessed on 1 December 2020.

References

Adamski A (2000) Prawo karne komputerowe, Warsaw

Adamski A (2001) Przestępczość w cyberprzestrzeni. Prawne środki przeciwdziałania zjawisku w Polsce na tle projektu konwencji Rady Europy, Toruń

Adamski A (2011) Cyberprzestępczość – rozwój regulacji prawnej w Europie. Doświadczenia krajowe na tle implementacji prawnych instrumentów zwalczania cyberprzestępczości, London, 11–12 November 2010). Prokuratura i Prawo 6

Chałubińska-Jentkiewicz K (2019) Cyberodpowiedzialność, Toruń

Gercke M (2011) Understanding Cybercrime: A Guide for Developing Countries. https://www.itu.int/ITU-D/cyb/cybersecurity/docs/ITU_Guide_A5_12072011.pdf. Accessed 10 Oct 2020

Hubbard AM, Schjølberg S. Harmonizing national legal approaches on cybercrime. http://www.itu.int/osg/spu/cybersecurity//docs/Background_Paper_Harmonizing_National_and_Legal_Approaches_on_Cybercrime.pdf. Accessed 10 Oct 2020

Kubicka J (2007) International organizations – The United Nations Organization – its activity and reforms. Dąbrowa Górnicza

Łoś-Nowak T (2009) (ed) Organizacje w stosunkach międzynarodowych. Istota – Mechanizmy działania – Zasięg, Warsaw

Radoniewicz F (2016) Odpowiedzialność karna za hacking i inne przestępstwa przeciwko danym komputerowym i systemom informatycznym, Warsaw

Radoniewicz F (2019) In: Kitler W, Taczkowska-Olszewska J, Radoniewicz F (eds) Ustawa o krajowym systemie cyberbezpieczeństwa. Komentarz, Warsaw

Schjølberg S. The History of Global Harmonization on Cybercrime Legislation – The Road to Geneva, http://www.cybercrimelaw.net. Accessed 10 Oct 2020

Sieber U (1998) Legal Aspects of Computer-Related Crime in the Information Society – Comcrime-Study, Würzburg

Tarnogórski R (2009) Konwencja o cyberprzestępczości – międzynarodowa odpowiedź na przestępczość ery informacyjnej. In: Madej M, Terlikowski M (eds) Bezpieczeństwo teleinformatyczne państwa, Warsaw

Filip Radoniewicz PhD; legal advisor; adjunct in the Department of Cybersecurity Law and New Technologies at the Institute of Law, War Studies University, Warsaw; expert at the Academic Centre for Cybersecurity Policy, (War Studies University) and in the Ministry of Justice; he worked as an assistant judge (in the Fourth Criminal and Sixth Penitentiary Department of the Regional Court in Lublin); graduate of post-graduate studies: "European Union Law" at the Jagiellonian University, "Human Rights and Freedoms", co-organized by the Institute of Legal Sciences of the Polish Academy of Sciences and the Helsinki Foundation for Human Rights, and "Computer Network Administration" at the Lublin University of Technology; author or co-author of approximately fifty publications, mainly in the field of broadly understood criminal law, new technology law and human rights. Selected publications: F. Radoniewicz (2016) Odpowiedzialność karna za hacking i inne przestępstwa przeciwko danym komputerowym i systemom informatycznym/Criminal liability for hacking and other offences against computer data and information systems/, Wolters Kluwer, Warszawa; Ustawa o krajowym systemie cyberbezpieczeństwa. Komentarz /Act on the National Cybersecurity System. Commentary/ (2019) ed. W. Kitler, J. Taczkowska-Olszewska, F. Radoniewicz, CH. Beck, Warszawa.

Cybersecurity in the European Union Law

Filip Radoniewicz

Abstract The first legal acts adopted within the framework of the European Communities were adopted in the early nineties. However, they were not binding. They contained calls for appropriate actions, identification of some solutions, proposals for draft legal acts, strategies and action plans to improve network security.

This chapter, however, highlights the most important binding acts: the first binding EU legal instrument to combat computer crime: Council Framework Decision 2005/222/JHA of the 24th of February 2005 on attacks against information systems, Directive 2013/40/EU of the European Parliament and of the Council of the 12th of August 2013 on attacks against information systems and replacing Council Framework Decision 2005/222/JHA and Directive (EU) 2016/1148 of the European Parliament and of the Council of the 6th of July 2016 concerning measures for a high common level of security of network and information systems across the Union.

1 Introduction

When discussing European Union activities in the field of cybersecurity and combating cybercrime, it appears advisable to go back to the 1990s, when the first non-binding legal Acts were adopted to regulate these matters. They called for the implementing of the appropriate measures, indicating specific solutions or proposals for the draft legal Acts, as well as the developing of strategies and action plans to improve network security. In this context, the following documents are worth noting:

F. Radoniewicz (✉)
Akademickie Centrum Polityki Cyberbezpieczeństwa/Academic Center for Cybersecurity Policy, Akademia Sztuki Wojennej w Warszawie/War Studies University in Warsaw, Warsaw, Poland
e-mail: filip.radoniewicz@radoniewicz.eu

K. Chałubińska-Jentkiewicz et al. (eds.), *Cybersecurity in Poland*,
https://doi.org/10.1007/978-3-030-78551-2_6

1. Council Decision 92/242/EEC of the 31st of March 1992 in the Field of Security of Information Systems;[1]
2. Council Recommendation 95/144/EC of the 7th of April 1995 on Common Information Technology Security Evaluation Criteria;[2]
3. Communication COM(2000)890 EU from the Commission to the Council, the European Parliament, the Economic and Social Committee and the Committee of the Regions of the 26th of January 2001: Creating a safer information society by improving the security of information infrastructures and combating computer-related crime (the so-called Communication on Cybercrime);
4. The Resolution of Parliament of the 19th of May 2002 Calling for Legislative Measures Against High-Tech Crime;[3]
5. Communication COM(2001)298 from the Commission to the Council, the European Parliament, the Economic and Social Committee and the Committee of the Regions, of the 6th of June 2001: Network and information security: Proposal for a European policy approach;[4]
6. Council Recommendation of the 25th of June 2001 on Contact Points Maintaining a 24-h Service for Combating High-Tech Crime;[5]
7. The Council Resolution of the 28th of January 2002 on a Common Approach and Specific Actions in the Field of Network and Information Security;[6]
8. Communication COM (2006)251 from the Commission to the European Parliament, the Council, the Economic and Social Committee and the Committee of the Regions, of the 31st of May 2006: A strategy for a secure information society: Dialogue, partnership and empowerment;
9. Communication COM (2006)288 from the Commission to the European Parliament, the Council, the Economic and Social Committee and the Committee of the Regions, of the 15th of July 2006 on counteracting spam, spyware and malicious software;
10. Communication COM (2007)267 from the Commission to the European Parliament, the Council and the Committee of the Regions of the 22nd of May 2007: Towards a general policy on the cybercrime prevention, extending the so-called Communication on Cybercrime of 2001;

---

[1]Council Decision 92/242/EEC of 31 March 1992 in the Field of Security of Information Systems (OJ EU L 123/19).

[2]Council Recommendation 95/144/EC of 7 April 1995 on Common Information Technology Security Evaluation Criteria, OJ EC 1995 C 93/27.

[3]The Resolution of Parliament of 19 May 2002 Calling for Legislative Measures Against High-Tech Crime, Unpublished.

[4]Unauthorised access to information systems, disruptive attacks on information systems, malicious software, misrepresentation (using other person's data with fraudulent intentions—this not only concerned identity theft but also spoofing).

[5]Council Recommendation of 25 June 2001 on Contact Points Maintaining a 24-h Service for Combating High-Tech Crime Official Journal C 187 of 3.07.2001, p. 5.

[6]The Council Resolution of 28 January 2002 on a Common Approach and Specific Actions in the Field of Network and Information Security, OJ EC 2002 C 43/2.

11. Communication COM (2009)149 from the Commission to the European Parliament, the Council, the Economic and Social Committee and the Committee of the Regions of the 30th of March 2009 on Critical Information Infrastructure Protection: Protecting Europe from large scale cyber attacks and disruptions: enhancing preparedness, security and resilience" together with a report on multi-annual wide-scale European consultations regarding network security;[7]
12. Commission Staff Working Document—Assessment of the EU 2013 Cybersecurity Strategy;[8]
13. Council Decision of the 23rd of September 2013 on the Security Rules for Protecting EU Classified Information (2013/488/EU);[9]
14. Joint Communication to the European Parliament, the Council, the Economic and Social Committee and the Committee of the Regions: Cybersecurity Strategy of the European Union: An Open, Safe and Secure Cyberspace.[10]
15. The *eEurope – An Information Society for All* initiative was launched at the end of 1999.[11] The Communication regarding the Commission's initiative was prepared for the special meeting of the European Council in Lisbon on the 23rd–24th of March 2000, the objective of which was to streamline the activities facilitating the creation of an information society. It was stressed in the Communication that the computerisation process must cover all aspects of European residents' lives, including in particular work, home, school, university, healthcare, transport, and contacts with public administration. The document identified ten fields on which special emphasis should be placed with a view to building an information society. According to Kuliński, these fields can be divided into three groups, centred on infrastructure (ensuring low-cost access to the Internet, and building fast Internet connections intended for scientific and academic circles),
16. research and education (in particular, providing Internet connections in schools, and supporting small and medium-sized enterprises in implementing advanced technologies),
17. applications (accelerating the development of e-commerce, smart cards, e-health, e-government, smart transport).[12]

At the aforementioned special meeting of the European Council, which took place in Lisbon on the 23rd–24th of March 2000, the eEurope programme was

[7]Radoniewicz (2016), pp. 233–236.

[8]Commission Staff Working Document—Assessment of the EU 2013 Cybersecurity Strategy SWD (2017) 295 final of 13.9.2017.

[9]Council Decision of 23 September 2013 on the Security Rules for Protecting EU Classified Information (2013/488/EU), OJ EU 2012 L 27/1.

[10]Communication to the European Parliament, the Council, the Economic and Social Committee and the Committee of the Regions: Cybersecurity Strategy of the European Union: An Open, Safe and Secure Cyberspace JOIN(2013) 1 final.

[11]Commission Communication COM (1999) 687: *eEurope – An Information Society for All.*

[12]Kuliński (2010), pp. 23–24. Cf. Chałubińska-Jentkiewicz (2019), pp. 266–269.

approved, and the so-called Lisbon Strategy was adopted. The Lisbon Strategy was a long-term socio-economic development programme for the European Union, the purpose of which was to make Europe the most dynamic and competitive economic region in the world by building the knowledge-based economy (i.e. an economy directly based on production, distribution, and the use of information and knowledge).[13]

In June 2000, at the meeting in Santa Maria de Feira, *eEurope 2002 – An Information Society for All. Action Plan* was adopted.

The measures implemented within the framework of the eEurope 2002 programme were maintained in the eEurope 2005 programme, and then in the i2010 Strategy announced in Commission Communication COM(2005)229 of the 1st of June 2005: *i2010 – A European Information Society for Growth and Employment. Europe 2020 – A strategy for smart, sustainable and inclusive growth* (COM (2010)2020), which was approved by the European Council on the 17th of June 2010, serves as a follow-up to the i2010 programme. It is within its framework that the European digital agenda has been implemented. Its objective is to develop a uniform digital market enabling EU Member States to derive permanent economic and social benefits.

At the meeting of the European Council which took place on the 4th–5th of November 2004 in Brussels, an action plan in the fields of justice and internal affairs was adopted. It was referred to as the Hague Programme, as it was developed during the Netherlands' Presidency of the Council of the European Union.

The Hague Programme's implementation was continued in the so-called Stockholm Programme—*An Open and Safe Europe Serving and Protecting Citizens*—adopted during Sweden's Presidency at the meeting in Brussels on the 10th–11th of December 2009. It was implemented within the framework of the action plan adopted by the Commission on the 20th of April 2010. It recommended that an internal security strategy be developed for the EU, directed at increasing the protection of citizens and at effectively combating serious crime, organised crime, and terrorism, by strengthening cooperation between the police and the judicial services in criminal cases, and Member States' cooperation in the field of border management, citizen protection and assistance in the event of natural disasters or catastrophes. Other guidelines regarding the development planning of the AFSJ (the area of freedom, security and justice) were laid down by the European Council on 26th–27th of June 2014. However, these were not turned into a programme, as had been done with previous guidelines, but were included in the European Union conclusions. In the document entitled *The Continuation of Work on a Comprehensive Approach to Cybersecurity and Cybercrime,* ensuring cybersecurity was considered a principal measure directed at providing EU citizens with real security space.[14]

[13]See more e.g. Radoniewicz (2019a), pp. 13–14.

[14]Chałubińska-Jentkiewicz (2019), pp. 269–270.

On the 6th of May 2015, *A Digital Single Market Strategy*[15] was adopted, its purpose being to develop a uniform legal framework for the EU digital market.

2 Council Framework Decision 2005/222/JHA of the 24th of February 2005 on Attacks Against Information Systems

Council Framework Decision 2005/222/JHA of the 24th of February 2005 on attacks against information systems[16] was the first binding EU legal instrument the objective of which was to combat computer crime. In principle, the document included definitions of the most pertinent concepts ("information system," "computer data," "legal person" and "without right"), and obliged Member States to consider illegal access to information systems and illegal system interference as punishable offences. Reference was also made to the liability of legal persons, jurisdiction, and the establishing of a network of points of contact' maintaining a 24-h service, available 7 days a week, to facilitate the exchange of information on attacks against information systems. The limited number of crimes defined in Framework Decision 2005/222, along with the need to recognise new threats, as well as the intent to adjust the regulations to new EU initiatives in the field of cybersecurity, and to supplement them in order to arrive at a comprehensive regulation of this subject matter, eventually led to a decision on developing a new legal instrument concerning cybercrime. Work on the new regulation coincided with the adopting of the Treaty of Lisbon, which made it possible to use the directive for regulating cybercrime issues.

3 Directive 2013/40/EU of the European Parliament and of the Council of the 12th of August 2013 on Attacks Against Information Systems

In Directive 2013/40/EU of the European Parliament and of the Council of the 12th of August 2013 on attacks against information systems and replacing Council Framework Decision 2005/222/JHA,[17] the provisions of Framework Decision

[15] *A Digital Single Market Strategy* Communication COM (2015)192 from the Commission to the European Parliament, the Council, the Economic and Social Committee, and the Committee of the Regions. Cf. Radoniewicz (2019a), pp. 14–15.

[16] Council Framework Decision 2005/222/JHA of 24 February 2005 on attacks against information systems, OJ EU 2005 L 69/67.

[17] Directive 2013/40/EU of the European Parliament and of the Council of 12 August 2013 on attacks against information systems and replacing Council Framework Decision 2005/222/JHA, OJ EU 2013 L218/8.

2005/222 were generally upheld, but a number of new solutions were added. New types of criminal offences were envisaged (e.g. the illegal interception of computer data, and crimes involving "hacking tools"), and additional circumstances were defined, along with committing crime within a criminal organisation, as provided for in Framework Decision 2005/222 (though with more stringent sanctions), which Member States should obligatorily treat as increasing criminal liability. These included 'botnet' attacks, causing serious harm (such issues as causing serious harm or influencing material interests were also envisaged in the Framework Decision, but that provision was of a non-obligatory character), committing an offence against an information system with critical-infrastructure status, and another person's true identity's being used by the perpetrator.[18]

4 Directive 2017/541 (EU) of the European Parliament and of the Council of the 15th of March 2017 on Combating Terrorism

Directive 2017/541/EU of the European Parliament and of the Council, of the 15th of March 2017 on combating terrorism and replacing Council Framework Decision 2002/475/JHA[19] and amending Council Decision 2005/671/JHA,[20] is the major legal instrument whose purpose is to combat terrorism in the European Union. Under Article 3 of Directive 2017/541, in order for an illegal act to be considered a terrorist offence, it must meet the objective criterion of being one of the acts listed in the closed-ended list contained in that article, or involve a threat of such an act's being committed. In addition, it must satisfy at least one of the premises listed further in the definition, concerning the perpetrator's purpose, i.e. it must be committed with the intention of

1. seriously intimidating a population, or
2. unduly compelling a government or an international organisation to perform or abstain from performing any act, or
3. seriously destabilising or destroying the fundamental political, constitutional, economic, or social structures of a country or an international organisation.

The list referred to above contains, *inter alia*, the illegal acts as defined in Articles 4 and 5 of Directive 2013/40 (illegal system interference and illegal data interference, respectively) provided that any of the aggravating circumstances listed in the directive are found to have occurred (as regards the act defined in Article 4, when the

[18]See more e.g. Radoniewicz (2017), pp. 303–317.

[19]About Framework Decision 2002/475/JHA see e.g. Radoniewicz (2015), pp. 192–196.

[20]Directive 2017/541/EU of the European Parliament and of the Council, of 15 March 2017 on combating terrorism and replacing Council Framework Decision 2002/475/JHA and amending Council Decision 2005/671/JHA, OJ EU 2017 L 88/6.

perpetrator's action involving the use of hacking software affected a large number of information systems, or the act caused serious damage to or was directed against an information system with critical-infrastructure status; and as regards the act as defined in Article 5, when the act was committed against an information system with critical-infrastructure status).[21] Furthermore, Member States were obliged to take the necessary measures to ensure the prompt removal of online content constituting a public provocation to commit a terrorist offence, or to block access to such content when its removal is not feasible (Article 21 of Directive 2017/541).[22]

5 Directive 2008/114/EC of the 8th of December 2008 on the Identification and Designation of European Critical Infrastructures

With a view to raising the security level of critical infrastructures of supra-national significance, Council Directive 2008/114/EC of the 8th of December 2008 on the identification and designation of European critical infrastructures, and the assessment of the need to improve their protection, was adopted.[23] Under Article 2(a) of the Directive, "critical infrastructure" means an asset, system, or part thereof located in Member States, which is essential for the maintenance of vital societal functions: health, safety, security, the economic or social well-being of people, the disruption or destruction of which would have a significant impact on a Member State as a result of the failure to maintain those functions; and "The European critical infrastructure", or "ECI", as defined in Article 2(b) of the Directive, means a critical infrastructure located in Member States whose disruption or destruction would have a significant impact on at least two Member States. The significance of this impact is assessed in terms of cross-cutting criteria. These include the effects resulting from cross-sector dependencies on other types of infrastructure. Under Article 3(2) of the Directive, the cross-cutting criteria comprise the casualties' criterion, the economic-effects' criterion, and the public-effects' criterion. While the Directive is focused on the energy and transport sectors, its extension is planned to include other sectors, e.g. the information-and-communication-technology (ICT) sector.

[21] See more: Radoniewicz (2016), pp. 266–267.

[22] See more e.g. Radoniewicz (2019b), pp. 193–205.

[23] Council Directive 2008/114/EC of 8 December 2008 on the identification and designation of European critical infrastructures and the assessment of the need to improve their protection (Text with EEA relevance), OJ EU 2008 L 345/7.

6 Directive 2002/21/EC on a Common Regulatory Framework for Electronic Communications Networks and Services (A Framework Directive)

Directive 2002/21/EC of the European Parliament and of the Council of the 7th of March 2002 on a common regulatory framework for electronic communications networks and services (A Framework Directive)[24] lays down a common regulatory framework for electronic-communications networks, i.e. transmission systems, which permit the conveyance of signals by wire, radio, optical, or other electromagnetic means, including satellite networks, fixed and mobile terrestrial networks, electricity-cable systems, networks used for radio and television broadcasting, and cable-television networks, irrespective of the type of information conveyed, as well as for electronic-communications services, which consist of the conveyance of signals on those networks, and the associated equipment and services related to electronic-communications networks and services, which facilitate or support the provision of services by such networks. It also lays down tasks of national regulatory authorities, and establishes a set of procedures to ensure the harmonised application of the regulatory framework throughout the Community (Article 1(1) of Directive 2002/21/EC).

The issue of network security is discussed in Chapter IIIa of Directive 2002/21/EC, which was added by way of a directive 2009/140/EC of the 25th of November 2009,[25] which became effective on the 19th of December 2009.

Under Article 13a (1) of Directive 2002/21/EC, Member States were obliged to ensure that undertakings providing public-communications networks or publicly available electronic-communications services take the appropriate technical and organisational measures to properly manage the risks posed to the security of networks and services. These measures are expected to ensure a level of security commensurate to the risk presented, having regard to the state of the art. In particular, measures should be taken to prevent and minimise the impact of security incidents on users and interconnected networks.

Member States are also required to ensure that undertakings providing public-communications networks take all the appropriate steps to guarantee the integrity of their networks, and thus ensure the continuity of the supply of the services provided over those networks (Article 13a (2) of Directive 2002/21/EC), and that undertakings providing public-communications networks or publicly available electronic-

[24]Directive 2002/21/EC of the European Parliament and of the Council of 7 March 2002 on a common regulatory framework for electronic communications networks and services (Framework Directive), OJ EC 2002 L 108/33.

[25]Directive 2009/140/EC of the European Parliament and of the Council of 25 November 2009 amending Directives 2002/21/EC on a common regulatory framework for electronic communications networks and services, 2002/19/EC on access to, and interconnection of, electronic communications networks and associated facilities, and 2002/20/EC on the authorisation of electronic communications networks and services (OJ EU 2013 L 337/37).

communications services take the appropriate technical and organisational measures to properly manage the risks posed to the security of networks and services (Article 13a (3) of Directive 2002/21/EC).

With a view to implementing the provisions of Article 13a, the responsible national regulatory authorities need to be vested with the power to issue binding instructions, including those regarding time limits for implementation, to undertakings providing public-communications networks or publicly available electronic-communications services (Article 13b (1) of Directive 2002/21/EC).

Under Article 13b (2) of Directive 2002/21/EC, undertakings providing public-communications networks or publicly available electronic-communications services should be required to notify the responsible national regulatory authority of every breach of security or loss of integrity, which has had a significant impact on the operation of networks or services.

Member States are expected to ensure that the responsible national regulatory authorities have the power to require undertakings providing public-communications networks or publicly available electronic-communications services to

(a) provide the information needed to assess the security and/or integrity of their services and networks, including documented security policies; and
(b) submit to a security audit performed by a qualified independent body or a responsible national authority, and make the results thereof available to the national regulatory authority. The cost of the audit will be met by the undertaking (Article 13b (2) of Directive 2002/21/EC).

Article 13b (3) of Directive 2002/21/EC provides for vesting national regulatory authorities with all the powers necessary to investigate cases of non-compliance and the effects thereof on the security and integrity of networks.

7 Directive 2006/24/EC on the Retention of Data Generated or Processed in Connection with the Provision of Publicly Available Electronic Communications Services or of Public Communications Networks

Directive 2006/24/EC of the European Parliament and of the Council of the 15th of March 2006 on the retention of data generated or processed in connection with the provision of publicly available electronic communications services or of public communications networks and amending Directive 2002/58/EC,[26] aimed to

[26]Directive 2006/24/EC of the European Parliament and of the Council of 15 March 2006 on the retention of data generated or processed in connection with the provision of publicly available electronic communications services or of public communications networks and amending Directive 2002/58/EC, OJ EU 2006 L 105/54 (no longer in force).

harmonise Member States' provisions concerning the obligations of the providers of publicly available electronic-communications services or of public-communications networks in respect of the retention of so-called transmission data (i.e. traffic and location data, and related data necessary to identify the subscriber or registered user) which are generated or processed by them, in order to ensure that the data are available for the purposes of the investigation, detection, and prosecution of serious crimes, as defined by each Member State in its national law (Article 1). At the same time, the Directive (in Article 3) obliges Member States to adopt measures to ensure that these data (specified in detail in Article 5) are retained in accordance with the provisions thereof, to the extent that they are generated or processed by providers of publicly available electronic-communications services, or of a public-communications network within their jurisdiction, in the process of supplying the communications services concerned. The obligation to retain data includes the retention of data in the event of unsuccessful call attempts where those data are generated or processed and stored (as regards telephone data) or saved while users' logging in (as regards Internet data), by providers of publicly available electronic-communications services, or of a public-communications network within the jurisdiction of the Member State involved in the process of supplying the communications services concerned. Under Article 6, these categories of data are retained for periods of not less than six months and not more than two years from the date of the communication. This Directive was implemented by Member States (obviously including Poland) but it was then deemed invalid by the Court of Justice decision of the 8th of April 2014.[27] However, the decision did not cause all the provisions adopted in the course of the Directive transposition to be repealed. The basis for data retention in EU law is thus still provided by Article 15(1) of the Privacy Directive.

8 Regulation No 910/2014 on Electronic Identification and Trust Services for Electronic Transactions in the Internal Market (eIDAS)

Regulation (EU) No 910/2014 of the European Parliament and of the Council of the 23rd of July 2014 on electronic identification and trust services for electronic transactions in the internal market and repealing Directive 1999/93/EC[28] (eIDAS) lays down a new system of secure electronic interactions across the EU between businesses, citizens, and public authorities.

---

[27]Joined cases C-293/12 and C-594/12, Digital Rights Ireland Ltd vs. the Minister for Communications et al., ECLI:EU:C:2014:238.

[28]Regulation (EU) No 910/2014 of the European Parliament and of the Council of 23 July 2014 on electronic identification and trust services for electronic transactions in the internal market and repealing Directive 1999/93/EC, OJ EU 2014 L 257/73, (hereinafter referred as eIDAS).

1. It also lays down the conditions under which Member States recognise electronic-identification means of natural and legal persons falling under a notified electronic-identification scheme of another Member State,
2. It lays down the rules for trust services, in particular for electronic transactions, and
3. It establishes a legal framework for electronic signatures, electronic seals, electronic time stamps, electronic documents, electronic registered-delivery services, and certificate services for website authentication (Article 1).

Under the regulation on trust services, qualified and non-qualified trust-service providers[29] are obliged to take the appropriate technical and organisational measures, having regard to the latest technological developments, to manage the risks posed to the security of the trust services they provide, while also ensuring that the level of security is commensurate to the degree of risk. In particular, they are expected to take measures to prevent and minimise the impact of security incidents, and to inform stakeholders of the adverse effects of any such incidents.

Qualified and non-qualified trust-service providers must, without undue delay, but in any case within 24 h after having become aware of it, notify the supervisory body, and, where applicable, other relevant bodies, such as the authorised national body for information security or the data-protection authority, of any breach of security or loss of integrity which has a significant impact on the trust service provided, or on the personal data maintained therein. Furthermore, where the breach of security or loss of integrity is likely to adversely affect a natural or legal person to whom the trust service has been provided, the trust-service provider must also notify the natural or legal person of the breach of security or loss of integrity without undue delay. Where appropriate, in particular if a breach of security or loss of integrity concerns two or more Member States, the notified supervisory body is obliged to inform the supervisory authorities in the other Member States concerned, and ENISA (The European Network and Information Security Agency; currently—The European Union Agency for Cybersecurity).

[29]Under Article 3(19), in conjunction with Article 3(20) of the Regulation on trust services, the term "trust-service provider" means a natural or a legal person who provides one or more trust services, either as a qualified (i.e. satisfying certain additional requirements stipulated in the regulation) or as a non-qualified trust-service provider. "Trust service" means an electronic service normally for remuneration which consists of:

(1) the creation, verification, and validation of electronic signatures, electronic seals, or electronic time stamps, electronic registered delivery services and the certificates related to those services; or
(2) the creation, verification, and validation of certificates for website authentication; or
(3) the preservation of electronic signatures, seals, or certificates related to those services.

Finally, "qualified trust service" means a trust service which meets the applicable requirements laid down in the regulation on trust services.

9 Directive 2016/1148 Concerning Measures for a High Common Level of Security of Network and Information Systems Across the Union

The draft version of Directive (EU) 2016/1148 of the European Parliament and of the Council of 6 July 2016, concerning measures for a high common level of security of network and information systems across the Union (NIS Directive)[30] was presented in 2013 as a major element in the Cybersecurity Strategy, its underlying objective being to ensure a high level of security of network and information systems (hence the Directive is commonly abbreviated as the NIS Directive) at the EU level, i.e. to increase the security of tele-information systems forming the basis for the functioning of the modern societies and economies of EU Member States, which is to improve the functioning of the EU internal market. To this end, Article 2(1) of the NIS Directive provides for

1. laying down obligations for all Member States to adopt a national strategy on the security of network and information systems
2. creating a cooperation group in order to support and facilitate strategic cooperation and the exchange of information among Member States, and to develop trust and confidence amongst them creating a computer security incident response team (CSIRT) network in order to contribute to the development of trust and confidence between Member States, and to promote swift and effective operational cooperation
3. establishing security and notification requirements for operators of essential services and for digital service providers
4. laying down obligations for Member States to designate the responsible national authorities, single points of contact, and CSIRTs, with tasks related to the security of network and information systems.

The requirements concerning security and incident reporting, as stipulated in the NIS Directive, are not applicable to undertakings which are subject to the requirements arising from Articles 13a and 13b of Directive 2002/21/EC of the European Parliament and of the Council of 7 March 2002, on a common regulatory framework for electronic communications networks and services (A Framework Directive) (i.e. to undertakings providing public-communications networks or publicly available electronic-communications services), or to trust-service providers which are subject to the requirements arising from Article 19 of Regulation (EU) No 910/2014 of the European Parliament and of the Council of the 23rd of July 2014 on electronic identification and trust services for electronic transactions in the internal market and repealing Directive 1999/93/EC.

[30]Directive (EU) 2016/1148 of the European Parliament and of the Council of 6 July 2016 concerning measures for a high common level of security of network and information systems across the Union, OJ EU 2016 L 194/1, (hereinafter referred as "NIS Directive").

The NIS Directive is without prejudice to the actions taken by Member States to safeguard their essential state functions, in particular to safeguard national security, including actions protecting information whose disclosure Member States consider contrary to the essential interests of their security, and to maintain law and order, in particular to facilitate the investigation, detection, and prosecution of criminal offences (Article 2(6)). It should be stressed that it provides for minimum harmonisation, as, under Article 4, Member States may adopt or maintain provisions with a view to achieving a higher level of security of network and information systems.

For the purpose of the NIS Directive (Article 4(1)), "network and information systems" are defined as

(a) electronic-communications networks within the meaning of point (a) of Article 2 of Directive 2002/21/EC
(b) any devices or groups of interconnected or related devices, one or more of which, pursuant to a programme, perform automatic processing of digital data; or
(c) digital data stored, processed, retrieve or transmitted by elements covered under points (a) and (b) for the purposes of their operation, use, protection, and maintenance.

The security of network and information systems is understood as the ability of network and information systems to resist, at a given level of confidence, any action which compromises the availability, authenticity, integrity, or confidentiality of stored or transmitted or processed data, or the related services offered by, or accessible via, those network and information systems (Article 4(2)). The operator of essential services means a public or private entity of a type referred to in Annex II (energy, transport, banking, financial-markets infrastructure, healthcare, water-supply and digital infrastructure). Digital services were specified in Annex III (online marketplace, online search engine, cloud-computing services).

In compliance with the NIS Directive, Member States are obliged to identify the operators which are subject to the Directive within each of the sectors listed in Annex II. It is not required to identify all services, but only those of major significance to social and economic interests, and which could be subjected to significant disruptive effects. The significance of a disruptive effect is determined by taking into account the factors listed in Article 6 of the NIS Directive. These refer to the number of users relying on the service provided by the entity concerned, the dependency of other sectors (referred to in Annex II) on the service provided by that entity, the impact which incidents could have on economic and societal activities or public safety, the relative impact of social and economic interests, market share, geographical spread, etc. Chapter II governs the national frameworks on the security of network and information systems. Article 7 obliges each Member State to adopt a national-security strategy, while at the same time defining the issues to be considered therein. Article 8 obliges each Member State to designate competent authorities on the security of network and information systems (supervising their compliance with the provisions implementing the NIS Directive) and single points of contact. The

Directive provides for establishing computer security incident response teams (CSIRTs) (Article 9) charged with the management of risks and incidents in the sectors defined in Annex II, and in the services listed in Annex III. Furthermore, the NIS Directive provides for cooperation at the national level between competent authorities, single points of contact, and CSIRTs (Article 10). Cooperation between Member States was regulated in Chapter III, which envisages establishing a Cooperation Group (Article 11) composed of representatives of Member States, the Commission, and ENISA, and entrusted with providing strategic guidance for the activities of the CSIRT network, exchanging information and best practices, etc. Article 12 obliges Member States to establish a national CSIRT network, the principal duty of which will be to ensure coordinated response to incidents. The NIS Director provides for certain security and incident-reporting obligations to be imposed both on operators of essential services (Article 14) and on digital service providers (Article 16).[31]

There are numerous documents related to the NIS Directive, including legal Acts of a binding and non-binding character:

1. Commission Implementing Regulation (EU) 2018/151 of the 30th of January 2018 laying down the rules for the application of Directive (EU) 2016/1148 of the European Parliament and of the Council as regards further specification of the elements to be taken into account by digital service providers for managing the risks posed to the security of network and information systems, and of the parameters for determining whether an incident has a substantial impact.[32]
2. Commission Implementing Decision (EU) 2017/179 of the 1st of February 2017 laying down the procedural arrangements necessary for the functioning of the Cooperation Group, pursuant to Article 11(5) of Directive (EU) 2016/1148 of the European Parliament and of the Council, concerning measures for a high common level of security of network and information systems across the Union.[33]
3. Communication from the Commission to the European Parliament and the Council: Making the most of NIS—towards the effective implementation of

[31]Savin (2017), pp. 347–348.

[32]Commission Implementing Regulation (EU) 2018/151 of 30 January 2018 laying down rules for application of Directive (EU) 2016/1148 of the European Parliament and of the Council as regards further specification of the elements to be taken into account by digital service providers for managing the risks posed to the security of network and information systems and of the parameters for determining whether an incident has a substantial impact, OJ EU 2018 L 26/48.

[33]Commission Implementing Decision (EU) 2017/179 of 1 February 2017 laying down procedural arrangements necessary for the functioning of the Cooperation Group pursuant to Article 11(5) of the Directive (EU) 2016/1148 of the European Parliament and of the Council concerning measures for a high common level of security of network and information systems across the Union, OJ EU 2017 L 28/7.

Directive (EU) 2016/1148 concerning measures for a high common level of security of network and information systems across the Union.[34]
4. Commission Recommendation (EU) 2017/1584 of the 13th of September 2017 on coordinated responses to large-scale cybersecurity-incidents and crises.[35]
5. Joint Communication to the European Parliament and the Council—Resilience, Deterrence, and Defence: Building strong cybersecurity for the EU.[36]

10 Directive (EU) 2018/1972 Establishing the European Electronic Communications Code

Directive (EU) 2018/1972 of the European Parliament and of the Council of the 11th of December 2018 establishing the European Electronic Communications Code (Recast) (Text with EEA relevance)[37] recast and replaced Directives 2002/19/EC, 2002/20/EC and 2002/21/EC (with subsequent amendments), the provisions of which were meant to be transposed to the legal order of EU Member States by 2003. The new provisions included in Directive (EU) 2018/1972 should be implemented in the legal order of EU Member States by the 21st of December 2020, and will be deemed applicable from that date. The Directive entered into force on the 20th of December 2018.[38]

---

[34]Communication from the Commission to the European Parliament and the Council: Making the most of NIS—towards the effective implementation of Directive (EU) 2016/1148 concerning measures for a high common level of security of network and information systems across the Union COM(2017) 476 final 2.

[35]Commission Recommendation (EU) 2017/1584 of 13 September 2017 on coordinated response to large-scale cybersecurity incidents and crises, OJ EU 2017 L 239/36.

[36]Joint Communication to the European Parliament and the Council—Resilience, Deterrence, and Defence: Building strong cybersecurity for the EU JOIN(2017) 450 final.

[37]Directive (EU) 2018/1972 of the European Parliament and of the Council of 11 December 2018 establishing the European Electronic Communications Code (Recast) Text with EEA relevance. PE/52/2018/REV/1, OJ EU 2018L 321/36.

[38]Article 125 of the Code stipulates that Directives 2002/19/EC [Directive 2002/19/EC of the European Parliament and of the Council of 7 March 2002 on the access to and the interconnection of electronic communications networks and associated facilities (Access Directive) (OJ EC 2002 L 108/7], 2002/20/EC [Directive 2002/20/EC of the European Parliament and of the Council of 7 March 2002 on the authorisation of electronic communications networks and services (Authorisation Directive) (OJ EC 2002 L 108/21], 2002/21/EC [Directive 2002/21/EC of the European Parliament and of the Council, of 7 March 2002 on a common regulatory framework for electronic communications networks and services (A Framework Directive) (OJ EC 2002 L 108/33], and 2002/22/EC [Directive 2002/22/EC of the European Parliament and of the Council of 7 March 2002 on universal service and users' rights relating to electronic communications networks and services (Universal Service Directive) (OJ EC 2002 L 108/51], listed in Annex XII, Part A, will be repealed on 21 December 2020 without prejudice to the obligations of Member States relating to the time-limits for the transposition into national law and the dates of application of the Directives set out in Annex XII, Part B. Article 5 of Decision 243/2012/UE [Decision No 243/2012/EU of the European Parliament and of the Council of 14 March 2012 establishing a multi-annual radio spectrum policy

Directive 2018/1972 is a set of new or updated solutions regulating activities in the communications sector, i.e. issues pertinent to electronic-communications networks (tele-communications networks), communications services, and associated equipment and services. It also defines the expertise of national regulatory bodies and other responsible entities, and also envisages a range of procedures serving the purpose of harmonising the regulatory frameworks across the EU. Its aim is to promote the internal market in the field of electronic-communications networks and services, e.g. by stimulating competition and increasing investments in 5G and high-capacity networks, leading to the proliferation of such networks, the achievement of sustainable competition, the development of the interoperability of electronic-communications services, accessibility, network and services securing, and the provision of other benefits to end users, so as to ensure that all EU citizens and businesses can use high-quality communications, enjoy a guaranteed high level of consumer protection, and choose from a wide range of innovative digital services. This involves ensuring the provision, throughout the Union, of good-quality, affordable, publicly available services through effective competition and choice, to deal with circumstances in which the needs of end-users, including those with disabilities, in order to access the services on an equal basis with others are not being satisfactorily met by the market, and to lay down the necessary end-user rights (Article 1 (2) of Directive 2018/1972).

In compliance with Directive 2018/1972, national regulatory bodies and other responsible bodies, as well as BEREC,[39] the Commission, and Member States, should seek to attain the following general objectives.

1. To promote connectivity with and access to, and the take-up of, very-high-capacity networks, including fixed, mobile, and wire-less networks, by all citizens and businesses of the Union
2. To promote competition in the provision of electronic-communications networks and associated facilities, including efficient infrastructure-based competition, and in the provision of electronic-communications services and associated services
3. To contribute to the development of the internal market in the field of communications networks and services in the EU by

    (a) removing the existing obstacles to investments in electronic-communications networks, associated facilities and services, and electronic-communications services

programme. Text with EEA relevance (OJ EU 2012 L 81/7)] is removed, effective on 21 December 2020.

[39]The Commission, the Body of European Regulators for Electronic Communications (BEREC) is expected to ensure that EU regulations are complied with in a consistent manner to facilitate the efficient functioning of the single electronic-communications market across the EU. It provides advice to EU institutions, whether at their request or on its own initiative. BEREC includes the so-called regulatory authorities council, which is composed of heads of the national regulatory bodies from each EU Member State (or designated senior representatives of those bodies).

(b) rendering such networks and facilities accessible
(c) providing such services across the Union
(d) facilitating the consolidation of terms and conditions governing investments in such networks, facilities and services, as well as rendering them accessible and ensuring their provision

4. To develop common rules and predictable regulatory approaches as regards

(a) favouring the effective, efficient, and coordinated use of radio spectra
(b) open innovation
(c) the establishment and development of trans-European networks
(d) the provision, availability, and interoperability of pan-European services and end-to-end connectivity

5. To promote the interests of the citizens of the Union by ensuring connectivity and the widespread availability and take-up of very-high-capacity networks, including fixed, mobile, and wire-less networks, and of electronic-communications services by

(a) enabling the generating of maximum benefits in terms of choice, price, and quality, on the basis of effective competition
(b) maintaining the security of networks and services
(c) ensuring a high and common level of protection for end-users through the necessary sector-specific rules, and
(d) addressing the needs—such as affordable prices—of specific social groups, in particular end-users with disabilities, elderly end-users, and end-users with special social needs, and by providing choice and equal access for end-users with disabilities.

Member States were obliged to ensure that entities providing public-communications networks or publicly available electronic-communications services take appropriate and commensurate technical and organisational measures to manage the risks posed to the security of networks and services. These measures must ensure a level of security appropriate to the risk presented, having regard to the state of the art. In particular, measures, including encryption, where appropriate, are required to prevent and minimise the impact of security incidents on users, and on other networks and services (Article 40(1)). The coordination of Member States will be facilitated by ENISA in order to avoid diverging national requirements that might create security risks and barriers to the internal market (Article 40(2)).

11 Regulation (EU) No 2019/881 of the European Parliament and of the Council of 17 April 2019 on ENISA (The European Union Agency for Cybersecurity) and on Information and Communications Technology Cybersecurity Certification, and Repealing Regulation (EU) No 526/2013

Finally, two entities, i.e. the European Agency and the European Cybercrime Centre, are worth mentioning. The European Union Agency for Cybersecurity (ENISA) was set up as The European Network and Information Security Agency on the 15th of March 2004 by way of Regulation (EC) No 460/2004 of the European Parliament and of the Council of the 10th of March 2004 establishing the European Network and Information Security Agency.[40] Its objective is to provide assistance to EU Member States regarding broadly understood cybersecurity issues, and to drive the development of the information society. Under Article 27 of Regulation No 460/2004, the European Network and Information Security Agency was established for a period of five years, starting from the 14th of March 2004. Its duration was then extended twice by way of two subsequent regulations [Regulation No 1007/2008 of the European Parliament and of the Council of the 24th of September 2008 amending Regulation (EC) No 460/2004 establishing the European Network and Information Security Agency as regards its duration,[41] and Regulation (EC) No 580/2011 of the European Parliament and of the Council of the 8th of June 2011 amending Regulation (EC) No 460/2004 establishing the European Network and Information Security Agency as regards its duration[42]]. Then, the Agency operated under Regulation (EU) No 526/2013 of the European Parliament and of the Council of the 21st of May 2013 concerning the European Union Agency for Network and Information Security (ENISA),and repealing Regulation (EC) No 460/2004,[43] in

[40]Regulation (EC) No 460/2004 of the European Parliament and of the Council of 10 March 2004 establishing the European Network and Information Security Agency (Text with EEA relevance), OJ EU 2004 L 77/1.

[41]Regulation (EC) No 1007/2008 of the European Parliament and of the Council of 24 September 2008 amending Regulation (EC) No 460/2004 establishing the European Network and Information Security Agency as regards its duration (Text with EEA relevance), OJ EU 2008 L293/1.

[42]Regulation (EU) No 580/2011 of the European Parliament and of the Council of 8 June 2011 amending Regulation (EC) No 460/2004 establishing the European Network and Information Security Agency as regards its duration Text with EEA relevance, OJ EU 2011 L 165/3.

[43]Regulation (EU) No 526/2013 of the European Parliament and of the Council of 21 May 2013 concerning the European Union Agency for Network and Information Security (ENISA) and repealing Regulation (EC) No 460/2004 Text with EEA relevance, OJ EU 2013 L 165/4.

which its duration was envisaged to continue for seven years. As was rightly noted by C. Banasiński and W. Nowak, this limited duration, even if subsequently extended, significantly reduced the Agency's authority, hindering any long-term planning, and affecting in a negative way the situation of the entities to which its services were addressed. It was also contradictory to the NIS Directive which (see further comments) entrusted the Agency with certain tasks.[44] Regulation (EU) No 2019/881 of the European Parliament and of the Council of the 17th of April 2019 on ENISA (The European Union Agency for Cybersecurity) and on information and communications technology cybersecurity certification, and repealing Regulation (EU) No 526/2013,[45] put an end to the temporary character of the Agency. Not only did it envisage the Agency's duration to be unlimited, but it also vested new rights and duties in the Agency (*inter alia*, relating to certification and normalisation).

The Regulation, along with determining the objectives and duties of ENISA, and regulating its organisational matters, provides a framework for the establishment of European cybersecurity certification schemes, for the purpose of ensuring an adequate level of cybersecurity for ICT products, ICT services, and ICT processes in the Union, as well as for the purpose of preventing the fragmentation of the internal market with regard to cybersecurity certification schemes in the Union (Article 1(1)). The framework provides for a mechanism to establish European cybersecurity certification schemes, and to attest that ICT products, ICT services, and ICT processes, which have been evaluated in accordance with such schemes comply with specified security requirements for the purpose of protecting the availability, authenticity, integrity, or confidentiality of stored or transmitted or processed data, or the functions or services offered by, or accessible via, those products, services, and processes throughout their life cycle (Article 46(2)).

12 The European Cybercrime Centre (EC3)

In turn, the European Cybercrime Centre (EC3) established by way of the Communication from the Commission to the European Parliament, and the Council, "Tackling Crime in our Digital Age: Establishing a European Cybercrime Centre",[46] is in charge of coordinating EU efforts aimed at tackling cybercrime. In addition, it operates as a technical-expertise centre specialising in this field. Its capacities, therefore, overlap with those of ENISA.

---

[44]Banasiński and Nowak (2018), p. 151.

[45]Regulation (EU) 2019/881 of the European Parliament and of the Council of 17 April 2019 on ENISA (the European Union Agency for Cybersecurity) and on information and communications technology cybersecurity certification and repealing Regulation (EU) No 526/2013 (Cybersecurity Act) (Text with EEA relevance), OJ EU 219 L 151/15.

[46]Communication from the Commission to the Council and the European Parliament Tackling Crime in our Digital Age: Establishing a European Cybercrime Centre COM/2012/0140 final.

References

Banasiński C, Nowak W (2018) Europejski i krajowy system cyberbezpieczeństwa. In: Cyberbezpieczeństwo. Zarys wykładu, Warsaw

Chałubińska-Jentkiewicz K (2019) Cyberodpowiedzialność, Toruń

Kuliński M (2010) Regulacje komunikacji elektronicznej, Warsaw

Radoniewicz F (2015) Techniki implementacji do polskiego porządku prawnego postanowień decyzji ramowych Rady Unii Europejskiej dotyczących prawa karnego materialnego, Przegląd Prawa Konstytucyjnego 3

Radoniewicz F (2016) Odpowiedzialność karna za hacking i inne przestępstwa przeciwko danym komputerowym i systemom informatycznym, Warsaw

Radoniewicz F (2017) Ujęcie przestępstw przeciwko ochronie informacji w Kodeksie karnym a postanowienia dyrektywy 2013/40/UE dotyczącej ataków na systemy informatyczne – aspekty wybrane. In: Kitler W, Taczkowska-Olszewska J (eds) Bezpieczeństwo informacyjne. Aspekty prawno-administracyjne, Warszawa

Radoniewicz F (2019a) In: Kitler W, Taczkowska-Olszewska J, Radoniewicz F (eds) Ustawa o krajowym systemie cyberbezpieczeństwa. Komentarz, Warsaw

Radoniewicz F (2019b) Zwalczanie cybeterroryzmu w prawie UE – aspekty karnomaterialne. Cybersecurity and Law 2

Savin A (2017) EU internet law. Cheltenham–Northampton

Filip Radoniewicz PhD; legal advisor; adjunct in the Department of Cybersecurity Law and New Technologies at the Institute of Law, War Studies University, Warsaw; expert at the Academic Centre for Cybersecurity Policy, (War Studies University) and in the Ministry of Justice; he worked as an assistant judge (in the Fourth Criminal and Sixth Penitentiary Department of the Regional Court in Lublin); graduate of post-graduate studies: "European Union Law" at the Jagiellonian University, "Human Rights and Freedoms", co-organized by the Institute of Legal Sciences of the Polish Academy of Sciences and the Helsinki Foundation for Human Rights, and "Computer Network Administration" at the Lublin University of Technology; author or co-author of approximately fifty publications, mainly in the field of broadly understood criminal law, new technology law and human rights. Selected publications: F. Radoniewicz (2016) Odpowiedzialność karna za hacking i inne przestępstwa przeciwko danym komputerowym i systemom informatycznym / Criminal liability for hacking and other offences against computer data and information systems/, Wolters Kluwer, Warszawa; Ustawa o krajowym systemie cyberbezpieczeństwa. Komentarz /Act on the National Cybersecurity System. Commentary/ (2019) ed. W. Kitler, J. Taczkowska-Olszewska, F. Radoniewicz, CH. Beck, Warszawa.

National Cybersecurity System Act

Filip Radoniewicz

Abstract The Act of the 5th of July 2018 on the National Cybersecurity System (hereinafter referred to as "NCSA"), as indicated in the explanatory memorandum to this act, is on the one hand an attempt to comprehensively regulate the national cybersecurity system, which is a response to the constantly growing and dynamically changing cyber threats, which may affect the security of the state, the economy and society, and on the other hand it is the implementation of the Directive (EU) 2016/1148 of the European Parliament and of the Council of the 6th of July 2016 concerning measures for a high common level of security of network and information systems across the Union (the NIS Directive). The purpose of this chapter is a brief description of the act and a synthetic presentation of the solutions it contains, which will be discussed in detail later in the monograph.

1 Introduction

The Act of the 5th of July 2018 on the National Cybersecurity System[1] (hereinafter the NCSA), as indicated in the substantiation to its draft version is, on the one hand, an attempt at comprehensively regulating the national cybersecurity system, in response to the ever-growing and dynamically evolving cyber threats, which may potentially compromise the security of the State, the economy and society; on the other hand, it is intended to implement the above-mentioned NIS Directive.

The national cybersecurity system is organised to ensure cybersecurity at the national level, including the undisrupted provision of essential services and digital services, by attaining a sufficient level of security of information systems serving the

[1] Act of 5 July 2018 on the National Cybersecurity System, consolidated text Polish Journal of Laws of 2020 item 1369 as amended.

F. Radoniewicz (✉)
Akademickie Centrum Polityki Cyberbezpieczeństwa/Academic Center for Cybersecurity Policy, Akademia Sztuki Wojennej w Warszawie/War Studies University in Warsaw, Warsaw, Poland
e-mail: filip.radoniewicz@radoniewicz.eu

K. Chałubińska-Jentkiewicz et al. (eds.), *Cybersecurity in Poland*,
https://doi.org/10.1007/978-3-030-78551-2_7

purpose of providing such services, and by ensuring incident handling (Article 3 of the NCSA).

The Act regulates three problem areas: the organisation of the national cybersecurity system, and the duties and obligations of the entities, which form its part; the procedure for supervising and inspecting compliance with the provisions of the Act; and the scope of the Cybersecurity Strategy of the Republic of Poland (which is discussed in Chapter 13 of the NCSA).

The legislator has envisaged some exclusions in this respect, whether in whole or in part. Namely, providers of trust services and entities conducting treatment activities, established by the Head of the Internal Security Agency or the Head of the Intelligence service are wholly excluded from the Act, while telecommunications enterprises are excluded in the part regarding security and incident reporting requirements.

For the purpose of the NCSA, 19 definitions were formulated which, in view of the significance of this regulation, should be considered systemic definitions. First and foremost, the information system is understood as the ICT system (the teleinformation system) referred to in Article 3(3) of the Act of the 17th of February 2005 on the Computerisation of the Operations of Entities Performing Public Tasks, along with electronic data processed in that system (Article 2(14) of the NCSA). Second, cybersecurity is viewed as the ability of information systems to resist any action that compromises the confidentiality, integrity, availability and authenticity of processed data or related services rendered via such systems (Article 2(4) of the NCSA).[2]

In Article 2(5) of the NCSA, an incident is defined as an event, which has, or may have, an adverse impact on cybersecurity. The legislator has distinguished four categories of incidents: a critical incident (Article 2 (6) of the NCSA), a serious incident (Article 2 (7) of the NCSA), a substantial incident (Article 2 (8) of the NCSA), and an incident occurring within a public entity (Article 2 (9) of the NCSA):

1. serious incidents (Article 2 (7) of the NCSA), which cause, or may cause, serious detriment to quality or which result, or may result, in the discontinuation of the provision of an essential service (as defined in Article 14 (3) of the NIS Directive, incidents having a significant impact on the continuity of essential services);
2. substantial incidents (Article 2 (8) of the NCSA), which have a substantial impact on the provision of a digital service within the meaning of Article 4 of the Implementing Regulation 2017/151 (as defined in Article 16 (3) of the NIS Directive, incidents having a substantial impact on the provision of digital services);
3. incidents occurring within a public entity (Article 2 (9) of the NCSA), the classification of an incident to this category is not based on its significance (the impact threshold) but on the object of such impact, which is the ICT network used for the processing of data connected with the implementation of public duties, by public entities referred to in Article 4(7)-(15) of the NCSA, hence, all incidents, which cause, or may cause, serious detriment or discontinuation of a public duty;

[2]See more e.g. Radoniewicz (2019), pp. 27–51.

4. critical incidents (Article 2 (6) of the NCSA), which are incidents of the most serious character, resulting in serious detriment to security or public order, international interests, economic interests, activities of public institutions, civic rights and freedoms, or human life and health, classified by the relevant CSIRT MON, CSIRT NASK or CSIRT GOV.[3]

2 Entities of the National Cybersecurity System

The national cybersecurity system covers, in particular, operators of essential services (e.g. banks and enterprises from the energy sector), providers of digital services (e.g. entrepreneurs conducting activities via e-commerce platforms), authorities competent for cybersecurity, i.e. public institutions whose competences include supervising a given essential sector of economy (competent ministers, i.e. the minister competent for energy, the minister competent for transport, the minister competent for of maritime economy, the minister competent for inland navigation, the minister competent for health, the Minister of National Defence, the minister—competent for computerisation and the Polish Financial Supervision Authority), the Computer Security Incident Response Teams established within the Internal Security Agency (CSIRT GOV), the Research and Academic Computer Network, National Research Institute (CSIRT NASK), the Ministry of National Defence (CSIRT MON), sectoral cybersecurity teams, the Point of Single Contact for cybersecurity, the Government Plenipotentiary for Cybersecurity, the College for Cybersecurity, and public entities listed in Article 4 of the NCSA. The above-listed entities can be divided into:

1. administration entities—mainly serving supervisory and inspection functions (listed in Article 4 (17)-(20) of the NCSA) or coordinating incident handling (listed in Article 4 (3)-(6) of the NCSA);
2. participants: operators of essential services, digital service providers, and public entities listed in Chapter 5 of the NCSA;
3. other entities, entities difficult to unambiguously classify, e.g. providers of cybersecurity services.[4]

3 CSIRT MON, CSIRT NASK and CSIRT GOV

While implementing the provisions of the NIS Directive on establishing Computer Security Incident Response Teams (CSIRTs), new entities were not established, but the use was made of those already operating at the national level, on which the

[3]See more Chałubińska-Jentkiewicz et al. (2021), passim.

[4]Radoniewicz (2019), p. 54.

obligations arising from the Directive were imposed. These included: CERT.GOV. PL, MIL-CERT.PL and CERT POLSKA, i.e. currently CSIRT GOV, CSIRT MIL and CSIRT NASK, respectively.

CSIRT GOV, the Government Computer Security Incident Response Team, operating since January 2008 within the Internal Security Agency (as CERT.GOV. PL). It is in charge of coordinating the handling of incidents reported by the entities listed in Article 26 (7) of the NCSA (government administration, the National Bank of Poland, and Bank Gospodarstwa Krajowego). In addition, it is entrusted with identifying, preventing and detecting threats to security, which are important for ensuring the continuity of the functioning of the national ICT systems, utilised by public administration authorities or a system of ICT networks forming part of critical infrastructure. CSIRT MON (formerly MIL-CERT.PL), operating within the Computer Incident Response System of the Ministry of National Defence (SRnIK RON), performs duties in the field of coordinating the processes of preventing, detecting and responding to computer incidents in the ICT systems and networks of that Ministry. CSIRT MON coordinates the process of handling incidents reported by the entities subordinated to or supervised by the Ministry of National Defence, including entities whose ICT systems or networks are included in a consolidated register of facilities, installations, devices and services forming parts of critical infrastructure, referred to in Article 5b (7) (1) of the Act of the 26th of April 2007 on Crisis Management, and entrepreneurs of particular economic and defensive significance. NASK (the Research and Academic Computer Network) is a national research institute operating since 1993, which conducts scientific activities, runs the national (.pl) domains register, and provides advanced ICT services. Since 1996, CERT POLAND, currently CSIRT NASK, has been operating within its framework, coordinating the process of handling incidents, which violate network security in the "civil area" and, which occur within public networks, i.e. incidents reported by other entities (not classified to any of the above-mentioned groups), including by operators of essential services (excluding operators of critical infrastructure), digital services providers, and local government authorities. Generally speaking, CSIRT NASK's competences cover all incidents reported by those entities, which do not fall within the competences of CSIRT GOV and CSIRT MON (while the latter two are always, regardless of the category of the reporting entity, in charge of terrorist incidents, and CSIRT MON is also in charge of any incidents related to national defence). It is thus referred to as the CERT of last resort, being the entity to whom all citizens (or, more generally, all natural persons and organisational units) may report incidents. Furthermore, if an entity cannot establish direct contact or receive the expected support from the party directly involved in the incident, the reporting party files its query with the CSIRT as a last resort.[5] The tasks of, CSIRT MON, CSIRT NASK and CSIRT GOV are detailed described the chapter entitled "The main tasks of the team network to respond to computer security incidents in the light of the Act on the national cybersecurity system in Poland".

[5]See Banasiński and Nowak (2018), pp. 161–162; Trąbiński (2018), pp. 76–78.

4 The Competent Authorities for Cybersecurity

The competent authorities for cybersecurity are supreme authorities (i.e. competent ministers, depending on the sector indicated in Appendix I to the Act, in which a given operator of an essential service or a digital service provider conducts its activities, the minister competent for energy, the minister competent for transport, the minister competent for maritime economy, the minister competent for inland navigation, the minister competent for health, the Minister of National Defence, or the minister competent for computerisation), and one central authority (the Polish Financial Supervision Authority), issuing decisions on recognising an entity as the operator of an essential service (and also confirming the expiry of decisions made to that effect) and supervising those entities. Their duties are discussed in the chapter "The authorities competent for cybersecurity".

5 The Minister Competent for Computerisation and the Minister of National Defense

The minister competent for computerisation and the Minister of National Defense play a special role in the national cybersecurity system. The cited regulations referred to them are described in detail in separate chapters in part II of the monograph. The contact point run by the minister competent for computerisation ensures the exchange of information between various entities responsible for cybersecurity. Its duties include collecting serious or substantial incident reports from other EU Member States, and passing them to CSIRT MON, CSIRT NASK, CSIRT GOV or sectoral cybersecurity teams; passing serious or substantial incident reports concerning two or more EU Member States to other Member States; representing the Republic of Poland in the Cooperation Group; cooperating with the European Commission in the field of cybersecurity; coordinating the cooperation between authorities competent for cybersecurity and public authorities with the competent authorities in EU Member States; and ensuring information exchange for the Cooperation Group and CSIRT network purposes.[6]

[6]See more: chapter 16 "Role of Minister competent for computerisation in Cybersecurity system".

6 The Government Plenipotentiary for Cybersecurity

This is a single-person function appointed and recalled by the President of the Council of Ministers to coordinate activities and to implement the government's policy directed at ensuring cybersecurity. The Plenipotentiary's primary duties include:

(1) analysing and assessing the functioning of the national cybersecurity system based;
(2) supervising the risk management process within the national cybersecurity system based;
(3) reviewing governmental documents, including draft legal acts, pertinent to the implementation of cybersecurity-related duties;
(4) popularising new solutions and initiating activities to ensure cybersecurity at the national level;
(5) initiating cybersecurity training at the national level;
(6) issuing recommendations on the use of IT equipment or software at the CSIRT request (Article 62(1) of the NSC Act).

7 The College for Cybersecurity

The College for Cybersecurity is a collegial opinion-making and advisory authority, operating within the Council of Ministers, regarding cybersecurity issues and activities conducted in this field by CSIRT, the Ministry of National Defence, CSIRT NASK, CSIRT GOV, sectoral cybersecurity teams and authorities competent for cybersecurity. The College is led by the President of the Council of Ministers and is composed of the minister competent for internal affairs, the Minister competent for computerisation, the Minister of National Defence, the minister competent for foreign affairs, the Head of the Chancellery of the President of the Council of Ministers, the Head of the National Security Bureau, and the Minister competent for coordinating the activities of special forces. The College meetings are also attended by the Director of the Government Centre for Security, the Head or Deputy Head of the Internal Security Agency, the Head or Deputy Head of the Military Counterintelligence Service, and the Director of the Research and Academic Computer Network and the National Research Institute.

In addition, the College draws up recommendations for the Council of Ministers on the activities directed at ensuring cybersecurity at the national level (Article 65 (2) of the NCSA).

8 Incident Response Teams for a Given Sector or Subsector

The Act has envisaged the possibility for a computer security incident response team to be established by the authorities competent in cybersecurity, for any of the sectors or subsectors listed in the appendix to the Act (which is, therefore, not an obligatory body), i.e. a sectoral cybersecurity team (as referred to in Article 4 (6) of the NCSA) in charge of receiving serious incident reports within that sector or subsector. Such a team shall also be responsible for providing support in the handling of such incidents, supporting operators of essential services in performing their duties arising from the Act, analysing serious incidents, identifying associations between incidents, and formulating conclusions on incident handling, as well as for cooperating with the competent CSIRT (Article 44 (1) of the NCSA). Sectoral cybersecurity teams were not included in the initial draft act. A suggestion to include the possibility for these entities to be established was put forward during social consultations, and it appeared in numerous opinions, in which the fact that such teams would take account of the specificity of a given sector, thus enabling the support to be adjusted to operators of essential services, was seen as a major advantage. More about the Government Plenipotentiary and the College for Cybersecurity, see the chapter "The duties and legal status of the Government Plenipotentiary for Cybersecurity and the College for Cybersecurity".

9 Operators of Essential Services

These are entities whose organisational units are situated in the territory of the Republic of Poland, and in respect of whom the authority competent for cybersecurity has issued a decision on recognising them as operators of essential services (i.e. services of the highest significance for the maintenance of social or economic activities, included in the list of essential services), e.g. banks, enterprises from the energy sector, etc. It seems that a situation cannot be ruled out in which natural persons conducting business activities are classified as such, along with legal persons and organisational units without a legal personality whose legal capacity arises from separate provisions (e.g. commercial law companies and partnerships).

The authorities competent for cybersecurity issue a decision on recognising an entity as the operator of an essential service. The list of operators of essential services is maintained by the minister competent for computerisation. Operators of essential services are obligated, in particular, to ensure the security of the information systems they use for the provision of essential services, Operators of essential services cooperate with the sectoral cybersecurity team (if applicable). In addition, they are obliged to ensure the carrying out, at least on a biennial basis, the security audit of the information system used for the provision of the essential service.

With the purpose of performing their cybersecurity duties, operators of essential services establish internal structures responsible for cybersecurity or enter into agreements with third parties for the provision of cybersecurity services. The organisational and technical conditions for entities providing cybersecurity services, and internal structures responsible for cybersecurity, are determined by the minister competent for computerisation, by way of a regulation, which must consider the Polish Norms, along with the need to ensure the security of the internal structures responsible for cybersecurity, entities providing cybersecurity services to operators of essential services, and information processed within such structures or entities.

10 Digital Service Providers

Digital service providers are legal persons or organisational units without a legal personality with a registered office or management bodies in the Republic of Poland, or whose representatives operate organisational units in the territory of the Republic of Poland, and which provide digital services, i.e. services rendered electronically, within the meaning of the Act of the 18th of July 2002 on the Provision of Services Electronically (see more in the latter part of this article), as listed in Appendix 2 to the Act, i.e. e-commerce platforms, cloud computing services and search engines (Article 17 of the NCSA). Digital service providers take the appropriate and commensurate technical and organisational measures, as defined in Implementing Regulation 2018/151, to manage the risks posed to information systems used for the provision of digital services. These measures must guarantee cybersecurity commensurate with the actual risk. The obligations of operators of essential services and digital service providers and the liability of these entities are discussed in Part III of this monograph.

11 Entities Providing Cybersecurity Services

Entities providing cybersecurity services are entities, with which operators of essential services may conclude agreements with the purpose of performing their cybersecurity duties (the outsourcing of security services). These involve estimating the risk to essential services and managing that risk; implementing the appropriate technical and organisational measures, commensurate with the estimated risk; collecting information on threats and vulnerabilities; incident management; using preventive measures to limit the incident's impact on the security of the information system; using the means of communications enabling the proper and safe communication within the national cybersecurity system (Article 8); appointing a person in charge of contacts with authorities competent for cybersecurity, the competent CSIRT and the Point of Single Contact supervised by the minister competent for computerisation, and (if applicable) the sectoral cybersecurity team, and notifying these bodies of this fact; conducting educational activities addressed to users; providing the competent authority with information specifying in which EU Member

States these entities have been recognised as operators of essential services, and the date of termination of the provision of such services (Article 9 of the NCSA); developing, implementing and updating the required documentation (Article 10 (1)-(3) of the NCSA); handling incidents within their own systems; reporting serious incidents; cooperating in the handling of serious and critical incidents with the competent CSIRT, and (if applicable) the sectoral cybersecurity team; eliminating the identified vulnerabilities (Article 11(1)-(3) and Article 12 of the NCSA); and passing to the competent CSIRT information on other incidents, threats to cybersecurity pertinent to risk estimation, vulnerabilities and technologies used (Article 13 of the NCSA).

12 Entities Referred to in Article 4(7)-(15) of the Act on the National Cybersecurity System

Another group of entities included in the national cybersecurity system is indicated in Article 4(7) of the NCSA. These are, in the first place public finance sector units referred to in Article 9 (1)-(6),(8),(9),(11) and (12) of the Act of the 27th of August 2009 on Public Finance.[7]

The concept of the finance sector, rather than being expressly defined, has been described by reference to entities forming its part. Although the express legal definition is missing, major characteristic features of the finance sector entities may be outlined.[8]

More specifically, the finance sector is composed of organisational units set up under the applicable acts (the PF Act and specific acts) with the sole purpose of fulfilling public duties, which are financed from public resources and are subject to planning, balancing, control, accountancy and reporting, as well as discipline based on uniform principles. Some of the entities forming part of the public finance sector are listed by their names (the National Health Fund, the Social Insurance Institution, the Agricultural Social Insurance Fund, and the Polish Academy of Sciences) while others by their type (budgetary units, public authorities, State-owned or local government owned legal persons).[9]

The entities indicated (indirectly) in Article 4 (7) of the NCSA, i.e. public finance sector entities referred to in Article 9 (1)-(6), (8), (9), (11) and (12) of the PF Act, include:

(1) public authorities, including government administration bodies, State inspection and law enforcement bodies, as well as courts and tribunals,

[7] Act of 27 August 2009 on Public Finance consolidated text, Polish Journal of Laws of 2019, item 869, as amended (hereinafter: the PFA).

[8] Cilak (2020).

[9] Lipiec-Warzecha (2011), p. 84.

(2) local government bodies and their unions,
(3) budgetary units,
(4) local government-owned budgetary establishments,
(5) executive agencies,
(6) budget management institutions,
(7) the Social Insurance Institution and the resources it manages, as well as the Agricultural Social Insurance Fund and the resources managed by the President of the Agricultural Social Insurance Fund,
(8) the National Health Fund (in Polish: NFZ),
(9) state-owned higher education institutions, and
(10) The Polish Academy of Sciences and the organisational units it establishes.

Other entities, not previously discussed, listed in Article 4(7)-(15) of the NCSA:

(1) research institutes;
(2) the National Bank of Poland;
(3) Bank Gospodarstwa Krajowego;
(4) the Office of Technical Inspection;
(5) the Polish Air Navigation Services Agency;
(6) the Polish Centre for Accreditation;
(7) the National Fund for Environmental Protection and Water Management, and regional funds for environmental protection and water management;
(8) commercial law companies and partnerships performing public utility duties within the meaning of Article 1(2) of the Act of the 20th of December 1996 on Municipal Services.[10]

The regulations referred to public entities indicated in Article 4 (7)-(15) of the NCSA are described in the chapter "Obligations of public entities in the National Cybersecurity system" in III part of the monograph.

The compliance with the provisions of the NCSA is controlled and supervised[11] by:

1. the minister competent for computerisation, as regards the compliance of the entities providing cybersecurity services with statutory requirements;
2. authorities competent for Cybersecurity, as regards:
   (a) the performance of the statutory obligations to counteract cybersecurity threats and to report serious incidents by operators of essential services,
   (b) the compliance of digital service providers with security requirements as part of the digital services rendered by those entities, as defined in Implementing

[10]Act of 20 December 1996 on Municipal Services, consolidated text, Polish Journal of Laws of 2019, item 712, as amended.

[11]This matter is dedicated the chapter 20 "The system of control and supervision of operators of essential services, digital-service providers and entities providing cybersecurity services" in part III of the book.

Regulation 2018/151, the performance of their statutory obligations to report substantial incidents.

13 Penalties Provided for in the Act on the National Security System

Article 21 of the NIS Directive puts Member States under the obligation to envisage effective, proportionate and dissuasive penalties for the infringements of national provisions adopted pursuant to this Directive, and to take all measures necessary to ensure that they are implemented.

The Polish legislator has laid down regulation providing for administrative liability to be incurred by three groups of entities:

1. operators of essential services,
2. digital service providers, and
3. managers of operators of essential services.

In respect of operators of essential services and digital service providers, the legislator has only envisaged financial penalties, their amounts ranging from 1.00 PLN (where no lower limit of the penalty has been set) to 200,000 PLN. However, if the authority competent for cybersecurity, having conducted an inspection, finds that a given operator of an essential service or a given digital service provider violates the provisions of that Act, causing:

1. a direct and serious threat to cybersecurity in the field of defence, State security, security and public order, or human life and health,
2. a threat of causing a serious property damage or serious disruptions in the provision of essential services,

the authority competent for cybersecurity imposes a monetary penalty of up to 1,000,000 PLN (Article 73 (5) of the NSC Act).

Almost all violations for which penalties have been envisaged in the national cybersecurity system refer to the non-performance or improper performance by the operator of an essential service of the obligation imposed by the provisions of the Act (failure to report a serious incident to the responsible CSIRT MON, CSIRT NASK or CSIRT GOV within twenty four hours of its detection; therefore, an incident reported after the expiry of the said period will also be construed as a violation). Two other violations refer to hindering the inspection process and a failure to conform to post-inspection recommendations.

The proceedings regarding financial penalties imposed under the NCSA are governed by the provisions of the Code of Administrative Procedure,[12] which arises from the content of Article 189a of the CAP requiring the application of the

[12]Act of 14 June 1960—the Code of Administrative Procedure (consolidated text, Polish Journal of Laws of 2020, item 256, as amended (hereinafter: "CAP").

provisions of Section IVa of the CAP in respect of imposing or applying an administrative financial penalty or granting a relief from the enforcement of the penalty.[13]

14 The Cybersecurity Strategy

The Cybersecurity Strategy of the Republic of Poland is a document adopted by way of a resolution of the Council of Ministers, determining the strategic objectives, and the relevant political and regulatory measures directed at attaining and maintaining a high level of cybersecurity. It is developed for a five-year period with possible amendments throughout its duration (Article 68 and Article 69 (1) of the NCSA).[14] The draft Strategy is developed by the minister in charge of computerisation in cooperation with the Plenipotentiary, other ministers, and the responsible managers of central offices. The work on the draft version of the Strategy may also be attended by a representative of the President of the Republic of Poland.

The Strategy specifies, in particular:

(1) the objectives and priorities regarding cybersecurity;
(2) the entities engaged in the implementation of the Strategy;
(3) the measures directed at implementing the objectives assumed in the Strategy;
(4) the means for readiness, response and restoration, including principles of public-private cooperation;
(5) an approach to risk assessment;
(6) activities related to educational, informational and training programmes in the field of cybersecurity;
(7) activities related to research and development plans in the field of cybersecurity.

Strategy is dedicated the separate chapter in this part of the monograph.

15 Legal Acts Modified by the Act on the National Cybersecurity System

The Act on the National Cybersecurity System adjusts a number of legal acts to the provisions of the NIS Directive:

[13] More about monetary penalties—see chapter 21 “Monetary penalties in the National Cybersecurity System Act” in part III of this book.

[14] The currently binding strategy was adopted by way of Resolution No. 125 of the Council of Ministers of 22 October 2019 on the Cybersecurity Strategy of the Republic of Poland for 2019–2024 (Official Gazette of the Government of the Republic of Poland of 2019, item 1037).

(1) the Act of the 7th of September 1991 on the Education System;[15]
(2) the Act of the 4th of September 1997 on Branches of Government Administration;[16]
(3) the Act of the 24th of May 2002 on the Internal Security Agency and on the Intelligence Service;[17]
(4) the Act of the 29th of January 2004—Public Procurement Law;[18]
(5) the Act of the 16th of July 2004—Telecommunications Law;[19]
(6) the Act of 26 April 2007 on Crisis Management;[20]

Furthermore, in connection with the amendment to Article 5a (2) of the Act on Crisis Management introduced under the reference Act (see Article 82 of the NCSA), it was deemed necessary to amend the Agreement of the 19th of August 2010 on determining the detailed scope and means of cooperation of the Government Centre for Security and the Internal Security Agency.[21]

16 Legal Acts Issued Under the Authorisations Included in the Act on the National Cybersecurity System

Under the authorisations stipulated in the NCSA, seven implementing acts have been issued to date.[22]

1. The Regulation of the Council of Ministers of the 31st of October 2018 on serious incidents thresholds;[23]

[15] Act of 7 September 1991 on the Education System, consolidated text, Journal of Laws of 2020, item 13277, as amended.

[16] Act of 4 September 1997 on Branches of Government Administration, consolidated text, Polish Journal of Laws of 2020, item 1220, as amended.

[17] Act of 24 May 2002 on the Internal Security Agency and on the Intelligence Service, consolidated text, Polish Journal of Laws of 2020, item 27, as amended.

[18] Act of 29 January 2004—Public Procurement Law, consolidated text, Polish Journal of Laws of 2019, item 1843, as amended.

[19] Act of 16 July 2004—Telecommunications Law, consolidated text, Polish Journal of Laws of 2019, item 2460, as amended.

[20] Act of 26 April 2007 on Crisis Management, consolidated text, Polish Journal of Laws of 2020, item 1856, as amended.

[21] Official Journal of the ISA of 2010 No. 3, item 28, as amended.

[22] I.e. by 1 December 2020.

[23] The Regulation of the Council of Ministers of 31 October 2018 on serious incidents thresholds Polish Journal of Laws of 2018, item 2180.

2. The Regulation of the Council of Ministers of the 16th of October 2018 on documents regarding cybersecurity of the information system used for the provision of essential services;[24]
3. The Regulation of the Council of Ministers of the 2nd of October 2018 on the scope of activities and the working procedure of the College for Cybersecurity;[25]
4. The Regulation of the Council of Ministers of the 11th of September 2018 on a list of essential services and significance thresholds of the consequences of incidents disrupting the provision of essential services;[26]
5. The Regulation of the Minister of Digital Affairs of the 10th of September 2018 on the organisational and technical conditions for entities providing cybersecurity services, and internal structures responsible for cybersecurity;[27]
6. The Regulation of the Minister of Digital Affairs of the 12th of October 2018 on the list of certificates authorising the performance of audits;[28]
7. The Regulation of the Minister of Digital Affairs of the 4th of December 2019 on the organisational and technical conditions for entities providing cybersecurity services, and internal organisational structures of operators of essential services responsible for cybersecurity;[29]

Under Article 42 (1) (5), in connection with Article 41(3) and (7) of the NCSA, Ordinance No. 20 of the Minister of Maritime Economy and Inland Navigation of the 16th of April 2019 on the guidelines regarding the reporting of incidents within the national cybersecurity system in the water transport subsector, and in the potable water supply and distribution sector,[30] was issued.

In addition, under Article 52 (1) of the Act of the 6th of September 2001 on Road Transport,[31] in connection with Article 21 (1) of the NCSA, Ordinance No. 43/2018

[24]The Regulation of the Council of Ministers of 16 October 2018 on documents regarding cybersecurity of the information system used for the provision of essential services ,Polish Journal of Laws of 2018, item 2080.

[25]The Regulation of the Council of Ministers of 2 October 2018 on the scope of activities and the working procedure of the Committee for Cybersecurity Polish Journal of Laws of 2018, item 1952.

[26]The Regulation of the Council of Ministers of 11 September 2018 on a list of essential services and significance thresholds of the consequences of incidents disrupting the provision of essential services Polish Journal of Laws of 2018, item 1806.

[27]The Regulation of the Minister of Digital Affairs of 10 September 2018 on the organisational and technical conditions for entities providing cybersecurity services, and internal structures responsible for cybersecurity Polish Journal of Laws of 2018, item 1780.

[28]The Regulation of the Minister of Digital Affairs of 12 October 2018 on the list of certificates authorising the performance of audits Polish Journal of Laws of 2018, item 1999.

[29]The Regulation of the Minister of Digital Affairs of 4 December 2019 on the organisational and technical conditions for entities providing cybersecurity services, and internal organisational structures of operators of essential services responsible for cybersecurity Polish Journal of Laws of 2019, item 2479.

[30]Official Journal of the Ministry of Maritime Economy and Inland Navigation of 2019, item 20.

[31]Act of 6 September 2001 on Road Transport Polish Journal of Laws of 2017, item 2200, as amended.

of the Chief Inspector of Road Transport on appointing the Plenipotentiary for cybersecurity at the Chief Inspectorate of Road Transport of the 20th of September 2018 was issued.[32]

Under 175a(2)(a) of the Telecommunications Law, added by way of Article 80 of the NCSA, the Minister of Digital Affairs issued the Regulation of the 20th of September 2018 on the criteria of recognising the violation of security or integrity of networks or telecommunications services as a violation significantly affecting the functioning of networks or services.[33] At the same time, under Article 175a (2) of Telecommunications Law, the Minister of Digital Affairs issued a new Regulation of the 20th of September 2018 on the template form for providing information on the violation of security or integrity of networks or telecommunications services as a violation significantly affecting the functioning of networks or services,[34] which replaced the previously binding regulation bearing the same title. However, the authorisation granted in Article 32aa(9) of the Act on the Internal Security Agency and the Intelligence Service, added by way of Article 79 of the NCSA, that the President of the Council of Ministers determine, by way of a regulation, the conditions and procedure for conducting, coordinating and implementing the warning system, and in particular to determine the measures necessary for its establishment and maintenance, and the template agreement referred to in Par. 7 (in which the ISA makes arrangements with the critical infrastructure operator regarding the technical aspects of participation in the warning system and the system configuration model), driven by the need to ensure security of the ICT systems significant from the point of view of the continuity of the functioning of the State, has not been implemented yet.

Some other documents were issued under the NCSA, e.g.:

1. The Communication of the Minister of Digital Affairs of the 7th of January 2020 on the agreement between CSIRT GOV and CSIRT NASK regarding the delegation of duties;[35]
2. Communication No. 1 of the Head of the Internal Security Agency of the 29th of August 2019 regarding the conclusion of an agreement on the delegation of duties related to incidents reported by the Polish Air Navigation Services Agency;[36]
3. Communication No. 2 of the Head of the Internal Security Agency of the 28th of November 2019 regarding the conclusion of an agreement on the delegation of

[32]Official Journal of the Chief Inspector of Road Transport of 2018, item 43.

[33]Polish Journal of Laws of 2018, item 1830.

[34]Polish Journal of Laws of 2018, item 1831.

[35]Official Journal of the Ministry of Digital Affairs of 2020, item 1.

[36]Communication No. 1 of the Head of the Internal Security Agency of 29 August 2019 regarding the conclusion of an agreement on the delegation of duties related to incidents reported by the Polish Air Navigation Services Agency Official Journal of the Internal Security Agency of 2019, item 15.

duties related to incidents reported by the Research and Academic Computer Network to the National Research Institute;[37]

4. Communication No. 3 of the Head of the Internal Security Agency of the 28th of November 2019 regarding the conclusion of an agreement on the delegation of duties related to incidents reported by companies being members of the Capital Group of PGE Polska Grupa Energetyczna S.A.;[38]
5. Resolution No. 125 of the Council of Ministers of the 22nd of October 2019 on the National Policy Frameworks on Cybersecurity of the Republic of Poland for 2019–2024;[39]
6. The Communication of the Minister of Digital Affairs of the 19th of September 2019 on the agreement between CSIRT GOV and CSIRT NASK regarding the delegation of duties.[40]

References

Banasiński C, Nowak W (2018) Europejski i krajowy system cyberbezpieczeństwa. In: Cyberbezpieczeństwo. Zarys wykładu, Warsaw

Chałubińska-Jentkiewicz K, Karpiuk M, Kostrubiec J (2021) The legal status of public entities in the field of cybersecurity in Poland. Lex Localis Press, Maribor

Cilak M (2020) Komentarz do art. 9. In: Ofiarski Z (ed) Ustawa o finansach publicznych. Komentarz, LEX/el

Lipiec-Warzecha L (2011) Ustawa o finansach publicznych. Komentarz, Warsaw

Radoniewicz F (2019) In: Kitler W, Taczkowska-Olszewska J, Radoniewicz F (eds) Ustawa o krajowym systemie cyberbezpieczeństwa. Warsaw, Komentarz

Trąbiński P (2018) Podział kompetencji w zapewnianiu cyberbezpieczeństwa. In: Szpor G, Gryszczyńska A (eds) Internet. Strategie bezpieczeństwa, Warsaw

[37]Communication No. 2 of the Head of the Internal Security Agency of 28 November 2019 regarding the conclusion of an agreement on the delegation of duties related to incidents reported by the Research and Academic Computer Network—National Research Institute Official Journal of the Internal Security Agency of 2019, item 22.

[38]Communication No. 3 of the Head of the Internal Security Agency of 28 November 2019 regarding the conclusion of an agreement on the delegation of duties related to incidents reported by companies being members of the Capital Group of PGE Polska Grupa Energetyczna S.A Official Journal of the Internal Security Agency of 2019, item 23.

[39]Resolution No. 125 of the Council of Ministers of 22 October 2019 on the National Policy Frameworks on Cybersecurity of the Republic of Poland for 2019-2024 Official Gazette of the Government of the Republic of Poland of 2019, item 1037.

[40]The Communication of the Minister of Digitisation of 19 September 2019 on the agreement between CSIRT GOV and CSIRT NASK regarding the delegation of duties Official Journal of the Ministry of Digital Affairs of 2019, item 26.

Filip Radoniewicz PhD; legal advisor; adjunct in the Department of Cybersecurity Law and New Technologies at the Institute of Law, War Studies University, Warsaw; expert at the Academic Centre for Cybersecurity Policy, (War Studies University) and in the Ministry of Justice; he worked as an assistant judge (in the Fourth Criminal and Sixth Penitentiary Department of the Regional Court in Lublin); graduate of post-graduate studies: "European Union Law" at the Jagiellonian University, "Human Rights and Freedoms", co-organized by the Institute of Legal Sciences of the Polish Academy of Sciences and the Helsinki Foundation for Human Rights, and "Computer Network Administration" at the Lublin University of Technology; author or co-author of approximately fifty publications, mainly in the field of broadly understood criminal law, new technology law and human rights. Selected publications: F. Radoniewicz (2016) Odpowiedzialność karna za hacking i inne przestępstwa przeciwko danym komputerowym i systemom informatycznym/Criminal liability for hacking and other offences against computer data and information systems/, Wolters Kluwer, Warszawa; Ustawa o krajowym systemie cyberbezpieczeństwa. Komentarz /Act on the National Cybersecurity System. Commentary/ (2019) ed. W. Kitler, J. Taczkowska-Olszewska, F. Radoniewicz, CH. Beck, Warszawa.

The New National Security Strategy of the Republic of Poland

Jacek Sobczak

Abstract The approval of the new security strategy of the Republic of Poland in May 2020 required paying attention to the terminological aspects of the concepts used in this document, as well as to legal issues, which were mainly connected with the problem of whether this act should be formally countersigned or not. An equally important issue was to draw attention to the fact that, in practice, two strategies were being developed in Poland's legal system—one approved by the President of the Republic of Poland in his decision of May 12, 2020, and the other, which was in the form of a resolution of the Council of Ministers, applicable from 9 April 2013. The current strategy was preceded by earlier strategies and the White Paper on National Security of the Republic of Poland. The strategy of May 12, 2020 is a comprehensive document that sheds light on all elements of national security. Its content addresses such phenomena as hybridity, operation in cyberspace, the need for new technologies, and artificial intelligence.

1 Terminology Issues

Pursuant to Article 4a(1)(1) of the Act of 21 November 1967 on the Universal Duty to Defend the Republic of Poland,[1] the President of the Republic of Poland, to safeguard the sovereignty and security of the state, and the integrity and indivisibility of its territory, at the request of the Prime Minister, approves the National Security Strategy.[2] The legislator did not provide a precise definition of "security strategy"

[1]Act of 21 November 1967 on the Universal Duty to Defend the Republic of Poland, consolidated text, Polish Journal of Laws of 2019, item 1541, as amended.

[2]The text of Article 4a of the Act on the Universal Duty to Defend the Republic of Poland was introduced in the Act pursuant to Article 4(1) of the Act of 29 May 1989 on Transferring the Powers

J. Sobczak (✉)
Akademia Ekonomiczno-Humanistyczna w Warszawie/University of Economics and Human Sciences in Warsaw, Warsaw, Poland
e-mail: j.sobczak@vizja.pl

K. Chałubińska-Jentkiewicz et al. (eds.), *Cybersecurity in Poland*,
https://doi.org/10.1007/978-3-030-78551-2_8

and the "Political and Strategic Defence Directive of the Republic of Poland", leaving these issues to the legal commentators. In the literature, the term "strategy" refers to all measures taken to achieve a certain goal.[3] More precisely, "strategy" is a domain of military science, which involves preparation for and carrying out war operations, and the respective campaigns and battles.[4] A strategy specifies the quantity and quality of the resources needed to achieve military goals, and the quantity and quality of all types of reserves, in terms of both staff and materials, as well as the organisation and preparation methods of the armed forces, the devising of plans and their use in warfare, and the development of the areas of operations and strategic directions.[5] A strategy involves defining long-term objectives, and the methods for achieving them through adopting specific courses of action and distributing resources.[6]

A "national security strategy" is usually understood as "a choice made on the basis of intelligence and strategic analyses of the appropriate and essential measures available to the state in order to achieve its goals and fulfil the tasks specified in the security policy[7]". A strategy is also defined as "the theory and practice of state operations with a view to achieving set goals in the domain of security, general and long-term". It is also perceived as "a domain of the national strategy encompassing its creation and preparation, and the use of the state's potential in order to prevent any threats to its existence and development" and as "the theory and practice

---

Previously Held by the Council of State to the President of the Polish People's Republic and Other State bodies (Polish Journal of Laws of 1989, No. 34, item 178, 19 July 1989). The original Article 4a only stated that the President of the Polish People's Republic as Commander-in-Chief of the armed forces, at the request of the Minister of National Defence, specifies the main development directions for the armed forces and their preparation for state defence. After changing the name of the Polish State to the Republic of Poland, the name of the Head of the State was changed, and the name "President of the Republic of Poland" was introduced in the Act on the Universal Duty to Defend the Republic of Poland through the Act of 25 October 1991, amending the Act on the Universal Duty to Defend the Polish People's Republic and Certain Other Acts (Polish Journal of Laws of 1991, No. 113, item 491). The power to approve the national security strategy was granted to the President of the Republic of Poland in Article 35(1) of the Act of 29 August 2002 Martial Law and the Competences of the Commander-in-Chief of the Army and the Rules of the Commander-in-Chief's Subordination to the Constitutional Authorities of the Republic of Poland (Polish Journal of Laws of 2002, No. 156, item 1301). The same provision granted the President of the Republic of Poland the power to issue, at the request of the Prime Minister, by way of a decision, the Political and Strategic Defence Directive of the Republic of Poland, and other secondary documents to the security strategy.

[3]The term "strategy" derives from the word *strategos*, which means "army leader", i.e. a commander of an army or fleet. In colloquial language, "strategy" is defined as "a way of acting in order to achieve a specific goal, operating in line with developed assumptions, a forward-thinking action plan". See Dubisz (2003), pp. 1411–1412.

[4]See Szymczak (1989), p. 346; Olechnicki and Załęcki (1997), p. 205, define strategy as a planned and often practiced method of achieving a set goal.

[5]See *Wielka Encyklopedia Powszechna PWN*, Vol. 11, p. 39.

[6]Beaufre (1988), p. 161.

[7]Marczak (2008), p. 129.

oriented towards advancing and deploying the state's potential in order to achieve the objective of counteracting any threats to its existence and development, general and long-term[8]". W. Kitler views the national security strategy as "a national strategy domain understood as a choice made on the basis of the strategic analysis of the appropriate and necessary measures available to the state in order to achieve its goals and satisfy the interests specified in the national security policy, general and long-term".[9] D. Robertson points out that, unlike tactics, a strategy requires long-term preparations, and both terms can be used in each conflict situation. He emphasises that in the contemporary defence terminology, strategies are considered to be political, and tactics are viewed as purely technical decisions by the army aimed at a better achievement of the strategic goals set by the political leaders.[10] Some literature sources consider strategy as a praxeological category, i.e. serving to combine the available documents, instruments, and methods of efficient operations in order to achieve the set goal.[11]

In analysing the notion of "a national strategy", R. Kuźniar concluded that a strategy does not set political goals, and yet a strategic instinct and discipline, characteristic of the constraints of a strategic approach, is an obligatory (though insufficient) condition for the optimum realisation of the state's interests (security and development), which should not depend on the whims of politics.[12]

The notion of the "security of the state" was not defined in the Act itself. The legal commentators have pointed out that, despite the term's being universally associated with national security, it is not synonymous with it. In the literature, "national security" is defined as "an objective state of the certainty of physical survival and the freedom to develop, at the same time being a vital need, and thus also a national goal and interest (raison d'état), which assumes the securing and strengthening of vital values (. . .) achieved in the external and internal spheres".[13] "The security of the state" is understood as a guarantee of the territorial integrity of the state and its sovereignty,[14] as well as its political, social, and economic development.[15] It is also pointed out that "the security of the state" is "the state's and society's ability to ensure the conditions for its survival as a civic community institution, the biological survival of the population, territorial integrity, political independence, internal

[8]Słownik terminów zakresu bezpieczeństwa narodowego, Warsaw 2002, p. 131.

[9]Kitler (2011), p. 39.

[10]Robertson (2009), pp. 420–421.

[11]Brodie (1973), p. 452.

[12]Kuźniar (2004), p. 9.

[13]Stańczyk (1996), p. 21; Mickiewicz (2018), p. 35.

[14]On sovereignty, see Czaputowicz (2018), pp. 15–55.

[15]Czaputowicz (2013), p. 15. Cf. also Zięba (1997), pp. 8–22. He states that security of the state, formulated as a foreign policy objective, is an expression of the internal needs, interests, and values of a specific society (nation), and its political system. He notes, "the national security policy has the aim of protecting the state and society (the nation or nations in the case of a multinational state) from external threats. He agrees with US researchers that "national security may be defined as a nation's ability to protect its internal values from external threats". Berkowitz and Bock (1965), p. X.

stability, and quality of life" (...) it is shaped by activities including taking opportunities, undertaking challenges, reducing risk, and eliminating external and internal threats to ensure continuance, identity, functioning, and the freedom to develop for the state and the nation (society)".[16] Attention is drawn to the fact that security also has an international dimension.[17] Building a security strategy is a difficult task due to the dynamically changing international environment. Currently it is interpreted as a guarantee of meeting broadly defined needs, rights and aspirations of a nation (society) referring to the way and quality of life, systemic and cultural identity and development opportunities.[18]

2 The Countersignature Issue

The wording of Article 4a(1)(1) of the Act on the Universal Duty to Defend the Republic of Poland can raise doubts as to the nature of the Act, especially whether the authorisation referred to in these provisions has the nature of a countersignature. Undoubtedly, in line with Article 144 of the Constitution, the President's official acts issued exercising his/her constitutional and statutory powers require the signature of the Prime Minister, who, by such a signature, accepts responsibility therefor to the Sejm. There is no doubt that the President cannot issue state leadership acts without a suitable mandate in legal regulations. The basis of such a mandate can be the Constitution and the Acts. These official laws can take the form of regulations, decrees, and decisions, and the legal commentators agree on this matter. It is pointed out that not every action of the President expressed in the form of a specific document should be regarded as an official act, as the name "act" is reserved for documents for which the President resolves an issue. Not every time the President's activity takes a written form addressed to a specific group of recipients can one speak of a President's official act as stipulated in Article 144 of the Constitution. If such a document addressed to a specific group of recipients does not contain any Resolution on rights or responsibilities, it is not a President's official act but only a manifestation of his/her official activities as the Head of the State. These may include congratulatory letters, speeches, and so-called official addresses.[19] Therefore, P. Sarnecki distinguishes President's official acts and written acts of the Head of the State. Their shared feature is that they contain information on the Presidential office, but do not bear any characteristics of legally binding decisions.[20]

[16]Zając and Zięba (2011), p. 10 et seq.

[17]Słomczyńska (2007), pp. 21–88. Cf. also Zięba (2018), pp. 17–34.

[18]Nowakowski (2008), p. 75; Gołda-Sobczak (2017), pp. 129–152; Sobczak (2013), pp. 187–213; Sobczak and Kakareko (2017), pp. 842–862.

[19]Kozłowski (2016), p. 708.

[20]Sarnecki (2000), p. 59.

The situation described in Article 4a(1)(1) of the Act of 21 November 1967 on the Universal Duty to Defend the Republic of Poland differs significantly from that described in Article 144(2) of the Constitution, which states that a President's official act should be signed by the Prime Minister in order to be valid, whereas in the case of the National Security Strategy the President receives the text of the Strategy from the Prime Minister for approval. Thus, it is the Prime Minister who presents the strategy to the President for approval. The wording of the quoted provision of the Act of 21 November 1967 shows that the Strategy is not binding without approval, being only a draft. Assessing the legal situation, one can venture the statement that the President is the one who countersigns an Act presented to him/her by the Prime Minister. The literature emphasises that the President is not always the initiator of the issuing of an official act, as he/she may receive such an act from the Prime Minister. K. Kozłowski points out that most official acts of the Head of the State subject to countersignature are prepared by the government, and subsequently presented to the President for approval. As Kozłowski mentions, this also refers to defence in general. He also indicates, referring to the position presented by P. Sarnecki, "the countersignature requirement should not cover the actions of the President, being 'a continuation' of certain official acts clearly exempt from the countersignature requirement, i.e. such which can be referred to as 'secondary'[21]".

The approval of the National Security Strategy was not mentioned among official acts exempt from a countersignature, i.e. those identified in Article 144(3) of the Constitution, which specifies the powers of the President exercised outside the political control system of the Sejm. However, it is worth mentioning that the literature sources emphasise the fact that authorisations corresponding to any of the powers mentioned in the provision with the same *ratio legis* for their exclusion should also be excluded from the countersignature requirement, despite the lack of a specific provision in Article 144(3) of the Constitution.[22] It thus can be claimed that if the President's legislative initiative and the decree on the promulgation of an act is exempt from the countersignature obligation, the same should apply to the National Security Strategy. Another argument is that, without the decision of the Prime Minister on submitting a request to the President for the approval of the Strategy, the President is unable to approve the Strategy.[23] Also, the President is not authorised to announce a Strategy independently without the request of the Prime Minister. In practice, the National Security Strategy is approved by a decision of the

[21]Sarnecki (2000), pp. 57–58; Granat (2002), p. 95 et seq.

[22]Kozłowski (2016), pp. 709–710. Sarnecki (2000), pp. 57–58.

[23]The literature contains a highly questionable statement that the President countersigns the Security Strategy because Article 4a (1) (1) "emphasises this role in the Security Strategy, which is approved by the President and the Prime Minister". Sobera (2015), p. 184. It should be stressed that, contrary to W. Sobera's view, the Prime Minister does not approve the Security Strategy but submits a request to the President to approve it. The Prime Minister may of course have an impact on the content of the Strategy, and if he/she does not approve of the document, he/she may defer the submission of the request. It is also difficult to agree with the view that the President is the person who countersigns the Security Strategy. Such a situation is not provided for in the Constitution.

President of the Republic of Poland announced in the Official Gazette of the Government of the Republic of Poland. The Strategy document is appended to the decision.[24]

3 Security Strategies of the Republic of Poland 1990–2007

The literature sources emphasise that one of the most important and urgent challenges for Poland after 1989 was the formulation of a national strategy, and developing a suitable independent security policy, including a defence policy.[25] At the turn of 1990, the Defence Doctrine of the Republic of Poland was developed and adopted by Resolution of the State Defence Committee of 21 February 1990. A change in the political situation as a result of the dissolution of the Warsaw Pact and the fall of the Soviet Union resulted in the adoption of two documents at the State Defence Committee meeting on 2 November 1992: Assumptions in the Polish Security Policy and the Security and Defence Strategy Policy of the Republic of Poland. After becoming a member of NATO, Poland created a new holistic draft of a new security and defence strategy.[26] On 4 January 2000, the Council of Ministers adopted the Security Strategy, and 5 months later, on 23 May 2000, the Defence Strategy.[27] Both documents were announced within one year from accession, and the adoption of NATO's strategic concept at the Washington summit in 1999.

Another strategy entitled the National Security Strategy of the Republic of Poland was developed in 2003. However, it was assessed as a much-needed and useful document, coming up against the new trends in the domain of international and national security which began to form after 11 September 2001 (9/11), despite its undoubted flaws. The new Strategy was adopted at the session of the Council of Ministers in April 2007, and the President of the Republic of Poland approved it on 13 November 2007.[28] The document aimed at an integrated approach to national security, stating that Poland's security was impacted on by processes and events in the state, the region, and Europe. It indicated three tiers of national interests—vital, important, and significant. However, as stated by S. Koziej and A. Brzozowski, it does have structural shortcomings.[29] The National Security Strategy was met with a

[24]See the Decision of the President of the Republic of Poland of 12 May 2020 on the approval of the National Security Strategy of the Republic of Poland, Official Gazette of the Government of the Republic of Poland of 2020, item 413.

[25]Koziej and Brzozowski (2015), p. 19.

[26]Koziej (1998a, b), passim.

[27]As a result of the implementation of the Defence Strategy, the Council of Ministers passed implementing regulations to the Act on the Universal Duty to Defend the Republic of Poland, which, based on the Strategy's assumptions, specified certain elements in the state's defence system.

[28]The strategy was presented to the President by the Prime Minister as required in the Act, but, before the approval of the Strategy, the Prime Minister and his Government resigned.

[29]Koziej (1998a, b), passim.

lively response from legal commentators, and a quite-critical assessment from academic circles.[30]

The 2007 strategy was replaced by another, which on 5 November 2014 was approved by President Bronisław Komorowski. Before the strategy was developed, the Strategic National Security Review and the White Book on National Security were prepared in 2013.[31]

4 The White Book on the National Security of the Republic of Poland

The White Book on National Security was presented on 24 May 2013 in the Presidential Palace as the outcome of two years of work by almost 200 experts appointed in November 2010. The work was conducted within the Strategic National Security Review and Report, which ended in September 2012. The outcome of the work was the classified Report of the Committee on the Strategic National Security Review, and it contained key conclusions and recommendations on the security policy of the Republic of Poland, which constituted the basis of the White Book. Its primary role in principle was to disseminate knowledge on security and spreading public awareness in this area.

The book is an extensive study containing 265 pages, which began with a synthesis containing a diagnosis of the state of security, a projection of the security environment development, and a concept of preparing security systems. The next parts comprised an introduction explaining the methodology and the principles of the study, and four chapters. These included a diagnosis of the state of national security, with a quite detailed account of the historical evolution of Poland's security,[32] Poland's potential in the domain of security, national interests, and

[30]Żurawski vel Grajewski (2013), p. 111 et seq.; Nowakowski et al. (2014), pp. 479–543; Koziej and Brzozowski (2014), pp. 11–40.

[31]*Biała Księga Bezpieczeństwa Narodowego https://www.bialystok.ap.gov.pl/arch/teksty/biala_ksiega.pdf*. Accessed on 5 July 2020, 5:27 p.m.

[32]The evolution of the history of security was presented from the origins of Poland's statehood until the present times. However, no attempts to establish continuous patterns were made, only pointing to the necessity to pay special attention to the range and forms of cooperation between the two major Poland's neighbours, Russia and Germany. The assessment of the pre-partition period made it possible to infer that it is in Poland's vital interests to have the ability to organise and maintain an efficiently operating state. It was stressed that it is unacceptable to disrupt the balance between the freedom of individuals or groups and the responsibility of the state. Emphasis was placed on cultivating national identity and preventing the development of an unfavourable union of interests among neighbours. Referring to the period of the Second Polish Republic and World War II, it was indicated that in addition to observing a neighbours' policy it was necessary to modernise the defence potential of the country and carry out a rational calculation of the effectiveness of the established unions. Assessing the period of the Third Polish Republic, it was concluded that after 1989 Poland managed to reach most strategic goals, as it joined the North Atlantic Treaty

strategic goals in the field of security. The subsequent part presented a projection of the security environment development in the global, regional, and national dimensions and security conditions development scenarios. The third chapter presented the concept of strategic activities, i.e. operational strategies, discussing the basis of and the fundamental idea behind the operational strategies, and also the strategic tasks of subsystems: national security operational and support subsystems. The last chapter contained a formulation of the concept for the preparation of national security systems, i.e. a preparatory strategy. The discussed issues included the bases of and the fundamental ideas behind the preparatory strategies, and the preparation of three national security subsystems: national and operational security management, and support. The book ends with a summarised conclusion and is supplemented with an extract of the main strategic recommendations of the national security review, a list of the main conceptual categories, a list of primary laws relating to national security and a list of individuals participating in the strategic security review.

Without going into a detailed presentation of the content of the White Book, it is worth emphasising that, in addition to so-called hard security issues, covering state defence and protection, special attention is drawn to new social and economic domains and sectors, as well as cross-sector security fields which are bringing new challenges and threats to the state, associated with financial, energy, demographic, cybernetic, climate and environmental security. Attention should also be paid to the main conceptual categories, contained in Annex No. 2. A characterisation was provided, i.a., of the following notions: security,[33] security environment, the state's

Organisation (1999) and the European Union, and established a strategic partnership with the United States, engaging in subregional cooperation (the Weimar Triangle, the Visegrad Group, the Central European Initiative, the Council of the Baltic Sea States).

[33]**Security** in the White Book is considered a basic category, defined as the theory and practice of ensuring the possibility of survival (existence) and the realisation of an entity's own interests, including, in particular, by taking advantage of opportunities (favourable circumstances), facing challenges, reducing risks, and counteracting (preventing and opposing) all kinds of threats to the given entity and its interests. It emphasises that "contemporary security is integrated (comprehensive, multidimensional) in nature and can – depending on the adopted criteria – be subdivided into various types, fields, sectors, divisions and areas". As indicated in the publication, depending on the type of entity involved, the following types of security may be distinguished: individual (personal) security, group security, national security (including state and territorial security, at the province, district, and commune levels), international security (regional and global), including interstate security (alliances and coalition arrangements) and transnational security. It was noted that "depending on the subject (content) of security, it is possible to distinguish as many types, fields, sectors, divisions, areas etc. as many potential spheres of activity of the given entity are possible (security issues arise in every sphere of activity)". As emphasised in the White Book, within the framework of the integrated national security of the Republic of Poland (the security of the state) it is possible to distinguish two constitutional areas thereof: internal and external security, as well as four primary fields of security: defence (national defence, i.e. the military security of a state), protection (civilian, non-military security), and social and economic security (one may, in fact, also speak of "socio-economic security", including the social and economic support of security efforts). It was stated that within the above fields, one might distinguish—in accordance with the Polish state activity structure, encompassing a number of departments of public administration—national security sectors such as diplomacy for security, military issues, intelligence and counterintelligence,

strategic goals in the sphere of security, the national security strategy,[34] and the national security system.[35] This terminological arrangement seems quite crucial, taking into consideration the fact that scientific studies, political commentary journalism, and normative acts of law include a number of concepts and attempts to define specific notions. The volume limits of this article do not allow a presentation of all the definitions formulated in the White Book, obliging the author to focus on the most important ones.

Unfortunately, the White Book seems to be rather unfamiliar to the public, as well as to the specialists, lawyers, and academics dealing with national security. The expectations of the White Book's authors have not been fulfilled, as they hoped that its publication would contribute to and stimulate a broad social debate and transformational activities, strengthening the synergy of the national security system through the integration of the national security management subsystem.

5 National Security Strategy of the Republic of Poland 2014

The Strategy was developed by the Interdepartmental Group for the Development of the National Security Strategy of the Republic of Poland appointed by way of Decree No. 63 of the Prime Minister of 4 September 2013.[36] By establishing the Interdepartmental Group for the Development of the National Security Strategy of the Republic of Poland, the Prime Minister indicated that its task would be to define the national interests and strategic objectives of the Republic of Poland in the sphere

public security, emergency rescue, social security (including, inter alia, the protection of heritage, education for security, the media in the security system), economic security (including, inter alia, energy, financial and infrastructural security). Due to the very nature of integrated security there are also security areas which span multiple sectors or fields, such as cybersecurity. *Biała Księga*, p. 248. On cybersecurity, see Chałubińska-Jentkiewicz (2019), pp. 7–24. Cf. also Sienkiewicz (2009), p. 27; Worona (2020), pp. 27–136. On the function of the media in security protection, see Skrzypczak (2015), pp. 25–34; Jancz, pp. 57–66; Wiśniewski (2012), pp. 223–246.

[34]**National security (state security) strategy** was defined as the concept, adopted by the given state, of ensuring security, identifying, in particular, national interests and strategic objectives, evaluating the future development of the strategic security environment, and the rules and methods of attaining strategic objectives in the envisaged conditions (the implementation of operational objectives) as well as of the preparation (maintenance and transformation) of a national security system (the implementation of preparatory objectives). *Biała Księga*, p. 249. The conceptual categories also include definitions of the operational, preparatory, and sectoral national security strategy and also the state security strategic potential.

[35]**The national security (state security) system** was defined as the entirety of resources, means, and forces (entities) earmarked by the state for the performance of tasks in the field of security, organised (into subsystems and components), maintained and prepared in a manner requisite for the purpose of performing such tasks. It consists of a control system (subsystem) as well as a number of executive subsystems (systems), including operational subsystems (defence and protection subsystems) and support subsystems (social and economic). *Biała Księga*, p. 250.

[36]Official Gazette of the Government of the Republic of Poland of 2013, item 719.

of security, analysing and projecting the development of external and internal national security circumstances, and formulating the main directions and the operating methods of the state and the preparations of its security systems, with the objective of developing a draft national security strategy of the Republic of Poland, and submitting it to the Council of Ministers.

The National Security Strategy of the Republic of Poland is a quite extensive document divided into four chapters, each divided into smaller sections, and preceded by a brief introduction presenting the objective and the composition of the Strategy. The subsequent chapters present Poland as a subject of security, characterise Poland's security environment in the global, regional, and national dimensions, and the concept of strategic actions, i.e. operational strategy; the chapter discusses defensive actions, protective actions, as well as social and economic actions in the area of security. The last, fourth chapter, is devoted to the concept of strategic preparations, i.e. a preparedness strategy, discussing the national security management subsystem, and the concomitant defence, protection, social, and economic subsystems. The document ends with a brief conclusion identifying the entities responsible for the Strategy's implementation, and explaining that its content was developed in the Political and Strategic Defence Directive of the Republic of Poland and the Strategy of Development of the National Security System of the Republic of Poland, specifying the long- and mid-term strategy of the country's development. It was also stated that the verification of arrangements included in the document would take place as part of strategic national security reviews. The publication replaces the Strategy approved by the President of the Republic of Poland of 13 November 2007.[37]

The adopted framework of the study does not allow a thorough analysis or a more-detailed description of the content of the mentioned strategy, which has already been studied by legal commentators in the above-mentioned texts. It is also worth noting the considerable progress of the content of the subsequent documents, and that in each of the subsequent strategies the concept of the security of the state was rendered differently, which resulted, on the one hand, from a change in external conditions, and on the other, the situation of the western security structures of both NATO and the European Union.

[37]The National Security Strategy of the Republic of Poland https://www.bbn.gov.pl/ftp/SBN%20RP.pdf, Accessed on 5 July 2020, 4:10 p.m. The Strategy was analysed in detail by Kupiecki (2015), pp. 11–36.

6 National Security Strategy of the Republic of Poland 2020

The next National Security Strategy of the Republic of Poland was approved by way of the decision of the President of 12 May 2020.[38] At the same time, it was clearly stated that the National Security Strategy of the Republic of Poland 2014 had been rendered null and void. The text of the Strategy begins with an introduction, in which it is explained that the Strategy defines a comprehensive vision of shaping the national security of the Republic of Poland in all its dimensions. The Strategy takes into consideration the subject-oriented aspect, i.e. the internal dimension of national security, and the international community, i.e. regional cooperation, collaborations on the global scale and within international organisations. It stresses that it also takes into account the object-oriented aspect, encompassing all dimensions of the national security system. As emphasised in the document, national interests and strategic objectives within the domain of national security are expressed in line with the national values as stipulated in the Constitution of the Republic of Poland.[39] The strategy also states that "the provisions of the Strategy should be further extended and reflected in the national strategic documents pertaining to the national security and development of Poland". As noted, the Strategy considers the context of Poland's membership of the North Atlantic Treaty Organisation and the European Union.

The introduction to the Strategy determines the security environment, pointing out that the greatest threat is the neo-imperial policy of the authorities of the Russian Federation, pursued by means that include military force. It affirms that the aggression against Georgia, the illegal annexation of Crimea,[40] and the hostilities in eastern Ukraine, all violated the basic principles of international law, and undermined the pillars of the European security system. As noted in the document, the Russian Federation is intensively developing its offensive military capabilities, conducting large-scale military exercises based on scenarios assuming a conflict with the NATO Member States, activities of a hybrid nature below the threshold of war which pose the risk of the outbreak of a conflict, undertaking comprehensive actions using non-military means, including cyber attacks and disinformation, with the aim of rebuilding its power and spheres of influence.[41]

It is argued that the primary factor shaping Poland's security is its strong embedding in the transatlantic and European structures, and the development of

---

[38]Official Gazette of the Government of the Republic of Poland of 2020, item 413.

[39]This statement might raise some doubts. It should be stated, however, that the intended meaning is the axiological system forming the basis for the Constitution and the guaranteed liberties, rights, and obligations of individuals and citizens. More on the issue in Piechowiak (2020), passim; id., Piechowiak (2013), pp. 39–70; Brzozowski (2006), pp. 17–28; Complak (2007), pp. 23–27, 49–56; Garlicki (2010), p. 95 et seq.; Winczorek (1996), pp. 13–14; Sobczak and Sobczak (2017), pp. 38–63; Sobczak (2012), pp. 285–318.

[40]On cybersecurity, see Gołda-Sobczak (2016), pp. 192–236.

[41]See Eggert (2005), pp. 50–51 i 62.

bilateral and regional cooperation with key partners. As noted in the document, the bonds between the United States of America and its European allies are evolving, and there is a risk of undermining the coherence of positions and actions. Another risk factor is perceived in persistent regional and internal conflicts in the Southern European Neighbourhood, and the growing migration pressure. At the global level, a significant risk-posing phenomenon is that of the increasing strategic rivalry between the United States of America, the People's Republic of China, and the Russian Federation.

It is concluded that the development of new technologies, both civilian and military, contributes to a significant increase in the deployment of unmanned and autonomous systems, automated and robotised weapon platforms using artificial intelligence, and long-range precision weapon systems. The rapid development of digital technologies generates previously unknown threats. The strategy states that as fixed and mobile communication networks can pose a threat to security, it is necessary to develop modern and secure telecommunication networks. In the context of the digital revolution, it is asserted that the specific role of cyberspace and information space should be considered, as they create conditions for disinformation and the manipulation of information, which necessitate effective strategic communication activities.[42]

Ensuring energy security is considered of key importance for Poland, and the perceived challenge is to maintain the competitiveness of electricity production in Poland, in line with the climate and energy policies of the European Union.[43] The document highlights the significance of the state's financial security and economic stability. The identified threats include the long-term deficit in the replacement level fertility rate in Poland, and the significant increase in the number of elderly people, which present a challenge for public finance.

The strategy recognises threats to the healthcare system, and the necessity to counteract the effects of lifestyle diseases and eliminate social inequalities in access to healthcare. It identifies the accelerating climate change, prolonged droughts, pollution, and the emissions of harmful substances as threats to security. It also indicates the need to improve the management of national security and to integrate a number of fragmented solutions. The authors further argue that, faced with progressing globalisation, the Polish economy has to face up to increasingly strong competition on foreign markets. As stated in the document, the strength of the Polish economy translates into the strength of the state's defence potential. The strategy strongly emphasises that Poland should strive to reinforce the external pillars of its security through its membership of the North Atlantic Treaty Organisation and the European Union, and the strategic partnership with the United States of America, as

[42]More on information security in Liderman (2012), pp. 43–179; Oleksiewicz and Krztoń (2017), passim; Oleksiewicz et al. (2017), passim.

[43]On energy security, see Nowacki (2010), pp. 189–278; Mickiewicz and Sokołowska (2010), passim; Chmielewski (2009), pasim; Kaczmarski (2010), passim; Gawłowski et al. (2010), passim; Pronińska (2012), passim.

well as regional cooperation for security. It recognises the positive impact of the EU Common Security and Defence Policy and the EU's Permanent Structured Cooperation.[44] It concludes that Poland attaches great importance to the development of regional cooperation, e.g. within the Bucharest Nine, the Visegrad Group,[45] the Weimar Triangle, the Three Seas Initiative, and collaboration with the countries of the Baltic Sea region.[46]

The subsequent part of the Strategy presents values, national interests, and strategic objectives in the domain of national security. The abovementioned primary national interests in the field of national security include safeguarding independence, territorial integrity, sovereignty, and security of the state and its citizens. Other interests include shaping the international order, based on solidarity and respect for international law, strengthening national identity, and preserving national heritage, and ensuring conditions for sustainable and balanced social and economic development and environmental protection. The main values include the independence and sovereignty of the state, the security of its citizens, human and civil liberties and rights, human dignity, justice, national identity and heritage, the democratic state of law, solidarity, international order based on the principles of international law and environmental protection. Finally, the authors state that the said aspects of the national interest form the pillars of Poland's national security.

This concept inspires the subsequent part of the Strategy, which presents the first pillar as concerning the security of the state and its citizens, and the second as Poland's situation in the national security system. The third pillar is national identity and heritage, and the fourth involves social and economic development and environmental protection.

The issues within the first pillar include the necessity for integrating national security management, including state-defence management and the building of adaptation capabilities. The numerous elements in these activities cover attempts to integrate the national security management system and to develop the ability for swift adaptation to new challenges and threats.[47] This is to lead to creating an interagency coordination mechanism for the management of national security through setting up a committee of the Council of Ministers, responsible, at the strategic level, for dealing with issues in the sphere of policies, strategies, and programmes pertaining to national security management, in a manner ensuring their consistent and coherent implementation. The committee should be linked with the new role and responsibilities of the Government Crisis Management Team and the Government Centre for Security. It is stated as necessary to involve the Marshals (Speakers) of the Sejm and the Senate of the Republic of Poland in this preparation for the sake of managing national security, by adjusting the mechanisms and instruments supporting the President of the Republic of Poland in a way which

[44]Marczuk (2014), pp. 169–218.

[45]On the security of the Visegrad Group countries, see Bień-Kacała et al. (2016), pp. 59–70.

[46]Cf. Stolarczyk (2004), pp. 11–51; Maj et al. (2016), passim.

[47]Czachór (2016), pp. 175–192; Żebrowski (2009), pp. 213–246.

reflects changes in the spheres of security and defence, including state-defence management. It is also seen as necessary to adjust the national crisis management system to the NATO Crisis Response System, by also extending it to the field of political and military conflict, and facilitating the smooth transition from the state of peace to the state of crisis and war, as well as ensuring that it provides effective tools to prevent and combat threats, including hybrid situations.[48] Further, it is considered necessary to review, prioritise, and interlink strategy and planning documents, and also to implement mechanisms in the areas of national security and defence, and the socio-economic development of the country. It is posited that the preparation and implementation of a communication system is essential for the purpose of managing the national security system, including state-defence management; also for ensuring, within the framework of a comprehensive and integrated national security system, at all levels of government and local government administration, the cohesion of civil and defence planning, as well as the possibility of the selective implementation of tasks, as required. The document states that the Act on National Security Management will be developed to implement the above-described measures.

As part of further activities under the first pillar, i.e. the security of the state and its citizens, the Strategy focuses on state defence and common defence. It asserts that it is necessary to increase the state's resilience to threats by creating a system of common civil defence, based on the efforts of the entire nation, and building an understanding for the development of the Republic of Poland's resilience and defence capabilities. It places special emphasis on building a system of common civil defence and resilience to threats, including hybrid threats, through ensuring the universal nature of civil defence and the protection of the population.[49] The strategy sees it necessary to develop the capacity of the health system and public administration structures to fight against epidemic threats, especially against highly infectious and particularly dangerous diseases. As noted, it is also necessary to develop diagnostic facilities and the strategic reserve programme. The strategy recognises the need for the transfer of know-how and capacities allowing the shaping of national security, based on the broad involvement of public authorities, including local government, educational, higher educational and scientific institutions, and the economy. It approaches building social capital by developing cooperation skills, networks of formal and non-formal social organisations, and by shaping the community of values within Polish society. It identifies the need to redefine the civil-defence system and the population-protection system by making it universal, and to develop a law comprehensively regulating the subject matter of civil defence. The document describes plans of increasing resilience to threats by ensuring effective energy supplies, preventing the uncontrolled movement of people and the relocation of the population, and the collection, protection, and management of food and water resources. Further goals include the creation of resilient telecommunication

[48]On security in crisis situations see Koziński (2010), passim.

[49]On the common civil defence system, see Grosset (2011), passim; Aleksandrowicz (2014); Piasecka (2011), pp. 31–44.

networks and Information and Communications Technology systems, population information and alert systems, and resilient transport networks. This is associated with the assumption of implementing a homogeneous system of human resources management, including the administration of personnel reserves.

The document expresses the need to develop the state's capacity to prevent and respond to terrorist threats and to fight organised crime, including criminal activities in cyberspace. The authors consider it appropriate to strengthen legal certainty by ensuring effective legal protection for citizens, an efficient judiciary system, and the proper enforcement of court decisions. They recognise the necessity to continue to strengthen the counter-intelligence protection of the state authorities and critical infrastructure in a way commensurate with increasing activities of foreign intelligence services, in both the military and civilian domains.

The strategy states that it is crucial to develop the capacities of national intelligence services to identify risks at an early stage. It also points to the necessity to create conditions, in the area of spatial planning and development, allowing the effective and efficient analysis of the requirements of national security, and to provide optimal legal and organisational conditions for acting flexibly in the event of an external threat to state security in times of peace, crisis, and war.[50] The authors consider it appropriate to strengthen interagency coordination with a view to developing the capabilities of the national industrial and technological defence base within state security, including the selective launching of actions to mobilise the economy, and to meet the needs of the Polish Armed Forces. Finally, they identify the need to increase capabilities in the fields of cryptology and the production of telecommunication appliances equipped with cryptographic modules, and to build capacities for technological development and the production of strategic resources in times of peace, crisis and war.

Another issue discussed within the first pillar is the need to strengthen the Polish Armed Forces and their operational capabilities. The strategy assumes efforts to increase the growth rate of defence spending, to reach 2.5% of GDP in 2024. It points to the necessity of continuing the adaptation of the command structure of the Polish Armed Forces to reflect the needs resulting from changes in the security environment. It also describes it as vital to supplement the personnel and equipment of the Armed Forces, and to adapt training programmes and capabilities to conduct asymmetric operations. It provides for enhancing the mobility of troops and the efficiency of their support and logistics systems. The authors consider it essential to improve the management of personnel resources and to streamline the qualification and recruitment processes, as well as education and professional training. They stress that there is a necessity to build a national integrated situational awareness system, based on various means of reconnaissance, communication, command, and control, including national Earth observation satellite systems, and unmanned aerial vehicle systems. The strategy recognises the need to ensure the state's capability for effective air defence, as well as operational capabilities, including long-range missile

[50]Potrzeszcz (2013), passim; Sobczak (2013), pp. 187–213.

defences. It is also thought appropriate to develop the operational capabilities of the Polish Armed Forces, in particular of the Special Operations Forces. Another task is to gain operational capabilities to conduct military operations in cyberspace, and develop Cyber Defence Forces. The document points to the need to improve the mobilisation system, including the training of personnel reserves, also noting the necessity to build the operational capabilities of the Navy. It expresses the decision to implement the programme of building the Territorial Defence Forces, so that the Polish defence industry could meet the long-term needs of the Polish Armed Forces.

A lot of attention is paid to cybersecurity.[51] It was determined to increase resilience and information protection levels in the military sector, while promoting practices enabling citizens to better protect their information.

The strategy also declares that it is necessary to ensure the safe operation of the state and citizens in information space. This involves creating the ability to protect this space, and the systemic response to disinformation. It was thought necessary to create a uniform system of state strategic communication, simultaneously creating procedures defining cooperation to counteract disinformation.

As part of the second pillar, strengthening the capabilities of the North Atlantic Treaty Organisation and the European Union is considered necessary. Among numerous measures to attain this objective, the decision made to pursue the increase and consolidation of the military presence of NATO on its Eastern flank is worth noting. Maintaining a dual-track policy towards the Russian Federation within the framework of NATO, consisting of enhanced deterrence and defence, combined with the readiness to engage in a conditions-based dialogue, is considered advisable, and so is engaging in the development of the European Union's Common Security and Defence Policy, including within the framework of the European Union's Permanent Structured Cooperation and the European Defence Fund. The document declares that divisions among European Union Member States should be prevented.[52]

Within this pillar, the strategy also discussed the need to develop cooperation in bilateral, regional, and global formats, including with the United States and key European partners. It promises actions aimed at strengthening the independence, sovereignty, and territorial integrity of Ukraine, Georgia, and the Republic of Moldova, including support for their efforts to fulfil their European and Euro-Atlantic aspirations. It also raises the need to take steps to enhance the effectiveness of the United Nations and the Organization for Security and Co-operation in Europe.[53] It stresses that national interests will be pursued in the spirit of solidarity with allies and partners. Finally, it assumes expanding the transport network and

---

[51]On cybersecurity, see Banasiński (2018), passim; Gzicki (2013), pp. 44–45; Kosiński (2015), pp. 212–274.

[52]Aleksandrowicz (2011), pp. 68–102; Wawrzyk (2009), passim; Siupiński (2013), passim; Marczuk (2012), pp. 310–432 and 499–544.

[53]Zajadło (2005); Rudkowski (2006), pp. 99–237.

seaports, extending the inland waters development programme, and building the Solidarity Transport Hub.

As part of the third pillar, the document emphasises the need to strengthen national identity, rooted in the Christian heritage and universal values. It highlights the notions of shaping and developing patriotic attitudes, refining instruments and procedures for the protection of cultural heritage, and promoting the development and protection of traditional family values, Polish national identity, culture, and traditions. It promises to strengthen the links between the Polish diaspora and the home country, and also to strive to increase the involvement of the former in activities related to the promotion of Poland.

Another objective established within the pillar involves strengthening the positive image of the Republic of Poland, and its cultural and economic attractiveness. It is pointed out that this should be pursued through public and cultural diplomacy, along with social communication technology, taking into account the state's historical policy.[54] The document suggests it is vital to promote the Polish language, culture, science, and history, and the nation's Christian heritage. In addition, it recognises the need to strengthen the "brand" of the Polish economy and to support Polish companies in the process of internationalisation. Last but not least, the strategy highlights the need to improve cooperation with Polish community social organisations, in order to promote Polish culture and economy.

As part of the fourth pillar, the strategy holds as fundamental that steps should be taken to improve the conditions for the protection and development of families, and to increase the health security of citizens. It also identifies the need to take measures to improve the demographic situation, including an increase in the birth rate.[55] It concludes that a policy dedicated to senior citizens must be implemented to ensure social and health security for the elderly, and to mobilise this group to remain professionally active.[56] It points to the need of improving patient care in the healthcare system, including by increasing the quality and availability of healthcare services, together with taking action in illness prevention and health education, and early diagnosis and rehabilitation. The document recognises the need to increase the number of health professionals and enhance their expertise, while preventing their migration abroad.[57] Finally, the authors consider it essential to continue to develop physical culture, by ensuring universal access to sport, and by modernising the existing sports and leisure infrastructure, and constructing new facilities.

The document also draws attention to coordinating migration policy with the economic, social, and security policies by considering both the current and projected

---

[54]As regards diplomacy measures aimed at security, see Macioszek (2003), especially 11–43 and 119–156; Grab (2018), pp. 19–118 and 198–220.

[55]Serafin and Parszowki (2011), passim; Pływaczewski (2017), passim; Chojnowski (2018), see especially pp. 389–412; Cichy and Szyjko (2015), see especially pp. 228–263.

[56]Cf. Jagusiak (2015), especially pp. 48–141.

[57]Cf. Szuniewicz (2016), pp. 33–78; Kowalewski (2015), pp. 64–84; Wedel-Domaradzka (2013), pp. 108–125.

needs on the labour market. At the same time, it emphasises the need to integrate migrants within Polish society, to ensure social cohesion, and to counteract possible threats to public order and security related to migration processes.

Further elements in the fourth pillar include economic and energy security. In terms of economic security, the strategy aims to support measures to increase resilience to international financial crises, in particular by strengthening the stability of the public finance system. It highlights the need to continue working towards a change to the structure of public expenditure, and to increase resources for development-oriented activities. It recognises the importance of ensuring efficient cash flows in times of disruption to the functioning of the banking system. It promises to strengthen the supervisory capacity and ability to counter threats related to the destabilisation of financial markets, speculative attacks on the Polish currency, and capital drain.

The document also points to the need to ensure the energy security of the state, based on traditional energy sources, by creating the conditions for the development of alternatives. It assumes increasing the diversification of oil and gas supply sources, and expanding the existing natural gas import capacities. It considers it advisable to carry out further work on extending the transmission system, and to continue diplomatic, legal, and administrative efforts to halt the construction of the transmission infrastructure which is increasing the dependence of Central Europe on gas supplies from the Russian Federation.[58]

Moreover, as part of the fourth pillar, the strategy refers to the need to protect the natural environment.[59] It highlights the urgency to create the conditions for the effective enforcement of environment-related legislation, and to establish a coherent policy for the protection, restoring, and management of water resources. It also recognises the need to intensify efforts to combat air pollution, to develop electromobility, and to promote the use of alternative fuels. It stresses the necessity of adjusting national policies and actions to the climate objectives agreed on in the fora of international organisations and attempting to preserve all the functions of the natural environment, including forests as one of the key elements in the country's ecological safety.

It recognises the need to manage human capital, and scientific and technological potential for the economic development of the country. It promises to provide the conditions conducive to the development of innovation, to promote exact sciences in order to increase technological expertise, especially in the field of security, and to promote the development and implementation of modern technologies, and the use of their effects for national security.[60] The document also highlights the need to increase investment in research and development to reach the European average, and to enhance the effectiveness of the use and commercialisation of its results.

[58]See more in Banasik and Rogozińska (2019), pp. 199–212.

[59]On ecological security, see Korzeniowski (2012), p. 203; Stępniewska (2018), pp. 213–215.

[60]See Glińska and Kowalewska (2011), pp. 114–113.

In the concluding section of the strategy, the authors state that the mechanisms for the implementation of its provisions will be further defined in the Act on National Security Management. Pending its adoption, the strategy is intended to be implemented within the framework of the currently binding law. The persons implementing the provisions included in the strategy are obliged to consider the national interests and strategic objectives in the domain of national security in all projects planned for implementation, and in day-to-day operations.[61] It is stressed that the verification of the implementation of the tasks set out in this Strategy, and the development of proposals to update it, may take place as part of national security strategic reviews.

The mere fact that this strategy has been developed should be regarded as favourable, as it was quite clear that the provisions of the previous strategy (of 2014) were neither approved nor actually implemented by the government. This strategy, however, was not preceded by any debate involving non-governmental third-party experts or representatives of various political powers. This seems to contradict the obligation arising from the previous document, which envisaged a strategic review of national security. It can be noted that the National Security Strategy of 2020 has a slightly different layout and structure compared to the documents of 2007 and 2014. This seems to clash with the logic of a strategic cycle which assumes four stages of formulating a strategic concept, i.e. identifying national interests as the starting point for further discussions; assessing and projecting the security environment; developing a concept of the objectives and duties of an operational strategy, i.e. the means to ensure the implementation of national interests; and determining the concept of the so-called preparatory strategy, i.e. the means to prepare an independent security system. It is worth noting that the Strategy fails to specify the strategic measures which Poland could and should take under various threat scenarios. The national interests of the Republic of Poland can thus be only presumed. An unquestionable strength of the Strategy is the accurate definition of existing national, regional, and global military and economic threats. Another positive aspect is the fact that it addresses such phenomena as hybridity, activities in cyberspace, and the demand for new technologies, including artificial intelligence. The intent to build an integrated security management system, which was expressed in the Strategy, and issues regarding the state's resilience and defence universality, are also noteworthy. The duties regarding the capacities of the armed forces are fairly ambitious and justifiable, but there is no mention of the order in which they will be implemented. As regards the third pillar, one can get the impression that this is a presentation of some political agenda which has already been discussed many times. Given the purpose of this document, its frequent references to the Christian heritage appear quite striking. Moreover, in contrast to previous documents, it fails to refer to the Constitution and its axiological system, which can be regarded as an omission. Definitely too little space is devoted to what appears the most important in the long run, i.e. the armed forces and their defence

[61]Nowak and Nowak (2011), pp. 39–70 i 147–158.

capacities. Finally, the promise to develop the Act on National Security Management is noteworthy, but it should be preceded with a wider discussion, attended also by those who are perhaps the most concerned with this issue, i.e. the representatives of armed forces.

7 Conclusions

The new National Security Strategy is an interesting, yet not flawless, document, which was preceded by earlier documents dealing with the same issues. It imposes highly ambitious and interesting obligations whose justifiability is hard to question, in terms of both the government and society as a whole. However, while the Strategy is of much significance, its ranking within the normative acts system is rather low. The Act of 6 December 2006 on the Principles of Conducting the Development Policy[62] should also be borne in mind. Within the framework of their statutory duties, the Council of Ministers have passed a number of resolutions formulating development strategies for various fields of the state's functioning and economic sectors.[63] The objectives and duties envisaged in those strategies clearly correspond

[62] Act of 6 December 2006 on the Principles of Conducting the Development Policy, consolidated text, Polish Journal of Laws of 2019, item 1295. See Jaśkiewicz (2014).

[63] Resolution No. 102 of the Council of Ministers of 17 September 2019 on adopting the National Regional Development Strategy 2030, the Official Gazette of the Government of the Republic of Poland of 2019, item 1060; Resolution No. 123 of the Council of Ministers of 15 October 2019 on adopting the Strategy for Sustainable Rural Development, Agriculture, and Fisheries 2030, the Official Gazette of the Government of the Republic of Poland of 2019, item 1150; Resolution No. 105 of the Council of Ministers of 24 September 2019 on adopting the Strategy for Sustainable Transport Development 2030, the Official Gazette of the Government of the Republic of Poland of 2019, item 1054; Resolution No. 114 of the Council of Ministers of 1 October 2019 on adopting the Strategy for Capital Market Development, the Official Gazette of the Government of the Republic of Poland of 2019, item 1027; Resolution No. 6 of the Council of Ministers of 26 January 2017 on adopting the Polish Space Strategy, the Official Gazette of the Government of the Republic of Poland of 2017, item 203; Resolution No. 58 of the Council of Ministers of 15 April 2014 on adopting the Strategy for Energy Security and Environment – a perspective by 2020, the Official Gazette of the Government of the Republic of Poland of 2014, item 469, as amended; Resolution No. 104 of the Council of Ministers of 18 June 2013 on adopting the Strategy for Human Capital Development 2020, the Official Gazette of the Government of the Republic of Poland of 2013, item 640; Resolution No. 61 of the Council of Ministers of 26 March 2013 on adopting the Social Capital Strategy 2020, the Official Gazette of the Government of the Republic of Poland of 2013, item 378; Resolution No. 17 of the Council of Ministers of 12 February 2013 on adopting the Efficient State Strategy 2020, the Official Gazette of the Government of the Republic of Poland of 2013, item 136; Resolution No. 7 of the Council of Ministers of 15 January 2013 on the Innovation Strategy for Economic Efficiency – Dynamic Poland 2020" 2020, the Official Gazette of the Government of the Republic of Poland of 2013, item 73; Resolution No. 60 of the Council of Ministers of 30 April 2014 on adopting the Development Strategy for Western Poland by 2020, the Official Gazette of the Government of the Republic of Poland of 2014, item 452; Resolution No. 3 of the Council of Ministers of 8 January 2014 on adopting the Development Strategy for Southern Poland by 2020,

to those presented in the National Security Strategy of the Republic of Poland approved on 12 May 2020. Additionally, by way of the Resolution of the Council of Ministers of 9 April 2013, passed under Article 14(3) of the Act of 6 December 2006 on the Principles of Conducting the Development Policy, the Strategy of the Development of the National Security System of the Republic of Poland 2022[64] was adopted. It contains a diagnosis of the national security system in the context of internal and external conditions, along with the challenges, development trends, and visions of the national security system, the Strategy's objectives and interventions, the Strategy's implementation system, and the financial framework. In the author's opinion, the Strategy adopted by way of Resolution No. 67 is more detailed, and focused on the defensive potential, than the Strategy adopted on 12 May 2020, and there is the impression that both Strategies appear competitive to each other. At this point, any more detailed considerations on the subject matter can hardly be presented, but one cannot ignore a certain dualism resulting from the fact that the Strategy of 2013 was adopted by way of a Resolution of the Council of Ministers and the Strategy of 12 May 2020 was by way of the President's decision passed on the motion of the Council of Ministers. Clarifying potential doubts when the provisions of these two documents are found to be contradictory is likely to pose serious problems for lawyers.

References

Aleksandrowicz TR (2011) Bezpieczeństwo w Unii Europejskiej, Warsaw

Aleksandrowicz TR (2014) Świat w sieci. Państwa, społeczeństwa, ludzie w poszukiwaniu nowego paradygmatu bezpieczeństwa narodowego, Warsaw

Banasik M, Rogozińska A (eds) (2019) W aspekcie niemilitarnych instrumentów oddziaływania Federacji Rosyjskiej, Warsaw

Banasiński C (2018) Cyberbezpieczeństwo. Zarys wykładu, Warsaw

Beaufre A (1988) Wstęp do strategii. Odstraszanie i strategia, Warsaw

Berkowitz M, Bock PG (eds) (1965) American National Security. A reader in theory on policy. The Free Press, New York

Bień-Kacała A, Jirásek J, Ciulka J, Drinóczi T (eds) (2016) Kategoria bezpieczeństwa w regulacjach konstytucyjnych i praktyce ustrojowej państw Grupy Wyszehradzkiej, Toruń

Brodie B (1973) War and politics, New York

Brzozowski W (2006) Konstytucyjna zasada dobra wspólnego, Państwo i Prawo 61(11)

Chałubińska-Jentkiewicz K (2019) Cyberbezpieczeństwo – zagadnienia definicyjne. Cybersecurity and Law 2

Chmielewski A (2009) Bezpieczeństwo energetyczne państwa. Geopolityczne uwarunkowania, Warsaw

the Official Gazette of the Government of the Republic of Poland of 2014, item 152; Resolution No. 121 of the Council of Ministers of 11 July 2013 on adopting the updated Socio-Economic Development Strategy for Eastern Poland by 2020, the Official Gazette of the Government of the Republic of Poland of 2013, item 641.

[64]The Official Gazette of the Government of the Republic of Poland of 2013, item 377.

Chojnowski L (2018) Bezpieczeństwo człowieka i społeczeństw w procesie dziejowym, Słupsk
Cichy A, Szyjko CT (2015) Wybrane zagadnienia bezpieczeństwa społecznego w Unii Europejskiej, Warsaw
Complak K (2007) Normy I Rozdziału Konstytucji RP, Acta Universitatis Wratislaviensis (Prawo CCCI) 2956
Czachór ZD (2016) Sprawiedliwość oraz bezpieczeństwo wewnętrzne Unii Europejskiej i jej obywateli. Wybrane pola badawcze w ujęciu instytucjonalno – prawnym. In: Chabasińska A, Czapur Z (eds) Bezpieczeństwo narodowe Polski. Zagrożenia i determinanty zmian, Warsaw
Czaputowicz J (2013) Kryteria bezpieczeństwa międzynarodowego państwa – aspekty teoretyczne. In: Dębski S, Górka-Winter B (eds) Kryteria bezpieczeństwa międzynarodowego państwa, Warsaw
Czaputowicz J (2018) Suwerenność, Warsaw
Dubisz S (ed) (2003) Uniwersalny słownik języka polskiego, vol 3, Warsaw
Eggert D (2005) Transatlantycka wspólnota bezpieczeństwa, Żurawia Papers 5
Garlicki L (2010) Aksjologiczne podstawy reinterpretacji Konstytucji. In: Zubik M (ed) Dwadzieścia lat transformacji ustrojowej w Polsce. Ogólnopolski Zjazd Katedr i Zakładów Prawa Konstytucyjnego, 19–21 czerwca 2009, Warsaw
Gawłowski S, Listowska-Gawłowska R, Piecuch T (2010) Bezpieczeństwo energetyczne kraju, Koszalin
Glińska E, Kowalewska A (2011) Identyfikacja współczesnych zagrożeń bezpieczeństwa obywateli w świetle badań własnych z 2008 r. In: Guzik-Makaruk EM (ed) Poczucie bezpieczeństwa obywateli w Polsce. Identyfikacja i przeciwdziałanie współczesnym zagrożeniom, Warsaw
Gołda-Sobczak M (2016) Krym jako przedmiot sporu ukraińsko-rosyjskiego, Poznań
Gołda-Sobczak M (2017) Bezpieczeństwo kulturowe w sieci. In: Wojtaszek A (ed) Europa wobec problemów bezpieczeństwa w XXI wieku, Szczecin
Grab L (2018) Dyplomacja obronna w procesie kształtowania bezpieczeństwa RP, Warsaw
Granat M (2002) Opinia na temat konieczności kontrasygnaty aktu Prezydenta o wyznaczeniu Marszałka Seniora. Ekspertyzy i opinie prawne. Biuletyn Ekspertyz i Opinii Prawnych
Grosset R (2011) Tożsamość bezpieczeństwa wewnętrznego – miejsce, rola i funkcje, Warsaw
Gzicki W (2013) Państwo wobec cyberterroryzmu (2013). In: Podraza A, Potakowski P, Wiak K (eds) Cyberterroryzm zagrożeniem XXI wieku. Perspektywa politologiczna i prawna, Warsaw
Jagusiak B (2015) Bezpieczeństwo socjalne współczesnego państwa, Warsaw
Jancz J. Relacjonowanie wydarzeń w czasie rzeczywistym przez środki masowego przekazu, a bezpieczeństwo i proces podejmowania decyzji. In: Skarżyński M, Andruszkiewicz I (eds) Media w systemie bezpieczeństwa narodowego, Poznań
Jaśkiewicz J (2014) Ustawa o zasadach prowadzenia polityki rozwoju. Komentarz, LEX/el
Kaczmarski M (2010) Bezpieczeństwo energetyczne Unii Europejskiej, Warsaw
Kitler W (2011) Bezpieczeństwo narodowe RP. Podstawowe kategorie. Uwarunkowania. System, Warsaw
Korzeniowski P (2012) Bezpieczeństwo ekologiczne jako instytucja prawna ochrony środowiska, Łódź
Kosiński J (2015) Paradygmaty cyberprzestępczości, Warsaw
Kowalewski M (2015) Aspekty bezpieczeństwa narodowego Rzeczypospolitej Polskiej, Warsaw
Koziej S (1998a) Tezy i komentarze do prac nad Strategią Bezpieczeństwa i Obronności Rzeczypospolitej Polskiej, Warsaw-Toruń 1998
Koziej S (1998b) Szkic do dyskusji o przyszłej strategii poszerzonego NATO (spojrzenie z polskiej perspektywy), Warsaw-Toruń
Koziej S, Brzozowski A (2014) 25 lat polskiej strategii bezpieczeństwa, Bezpieczeństwo Narodowe 2
Koziej S, Brzozowski A (2015) Strategie Bezpieczeństwa RP 1990-2014. Refleksje na ćwierćwiecze. In: Kupiecki R (ed) Strategia Bezpieczeństwa Narodowego Rzeczypospolitej Polskiej. Pierwsze 25 lat, Wojskowe Centrum Edukacji Obywatelskiej im. płk. dypl. Mariana Porwita, Warsaw

Koziński M (2010) Bezpieczeństwo kryzysowe, Gdańsk
Kozłowski K (2016) In: Safjan M, Bosek L (eds) Konstytucja RP, vol II, Komentarz, Warsaw
Kupiecki R (2015) Strategia Bezpieczeństwa Narodowego RP 2014 jako instrument polityki państwa. Uwarunkowania zewnętrzne i aspekty procesowe, Bezpieczeństwo Narodowe 1
Kuźniar R (2004) Strategia państwowa. Zeszyty Akademii Dyplomatycznej 15
Liderman K (2012) Bezpieczeństwo informacyjne, Warsaw
Macioszek M (2003) Dyplomacja prewencyjna Unii Europejskiej w pozimnowojennej Europie, Toruń
Maj E, Mazurek K, Sokół W, Szwed-Walczak A (eds) (2016) Bezpieczeństwo Europy, bezpieczeństwo Polski, Lublin 2016
Marczak J (2008) Założenia polityki i strategii bezpieczeństwa narodowego. In: Jakubczak R, Skrabacz A, Gąsiorek K (eds) Obrona narodowa w tworzeniu bezpieczeństwa Polski w XXI wieku, Warsaw 2008
Marczuk KP (2012) Bezpieczeństwo wewnętrzne państw członkowskich Unii Europejskiej. Od bezpieczeństwa państwa do bezpieczeństwa ludzi, Warsaw
Marczuk KP (2014) Bezpieczeństwo funkcjonalne państw regionu Europy Północnej, Warsaw
Mickiewicz P (2018) System bezpieczeństwa narodowego w rozwiązaniach systemowych wybranych państw, Warsaw
Mickiewicz P, Sokołowska P (2010) Bezpieczeństwo energetyczne Europy Środkowej, Toruń
Nowacki M (2010) Prawne aspekty bezpieczeństwa energetycznego w UE, Warsaw
Nowak W, Nowak M (2011) Zarys teorii bezpieczeństwa narodowego, Warsaw
Nowakowski Z (2008) Bezpieczeństwo narodowe. Ewolucja pojęcia i zakresu. In: Jemioło T, Rajchel K (eds) Bezpieczeństwo narodowe i zarządzanie kryzysowe w Polsce w XXI wieku. Wyzwania i dylematy, Warsaw
Nowakowski N, Rajchel J, Szafran H, Szafran R (2014) Strategia bezpieczeństwa narodowego Polski na tle strategii bezpieczeństwa wybranych państw, Warsaw
Olechnicki M, Załęcki P (1997) In: Słownik socjologiczny, Toruń
Oleksiewicz I, Krztoń W (2017) Bezpieczeństwo współczesnego społeczeństwa informacyjnego w cyberprzestrzeni, Warsaw, passim
Oleksiewicz I, Michalski K, Sienkiewicz E (2017) Bezpieczeństwo w społeczeństwie informacyjnym. Zagadnienia w wymiarze online i offline, Warsaw
Piasecka P (2011) Zagrożenia ładu i bezpieczeństwa międzynarodowego we współczesnym świecie. In: Liedel K (ed) Transsektorowe obszary bezpieczeństwa narodowego, Warsaw
Piechowiak M (2013) Aksjologiczne podstawy polskiego prawa. In: Guz T, Głuchowski J, Pałupska M (eds) Synteza prawa polskiego od 1989 roku, Warsaw
Piechowiak M (2020) Preambuła Konstytucji Rzeczpospolitej Polskiej 6z 1997 r. Aksjologiczne podstawy prawa, Warsaw
Pływaczewski E (ed) (2017) Bezpieczeństwo obywateli. Prawa człowieka. Zrównoważony rozwój, Białystok
Potrzeszcz J (2013) Bezpieczeństwo prawne z perspektywy filozofii prawa, Lublin
Pronińska KM (2012) Bezpieczeństwo energetyczne w stosunkach UE – Rosja. Geopolityka i ekonomia surowców energetycznych, Warsaw
Robertson D (2009) Słownik polityki, Warsaw
Rudkowski D (2006) Interwencja humanitarna w prawie międzynarodowym, Warsaw
Sarnecki P (2000) Prezydent Rzeczypospolitej Polskiej. Komentarz do przepisów, Kraków
Serafin T, Parszowki S (2011) Bezpieczeństwo społeczności lokalnych. Programy prewencyjne w systemie bezpieczeństwa, Warsaw
Sienkiewicz P (2009) Terroryzm w cyberprzestrzeni. In: Jamioło T, Kisielnicki J, Rajchel K (eds) Cyberterroryzm – nowe wyzwania XXI wieku, Warsaw
Siupiński A (2013) Wspólna polityka bezpieczeństwa i obrony Unii Europejskiej. Geneza. Rozwój. Funkcjonowanie, Warsaw
Skrzypczak J (2015) Obowiązki mediów w sytuacjach nadzwyczajnych. In: Skarżyński M, Andruszkiewicz I (eds) Media w systemie bezpieczeństwa narodowego, Poznań

Słomczyńska J (2007) Europejska polityka bezpieczeństwa i obrony. Uwarunkowania, struktury, funkcjonowanie. In: Zięba LR (ed) Bezpieczeństwo międzynarodowe w XXI wieku, Warsaw
Słownik terminów zakresu bezpieczeństwa narodowego, Warsaw 2002
Sobczak J (2012) Aksjologiczne Podstawy Konstytucji RP. In: Miluska J (ed) Wartości w świecie polityki, Poznań
Sobczak J (2013) Wymiar sprawiedliwości w systemie bezpieczeństwa państwa. In: Wojciechowski S, Wejkszner A (eds) Kluczowe determinanty bezpieczeństwa Polski na początku XX wieku, Warsaw 2013
Sobczak J, Kakareko K (2017) Prawo do ochrony kultury w systemie prawnym w Unii Europejskiej. In: Babiusz H, Kapustka P, Michalska J (eds) Aktualne problemy Konstytucji. Księga Jubileuszowa z okazji 40-lecia pracy naukowej Profesora Bogusława Banaszaka, Legnica
Sobczak J, Sobczak W (2017) Aksjologia regionalnych aktów normatywnych stojących na straży praw człowieka. In: Jaskiernia J, Stryszak K (eds) Ochrona praw człowieka w wymiarze uniwersalnym. Aksjologia – instytucje – nowe wyzwania praktyka, Toruń
Sobera W (2015) Strategia Bezpieczeństwa Narodowego jako element polityki państwa, Rocznik Europeistyczny 1
Stańczyk J (1996) Współczesne pojmowanie bezpieczeństwa, Warsaw
Stępniewska P (2018) Współczesne bezpieczeństwo ekologiczne. Bezpieczeństwo. Teoria i Praktyka 30(1)
Stolarczyk M (2004) Wzrost kontrowersji w stosunkach transatlantyckich i ich implikacje dla bezpieczeństwa europejskiego. In: Stolarczyk M (ed) Bezpieczeństwo Polski i bezpieczeństwo europejskie na początku XXI wieku. Wybrane aspekty, Katowice
Szuniewicz M (2016) Ochrona bezpieczeństwa państwa jako przesłanka ograniczenia praw i wolności jednostki w świetle Europejskiej Konwencji Praw Człowieka, Warsaw
Szymczak M (1989) Słownik języka polskiego, vol III, Warsaw
Wawrzyk P (2009) Bezpieczeństwo wewnętrzne Unii Europejskiej, Warsaw
Wedel-Domaradzka A (2013) Wolność zgromadzeń a obowiązki zapewnienia bezpieczeństwa przez państwo. In: Jastrzębski M, Kuczur T (eds) Bezpieczeństwo państwa a wolność jednostki. Wybrane aspekty prawne i polityczne, Toruń
Wielka Encyklopedia Powszechna PWN, vol 11
Winczorek P (1996) Nowa Konstytucja Rzeczypospolitej Polskiej. Problem aksjologii, Przegląd Sejmowy 4
Wiśniewski P (2012) Radiofonia i telewizja jako elementy społeczeństwa informacyjnego w Polsce. Aspekt prawny. Zagadnienia wybrane. In: Misztal-Konecka J, Tylec G (eds) Wizja europejskiego społeczeństwa informacyjnego i jej realizacja w prawie polskim, Lublin
Worona J (2020) Cyberprzestrzeń a prawo międzynarodowe, Warsaw
Zając J, Zięba R (2011) Budowa zintegrowanego systemu bezpieczeństwa narodowego Polski. Ekspertyza na potrzeby realizacji średniozakresowej strategii rozwoju RP na lata 2014-2020, Warsaw
Zajadło J (2005) Dylematy humanitarnej interwencji, Gdańsk
Żebrowski A (2009) Instrumenty Rady Ministrów w realizacji polityki bezpieczeństwa państwa. In: Księżopolski KM (ed) Problemy bezpieczeństwa wewnętrznego i bezpieczeństwa międzynarodowego, Warsaw
Zięba R (1997) In: Bobrow DB, Haliżak E, Zięba R (eds) Bezpieczeństwo narodowe i międzynarodowe u schyłku XX wieku, Warsaw
Zięba R (ed) (2018) Bezpieczeństwo międzynarodowe w XXI wieku, Kraków
Żurawski vel Grajewski P (2013) Militarny wymiar strategii bezpieczeństwa narodowego Polski 2007 i program profesjonalizacji sił zbrojnych z 2008 roku a NATO. In: Czulda R, Łoś R, Reginia-Zacharski J (eds) NATO wobec wyzwań współczesnego świata, Warsaw-Łódź

Jacek Sobczak professor, retired judge of the Supreme Court; Institute of Legal Sciences of the University of Economics and Human Sciences in Warsaw. In the past, head of the Department of Intellectual Property Law at the University of Social Sciences and Humanities SWPS (2008–2019); head of the Department of Press Systems and Press Law at the Faculty of Political Sciences and Journalism of the University of Adam Mickiewicz (1987–2010). A member of many editorial boards of scientific journals, including "Themis Polska Nova" (editor-in-chief) and "Medyczna Wokanda" (deputy editor-in-chief). He is interested in issues of constitutional law, human rights, freedom of the press, copyright and press law, personal rights, as well as the history of legal doctrines. Author of 32 books and over 350 studies and articles. He was a supervisor of 64 completed doctoral dissertations, and a reviewer of 83 doctoral dissertations, 45 habilitation dissertations and 34 dissertations for conferring the title of professor.

The Cybersecurity Strategy of the Republic of Poland

Waldemar Kitler

Abstract Directive 2016/1148 obliged each Member State to have a national strategy in the field of network and information system security, defining strategic goals and specific policy actions to be implemented. The adoption of the "Cybersecurity Strategy of the Republic of Poland" is also a requirement to implement the provision of Article 68 of the Act of 5 July 2018 on the National Cybersecurity System.

The strategy for the years 2019–2024, which defines targets in the field of cybersecurity, set the main goal, i.e. increasing the level of resilience to cyber threats and increasing the level of information protection in the public, military, and private sectors and promoting knowledge and good practices enabling citizens to better protect their information.

As part of the activities planned in the Strategy until 2024, the Government of the Republic of Poland will systematically strengthen and develop the National Cybersecurity System. The activities include systemic organisational, operational, technological, and legal solutions, creating social attitudes and conducting scientific research in order to ensure compliance with high cybersecurity standards in the area of software, devices and digital services. Government activities will be undertaken with respect for the rights and freedoms of citizens and by building trust between individual market sectors and public administration.

W. Kitler (✉)
Faculty of National Defence, Akademia Sztuki Wojennej w Warszawie/War Studies University in Warsaw, Warsaw, Poland
e-mail: w.kitler@akademia.mil.pl

K. Chałubińska-Jentkiewicz et al. (eds.), *Cybersecurity in Poland*,
https://doi.org/10.1007/978-3-030-78551-2_9

1 Introduction

The adoption of the NIS Directive[1] by the European Parliament and the Council (EU) obligated Member States to develop their own national strategies on the security of network and information systems. Under Article 7(1) of the NIS Directive,

> Each Member State shall adopt a national strategy on the security of network and information systems defining the strategic objectives and appropriate policy and regulatory measures, with a view to achieving and maintaining a high level of security of network and information systems, and covering at least the sectors referred to in Annex 2 and the services referred to in Annex 3.

In consequence, on 27 April 2017 the National Framework of Cybersecurity Policy of the Republic of Poland for 2017–2022[2] was adopted by way of Resolution No. 52/2017 of the Council of Ministers, along with the accompanying document entitled "The Action Plan for Implementing the National Framework of Cybersecurity Policy of the Republic of Poland for 2017-2022." It is also worth noting that in the same year the Minister competent for Digital Affairs adopted a document entitled "The Cybersecurity Strategy of the Republic of Poland for 2017-2022." All the above-mentioned documents envisaged the continuation of measures implemented by the government administration with the aim of improving the level of security in the cyberspace of the Republic of Poland, as well as the document entitled "The Governmental Cyberspace Protection Programme of the Republic of Poland for 2009-2011 – assumptions," discussed on 9 March 2009 by the Standing Committee of the Council of Ministers, and the Cyberspace Protection Policy of the Republic of Poland adopted by the Government in 2013.[3] It should be stressed at this point that, before the entry into force of the Cybersecurity Strategy of the Republic of Poland for 2019–2024, the role of a similar-stature document had been played by the National Framework of Cybersecurity Policy of the Republic of Poland for 2017–2022, adopted by way of Resolution No. 52/2017 of the Council of Ministers of 27 April 2017 on the National Framework of Cybersecurity Policy of the Republic of Poland for 2017–2022.

Two years after the adoption of the NIS Directive, the Polish Sejm passed the Act of 5 July 2018 on the National Cybersecurity System,[4] following which, under

[1]Directive 2016/1148 of the European Parliament, and of the Council (EU), of 6 July 2016, concerning measures for a high common level of security of network and information systems across the Union (OJ EU 2016 L 194/1).

[2]Resolution No. 52/2017 of the Council of Ministers of 27 April 2017 on the National Framework of Cybersecurity Policy of the Republic of Poland for 2017-2022 (KPRM), RM-111-52-17.

[3]Resolution No. 111/2013 of the Council of Ministers of 25 June 2013 on the Cyberspace Protection Policy of the Republic of Poland, KPRM, RM-111-103-13.

[4]Polish Journal of Laws of 2018, item 1560 as amended.

Article 68 thereof, the legislator developed formal grounds for the adoption of the Cybersecurity Strategy of the Republic of Poland by the Council of Ministers.[5]

2 The Cybersecurity Strategy vs. Normative Acts and Strategic Documents

The provisions of the Constitution of the Republic of Poland stipulate that the Council of Ministers shall conduct the internal affairs and foreign policy of the Republic of Poland (Article 146(1)), and to the extent, and in accordance with, the principles specified by the Constitution and Acts, it shall, in particular, guarantee the implementation of Acts (Article 146(4)(1)); safeguard the internal security of the state and public order (Article 146(4)(7)); and ensure the external security of the state (Article 146(4)(8)). The national security of the Republic of Poland, in both the subjective and objective scopes, is dependent on the undisrupted functioning of cyberspace, to the same extent as its very existence and development. In consequence, ensuring the resilience of information systems against actions which compromise the confidentiality, integrity, availability and authenticity of processed data, or the related services provided by those information systems, is among the major challenges faced by the Polish administration, in particular at the central level.

Cybersecurity, including the national cybersecurity system which is being constructed to secure the accomplishment of the set objectives, is now a key sphere of national security, in its both internal and external dimensions. In addition, considering the increasingly blurred boundaries between these two dimensions, the strategy must take into account any actions, regardless of state borders, which violate the confidentiality, integrity, availability, and authenticity of the processed data or related services provided through network and information systems.

The strategy, by outlining the mode of accomplishing the security policy objectives regarding cyberspace, determines the directions of the state's activities and the method of fulfilling its potential. However, certain doubts can arise in connection with its normative status, despite its being developed and adopted under the NCSA.

The draft version of that document, which, at the request of the Minister competent for computerisation, was developed in cooperation with the Government Plenipotentiary for Cybersecurity[6] other Ministers and the appropriate managers of central governmental offices (see Article 70 of the NCSA), is to be adopted by the Council of Ministers by way of a Resolution. In compliance with Article 68 of the

---

[5]The name adopted in the said Act (see Article 45(1)(1)). It was also used in the title of the draft Act in *"The list of the legislative and programme work of the Council of Ministers,"* reading as *"A draft Act of the Council of Ministers on the Cybersecurity Strategy of the Republic of Poland,"* draft No. ID210. Eventually, that name was also used in Resolution No. 125 of the Council of Ministers of 22 October 2019 on the Cybersecurity Strategy of the Republic of Poland for 2019-2024 (The Official Gazette of the Government of the Republic of Poland of 30 October 2019, item 1037).

[6]Hereinafter referred to as "the Plenipotentiary",

NCSA, the strategy is to be adopted by the Council of Ministers under an internal legal act, i.e. by way of a Resolution. However, the Polish legislators did not adopt a legal definition of the term *cybersecurity strategy* (of the Republic of Poland), but it indicated, by way of an Act, the elements which this document should feature (Article 69(2) of the NCSA) and determined its legal form. Among other documents related to national security of strategic importance, this is one of the few examples of making a strategy a state-level document. In the vast majority of cases, the legislator merely authorised the responsible bodies to develop, announce, and adopt specific strategies. The latter situation involved the National Security Strategies of the Republic of Poland of 2007 and 2014, for which the legal grounds were provided by Article 4a(1)(1) and Article 6(1)(1) of the Act of 21 November 1967 on the Universal Duty to Defend the Republic of Poland,[7] the Strategy for the Development of the National Security System of the Republic of Poland 2022, and the Strategy for Responsible Development by 2020 (including a 2030 perspective), both adopted by way of Resolutions of the Council of Ministers under Articles 9 and 12a of the Act of 6 December 2006 on the Principles of Conducting the Development Policy.[8] As a result, the executive authorities, and in particular the Government authorities, used to have a decisive voice when it came to the structure of the strategic documents of this stature. This time, however, the legislator determined the framework of the substantive structure of the Strategy, although this decision was somewhat imposed to ensure compliance with the requirements laid down in Article 7(1) of the NIS Directive.

In connection with the above, the legal effect of the directives (which have the character of programmatic norms) included in the Strategy can be questioned, *inter alia*, due to the fact that their provisions regarding purpose and content might not be directly binding on public authorities, or other entities in the national cybersecurity system, which, in compliance with the Constitution of the Republic of Poland, operate on the basis of and within the law. Resolutions and other internal legal acts form a separate set of normative acts, and govern only the relationships between the organisational units forming part of the apparatus supervised by the body which issues a given Resolution or internal legal act. Resolutions of the Council of Ministers may be addressed to subordinate units, and, thus, any strategies adopted on that basis bind only those subordinate units (Article 93(1) of the Constitution of the Republic of Poland), and they may not serve as the basis for decisions taken in respect of citizens, legal persons, or other entities (Article 93(2) thereof). Given the substantive content of the Strategy (Article 69 of the NCSA) and some elements included in the national cybersecurity system (Article 4), the above doubts can be justified. This concerns in particular the National Bank of Poland, Bank

[7]Act of 21 November 1967 on the Universal Duty to Defend the Republic of Poland, consolidated text, Polish Journal of Laws of 2019, item 1541, as amended.

[8]Act of 6 December 2006 on the Principles of Conducting the Development Policy, Polish Journal of Laws of 2009 No. 84, item 712, as amended.

Gospodarstwa Krajowego, companies and partnerships, and some entities performing cybersecurity services.

It can be concluded, therefore, that the national cybersecurity system includes some entities which cannot be subject to the provisions of the Strategy. Under Article 4 of the NCSA, the national cybersecurity system consists of: operators of essential services—digital service providers; CSIRT MON; CSIRT NASK; CSIRT GOV; sectoral cybersecurity teams; units operating within the public-finance sector referred to in Articles 9(1-6), (8), (9), (11) and (12) of the Act on Public Finance; research institutes; the National Bank of Poland; Bank Gospodarstwa Krajowego; the Office of Technical Inspection; the Polish Air Navigation Services Agency; the Polish Centre for Accreditation; the National Fund for Environmental Protection and Water Management, and regional funds for environmental protection and water management; companies and partnerships performing public-utility duties within the meaning of Article 1(2) of the Act on Municipal Services; entities providing services in the field of cybersecurity; bodies in charge of cybersecurity;[9] the Single Point of Contact for cybersecurity;[10] the Government Plenipotentiary for Cybersecurity; and the College for Cybersecurity.[11]

It can be concluded that, given the status of the Strategy, it can have a direct impact on government administration authorities, and, given its legal status in relation to generally applicable law, its impact on other public authorities, entrepreneurs, and citizens is only indirect.

It should also be stressed that several government administration bodies were appointed by the legislator for the purpose of developing, and then adopting, the Strategy. These included the Minister competent for computerisation, who was obliged to cooperate with the Plenipotentiary, other Ministers, and the appropriate managers of central offices (in developing the draft version of the Strategy), and the Council of Ministers (passing a Resolution on adopting the Strategy). The mere fact of finalising the draft version of the Strategy reflects the good will and agreement of the authorised bodies as to its content, by which they express their standpoint on the

[9]The competent bodies in the field of cybersecurity are as follows: for the energy sector—the Minister competent for energy; for the transport sector excluding the water-transport subsector—the Minister competent for transport; for the water-transport subsector—the Minister competent for the maritime economy and the Minister competent for inland shipping; for the banking sector and the financial-market infrastructure—the Polish Financial Supervision Authority; for the healthcare sector, excluding the entities referred to in Article 26(5)—the Minister competent for health; for the healthcare sector including the entities referred to in Article 26(5)—the Minister of National Defence; for the potable-water supply and distribution sector—the Minister competent for water management; for the digital-infrastructure sector, excluding the entities referred to in Article 26 (5)—the Minister competent for computerisation; for the digital infrastructure sector, including the entities referred to in Article 26(5)—the Minister of National Defence; for digital service providers, excluding the entities referred to in Article 26(5)—the Minister competent for computerisation; and for digital service providers, including the entities referred to in Article 26(5)—the Minister of National Defence (Article 41 of the NCSA).

[10]Hereinafter referred to as "the Single Point of Contact".

[11]Hereinafter referred to as "the College".

subject matter. The ultimate Act, for it to be adopted, engages the whole Council of Ministers, and requires a consensus to be reached by way of discussions attended by the majority of the Council of Ministers at Council meetings (§ 15(1) and (2) of the Resolution of the Council of Ministers of 29 October 2013 *Internal Working Regulations of the Council of Ministers*).[12] The Resolution of the Council of Ministers becomes binding on all its members who "[. . .] shall be collectively responsible to the Sejm for the activities of the Council of Ministers" (Article 157 (1) of the Constitution of the Republic of Poland).

Summing up, it can be stated that, in view of the current legal status, the Strategy adopted by the Council of Ministers can be applicable across the Government's administration, but without covering other public entities or institutions, local government authorities, businesses not owned by the state, or non-governmental organisations.

3 The Vision, Main Goal, and Specific Objectives of the Strategy

In compliance with Article 60(1) of the NCSA,

> The Strategy determines the strategic objectives, and the appropriate political and regulatory measures, aimed at attaining and maintaining a high level of cybersecurity. The Strategy shall cover the sectors referred to in Annex 1 hereto, and the digital services and the public entities referred to in Article 4(7)-(15).

The Council of Ministers, in adopting the Resolution on the Cybersecurity Strategy of the Republic of Poland for 2019-2024, strengthened the strategic objectives by introducing the heading "Vision, main goal, specific objectives."

The vision assumes that

> The efficient and safe operation of information systems and means of electronic communication are related to the successful growth of the Republic of Poland, the increasing wealth and effectiveness of the economy, and the performance of its institutions and entities, including the social activities and everyday functioning of individual members of society. Therefore, as part of the actions planned in the Cybersecurity Strategy by 2024, the Government shall systematically enhance and develop the national cybersecurity system. The said actions include systemic organisational, operational, technological, and legal measures, as well as the shaping of social attitudes, and conducting research and development projects, to ensure the achievement of high cybersecurity standards of software, hardware, and digital services. The Government shall take these actions by building confidence between the private sector and the public administration, while respecting the rights and freedoms of the citizens—(Point 4.1 of the Strategy).

[12]The Resolution of the Council of Ministers of 29 October 2013 *Internal Working Regulations of the Council of Ministers*. The Official Gazette of the Government of the Republic of Poland of 2016, item 1006, as amended.

In Article 69(1) of the NCSA, the legislator stipulated that the Strategy should determine the strategic objectives and the appropriate political and regulatory measures, aimed at attaining and maintaining a high level of cybersecurity. This resulted from the provisions of the NIS Directive which, in the definitions section, *stipulated*

> the 'national strategy on the security of network and information systems' entails a framework providing strategic objectives and priorities on the security of network and information systems at the national level—(Article 4(3)).

Furthermore,

> Each Member State shall adopt a national strategy on the security of network and information systems, defining the strategic objectives and the appropriate policy, and regulatory measures, with a view to achieving and maintaining a high level of security of network and information systems, and covering at least the sectors referred to in Annex 2 and the services referred to in Annex 3. (Article 7(1), sentence 1).

Such an approach is consistent with the prevailing view of the essence of the strategy as such, which J. Penc defined as a concept of

> [...] systemic action (an action plan) which involves formulating a set of long-term business objectives, and modifying these objectives, depending on changes occurring in the business environment, and determining the resources and means for these objectives to be fulfilled (...).

A similar way of reasoning regarding the Strategy was adopted when implementing the national development policy, in which it was defined as "[...] a process of creating and implementing a long-term plan, attaining a certain standing, and securing a relatively permanent operational model," and the strategy of an organisation as "a set of non-concurrent operating modes, adjusted to its potential and circumstances, enabling its long-term objectives to be fulfilled." In consequence, developing a strategy implies

> [...] selecting the field of operation in which the organisation is seeking to establish its presence, and determining the means necessary for its survival and development, i.e. for gaining a stronger competitive edge within the sectors, and on the markets, in which it is pursuing its activities.

The state is to ensure the national existence and development conditions which are free from disruptions (and, in particular, threats), which fact was reflected in Article 5 of the Constitution of the Republic of Poland, reading

> The Republic of Poland shall safeguard the independence and integrity of its territory, and ensure the freedoms and rights of persons and citizens, the security of its citizens, safeguard the national heritage, and shall ensure the protection of the natural environment, pursuant to the principles of sustainable development.

Also, numerous legislative acts contain the standards defined by the legislators in laying down the duties of public authorities, and other public entities and institutions, businesses, social organisations, and citizens, regarding the state's (or national) security. All these regulations involve, to a large extent, the fulfilment of the state's external and internal functions, including, in particular, law-enforcement, organisational, executive, regulatory and planning functions.

In determining the strategic objectives, the Council of Ministers lays down the cybersecurity goals which are expected to be attained in the future. These correspond to the anticipated operational outcomes expressed through programmatic norms and directives which cannot be made into legal norms. For this reason, the Strategy may be neither an Act nor a regulation, as its provisions govern a certain operational programme of public administration, within the framework of the national cybersecurity strategy, but they are rather unspecific and imprecise, while their legal enforcement would be hindered.

An illustration of the determining of strategic objectives is provided in Article 3 of the NCSA, reading

> The national cybersecurity system is aimed at ensuring cybersecurity at the national level, including the undisrupted provision of essential services and digital services, by attaining a sufficient level of security of information systems serving the purpose of providing such services, and by ensuring incident handling.

Notwithstanding the foregoing, one should note that, in determining the strategic objectives, the Council of Ministers is driven by substantive factors and the principles of defining the organisation's goals. In the first case, this refers to following the provisions of both the NIS Directive and the NCSA and the EU Internal Security Strategy and national strategies (regarding security and development).

The Strategy for 2019–2024, determining the cybersecurity objectives, also contains the main goal, i.e.

> Increasing the level of resilience to cyber threats and the protection of information in the public, military and private sectors, as well as promoting knowledge and good practices to enable the public to better protect information.

The main goal is followed by five specific objectives.[13]

- Specific objective 1—The development of the national cybersecurity system, (including the implementation and evaluation of the functioning of the provisions regarding the national cybersecurity system; enhancing the efficiency of the functioning of the national cybersecurity system; the development of an information sharing system for the purpose of national security management; enhancing the cybersecurity of essential and digital services and critical infrastructure; the development and implementation of a risk assessment methodology at the national level; and increasing the capacity to counteract cybercrime, including cyber espionage and incidents of a terrorist nature).
- Specific objective 2—Increasing the resilience level of information systems of the public administration and private sectors, and building the capacity to effectively prevent and respond to incidents (including the development and implementation of National Cybersecurity Standards, and the dissemination of good practices and recommendations; supply chain security; and security tests and audits).

[13]See The Cybersecurity Strategy of the Republic of Poland for 2017-2022, Appendix to Resolution No. 125 of the Council of Ministers of 22 October 2019 Official Gazette of the Government of the Republic of Poland of 2019, item 1037.

- Specific objective 3—Increasing the national capacity in the sphere of cybersecurity technology (including the development of industrial and technological resources for the purposes of cybersecurity; focus on developing public-private cooperation; stimulating research and development in the field of cybersecurity; and building the capacity to perform a full spectrum of military operations in cyberspace);
- Specific objective 4—Enhancing public awareness and skills in the field of cybersecurity (including increasing the expertise of the staff of entities applicable to ensuring the cybersecurity of the Republic of Poland; creating conditions for the safe use of cyberspace by citizens; and developing public awareness towards the safe use of cyberspace);
- Specific objective 5—Establishing a strong international position of the Republic of Poland in the sphere of cybersecurity (including: active international cooperation at the strategic and political levels; and active international cooperation at the operational and technical levels).

4 The Means for Fulfilling the Strategy's Objectives and the Entities Involved in Its Implementation

The legislators obligated the Council of Ministers to determine the means for achieving the Strategy objectives. These should, in principle, ensure the level of security of network and information systems commensurate with the risk presented, by preventing and minimising the impact of incidents on the security of the network and information systems which are used for the provision of essential services. These will be technical and organisational measures, accompanied by normative (legal) and administrative measures ensuring that the authorised bodies, the operators of essential services, and providers of essential services, are vested with the necessary rights. These are contained, to a greater or lesser extent, in the specific objectives.

The means for accomplishing the objectives are determined both via programmatic norms and technical directives, as the former are intended to set the goals to be fulfilled, and the latter specify various entities, priorities, means, and other activities, in accordance with Article 69(2) of the NCSA. This aspect of the strategy is reflected in the current achievements and traditions related to developing strategic documents, and in the content of the National Framework of Cybersecurity Policy of the Republic of Poland[14] for 2017–2022[15] adopted by way of Resolution No. 52/2017 of the Council of Ministers of 27 April 2017.

If we assume that policy measures are any activities undertaken by public authorities with a view to attaining the set objectives, then attention should be paid to the fact that, in the reference Strategy, the Council of Ministers designates, in

[14]hereinafter "the National Framework".

[15]KPRM/RM-111-52-17.

varying degrees, activities at the international and national levels (economic, military, educational, scientific and technical, normative, and special), in compliance with the NCSA.

In turn, regulatory measures are implemented to ensure compliance with both the NIS Directive and the NCSA, in order to attain and maintain a high level of cybersecurity. Therefore, the regulations should seek, under the NCSA, *inter alia*, to ensure the consistency of the developed cybersecurity system as regards supervision over financial markets, the adjustment of the banking sector's and the financial markets' infrastructure, the conclusion of agreements for the provision of essential ICT services, and the security of network and information systems of operators of essential services and digital service providers.

Prior to entry into force of the NIS Directive and the NCSA, the national regulatory framework for electronic communications networks and services had been defined in Directive 2002/21/EC of the European Parliament and of the Council of 7 March 2002 on a common regulatory framework for electronic communications networks and services (Framework Directive).[16] The Directive lays down a common legal framework for the provision of electronic communications services, electronic communications networks, and associated facilities and services. It also lays down the tasks of national regulatory authorities, and establishes a set of procedures to ensure the harmonised application of the regulatory framework throughout the Community (Article 1(1) of Directive 2002/21/EC).

Similar to political measures, regulatory measures should also ensure the attaining and maintaining of a high level of cybersecurity.

Under Article 69(1), the Strategy shall cover the sectors referred to in Annex 1 hereto, and the digital services and the public entities referred to in Article 4(7)-(15) (Official Journal EU L 194/1 of 19.07.2016, p 1). Considering that the NIS Directive lays down the obligations serving the purpose of ensuring the cybersecurity of information systems in the services sectors which are essential for the maintenance of social and economic activities, the legislators, by performing minor substantive modifications, indicated (Annex 1 to the NCSA) the sectors, subsectors and types of entities in respect of which the body in charge of cybersecurity has issued a decision on recognising an operator of essential services (see Article 5(2)). These are energy, transport, banking, financial market infrastructure, healthcare, water supply and digital infrastructure. The sectors, subsectors, and types of entities providing essential services were defined in further detail, together with significance thresholds of the consequences of incidents disrupting the provision of essential services, in an Annex to the Regulation of the Council of Ministers of 11 September 2018, a list of essential services and significance thresholds of the

[16]Directive 2002/21/EC of the European Parliament and of the Council of 7 March 2002 on a common regulatory framework for electronic communications networks and services (Framework Directive), OJ EC 2002 L 108/33 (hereinafter: Directive 2002/21/EC).

consequences of incidents disrupting the provision of essential services.[17] The Regulation, within its scope of application, serves the purpose of implementing the NIS Directive.

The entities involved in the Strategy implementation, which need to be indicated in its provisions, are in fact listed in the Act. These are the entities which, under Article 4 of the NCSA, comprised the national cybersecurity system, i.e. the operators of essential services listed in Annex 1 to the said Act; digital service providers (see the commentary to Chapter 4); CSIRT MON; CSIRT NASK; CSIRT GOV; sectoral cybersecurity teams; units operating within the public finance sector referred to in Article 9(1-6), (8), (9), (11) and (12) of the Act on Public Finance; research institutes; the National Bank of Poland; Bank Gospodarstwa Krajowego; the Office of Technical Inspection; the Polish Air Navigation Services Agency; the Polish Centre for Accreditation; the National Fund for Environmental Protection and Water Management, and regional funds for environmental protection and water management; companies and partnerships performing public utility duties within the meaning of Article 1(2) of the Act of 20 December 1996 on Municipal Services; entities providing services in the field of cybersecurity; competent authorities for cybersecurity; the Single Point of Contact; the Government Plenipotentiary for Cybersecurity; and the College for Cybersecurity.

5 The Means for Readiness, Response and Restoration

The specification of the means for readiness, response, and restoration, including the principles of public-private cooperation, constitutes another element of the Strategy. Their description was also, though to a minor extent, included in the content of the specific objectives.

The entire set of the means for readiness, response, and restoration had been previously implemented in the field of the state's defensive readiness and alert levels, as well as in crisis management. However, systemic cybersecurity solutions were lacking. In the statement of grounds for the Act, it was stated that Poland had no "[...] statutory provisions determining the detailed scope of the competences of specific bodies in the field of cybersecurity, in relation to sectors defined in the Directive[18]". Prior to adopting the Act, the National Framework envisaged the determining of the scope of responsibilities, obligations, and rights of the system participants, and the ways of interacting with and between other system participants. More specifically, they assumed the defining of the competences of the appropriate

[17]Regulation of the Council of Ministers of 11 September 2018, a list of essential services and significance thresholds of the consequences of incidents disrupting the provision of essential services, Polish Journal of Laws of 2018 r., item. 1806.

[18]Statement of grounds, p. 11, http://www.sejm.gov.pl/Sejm8.nsf/druk.xsp?nr=2505 Accessed on 10.10.2020.

bodies in charge of supervising information systems in the sectors within which essential services and digital services are provided.[19] Nonetheless, one should bear in mind that the National Framework was not a national product, but its development was based on the draft version, and then the final version, of the NIS Directive. The Act merely sanctioned, at the appropriate level, the provisions of the document adopted by the Council of Ministers, by way of a Resolution.

Despite the benefits of adopting the new Act and determining the means for readiness, response, and restoration, the need to allocate competence between several legal administrations, i.e. the state's defensive readiness, crisis management, and the three states of emergency (natural disaster, the state of exception, and martial law), must be borne in mind.

Ensuring cyberspace security requires concerted efforts from the private and public sectors. Building an effective public-private partnership system based on trust and shared responsibility can constitute a major security pillar in cyberspace.

> The public administration shall, at the same time, improve its potential to advise market sectors in the field of ICT security. The government shall also actively engage in the existing and emerging forms of European public-private cooperation, and thus promote Polish business at the international level.[20]

As stressed by M. Ganczar

> The EU legislators have noted that most of the network and information systems are utilised by private entities; therefore, it has been continually implementing the previous assumptions regarding the creation of a contractual public-private partnership for cybersecurity.[21]

The author also stressed that the operators and providers of essential services should be encouraged to create their own and informal cooperation mechanisms in this field.

6 Risk Assessment

The risk-assessment approach constitutes a major element of the Strategy, which results from the requirements laid down in the EU directive and the national Act. As stipulated in the NIS Directive, "Risk-management measures include measures to identify any risks of incidents, to prevent, detect and handle incidents, and to mitigate their impact" (recital 46, sentence 1 of the NIS Directive). It should also be stressed that, from the point of view of the EU legislators,

> In practice, the degree of risk for operators of essential services, which are often essential for the maintenance of critical societal and economic activities, is higher than for digital service providers. Therefore, the security requirements for digital service providers should be less

[19] Ibidem.

[20] The National Framework..., Point 7.2.

[21] M. Ganczar (2017), p. 87.

> stringent. Digital service providers should remain free to take measures they consider appropriate to manage the risks posed to the security of their network and information systems. Because of their cross-border nature, digital service providers should be subject to a more harmonised approach at the Union level. Implementing acts should facilitate the specification and implementation of such measures—(recital 49).

From the legislators' point of view, risk is "[. . .] a combination of the likelihood of the occurrence of an adverse event and its consequences," whereas risk management means "[. . .] coordinated activities in the field of cybersecurity management in relation to the estimated risk" (Article 2(12) and Article 2(19) of the NCSA, respectively). Such a risk interpretation is characteristic of almost all legal regulations, *inter alia*, those concerning crisis management and the protection of classified information.

The risk-assessment approach is an integral element of risk management which, according to the generally acceptable standards, includes risk assessment which covers risk identification; risk analysis and evaluation; decision-making; risk handling; and monitoring and reviewing, whereas

> This process concerns any risk and must form an integral part of an organisation's practical activities, and must have an executor capable of providing the appropriate methods and tools for its implementation.[22]

Risk assessment (or risk estimation, as in Article 2(13) of the NCSA), according to the generally applicable rules, should thus cover selecting risk sources (incidents) or threats which have or could have an adverse impact on cybersecurity; identifying and creating a list of risks influencing cybersecurity objectives; determining the consequences for information systems of any actions which violate confidentiality, integrity, availability, and authenticity of processed data or the related services provided through such systems; defining the causes of the sources of risks and threats; assessing the efficiency of existing security systems; determining the location, time, and circumstances of risk occurrence; and risk classification in comparison with acceptable values.[23]

The development and implementation of a risk-assessment methodology at the national level is considered a priority in the specific objective of the Strategy regarding the establishing of a National Cybersecurity System. Accordingly, "A joint static and dynamic risk-assessment methodology which takes into account the specificity of individual sectors, critical-infrastructure operators, operators of essential services, and digital service providers, shall be introduced for the purpose of cybersecurity management at the national level. This shall ensure the comparability of estimates, also regarding risk levels, in particular for the purpose of national--security-risk reports, developed in accordance with the crisis-management regulations. Risk assessment shall become a continuous process which will enable the identifying of the risk level in near real time.

---

[22]See D. Wróblewski (2015), p. 37.

[23]More on the issue, ibid., pp. 44–48.

The methodology and tools facilitating static and dynamic risk assessment in communication and information systems are being developed as part of the National Cybersecurity Platform, a project funded by the National Centre for Research and Development; the completion of this work has been scheduled for the end of 2020.[24]

7 Educational, Informational and Training Programmes in the Field of Cybersecurity

Activities related to educational, informational, and training programmes in the field of cybersecurity constitute an integral part of the Strategy. This wording has been slightly altered, and seems less precise, compared to the provisions of the NIS Directive, as the latter stipulates that it concerns guidelines referring to programmes developed in this field. In fact, this definition is *more* specific, as these are executive bodies which conduct specific educational, informational, and training activities consistent with their range of competence. The Council of Ministers should provide indications, within the Strategy, regarding the general principles of implementing various undertakings in this area.

The legislators have entrusted duties in the reference scope to numerous entities in the national cybersecurity system, in accordance with their expertise. The major players include the Minister competent for computerisation (see the commentary to Article 45(1)); the Single Point of Contact (Article 49(1)); CSIRT MON, CSIRT NASK and CSIRT GOV (Article 26(3)); and the Minister of National Defence (Article 51).

Cybersecurity tests and audits will be a no-less-important undertaking, and a vehicle for implementing the Strategy. Periodic audits are among measures which allow the assessment of the effectiveness of the currently implemented information security management systems, and the adequacy of the safeguards introduced. Audit methodologies should take into account the applicable standards, good practices, and specificity of the respective sectors. The aim of such an approach is to achieve comparability in audit outcomes. Periodic tests (including penetration testing), which provide for a real assessment of the system's resilience to threats, are another security assessment measure. The outcomes of these tests are the basis for the verification of the safeguards deployed. In order to utilise the public capacity in the sphere of cybersecurity, so-called bug bounty testing will be disseminated, which is a search for software vulnerabilities conducted by people not associated with the software developer, usually with the general consent of the developer.

[24]See the Cybersecurity Strategy of the Republic of Poland for 2019-2024...op. cit., p. 13.

8 Developing, Reviewing and Updating the Strategy

Article 69 indicates that the Strategy was to be developed for a five-year period with possible amendments throughout its duration. While the document will remain in force for 5 years, it is to be reviewed (in terms of up-to-dateness) every 2 years. At the strategic level, the process of developing long-term tactics oriented towards identifying and implementing organisations' objectives usually takes no less than 5 years, at the tactical level 2–5 years, and at the operational level up to 2 years. The Strategy, reflecting the arrangements made by leading entities in the field of cybersecurity, including the Council of Ministers, which has adopted it by way of a Resolution, is a document of strategic significance. Hence, its duration is 5 years. The legislator, however, has envisaged amendments to be made within its content, on an as-needed basis, and at any time, and its review at an arbitrarily set time, i.e. every 2 years (Article 71 of the NCSA).

It should be stressed once more that, in the case of this Strategy, we are dealing with quite an innovative approach by the legislator in assigning a status to a document which had not previously occurred in the processes of developing and announcing cybersecurity strategies. To date, a similar requirement to determine strategic objectives, and the appropriate political and regulatory measures, to indicate the sectors referred to in Annex 1 to the Act, as well as digital services and public entities, and to specify the leading specific content of the Strategy, its duration and reviews, has not been included in any other strategies regarding national security, national defence, or military strategies.

In 2015, following amendments to the Act of 4 September 1997 on Government Administration Departments,[25] the scope of this department was made to include cybersecurity issues. Following the adoption of the NCSA, another amendment was made to the Act on Government Administration Departments, which involved new wording for Article 12a(1)(10). In consequence, the scope of the computerisation department was limited to civil matters related to cybersecurity,[26] while its military aspects became the domain of the defence department.

This way, the Minister's leading role in Strategy development arises from the duties assigned to the Ministers chairing specific government administration departments, which involve initiating and developing the Council of Ministers' policies for given departments, and submitting initiatives, draft assumptions, draft Acts, and draft versions of normative Acts, at Council of Ministers meetings, on the principles and according to the procedure defined in the Internal Work Regulations of the Council of Ministers (Article 34(1) of the GAD Act). We are, therefore, dealing with the principle of competency, according to which each body has a set of rights and obligations determined in systemic regulations.

[25] Act of 4 September 1997 on Government Administration Departments, Consolidated text Polish Journal of Laws of 2020, item 1220, as amended.

[26] See Article 12a (1) and Article 19(1)(1a) of the Act on Government Administration Departments.

The Act indicates the Minister competent for computerisation as the leading body entrusted with developing draft versions of the Strategy. However, given the systemic expertise of the Government Plenipotentiary, other Ministers, and the authorised managers of central offices, and in particular their responsibilities within the national cybersecurity system, cooperation with them is justified for substantive reasons, and in view of the related scope of responsibilities of administration bodies in this field. The Minister can also collaborate with members of the Council of Ministers and government administration authorities to act for the common good and in the public interest, on the principles and according to the procedure defined in the NCSA.

It is also worth stressing that, although the legislators have not specified this issue in the Act, the NIS Directive, and more specifically Article 7(2) thereof, stipulates that Member States may request the assistance of ENISA (the European Union Agency for Cybersecurity) in developing national strategies on the security of network and information systems.

While the work on the draft version of the Strategy can also be attended by a representative of the President of the Republic of Poland, the legislators have not determined who, and under which procedure, decides on the need for the President's representative to be involved. Nor has it been expressly stated that the role of that representative should be fulfilled by the Head of the National Security Bureau.

Under Article 126 of the Constitution of the Republic of Poland, the President is the supreme representative of the Republic of Poland, and the guarantor of the continuity of state authority, who ensures the observance of the Constitution, and safeguards the sovereignty and security of the state, as well as the inviolability and integrity of its territory. Our interest, however, focuses especially on the President's role in the international affairs of the Republic of Poland, as an authority safeguarding national security. Also in this field, the President collaborates with the Council of Ministers as a whole, and with individual Ministers as Council members. Due to the convergence of capabilities, and at the same time their separation, the Minister competent for computerisation, by inviting a representative of the President of the Republic of Poland to attend work on the draft version of the Strategy, contributes to a reliable and efficient operation of public institutions.

The Strategy is of key significance for national security, and for compliance with international obligations. As a result, given the stature of the body which adopts it (the Council of Ministers) and the competences of the President of the Republic of Poland regarding national security, and the cooperation obligation of executive bodies, including when they act through their representatives, in the field of national and EU cybersecurity policies, reflects the implementation of the constitutional principle of collaboration, and avoidance of competition between, public authorities.

Article 71 of the NCSA stipulates that the Minister competent for computerisation, in cooperation with the Plenipotentiary, other Ministers, and the appropriate managers of central offices, shall review the Strategy every 2 years. The authority of this body arises from its being entrusted by the legislator with a mission to develop the draft version of the Strategy in cooperation with the entities indicated in Article 70 of the said Act.

In addition, the periodic character of the Strategy reviews arises from the provisions of the NIS Directive, *inter alia*, on updating the list of identified digital service providers (at least every 2 years), and on the reviewing of the Directive by the European Commission, and reporting to the European Parliament and the Council.

Article 7(3) of the NIS Directive stipulates "Member States shall communicate their national strategies on the security of network and information systems to the Commission within three months from their adoption." As a result, the Polish legislator has obligated, under Article 72 of the NCSA, the Minister competent for computerisation to submit the Strategy to the European Commission within 3 months of its being adopted by the Council of Ministers.

References

Ganczar M (2017) Umowne partnerstwo publiczno-prywatne w kontekście bezpieczeństwa sieci i informacji administracji publicznej in: Internet. Strategie bezpieczeństwa, ed. G. Szpor, A. Gryszczyńska, Warsaw

Wróblewski D (ed) (2015) Zarządzanie ryzykiem - przegląd wybranych metodyk, Józefów

Waldemar Kitler Professor, Eng., full professor at the National Security Faculty of the War Studies University. In scientific activity, he deals with issues of national security, national defense and crisis management as well as selected legal and administrative aspects of security and defense of the Republic of Poland. He has extensive professional experience, including work in universities and central administration. The most important experiences include work at the National Defense University, the Department of Defense System of the Ministry of National Defense, the Office of Crisis Management and Civil Protection and the National Headquarters of the State Fire Service. In the years 2010–2011 he managed the Cathedral of Law and Administration. From 2011, he was the Vice-Dean of the Faculty of National Security for Scientific Affairs. In the years 2015–2016 he was the head of the Cathedral of National Security Law, and in the years 2017–2019 the director of the Institute of Law and Defense Administration. Currently, he is the director of the Institute of State Security. The professor promoted 16 doctors and his scientific achievements include over 260 publications, including over 80 articles and scientific papers, 25 original creative works (including 10 monographs), about 60 scientific and research papers, 8 textbooks and academic scripts, 90 reviews and scientific opinions.

The Functioning of State Power Structures and Cybersecurity

Marzena Toumi

Abstract The national security of Poland in the twenty-first century is strongly influenced by the processes taking place in the contemporary global security environment. These changes are characterised by high dynamics and complexity as well as the occurrence of asymmetric threats, among which the most dangerous are threats in cyberspace. The functioning of the state and the implementation of its constitutional obligations are increasingly dependent on the development of modern technologies, the information society and the smooth functioning of cyberspace, which is largely dependent on the security of the ICT infrastructure, which allows the use of cyberspace, information resources and services accumulated therein. Rapid progress in the field of digital technologies necessitates the effective use of the latest technologies while creating an opportunity for the Polish state to leave the role of only a user and join the group of countries with an effectively functioning digital economy, providing solutions and co-creating international standards. To meet these expectations, the President of the Republic of Poland signed the Act on the National Cybersecurity System on 1 August 2018, implementing Directive 2016/1148 (NIS Directive).

State power is a form of universal or general power over the whole population in a given territory. It is exercised by a special power apparatus elected from among society as a whole.

In the literature on the subject matter, the features of state power include its primary character, indivisibility, permanency, exercisability under legal regulations, implementation only in an organised manner, the possibility to legally use coercive measures (also direct), and exercisability in a given territory.[1]

[1]Representatives of state power, in order to gain citizens' endorsement, use various arguments which are meant to legitimise their powers. These arguments pertain both to the sources of power

M. Toumi (✉)
Instytut Prawa/Institute of Law, Akademia Sztuki Wojennej w Warszawie/War Studies University in Warsaw, Warsaw, Poland
e-mail: m.toumi@akademia.mil.pl

K. Chałubińska-Jentkiewicz et al. (eds.), *Cybersecurity in Poland*,
https://doi.org/10.1007/978-3-030-78551-2_10

State authority in a democratic system has a collective character, as it comprises both direct state authority and social (ultimate) authority.

Direct authority is composed of the political personnel of state bodies and public servants (bureaucracy). The managing bodies of a state organisation, political parties, interest groups, and mass media, constitute the power elite. Direct state authority ensures both internal and external security, protects socio-economic relations, and creates the conditions conducive to self-assembly, e.g. through social governance. Social authority is exercised by the nation, i.e. all citizens who participate in electing the political leadership and influencing its rule.

State authority can, therefore, be said to jointly cover the power elite and the nation. There is no single sovereign entity which would finally and ultimately decide on the ways state power should be exercised (the rule of the people exercised by the elites they elect).

The major powers vested in state authority include legislative powers, i.e. the powers to enact universally binding legal regulations under the Constitution, i.e. without violating any constitutional civic rights and freedoms; to take measures to amend the obligations arising from already enacted regulations (administrative decisions made by the government, general administration, and specialised services); and to impose sanctions on those infringing the legal regulations (via the judiciary and direct coercion bodies, such as the army, the police, and the prison service).

The bodies vested with decision-making powers constitute the state power apparatus, i.e. a system of state bodies, interrelated in terms of organisation, along with offices and institutions which serve the central decision-making authority (e.g. the government) in implementing current state policies.[2]

State power should fulfil the following four core functions: integrative, distributional, security-making, and structure-building. This article focuses, in particular, on the third function.

One of the duties of state power is, therefore, to create a "security umbrella", to protect those who fall within the impact of the state's decision-makers and

(legal power) and also, increasingly, to the ways in which it is exercised (efficient and competent) as well as to the consequences of their actions (successful, meeting social needs), cf. Kuciński (2008), p. 113.

[2]The state apparatus includes (1) legislative bodies (the Sejm and the Senate) (2) executive bodies (the President and the Council of Ministers), which are entrusted with performing state duties aimed at implementing the Law. government administration authorities are also endowed with executive power. The National Broadcasting Council, whose powers are provided for in the Constitution of the Republic of Poland, is also an executive body, and has the right to issue regulations. In the Election Code, the National Electoral Commission was appointed as the *sui generis* executive body (although its powers are not provided for in the Constitution of the Republic of Poland, and it does not have the right to issue regulations, it may issue instructions binding on lower-level electoral bodies) (3) coercion bodies (e.g. the police, the army)—a group of state bodies whose aim is to ensure the implementation of the Law. They are in charge of maintaining public order, as well as of ensuring the external and internal security of the country (4) judicial bodies—the Supreme Court, common courts, military courts, and administrative courts (5) inspection bodies (e.g. the Supreme Chamber of Control) which supervise compliance with the Law.

authorities. The latter fulfil their security functions by employing various decision-making tools, and with a considerable use of legal instruments.[3]

The national security system is understood as the entirety of resources, means, and forces (entities) earmarked by the state for the performance of tasks in the field of security, organised (into subsystems and components), maintained and prepared in a manner capable of fulfilling the purpose of performing such tasks.[4] The objective of the National Security Strategy is to counteract emerging threats to the survival of both the nation and the state, to territorial integrity, to political independence and sovereignty, to the efficient functioning of state institutions, and to socio-economic development. It covers elements of both external and internal security, oriented towards ensuring nationwide security in combination with the socio-economic development of the country.[5]

The national security system comprises all the bodies and institutions constituting legislative, executive, and judicial powers, which are in charge of ensuring security in the light of the Constitution of the Republic of Poland and other relevant acts. These include Parliament, the President of the Republic of Poland, the President of the Council of Ministers, the Council of Ministers, central government administration authorities, and other central state bodies and public institutions. The armed forces, as well as government services and institutions, also form crucial elements in the national security system. They are obliged to prevent and counteract external threats, to ensure public security, to conduct rescue operations, and to protect people and property in extraordinary situations. In addition, the system covers local government authorities and other legal entities, including entrepreneurs who form the industrial defence potential, and implement duties in the field of national defence.

The national security system consists of the national security control subsystem, and several executive subsystems. The control subsystem is formed by public authorities and managers of organisational units implementing duties related to national security, and command authorities of the Armed Forces of the Republic of Poland. Executive subsystems are the means and forces earmarked for the Ministers leading government administration departments, central-government administration authorities, province governors (voivodes), local government authorities, and other public institutions and entities responsible for implementing duties in the field of national security as arising from the applicable Acts.[6]

Processes occurring in the contemporary global security environment have a material impact on the national security of Poland in the twenty-first century. These are characterised by powerful dynamics and complexity of changes, and by the emergence of asymmetric threats, the most serious including terrorism, the

[3]Kuciński (2008), pp. 108–109.

[4]*The White Book on the National Security of the Republic of Poland*, Warsaw 2013, p. 36.

[5]*The Strategy of the Development of the National Security System of the Republic of Poland 2022 (2013)*, adopted by way of Resolution No. 67 of the Council of Ministers of 9 April 2013, Journal Monitor Polski 2013, item 377.

[6]Dubiel (2018), Accessed on 20 September 2020.

proliferation of weapons of mass destruction and the means of their delivery, international organised crime, and threats in cyberspace.[7] The functioning of the state and the performance of its constitutional duties increasingly depends on the development of modern technologies, the information society, and the uninterrupted functioning of cyberspace. The last of these, in turn, is largely dependent on the security of the communications infrastructure which facilitates the use of cyberspace, and of information resources and services which function within it.

Cyberspace is understood as "a space for the processing and exchange of information created by information and communication systems," as defined in Article 3 (3) *of the Act of 17 February 2005 on the Computerisation of the Operations of Entities Performing Public Tasks,*[8] "including the links between them and their relations with users." Virtual space also tends to be increasingly treated as the territory of a given country. The cyberspace of the Republic of Poland is the cyberspace within the territory of Poland and outside, and basically covers any places where representatives of the Republic of Poland operate (e.g. diplomatic posts or military contingents).[9]

In the contemporary world, cyberspace is a major channel of information exchange, and the issues of electronic data transfer are increasingly pertinent to public institutions.[10] This is due to the progressing digitisation of offices and public institutions, as a result of which the computerisation of office infrastructures is triggering the growing use of information technologies in the electronic collecting, processing, and transferring of confidential information between entities in the national economy. This also involves the computerisation of the processes utilising the resources of the personal data of the customers served by these economic entities, and of citizens' data available to offices and public institutions.[11]

As part of the state's digitisation process, such technologies are used by public institutions (government and local government administration institutions, as well as legislative, executive, and judicial bodies), specialised services (e.g. the police, the emergency services, and the fire service), and media, banking, and finance institutions as part of their service portfolios, transport (by air and rail), and energy and

[7]*The Strategy* .... (2013), p. 4.

[8]Act of 17 February 2005 on the Computerisation of the Operations of Entities Performing Public Tasks, consolidated text Polish Journal of Laws of 2020, item 346, as amended.

[9]*The Cyberspace Protection Policy of the Republic of Poland*, a document adopted by the Ministry of Administration and Digitisation and the Internal Security Agency (2013), Warsaw, p. 5. Such a definition of the cyberspace of the Republic of Poland does not cover the storage and processing of information, e.g., in a cloud, which is not necessarily located within the Polish territory. This provision is exclusive of new technologies, e.g. data storage in Azure, AWS (cf. *The Cyberspace Protection Policy of the Republic of Poland (departmental comments by ISSA Poland)* in: http://mac.gov.pl/wp-content/uploads/2012/09/polityka-CBR-stan-na-18-09-2012-konsultacje-resortowe-.pdf, accessed on 10 October 2020.

[10]Borkowski (2013), pp. 112–134.

[11]Gołębiowska (2015), p. 29.

water supply networks.[12] Most of these fields form part of the so-called critical infrastructure, which is understood as a network of interrelated systems enabling public, economic, and social institutions to fulfil their basic duties, such as maintaining security and public order, and rendering core social services.[13]

The use of e-government[14] brings numerous benefits both for the administration system itself, such as improved communication (both internal and external), and increased operational transparency, which results, *inter alia*, from services standardisation and procedures automation (eliminating the human factor), and for individual citizens and society—a faster and more efficient handling of official matters increases customer satisfaction and contributes to building a positive image of public administration. E-government provides employees with easier access to information and facilitates information exchange, both within a unit (a given office) and between various units. It also makes it quicker to gather (in one place) voluminous information regarding an entity (e.g. its public-law obligations; tax arrears or no tax arrears; payments of premiums to the Social Insurance Institution, etc.), which then facilitates prompt verification of the information (data) submitted to the institution, and, in consequence, the prompt detection of irregularities, and, where necessary, the instituting of explanatory proceedings.[15]

In compliance with the provisions included in the government's strategic document *The Strategy for Responsible Development,* adopted by the Council of Ministers in 2017, e-government was seen as a factor determining a well-functioning state.[16] The use of digital technologies is a key element in ensuring the transparency and effectiveness of tasks implemented by public administration.[17] Despite all its benefits, digitisation also involves the risk of a much greater susceptibility to attacks launched by cybercriminals,[18] who can include both criminal groups operating for profit-oriented or terrorist motives and groups led by foreign states. Such activities are aimed at obtaining information, effecting political or economic destabilisation, or

---

[12]Suchorzewska (2010), pp. 318–338.

[13]Dawidziak et al. (2009), pp. 55–56.

[14]The term *e-government*, i.e. electronic public administration, describes a system (and, more specifically, an organisational, legal, institutional, and computer system) which makes it possible to handle administrative matters electronically, Ejdys (2018), p. 5.

According to the European Commission, e-government stands for the use of IT tools and systems in order to provide better-quality public services for citizens and enterprises, Glossary of the European Commission https://ec.europa.eu/digital-single-market/en/glossary#letter_e, accessed on 14. September 2020.

[15]Mituś (2013). *Sprawne i skuteczne funkcjonowanie e-administracji przynosi korzyści na trzech poziomach: ludności i podmiotów gospodarczych, organów administracji oraz społeczeństwa i gospodarki jako całości*, cf. Lulkiewicz, *E-administracja (*2013*)*, p. 217.

[16]*A Strategy for Responsible Development (2017)*, the Council of Ministers, Warsaw 2017, p. 226.

[17]See: Śledziewska et al. (2016), pp. 119–130.

[18]According to Interpol, cybercrime is currently a more-profitable activity than drug trafficking (with revenue from such activity in some countries exceeding 1% of GDP), cf. D. Bałut, K. Budek, *Cyberbezpieczeństwo dla przedsiębiorców: Nowa era zagrożeń*, https://marketingibiznes.pl/it/cyberbezpieczenstwo/; accessed on 9 September 2020.

causing social discontent.[19] Notably, any act of disturbing the functioning of cyberspace, whether global or local, affects economic security, the sense of security among citizens, the effective functioning of public-sector institutions, the course of production and service processes, and, in consequence, overall national security.[20]

Therefore, more intensified measures in the field of cybersecurity (i.e. ensuring the protection of the domain of information processing and of interactions within tele-information networks) are indispensable to responding to the growing threat from cybercriminals.[21] It is public administration's duty, in the age of information, to synchronise activities performed by entities operating within various sectors to manage complex networking sites, and to adapt its operational mode so as to be able to explore new technologies, as it is one of the major users of new tools and tele-information technologies, and its functioning is based on the processing of information which forms the principal resource of administration,[22] while information security issues are an element in the laws on national security.[23] For this reason, the public duties (viewed as legal obligations) oriented towards security in cyberspace are a significant aspect of the secure and efficient functioning of the state, and are implemented by way of cooperation between public services and entities in charge of cybersecurity, both at the national (the private sector and NGOs), and international, levels (NATO, the European Union, the UN and supranational associations).[24] Such cooperation plays a major role in the fight against the growing number of incidents being caused by illegal actions in cyberspace, which precipitate financial and image losses.

[19]As e-Government primarily utilises websites as the domain for the exchange of information between administration bodies and citizens, these should meet basic security requirements, i.e. ensure adequate access, integrity and data confidentiality. Otherwise, information might become inaccessible, or might lose its integrity and confidentiality, as a result of impacts originating from various sources, e.g. targeted measures aimed at distributing *malware,* which performs actions on a computer without the consent or knowledge of its user, for the benefit of a third party; disguising oneself as a trustworthy entity, e.g. a renowned institution or person, with the aim of fraudulently obtaining sensitive information (*phishing* and *pharming*); *cross-site scripting,* which involves injecting a malicious code into a given website which takes the user to another website; *SQL Injection,* which involves criminals exploiting various vulnerabilities, e.g., in apps which allow access to personal data to be obtained by unauthorised persons; or *ransomware,* the purpose of which is to take over and encrypt a user's data, and then provide such data to the user on condition that "a ransom" is paid.

[20]*The Cybersecurity Strategy of the Republic of Poland for 2017–2022*, Warsaw 2017, p. 4.

[21]It should be a requirement for public administration to use only the type of electronic equipment which has obtained a special national security certificate. A major element in ensuring a so-called safe supply chain is to assess and certify products, with the establishing of a "national evaluation system" being considered a priority. *Cyberbezpieczeństwo w Polsce: ochrona urządzeń końcowych przed cyberatakami. Analiza sytuacji i rekomendacje działań*, A report prepared by Cyfrowa Polska, Warsaw 2019, pp. 10–11.

[22]Szczepaniuk (2016), p. 26.

[23]Cf. Kamiński (2019b), pp. 57–76; Kamiński (2019a), pp. 28–34.

[24]Bączek (2016), p. 244.

In the Republic of Poland, duties in the field of cyberspace security are implemented by public authorities (legislative, executive, and judicial), and their subsidiary administrative authorities.[25] A significant role of the legislative authorities (the Sejm and the Senate) regarding cybersecurity is to develop legislation and to determine the principal directions of the state's activities.[26] The judicial authorities are entrusted with administering justice in criminal cases, which often involve generally understood national security, and its trans-sectoral domain, i.e. cyberspace security, which is subject to the regulations determining the rules of conduct.[27] The key role in this respect is ascribed to the executive power. The Council of Ministers leading the government's administration, by performing duties to foster the protection of cyberspace, fulfils its constitutional obligations, and bears the main responsibility for ensuring the appropriate level of security for cyberspace and the citizens who function within it.[28]

On 1 August 2018, the President of the Republic of Poland signed the Act on the national cybersecurity system thus implementing within the Polish legal system the Directive of the European Parliament and of the Council (EU) concerning measures for a high common level of security of network and information systems across the Union (Directive 2016/1148).[29] The full implementation of NIS Directive also required adopting two regulations by the Council of Ministers, i.e. on serious incident thresholds,[30] and on a list of essential services and significance thresholds for the consequences of incidents disrupting the provision of essential services.[31]

The national cybersecurity system so established is aimed at ensuring cybersecurity at the national level, including in particular the uninterrupted provision of essential services and digital services, by attaining a sufficiently high level of security of information and communication systems serving the purpose of providing such services, and by ensuring incidents handling.[32]

The system covers operators of essential services[33] (e.g. in the energy, transport, healthcare, and banking sectors), digital service providers, CSIRTs (Computer

[25]Chałubińska-Jentkiewicz (2019), p. 360.

[26]Kitler (2011), pp. 76–77.

[27]Chałubińska-Jentkiewicz (2019). pp. 360–361. See more: Radoniewicz (2016).

[28]Chałubińska-Jentkiewicz (2019), p. 353.

[29]Official Journal EU L 194/1.

[30]The Regulation of the Council of Ministers of 31 October 2018 on serious incidents thresholds (Polish Journal of Laws of 2018, item 2180).

[31]The Regulation of the Council of Ministers of 11 September 2018 on a list of essential services and significance thresholds of the consequences of incidents disrupting the provision of essential services (Polish Journal of Laws of 2018, item 1806).

[32]Article 3 of NCSA.

[33]Operators of essential services, and companies and institutions rendering services in one of the six critical areas, from the point of view of the national economy, i.e. energy, transport, banking, healthcare, potable water supply (and distribution), and the digital infrastructure.

An essential service is considered to be dependent on IT systems. Under Article 17 of the Act on the national cybersecurity system, a digital service provider (DSP) is a legal person or an

Security Incident Response Teams) at the national level, sectoral cybersecurity teams, entities providing services in the field of cybersecurity, responsible bodies in the field of cybersecurity, and single points of contact within the framework of EU cooperation in the field of cybersecurity.

The Act indicates three CSIRTs established at the national level: CSIRT NASK (operating within the Research and Academic Computer Network—the National Research Institute in Warsaw), CSIRT GOV (operating within the Internal Security Agency), and CSIRT MON (operating within the Ministry of Defence). Each CSIRT at the national level has a clearly determined constituency—entities which have a reporting obligation towards that CSIRT, and to which it provides support.

CSIRT MON coordinates the process of handling incidents reported by bodies subordinated to, or supervised by, the Ministry of Defence, including entities whose information and communication systems or networks are included in a consolidated register of facilities, installations, devices, and services forming parts of critical infrastructure, and enterprises of particular economic and defensive significance, for which the Minister of Defence acts as the entity organising and supervising state defence duties.[34]

CSIRT GOV[35] coordinates, on incidents reported by the government administration, units operating within the public finance sector, the National Bank of Poland, Bank Gospodarstwa Krajowego, and operators of critical infrastructure.[36]

CSIRT NASK coordinates on incidents reported by other entities, including operators of essential services (other than operators of critical infrastructure), digital service providers, and local governments.[37] CSIRT NASK can also be referred to as a CERT of last resort, as it is the entity to whom also natural persons (irrespective of their citizenship status or lack of citizenship) and organisational units (irrespective of

computerization unit providing a digital service which does not have legal personality, has its base or management on the territory of Poland, or whose representative runs an computerization unit on the territory of Poland. Small and microenterprises have been excluded from that Act. A list of operators of essential services is maintained by the Minister competent for digital affairs. Operators are entered in and removed from the list at the request of a body responsible for cybersecurity; more on the issue: Radoniewicz (2019), p. 55.

[34]https://www.gov.pl/web/cyfryzacja/zespol-reagowania-na-incydenty-bezpieczenstwa-komputerowego-csirt, accessed on 28 August 2020.

[35]Operating since January 2008 within the Internal Security Agency as CERT.GOV.PL.

[36]In compliance with the Act of 26 April 2007 on Crisis Management, Polish Journal of Laws of 2007 No. 89, item 590, as amended and the Act of 27 August 2009 on public finance, Polish Journal of Laws of 2009 No. 157, item 1240, as amended. CSIRT GOV is mainly entrusted with identifying, preventing, and detecting threats to security, which are important for ensuring the functional continuity of the national tele-information systems utilised by public-administration bodies, or a system of tele-information networks included in a consolidated register of facilities, installations, devices, and services forming parts of the critical infrastructure, as well as tele-information systems of owners and holders of facilities, installations, and devices forming parts of the critical infrastructure, https://www.gov.pl/web/cyfryzacja/zespol-reagowania-na-incydenty-bezpieczenstwa-komputerowego-csirt, accessed on 28 August 2020.

[37]See: *The Deployment of the Baseline Capabilities of National/Governmental CERTs*, ENISA – www.enisa.europa.eu; see also Banasiński and Nowak (2018), pp. 161–162.

their base) can report incidents if no other CSIRTs are considered competent in their case.

Furthermore, CSIRT MIL and CSIRT GOV (in compliance with the Act on Anti-Terrorist Activities and the Act on the Military Counterintelligence Service and the Military Intelligence Service) are competent for handling incidents which constitute acts of terrorism.[38] When it comes to incidents related to national defence, CSIRT MON is always the competent body.

Close cooperation between the CSIRTs established at the national level is the principal assumption of the Act. All the CSIRTs established at the national level are obliged to cooperate both with one another and with competent authorities in the field of cybersecurity, the Minister competent for computerisation, and the Plenipotentiary for Cybersecurity, as well as to ensure a consistent and complete risk management system at the national level, to perform duties related to counteracting cybersecurity threats of a supra-sectoral and cross-border character, and to ensure the coordinated handling of reported incidents (Article 26(1)).

Another major element introduced by the Act on cybersecurity is the possibility of the performing of equipment and software inspections by CSIRTs, with a view to identifying any vulnerabilities which might be used to threaten the integrity, confidentiality, accountability, authenticity, or accessibility of processed data, which might then affect public security or significant national security interests. Based on such inspections, CSIRTs can present recommendations for removing such vulnerabilities in the equipment or software used by entities operating within the national cybersecurity system.[39]

Operators of essential services are also obliged to implement effective security measures, to estimate cybersecurity-related risks, to provide information on major incidents, and to handle such incidents in cooperation with the CSIRTs established at the national level. The entities listed are also obliged to appoint persons responsible for the cybersecurity of the provided services, for incident reporting and handling, and for the dissemination of information on cybersecurity. The national cybersecurity system also includes public administration authorities and telecommunications companies.

In addition, the requirements regarding cybersecurity have been extended to cover digital service providers, i.e. e-commerce platforms, cloud-computing services, and search engines. Given the international nature of these entities, the obligations binding on digital service providers are covered by the regulatory régime harmonised at the EU level (at this point, the Act relates to the relevant Commission Implementing Decision).

[38] Act of 10 June 2016 on Anti-Terrorism (Polish Journal of Laws of 2019, item 796); the Act of 9 June 2006 *on the Military Counterintelligence Service and the Military Intelligence Service*, (Polish Journal of Laws of 2006, No. 104, item 709).

[39] https://www.gov.pl/web/cyfryzacja/zespol-reagowania-na-incydenty-bezpieczenstwa-komputerowego-csirt, accessed on 28 August 2020.

The national cybersecurity system also includes public entities such as the National Bank of Poland, Bank Gospodarstwa Krajowego, the Office of Technical Inspection, the Polish Air Navigation Services Agency, the Polish Centre for Accreditation, the National Fund for Environmental Protection and Water Management, and regional funds for environmental protection and water management, as well as research institutes and commercial law companies performing public-utility duties.

Under Article 21 of the Act on the national cybersecurity system, each of these entities is obliged to appoint a person in charge of maintaining contacts with entities operating within the national cybersecurity system, as regards public duties dependent on IT systems.

Furthermore, each public entity is obliged to manage incidents within its structures, and to ensure that they are properly handled. Any major incidents must be reported to the competent CSIRT within 24 hours of their being identified (Article 11 (4)). Any decisions made to this end shall require prior consultation with the operator of essential services or the digital service provider which has reported an incident.

CSIRT MON, CSIRT NASK or CSIRT GOV, acting via Single Points of Contact, shall inform other EU Member States of any major incident, as long as it involves two or more EU Member States (Article 29).

The Act has also introduced a formula for Critical Incident Response Teams which act as auxiliary bodies in matters of handling critical incidents, and which comprise the CSIRTs established at the national level and the Government Centre for Security (as a secretariat), to facilitate cooperation with the Government Centre for Crisis Management. Representatives of the competent bodies can also be invited to participate in the work of these Teams.

In compliance with the said Act, information on vulnerabilities and incidents, and the risks of their occurrence, as well as cybersecurity threats, is not subject to the Act on Access to Public Information.[40] Nonetheless, the competent CSIRT MON, CSIRT NASK and CSIRT GOV may publish such information (to the extent necessary) on the websites of the Public Information Bulletin of the Minister of Defence, the Research and Academic Computer Network—National Research Institute, or the Internal Security Agency, as appropriate, if such a transfer of information is likely to contribute to increasing the cybersecurity of the IT systems used by citizens and entrepreneurs, and to ensuring the secure operation of such systems. No published information may, however, violate the provisions on the protection of confidential information or other legally protected secrets, or the provisions on personal-data protection. (Article 35(5)).

Each of the key sectors of the economy is supervised by the competent body in the field of cybersecurity. These include Ministers competent for individual

[40]Act of 6 September 2001 on access to public information (consolidated text Polish Journal of Laws of 2019, item 1429, as amended).

administration departments,[41] who, by way of memoranda of understanding, can entrust some of their duties to subsidiary or supervised units. In practice this means that sectoral regulators (if any) may fulfil such functions instead of the competent Ministers.

The competent body in the field of cybersecurity is in charge of analysing entities operating in a given sector, and issuing decisions on the recognition of operators of essential services. In addition, it prepares recommendations on actions to strengthen the cybersecurity of that sector, and is in charge of calling on operators to remove any vulnerabilities which could lead, or could have led, to serious incidents, conducting inspections of operators of essential services, cooperating with other EU Member States via Single Points of Contact, participating in training, and processing personal data necessary for its duties to be fulfilled.[42]

In justified cases, the authorities competent for cybersecurity and the Single Point of Contact cooperate with law enforcement authorities and the entity competent for personal data protection (Article 42(7)).

The civil aspects of the cybersecurity of the Republic of Poland remain within the remit of the Minister competent for computerisation. That Minister, in cooperation with the Plenipotentiary for Cybersecurity, and other Ministers, is responsible, *inter alia*, for developing the Cybersecurity Strategy,[43] implementing information policies regarding the national cybersecurity system, fulfilling reporting obligations towards EU institutions, and launching, as of 1 January 2021, an information and communication system enabling automated incident reporting and handling, ICT

[41]Under Article 41 of the NCSA, the competent authorities in the field of cybersecurity are as follows: for the energy sector—the Minister competent for energy; for the transport sector, excluding the water-transport subsector—the Minister competent for transport; for the water-transport subsector—the Minister competent for the maritime economy and the Minister competent for inland shipping; for the banking sector and the financial-market infrastructure—the Polish Financial Supervision Authority; for the healthcare sector—the Minister competent for health; and for the potable-water supply and distribution sector—the Minister competent for water management. In addition. for the digital infrastructure sector and digital service providers—the Minister competent for computerisation; and for healthcare, digital infrastructure and digital service providers (to the extent as defined in the Act)—the Minister of Defence (entities subordinated to the Minister of Defence and companies of particular economic and defense significance).

[42]The Act on the National Cybersecurity System in: https://cyberpolicy.nask.pl/ustawa-o-krajowym-systemie-cyberbezpieczenstwa, accessed on 10 September 2020.

[43]The Security Strategy lays down the strategic objectives, and the appropriate political and regulatory measures which make it possible to attain (and maintain) a high level of cybersecurity. The Security Strategy also specifies the priorities, the entities engaged in its implementation, and the activities regarding educational and informational programmes, as well as research-and-development plans. It is adopted by way of a Resolution by the Council of Ministers. On 22 October 2019, the Council of Ministers adopted a Resolution on the Cybersecurity Strategy of the Republic of Poland for 2017-2022 (Official Gazette of the Government of the Republic of Poland of 2019, item 1037). The document has been in force since 31 October 2019, replacing *the National Framework of Cybersecurity Policy of the Republic of Poland for 2017-2022*. The Minister competent for computerisation, in cooperation with other members of the Council of Ministers, is responsible for implementing the provisions of the said document, and for presenting, by 30 March of each year, information on the implementation of the Strategy.

risk estimation, and warnings about cybersecurity threats, recommending fields of cooperation with the private sector, implementing information measures regarding good practices, educational programmes, campaigns and training courses aimed at expanding knowledge on and raising awareness of cybersecurity. The Minister also runs the Single Point of Contact, which is responsible for cooperating with the European Commission and submitting annual reports; it also cooperates with other Member States in the field of cybersecurity, and coordinates cooperation between competent national authorities (Articles 45–50).

The major duties of the Minister of Defence include facilitating international cooperation between the Armed Forces of the Republic of Poland and the responsible bodies of NATO, the EU, and other international organisations, in the field of defence, and, more specifically, cybersecurity. The Minister of Defence is also responsible for guaranteeing the capabilities of the Armed Forces of the Republic of Poland, within the national, alliance, and coalition systems; for conducting military activities in the event of a cybersecurity threat's triggering the need for defence measures; for developing the abilities of the Armed Forces of the Republic of Poland of ensuring cybersecurity by launching specialised training initiatives; for acquiring and developing tools for building capabilities for ensuring cybersecurity in the Armed Forces of the Republic of Poland; for assessing the impact of incidents on the national defence system; and for managing activities related to incident handling during martial law (Articles 51–52).

As the cybersecurity issues are horizontal, i.e. they involve several Ministries and governmental agencies, the Act envisaged establishing the College for Cybersecurity and the Plenipotentiary for Cybersecurity, for the purpose of coordinating related policies on the national scale. The Plenipotentiary is to pursue international cooperation, to support the scientific research and development of technologies in the field of cybersecurity, to take measures to raise the public's awareness of cybersecurity threats, and to promote the safe use of the Internet. That person is also entrusted with analysing and assessing the functioning of the national cybersecurity system, supervising the process of risk management within the national cybersecurity system, issuing opinions on governmental documents, including draft legal Acts appropriate for the implementation of cybersecurity duties, and issuing recommendations on the use if IT tools or software at the request of the responsible CSIRT.

The Plenipotentiary is appointed and dismissed by the President of the Council of Ministers from among secretaries or under-secretaries of state, and is accountable to the Council of Ministers (Articles 60–63).

The College for Cybersecurity is an opinion-making and advisory body to the Council of Ministers regarding cybersecurity issues and activities conducted in this field by CSIRTs, the Ministry of Defence, CSIRT NASK, CSIRT GOV, sectoral cybersecurity teams, and authorities competent for cybersecurity (Article 64). The Committee is led by the President of the Council of Ministers, and is composed of the Minister competent for internal affairs, the Minister competent for computerisation, the Minister of Defence, the Minister competent for foreign affairs, the Chancellery of the President of the Council of Ministers, the Head of the National Security Bureau, and the Minister competent for coordinating the activities of special forces. Committee meetings are also attended by the Director of the Government Centre for Security, the Head or Deputy Head of the Internal Security Agency, the Head or Deputy Head of the Military Counterintelligence Service, and the Director of the Research and Academic Computer Network—National Research Institute (Article 66). The scope of responsibilities of the College for Cybersecurity was outlined in Article 65 of the Act.[44]

The implementation of the National Cybersecurity System Act is a challenge both for the administration and private sectors. Constructing an efficiently functioning system in various sectors is another huge challenge arising from that Act (as it entails establishing sectoral cybersecurity teams and amending sector-specific provisions). The competent bodies must, in the first place, develop expertise regarding supervision over cybersecurity issues. The incident-reporting obligation is a major change for the private sector, which also becomes challenging for the administration when it comes to developing specific tools[45]—e.g. an information and communication system—which, in principle, is to support the national cybersecurity system. The practical implementation of these activities will be crucial for the safe functioning of the state's power structures.

The rapid development of the Internet, coupled with ICT expansion, have caused, *inter alia*, the globalisation of economic, social and political phenomena.

The functioning of the state and the implementation of its constitutional duties increasingly depends on the development of modern technologies, the information society, and the uninterrupted functioning of cyberspace. The last of these, in turn, is largely dependent on the security of the ICT infrastructure which facilitates the use of cyberspace, and the information resources and services which function within it. Continuous education and raising the awareness of public servants regarding issues related to cyberspace security, and in particular appropriate and effective protection, should be a major responsibility of the state. Special attention should be paid to educating those in charge of public procurement in offices and public institutions. Ultimately, entities ordering equipment and services which can potentially be threatened by cyber attacks should choose such solutions which guarantee digital safety.

The results of inspections regarding the management of information security in local government units, conducted by the Supreme Chamber of Control in 2018, showed that awareness among persons fulfilling major functions in the National Cybersecurity System regarding the importance of information security issues was insufficient. The shortage of both financial resources to implement major undertakings, and of information security experts, was also brought to light, these being two major aspects which the national authorities should seek to address.

Security in cyberspace is the newest, and currently the most demanding, field of national security, which combines defence and protection, civil and military, and

[44]See also: Brzostek (2019), pp. 146–147.

[45]This is quite a novelty in the Polish legal order, as previously—except for the communications sector—there was no obligation to report incidents.

also public and private, aspects. Ensuring cybersecurity in Poland, and constructing a system resistant to threats, constitute an ongoing process, which, as should be noted, is becoming more deliberate and planned, despite the emerging challenges and difficulties which were not known before.

References

Bączek P (2016) Zagrożenia informacyjne a bezpieczeństwo państwa polskiego, Toruń

Bałut D, Budek K. Cyberbezpieczeństwo dla przedsiębiorców: Nowa era zagrożeń. https://marketingibiznes.pl/it/cyberbezpieczenstwo/. Accessed 10 Oct 2020

Banasiński C Nowak W (2018) Europejski i krajowy system cyberbezpieczeństwa in: Cyberbezpieczeństwo. Zarys wykładu, Warsaw

Borkowski M (2013) Cyberprzestrzeń a bezpieczeństwo jednostki, Warsaw

Brzostek A (2019) Polityka ochrony cyberprzestrzeni administracji publicznej na przykładzie organów administracji rządowej wskazanych w ustawie o Krajowym Systemie Cyberbezpieczeń. In: Kitler W, Chałubińska-Jentkiewicz K, Badźmirowska-Masłowska K (eds) System bezpieczeństwa w Cyberprzestrzeni RP. Warszawa

Chałubińska-Jentkiewicz K (2019) Cyberodpowiedzialność, Toruń

Dawidziak P Łęcki B Stolarski M (2009) Sieć Internet – znaczenie dla nowoczesnego państwa oraz problemy bezpieczeństwa. In: Madej M, Terlikowski. Bezpieczeństwo M (eds) Teleinformatyczne państwa, Warsaw

Dubiel AJ (2018) System Bezpieczeństwa Narodowego. https://mil.link/en/wp-content/uploads/2018/01/SBN.pdf. Accessed 10 Oct 2020

Ejdys J (2018) Zaufanie do technologii w e-administracji. Białystok

Gołębiowska A (2015) Local Government in the Constitution of the Republic of Poland of 1997. Ius Novum 2(29)

Kamiński MA (2019a) Military law in the Republic of Poland. Safety Defence 5

Kamiński MA (2019b) Prawo bezpieczeństwa narodowego. Wiedza Obronna 3(268)

Kitler W (2011) Bezpieczeństwo narodowe RP. Podstawowe kategorie, uwarunkowania, system, Warsaw

Kuciński J (2008) Nauka o państwie i prawie, Warsaw

Lulkiewicz E, E-administracja (2013) Korzyści i zagrożenia. In: Stanisławski T, Przywora B, Jurek Ł (eds) E-administracja. Szanse i zagrożenia, Lublin

Mituś A (2013) E-administracja: korzyści i zagrożenia. In: Suwaj JP, Zimmerman J (eds) Wpływ przemian cywilizacyjnych na prawo administracyjne i administrację publiczną, Lex/el 2013

Radoniewicz F (2016) Odpowiedzialność karna za hacking i inne przestępstwa przeciwko danym komputerowym i systemom informatycznym, Warsaw

Radoniewicz F (2019) Article 4 (The scope of application). In: Kitler W, Taczkowska-Olszewska J, Radoniewicz F (eds) The Act on the national cybersecurity system. Commentary. Warsaw

Śledziewska K Levai A Zięba D (2016) Use of e-Government in Poland in comparison to other European Union Member States. Information Systems in Management 1(5)

Suchorzewska A (2010) Ochrona prawna systemów informatycznych wobec zagrożenia cyberterroryzmem, Warsaw

Szczepaniuk E (2016) Bezpieczeństwo struktur administracji w warunkach zagrożeń cyberprzestrzenią państwa, Warsaw

Marzena Toumi dr hab., associate professor at the War Studies University in Warsaw; advocate; a graduate of Faculty of Law, Canon Law and Administration at the John Paul II Catholic University of Lublin and a graduate of the 4th edition of the Annual Diplomatic Program of the Academy of Foreign Affairs—House of Diplomacy. Director of the Institute of Law and Head of the Department of History and Theory of Law at the War Studies University in Warsaw. Vice President of the Association of the Center for Comparative Studies. Author of monographs, textbooks and publications, including in the field of history of law as well as constitutional and legal systems of modern countries.

Personal Data Protection in the Context of the Act on the National Cybersecurity System

Monika Nowikowska

Abstract The dynamic development of technology has led to significant changes in the concept of cyberspace. Currently, it is primarily a virtual space in which we communicate with each other using computers, phones and tablets connected by a network. Cyberspace protection has now become one of the most frequently discussed security-related topics. At a time when information systems allow the collection of huge amounts of information, supervision over data security is one of the key challenges of each country and individual network users. This article describes the principles of personal data protection by national CSIRTs, which are responsible for handling and responding to computer security incidents.

The principles of personal data protection in cyberspace have been regulated under Polish law in several legal acts. The fundamental act which stipulates the protection of personal data, is the Constitution of the Republic of Poland of 2 April 1997.[1] The right to personal data protection is a unique legal construct intended to protect the values referred to in Article 47 of the Constitution of the Republic of Poland. The Constitution provides that everyone is entitled to the legal protection of his or her private life, family life, honour, and reputation, as well as the right to decide on their personal life.[2] In the relevant literature, the individual's right to the protection of his or her personal data is referred to as "information autonomy".[3] The right to the protection of personal data is categorically associated with the right to privacy, recognising it as its unique form.[4]

[1]The Constitution of the Republic of Poland of 2 April 1997, Polish Journal of Laws No. 78, item 483, as amended.

[2]Nowikowska (2018), p. 165.

[3]Safjan (1999), p. 9.

[4]Polok (2008), p. 26.

M. Nowikowska (✉)
Instytut Prawa/Institute of Law, Akademia Sztuki Wojennej w Warszawie/War Studies University in Warsaw, Warsaw, Poland
e-mail: m.nowikowska@akademia.mil.pl

K. Chałubińska-Jentkiewicz et al. (eds.), *Cybersecurity in Poland*,
https://doi.org/10.1007/978-3-030-78551-2_11

Regulation (EU) 2016/679 of the European Parliament and of the Council of 27 April 2016 on the protection of natural persons with regard to the processing of personal data and on the free movement of such data, and repealing Directive 95/46/EC (The General Data Protection Regulation) (GDPR), is also of fundamental importance in this regard.[5] The issue of personal data is also governed by the Act of 10 May 2018 on personal data protection,[6] which repealed several provisions of the former Act, and introduced new ones, which regulate, inter alia, the status of the President of the Personal Data Protection Office, as well as the procedure for initiating and conducting proceedings in connection with the infringement of personal data in the common courts, and the Act. The group of legislative acts regulating the principles of personal data processing in cyberspace also includes the Act on the National Cybersecurity System.

According to Article 1 of the GDPR, the EU legislators, when determining the adoption and application of uniform solutions for the processing of personal data in all EU Member States, pursue two equally important objectives: first, they protect the fundamental rights and freedoms of natural persons, and in particular the right to the protection of their personal data; and second, they ensure the free transfer of personal data between Member States.

According to the GDPR, "personal data" refers to any information concerning an identified or identifiable natural person (data subject); an identifiable natural person is one who can be identified, directly or indirectly, in particular by reference to an identifier such as a name, an identification number, location data, an internet identifier, or one or more factors specific to the physical, physiological, genetic, mental, economic, cultural, or social identity of a natural person.[7]

Polish literature sources emphasise that it is irrelevant to the principles of personal-data processing (including the determination of the scope and type of obligations incumbent on processors and personal-data controllers) that the processing of the data occurs in cyberspace.[8] Ensuring cybersecurity is understood as ensuring the security of data and services, and, consequently, providing confidentiality, integrity, availability and authenticity. These characteristics are included in the literature as attributes of information security. Data confidentiality means the protection of communications or stored data against interception and reading by unauthorised persons. Data integrity is the confirmation that the data sent, received, or stored, are complete and unchanged. The concept of accountability is understood as ensuring that the activities of an entity can be unambiguously attributed only to that entity.

---

[5]Regulation (EU) 2016/679 of the European Parliament and of the Council of 27 April 2016 on the protection of natural persons with regard to the processing of personal data and on the free movement of such data, and repealing Directive 95/46/EC (The General Data Protection Regulation), OJ EU 2016 L 119/1, as amended.

[6]Act of 10 May 2018 on personal-data protection, consolidated text Polish Journal of Laws of 2019, item 1781, as amended.

[7]Taczkowska-Olszewska and Nowikowska (2019), p. 245.

[8]Taczkowska-Olszewska (2019), p. 76.

Thus, the information/security attributes indicated in the Act fulfil a twofold function—i.e. they determine the standard of security in cyberspace, and simultaneously constitute a criterion for assessing the level of cybersecurity. The absence of any of the attributes indicated in the Act, or any infringement of the required standard of protection of confidentiality, integrity, availability, and authenticity, means the occurrence of an incident which, within the meaning of the Act, is an event which has or might have an adverse effect on Cybersecurity.[9]

Pursuant to the adoption on 6 July 2016 by the European Parliament and the Council of the European Union of Directive 2016/1148,[10] all Member States were required to adopt a national strategy for the security of network and information systems. The preamble of the NIS Directive emphasises that IT networks, systems, and services perform an important role in society. Their reliability and security are crucial for economic and social activities, in particular for the functioning of the internal market. The scale, frequency, and impact of security incidents are increasing, and are posing a serious threat to the functioning of network and information systems. These systems can also become the object of deliberate harmful actions aimed at damaging or disrupting their operation. Moreover, these types of incident can hinder business activity, cause significant financial losses, undermine user confidence, and result in serious losses to the Union's economy.

In numerous cases there is a risk of personal data's being compromised as a result of incidents. In such a context, cybersecurity authorities and the President of the Personal Data Protection Office should cooperate and exchange information on all relevant issues in order to address any personal-data breaches resulting from such incidents.[11] Furthermore, the exchange of information on risks and incidents within the CSIRT cooperation group and network can involve the processing of personal data.

Such processing should generally be in accordance with the GDPR. However, it should be noted, in accordance with Article 2(2)(d) of the GDPR, that the processing of personal data in matters relating to national security is not governed by this Regulation. The Regulation does not apply to the processing of personal data by competent authorities for the purposes of the prevention, investigation, detection, and prosecution of prohibited acts, or the enforcement of penalties, including protection against and the prevention of threats to public security.[12]

The principles of sharing information and processing personal data in the national cybersecurity system are regulated in detail in Chapter 7 of the Act on the National Cybersecurity System. In terms of information sharing, the legislators have introduced the principle that information about vulnerabilities, cybersecurity incidents

---

[9]Sieńczyło-Chlabicz et al. (2019), p. 145 et seq.

[10]Directive (EU) 2016/1148 of the European Parliament and of the Council of 6 July 2016 concerning measures for a high common level of security of network and information systems across the Union, OJ EU 2016 L 194/1.

[11]Szostek (2017), p. 257 et seq.

[12]Nowikowska (2019), p. 163.

and threats, as well as the level of risk of an incident, for reasons of state security, and for the protection of the legally protected confidentiality of the providers of essential services and digital-services suppliers, are excluded from the scope of the Act on Access to Public Information. The relevant CSIRT MON, CSIRT NASK, or CSIRT GOV may, following consultation with the notifying providers of essential services, publish on the website of the Public Information Bulletin of the Minister of National Defence, the Scientific and Academic Computer Network—the State Research Institute, or the Internal Security Agency information concerning serious incidents, when it is necessary to prevent the occurrence of the incident or ensure dealing with it. A similar solution was adopted for reports of significant incidents from digital service providers. In the latter case, CSIRT MON, CSIRT NASK or CSIRT GOV may request the Cybersecurity Authority to oblige the digital service provider to make that information public when this is necessary to prevent the incident, or to effect dealing with the incident, as well as when, for any other reason, disclosure of the incident is in the public interest.

The divulging of such information must not violate the regulations on the protection of classified information, or of other legally protected secrets, or the regulations on personal data protection. Following the May 2018 entry into force of Regulation 2016/679, the NCSA legislators took into account the requirements of the GDPR for entities included in the national cybersecurity system, particularly with regard to the processing of data by CSIRTs, and by sectoral cybersecurity teams in connection with the support and coordination of incident handling. In order to perform tasks such as the monitoring of cybersecurity threats and incidents at the national level, the risk assessment of an identified threat, or issuing communications about identified cyber threats, CSIRT MON, CSIRT NASK, CSIRT GOV, and sectoral cybersecurity teams, may process data obtained in connection with cybersecurity incidents and threats, including sensitive personal data, within the scope, and for the implementation, of these tasks. These entities may process personal data obtained in connection with cyber incidents and threats

(1) concerning users of information systems and telecommunications terminal equipment
(2) concerning telecommunications equipment intended to be connected directly or indirectly to network terminals
(3) collected by providers of essential services and digital service providers, for the purposes of the provision of services
(4) collected by public entities in the implementation of public tasks, concerning the entities reporting the incident.

For the purposes of performing the tasks specified in the Act on the National Cybersecurity System, CSIRT MON, CSIRT NASK, CSIRT GOV, and other sectoral cybersecurity teams, may transfer data to each other to the extent necessary to perform these tasks, and to cooperate with the President of the Personal Data Protection Office. The data are deleted or anonymised as soon as it is determined that they are not essential for the performance of the assignment, or within 5 years from the end of the incident to which they relate. Insofar as the processing of data is unrelated to national security, the Act provides for restrictions on the scope of certain obligations and rights for the controller or processor of personal data. Such restrictions include, but are not limited to, the data subject's right of access, the right of rectification, the right to limit the processing in the event when the accuracy of the data is challenged, and, in the event of an objection, the notification of the data subject about the recipients informed of the rectification or deletion of the personal data, where the exercise of this right would prevent CSIRT from accomplishing its tasks.

To summarise the above, it can be stated that the main task of CSIRTs is not to collect and process personal data—this is a secondary activity emanating from other tasks. In the course of monitoring cybersecurity incidents and threats or analytical activities, CSIRTs might encounter data which are generally non-personal data, but, as a result of the appropriate correlation of the information, might *become* such data, and be used to identify the perpetrator of an incident. Personal data which might be generated during the handling of an incident can include network-traffic content, data provided during the incident report, databases obtained as part of computer forensics, as well as logs and event logs. Due to the specificity of CSIRT, it is not possible to create an exhaustive list of the processed data. The explanatory memorandum of the Act emphasises that CSIRTs have no interest in personal data per se, but can be part of other data processing activities, especially with regard to a broad understanding of what personal data is. In such a case, intervention seems justified and proportionate.[13]

References

Nowikowska M (2018) Ochrona danych osobowych w dokumentach kontrolnych. In: Taczkowska-Olszewska J, Nowikowska M, Brzostek A (eds) Reforma ochrony danych osobowych. Cel, narzędzia, skutki. Poznań

Nowikowska M (2019) Zasady udostępniania informacji i przetwarzania danych osobowych. In: Taczkowska-Olszewska J, Chałubińska-Jentkiewicz K, Nowikowska M (eds) Retencja, migracja i przepływ danych w cyberprzestrzeni. Ochrona danych osobowych w systemie bezpieczeństwa państwa, Warsaw

Polok M (2008) Bezpieczeństwo danych osobowych. Warsaw

Safjan M (1999) Ochrona danych osobowych – granice autonomii i informacji. In: Wyrzykowski M (ed) Ochrona danych osobowych. Warsaw

[13]Nowikowska (2019), p. 165.

Sieńczyło-Chlabicz J, Zawadzka Z, Nowikowska M (2019) Prawo prasowe, Warsaw
Szostek I (2017) Prawo do informacji publicznej a ochrona danych osobowych w polskim systemie prawnym. In: Kitler W, Taczkowska-Olszewska J (eds) Bezpieczeństwo informacyjne. Aspekty prawno-administracyjne. Warsaw
Taczkowska-Olszewska J (2019) Dane osobowe w cyberprzestrzeni. In: Taczkowska-Olszewska J, Chałubińska-Jentkiewicz K, Nowikowska M (eds) Retencja, migracja i przepływ danych w cyberprzestrzeni. Ochrona danych osobowych w systemie bezpieczeństwa państwa, Warsaw
Taczkowska-Olszewska J, Nowikowska M (2019) Prawo do informacji publicznej, Informacje niejawne. Ochrona danych osobowych, Warsaw

Monika Nowikowska PhD, adjunct at the Department of Cybersecurity Law and New Technologies of the Institute of Law of the War Studies University. Author of several dozen scientific publications in the field of intellectual property law and the media. He also specializes in issues related to security, such as audit, protection of classified information and personal data. Internal auditor, legal advisor.

Space Security and Cybersecurity in Poland

Małgorzata Polkowska

Abstract This article refers to the definitions of: "space security" and "cybersecurity". Both terms are strictly connected to the national defense and can be part of international law and national law of security. It seems that those two aspects of security are well regulated in Europe and Poland. Making such a regulation on international level is still a challenge. Poland is more active in space and legislation since the Polish Space Agency was created. The Security in Space began the very important factor for the national defense. Polish entrepreneurs involved in space business should be aware of this while undertaking space activities. Space has reached an easy access and became the target for intruders. That is why the regulators of cybersecurity and space security should be aware of this new threat and cooperate together in case to make the law practicable and effective.

1 Introduction

In such a broad term as "security", both: "space security" and "cybersecurity" aspects can be found. Both terms are strictly connected to the national defense and can be part of international law and national law of security. It seems that those two aspects of security are well regulated in Europe and Poland. Making such a regulation on international level is still a challenge. While talking about cybersecurity (which seems more Earth oriented issue) we cannot forget about space security (connected to Outer Space) and all regulations connected.

M. Polkowska (✉)
Instytut Prawa/Institute of Law, Akademia Sztuki Wojennej w Warszawie/War Studies University in Warsaw, Warsaw, Poland
e-mail: m.polkowska@akademia.mil.pl

K. Chałubińska-Jentkiewicz et al. (eds.), *Cybersecurity in Poland*,
https://doi.org/10.1007/978-3-030-78551-2_12

2 Polish Space History and Polish Space Business

The history of Space in Poland is much longer than expected. The beginnings of Polish astronomical activity date back to the fifteenth Century and the Copernican revolution. The most famous figure of this period was Nicolaus Copernicus, whose work "On the rotation of celestial spheres" presented in detail the heliocentric vision of the planetary system. In the sixteenth and seventeenth centuries, Jan Hevelius (mathematician, astronomer) and Kazimierz Siemienowicz (engineer, rocket constructor) contributed to the development of Polish cosmic thought. In the twentieth Century, Polish scientists were involved in cooperation with the USSR, among others, in the Interkosmos programme. The first Polish device for measuring solar radiation was sent into orbit on board of the Copernicus satellite—500 (in 1973). Other achievements include the experiment of crystallization in microgravity conditions. Three years later the Space Research Centre of the Polish Academy of Sciences (CBK) was established for space exploration and development of space technologies. In the 1970s, the practical use of satellite images and satellite communications in Poland also began. The 1970s also saw participation in several space missions (by 1999, a total of 60 Polish devices for performing experiments in physics had been deployed). In 1978, the Polish astronaut Mirosław Hermaszewski travelled in Space on board the Soviet ship Soyuz-30. The purpose of the journey was an 8-day mission to carry out experiments at the Soviet station Salut-6.

The research of Polish scientists included mainly astrophysics (solar system), the study of planets and small celestial bodies of the solar system, the study of the sun, the study of phenomena occurring in space plasma in interplanetary and periplanetary space, Earth exploration by satellite geodesy and satellite remote sensing (checking the degree of pollution of ponds, forests, soil moisture, weather forecasts), the discovery of planets outside the sun, cooperation in the construction of a telescope in South Africa.

After 1989, political changes made it possible to develop cooperation with countries outside the Eastern bloc. In 1994, Poland signed an agreement with ESA on cooperation in the peaceful use of space, which was extended in 2002. On its basis, Poles could participate in ESA's scientific programmes, which resulted in the presence of Polish devices on most of ESA's flagship research missions (Cassini-Huygens, Integrat, Mars Express, Rosetta, Venus Express and Herschel). The beginning of the twenty-first Century and Polish accession to the EU brought an intensification of cooperation with ESA. In 2007, an agreement on a European Collaborating State (PECS) was signed with ESA, and thanks to the creation of this mechanism, 45 projects were financed by Polish companies, research institutions and universities in cooperation with ESA[1] Space activities like few other areas of economic activity require extremely intensive international cooperation. For Poland, the main direction of such cooperation is Europe, where, apart from

[1]Polkowska and Ryzenko (2016), p. 339.

individual countries, space activities are conducted by the European Union (EU) and a dedicated organization-ESA.

In the 2007–2013 financial perspective, the EU allocated about EUR 4.9 billion for space projects, i.e. EUR 700 million annually. Poland, with its share of about 3.2% in the general EU budget, proportionally co-financed EU space programmes with the amount of about 22.4 million Euro annually. In the current financial perspective 2014–2020, the EU plans to spend a total of approximately EUR 11.8 billion on space activities (nearly 2.5 times more than in the previous one), of which the estimated share of Poland will amount to approximately EUR 378 million.

These figures show Poland's relatively large financial involvement in the financing of European space-related activities. However, until recently, there were no mechanisms to facilitate access to these funds for space activities in Poland. This was mainly due to the fact that EU space projects are implemented within the framework of industrial cooperation, which is shaped in the programmes of a separate organisation—ESA. As a result, the possibilities of actual participation in EU projects are extremely limited for countries that are not members of ESA.

In November 2012 Poland joined ESA, which opened the way for faster development of space technologies and satellite techniques through the possibility of full participation in most of the Agency's programmes. Poland has become the 20th member of ESA, paying a contribution of around €30 million per year. Poland's membership in ESA provides an opportunity to create and strengthen the relevant skills and potential of Polish industry, develop cooperation between the environment, access to joint programmes, ensure coherence between ESA and Poland.

At the same time, the possibility to engage in industrial cooperation in ESA programmes has opened the way to real participation in EU space projects. It is fully understandable that the opportunity to ensure a partial flow of Polish investment in the EU space programme back to Poland, in the form of investment in cutting-edge sectors of the economy, is of great importance for Polish economic policy.

Currently, the Polish space policy community, based on 6 years of experience of actual implementation of international cooperation with ESA, still formulates a similar answer to the question "why should Poland invest in space?"

In the context of these considerations, it is necessary to present the way in which expectations in relation to measurable benefits from Polish membership in ESA are determined. The following elements should be taken into account:

(1) geographical return—return to Poland of the majority of funds transferred to ESA;
(2) inflow of EU funds allocated to space programmes;
(3) growth in sales of Polish companies participating in ESA programmes;
(4) increase in the number of new jobs in the area of high technologies;
(5) increase in the level of innovativeness of the participating entities—secured intellectual property rights and the effects of their commercialisation

A large number of companies interested in participating in ESA programmes confirms that Poland has a significant potential of innovative enterprises, and at the same time these companies are interested in the development of new technologies—

on condition that it is possible to obtain public support. It is still too early to assess the effectiveness of these mechanisms. The translation of such works into actual market sales of these companies will take place at the earliest after 3–4 years, and in the case of companies developing strictly space technologies even after several years.

Cooperation with ESA is aimed at increasing the competence of the Polish industry and consequently its greater involvement in the implementation of the European space programme. Poland's participation in ESA programmes gives wider access to technology, the possibility of transferring new technologies to industry, participation in expenditures on modern industries and opens up opportunities for scientific cooperation. It is extremely important that ESA has a geographical return, so contracts are allocated in proportion to the share of the Agency's funding.

3 Polish Space Legislation

Poland is more active in space and legislation since the Polish Space Agency was created (POLSA). This Agency is a governmental executive body, subject to the Prime Minister. It consists of civilian and military personnel. It was established by the Act of 26 September 2014 and became fully operational at the end of 2015.[2] This act has been amended in 2018. The agency participates in fulfilling the strategic goals of the Republic of Poland by supporting the utilization of satellite systems and the development of space technologies. The main tasks of POLSA cover the following 5 areas: coordinating the activity of the Polish space sector on the national and international level, representing Poland in relations with international space sector organizations, supporting national science and business projects associated with space technologies, popularizing the use of satellite data by public administration and increasing the defensive capabilities of the country. The agency is executive in nature in accordance with the Act from 27 August 2009 in public financing (Article—Act of 26 September 2014) and it can create local branches of the agency. The headquarters of the Agency is located in Gdansk (Article 3. The activities of the Agency are under the auspice of the President of the Council of Ministers (Article 2). The duties of the agency are described in Article 3. The President of the POLSA Council is composed of representatives of the government- one from each administration and four representatives of scientists and the industry with recognized achievements in research or business and chosen based on their knowledge competence in areas concerning POLSA activities (Article 14).[3]

Polish Space law is still waiting for the Parliamentary approval. Several versions of the draft have been developed; at present, the Government Legislation Centre

[2] Act on Polish Space Agency, Polish Journal of Laws of 2014, item 1533.

[3] Polkowska (2016), pp. 68–69.

website has published a draft law on space activities and the National Register of Space Objects. The Act regulates: the rules of performing space activities and the rules of maintaining the National Register of Space Objects. Earlier, however, the amendment of the Act on POLSA will be processed. The changes proposed in the draft act are aimed at: to streamline and clarify the scope of tasks of the Polish Space Agency, as an executive agency to provide the necessary expert support and technological knowledge to other public administration bodies involved in space activities, and responsible for the preparation and coordination of the implementation of the National Space Programme; and to adapt the supervision of POLSA to the solutions in force in other European countries, especially in the Member States of the European Space Agency (ESA), as well as to introduce improvements in the organisation of POLSA.

Polish Space Strategy was published by the Polish Ministry of Economic Development in February 2017. The objectives are: increasing competitiveness of the Polish space sector and its share in turnover (increasing participation in the EU space programmes: SST Support Framework), development of satellite applications, strengthening capacities in the area of security and defense using space (establishment of Space Situational Awareness System), creating favorable conditions for the development of space sector in Poland, building human resources for the Polish space sector. The strategic issue is to obtain 3% of the EU market in 2030. National Space Plan (2019–2021) from 2018 states about the establishment, development and operation of a National Space Situational Awareness System (SSA) in cooperation with the EU SST consortium. The objective of the project is to enhance the security of citizens and infrastructure (Earth and space) in the context of space threats, to build national Space Situational Awareness (SSA) capabilities and to prepare for commercial exploitation of services provided in the area of SSA. The first stage of the activity is to launch basic functionalities of the national SST system (Space Surveillance and Tracking), inter alia, through the development of infrastructure and capabilities enabling the implementation of tasks envisaged within the framework of Poland's future membership in the European SST consortium. 19th of December 2018- Poland joined the European SST Consortium related to the tracking of space debris threatening infrastructure in space and on Earth.[4]

Poland has become a full member of the European Space Surveillance and Tracking Consortium. The accession agreement was signed on 19 December 2018 at the seat of the Polish Space Agency in Warsaw. Joining the consortium will enable national entities to participate in projects financed by the EU, whose budget in the current and future financial perspective may amount to more than EUR 350 million. Membership in the consortium will allow for faster development of the Polish SST system, which will provide our country with data necessary to protect the planned missions of Polish satellites and will support national security and defense in monitoring threats from artificial space objects. Participation in the European programme also brings great scientific and business potential. Ensuring the

[4]Polkowska (2019).

operability of the observation sensors forming the Polish SST infrastructure, the possibility of their modernization and the demand for new ones—all this will facilitate a faster growth of competence in the area of SST and optical and radar observations for Polish entities, which already today gain experience by implementing projects under the optional SSA programme in ESA.

In view of the progressing commercialization of products related to situational awareness in space, domestic entities providing solutions and services in this area will be able to direct their offer also to the global market, which will grow as a result of the New Space trend, the increasing number of micro and smaller satellites, the planned development of mega-constellations and new areas such as satellite in-orbit servicing or, in the longer term, the sourcing of raw materials from celestial bodies.[5] The Polish National Space Programme comes from December 2018 and still is in public consultations. Polish Space Agency (POLSA)[6] will be responsible for the implementation of the programme. POLSA has considered a few areas of public support within the programme, such as, "Development of satellite systems"—with one of the priority projects: "Space Situational Awareness System". The vital goal of the project is to provide a long-term access to the European and national space infrastructure and the services crucial for securing its operations. As a consequence, a network of sensors (telescopes, lasers, radars) responsible for space object observation and tracking is to function on the territory of Poland and staff is to be trained in order to perform tasks in the frame of SST.[7]

4 Polish and the European Approach in SSA: Rising Stakes for Civilian Space Programmes

The European Space Situational Awareness System (SSA) consists of three separate segments: Space Surveillance and Tracking, especially in the context of Space Debris (Space Weather) and Near Earth Orbit (NEO) observation. The European SSA system has dual-use civilian and military applications. Additional components to the SSA system may be added in the near future. They are built on the basis of military requirements and compiled by the European Defence Agency (EDA). The conference also devoted a lot of space to the development of the STM (Space Traffic Management)[8] system, which does not yet exist in Europe, unlike the USA. The goals for Space Situational Awareness are the following: society heavily dependent on critical space and ground assets, critical assets need to be protected against

[5]www.polsa.gov.pl.

[6]The Polish National Space Programme (www.polsa.gov.pl).

[7]Polkowska (2019).

[8]"Space Traffic Management (STM) is the set of technical and regulatory provisions for promoting safe access into outer space, operations in outer space and return from outer space to Earth free from physical or radio-frequency interference."

adverse effects from space, SSA Programme Declaration calls for independent European access to SSA data and services. There are three main areas: Space Weather, Near Earth Objects, Space Debris clean space. The participants in ESA SSA programs are 19 participating states. The good progress in the development of a SSA system in Europe has been observed and many actors involved: Member States, ESA, and EU. Distribution of roles needs to be finalized: development vs exploitation. There is still a performance gap in surveillance radars that is why there is a need to agree on a suitable governance scheme for the exploitation of future high performance European surveillance radar. There is a development of a high performance radar can be achieved within 3 years SWE and NEO systems will reach pre-operational status by 2020.[9]

Thus, Europe has started its own preparatory programme of the SSA. International negotiations on permanent exchange of information and coordination, mainly with the USA, are also foreseen. Poland should also participate in these studies, which this year is to eventually become a member of the European SSA Consortium, where they play the biggest role: France, Germany, Great Britain (not in Consortium after Brexit) and Italy.[10] Much of the data to be dealt with by the established Consortium can be found in public satellite catalogues created by the USA and other countries, which are available on the Internet and can be freely used. That is why transatlantic cooperation is so crucial. Orbital paths are constantly changing or are disturbed by a number of factors, such as inconsistent degrees of attraction, solar activity or the effects of gravity of other orbital objects. International cooperation on SSA data sharing is weakened by issues such as liability and property concerns, data formatting standards and compliance with catalogued tools, and finally security (some satellites do not provide data to the public). These issues are still being discussed in various international fora, including UN COPUOS (United Nations Committee on the Peaceful Uses of Outer Space). The author follows these discussions on an ongoing basis and makes use of them in her scientific work. Space security has a multidimensional concept. It can be understood as Security in Outer Space, Outer Space for Security or Security for Space. The first means the protection of the space infrastructure against natural and man-made threats or risks, ensuring the safety and sustainability of space activities. The second means the use of space systems for security and defence purposes. Security for Space means the protection of human life and the Earth environment against natural threats and risks coming from space.

There are also several meanings of such definitions as: Space Situational Awareness (SSA) which can be understood as current and predictive knowledge and understanding of the outer space environment including space weather and location of natural and manmade objects in orbit around the Earth; SEPP (Space Environment

[9]N. Bobrinsky, *Forging ahead: from SSA to space safety, presentation at the 12th ESPI Autumn Conference*, Vienna, September 2th 2018.

[10]P. Faucher, SST Support Framework: Safeguarding European space infrastructure. Overview, governance model, security relevance and future perspectives, presentation at the EUSST webinar 16 November 2020.

Protection and Preservation), which is preventive and curative mitigation of negative effects of human activity in outer space on the safety and sustainability of the outer space environment and Space Infrastructure Security (SIS) as assurance of the infrastructure ability to deliver a service that can justifiably be trusted despite a hazardous environment.

There are some challenges to space infrastructure security, such as unintentional hazards (space debris, accidental interferences), intentional threats (ASAT, malicious interferences, and cyber attacks), Space weather hazards (geomagnetic storms, solar storms).

There are rising challenges to space infrastructure security. Space is an increasingly congested and contested resource. Space is multiple and diverse, there are different mitigation and protection measures. There are many actors playing in the Space, so interdependence between them has been noticed. There are various trends in Space, such as increasing space activity, new concepts, connected space, strategic target, "space control" capabilities, etc. The most important is growing dependence on space for society and economy at large.[11]

Growing security threats to civilian space programmes (access to space, cybersecurity in space, safe operations in space). Space is a critical infrastructure: satellites (jamming, spoofing, blinding), ground stations (hacking). Threats (military, non-military, natural) are understood and accepted and now are more properly and precisely assessed. Readiness to face and respond to threats is growing in governments and private sector. It seems that there is a possibility to invest in handling threats are developing and to find political solutions in managing threats.[12]

5 Space and Cyber Security

The constant growth in Space industry due to the globalization was one of the factors, which changed the meaning of the definition of "space security". The new emerging trends in "NewSpace" era caused the big amounts of risks. Launches are getting cheaper, satellites are getting smaller and more capable, venture capitalist funded private sector companies are entering the space market, new applications and services are driving the commercial market for connectivity, civil space spending is increasing. These factors are connected to the cyber threats as well. If the sector is to realize the government's aspiration of taking 10% of the global market by 2030, the foundations must be safe, secure and sustainable—and therefore address cybersecurity. From a cybersecurity perspective this will result in a larger attack surface both in the space and ground segments and demonstrate a growing need to assure the

[11] S. Moranta (2018), Security in Outer Space: Perspectives on Transatlantic Relations, presentation at the 12th ESPI Autumn Conference Vienna, September 27th 2018.

[12] K. Uwe Schrögl (2018), Security in Outer Space: Rising Stakes for Civilian Space Programmes, 8 presentation at the 12th ESPI Autumn Conference Vienna, September 27th 2018.

security of the integrated network, the manufacturing supply chain and the information transmission, analysis and storage.[13]

Governments, critical infrastructure, and economies rely on space-dependent services—for example, the Global Positioning System (GPS)—that are vulnerable to hostile cyber operations. However, few spacefaring states and companies have paid any attention to the cybersecurity of satellites in outer space, creating a number of risks.[14] The commercialization of space provided the cybersecurity concerns for many reasons, including market incentives to lower costs and innovate quickly, often at the expense of software and hardware security. For example, networks of linked small-satellites can provide internet access, communications, data storage and transmission, imaging, and remote sensing. This next generation of satellites harnesses innovations in computing, electronics, miniaturization, imaging, sensors, big data, and artificial intelligence. Satellite services for Earth observations from space are growing. They support many policy and commercial purposes and contribute to agricultural productivity, transportation efficiency, and environmental monitoring. Commercial space activities use cutting-edge technologies and produce valuable data and are, thus, targets for cyber espionage, including economic cyber espionage, and cybercrime.[15]

This situation is challenging. Some international agencies are involved in the project related to cybersecurity in space, such as the Space Generation Advisory Council (SGAC) in support of the United Nations Programme on Space Applications.[16] One of the projects of the group refers to cyber risks in space. The objective of the project is referring to safety and security of the state. Satellite provide information and services to support global communications, the economy, security and defense, safety and emergency management, the environment and health. Their strategic value inevitably raises the issue of cybersecurity. The information they provide thus becomes a lucrative and enticing prospect for hackers. No more, considering how satellites and their associated infrastructure are critical to sustaining an increasingly globalised, and interconnected world. The space sector is unique in the field of cybersecurity. It is an industry where civil, commercial and military

---

[13] Bailey et al. (2019), (Accessed 3-12-2020), p. 7.

[14] https://www.cfr.org/report/cybersecurity-and-new-era-space-activities Accessed on 4 October 2020.

[15] https://www.cfr.org/report/cybersecurity-and-new-era-space-activities Accessed on 4 October 2020.

[16] SGAC is a global non-governmental, non-profit organisation and network which aims to represent university students and young space professionals ages 18–35 to the United Nations, space agencies, industry, and academia, representing many states, including Poland. SGAC was conceived at UNISPACE III in 1999, whereby states resolved, as part of the Vienna Declaration, "To create a council to support the United Nations Committee on the Peaceful Uses of Outer Space, through raising awareness and exchange of fresh ideas by youth. SGAC holds Permanent Observer status at the United Nations Committee on the Peaceful Uses of Outer Space (UN COPUOS) and regularly takes part in the annual meeting, as well as its Legal and Scientific and Technical Subcommittees.

applications seamlessly co-exist, creating a haphazard situation for cybersecurity experts and telecommunication engineers.[17]

6 Concluding Remarks

Poland has been much involved in Space. That is why the Space Agency was created. Due to the big interest in Space industry the cooperation in Space is growing. Security in Space began the very important factor for the national defense and sovereignty as well. It seems that the cybersecurity issues are closely related to the security in Space. The Polish entrepreneurs involved in Space business should be aware of this while undertaking space activities. Space has reached an easy access and became the target for intruders. That is why the regulators of cybersecurity and space security should be aware of this new threat. The scope of the regulations of cyber threats has been broadened since the New Space era begun (smaller satellites and cheaper access to space for the public). This factor should be definitely taken into account for those, responsible for making national policies and strategies or security regulations in Poland.

References

Bailey B Speelman RJ Doshi PA Cohen NC Wheeler WA (2019) Defending spacecraft in the cyber domain in https://aerospace.org/sites/default/files/2019-11/Bailey_DefendingSpacecraft_11052019.pdf. Accessed 4 Oct 2020

Moranta S (2018) Security in Outer Space: Perspectives on Transatlantic Relations. Presentation at the 12th ESPI Autumn Conference Vienna, September 27th 2018

Polkowska M (2016) Polish space agency pursues task of developing country's space expertise, Room. The Space Journal 2(8)

Polkowska M (2019) European challenges in SSA. Poland example. Presentation at the Space Situational Awareness Workshop: Perspectives on the Future, Directions for Korea, Seoul 24-25 January 2019

Polkowska M, Ryzenko J (2016) Aktywność Polski w przestrzeni kosmicznej - nauka, polityka i prawo. Stan obecny, Gdańskie Studia Prawnicze XXXVI

Małgorzata Polkowska dr hab., associate professor at the War Studies University in Warsaw, specialist in Aviation and Space law, Security and Defense. In the years 2003–2017 an expert in the Civil Aviation Authority, since 2002 a lecturer at the University of War Studies and visiting professor of the University of Gdańsk and Rzeszów University of Technology. In 2013–2016, she was the first permanent Council Representative of the International Civil Aviation Organisation for Poland and the Central European Rotation Group (CERG); Lecturer at Polish and foreign

[17] https://spacegeneration.org/projects/space-cybersecurity, Accessed on 4 October 2020.

universities (including McGill University in Montreal, Canada, de Paul in Chicago, US, ENAC in Toulouse, France and University City of London, UK); speaker and moderator of a number of Aviation and Space conferences. Author of over 120 publications in Polish and English on International law, including air and space.

Part II
Competences, Obligations and Tasks of Entities Responsible for Ensuring Cybersecurity Under the National Cybersecurity System ("Imperious Entities")

Cybersecurity as a Public Task in Administration

Katarzyna Chałubińska-Jentkiewicz

Abstract Contemporary models of public administration have been formed by various political, social and economic conditions. Public tasks are carried out on the basis of legal provisions under the conditions of applying specific decision-making rules and organisational techniques, which include specific principles, procedures and practice—experience. These features characterise public administration as a system of operations, also in relation to cyberspace. The transformations associated with the computerisation and dissemination of information and communication technologies have meant that the duty of public administration in the information age is, on the one hand, to synchronise the activities of entities belonging to different sectors, and on the other, to manage complex networks, as well as to adapt the functioning of public administration to using new technologies. The goal of cybersecurity management is to provide optimal cost protection; to determine which risks can be avoided and how, using both organisational and technical solutions, the risk can be minimised to an acceptable level.

1 General Remarks

Numerous processes have shaped the contemporary public administration environment in Poland. The political transformation which took place in Central and Eastern Europe after 1989 consisted of the simultaneous creation of new foundations for political freedoms, private property, and market economy conditions, as well as of the values and mechanisms of the civil state. Various political, social, and economic conditions have shaped the contemporary public administration models. The state system and political considerations have contributed to the transformation of the centrally planned economy into a free market economy. After new governance

K. Chałubińska-Jentkiewicz (✉)
Akademickie Centrum Polityki Cyberbezpieczeństwa/Academic Center for Cybersecurity Policy, Akademia Sztuki Wojennej w Warszawie/War Studies University in Warsaw, Warsaw, Poland
e-mail: k.jentkiewicz@akademia.mil.pl

K. Chałubińska-Jentkiewicz et al. (eds.), *Cybersecurity in Poland*,
https://doi.org/10.1007/978-3-030-78551-2_13

standards were implemented, a demand developed for high-quality public services provided within public administration structures. This stems from the actual function of administration. The term 'administration' derives from the Latin '*ministrare*', which means to lead, serve, manage[1] (and the prefix 'ad' emphasises the service-related aspect).[2] One of the first definitions was put forward by W. Jellinek. It dates back to the time when the canon of the rule of law was born, and it refers to the tripartite separation of powers in the state. It proclaimed that "[. . .] administration is an activity of the state which is neither legislation nor justice".[3] In recent years, there has been a general trend towards a shift from the administration to the management of public affairs, which is reflected in the introduction of the concept of "good governance" in the public sector.[4]

The modern state, whose administration relies on new technical solutions, has become susceptible to disruptions in the operation of hardware, IT networks, systems, databases, and the information processes based on these solutions. Nowadays, ensuring the security of information resources and systems which serve, in particular, to fulfil public tasks, has emerged as a serious issue. The efficient operation of public-sector entities is conditional, among other things, on the efficient performance of public tasks related to ensuring cybersecurity at every stage of the activities of public institutions.[5]

Public administration is extensively defined by legal commentators, but all these definitions relate to the state (or local government), society, and the citizen. J. Starościak[6] describes it as

> [. . .] an organisational function with features such as the initiating nature of activities, solving specific situations, and carrying out organisational work, not only by creating binding norms within the legal order, specific legally defined forms of administrative activity of the state.[7]

According to H. Izdebski and M. Kulesza,

> Public administration is understood as a set of activities, operations and undertakings, both organisational and executive (the functional element), carried out in the public interest (the object element) by various entities, authorities, and institutions (the subject element) on the basis of Acts, and in the forms specified by law (functional element).[8]

Most generally, citing E. Ochendowski,[9] this term is understood to mean any organised activity aimed at achieving specific objectives. On the other hand, according to J. Boć

---

[1]Latin *administratio*—administrating, managing; *administrare*—to be of assistance.

[2]Ochendowski (2002), p. 18; Izdebski and Kulesza (2004), p. 23, and Hausner (2005).

[3]Szczepaniuk (2016), p. 11.

[4]Szczepaniuk (2016), p. 8.

[5]Szczepaniuk (2016), p. 7.

[6]J. Starościak (1975), p. 10.

[7]Lisiak-Felicka and Szmit (2016), p. 55.

[8]Izdebski and Kulesza (2004), p. 93.

[9]Ochendowski (2002), p. 19.

> Public administration is the fulfilment of the collective and individual needs of citizens, resulting from the coexistence of individuals in communities, by the state and its dependent authorities, as well as by local and regional authorities.[10]

Public administration is defined as a set of activities, operations, and organisational and executive undertakings carried out in the public interest by various entities, authorities and institutions, on the basis of Acts and in the forms established by law. It serves the general public, and covers the scope of matters of a public nature.[11] In defining public administration, we therefore refer to functions and actions which link the administration to its active and state-dependent activities. State and local government authorities create organisational structures to meet the needs of citizens. The computerisation process, which is being introduced with a view to facilitating the effective performance of public services and tasks, is a means by which modern administration intends to meet such needs.

Public tasks are performed pursuant to the law in compliance with certain rules of decision making and organisational techniques, which consist of certain rules, procedures and practice—experience. These characteristics define public administration as a system of operations.[12] The efficient and effective functioning of public administration depends to a significant extent on its organisational structure, which consists of various units vested with the powers specified in the Acts, and forming a specific organisational system to perform public tasks.[13]

The transformations associated with computerisation and the popularity of information and communication technologies[14] have resulted in, among other things, the convergence of economic, social, and political phenomena. On the one hand, the duty of public administration in the information age is to synchronise the activities of entities belonging to various sectors, to manage complex social networks, and to adapt the functioning of public administration to the use of new technologies. On the other hand, it should be noted that administrative authorities are some of the most important users of modern ICT tools and techniques, since the functioning of the administration involves, or is based on, the processing of information; information is therefore an essential resource for administration.[15] In a democratic state of law, public-administration tasks have the status of legal obligations. In a state of law, the administration can influence the shape of legal acts which contain the legal norms characterising its tasks; however, it may not decide what its tasks are. It might have some freedom and influence on the shape and scope of the tasks to be carried out, but

---

[10] Boć (2004), p. 16.

[11] Monarcha-Matlak (2008), p. 19.

[12] Monarcha-Matlak (2008), p. 19.

[13] Lang (1997), p. 15.

[14] Information and communication technologies (ICT)—all activities relating to the manufacture and use of telecommunications- and information-technology equipment and associated services, and the collection, processing, and provision, of information in electronic form using digital technologies and any electronic communication tools. http://lawp.eu/pdf/ict_definicja.pdf, accessed 10 September 2020.

[15] Szczepaniuk (2016), p. 26.

the sources and limits of that freedom always stem from legislation adopted by the responsible legislative bodies. The state performs its tasks through public authorities. Central and local government authorities and other state authorities are responsible for public tasks. This is a statutory procedure, carried out in the public interest. Polish legislation does not offer a legal definition of public tasks. However, many definitions can be found in academic papers.[16] On the basis of the definition of public administration presented by J. Boć, it is possible to derive the term 'public tasks', as tasks assumed by the state, consisting of meeting collective and individual human needs resulting from the coexistence of people in communities. The development of communities and the changing reality is enforcing changes to the field of the tasks taken over by the state. These tasks are implemented on the basis of the provisions of the law.[17]

According to A. Błaś:

> [...] the performance of administrative tasks is the duty of the public administration authority to which they have been entrusted by law to take up an active role in the implementation of these tasks.[18]

The literature on the subject stresses that administrative tasks should be supported by the very-broadly defined rule of good governance. It is also worth mentioning the understanding of

> [...] public administration as a set of activities, operations, and organisational and executive undertakings, carried out in the public interest by various entities, authorities, and institutions, on the basis of Acts, and in the forms established by law.[19]

According to S. Biernat,

> Public tasks may be carried out by public entities without any powers of authority, or even by non-public entities. The main criterion for defining a task as a public task is the fact that the state or local authority is legally responsible for its implementation. The mere performance of tasks within the organisational structures of the state or local government is not a criterion which qualifies it as public tasks. The responsibility of the authorities is maintained when other entities are authorised to carry out public tasks, but the forms of activity and their scope change.[20]

P. Schmidt defines public tasks as "a set of activities, operations, and organisational and executive undertakings carried out in the public interest by various entities, authorities, and institutions, on the basis of Acts and in forms established by law".[21] On the other hand, T. Kocowski describes public tasks as "a legal obligation for an entity clearly indicated in legal norms to achieve or

---

[16] Chałubińska-Jentkiewicz (2014), p. 20.

[17] Boć (2004), p. 17.

[18] Boć (2004), p. 44.

[19] The definition according to Izdebski and Kulesza (2004), p. 79.

[20] Biernat (1994), pp. 29–30.

[21] P. Schmidt, *Prywatyzacja zadań publicznych w zakresie zapewnienia dostępu do kultury*, followed by K. Chałubińska-Jentkiewicz in: K. Chałubińska-Jentkiewicz (2014), p. 20.

maintain a certain state which is important and desirable in terms of the public interest".[22] These two definitions, though different in content, have many compatible properties. Public tasks is a collective term for tasks carried out by the state, which performs them through public administration. On the basis of the applicable regulations, public tasks are implemented through planned and rational action aimed at reaching specific objectives.[23]

In J. Zimmermann's view, the main indicator for considering a task public is where the state or local and regional authorities are responsible under law for carrying it out.[24] According to M. Stohl, the concept of a "public task" is associated with public (public-utility) objectives to be achieved by the administration. In turn, these objectives are identified with the public interest.[25] According to E. Knosala, there are currently no clear criteria for distinguishing between the public and the private domain. This means that the outlines of public tasks are no longer as clearly defined as in the past.[26] Public tasks are those which serve to meet collective needs and the needs of a particular community.[27] Public tasks are generally attributed to the state, but under the influence of political factors it decides which tasks will be performed by its authorities on an exclusive basis, which can (and must) be entrusted to other public authorities, and which can be performed by non-public entities.[28]

A typical feature of public tasks is that their performance is an obligation of public authorities, not an entitlement. This concept is determined by individual legal norms, which are indeterminate, due to the fact that it is the state that decides independently and ultimately whether a given function is a public task or not. It is not necessary for public tasks to be implemented within the structure of public administration (e.g. if the performance of a public task has been privatised). The law provides a legal basis for public administration, and sets out a framework for the performance of public tasks. Respect for the law is based on the constitutional principle of legalism (the rule of law) expressed in Article 7 of the Constitution of the Republic of Poland. Public tasks cited in the Constitution include guaranteeing

---

[22]T. Kocowski, *Prywatyzacja zarządzania majątkiem publicznym, prywatyzacja majątkowa, prywatyzacja zadań publicznych i prywatyzacja wykonania zadań publicznych* followed by K. Chałubińska–Jentkiewicz in: K. Chałubińska–Jentkiewicz (2014), p. 20.

[23]A.K. Mikicka, *Partnerstwo publiczno-prywatne jako prywatyzacja sensu largo zadań publicznych jednostek samorządu terytorialnego* followed by K. Chałubińska–Jentkiewicz in: K. Chałubińska–Jentkiewicz (2014), p. 20.

[24]J. Zimmermann, *Prawo administracyjne* followed by K. Chałubińska–Jentkiewicz in: K. Chałubińska–Jentkiewicz (2014), p. 20.

[25]J. Zimmermann (ed.), *Cele publiczne i zadania publiczne, Koncepcja systemu prawa administracyjnego* followed by K. Chałubińska–Jentkiewicz, in: K. Chałubińska–Jentkiewicz (2014), p. 20.

[26]E. Knosala, *Zarys nauki administracji* followed by K. Chałubińska–Jentkiewicz: (2014), p. 20.

[27]Chałubińska–Jentkiewicz (2014), p. 20.

[28]Dobkowski (2004), p. 106.

the security and inviolability of the territory of the Republic of Poland, freedom, human and civil rights, the security of citizens, and environmental protection;[29]

Government administration authorities and local government units, and other state authorities, are responsible for public tasks, i.e. legally defined conduct postulated for the sake of common good.

> According to legal commentators, public tasks may be performed by public entities without any powers of authority, or even by non-public entities. The main criterion for considering a given task as public is that the state or local authority is legally responsible for its implementation.[30]

The Constitutional Tribunal[31] (TK), in its Resolution of 27 October 1994, case file No. W 10/93,[32] ruled that all tasks of local government which serve to satisfy the collective needs of local communities, as well as national needs, were public tasks. According to the TK, "Both commissioned tasks and local government's own tasks are public tasks as defined by the applicable law".

In the opinion of the Constitutional Tribunal, the definition of the commune's own tasks as public tasks is not inconsistent with the undoubted fact that the commune, as an entity responsible for the municipal assets, manages it in a manner appropriate for the performance of its own tasks.[33] It should be mentioned here that the set of systems which constitute critical infrastructure is also part of municipal assets. Special tasks in the field of cybersecurity are entrusted to local government entities under, i.a., the Act of 26 April 2007 on Crisis Management. According to Article 3 (2) of the Act on Crisis Management, critical infrastructure should be understood as systems and functionally integrated facilities, including installations, devices, building structures, and services crucial for the security of the state and its citizens, and serving to guarantee the efficient functioning of public administration authorities, as well as of institutions and enterprises.[34]

Therefore, public tasks for the security of cyberspace have high priority in the safe and efficient functioning of the state. The responsibility for ensuring cybersecurity rests with all network users, but public administration authorities have a particularly important role to play, as their priorities include ensuring security and public order. The Council of Ministers, in leading Government administration, performs its constitutional duties by carrying out tasks for the protection of

[29]See Article 126(2) of the Constitution of the Republic of Poland. See more Chałubińska-Jentkiewicz et al. (2021), *passim*

[30]Martysz et al. (2015), p. 10190.

[31]Hereinafter referred to as the "TK".

[32]Resolution of the Constitutional Tribunal of 27 October 1994, case file No. W 10/93 OTK 1994, No. 2, item 46.

[33]M. Kłaczyński, *Komentarz do ustawy z dnia 6 września 2001 r. o dostępie do informacji publiczne,* followed by K. Chałubińska-Jentkiewicz (2014), p. 21.

[34]Chałubińska-Jentkiewicz (2014), p. 21.

cyberspace. It also has the primary responsibility for ensuring a high level of security for cyberspace and the citizens functioning within it.[35]

The expansion of modern communication and information technologies has meant that the administration is responsible for the quality and maintenance of communication routes and road networks, and nothing has changed in this respect. It is clear that the creation of the technical infrastructure and the system of access to it by specific users requires substantial financial resources, which can only be provided by private entities interested in benefitting financially from these activities. In this respect, the function of public administration is to ensure the security of IT systems and networks, and to select entities which ensure continuity and a high quality of services, while guaranteeing access conditions for the widest-possible range of recipients.[36]

As has already been mentioned, one of the basic public tasks is to ensure a safe and efficient state, including the security of cyberspace. Cybersecurity is all the more important because the dangers in cyberspace can adversely affect national security, which in turn is the foundation of public tasks.[37]

> National security is also the most important value, national need, and priority objective, of the activities of the state, individuals, and social groups, and at the same time a process comprising a variety of measures to ensure sustainable, unhindered, national (state) existence and development, including the defence of the state as a political institution and the protection of individuals and society as a whole, as well as their assets and the natural environment, from threats which significantly restrict its functioning or pose a threat to fundamental rights.[38]

The key national needs include needs of a systemic nature (e.g. strengthening the social and economic system and legal order), social needs (ensuring health protection, social security, and counteracting all forms of discrimination), economic needs (e.g. national development, economic growth), ecological needs (environmental protection), and cultural needs (nurturing national heritage, respect for differences in outlooks on life, and ethnicity).[39] Each of these national needs can be adversely affected by cyber threats, which is why the security of cyberspace is so important for the proper functioning of the state.[40]

State administration, as a complex structure, performs public tasks in the field of cybersecurity through a set of activities, actions, and organisational undertakings. The administration's primary tasks include efforts to guarantee public safety and order. The administration ensures the security of IT systems and networks and selects entities ensuring continuity and high service quality, while guaranteeing access conditions for the widest-possible audience; it secures the functioning of

[35]Chałubińska–Jentkiewicz (2014), p. 26.

[36]Jaxa-Dębicka (2008), p. 267208.

[37]Chałubińska–Jentkiewicz (2014), p. 22.

[38]Kitler (2011), pp. 22–31.

[39]Kitler (2011), p. 37.

[40]Bączek (2006), p. 244.

the national trust service infrastructure and supervises trust service providers. It is the executive sector of the state which carries out activities to pursue the public interest through cooperation between public authorities and services. These authorities are responsible for ensuring a high level of security for cyberspace and its users.

It should be stressed that the adopted policy is an important instrument for implementing public tasks in cyberspace.

Generally speaking, a policy is a set of coherent, precise, and lawful rules, principles, and procedures, according to which a given organisation, or administration, builds, manages, and provides information resources.[41]

2 The Main Benefits of a Well-Designed Security Policy

- Allocating responsibility for system development to a separate group of people, so that no one has full authority within the system
- Establishing organisational structures responsible for managing information security
- Controlling the process of issuing cards and codes' not being left to programmers/developers who have access to account data
- Introducing a distinction into open and protected information
- Distributing operational functions between different people
- Effective programming of information-security principles among the management and employees of the organisation
- Documenting changes in the system to facilitate its periodic checks
- Supervising software modifications and system testing
- Regular training of users on information security
- Backups' being stored in a different room than the one in which the server is located
- Monitoring the system and detecting any anomalies.[42]

As can be seen, the issue of cybersecurity in today's administration is of crucial importance. Therefore, the information-security and cybersecurity management system is part of the organisation-management system. It is often based on an approach related to business risk, and refers to the establishment, implementation, monitoring, maintenance, and improvement of information security in particular.

> The aim of cybersecurity management is to provide optimal protection in terms of cost; to identify which risks can be avoided and how, using both organisational and technical solutions, risks can be minimised to an acceptable level[43]

At every institution covered by the National Cybersecurity System Act, the unit's head must establish a cybersecurity management system based on the existing standards and best practices. These should define, among other things, the roles of the administrators and security inspectors of information processed on open communication and information systems and networks. The information-security

---

[41]Wojciechowska-Filipek and Ciekanowski (2016), p. 157.

[42]Matuszczyk and Matuszczyk (2006), pp. 99–101.

[43]Liderman (2002), p. 78.

management system will thus become an integral part of the institution's security policy.[44] Public entities modify, develop, and implement, as appropriate, security policies for the communication and information systems used by these entities to perform public tasks.[45] In drafting their security policies, public entities take into account the responsibilities stipulated by the Act of 17 February 2005 on the Computerisation of the Operations of Entities Performing Public Tasks,[46] regarding the minimum information security requirements for communication and information systems.[47] A public entity should also take into account the provisions of the Polish Standards in the field of information security, in particular the group of standards in the PN ISO/IEC 27000 series, along with other related standards.[48] Coordinating the information-security policy of organisational units will ensure a common minimum level of security. All institutions, when taking into account cybersecurity, are obligated to establish, implement, monitor, operate, review, maintain, and improve their Information Security Management Systems[49] (see further comments).[50] The Minister competent for computerisation, in accord with the Ministry of National Defence (the MON), the Internal Security Agency (the ABW), and the Military Counterintelligence Service (the SKW), with the intention of guaranteeing a uniform information security policy for organisational units, has the power to draw up guidelines for cybersecurity management systems.[51]

When the appropriate regulations are implemented at the statutory level, the following will be ordered.

- Reporting on cybersecurity incidents to a designated governmental centre on cybersecurity;
- Drawing up Disaster Recovery Plans (DRPs) and Business Continuity Plans (BCPs), after the occurrence of an incident, including national standards or, in the absence thereof, international standards, acceptable principles not included in official standards, or widely recognised good practices

---

[44] *Strategia Cyberbezpieczeństwa Rzeczypospolitej Polskiej na lata 2017-2022*. https://mc.gov.pl/aktualnosci/strategia-cyberbezpieczenstwa-rzeczypospolitej-polskiej-na-lata-2017-2022 Accessed on 24.05.2020.

[45] *Rządowy Program Ochrony Cyberprzestrzeni RP na lata 2011-2016*. http://bip.msw.gov.pl/bip/programy/19057,Rządowy-Program-Ochrony-Cyberprzestrzeni-RP-na-lata-2011-2016.html Accessed on 28 May 2020.

[46] Consolidated text, Polish Journal of Laws of 2017, item 570.

[47] *Polityka Ochrony Cyberprzestrzeni*, Warsaw 25.06.2013. https://mac.gov.pl/files/polityka_ochrony_cyberprzestrzeni_rp_wersja_pl.pdf Accessed on 24.05.2020.

[48] *Rządowy Program Ochrony Cyberprzestrzeni RP na lata 2011–2016*. http://bip.msw.gov.pl/bip/programy/19057,Rządowy-Program-Ochrony-Cyberprzestrzeni-RP-na-lata-2011-2016.html Accessed on 28.05.2020.

[49] The "ISMS".

[50] *Strategia Cyberbezpieczeństwa Rzeczypospolitej Polskiej na lata 2017–2022*. https://mc.gov.pl/aktualnosci/strategia-cyberbezpieczenstwa-rzeczypospolitej-polskiej-na-lata-2017-2022 Accessed on 24.05.2020.

[51] *Polityka Ochrony Cyberprzestrzeni*, Warszawa 25.06.2013. https://mac.gov.pl/files/ polityka_ochrony_cyberprzestrzeni_rp_wersja_pl.pdf Accessed on 24.05.2020.

- Managing the cybersecurity of information and the introduction of safeguards, including national standards or, in the absence thereof, international standards, acceptable principles not included in official standards, or widely recognised good practices;
- Operating within a network of information about hazards.[52]

The ISMS (Information Security Management System) is understood (as defined in the ISO/IEC 27000 series of standards) as a part of the management system, based on the concept of business risk management, responsible for establishing, monitoring, implementing, operating, reviewing, maintaining, and improving information security,[53] the management system itself being understood as a set of guidelines, policies, procedures, processes, and related resources (i.e. material resources—such as computers and machines; human resources—such as employees, with their skills and experience; and intangible resources—such as computer programs and organisational culture) aimed at ensuring that the organisation completes its tasks.[54] At least two elements in the normative definitions should be stressed:[55]

- The systemic approach, in particular as the information security management system is composed not only of "paper" records (procedures, standards, ordinances, etc.) but also of all the resources relating to information security
- Basing information security on the business risk management concept.[56]

According to § 20(1) of the Regulation of the Council of Ministers of 12 April 2012 on the National Interoperability Framework (KRI), the minimum requirements for public records and the exchange of information in electronic form, and the minimum requirements for communication and information systems[57] the entity performing public tasks develops and establishes, implements and operates, monitors and reviews, and maintains and improves, an information security management system, ensuring the confidentiality, availability, and integrity of information, taking into account such attributes as authenticity, accountability, non-repudiation, and reliability. The requirements for the information security management system in the KRI Regulation are considered to be fulfilled if the system

[52]*Strategia Cyberbezpieczeństwa Rzeczypospolitej Polskiej na lata 2017–2022*. https://mc.gov.pl/aktualnosci/strategia-cyberbezpieczenstwa-rzeczypospolitej-polskiej-na-lata-2017-2022 Accessed on 24.05.2020.

[53]ISO/IEC 27000:2014 Information technology – Security techniques – Information security management systems – Overview and vocabulary.

[54]Gillies (2011), pp. 367–376; Humphreys (2007), pp. 11–44.

[55]Lisiak-Felicka and Szmit (2016), p. 62.

[56]PN-ISO/IEC 31000:2012 – Zarządzanie ryzykiem – Zasady i wytyczne. http://pbsg.pl/polski-komitet-normalizacyjny-pbsg-polrisk-i-zakonczyly-z-sukcesem-prace-nad-opracowaniem-pierw/ Accessed on 22.05.2020).

[57]Regulation of the Council of Ministers of 12 April 2012 on the National Interoperability Framework (KRI), the minimum requirements for public records, the exchange of information in electronic form, and the minimum requirements for communication and information systems, consolidated text, Polish Journal of Laws of 2017, item 2247, as amended, the "KRI Regulation".

has been developed on the basis of the Polish Standard PN-ISO/IEC 27001, and the establishment of safeguards, risk management, and auditing is carried out on the basis of Polish Standards related to this standard, including:

- PN-ISO/IEC 17799168—with regard to the establishment of safeguards
- PN-ISO/IEC 27005—with regard to risk management
- PN-ISO/IEC 24762—with regard to IT-disaster recovery within business continuity planning.[58]

As regards the information security management system, the most important standards are

- PN-ISO/IEC 27001:2014–12 – Information technology – Security techniques – Information security management systems – Requirements: specifies the requirements for the establishment, implementation, maintenance, and continuous improvement of the information security management system with regard to its organisation. It also includes the requirements for estimating and handling information-security risks
- PN-ISO/IEC 27002:2014-12 – Information technology – Security techniques – Code of practice for information security controls, contains recommendations for information-security standards in organisations, and information security management practice, including the selection, implementation, and management of security, taking into account the environment(s) in which information-security risks are present in the organisation. Chapters 5 to 18 relate to the safeguards listed in Annex A of the 27001 security standard.[59]

It should be noted that the new possibilities for the administration's operation, and, in particular, the virtualisation of its activities, also generate an ever-increasing risk of interference with information security. Risk management is the element of key importance in the process of protecting cyberspace. It determines and justifies measures taken to reduce the risk to an acceptable level. The first stage in risk management is the identification of all cases of hazards, and the identification of their sources and impacts. Each identified risk should then be evaluated and categorised, using the defined risk categories and parameters, and prioritised.[60] This is very important in the context of taking potential preventive action against key risks, in line with the risk management and implementation strategy adopted in order to regularly monitor the status of each risk.[61] The adopted action plan will direct most of the resources (technical and non-technical) against the most likely risks. Information-security risk assessment should be performed repeatedly during business operations. It should be stressed that risk management is not intended to provide total protection, but to ensure a level of protection proportionate to the importance of the resources being protected. Risk management is a process which consists of both identifying hazards and assessing risks, by deciding which risks are to be avoided, and which ones to control, and how. An organisation, such as an administrative unit, can take action to avoid risks by refraining from high-risk operations, such as, for example, introducing "top secret" information into the system. It can also transfer the

[58]Lisiak-Felicka and Szmit (2016), p. 64.

[59]Lisiak-Felicka and Szmit (2016), p. 64.

[60]Wojciechowska-Filipek and Ciekanowski (2016), p. 160.

[61]Crapko (2012), pp. 215–266.

risk to another entity with the use of a legal mechanism, e.g. to insure itself against a given risk. The administration can also consciously control risks in two ways.[62]

One of these is to minimise risk by implementing business continuity plans to ensure that users have access to the most important organisational functions in an emergency situation. In the event of a crisis situation, organisations should apply data- and information-security procedures.

- Have a backup archive at another location if possible
- Data stored on hard drives should be copied to two independent external media, and regularly returned and stored in a safe place
- If you have important paper documents, you should photocopy or scan them, and store them in a safe place, such as a safety deposit box
- Prepare precise instructions in the event of an emergency shutdown of equipment, especially computer hardware.[63]

The second way to control risk is prevention by using safeguards.
Ways of reducing risk:
The second way to control risk is risk prevention by using safeguards.
Ways of reducing risk:

- Risk avoidance
- Risk control
- prevention through safeguards
- non-technical safeguards
- technical safeguards
- minimising by implementing business continuity plans
- Risk transfer.[64]

On the last day of January of each year, with the intention of achieving an acceptable level of security, all government administration units referred to in Point 1.4 (sub-points 1–4) of the Polish Cyberspace Protection Policy[65] provide the Minister competent for computerisation with a report summarising the results of risk assessment (according to the model developed by the Minister competent for computerisation). The report includes general data relating to the hazards, risks, and vulnerabilities identified in each of the sectors in which the institution operates and for which it is responsible. The report also presents information on methods for dealing with risk. The Minister competent for computerisation, in cooperation with the institutions involved, formulates a uniform methodology for conducting risk analyses. This methodology is obligatory for Government administration institutions. The Governmental Computer Security Incident Response Team CERT.GOV. PL submits to the Minister competent for digital affairs, with a view to achieving a

[62]Wojciechowska-Filipek and Ciekanowski (2016), p. 160.

[63]Murdoch (2003), p. 22.

[64]Murdoch (2003), p. 22.

[65]*Polityka Ochrony Cyberprzestrzeni*, Warszawa 25.06.2013. https://mac.gov.pl/files/polityka_ochrony_cyberprzestrzeni_rp_wersja_pl.pdf, hereinafter "**the Policy**" Accessed on 24.05.2020.

unified approach, catalogues covering vulnerabilities which undermine cybersecurity, and the specification of possible threats.[66]

Authorised representatives for cybersecurity (hereinafter referred to as **the PBC**) have been appointed within government-administration units.

The PBC performs the following tasks regarding cybersecurity.

- Drawing up and launching procedures for responding to computer incidents, which will function within the organisation
- Developing contingency plans and their testing
- Performing tasks resulting from the provisions of legal acts dedicated to ensuring security in cyberspace
- Identifying and conducting periodic risk analyses
- Preparing procedures to ensure the notification of the appropriate CERTs.[67]

The position of the Cybersecurity Representative within the structure of the organisational unit is not indicated by the Policy; however, this role should be performed by a person responsible for the implementation of the ICT-security process.[68]

In summary, a cybersecurity policy is a set of precise and consistent procedures and rules, according to which a given public-administration institution manages, builds, and makes available information and communication resources and systems. It determines which resources are to be protected and the methods applied to this end. The ISMS, on the other hand, is a continuous process which must be constantly improved and adapted to changing circumstances. Each stage is divided into activities which involve security policy, risk management, and resources. Combining all activities into a continuous process of secure information management facilitates secure functioning in the new digital reality.

In the Republic of Poland, cybersecurity tasks, like other security tasks, are carried out by public authorities and their subsidiary administrative authorities. According to constitutional division, a public authority possesses legislative, judicial, and executive powers.[69]

These tasks arise from the general public task of ensuring national security. W. Kitler cites, inter alia,

> the protection of the constitutional order, understood as the activities of state authorities and institutions, and the system of legal rules guaranteeing the continuity of the constitutional state system, including the protection of the state as a legal and political organisation, as well as the protection of freedom and human and civil rights, and the protection of classified information and personal data; the protection of the life and health of the people, and of goods and the environment, from the negative effects of human activities, technical failures and natural forces.[70]

---

[66] *Polityka Ochrony Cyberprzestrzeni.* …., p. 160.

[67] *Polityka Ochrony Cyberprzestrzeni.* …., p. 161.

[68] *Polityka Ochrony Cyberprzestrzeni.* …., p. 162.

[69] See Article 10(1) of the Constitution of the Republic of Poland.

[70] Kitler (2011), pp. 76–77.

It should be noted that all these values can be affected by the risks arising from the use of cyberspace. The role of the legislative authority, which includes the Sejm, the lower House of the Polish Parliament and the Senate, in the field of cybersecurity, mainly arises from its system-forming functions, including legislation. This encompasses legislation and the definition of the main directions of the state's activities,[71] which is related to the effectiveness of the Polish legal system and the activities carried out by administrative bodies.

Public authorities also include the judiciary. Its main tasks, which it also carries out within the ambit of cybersecurity, include the administration of criminal justice. These often relate to national security in general, as well as to its trans-sectoral field, that is to say, cybersecurity, with its rules of conduct.

However, the executive branch plays the key role in the field of cybersecurity. Its responsibilities relate to managing cybersecurity, through "influencing the behaviour of others and supervising their actions, but also by taking specific measures, having the tools and managing the assets related to the achievement of its objectives".[72] The Constitution of the Republic of Poland states that executive power in Poland is held by the President and the Council of Ministers.[73] Pursuant to Article 126(2) of the Constitution of the Republic of Poland, "The President of the Republic of Poland shall ensure observance of the Constitution, safeguard the sovereignty and security of the state as well as the inviolability and integrity of its territory".[74] This provision is general, but a more specific function follows from Article 230 (1), which states

> In the case of threats to the constitutional order of the state, to security of the citizenry or public order, the President of the Republic may [...] introduce for a definite period no longer than 90 days, a state of emergency in a part of or upon the whole territory of the state.

This is all the more important, as, under the State of Emergency Act, these threats can be caused by actions in cyberspace.[75]

A special role in ensuring the security of cyberspace lies with the Council of Ministers, consisting of the Prime Minister and Ministers. As noted by W. Kitler, "The Council of Ministers is the 'leader' of the public administration",[76] as it is responsible for implementing laws and controlling and coordinating the activities of government administration bodies. The Council of Ministers is responsible for external security, internal state security, and public order, which includes the implementation of cybersecurity tasks. Other tasks related to cybersecurity include crisis management on the territory of the Republic of Poland, actions for the protection of critical infrastructure, and, in situations of special threat, including those arising from cyberspace, which cannot be removed by ordinary constitutional

---

[71] Kitler (2011), p. 195.

[72] Kitler (2011), p. 207.

[73] Article 10(2) of the Constitution of the Republic of Poland.

[74] Article 126(2) of the Constitution of the Republic of Poland.

[75] Article 2(1) of the Act on the State of Emergency.

[76] Kitler (2011), p. 212.

means, the Council of Ministers may adopt a Resolution to request the President to impose a State of Emergency or Martial Law, and in certain cases it may itself impose a State of Natural Disaster.[77] The leading role in the Council of Ministers is played by the Prime Minister, who presides over the Council of Ministers, that is to say, exercises leadership, coordination, and control tasks in respect of it. The second body of the Council of Ministers is made up of the Ministers themselves, who head the various departments. They define the principles, methods, and ways of performing public tasks, in the offices and organisational units subsidiary to them.

Cybersecurity as a trans-sectoral field involves all administrative authorities. Public tasks focused on this field are performed by various types of state entities, guards, services, and inspections subordinate to the Prime Minister or individual Minister. Given the responsibilities assigned, the leading role in this respect is played by the Internal Security Agency, the Ministry competent for Digital Affairs, the Minister of the Interior and Administration, and the Minister of National Defence.

The most important bodies responsible for cybersecurity include the Internal Security Agency (the ABW), whose Head reports directly to the Prime Minister. The ABW is competent for the internal security of the state and its constitutional order.[78] These responsibilities also include cybersecurity, including tasks which the ABW performs through the Department of Information and Communication Security and the Department of Classified Information Protection. The former includes the Governmental Computer Security Incident Response Team, which is the main state entity responsible for identifying, combating, and neutralising cyber threats.[79] It was modelled on European and American units operating in the field of computer incidents.

The next important institution in the protection of cyberspace is the entity established on 5 July 2016—the National Cybersecurity Centre.[80] The Centre functions as an early-warning unit, which, working on a 24/7/365 basis, manages and monitors the procedure of issuing information about network threats (Dyżurnet.pl[81]). The NC Cyber is developing a national-protection plan, in cooperation with the administration, business, and the scientific communities. The NC Cyber operates within the structures of the NASK, and consists of four divisions—Operations, Research & Development, Analysis, and Training. Within the Operations Division there is the National CERT team, i.e. a group which, among other things, responds to network security incidents, constantly monitors threats in cyberspace, and anticipates upcoming trends and threats. Thanks to cooperation with such entities as

[77]Article 228-232 of the Constitution Republic of Poland.

[78]Article 1 of the Act of 24 May 2002 on the Internal Security Agency and on the Intelligence Service, Polish Journal of Laws of 2020, item 27, as amended.

[79]P. Borkowski, *Polska wobec zjawiska cyberterroryzmu*, http://www.psz.pl/116-bezpieczenstwo/piotr-borkowski-polska-wobec-zjawiska-cyberterroryzmu Accessed 4 December 2020.

[80]"The NC Cyber".

[81]Dyżurnet.pl is the point of contact for receiving reports of illegal content on the Internet (in practice, most of it relates to paedophilia and child pornography, but there are also those which involve racial, ethnic and religious hatred).

banks, mobile-phone operators, power-line managers, energy distributors, etc., CERT specialists have direct access to the IT infrastructure of the whole country. If a cyber attack from outside is detected, it is intended to make it easier to defend against it at the Polish IT border. As part of their cooperation with the NC Cyber, the individual institutions have deployed their specialists, who monitor the situation in cyberspace 24 hours a day, to its Headquarters. Their presence is designed to facilitate rapid response in the event of an adverse situation.[82]

The NC Cyber acts as a security operation centre (SOC) in the field of cybersecurity, carries out audits of companies and public administration authorities which encompass critical infrastructure, and issues orders and recommendations. The NCC NASK is the place where information on threats from the various actors involved in the project is collected as part of the National Cyberspace Protection System. The NASK's NC Cyber specialists conduct analyses and make recommendations on the basis of this information. The NC Cyber develops contingency plans, organises training and exercises for persons responsible for the security of the state administration, and stipulates minimum security requirements for institutions. The NC Cyber will prepare incident-reporting schemes, which will include critical-infrastructure managers, banks, and other business sectors.[83] The Centre plays a key role in the process of implementing the EU NIS Directive in Poland.

3 Conclusions

In conclusion, in recent years we have seen a spike in interest in cybersecurity, resulting in an increasing number of individuals and organisations emerging to deal with this problem. However, in order to carry out public tasks in this area more effectively, it is necessary for administrative, military, and civil fields to cooperate and exchange information. It is also essential in these fields to build structures and systems protecting the information which forms the basis of their operations.

A key role for the security of cyberspace is played by the Minister of National Defence, one of whose main tasks in peacetime is to lead the Armed Forces of the Republic of Poland. The Armed Forces are not only responsible for cybersecurity, but they themselves could become the target of potential attacks, which could lead to losses for the whole country. The Armed Forces have also been subject to computerisation and digitisation activities, resulting in the emergence of cyber-sensitive vulnerabilities.[84] New technologies and networks are being used more and more often in operational reconnaissance,[85] or in the information war. These

[82]https://mc.gov.pl/aktualnosci/ncc-na-strazy-cyberbezpieczenstwa Accessed on 24.05.2020.

[83]http://www.cyberdefence24.pl/398863,na-bazie-cert-polska-rusza-narodowe-centrum-cyberbezpieczenstwa Accessed on 01.12.2020.

[84]Bączek (2006), p. 136.

[85]Sadlok (2011), Accessed on 04.05.2020.

processes are intensifying with the development of nanotechnologies and automated and robotic devices. Military operations are also permeating cyberspace, which means that more countries are deciding to develop offensive capabilities to deter potential aggressors.[86] The changes related to digitisation have led to the creation of special units dealing with cybersecurity within the structures of the Polish Armed Forces.

References

Bączek P (2006) Zagrożenia informacyjne a bezpieczeństwo państwa polskiego, Toruń

Biernat S (1994) Prywatyzacja zadań publicznych, Warsaw – Cracow

Boć J (ed) (2004) Prawo administracyjne, Wrocław

Borkowski P Polska wobec zjawiska cyberterroryzmu, http://www.psz.pl/Piotr-Borkowski-Polska-wobeczjawiska-cyberterroryzmu. Accessed 22 May 2020

Chałubińska–Jentkiewicz K (2014) Bezpieczeństwo cyberprzestrzeni jako zadanie publiczne w systemie bezpieczeństwa narodowego RP. Zeszyty Naukowe AON, 3(2)

Chałubińska–Jentkiewicz K, Karpiuk M, Kostrubiec J (2021) The legal status of public entities in the field of cybersecurity in Poland. Lex Localis Press, Maribor

Crapko M (2012) CMMI. Doskonalenie procesów w organizacji

Dobkowski J (2004) Struktura interesu publicznego a zasady rozdzielenia odpowiedzialności publicznoprawnej w Administracji. In: Jednostka – państwo – Administracja. Nowy wymiar, Rzeszów,

Gillies A (2011) Improving the quality of information security management systems with ISO27000. The TQM Journal: the international review of organizational improvement 23(4)

Grzelak M, Lidel K (2012) Bezpieczeństwo w cyberprzestrzeni. Zagrożenia i wyzwania dla Polski – zarys problemu. Bezpieczeństwo Narodowe 22

Hausner J (2005) Administracja publiczna, Warsaw

Humphreys E (2007) Implementing the ISO/IEC 27001 Information Security Management System Standard. Artech House, Norwood

Izdebski H Kulesza M (2004) Administracja publiczna – zagadnienia ogólne, Warsaw

Jaxa-Dębicka A (2008) Sprawne państwo, Warszawa, LEX/el

Kitler W (2011) Bezpieczeństwo narodowe RP. Podstawowe kategorie, uwarunkowania, system, Warsaw

Lang J (1997) Zagadnienia wstępne. In: Wierzbowski M (ed) Prawo administracyjne. Warsaw

Liderman KK (2002) Bezpieczeństwo teleinformatyczne, Wyższa Szkoła Informatyki Stosowanej i. Zarządzania, Warsaw

Lisiak-Felicka D, Szmit M (2016) Cyberbezpieczeństwo administracji publicznej w Polsce. Wybrane zagadnienia, Kraków

Martysz Cz, Szpor G, Wojsyk K (eds) (2015) Ustawa o informatyzacji działalności podmiotów realizujących zadania publiczne. Komentarz. LEX/el

Matuszczyk A, Matuszczyk P (2006) Instrumenty bankowości elektronicznej, Warsaw

Monarcha-Matlak A (2008) Obowiązki administracji publicznej w komunikacji elektronicznej, Warsaw

Murdoch A (2003) Komunikowanie w kryzysie. Jak ratować wizerunek firmy, Warsaw

Ochendowski E (2002) Prawo administracyjne – część ogólna, Toruń

[86]Grzelak and Lidel (2012), p. 128.

Sadlok M (2011) Cyberterroryzm, cyberprzestępczość - wirtualne czy realne zagrożenie? http://www.racjonalista.pl/kk.php/s,846. Accessed 22 May 2020
Starościak J (1975) Prawo administracyjne, Warsaw
Szczepaniuk E (2016) Bezpieczeństwo struktur administracyjnych w warunkach zagrożeń cyberprzestrzeni państwa, Warsaw
Wojciechowska-Filipek S, Ciekanowski Z (2016) Bezpieczeństwo funkcjonowania w cyberprzestrzeni jednostki – organizacji - państwa, Warsaw

Katarzyna Chałubińska–Jentkiewicz dr. hab. of legal sciences (University of Warsaw and the Jagiellonian University), legal advisor, associate professor, and head of the Department of Cybersecurity Law and New Technologies at the Institute of Law in the Faculty of National Security at the War Studies University in Warsaw. She is also a lecturer at the SWPS University and director of the Academic Center for Cybersecurity Policy. In the years 1996–2010, she worked as a lawyer in the National Broadcasting Council and with the public broadcaster TVP S.A. Between 2011 and 2017, she was deputy director of the National Audiovisual Institute (her competence centered on the field of digitization). As a scientist, she conducts research on cybersecurity, information security threats, the development of electronic media law, protection of intellectual property, and the impact of new technologies on the development of the state and the legal situation of the individual. Katarzyna Chałubińska–Jentkiewicz is the author of monographs and numerous articles, which include topics such as new technologies law, cyber responsibility, information security law, and audiovisual media: Regulatory conflict in the age of digitization, Audio visual media services; Regulation in the conditions of digital conversion; Information and computerization in public administration; Cultural Security Law and Reuse of public sector information. She is head of the Ministry of Science's research project "Polish cybersecurity system – a model of legal solutions."

The Authorities Competent for Cybersecurity

Agnieszka Brzostek

Abstract Authorities competent for cybersecurity matters are indicated in Article 41 of the NCSA. The legislator created a catalogue of organs, at the same time specifying the scope of their properties. The legislator, while creating the catalogue of competent authorities, indicated among them ministers managing government administration departments. The Polish Financial Supervision Authority is an exception.

Various legal doubts arise in analysing the legal status of authorities and the scope of their tasks. First of all, the authorities competent for cybersecurity were explicitly indicated as an element of the National Cybersecurity System, but their exact indication as public entities was missing.

Secondly, attention should be paid to the overlapping of competences of authorities competent for cybersecurity with the competent authorities in the field of crisis management.

The specified catalogue of the scope of tasks of the organs was limited to listing their individual tasks. In the implementation of tasks, public administration bodies use their imperious forms of activity.

It is also worth noting that the competent authorities consult and cooperate with relevant national law enforcement and national data protection authorities. The presence of various legal problems and issues was the motivation behind this article.

According to Article 8 of the NIS Directive, each Member State shall designate one or more national authorities competent for the security of network and information systems, covering at least one sector. Member States may assign this role to an existing authority or authorities. Their task is to monitor the application of the Directive at the national level. The Polish legislators have named a list of these

A. Brzostek (✉)
Instytut Prawa/Institute of Law, Akademia Sztuki Wojennej w Warszawie/War Studies University in Warsaw, Warsaw, Poland
e-mail: a.brzostek@akademia.mil.pl

K. Chałubińska-Jentkiewicz et al. (eds.), *Cybersecurity in Poland*,
https://doi.org/10.1007/978-3-030-78551-2_14

authorities.[1] By identifying successively the sectors related to cybersecurity, their responsibility has been defined and assigned to successive Ministers.

The position of a Minister as a member of the Council of Ministers is emphasised in Article 149 of the Constitution of the Republic of Poland. It has been specified that the tasks of Ministers in charge of departments of government administration are defined by the appropriate Acts.[2] As P. Czarny stressed, the Constitution does not explicitly state that a given department should cover similar or related matters, which constitute a certain part of the government administration's activities under the authority of a single Minister.[3] However, Article 149(1) provides for the principle of one-person management by a Minister within the department entrusted to him or her. This is combined at the constitutional level with individual responsibility before the Sejm for matters falling within its ambit, pursuant to Article 157(2) of the Constitution of the Republic of Poland.[4] It should be stressed that a department is managed in accordance with the provisions of the Acts governing the activities of individual government administration institutions, which define more precisely the specific powers of a Minister towards them. Due to the general nature of the concept of management, it may also be of a controlling, supervisory (both in substantive and personal terms), and coordinating nature. However, such provisions cannot be interpreted restrictively. The concept of management implies a general power to influence the activities of subsidiary institutions, except for the use of instruments prohibited by law. The law should also provide for the possibility of assigning certain powers, within the scope of the broadly understood management of organisational units subsidiary to a Minister, to the Council of Ministers or the Prime Minister. The independence of a Minister in managing a department is limited not only by the provisions of the Acts, but also by Article 146(1) and (3) and Article 148(4) of the Constitution. A Minister is also bound by the "political line" established by the Council of Ministers, and the methods of its implementation specified by the Prime Minister.[5] It should be stressed that management is a standard administrative-law scenario of an administrative authority. As part of it, a Minister may apply numerous and various authoritative means of influence on the managed entities, which do not benefit from legally guaranteed independence. These means do not have to be laid down by law, although they must not conflict with the law. The choice of these means depends on the will of the managing authority. Open means can also be applied.[6] The essence of management is that it exists only in a centralised system, in which, as part of management, a superior authority may use all means of influence, e.g. an official order, by which it determines the substance of the action to

[1] Article 41 of the NCSA.

[2] Act of 4 September 1997 on Government Administration Departments (consolidated text, Polish Journal of Laws of 2020, item 1220, as amended).

[3] Czarny (2019).

[4] Czarny (2019).

[5] Czarny (2019).

[6] Góralczyk Jr (2016), pp. 126–132.

be taken by a managed entity, but it is the superior authority which bears full legal responsibility for its implementation. The absence of legal indications as to the scope of management and the means of its implementation could give rise to a presumption of unlimited action affecting a subsidiary authority. This perception is limited by virtue of the powers which only the law may confer on individual authorities. A managing authority does not have the right to withdraw or take over these powers, but can only determine the manner in which they are to be exercised.[7]

The Act on Government Administration Departments, by identifying public administration departments, also defined their scope of action. This indication is reiterated in the National Cybersecurity System Act, except that this specification points to the authorities competent for cybersecurity.[8] The following sectors and authorities were identified.

1. The energy sector—the Minister competent for energy.
2. The transport sector, excluding the water transport subsector—the Minister competent for transport.
3. The water transport subsector—the Minister competent for the maritime economy and the Minister competent for inland navigation.
4. The banking sector and financial-markets infrastructure sector—the Polish Financial Supervision Authority (KNF).
5. The healthcare sector—the Minister competent for health.
6. The healthcare sector[9]—the Minister for National Defence.
7. The drinking water supply and distribution sector—the Minister competent for water management.
8. The digital infrastructure sector—the Minister competent for computerisation.
9. The digital infrastructure sector—the Minister for National Defence.
10. For digital service providers—the Minister competent for computerisation.
11. For digital service providers—the Minister for National Defence.

Each of the entities indicated (apart from KNF) is a Minister managing a department of government administration, with a strictly defined material brief and position within the structure of public administration. It is not specified what is meant by the indicated responsibility of these authorities as authorities accountable

---

[7]Zimmermann (2016), p. 227.

[8]Article 41 of the NCSA.

[9]In points 5, 6, 8, 9, 10, 11, only in respect of the entities specified in Article 26(5) of the National Cybersecurity System Act. The tasks of the CSIRT MON include the coordination of handling incidents reported by: entities subordinate to or supervised by the Minister of National Defence, including entities whose communication and information systems or networks are covered by the uniform list of facilities, installations, devices, and services comprising the critical infrastructure referred to in Article 5b(7)(1) of the Act of 26 April 2007 on Crisis Management; enterprises of particular economic and defence importance in respect of whom the authority organising and supervising the performance of tasks for the defence of the state within the meaning of Article5 (3) of the Act of 23 August 2001 on the Organisation of Tasks for State Defence Performed by Enterprises (consolidated text, Polish Journal of Laws of 2020, item 1669) is the Minister for National Defence.

for cybersecurity. According to the theory of administrative law, it can be assumed that this is a material competence. Pursuant to Article 20 of the Code of Administrative Procedure (CAP)[10] the material competence of a public administration authority shall be defined by the regulations on the sphere of its activities. The legal provisions on the sphere of activities to which the National Cybersecurity System Act refers are provisions belonging to substantive administrative law, authorising or obligating public administration authorities to resolve individual matters cited in these provisions by way of decisions.[11]

According to the Constitution, Ministers manage specific departments of government administration, or carry out the tasks assigned to them by the Prime Minister.[12] Pursuant to Article 34(1) of the Act on Government Administration Departments, a Minister is obliged to initiate and prepare the policy of the Council of Ministers relating to the department which is headed by the Minister, as well as to submit draft laws and normative acts to the meetings of the Council of Ministers in this respect in accordance with the Rules of Procedure of the Council of Ministers. Within the department headed, the Minister implements the policy of the Council of Ministers and coordinates its implementation by the authorities, institutions, and organisational units subsidiary to or supervised by the Minister.[13] As part of their powers, any Minister heading an administrative department may issue regulations and orders. A regulation of a Minister, issued pursuant to Article 149(2) of the Constitution, as well as regulations of the Council of Ministers and the Prime Minister, is used as an act of management only in exceptional circumstances. Much more often such a role is played by an order of a Minister issued pursuant to Article 93(1) of the Constitution of the Republic of Poland. The difference between the orders of the Prime Minister and those of Ministers is that the binding force of the orders of the Prime Minister is greater than that of a Minister's, and that the scope of the potential addressees of the orders of a Minister is much narrower. It covers only those entities falling under the management of a given Minister, whereas orders of the Prime Minister could concern the entire government administration.[14]

The fact that the Polish Financial Supervision Authority (KNF) is included in the list of competent authorities indicated in the National Cybersecurity System Act requires clarification. Pursuant to Article 3 of the Act on Financial Supervision,[15] the Polish Financial Supervision Authority is the supervisory authority responsible for the capital market, and the market for financial instruments which are the subject of

---

[10] Act of 14 June 1960—the Code of Administrative Procedure, consolidated text, Polish Journal of Laws of 2020, item 256, as amended.

[11] Wróbel (2020b).

[12] Zimmermann (2016), p. 242.

[13] More on the political position of a Minister heading a department of government administration—Opaliński (2013), pp. 26–27.

[14] Góralczyk Jr (2016), pp. 126–132.

[15] Act of 29 July 2005 on Capital Market Supervision, Polish Journal of Laws of 2020, item 1400, consolidated text.

requests for admission to trading on the market.[16] The Chair of the KNF manages the operations of the KNF. There is no uniform view in the literature on the subject assessing the legal status of the KNF. As noted by L. Góra, some of the authors rank the KNF as a central-government administration authority, while others indicate that the KNF does not have the status of a government administration authority.[17] Also, the case law of the administrative courts remains inconsistent. The view that the Polish Financial Supervision Authority has the status of a state administration authority prevails, although

> the Act does not explicitly state that the Polish Financial Supervision Authority is a central authority (headed by a Minister within the meaning of the provisions of the CAP), such a conclusion should be drawn from a comprehensive analysis of the provisions of the Act on Financial Supervision.

At the same time, the Supreme Administrative Court noted

> no other state authority has been designated which would be responsible for matters falling within the scope of the Polish Financial Supervision Authority, and, in particular, no other authority has been designated which would be a higher-instance authority, superior to the Polish Financial Supervision Authority, with a power to decide on the validity of KNF's decisions.[18]

The legal assessment of the KNF in the literature has been significantly influenced by the judgment of the Constitutional Tribunal, in which it stated that

> the specific links with other state authorities resulting from the legal provisions which could determine whether that authority is subject to the jurisdiction of the Council of Ministers, the Prime Minister, or a responsible Minister heading a department of government administration, are essential for determining the position of the Polish Financial Supervision Authority within the structure of state authorities[19].

According to the analysis made by the Tribunal as regards the statutory tasks of the KNF, and of the legal forms of action the KNF may use, it can be concluded that the authority is part of the executive. The Constitutional Tribunal noted

> in the light of the provisions of the Constitution, the Act on Financial Market Supervision, and other Acts, it should be stated that the Polish Financial Supervision Authority is a special public state-administration authority, but located outside the government administration structure.[20]

In the case of the KNF, with the existence of certain statutory links, the status of the KNF is characterised by a considerable degree of autonomy and independence, greater than that of the regulatory authorities defined by law as central-government administration authorities.[21] The argument by P. Wajda that the Polish Financial

[16]Article 3(1) of the Act on Capital Market Supervision.

[17]Góral (2012).

[18]The Supreme Administrative Court in its judgment of 21 February 2012, II GSK 67/11.

[19]The judgment of the Constitutional Tribunal of 15 June 2001, K 2/09, OTK-A 2011/5/42.

[20]The judgment of the Constitutional Tribunal of 15 June 2001, K 2/09, OTK-A 2011/5/42.

[21]Góral (2012).

Supervision Authority, due to its appointment to perform the tasks of public administration specified in legal acts, within its territorial responsibility covering the whole country, should be included in a collective group of administrative entities, which form the so-called central administration, may be accepted. Within this broad category, the KNF, due to the fact that it has not been granted the position of supreme authority, should be classified in a subcategory of central offices.[22] It should also be emphasised that to decisions by the *Polish Financial Supervision Authority* on the basis of Article 11(6) of the Act on Financial Market Supervision, Article 127§3 of the CAP should be applied accordingly, which results in the KNF's being considered a Minister within the meaning of Article 5§2(4) of the CAP, as such a legal measure is available in respect of decisions by a Minister or a local government appeal court issued in the first instance.[23]

In the Cybersecurity System Act, the legislators have created a list of tasks for cybersecurity authorities.[24] This fragmented list can be divided into several aspects of the operation of the authorities.

The first of these concerns the situation in which a Minister, as a public administration authority, conducts administrative proceedings in accordance with the CAP, and issues administrative decisions on recognising an entity as an operator of essential services, or decisions stating that rulings on recognising entities as operators of essential services have expired.

The second group comprises the authorities' powers to supervise and monitor the activities of the operators of essential services.

The third group entails the authorities' tasks regarding the formulation of conclusions and recommendations.

The next group of actions includes cooperation with EU bodies.

The last group comprises the powers to process information, including personal data, concerning the provision of essential and digital services, and operators of essential services or digital service providers.

While analysing the separate first group of tasks, it should be noted that each designated authority may conduct administrative proceedings in the field of the recognition of an entity as an operator of essential services. According to Article 1 (1) of the CAP, proceedings before public administration authorities in individual cases falling within the responsibility of these bodies shall be settled by means of administrative decisions, or settled tacitly. A legal definition of an administrative authority classifies, in Article 5§2 of the CAP, a Minister as a public-administration authority within the meaning of the CAP. Pursuant to the provisions of the National Cybersecurity System Act, the authority carries out an ongoing analysis of entities in a given sector or subsector, in terms of their recognition as an operator of essential services, or failure to meet the conditions classifying an entity as an operator of

[22]Wajda (2009), p. 139.

[23]Chróścielewski (2015), p. 13.

[24]More on the public administration authorities responsible for cybersecurity in Chałubińska-Jentkiewicz (2019), pp. 360–375.

essential services, and issues decisions on the recognition of an entity as an operator of essential services, or decisions stating that the ruling on recognising an entity as an operator of essential services has expired. Such an indication precludes tacit decisions. The authority carrying out the aforementioned analysis conducts administrative proceedings, as evidenced by the fact that the proceedings are terminated with the issue of an administrative decision. When applying the CAP to the issue of this decision, the operators of essential services become parties to the proceedings, using all the statutory rights of such parties. A Minister as a public-administration authority issues a decision, and, pursuant to Article 127§3 of the CAP, no appeal may be brought against this decision.[25] However, any party dissatisfied with the decision may ask the authority to re-examine the case, and the regulations regarding appeals against decisions apply in such a case. A request for re-examination of the case as regards a first-instance decision issued by a Minister is treated in the literature on the subject as a form of a standard appeal, although it serves as a final decision. A request for the re-examination of a case differs from an appeal in that it does not have a devolutive effect, i.e. it does not refer the case to a higher authority.[26] It should be noted that a request for the re-examination of a case will also be admissible when specific provisions introduce the possibility of bringing an action before a court in respect of a particular type of decision.[27]

Immediately after issuing a decision on recognising an operator of essential services, or a ruling stating the expiry of a decision on recognising an operator of essential services, the competent authority forwards requests to the Minister competent for digital affairs for inclusion in the list of operators of essential services, or removal from that list.[28]

It was further stated that authorities competent for cybersecurity should monitor the application of the provisions of the Act by operators of essential services, and digital service providers.[29] The use of the verb "monitor" ("monitoruje") by the legislators creates some ambiguity in its interpretation. The use of this term results from a direct translation of the terminology of the NIS Directive. It would be more appropriate to use the term "nadzór" ("supervision"). This provision would then correlate with the next task, namely that the competent authority, at the request of CSIRT NASK, CSIRT GOV, or CSIRT MON, calls on the operators of essential services or digital service providers to remove, within a specified time frame, the vulnerabilities which have led or could lead to a serious, significant, or critical

[25]According to B. Adamiak, an appeal against a decision is one of the legal remedies, which should be understood as "procedural institutions standardize which authorised entities may request the verification of administrative decisions with a view to their cassation or amendment". Adamiak (1996), p. 544. For more information on a request for re-examination of the case, cf. Piszczek and Piszczek (2008), pp. 62–77.

[26]Wróbel (2020a). More on the devolutive effect of a request for the re-examination of the Z. Kmieciak case, Kmieciak (2008), pp. 19–35.

[27]Przybysz (2019).

[28]Article 42(1) (3) of the NCSA.

[29]Article 42(1) (6) of the NCSA.

incident.[30] The literature indicates that supervision occurs in a centralised and decentralised authority structure. The concept of supervision is connected with subsidiarity, in which a supervisory authority has overseeing powers, and the essence of supervision is the ability to draw consequences from the behaviour of a subsidiary authority, observed by the supervisory authority from the point of view of a specific, selected criterion.[31] The literal use of the concept of supervision in this form is justified in the later part of the list of tasks assigned to the authorities compe for cybersecurity, in which the authorities submit requests for a change to the data in the list of operators of essential services, no later than 6 months after the change of such data, and monitor the application of the provisions of the Act by the operators of essential services and digital service providers.[32] In Chapter 11 of the Act, the Polish legislators indicated the principles and manner of exercising supervision over the operators of essential services and digital service providers.

The concept of supervision is connected with the notion of control. Control should be understood as the examination of the compliance of the existing state with the requested state, the determination of the scope and causes of discrepancies, the communication of the results of this determination, and sometimes the resulting instructions to both the controlled entity and the superior entity.[33] Control is a basic element of supervision, and also an element of management. According to J. Zimmermann, supervision is, precisely, control carried out within the administrative system, enhanced by an element of administrative power, which makes it possible to derive consequences from the deficiencies in the activities of an administrative authority or other entity identified during the control. This means that control occurs as a stage in the supervisory procedure, or as a stage in the management procedure, and can occur as independent control.[34] The legislators specified in Article 42(1)(8) that the authorities carry out the control of the operators of essential services and digital service providers. In accordance with Article 15(1) of the NIS Directive, Member States shall ensure that the competent authorities have the necessary powers and means to assess the compliance of the operators of essential services with their obligations. Article 17(1) of the NIS Directive stipulates that Member States shall ensure that the competent authorities take action, if necessary, through *ex post* supervisory measures, when provided with evidence that a digital service provider does not meet the requirements laid down in Article 16. Such evidence may be submitted by a competent authority of another Member State in

[30] Article 42(1) (7) of the NCSA.

[31] Zimmermann (2016), p. 228. The most common supervision measures used include legality, i.e. compliance with the law, expediency, cost-effectiveness, reliability, and validity. These are repressive supervision measures. Preventive supervision, carried out before the supervised authority takes action, i.e. agreement or opinion on an act. Zimmermann (2016), p. 228.

[32] Article 42(1) (4) of the NCSA.

[33] Boć (2003), p. 327.

[34] Zimmermann (2016), p. 229.

which the service is being provided.[35] The detailed scope of control is set out in Chapter 11 of the National Cybersecurity System Act.

The competent authorities, using their powers, in cooperation with CSIRT NASK, CSIRT GOV, CSIRT MON, and sectoral cybersecurity teams, prepare recommendations for action to strengthen cybersecurity, including sector-specific guidelines on incident reporting.[36] Recommendations for action to strengthen cybersecurity, including sector-specific guidelines on incident reporting, referred to in paragraph 1(5), are prepared, taking into account, in particular, Polish standards transposing European standards, common technical specifications, understood as ICT technical specifications defined in accordance with Articles 13 and 14 of the Regulation of the European Parliament and of the Council (EU).[37]

As part of their powers, the competent authorities may cooperate with the authorities of the Member States of the European Union, and a Single Point of Contact.[38] As a general rule, cooperation between authorities should take place through a single point of contact. However, it cannot be excluded that a Polish competent authority might establish direct contact with its counterpart in another Member State. A Single Point of Contact should, however, be informed of such cooperation on a case-by-case basis, so that it is fully informed of the consultations which are taking place, and which will facilitate the proper coordination of activities.[39]

When a legal person or an organisational unit without legal personality providing digital services does not have its registered office or management board on the territory of the Republic of Poland, or has not appointed a representative on the territory of the Republic of Poland, but its information systems are located on the territory of the Republic of Poland and does not comply with the requirements set out in Implementing Regulation 2018/151, the authority competent for cybersecurity for digital service providers may transmit information and request action to the competent authority in another Member State of the European Union on the territory in which it has its registered office or management board, or has appointed a representative.[40]

The legislators have allowed the authorities competent for cybersecurity to delegate their tasks. This means that the authority may entrust the performance, on

[35]Prusak-Górniak and Silicki (2019a).

[36]Article 42(1)(5) of the NCSA.

[37]Articles 13 and 14 of Regulation (EU) No. 1025/2012 of the European Parliament and of the Council of 25 October 2012 on European standardisation, amending Council Directives 89/686/EEC and 93/15/EEC and Directives 94/9/EC, 94/25/EC, 95/16/EC, 97/23/EC, 98/34/EC, 2004/22/EC, 2007/23/EC, 2009/23/EC, and 2009/105/EC of the European Parliament and of the Council and repealing Council Decision 87/95/EEC and Decision No. 1673/2006/EC of the European Parliament. and of the Council (OJ EU 2012 L 316/12). and the guidelines of the European Commission and the European Network and the Information Security Agency (ENISA).

[38]Article 42(1)(9) of the NCSA.

[39]Prusak-Górniak and Silicki (2019b).

[40]Article 42(2) of the NCSA.

its behalf, of certain tasks to entities which are subsidiary to, or supervised by, the authority.[41] Tasks are entrusted on the basis of an agreement between the competent authority for cybersecurity and the entities. This agreement sets out the rules for the exercise of control by the competent authority for cybersecurity over the proper performance of the tasks entrusted. The communication on the conclusion of the agreement is published in the official journal of the competent authority for cybersecurity. The Act specifies what information such a communication should contain.[42]

Each competent authority processes information, including personal data concerning the provision of key and digital services and digital service operators or providers, to the extent necessary to carry out its statutory tasks. The right to process information, including personal data, should be derived from provisions indicating the specific tasks for which such processing is required. As noted by K. Prusak-Górniak and K. Silicki, the processing of information may take place only to the extent justified by the performance of a specific task, hence it seems excessive to include provisions indicating the general right to process information, including personal data.[43]

The legislators have provided the possibility of requesting information by creating a simplified procedure.[44] As a result, the authority competent for cybersecurity may, without initiating proceedings for recognising an entity as an operator of essential services, request information to enable a preliminary assessment of whether the entity meets the conditions to be recognised as an operator of essential services.[45] The same applies to procedures to carry out an inspection. The competent authority may, without initiating an inspection, request information from an operator of essential services which will make it possible to determine the need for an inspection, and may, without initiating proceedings, request information from an operator of essential services which will make it possible to make a preliminary assessment of whether the entity no longer meets the conditions to be recognised as an operator of essential services.[46]

The authority competent for cybersecurity, when making a request for information to the appropriate entity or operator of essential services, indicates when the information is to be provided. The deadline set may not be less than 14 days from the date of the receipt of the request by the entity or the operator of essential services.[47] The competent authority addresses the entity in the form of a simple letter containing

[41] Article 42(3) of the NCSA.

[42] Article 42(4)-(6) of the NCSA. The information refers to the address of the website on which the agreement will be published, together with its integral annexes, and the date from which the agreement will be effective.

[43] Prusak-Górniak and Silicki (2019a).

[44] Walczuk (2019), pp. 274–275.

[45] Article 43(1) of the NCSA.

[46] Article 43(2) of the NCSA.

[47] Article 43(3) of the NCSA.

questions which will allow a preliminary assessment of the legitimacy of initiating a formal procedure based on the provisions of the Code of Administrative Procedure.[48] The entity requested by the authorities may provide information on the matter to which the request relates, or decline to provide information.[49] A request for information followed by the failure to provide information does not affect the possibility of initiating administrative proceedings or inspections, but might constitute evidence in administrative proceedings or inspections initiated. The failure to provide information does not affect the procedural situation of the party or the inspected entity, nor does it affect the administrative proceedings or inspection initiated.[50]

The National Cybersecurity System Act also indicates the possibility of the competent authority's creating a sectoral cybersecurity team for specific sectors or subsectors. Such a team is responsible, in particular, for receiving reports of serious incidents and assisting in the handling of those incidents, supporting the operators of essential services in carrying out their duties, analysing serious incidents, finding links between incidents, preparing conclusions of incident handling, and cooperating with the appropriate CSIRT MON, CSIRT NASK, or CSIRT GOV in coordinating the handling of serious incidents.[51] It should be noted, as did K. Walczuk, that the tasks mentioned above do not form an exhaustive list; on the contrary—they rather constitute a sample task list.[52]

A sectoral cybersecurity team may transmit to, and receive from, other states, including Member States of the European Union, information on serious incidents, including those involving two or more Member States of the European Union. A sectoral cybersecurity team may receive reports of a serious incident from another Member State of the European Union involving two or more Member States of the European Union. A sectoral cybersecurity team forwards these reports to the appropriate CSIRT MON, CSIRT NASK, or CSIRT GOV, and a Single Point of Contact.[53] When a sectoral cybersecurity team is established, the authority competent for cybersecurity informs the operators of essential services in the appropriate sector, and CSIRT MON, CSIRT NASK, and CSIRT GOV, of the establishment of that team, and the scope of the tasks carried out.[54] Sectoral cybersecurity teams may operate in addition to CSIRTs which are mandatory at the national level.[55]

The legislators have defined the responsibility of the authorities in a fairly short and general chapter, while at the same time providing the opportunity to extend this responsibility in the other chapters discussed in this publication. The indicated list of

[48]Prusak-Górniak and Silicki (2019a).

[49]Article 43(4) of the NCSA.

[50]Article 43(6) of the NCSA.

[51]Article 44(1) of the NCSA.

[52]Walczuk (2019).

[53]Article 44(2) and (3) of the NCSA.

[54]Article 44(4) of the NCSA.

[55]Walczuk (2019).

tasks of the authorities competent for cybersecurity is limited to mentioning the individual tasks of these authorities. Public-administration authorities use their own authoritative forms of action to perform their tasks. What is important is that in the case of doubts as to the legitimacy of initiating proceedings, the competent authorities may use the measure provided for in Article 43 of the National Cybersecurity System Act to request information, without the need to formally initiate the procedure. It is also worth noting that the competent authorities, with regard to Article 8 (6) of the NIS Directive, consult and cooperate with the appropriate national law enforcement authorities and national data protection authorities. However, it should be stressed that the statutory assumptions will only be verified as time goes by. The presentation of the activities of the authorities competent for cybersecurity as outlined above follows from the recommendations set out in the NIS Directive, and from political considerations and consultations. It is intended to provide for the possibility of applying these provisions to the widest possible extent, but the period which has elapsed since the adoption of the Act (2 years) does not yet enable a full assessment of their application in practice. What remains is the practice of the authorities, which might resolve a number of interpretation doubts.

References

Adamiak B (1996) Komentarz do Kodeksu postępowania administracyjnego, Warsaw

Boć J (2003) Administracja publiczna, Wrocław

Chałubińska-Jentkiewicz K (2019) Cyberodpowiedzialność, Toruń

Chróścielewski W (2015) Postępowanie administracyjne – Komisja Nadzoru Finansowego – wyłączenie od udziału w sprawie. Glosa to the Judgment of the Polish Supreme Administrative Court (NSA) of 29 April 2014 r., II GSK 320/13 – a partly critical gloss

Czarny P (2019) Commentary on Article 149 Konstytucji RP. In: Tuleja P (ed) Konstytucja Rzeczypospolitej Polskiej. Komentarz, Wolters Kluwer, Warsaw, LEX/el

Góral L (2012) Commentary on Article 3 w: Ustawa o nadzorze nad rynkiem finansowym. Komentarz, LEX/el

Góralczyk W Jr (2016) Kierownictwo w prawie administracyjnym, Warsaw

Kmieciak Z (2008) Wniosek o ponowne rozpatrzenie sprawy w KPA (Odwołanie czy remonstracja?), Państwo i Prawo 3

Opaliński B (2013) Prawnoustrojowe uwarunkowania struktury Rady Ministrów, Przegląd Legislacyjny 1

Piszczek K, Piszczek P (2008) Wniosek o ponowne rozpatrzenie sprawy – kontrowersje wokół jego istoty. Prokuratura i Prawo 11

Prusak-Górniak K, Silicki K (2019a) Commentary on Article 42. In: Czaplicki K, Gryszczyńska A, Szpor G (eds) Ustawa o Krajowym Systemie cyberbezpieczeństwa. Komentarz, Warsaw, LEX/el

Prusak-Górniak K, Silicki K (2019b) Commentary on Article 26. In: Czaplicki K, Gryszczyńska A, Szpor G (eds) Ustawa o Krajowym Systemie cyberbezpieczeństwa. Komentarz, Warsaw, LEX/el

Przybysz P (2019) Commentary on Article 127. In: Przybysz P (ed) Komentarz do kodeksu postępowania administracyjnego, Komentarz aktualizowany, LEX/el

Wajda P (2009) Pozycja prawnoustrojowa i skład Komisji Nadzoru Finansowego – kilka uwag krytycznych, Przegląd Prawa Publicznego 7–8

Walczuk K (2019) Commentary on Article 43. In: Kitler W, Taczkowska-Olszewska J, Radoniewicz F (eds) Ustawa o krajowym systemie cyberbezpieczeństwa. Komentarz, Warsaw
Wróbel A (2020a). Komentarz do art. 20 KPA. In: Jaśkowska M, Wilbrandt-Gotowicz M,Wróbel A (eds) Komentarz zaktualizowany do Kodeksu postępowania administracyjnego, Warsaw, LEX/el
Wróbel A (2020b). Komentarz do art. 127 KPA. In: Jaśkowska M, Wilbrandt-Gotowicz M,Wróbel A (eds) Komentarz zaktualizowany do Kodeksu postępowania administracyjnego, Warsaw, LEX/el
Zimmermann J (2016) Prawo administracyjne, Warsaw

Agnieszka Brzostek PhD, adjunct at the Institute of Law of the War Studies Academy. She is a lecturer of law and administrative procedure at studies in the field of law and administration. Scientific interests focus on administrative law and administrative procedure, as well as on the functioning of public administration, in particular on the activities of public administration bodies in the field of security and cybersecurity. Scientific interests focus on administrative law and administrative proceedings, as well as on the operation of public administration, in particular on the operation of public administration bodies in the field of security and cyber security. She is the author or co-author of numerous chapters in monographs and scientific articles.

The Main Tasks of the Network of Computer Security Incident Response Teams in the Light of the Act on the National Cybersecurity System in Poland

Monika Nowikowska

Abstract Computer Security Incident Response Teams (CSIRTs) are specialised entities established to handle network and information system security incidents and cooperate with similar entities around the world, both in terms of operational, as well as research and implementation activities. The main tasks of CSIRTs include: recognition, prevention, recording and handling of events that breach network security, active response in the event of direct threats, cooperation with other CSIRT teams, and, finally, participation in national and international projects related to information security and research activities on the scope of methods for detecting security incidents. The article analyses the detailed tasks established on the basis of the Act of 5 July 2018 on the National Cybersecurity System of three CSIRTs operating in Poland: CSIRT MON, CSIRT NASK and CSIRT GOV.

Subsequent to the adoption on 6 July 2016 by the European Parliament and by the Council of the European Union of Directive 2016/1148 concerning measures for a high common level of security of network and information systems across the Union (the NIS Directive) all Member States were required to adopt a national strategy for the security of network and information systems, including the establishment of networks of Computer Security Incident Response Teams, known as CSIRT networks. The Preamble to the NIS Directive indicates that network and information systems and services play an important role in society. Their reliability and security are essential for economic and social activities, in particular for the functioning of the internal market.

The scale, frequency, and impact of security incidents are increasing, and constitute a serious threat to the functioning of network and information systems. These systems can also become the object of intentional harmful operations designed to

M. Nowikowska (✉)
Instytut Prawa/Institute of Law, Akademia Sztuki Wojennej w Warszawie/War Studies University in Warsaw, Warsaw, Poland
e-mail: m.nowikowska@akademia.mil.pl

K. Chałubińska-Jentkiewicz et al. (eds.), *Cybersecurity in Poland*,
https://doi.org/10.1007/978-3-030-78551-2_15

damage or interrupt their performance. Such incidents can hamper business activities, cause significant financial losses, undermine user confidence and result in serious damage to the Union's economy.

In view of the differences between national management structures, the Member States were authorised to designate responsible national authorities (more than one) to be in charge of implementing tasks related to the security of network and information systems belonging to operators of essential services and digital service providers. Furthermore, for the purpose of facilitating cross-border cooperation and communication, each Member State is required to designate a national single point of contact responsible for coordinating issues relating to the security of network and information systems and cross-border cooperation at the Union level. The NIS Directive therefore provided the states with the flexibility to determine the number of CSIRTs, with the reservation that operators of essential services and digital service providers will have a designated CSIRT to which they will report. The Polish legislators have designated three national-level CSIRTs: the CSIRT MON, CSIRT NASK, and CSIRT GOV.

In the National Cybersecurity System Act the legislators established the CSIRT structure and the responsibilities of individual CSIRTs. The CSIRT MON, CSIRT NASK, and CSIRT GOV are obliged to cooperate with each other, with the authorities competent for cybersecurity matters, the Minister competent for computerisation, and the Plenipotentiary, ensuring a cohesive and complete system at the national level, performing tasks for counteracting cybersecurity threats of a cross-sectoral and cross-border nature, as well as ensuring the coordination of handling reported incidents. The entities have been obligated to jointly develop a procedure for dealing with incidents, the coordination of which requires CSIRT cooperation. Chapter 6 of the National Cybersecurity System Act implements Articles 9 and 10 of the NIS Directive.

Pursuant to Article 9 of the NIS Directive, each Member State shall designate one or more CSIRTs, which shall comply with the requirements set out in point (1) of Annex I covering at least the sectors referred to in Annex II and the services referred to in Annex III, responsible for risk and incident handling in accordance with a well-defined process. CSIRTs may be established within a competent authority. The Polish legislators adopted the second option, indicating three parallel CSIRTs. CSIRTs, also known as CERTs, are computer emergency response teams which comply with essential requirements to guarantee effective and compatible capabilities to deal with incidents and risks, and to ensure efficient cooperation at the Union level. The CSIRTs are expected to contribute to developing trust and confidence between the Member States, and to promote prompt and effective operational cooperation. The CSIRTs should be able to instruct the single point of contact to forward incident reports to the single points of contact in other Member States affected by the incident.

The states are required to ensure that the competent authorities and the single points of contact are adequately equipped in terms of both technical and organisational capabilities. It is intended to ensure the effective and efficient prevention, detection, response, and mitigation of network and information system incidents and risks.

In Poland, a model based on three CSIRTs has been adopted: CSIRT GOV—a Computer Security Incident Response Team operating at the national level, managed by the Head of the Internal Security Agency, CSIRT MON—a Computer Security Incident Response Team operating at the national level, managed by the Minister of National Defence, and CSIRT NASK—a Computer Security Incident Response Team operating at the national level, managed by the Research and Academic Computer Network—the National Research Institute. These designated CSIRTs cover all the sectors referred to in Annex II of the NIS Directive.

The three parallel CSIRTs represent the technical level of coordination of incident handling, and demonstrate that the Polish legislators have adopted a de-centralised system for the functioning of the CSIRTs. For the purpose of avoiding conflicts of competence, the legislators have defined the briefs of computer incident response teams. The tasks of CSIRTs take into consideration the responsibilities assigned to each CSIRT for the management of the state's cybersecurity, and include directories of the entities supported forming the national cybersecurity system. The competence scope is of a subjective and objective nature.

Among the tasks of the CSIRT MON is the coordination of handling incidents reported by the entities subordinate to or supervised by the Minister of National Defence, including those whose information and communication systems or networks are covered by the uniform list of facilities, installations, devices, and services constituting the critical infrastructure, as drawn up by the Director of the Government Centre for Security, pursuant to the Act on Crisis Management. The tasks of the CSIRT MON also involve coordinating the handling of incidents reported by enterprises of particular economic and defence significance, in relation to which the Minister of National Defence is the authority organising and supervising the performance of tasks for national defence, as well as in the field of incidents related to events of a terrorist nature which undermine the security of the defence potential of the state, the Polish Armed Forces, and the organisational units of the Ministry of National Defence.

The CSIRT GOV operates within the structures of the Internal Security Agency. The CSIRT GOV's tasks encompass the coordination of incident handling in the sphere of government administration and critical infrastructure.

The CSIRT NASK operates within the Research and Academic Computer Network—the National Research Institute, supervised by the Minister competent for computerisation. NASK operates in accordance with the Act of 30 April 2010 on Research Institutes.[1] The tasks of CSIRT NASK are a continuation of CERT Polska, which was established in 1996 as the first incident response team in Poland.

The first set of tasks of CSIRTs is to cooperate with each other, with the authorities competent for cybersecurity, the Minister competent for computerisation, and the Plenipotentiary, ensuring a cohesive and complete risk-management system at the national level.

---

[1]Act of 30 April 2010 on Research Institutes, consolidated text, Polish Journal of Laws of 2020, item 1383, as amended.

The second group of responsibilities is to implement measures to counteract threats to cybersecurity. The CSIRTs operate to counter cybersecurity threats of a cross-sectoral and cross-border nature. Cybersecurity hazards of a cross-sectoral nature are those which go beyond a single sector listed in the Act. For the prevention of threats of a cross-border nature, CSIRTs shall cooperate within the framework of the CSIRT network, consisting of representatives of CSIRTs of the European Union Member States. Under this cooperation, the Single Point of Contact provides information on cross-border incidents.

The Single Point of Contact is required to submit summary reports to the Cooperation Group, which should be anonymised in order to preserve the confidentiality of the notifications and the identity of the operators of essential services and digital service providers. It is indicated that information on the identity of the notifying entities is not required for the exchange of best practices within the Cooperation Group. The summary report should therefore include information on the number of notifications received, as well as information on the nature of the reported incidents, such as the types of security breaches, their seriousness, and their duration. The Single Points of Contact should not receive any incident notifications directly, unless they also function as a competent authority or a CSIRT.

CSIRTs are obligated to receive, analyse and coordinate incident notifications. The CSIRT MON, CSIRT GOV, and CSIRT NASK obtain incident reports from operators of essential services, digital service providers, and public entities, according to their competence. Pursuant to Article 26(2) of the NCSA, CSIRTs, in justified cases, are also obligated to provide incident-handling support at the request of operators of essential services, digital service providers, public entities, sectoral cybersecurity teams or owners, owner-like possessors, or holders bound by obligations towards owners, of facilities, installations, and equipment or services forming part of the critical infrastructure. Therefore, the principle should be that the incident must be handled by persons connected with the affected entity, or working for it. The reliable handling of incidents requires knowledge of the specific system under attack, and its functionality and design, which their administrators have. The operators of essential services should not expect the appropriate CSIRT team to provide support in every case. The granting of support might depend on the scale of the threat, the degree of impact, and other relevant factors. It should be emphasised that the CSIRT support or its handling of serious incidents which have affected operators of essential services and other entities can occur under two conditions: in justified cases, and at the request of these entities.

The coordination of incidents is the primary task of the CSIRT teams. This is essential for the proper performance of tasks, in particular when the incident is of a cross-sectoral nature. Under this cooperation, the CSIRT teams exchange information concerning threats. In Article 26(3) of the NCSA, the legislators defined the responsibilities shared by all three national-level CSIRTs. The monitoring of cybersecurity threats and incidents at the national level is listed as the first task. Incident management involves responding to a reported incident. Incident handling involves verification and classification, collection of information, documentation, coordination, and, if incident management requires CSIRT cooperation, reporting or communication with the media. As part of incident management, the CSIRT classifies incidents, including those which are serious and significant, as critical incidents, and coordinates the handling of critical situations, as well as reclassifies serious and significant ones. Serious and significant incidents involving two or more countries shall be forwarded to the Single Point of Contact for further transmission to the relevant Member States.

The common responsibilities of CSIRTs include the assessment of the risks associated with identified cybersecurity threats and incidents, including dynamic risk analysis. The analysis of the incident is one of the crucial steps in dealing with the occurrence. Its proper implementation can and should serve to draw conclusions and tighten the security of systems. The proceedings during this stage should include securing evidence and preparing documentation on the event, on the basis of which further actual analysis of the incident will be performed.

CSIRTs have been obligated to report incidents and risks to the national cybersecurity system, and to issue communications about identified cybersecurity threats.

For cross-sectoral incidents, the legislators have ordered that technical information concerning the incident, the coordination of which requires CSIRT cooperation, must be transmitted to the appropriate CSIRT.

Where appropriate, CSIRTs have been required to conduct examinations of IT devices or software in order to identify the vulnerabilities whose exploitation can threaten, in particular, the integrity, confidentiality, accountability, authenticity, or availability of the data processed, and which can affect public security or the essential interests of national security; they must also submit proposals or recommendations to the entities of the national cybersecurity system in respect of the use of IT equipment or software, in particular with regard to the impact on public security or essential interests of national security. The concept of accountability is understood as ensuring that the actions of an entity can be unambiguously attributed only to that entity. Data integrity means confirmation that the data transmitted, received, or stored is complete and unaltered. Data confidentiality relates to the protection of communications or stored data against interception and reading by unauthorised persons. Furthermore, it should be noted that the legal regulations strictly define the basic safety conditions to be met by IT devices and software.

The Polish legislators have obligated CSIRTs to provide, by 30 May each year, to the Single Point of Contact, a list of serious incidents notified in the previous calendar year by operators of essential services which have affected the continuity of their essential services in the Republic of Poland and the continuity of their provision of essential services in the Member States of the European Union, as well as a summary of significant incidents notified by digital service providers in the previous calendar year, including those involving two or more Member States of the European Union. Moreover, the CSIRT teams must collectively prepare and submit to the Minister competent for digital affairs the part of the report on national security threats referred to in the Act on Crisis Management concerning cybersecurity.

National-level CSIRTs provide analytical and R&D facilities for the national cybersecurity system. This involves conducting advanced malware and vulnerability analyses, monitoring cyber threat indicators, developing tools and methods for detecting and combating cyber threats, conducting analyses and developing standards, recommendations, and good practices in the field of cybersecurity, supporting entities of the national cybersecurity system in building cybersecurity capacities and capabilities, and conducting awareness-building activities in the sphere of cybersecurity.

The CSIRT tasks defined in the NCSA are compliant with the requirements for Computer Security Incident Response Teams as defined in Annex I to the NIS Directive. The EU legislature has included among these tasks monitoring incidents at the national level, providing early warnings to the relevant stakeholders, issuing alerts, publishing announcements and disseminating information to the stakeholders regarding risks and incidents, responding to incidents, providing dynamic risk and incident analysis and situational awareness, participating in the CSIRT network, and establishing cooperation with the private sector.

The Polish legislators, in Article 26(8) of the NCSA, also regulated the rules for forwarding incident notifications by the inappropriate CSIRT according to competence. The CSIRT MON, CSIRT NASK, or CSIRT GOV which has received an incident notification, but is not responsible for coordinating its handling, shall immediately forward this notification to the competent CSIRT, along with the information received. These entities may also entrust each other with the performance of tasks in respect of certain types of entity on the basis of an agreement. Should such an agreement be made, the CSIRT shall inform the entity in respect of which there has been a change of subsidiarity. Additionally, the announcement of the conclusion of the agreement shall be published in the Official Journal of the Minister of National Defence, the Minister for Digital Affairs, or the Internal Security Agency, respectively, indicating the address of the website on which the content of the agreement is published, and the date from which the agreement is binding. Whenever it is determined that the incident, the handling of which is coordinated by the responsible CSIRT MON, CSIRT NASK, or CSIRT GOV, is related to an event of a terrorist nature or to a terrorist act detrimental to the security of the state's defence capabilities, the Polish Armed Forces and the organisational units of the Ministry of National Defence, the coordination of incident handling is assumed by the responsible CSIRT MON or CSIRT GOV.

It is important to note that information regarding incidents is becoming increasingly valuable to the general public and businesses. Therefore, it is important that such information should not only be focused on incidents and events with a national range, but must also be provided in an aggregated form at the Union level. This is due to the fact that small and medium-sized enterprises in particular are increasingly operating across borders and the citizens are using online services. The EU legislators encourage CSIRTs to provide, on a voluntary basis, information to be published on websites, without including confidential or sensitive information. When information is considered confidential according to national laws, it must be kept confidential. At the same time, the authorities are obligated to devote due attention to safeguarding informal and trusted channels of information-sharing. Decisions concerning the provision of information to the public about incidents should be taken with a reasonable balance between the public interest, according to which the public should be informed of the threats, and the risk of the reputational and commercial damage to which the operators of essential services and digital service providers reporting incidents are exposed. While fulfilling their incident-notification obligations, the competent authorities and the CSIRTs should pay particular attention to the need to maintain strict confidentiality with regard to information relating to product vulnerabilities until the appropriate security fixes are released.

In identifying the right CSIRT, priority shall be given to examining whether an entity belongs to the category of entities for which the CSIRT MON is appropriate. The NCSA identifies two entity categories. First, entities subordinate to or supervised by the Minister of National Defence, including those whose communication and information systems or networks are covered by the uniform list of facilities, installations, devices, and services included in the critical infrastructure, referred to in Article 5b(7)(1) of the Act of 26 April 2007 on Crisis Management; Second, the enterprises of special economic and defence importance in respect of which the Ministry of National Defence is the authority organising and supervising the performance of tasks for state defence within the meaning of Article 5(3) of the Act of 23 August 2001 on the Organisation of Tasks for State Defence Performed by Enterprises.[2] If a given entity is part of one of these two groups, it is obligated to report to, or liaise with, the CSIRT MON response team. The CSIRT MON is exclusively responsible for implementing the tasks laid down in the NCSA in relation to the entities listed below. The scope of the entities subordinate to or supervised by the Minister of National Defence was defined in the Notice of the Minister of National Defence of 16 January 2019.[3] Furthermore, it should be indicated that the CSIRT MON's jurisdiction *ratione personae* extends to critical-infrastructure entities which are also subsidiary to the Minister of National Defence. Essentially, the CSIRT GOV will be the responsible entity for critical infrastructure. The legislators have thus decided that, as far as critical infrastructure is concerned, entities under the authority of the Minister of National Defence, and supervised by him or her, would be covered by the CSIRT MON's responsibility. The second group of entities within the responsibility of the CSIRT MON includes enterprises of particular economic and defence importance, in respect of which the Minister of National Defence is the authority organising and supervising the performance of tasks for state defence.

Within the scope of the CSIRT NASK's responsibilities, the legislators have adopted both a subjective and an objective scope. In addition to the category of entities which are within the responsibility of the CSIRT NASK, two functions have been identified, which remain within the exclusive ambit of the CSIRT NASK. In the subjective aspect, the tasks of the CSIRT NASK include the coordination of handling incidents reported by units subsidiary to or supervised by

[2]Act of 23 August 2001 on the Organisation of Tasks for State Defence Performed by Enterprises, consolidated text, Polish Journal of Laws of 2020, item 1669.

[3]Notice of the Minister of National Defence of 16 January 2019, The Official Gazette of the Government of the Republic of Poland of 2019, item 48.

government-administration authorities, except for units subsidiary to or supervised by the Prime Minister, research institutes, the Office of Technical Inspection, the Polish Air Navigation Services Agency, the Polish Centre for Accreditation, the National Fund for Environmental Protection and Water Management, and provincial funds for environmental protection and water management, commercial law companies performing public service tasks intended to meet, on an ongoing and continuous basis, the collective needs of the population through the provision of open services, natural persons, digital service providers, in so far as they are not critical infrastructure operators, the operators of essential services, with the exception of those operators which are assigned to the CSIRT MON and the CSIRT GOV, and other entities which are outside the responsibility of the CSIRT MON and the CSIRT GOV. Therefore, incidents may be reported to the CSIRT NASK by all entities not classified in any of the above-mentioned categories of entity. This means that anyone can report incidents to the CSIRT NASK.

Among the additionally indicated exclusive tasks of the CSIRT NASK are the creation and provision of tools for voluntary cooperation, and the exchange of information on cybersecurity threats and incidents. The EU legislators encourage the creation by other organisations of their own informal cooperation mechanisms to ensure the security of network and information systems, recognising the need for cooperation between the public and the private sectors. The Cooperation Group should invite relevant stakeholders for discussion. In order to effectively encourage the sharing of information and best practices, it is necessary to ensure that operators of essential services and digital service providers participating in such exchanges do not bear the consequences arising from the mere fact of cooperating. Moreover, it should be stressed that the CSIRT NASK's activities are financed in the form of an earmarked subsidy from the part of the state budget at the disposal of the Minister competent for computerisation.

The second function of the CSIRT NASK is to provide a telephone or Internet service for those who are active in reporting and analysing the distribution, dissemination, or transmission of child pornography through information and communication technologies. This task is performed on the basis of Directive 2011/92/EU of the European Parliament and of the Council of 13 December 2011 on combating the sexual abuse and sexual exploitation of children and child pornography.[4]

The categories of content covered by the CSIRT NASK response procedure include child sexual abuse material, hard pornography, racism, and xenophobia, but also other illegal content which does not relate to either of these categories. All materials (photos and videos) displaying the sexual abuses of children are transferred to the ICCAM database to identify the victims and perpetrators. ICCAM is an integrated database for the exchange of information on CSAM (child sexual abuse materials). The legislators, in the discussed provision, explicitly indicated that the

[4]Directive 2011/93/EU of the European Parliament and of the Council of 13 December 2011 on combating the sexual abuse and sexual exploitation of children and child pornography, and replacing Council Framework Decision 2004/68/JHA, OJ EU 2011 L 335/1.

task of the CSIRT NASK was to undertake activities in the field of the analysis of cases of the distribution, dissemination, or transmission of child pornography by means of information and communication technologies. In order to fulfil this obligation, employees are allowed to be in possession of pornographic content. It should be stressed that the CSIRT NASK's activities will be within the limits of its statutory entitlements and obligations, and will not constitute a breach of Article 202 § 4a and 4b of the Penal Code. If the material featuring the sexual abuse of a child is on a server located in Poland, the information is forwarded to the National Police Headquarters. If the child sexual abuse material is located in a country covered by the operations of INHOPE Association, the information is forwarded to the response team of the country where the server is located, as well as to Interpol. If the child sexual abuse material is out of the reach of INHOPE, the information is forwarded to the National Police Headquarters and to Interpol.

This task is implemented by the CSIRT NASK through Dyżurnet.pl, a team of CSIRT NASK experts. This team belongs to the International Association of Internet Hotlines (INHOPE). More than 50 response teams from all over the world are members of the Association. The operations of all response teams and the law-enforcement agencies cooperating with them aim to identify the perpetrator and victim of sexual abuse as quickly as possible. The notification by the user and immediate action by the administrator facilitates a significant reduction in the dissemination of the material and a reduction in secondary victimisation.

The Polish legislators have defined the categories of entities and specific, named, entities for which the CSIRT GOV is competent. The tasks of the CSIRT GOV include the coordination of handling incidents reported by selected public finance sector entities: public authorities, including government-administration bodies, state control and law protection institutions and courts and tribunals, the Social Insurance Institution and funds managed by it, the Agricultural Social Insurance Fund and funds managed by the President of the Agricultural Social Insurance Fund, and the National Health Fund. Additionally, the CSIRT GOV is responsible for entities subordinate to or supervised by the Prime Minister, the National Bank of Poland, Bank Gospodarstwa Krajowego, and other entities whose communication and information systems or networks are covered by the uniform list of facilities, systems, equipment, and services included in the critical infrastructure prepared by the Director of the Government Centre for Security pursuant to the Act on Crisis Management, with the exception of entities whose incident handling is performed by the CSIRT MON.

The CSIRT GOV has jurisdiction over all critical infrastructures. The legislators have indicated that the entities whose incident handling is coordinated by the CSIRT NASK, if the incident involves information and communication systems or networks covered by the uniform list of facilities, systems, equipment, or services which are part of the critical infrastructure, prepared by the Director of the Government Centre for Security under the Crisis Management Act, fall within the competence of the CSIRT GOV. When determining the scope of the CSIRT GOV's competence in relation to critical infrastructure entities, it should be stressed that the principle is the

CSIRT GOV's competence, excluding entities subject to or supervised by the Minister of National Defence.

The legislators have obligated CSIRT teams to respect the range of their competence. In the event that the CSIRT MON, CSIRT NASK, or CSIRT GOV receives an incident notification from an entity for which it does not have an assigned coordination capability, it shall immediately forward that notification to the appropriate CSIRT, along with any information received. The notifier should also be informed of the transmission of the notification by virtue of the obligations incumbent on them. The National Cybersecurity System Act also provides for the possibility of the CSIRTs' entering into agreements under which the general responsibility of an individual CSIRT can be modified. These entities may also entrust each other with the performance of tasks in relation to certain entity types by agreement. When such an agreement is made, the CSIRT shall inform the entity in respect of which there has been a change of subordination. The notification should contain, in particular, the parties to the agreement, a list of entities in relation to which the CSIRT has been changed, and the effective date of the agreement, the obligation for the CSIRT to inform the entities concerned that the agreement has been made, and the address of the website on which the text of the agreement will be published.

Pursuant to Article 27 of the National Cybersecurity System Act, the CSIRT GOV and CSIRT MON are exclusive in relation to incidents linked to terrorist acts. The statement of reasons to the Act indicates that the purpose of introducing the provision was to maintain the consistency of the provisions of the NCSA with the provisions of the Act on Anti-Terrorism. Incidents associated with a terrorist act have been treated in a unique way, due to the seriousness of the threat. **The primary objective of the regulation is to increase the effectiveness of the Polish cybersecurity system, and thus to increase the security of all Polish citizens, by strengthening the mechanisms for coordinating actions, clarifying the tasks and responsibilities of the various CSIRTs and the rules of cooperation between them, and ensuring that effective action can be taken in the event of an incident related to a terrorist act.**

Whether a specific incident is related to terrorist activities might be difficult to identify during the notification phase. Here it is important to analyse in detail the causes of the incident and to exchange information between the CSIRT teams. In fact, only the CSIRT to which the incident has been reported may conduct an analysis of the incident, and it is the one which remains responsible for the correct classification. The CSIRT GOV is competent for incidents related to terrorist activities. The event of a terrorist nature is a situation which is suspected to have arisen as a result of an offence as specified in Article 115(20) of the Act of 6 June 1997—the Penal Code.[5] Pursuant to Article 115(20) of the Penal Code, a terrorist offence is a prohibited act with the aim of seriously intimidating a large number of people, to compel a public authority of the Republic of Poland or another state or an

[5] Act of 6 June 1997—the Penal Code, consolidated text, Polish Journal of Laws of 2020, item 1444, as amended.

authority of an international organisation to undertake or refrain from undertaking any specific act, or to cause any serious disruption to the system or the economy of the Republic of Poland or another state or international organisation, or threaten to commit any such act.[6] It is punishable by a maximum term of imprisonment of at least five years.

The CSIRT MON is competent for incidents related to events of a terrorist nature which compromise the security of the state's defence capabilities, the Armed Forces of the Republic of Poland, and organisational units of the Ministry of National Defence. Whenever an incident, the handling of which is coordinated by the responsible CSIRT MON, CSIRT NASK, or CSIRT GOV, is related to events of a terrorist nature, the coordination of incident handling will be assumed by the responsible CSIRT MON or CSIRT GOV, depending on the nature of the incident.

The Polish legislators have imposed an obligation on CSIRT MON, CSIRT NASK, and CSIRT GOV teams to inform other European Union Member States of incidents which affect them. This obligation relates to serious incidents reported by the operators of essential services. The information is transmitted through the Single Point of Contact, which is used for communication within the European Union. The exchange of information between EU Member States contributes to the objectives of the NIS Directive to achieve a high common level of security of network and information systems in the EU. The Single Point of Contact shall forward, at the request of the appropriate CSIRT MON, CSIRT NASK, or CSIRT GOV, notifications of a serious incident or an incident involving two or more Member States of the European Union to Single Points of Contact in other Member States of the European Union. It is also obligated to receive notifications of a serious incident involving two or more Member States of the European Union from the Single Points of Contact in other Member States of the European Union, followed by the transmission of these notifications to the CSIRT MON, CSIRT NASK, CSIRT GOV, or sectoral cybersecurity teams. A serious incident, reported by an operator of essential services, will be one associated with a serious deterioration or disruption to the provision of an essential service.

The appropriate CSIRT MON, CSIRT NASK, or CSIRT GOV may request from the Single Point of Contact that a report of a serious incident be forwarded to the Single Points of Contact in the other Member States of the European Union affected by such an incident. This obligation relates to serious incidents. The information is transmitted through the Minister for Digital Affairs, who performs the tasks of the Single Point of Contact.

Article 29 of the NCSA establishes the obligation for the responsible CSIRT to inform other EU Member States of incidents involving two or more Member States. This obligation has been imposed on all CSIRTs. Article 29 reflects the provisions laid down in Article 16(6) of the NIS Directive. In accordance with this Article, when a significant incident involves two or more Member States, the appropriate authority or CSIRT shall inform the other affected Member States. In so doing, the

[6] Węglowski (2018).

competent authorities, CSIRT, and Single Points of Contact shall protect the security and commercial interests of the digital service provider, as well as the confidentiality of the information transmitted. This obligation concerns significant incidents. A significant incident is an incident which has a substantial impact on the provision of a digital service. These are incidents which are reported by digital service providers. Digital service providers shall, without undue delay, report to the appropriate CSIRT any incident having a significant impact on the provision of a service afforded by those providers in the Union. These notifications must contain information enabling the appropriate CSIRT to determine the significance of the cross-border impact. The notification must not expose the notifying party to increased liability.

Digital service providers should ensure a level of security commensurate with the level of risk to which the security of their digital services is exposed, considering the importance of those services for the activities of other businesses in the Union. This article is applicable to digital service providers. The EU legislators have noted that the degree of risk to the operators of essential services—which are often crucial for maintaining critical societal and economic activities—is higher than for digital service providers. The security requirements for digital service providers should therefore be reduced. Digital service providers should be permitted to adopt measures they consider appropriate to manage the risks to which the security of their network and information systems might be exposed. The CSIRT MON, CSIRT NASK, or CSIRT GOV shall inform the other Member States of the European Union about the incident via the Single Point of Contact.

The NCSA also defines the rules for incident notification to the CSIRT NASK by entities other than operators of essential services and digital service providers, including individuals. For the purpose of receiving voluntary incident notifications, the CSIRT NASK is the responsible entity. Entities not identified as operators of essential services and which are not digital service providers may, on a voluntary basis, report incidents which have a significant impact on the continuity of the services they provide. A voluntary notification may not result in the imposition of any obligations on the notifying party to which they would not be subject if they had not done this notification. The entity which voluntarily reports an incident to the CSIRT NASK is required to provide its name, or details of the information system in which the incident occurred. Secondly, it should describe the incident, which must be an event which has an adverse effect on cybersecurity. The notification is made by filling in the form available on incydent.cert.pl, and specifying the category. These categories are grouped into (1) suspicious e-mails (suspicious attachments, phishing, blackmail), (2) attempts at fraud (fake online shops and other attempts at impersonation), (3) malware (virus samples or ransomware-encrypted files), (4) vulnerabilities (errors in software or web applications), (5) illegal content (notifications intended for the Dyżurnet.pl team), (6) and other (all incidents not matching the previous categories).

The notification shall contain all the appropriate information on the incident. This information should be useful for the CSIRT. As an example, the source from which the applicant learned about the site, and the bank account number for transferring money may be mentioned. Information which is legally protected, including trade secrets, should be clearly identified in the notification. The legislators, in Article 30 (2) of the NCSA, stipulated that the CSIRT NASK should deal with incident reports from operators of essential services and digital service providers, i.e. mandatory notifications as a priority over voluntary notifications. Voluntary notifications are examined only if such an examination does not impose a disproportionate or excessive burden on the Member States involved. In this context, it should be recognised that anyone who is concerned about a specific cybersecurity incident may report the incident to the CSIRT NASK.

The Polish legislators have granted individual CSIRTs the responsibility to determine how notifications should be submitted. It should be noted that the CSIRT MON, CSIRT NASK, and CSIRT GOV have been responding to incidents for several years, maintaining cybersecurity. The legislators have recognised that the solutions developed by individual CSIRTs in the field of incident notification and communication with their entities, taking into consideration the specificity of each entity's operations, may still be implemented. Pursuant to Article 31, it is possible to determine the manner in which notifications are to be made and information provided in electronic form.

The independence of a CSIRT in respect of the entities for which it is responsible concerns

(1) serious incidents which must be reported by the operators of essential services
(2) significant incidents which must be reported by digital service providers
(3) incidents in a public entity, to be reported by the public entities
(4) information from the operators of essential services, digital service providers, and public entities on other serious incidents, cyber threats, risk estimation, vulnerabilities and technologies used
(5) other than the above-mentioned incidents, which may be reported by entities not covered by the obligation to notify of incidents, on a voluntary basis.

The legislators reserve within the ambit of the CSIRT MON, CSIRT NASK, and CSIRT GOV the technical issues of notifications. These notifications may be submitted by electronic means as well as by other communication media where it is not possible to submit the notification or to transmit it by electronic means. The manner of notification and communication should be specified in the communication. The notice is published on the website of the Public Information Bulletin of the Minister of National Defence, Research and Academic Computer Network—the National Research Institute, or the Internal Security Agency, respectively.

Electronic incident notification for the CSIRT MON is made by filling in the Incident Notification Form. As regards the CSIRT NASK, the electronic incident notification takes place using the form available on the incydent.cert.pl website. The form is completed under one of these categories: (1) suspicious e-mails, (suspicious attachments, phishing, blackmail), (2) attempts at fraud (fake online shops and other attempts at impersonation), (3) malware (virus samples or ransomware-encrypted files), (4) vulnerabilities (errors in software or web applications), (5) illegal content (notifications intended for the Dyżurnet.pl team), (6) other (all incidents not falling into the previous categories). The electronic reporting of an incident in the case of the CSIRT GOV is made via the form available on csirt.gov.pl.

The Polish legislators have introduced the principle that the CSIRT MON, CSIRT NASK, or CSIRT GOV may conduct an inspection of an IT device or software to identify vulnerabilities, the use of which might, in particular, jeopardise the integrity, confidentiality, accountability, authenticity, or availability of the data processed, and which may affect public security or vital national security interests. The subject of the inspection may be an IT device or software. The purpose of the investigation is to identify vulnerabilities which, in particular, can jeopardise the integrity, confidentiality, accountability, authenticity, or availability of the data processed, where such vulnerability might affect public security or a substantial national security interest.

Data integrity is the confirmation that the data sent, received, or stored are complete and in an unaltered state, and that the resources of the information system have not been unlawfully modified. Data confidentiality is a property which ensures that information is not disclosed to unauthorised persons. It means protecting communications or stored data against interception and reading by unauthorised persons. Accountability means the property of a system which allows specific activities to be assigned to a person or process and placed in time. Authenticity refers to the feature that the data content or origin is as declared. The last feature, the availability of the processed data, is the property determining that the data may be used on request, within the assumed period of time, by an entity authorised to work in a communication and information system.

The legislators have established in Article 33(2) of the NCSA an obligation to declare the fact of undertaking an inspection of an IT device or software. If one of the CSIRTs initiates an inspection of an IT device or software, it shall inform the other CSIRTs. The information should indicate which specific IT device or software is being tested. This solution is designed to prevent the duplication of activities by the individual CSIRT teams. The CSIRT MON, CSIRT NASK, or CSIRT GOV informs the other CSIRTs of the results.

Following the testing of an IT device or software, the CSIRT should prepare a report which includes its findings and conclusions. Where it is established that there is a vulnerability whose use can have an impact on public security or a substantial national security interest, the CSIRT shall request a recommendation for the use of a given IT device or software. The request is addressed to the Plenipotentiary for Cybersecurity.

Recommendations shall be issued by the Plenipotentiary after obtaining the approval of the College for Cybersecurity. The Plenipotentiary is also entitled to change and cancel the recommendation concerning the use of IT devices or software. Both the amendment and the withdrawal of the recommendation require the approval of the College. Recommendations are not administrative decisions. The statement of reasons to the Act indicates that recommendations are a positive measure, which means that they may recommend the software in question or consider it undesirable. Recommendations should also be a voluntary measure, which means that they cannot bind private entities. It is designed to raise user awareness, supporting the safe use of hardware and software. Recommendations are of an abstract nature, which means that the Plenipotentiary should inform all entities of the national cybersecurity system which might be affected by the vulnerability when the recommendation is issued.

An entity of the national cybersecurity system may raise objections to the Plenipotentiary's recommendations concerning the use of IT devices or software, on the grounds of their negative impact on the service provided, or the public task being performed, no later than within 7 days of the receipt of the recommendation. The Plenipotentiary should address the concerns received from the national cybersecurity system operator without delay, but no later than 14 days after receipt. As a result of examining the objections, the Plenipotentiary may uphold the recommendations concerning the use of IT equipment or software, or issue amended recommendations. If the objections are deemed justified, the amended content of the recommendation shall be subject to the approval of the College. If the recommendations concerning the use of IT equipment or software are not taken into consideration, the Plenipotentiary is entitled to apply to the authority supervising the entity to which the recommendation relates for them to be disregarded. The supervisory authority, within the scope of its responsibilities, may take supervisory measures.

The NCSA has established the principle of cooperation between the CSIRT MON, CSIRT NASK, CSIRT GOV and sectoral cybersecurity teams and service providers, with law enforcement authorities, as well as with the justice and intelligence services, in the performance of their statutory tasks. The legislators have thus highlighted that the CSIRT teams play an extremely significant role in counteracting cybercrime. This might arise from the fact that these entities have knowledge and experience in incident analysis. The CSIRT MON, CSIRT NASK, and CSIRT GOV, while coordinating incident handling, are obligated to determine whether an incident involves personal data. If the incident is found to have resulted in a personal data breach, the CSIRT is required to cooperate with the authority responsible for personal data protection.

Operators of essential services, digital service providers, and public entities, in the case of an incident resulting in a personal data breach, in addition to the obligation to notify the appropriate CSIRT of the incident, pursuant to the GDPR regulation, are also obligated to report such a violation to the President of the Personal Data Protection Office.

According to Article 31 of the GDPR, the controller and processor shall cooperate with the supervisory authority in the performance of their tasks. In the case of a personal data breach, the controller shall, without undue delay, where possible not later than 72 h after having established the breach, report it to the supervisory authority, unless the breach is unlikely to result in a risk of jeopardising the rights and freedoms of natural persons. Where the notification to the supervisory authority is not made within 72 h, it shall be accompanied by reasons for the delay (Article 33 (1) of GDPR).

Under Article 35 of the NCSA, the legislators provided for a specific category of incidents, i.e. critical incidents. These are incidents with the most significant importance, resulting in considerable damage to public safety or order, international interests, economic interests, the operation of public institutions, civil rights and freedoms, or the lives and health of people. Each time an incident is classified as critical by the CSIRT team, and the identification of such an incident by each CSIRT is related to the requirement to inform the other CSIRTs about the incident and to notify the Government Centre for Security. The information should include a preliminary analysis of the potential effects of the incident. This analysis should identify the number of users affected by the incident (especially if it disrupts the provision of an essential service), the moment when the incident occurred and was detected, and its duration, as well as the geographical coverage of the affected area. The information should include a description of the incident, specifying its nature, course, and technical characteristics.

The information may include a recommendation to establish a Government Crisis Management Team. It is a consultative and advisory authority responsible for initiating and coordinating crisis management activities, operating within the structures of the Council of Ministers. The team is composed of the Prime Minister, as the Chairperson, the Minister of National Defence and the Minister competent for public administration, the Minister of Foreign Affairs and the Minister Coordinator of Special Services. The tasks of the Government Crisis Management Team include preparing proposals for the use of the forces and resources necessary to manage a crisis situation, and advising on the coordination of actions by government administration authorities, state institutions and services in crisis situations, as well as providing opinions on the final reports on actions taken regarding crisis management.

The Act also provides for the possibility of including in the information a request to convene a Critical Incidents Team. Apparently, a critical incident event may be qualified as a crisis situation as referred to in the Act on Crisis Management. A crisis situation is defined as any situation which adversely affects the level of security of individuals, property of substantial size, or the environment, causing significant constraints on the operation of the responsible public authorities due to the inadequacy of the forces and the resources available. Immediate cooperation, together with the exchange of information and the coordination of actions, are essential elements in the event of a critical incident. The CSIRT which has classified an incident as critical transfers information to the other CSIRT teams. All CSIRT teams are authorised to inform each other in the event of intelligence on cybersecurity threats. These are potential sources of incidents. Moreover, this appears to refer to cybersecurity threats that might contribute to a critical incident. Therefore, it would be inappropriate to communicate all the threats identified by individual CSIRTs. The CSIRT may also inform the Government Centre for Security on these threats. The Government Centre for Security is the state entity established under Article 10 of the Act on Crisis Management. It reports to the Prime Minister. One of the tasks of the Government Centre for Security is to support the Critical Incidents Team.

All CSIRTs have also been authorised to publish on the website of the Public Information Bulletin of, respectively, the Minister of National Defence—the CSIRT MON, the Research and Academic Computer Network—the National Research

Institute—the CSIRT NASK, or the Internal Security Agency—the CSIRT GOV, information, to the extent necessary, on vulnerabilities, critical incidents, and threats to cybersecurity, provided that the provision of the information contributes to increasing the cybersecurity of the information systems used by citizens and businesses, or to ensuring the safe use of those systems. The information disclosed may not violate the regulations on the protection of classified information and other legally protected secrets, or the regulations on personal data protection. The publication of information on vulnerabilities, critical incidents, and threats to cybersecurity should contribute to increasing the security of systems and public awareness of the hazards. Such publication may be accompanied by information relating to risk prevention and advice.

The adoption by the Polish legislators of several entities responsible for performing duties related to the security of networks and IT systems owned by operators of essential services and digital service providers—three national level CSIRTs: the CSIRT MON, CSIRT NASK, and CSIRT GOV—resulted in the obligation to establish a team which would coordinate the activities undertaken by the CSIRT MON, CSIRT NASK, CSIRT GOV, and the Government Centre for Security. In the article discussed, the legislators appointed the Critical Incidents Team, which coordinates the activities of the three CSIRTs, and exchanges information in the event of a critical incident.

It is composed of representatives of the CSIRT MON, the CSIRT NASK, the Head of the Internal Security Agency implementing the tasks of the CSIRT GOV, and the Government Centre for Security. The Team's work is managed by the Director of the Government Centre for Security. The Centre also supports the operations of the Team. According to the statement of reasons for the Act, this is an auxiliary body which should provide organisational and technical assistance for critical incidents. This Team is therefore not a decision-making unit. The work of the Team is convened by the Director of the Government Centre for Security. The Director is obligated to convene the Team on his or her own initiative after being notified of the occurrence of a critical incident, at the request of a Team member, and if the request to call the Team results from CSIRT information on the occurrence of the said incident. The Director of the Government Centre for Security shall immediately notify the members of the Team of the date and venue of the Team's meeting. Participation in the meeting of the Group may take place by electronic means of communication. Electronic-communication means shall be understood not only as technical solutions, but also as information and communication devices and associated software tools enabling individual communication at a distance using data transmission between communication and information systems, in particular e-mail.

The actions taken by the Team at meetings include unanimously designating the CSIRT coordinating critical incident handling, and defining the roles of the other CSIRTs and the Government Centre for Security in dealing with the incident. The designation of the leading entity enables all information to be gathered in one place. The Team also determines the manner in which technical information on the critical incident shall be exchanged between the CSIRT MON, CSIRT NASK, or CSIRT GOV. The Team's responsibility also includes adopting decisions requiring the

Director of the Government Centre for Security to submit a request to the Prime Minister to convene the Government Crisis Management Team. The decision to call the Government Crisis Management Team relates to situations in which such critical incidents might result in crisis situations within the meaning of the Act on Crisis Management. Where a critical incident might result in the threat of a terrorist act involving the information and communication systems of public authorities, or information and communication systems which form a critical infrastructure, the Team prepares information and conclusions on such an incident for the Minister competent for the Interior and the Head of the Internal Security Agency. According to the information provided, CRP alert levels (alerts related to threats in the cyber-space) may be announced.

CRP alert levels are introduced pursuant to Article 15(2) of the Act of 10 June 2016 on Anti-Terrorism. There are four CRP alert levels. Where there is a threat of a terrorist incident involving information and communication systems of public administrations, or information and communication systems which are part of the critical infrastructure, or where such an event occurs, one of the four CRP alert levels may be introduced.

(1) First CRP alert level (ALFA-CRP level);
(2) Second CRP alert level (BRAVO-CRP level);
(3) Third CRP alert level (CHARLIE-CRP level);
(4) Fourth CRP alert level (DELTA-CRP level).

The first alert level may be introduced when there is intelligence on the possibility of a terrorist event, the type and extent of which is difficult to predict. The second alert level may be introduced in the event of an increased and foreseeable threat of a terrorist act, although the specific target of the attack has not been identified. The third alert level may be introduced in the event of an occurrence of incidents confirming the probable target of a terrorist attack which is detrimental to the security or public order or safety of the Republic of Poland, or the security of another state or international organisation, and poses a potential threat to the Republic of Poland; or in the event of obtaining reliable and confirmed information about a planned terrorist event on the territory of the Republic of Poland; or in the event of obtaining reliable and confirmed evidence of a planned terrorist act, the consequences of which might affect Polish citizens residing abroad or Polish institutions or Polish infrastructure located outside the Republic of Poland. The fourth level may be introduced in the event of the occurrence of any event of a terrorist nature which causes a threat to public security or order, or to the security of the Republic of Poland, or to the security of another country or international organisation, and poses a threat to the Republic of Poland intelligence being obtained indicating an advanced stage of preparation for a terrorist event on the territory of the Republic of Poland, intelligence being obtained indicating an advanced stage of preparation for a terrorist event which is to be targeted at Polish citizens residing abroad, or at Polish institutions or Polish infrastructure located outside the borders of the Republic of Poland, whereas the information obtained indicates the inevitability of such an event.

The alert levels are introduced, modified, or cancelled by way of an Order—depending on the type of threat posed by the terrorist event—by the Prime Minister, following consultation with the Minister competent for internal affairs and the Head of the Internal Security Agency, and, in urgent cases, by the Minister competent for internal affairs after consulting the Head of the Internal Security Agency, informing the Prime Minister promptly.

Reference

Węglowski MG (2018) Działania antyterrorystyczne. Komentarz, Warsaw

Monika Nowikowska PhD, adjunct at the Department of Cybersecurity Law and New Technologies of the Institute of Law of the War Studies University. Author of several dozen scientific publications in the field of intellectual property law and the media. He also specializes in issues related to security, such as audit, protection of classified information and personal data. Internal auditor, legal advisor.

Tasks of the Minister of National Defence in the Field of Cybersecurity

Krzysztof Wąsowski

Abstract This article is an attempt to analyse the legal position of the Minister of National Defence of the Republic of Poland in the sphere of the national cybersecurity system. The author distinguishes a large number of types of functions of this public administration entity. On the other hand, the author conducts an analysis of cybersecurity competence of the independent bodies responsible for the cyberspace system security in Poland. The author demonstrates that the Minister of National Defence plays a crucial role in the Polish cybersecurity system in the context of the state's external security.

1 The Notion of a Task Within the Domain of Public Administration—The Responsibilities Associated with the Activities of a Public-Administration Authority

The tasks involved in the activities carried out by a public administration authority are described by administrative law commentators as the notion of competence within which a given public administration authority should operate. In this sense, a "task" is often identified with the so-called material competence of a public administration authority.[1] However, the issue of the material responsibility of a public administration authority is worth analysing from a broader perspective. As Z. Cieślak suggests,

> (...) the notion of "competence" in this context goes beyond legal categories, because it relates to the fundamentals of creating administrative structures (the organisational structure

[1] Cf. Cieślak (2013), p. 81.

K. Wąsowski (✉)
Akademickie Centrum Polityki Cyberbezpieczeństwa/Academic Center for Cybersecurity Policy, Akademia Sztuki Wojennej w Warszawie/War Studies University in Warsaw, Warsaw, Poland
e-mail: k.wasowski@akademia.mil.pl

K. Chałubińska-Jentkiewicz et al. (eds.), *Cybersecurity in Poland*,
https://doi.org/10.1007/978-3-030-78551-2_16

of public administration reflects the structure of its administrative objectives, tasks, and affairs) and the rules of their functioning (. . .).[2]

According to the author, "competence" in its broader perspective may be characterised as "the sum, type, and content of affairs encompassed by the legally non-indifferent activities of an entity."[3] On the other hand, from a strictly procedural perspective, competence is interpreted as only a specific "range of matters" assigned by Acts, which a given entity (a public administration authority or judicial authority) should resolve within its statutory powers.[4] Therefore, legal procedure experts associate the powers and obligations (competence) of a specific authority with the notion of the "legal capacity of authorities", defining it as a "set of premises exerting a decisive impact on the capacity to take procedural steps in administrative proceedings", and these premises, in turn, are determined by the norms of procedural law.[5]

Traditionally administrative law commentators generally linked the notion of the "scope of the activities" (competence, or powers and obligations) of a specific authority to the so-called "task norms" regulating the tasks which should be carried out by a specific administrative authority. This approach was linked to the normative system of a specific public administration authority.[6] Task norms show the subjective correlation between the activities carried out by public administration authorities and the legal forms of conduct attributed to such activities. Therefore, administrative law norms combine a significance for the state political system with the obligations of a substantive law nature. It should also be stressed that when the tasks in the domain of public administration are carried out in specific matters, they are based on "competence norms".[7] In the light of the constitutional principle of legality, concerning the activities of public administration authorities (defined in Article 7 of the Constitution of the Republic of Poland[8]), the responsibility of a public administration authority must arise from the provisions of generally applicable law. Structural legal norms regulating competence—whether defined in a broader, political-system-related, or strictly procedural context—should encompass the four basic

---

[2]Cieślak (2013), p. 81.

[3]*Ibidem*; The same author defines "competence" in the context of the administration theory (as opposed to the legal approach) as the "notion describing the static-structural foundations of conduct, the so-called who and what components". Obviously, this definition is not sufficient within the state-administration system, and must always be accompanied by a description of the functional-dynamic components, because the ability to act (operational capacity) is never equal to the performance (execution). These two actual aspects of conduct, complementing each other, are reflected in the normative approach, and—strictly speaking—in the types of legal norms—see Cieślak (1992), p. 28.

[4]Compare Adamiak (1998), pp. 119–120.

[5]Also, Adamiak (1998), p. 119.

[6]This issue is presented as such by, i.a. Dawidowicz (1974), p. 57 or Filipek (1974), p. 44.

[7]Similarly, Borkowski (1980), also Dawidowicz (1989), p. 18.

[8]Article 7 of the Constitution of the Republic of Poland states "The bodies of public authority shall function on the basis of, and within the limits of, the law."

components: time, place, subjective features, and the subject of the activities. The essence of the time criterion in the reconstruction of competence (powers and obligations) of the activities of a public administration authority is the basis for the reconstruction of the "rules updating the capacity for action by an individualised entity.[9]"

2 The Position of the Minister of National Defence in the State System

The Minister of National Defence is the central public administration authority, managing the activities carried out by the department of government administration called "national defence",[10] and a monocratic component of the central collective authority, namely, the Council of Ministers.[11] In the light of the Constitution, the Minister of National Defence acts as an intermediary in the authority of the President of the Republic of Poland over the Polish Armed Forces in peacetime.[12] In a hierarchical structure, the role of the Minister of National Defence is threefold. First of all, the Minister of National Defence is an independent authority of the government administration with independent responsibilities and tasks (arising from the Act on the Authority of the Minister of National Defence and the Act on the Tasks of Government Administration[13]). Second, it acts as an entity, being part of a collective authority that is the Council of Ministers subject to the authority of the Prime Minister.[14] Third, the Minister of National Defence is subject to a certain form of command of the President of the Republic of Poland in terms of having power

[9]Similarly, Cieślak (1992), p. 56.

[10]See Article 1(1) of the Act of 14 December 1995 on the Authority of the Minister of National Defence, Polish Journal of Laws of 2019, item 196, as amended; ("the AAMND").

[11]Cf. Article 1 of the Act of 8 August 1996 on the Council of Ministers, Polish Journal of Laws of 2019, item 1171, as amended; ("the ACM").

[12]See Article 134(2) of the Constitution of the Republic of Poland, and Article 1(1) of the AAMND—it should also be noted that neither the Constitution of the Republic of Poland nor the AAMND refer to the essence of the role of intermediation of the Minister of National Defence in the command of the President of the Republic of Poland over the Armed Forces of the Republic of Poland in peacetime, or to the forms and courses of the performance of this legal relation. The authorisation to file applications to the President of the Republic of Poland for the conferring of a military rank specified in the Act is the second constitutional duty—attributed strictly to the Minister of National Defence.

[13]The Act on Government Administration Departments (the GAD Act), which uses both the terms "Minister competent for matters of national defence" (Article 19(2) of the GAD Act) and "Minister of National Defence" (Article 19(3) of the GAD Act).

[14]See Article 148(2) of the Constitution of the Republic of Poland and Article 6(1) *a contrario* the ACM.

over the Polish Armed Forces in times of peace[15] and conferring the military ranks.[16] On the other hand, as regards the activities of an entity mentioned in the legal norms defining the responsibilities of the Minister of National Defence (apart from the task of "intermediation" in the authority of the President of the Republic of Poland over the Polish Armed Forces in peacetime), its role is limited only to managing the department of government administration called "National Defence".[17] According to the GAD Act, the National Defence Department (limited in time—which is quite unique in comparison to other departments of government administration—to the "time of peace") encompasses the following affairs: state defence, the Armed Forces of the Republic of Poland, the security of the cyberspace in the military dimension, the participation of the Republic of Poland in the military projects of international organisations, and fulfilling the military tasks arising from international agreements and offset agreements.[18] The task norm—defining the scope of activities—entrusts to the Minister of National Defence a wide scope of matters, from managing (in peacetime) the entire operations of the Armed Forces through the operational, executive, and personnel matters concerning the performance of state defence tasks, by implementing the commitments arising from the military obligations undertaken by the Council of Ministers, to the performance of tasks as *statio fisci,* a state or local government organisational unit acting for and on behalf of the State Treasury.[19]

3 The National Cybersecurity System

Undoubtedly, globally noticeable technological advancements have taken place in the recent decades, especially in the field of telecommunications and information technologies, which have had an increasing (nearly decisive) impact, not only on the economic life of societies, but also on matters of the security of citizens, including national defence and security. Digital technologies provide not only huge opportunities but also pose significant risks, as reflected in the growing number of what is known as computer incidents.[20] The situation has been addressed at the supranational level. In particular, in 2013, the European Commission and the High

[15] Article 134(2) of the Constitution of the Republic of Poland.

[16] Article 134(5) of the Constitution of the Republic of Poland.

[17] See Article 1(1) of the AAMND.

[18] See Article 19(1) of the GAD Act. The specific statutory proviso, making the attribution of this jurisdiction to the Minister of National Defence conditional on the autonomous responsibilities of the President of the Republic of Poland or other state authorities, forming, at the same time, a rule concerning conflict if any doubts about interpretations arise in the case of so-called overlapping of responsibilities of individual authorities, is worth noting.

[19] Cf. Article 2, (1)–(23) of the AAMND.

[20] The issue has been more extensively discussed in numerous studies and reports, i.e. *The security landscape of the Polish Internet 2016. The annual report on the activities of CERT Polska*, NASK, https://www.cert.pl/PDF/Raport_CP_2016.pdf. Accessed 11 June 2020.

Representative of the Union for Foreign Affairs and Security Policy published the Communication on a Cybersecurity Strategy of the European Union—An Open, Safe and Secure Cyberspace,[21] accompanied by a legislative proposal for a Directive concerning cybersecurity. Directive (EU) 2016/1148 of the European Parliament and of the Council concerning measures for a high common level of security of network and information systems across the Union was adopted on 6 July 2016. It imposed on all Member States the obligation to create a system capable of ensuring the necessary level of cybersecurity in information systems in service sectors of key importance for the maintenance of critical societal and/or economic activities, such as energy, transport, banking, financial institutions, health protection, water supply, and digital infrastructure. The specified administrative system, encompassing specialised public administration authorities and related administrative entities (such as Computer Security Incident Response Teams[22]), acting in line with the principle of a single point of contact responsible for the cybersecurity, is intended to be the mechanism supporting and coordinating the functioning of the entire system. The NIS Directive obliged the Member States of the European Union to implement its provisions until 9 May 2018 (however, it is an example of so-called minimum harmonisation, not preventing the Member States from extending the level of cybersecurity required under the Directive). While implementing the obligations imposed under the above-mentioned Directive, Poland began legislative action in April 2017 when the Council of Ministers issued Resolution No. 52/2017 adopting a strategic document on cyberspace in the form of the National Framework of Cybersecurity Policy of the Republic of Poland for 2017–2022. At that time, the Ministry of Digital Affairs started work on the draft of the Act implementing the NIS Directive. The process of inter-Ministry agreements and consultations,[23] completed with the decision of the Council of Ministers' handing over the draft of the Act for parliamentary debate, was started on 8 January 2018.[24] The bill was submitted to the Sejm on 30 April 2018,[25] which adopted the National Cybersecurity System Act.

The main objective of the Act, in force as of 28 August 2018, was to organise and define the functioning of the National Cybersecurity System.[26] The statutory objective was reached in the form of a direct regulatory effect encompassing the named

[21]Join (2013) 1 Final, 07.02.2013.

[22]CSIRT—Eng. Computer Security Incident Response Teams.

[23]The detailed course of the process, and the documentation referring to it, are published on the website of the Government Legislation Centre (Rządowe Centrum Legislacji)—https://legislacja.rcl.gov.pl/projekt/12304650/katalog/12466714#12466714. Accessed 11 June 2020.

[24]See Memorandum of Understanding No. 17/2018 of the meeting of the Council of Ministers held on 26 April 2018 (RM-000-17-18) https://legislacja.rcl.gov.pl/docs//2/12304650/12466740/12466745/dokument341423.pdf. Accessed 11 June 2020.

[25]The Sejm document was given the number 2505. For the detailed course of the Parliamentary work, see http://www.sejm.gov.pl/Sejm8.nsf/PrzebiegProc.xsp?nr=2505. Accessed 11 June 2020.

[26]See the impact assessment of a legal Act concerning the draft of the National Cybersecurity System Act—https://legislacja.rcl.gov.pl/projekt/12304650/katalog/12466714#12466714. Accessed 11 June 2020.

sectors of the national economy, defining the criteria for the identification of the operators of essential services, defining the minimum requirements for the information and communications security of the information systems belonging to operators of essential services and digital service providers, and stipulating the statutory requirements and responsibilities of the Computer Security Incident Response Teams in the field of cybersecurity. Undoubtedly, the test concerning the performance of control and supervisory functions of the responsible public administration authorities defined in the law, regardless of whether their status is of a systemic or just functional nature, will be of key importance for the reliable functioning of the system (administrative structure) from the praxeological point of view.

The systematics of the Act was established on the basis of a model entailing a link between a specific state system hierarchy of various categories and functions of public administration authorities and other administrative entities with tasks attributed to them, and correlated with the responsibilities of the administered entities, defined in the law and characteristic for regulatory legal acts. Customarily, the legislators have separated the control powers (slightly excessively combining them with control responsibilities) of the authorised staff of broadly defined administrative entities. The relatively modern penalty system in the form of financial administrative penalties was additionally implemented, and this will undoubtedly strengthen the importance and "effectiveness" of the control procedure. On the other hand, the "penal-administrative" procedure will definitely be the basic instrument for the implementation of the supervisory (*ex-post*) competences, and together with *ex-ante* supervision instruments (especially, involving decisions on permits) should result in a variety of regulating tools allowing the effective stimulation of the conduct of entities functioning on relevant markets.

4 The Task Norms of the Minister of National Defence Within the Framework of the National Cybersecurity System

In the National Cybersecurity System Act, the Minister of National Defence is mentioned in at least four basic state system dimensions. First of all, as the authority competent for these matters and a component of the National Cybersecurity System.[27] Second, as an independent coordination-control-management authority having the separate tasks entrusted to it by the legislators.[28] Third, as an authority supervising[29] the Computer Security Incident Response Team (the CSIRT MON) functioning at the national level. Fourth, as a member of the collegial body (the College for Cybersecurity), being an advisory and opinion-forming authority of the

[27]See Article 4(17) in conjunction with Article 41(6), (9) and (11) of the NCSA.

[28]Cf. Chapter 10 of the NCSA.

[29]This follows directly from Article 2(2) of the NCSA.

Council of Ministers on cybersecurity.[30] It should also be noted that the adoption of the law on the National Cybersecurity System modified the Act on the Departments of Government Administration[31] to some extent, dividing a subdivision component of "cyberspace security", into a unit functioning within the "civil dimension" (attributing this component to the department of "digitisation")[32] and one functioning in the "military dimension" (attributing this component to the department of "national defence").[33]

As mentioned earlier, the Minister of National Defence is a component of the national security system due to being named in the law as the authority responsible for the cybersecurity of the following sectors: (1).The health-protection sector—encompassing entities subordinate to or supervised by the Minister of National Defence, including entities whose information and communication systems and networks are included in a uniform list of facilities, installations, equipment, and services forming critical infrastructure,[34] and encompassing enterprises of special economic and defence importance and their performance of tasks in the field of the national defence, as organised and supervised by the Minister of National Defence;[35] (2) The digital infrastructure sector—for entities listed in the same way;[36] (3) digital service providers encompassing the same entities as defined above.[37]

Within the named sectors and in respect of the said digital service providers, due to their status as "authorities competent for cybersecurity", the legislators entrust to the Minister of National Defence the authority of a superior ("imperial") nature, encompassing, in particular, (1) the competence to issue decisions on recognising a specific entity as an operator of essential services;[38] (2) the competence to issue decisions on the annulment of decisions recognising an entity as an operator of essential services;[39] (3) the establishment of a cybersecurity team for a given sector or subsector[40] (however, in discharging this duty, the authority competent for cybersecurity is obliged to provide information to the operators of essential services in a given sector and to the CSIRT MON, CSIRT NASK, and CSIRT GOV);[41]

[30]See Article 64 in conjunction with Article 66(1)(4)(c) of the NCSA.

[31]See Article 78 of the NCSA.

[32]See Article 12a(1) (10) of the GAD Act.

[33]See Article 19(1) (1a) of the GAD Act.

[34]See Article 41(6) in conjunction with Article 26(5) of NCSA in conjunction with Article 5b (7) (1) of the Act on Crisis Management.

[35]See Article 41(6) in conjunction with Article 26(5) of NCSA in conjunction with Article 5(3) of the Act on Organisation of National Defence Tasks Performed by Entrepreneurs.

[36]See Article 41(9) in conjunction with Article 26(5) of NCSA.

[37]See Article 41(11) in conjunction with Article 26(5) of NCSA.

[38]See Article 5(1) in conjunction with Article 42(1)(2) of NCSA.

[39]See Article 5(6) in conjunction with Article 42(1)(2) of NCSA.

[40]See Article 44(1) of NCSA.

[41]See Article 44(4) of NCSA.

(4) the competence to impose administrative financial penalties[42] forming instruments of supervision exercised in respect of operators of essential services and digital service providers, and, under exceptional circumstances, also in respect of the head of an operator of an essential service.[43] In addition to the clearly defined tasks performed in the capacity of a superior authority, the legislators have entrusted to the Minister of National Defence, being the authority competent for cybersecurity, an entire set of tasks to be carried out in a non-superior, substantive, and technical or organisational capacity, arising from the control and information tasks.[44]

The legislators have entrusted a separate group of tasks to the Minister of National Defence as a specialised, autonomous public administration authority distinguished in the National Cybersecurity System Act.[45] Within these tasks, the Minister of National Defence was entrusted with various competences, within the scope of the performance of these "superior",[46] legal forms of activity, and those of a "non-superior"—control[47] or strictly organisational[48] or substantive and technical

[42]See Article 53(2)(2) in conjunction with Article 74(1) of NCSA.

[43]See Article 75 of the NCSA.

[44]Examples of such tasks-powers-responsibilities can be found in Article 42(1) of the NCSA, in which the legislators included the possibility of "entrusting certain tasks to be carried out on its behalf (...) to entities subordinate to or supervised by the authority" (Article 42(3) of the NCSA), also including in the form of an "agreement", (Article 42(4) of the NCSA), in which "the principles for carrying out the supervision over the proper performance of entrusted tasks by the authority responsible for cybersecurity" should be defined (Article 42(5) of the NCSA). To learn more about the issue of the canonical-theoretical concept of an administrative agreement as the legal form of the activities of public-administration authorities, see Cieślak (1982).

[45]See Chapter 10 of the NCSA—"The Tasks of the Minister of National Defence."

[46]This pertains, *inter alia*, to the superior competence for managing activities concerning incidents in times of a state of emergency (see Article 51(5) of the NCSA) or the operations of the National Contact Point for cooperation with the North Atlantic Treaty Organisation (see Article 52 of the NCSA).

[47]In particular, the procurement of tools for capacity-building for ensuring cybersecurity in the Polish Armed Forces (see Article 51(4) of the NCSA), the assessment of the impact of incidents on the state defence system (see Article 51(6) of the NCSA), the assessment of hazards to cybersecurity in times of a state of emergency (see, *in principio*, Article 51(7) of the NCSA) or the development of the systems for sharing information on cybersecurity in the sphere of national defence (see Article 52(4) of the NCSA).

[48]*Inter alia*, cooperation between the Armed Forces of the Republic of Poland and the appropriate authorities of the North Atlantic Treaty Organisation, the European Union, and international organisations in the field of state defence in terms of cybersecurity (see Article 51(1) of the NCSA); providing the Armed Forces of the Republic of Poland with the capacities to carry out military actions within the national, coalition, and allied systems, when there is a threat to cybersecurity introducing the need to undertake defensive measures (see Article 51(2) of the NCSA); developing the skills of the Armed Forces of the Republic of Poland in ensuring cybersecurity by organising special training projects (see Article 51(3) of the NCSA); and developing tools for capacity-building involving the assurance of cybersecurity in the Armed Forces of the Republic of Poland (see Article 51(4) of the NCSA).

character.[49] The legislators entrusted the Minister of National Defence with responsibilities involving tasks in the field of cybersecurity in a specific manner.

The legislators have specified the performance of tasks entrusted to the Minister towards the newly established entity, namely, the CSIRT MON, in an extensive and open manner. Apart from the task of "operating" the CSIRT MON (specified in an extensive and open manner), the legislators do not regulate the mutual relations between these two entities, which are critical for the reliability of the cybersecurity system in the sphere of defence. The issue of the status of the CSIRT MON in the state system goes beyond the framework of this study. It may be even said that a specific kind of "discretion" by the Minister in the performance of this task has been sanctioned, to some extent.

On the other hand, the fact that no other powers have been entrusted to the Minister of National Defence as a member of the collegial body, namely, the College for Cybersecurity, recognised as an opinion-forming and advisory authority of the Council of Ministers, is not surprising, because this "gap" results from the essence of the activities of the collegial authority within the framework of which separate responsibilities are attributed only to the chairs of such authorities.[50]

5 Summary

It is hard to resist the impression that the diversity and multiplicity of tasks attributed to the Minister of National Defence within the framework of the National Cybersecurity System can raise many doubts concerning interpretation within the activities of this supreme (constitutional) public administration authority, which can have unpredictable consequences, especially taking into account its undoubtedly highly responsible function within the public-administration system (directly involving state security). In the field of the cybersecurity of the state, special attention should be drawn to building such legal relations that will be an efficient instrument for the prompt making of correct key decisions. They should be characterised by the maximum elimination of any doubts over interpretation, and the avoiding of any overlapping individual tasks and responsibilities. In the field of cybersecurity, the legislators have expressed a precise definition of the tasks entrusted to the Minister of National Defence only in a limited scope, and have allocated to them a specific set

[49]For instance, participation in achieving the objectives of the North Atlantic Treaty Organisation in the fields of cybersecurity and cryptology (see Article 52(5) of the NCSA) or submitting to the competent authorities proposals concerning defensive measures (see *in fine*, Article 51(7) of the NCSA).

[50]The Chair of the National Broadcasting Council who is the Chair of a collegial body, namely, the National Broadcasting Council, and at the same time has separate, independent, and superior responsibilities to issue concession decisions within the framework of the procedures carried out in cooperation (under specific collaborations) with the National Council *in corpore*, is so far the most characteristic example of such "functioning" within the framework of a collegial body.

of legal instruments in the form of appropriate legal actions. Clearly, numerous doubts concerning interpretation can be resolved and eliminated in the course of the authority's practical performance of activities.

References

Adamiak B (1998) Właściwość organów. In: Adamiak B, Borkowski J (eds) Kodeks postępowania administracyjnego. Komentarz, Warsaw
Borkowski J (1980) Zakres przedmiotowy kodeksu postępowania administracyjnego w świetle nowelizacji, Państwo i Prawo 5
Cieślak Z (1982) Porozumienie administracyjne, Warsaw
Cieślak Z (1992) Zbiory zachowań w administracji państwowej. Zagadnienia podstawowe, Warsaw
Cieślak Z (2013) Podstawowe instytucje prawa administracyjnego. In: Niewiadomski Z (ed) Prawo administracyjne, Warsaw
Dawidowicz W (1974) Wstęp do nauk prawno-administracyjnych, Warsaw
Dawidowicz W (1989) Zarys procesu administracyjnego, Warsaw
Filipek J (1974) Rola prawa w działalności administracji państwowej, Warsaw-Cracow

Krzysztof Wąsowski PhD, advocate. Graduated from the Faculty of Law and Administration at the University of Warsaw, Poland and ARGO Top Public Management at the IESE Business School in Barcelona, Spain. Adjunct at the Department of Cybersecurity and New Technologies and an expert at the Academic Center for Cybersecurity Policy at the War Studies University in Warsaw. Partner of the law firm "WLP Legal" in Warsaw, Poland.

Role of the Minister Competent for Computerisation in the Cybersecurity System

Katarzyna Chałubińska-Jentkiewicz

Abstract A public administration authority, as a functional unit of public administration, is responsible for the implementation and quality of public services. The areas of competence of administrative authorities often refer to a specific field. This is also the case with computerisation. The processes it involves are closely related to innovation, new technologies and science. Computerisation has formed the substantive area of activities of various ministries. The minister competent for computerisation performs a range of organisational and reporting tasks and is responsible for the monitoring the implementation of the Cybersecurity Strategy of the Republic of Poland and the performance of action plans for its implementation. The minister prepares annual reports on significant incidents reported by operators of essential services and substantial incidents reported by digital service providers, being responsible for monitoring the strategic dimension of cybersecurity.

Military and civil security issues are central in the activities of public administration authorities related to cybersecurity and the fulfilment of responsibilities in this field involves both the public and the private sectors. It is the public administration authority as a functional unit that is responsible for the delivery and quality of public services. The spheres of responsibility of administrative authorities often involve a specific sector. The same applies to computerisation. Computerisation processes are closely related to innovation, new technologies, and science. Computerisation has been one of the core objectives of various Ministries. Changes to this arrangement, and consequently to the responsibility for this aspect of state and public-administration functioning, have been commensurate with the transformation of public administration itself, and the processes related to it. Therefore, the Regulation of the Council of Ministers of 18 March 2003 on the establishing of the Ministry of Science and Computerisation, and the abolition of the office of the Scientific

K. Chałubińska-Jentkiewicz (✉)
Akademickie Centrum Polityki Cyberbezpieczeństwa/Academic Center for Cybersecurity Policy, Akademia Sztuki Wojennej w Warszawie/War Studies University in Warsaw, Warsaw, Poland
e-mail: k.jentkiewicz@akademia.mil.pl

K. Chałubińska-Jentkiewicz et al. (eds.), *Cybersecurity in Poland*,
https://doi.org/10.1007/978-3-030-78551-2_17

Research Committee,[1] introduced the concept of computerisation to the Ministry of Science and Computerisation which was being formed at the time. From 2005, public administration, computerisation, internal affairs, religious denominations, and national and ethnic minorities were the domain of the Minister of Internal Affairs and Administration.[2] In accordance with the principle of the division of responsibilities between the Ministries, the objectives related to computerisation were assigned by law. Pursuant to the Act on Government Administration Departments, the legislators made distinctions by subject matter. The Minister competent for digital affairs is responsible for matters of computerisation. In accordance with Article 12a of the Act, the computerisation department deals with issues involving:

(1) the computerisation of public administration and entities performing public tasks
(2) information and communication systems and networks of public administration
(3) support for computerisation projects
(4) the fulfilment of the international obligations of the Republic of Poland in the fields of computerisation and telecommunications
(5) participation in developing the European Union's computerisation policy
(6) the development of the information society, and counteracting digital exclusion
(7) the development of services provided by electronic means
(8) the development of state policy on personal data protection
(9) telecommunications
(10) **the civil aspect of cyberspace security**
(11) the PESEL register, Register of Identity Cards, Civil Registry, and the Central Register of Issued and Cancelled Passport Documents
(12) the vehicle register, drivers' register, and parking-card holders' register
(13) the supervision over the provision of trust services within the meaning of trust-services regulations
(13a) electronic identification.

The Prime Minister determines, by way of a regulation, the detailed scope of a Minister's activities, and designates a Ministry or other government administration office to assist the Minister. The Prime Minister, in specifying the detailed scope of the Minister's activity (in the case of a Minister managing a specific department of government administration), designates the department or departments which the Minister manages, and defines the scope of the Minister's rights as the administrator of a separate part or separate parts of the state budget.

Pursuant to the Regulation of the Prime Minister of 22 September 2014 on the detailed scope of activities of the Minister for Administration and Digital Affairs,

[1]Regulation of the Council of Ministers of 18 March 2003 on the establishing of the Ministry of Science and Computerisation, and the abolition of the office of the Scientific Research Committee, Polish Journal of Laws of 2003 No. 51, item 443 (no longer in force).

[2]The Regulation of the Prime Minister of 31 October 2005 on the detailed scope of activities of the Minister for Internal Affairs and Administration.

Article 1 (1) stipulates that the scope of activities of the Minister for Administration and Digital Affairs should include matters concerning public administration and computerisation. Pursuant to Order No. 43 of the Prime Minister of 15 July 2014 on granting a charter to the Ministry of Administration and Digital Affairs, a provision was introduced which, pursuant to Article 39 (5) of the Act of 8 August 1996 on the Council of Ministers, the Ministry for Administration and Digital Affairs was duly assigned the charter, which was an annex to the Order, the aim being to support the responsible Minister of Administration and Digital Affairs on the basis of the Regulation of the Prime Minister of 22 September 2014 on the detailed scope of activities of the Minister of Administration and Digital Affairs, which involved public administration and computerisation.

Next, under the Regulation of the Council of Ministers of 7 December 2015 on the Establishment of the Ministry for Digital Affairs under Article 39 (1) of the Act of 8 August 1996 on the Council of Ministers, the creation of the Ministry of Digital Affairs was ordered by way of the reorganisation of the existing Ministry of Administration and Digital Affairs. The reorganisation involved the exclusion from the existing Ministry of Administration and Digital Affairs—responsible for the departments of public administration, computerisation, communication, and religious denominations, and national and ethnic minorities—the organisational units supporting the departments of public administration, communication, and religious denominations, as well as national and ethnic minorities and employees working for those departments. In accordance with the Regulation of the Prime Minister of 13 December 2017 on the detailed scope of activities of the Minister of Digital Affairs, the Minister manages the department of Government Administration—computerisation.[3] Consequently, he or she would be the administrator of part 27 of the State budget. The services for the Minister were to be provided by the Ministry of Digital Affairs.

Currently the Minister for Digital Affairs does not have his own organizational unit (ministry), but is supported by the Chancellery of the Prime Minister.[4]

Article 45 of the National Cybersecurity System Act defines the competences of the minister competent for computerisation, who is competent for:

(1) monitoring the implementation of the Cybersecurity Strategy of the Republic of Poland, and associated action plans;
(2) recommending the spheres of cooperation with the private sector in order to increase the cybersecurity of the Republic of Poland;
(3) preparing annual reports regarding:

[3]Regulation of the Council of Ministers of 13 December 2017 on the detailed scope of activities of the Minister of Digital Affairs, Polish Journal of Laws of 2017 item 2327.

[4]Regulation of the Council of Ministers of 6 October 2020 on the detailed scope of activities of the Minister of Digital Affairs, Polish Journal of Laws of 2020 item 1716.

   (a) serious incidents notified by operators of essential services affecting the continuity of their essential services in the Republic of Poland and in the Member States of the European Union;
   (b) significant incidents notified by digital service providers, including those involving two or more European Union Member States;

(4) conducting informational activities on good practices, educational programmes, campaigns, and training, to expand knowledge and build awareness of cybersecurity, including the safe use of the Internet by various categories of users
(5) collecting information on serious incidents which concerns, or has been provided by, another Member State of the European Union
(6) providing information and good practices related to the reporting of serious incidents by operators of essential services, and significant incidents by digital service providers, obtained from the Cooperation Group, including

   (a) incident-management procedures
   (b) risk-management procedures
   (c) the classification of information, risks, and incidents

The Act imposes a range of organisational and reporting obligations on the Minister competent for computerisation. The Minister competent for computerisation is responsible for monitoring the implementation of the Cybersecurity Strategy of the Republic of Poland and associated action plans, and preparing annual reports on serious incidents notified by operators of essential services and significant incidents notified by digital service providers, with responsibility for the strategic monitoring cybersecurity at the national level. It is important to add that these responsibilities, according to the division between government departments, also include issues of cybersecurity in the civil dimension. Accordingly, the Minister of National Defence is responsible for the security of cyberspace in the military sphere, indicated as part of the national defence department.

The responsibilities provided for in the said provision relate to the following obligations of the Member States as defined in the Directive:

(1) **Monitoring the implementation of the Cybersecurity Strategy of the Republic of Poland, hereinafter referred to as "the Strategy", and the delivery of action plans for its introduction**

This includes supervision over the implementation of Poland's strategic cybersecurity objectives. The strategy builds on the actions undertaken previously by government administration, aimed at increasing the level of security in the cyberspace of the Republic of Poland. Following strategic assumptions, both national-development strategies and those relating to the sphere of public order and national security make their success conditional on the use of communication and information systems. Not only is digitisation a source of development and innovation, but it also creates risks associated with the growing number of online threats. Considering these new threats, the extensive architecture of communication and information systems, and the growing dependence of society and entrepreneurs on these systems, it is necessary to expand the national cybersecurity system and ensure a coherent approach across the country. The main objective of the Strategy is to define a framework of actions aimed at achieving a high level of resilience for national communication and information systems, operators of essential services, critical infrastructure operators, digital service providers, and public administration, to incidents in cyberspace. Furthermore, the proposed strategic policies are also expected to increase the effectiveness of law-enforcement agencies and the judiciary in detecting and combating crimes and terrorist and spying activities in cyberspace. The strategic objectives include specific goals, such as gaining the ability to coordinate nationwide activities aimed at preventing, detecting, combating, and minimising the effects of incidents which compromise the security of communication and information systems central to the functioning of the state, reinforcing the ability to counteract cyber threats, improving national capabilities and expertise in the field of cybersecurity, and developing a strong international position for Poland in the field of cybersecurity.

Moreover, it is essential to achieve a capacity for nationally coordinated actions to prevent, detect, combat, and minimise the effects of security incidents on communication and information systems central to the functioning of states, and to adapt the legal environment to the requirements and challenges in the field of cybersecurity.

(2) **Recommending areas of cooperation with the private sector in order to improve the cybersecurity of the Republic of Poland.**

The need for cross-sectoral cooperation was indicated by the European Union's Cybersecurity Strategy: an open, secure, and protected cyberspace enhances private-sector readiness and engagement. This strategy stressed the fact that the vast majority of network and information systems are independently owned and operated by private entities, and that the deeper involvement of the private sector in the efforts to enhance cybersecurity is essential. The private sector should develop its own cyber resilience capabilities at the technical level, and ensure the exchange of best practices between different industries. Equally, the public sector should benefit from the instruments developed by the industry to respond to incidents, identify causes, and conduct forensic analyses. The purpose of the discussed regulation is, therefore, to create a situation in which entities operating in many critical areas (energy, transport, banking, stock exchanges, and technologies facilitating the provision of essential online services, as well as public-administration authorities) assess the cybersecurity threats they are exposed to, ensure the reliability and resilience of the network and information systems employing the appropriate risk-prevention strategies, and exchange information with the competent network and information-security authorities. The European Public-Private Partnership for Resilience was launched in accordance with document COM (2009) 149.[5] This platform has

[5]Communication from the Commission to the European Parliament, the Council, the European Economic and Social Committee and the Committee of the Regions on Critical Information Infrastructure Protection *Protecting Europe from large scale cyber-attacks and disruptions: enhancing preparedness, security and resilience,* COM (2009) 149.

initiated activities by and increased cooperation between the public and private sectors in identifying key resources, means, functions, and baseline requirements for resilience, as well as the demand for cooperation and mechanisms for responding to large-scale electronic-communications disruptions. Communication from the Commission: Joint Communication to the European Parliament and the Council—Resilience, Deterrence and Defence: Building strong cybersecurity for the EU, Brussels, 13.9.2017. JOIN(2017) 450 final, emphasised that the effectiveness of traditional law-enforcement mechanisms has been undermined by the characteristics of the digital world, which consists mainly of privately owned infrastructures and multiple entities operating within various jurisdictions. In consequence, cooperation with the private sector, including industry and civil society, is fundamental to the public authorities' effective fight against crime. However, the role as defined above is the implementation of the aforementioned guidelines at the level of government administration.

(3) **Preparing annual reports regarding:**

  (a) serious incidents reported by operators of essential services affecting the continuity of their essential services in the Republic of Poland and the continuity of their essential services in the Member States of the European Union
  (b) significant incidents notified by digital service providers, including incidents involving two or more Member States of the European Union.

(4) **conducting informational activities on good practices, educational programmes, campaigns, and training, to increase knowledge and build awareness of cybersecurity, including the safe use of the Internet by various categories of users**
(5) **collecting information on serious incidents which involves or has been provided by another Member State of the European Union**
(6) **providing information and good practices related to the reporting of serious incidents by operators of essential services, and significant incidents by digital service providers, obtained from the Cooperation Group, including**

  (a) incident-management procedures
  (b) risk-management procedures
  (c) the classification of information, risks, and incidents.

Strategic cooperation between Member States, and the exchange of information, experience, and best practices concerning the security of network and information systems are essential to respond effectively to the challenges posed by security incidents and threats to those systems across the Union. These tasks also apply to cross-sectoral information exchange, especially in the field of educational activities and the application of good practices. These responsibilities are supported by extensive reporting. This reporting includes issues related to the duties referred to in recital 61 of the NIS Directive, according to which competent authorities should have the necessary means to perform their duties, including the power to obtain sufficient information to assess the security level of network and information systems. The NIS Directive defines such a concept as "an incident", which means any event which has a genuinely adverse impact on the security of network and information systems; "incident handling", which means all procedures for detecting, analysing, containing, and responding to an incident; and **"risk", which means any reasonably identifiable circumstance or event which has a potentially adverse impact on the security of network and information systems**. According to the definitions provided in the Act: an "incident"—an event which has or might have an adverse effect on cybersecurity; a "critical incident"—one which results in significant damage to public security or order, international interests, economic interests, the operation of public institutions, civil rights and the freedoms or the lives and health of the people, as classified by the respective CSIRT MON, CSIRT NASK, or CSIRT GOV; a "serious incident"—an occurrence which causes or is likely to cause a significant deterioration in or disruption to the provision of an essential service; and a "significant incident"—an event which has a serious impact on the provision of a digital service within the meaning of Article 4 of Commission Implementing Regulation (EU) 2018/151 of 30 January 2018 laying down rules for application of Directive (EU) 2016/1148 of the European Parliament and of the Council as regards further specification of the elements to be taken into account by digital service providers for managing the risks posed to the security of network and information systems and of the parameters for determining whether an incident has a substantial impact.[6] Risk, in turn, means a combination of the probability of an undesirable event and its consequences, and risk estimation means the overall process of risk identification, analysis, and evaluation. Therefore, reporting includes gathering information on the incidents themselves, as well as providing information obtained from the Cooperation Group—within the scope of developed cybersecurity procedures, as well as the measures applied and all kinds of regulations on preventive actions related to the application of so-called good practices in incident response. The second pillar of the NIS Directive primarily involves cooperation between Member States. The NIS Directive introduces cooperation mechanisms on two levels: technical, and political-strategic. Technical cooperation is to be provided by the European CSIRT Network and the creation of mechanisms for the exchange of information on cross-border incidents between CSIRTs designated for operators of essential services and digital service providers. Cooperation at the political and strategic levels is to be implemented through the creation of a Cooperation Group which will work on the development of common strategic concepts and will receive, among other things, annual reports from the appropriate authorities. In accordance with recital 4 of the preamble to the Directive, a Cooperation Group composed of representatives of Member States, the Commission and the European Union Agency

[6]Commission Implementing Regulation (EU) 2018/151 of 30 January 2018 laying down rules for application of Directive (EU) 2016/1148 of the European Parliament and of the Council as regards further specification of the elements to be taken into account by digital service providers for managing the risks posed to the security of network and information systems and of the parameters for determining whether an incident has a substantial impact, OJ EU 2018 L 26/48 (hereinafter referred to as "Implementing Regulation 2018/151).

for Network and Information Security (nowadays: the European Union Agency for Cybersecurity; hereinafter referred to as "ENISA") should be established to promote and facilitate strategic cooperation between Member States on the security of network and information systems. In order for this group to be effective and accessible to all, it is essential that all Member States have at least the minimum capabilities, and strategy, to ensure a high level of security of network and information systems on their territory. Additionally, security and incident-reporting requirements should apply to operators of essential services and digital service providers for the promotion of a risk-handling culture, and to ensure that the most serious incidents are reported. Article 11 of the NIS Directive establishes a Cooperation Group composed of representatives of the Member States, the Commission, and ENISA. According to Article 11 of the NIS Directive, the Cooperation Group is to perform its tasks on the basis of biennial work programmes. The responsibilities of the Group include providing strategic guidance on the activities of the computer security incident response teams network, exchanging information and best practices, and discussing Member States' capabilities and preparedness. The Cooperation Group is also obliged to submit, every year and a half, a report evaluating the experience gained in its strategic cooperation. It is also responsible for discussing, at the request of a Member State, specific draft national measures by that Member State concerning the identification of operators of essential services in a particular sector. According to Article 14(7) of the NIS Directive, competent authorities, acting jointly within the framework of the Cooperation Group, may develop and adopt guidelines on the circumstances in which operators of essential services are required to report incidents, including guidelines on parameters to determine the significance of the impact of an incident. The Cooperation Group should be presided over by a representative of the Member State holding the Presidency of the Council of the European Union. The Chairperson should be assisted in the performance of his or her duties by a representative of the Member State holding the previous Presidency of the Council of the European Union, and a representative of the Member State which will hold the next Presidency. The Chairperson may indicate the duties in respect of which he or she will need such support. In the event that the Member State holding the Presidency of the Council decides not to preside over the Group, a two-thirds majority of the members of the group shall elect a replacement Chairperson.

The responsibilities of the Cooperation Group as defined in the Directive are:

(a) providing strategic guidance on the activities of the CSIRTs network;
(b) exchanging best practice on information exchange related to incident reporting
(c) exchanging best practice between Member States, and, in collaboration with ENISA, assisting Member States in capacity building with a view to ensuring the security of network and information systems
(d) discussing Member States' capabilities and preparedness, and, on a voluntary basis, assessing national strategies for network and information system security and the effectiveness of CSIRT, and identifying best practice
(e) exchanging information and best practices on awareness raising and training
(f) exchanging information and best practices on research and development relating to the security of network and information systems

(g) where relevant, exchanging experiences on matters relating to the security of network and information systems with the relevant Union institutions, bodies, offices, and agencies
(h) discussing the standards and specifications with representatives from the relevant European standardisation organisations
(i) collecting information on best practice for risks and incidents
(j) examining the summary reports on an annual basis
(k) discussing the work undertaken with regard to exercises on network and information-systems security, education programmes and training, including the work performed by ENISA
(l) with the assistance of ENISA, exchanging best practice with regard to the identification of the operators of essential services by the Member States, including in relation to cross-border dependencies, regarding risks and incidents
(m) discussing the rules on incident reporting.

In performing his or her duties, the Chairperson should be guided by the principles of inclusiveness, commitment, respect for diversity, and the pursuit of consensus. In accordance with Article 11(2) of the NIS Directive, the Cooperation Group may, where appropriate, invite representatives of influential stakeholders to participate in its meetings. In order to ensure that acceding countries meet the requirements specified in the NIS Directive from the date of their accession, representatives of these countries should be invited to participate in the meetings of the Cooperation Group from the date of signing the Treaty of Accession to the EU. The decision to invite representatives of important stakeholders or experts to participate in a meeting, or part of a meeting, of the Group, should be taken by the Chairperson, unless a simple majority of members oppose the participation in the meeting or part of it by the representative or expert concerned. In order to facilitate its activities, the Cooperation Group should be able to create subgroups. The meetings of the Group are convened by the Chairperson, either on his or her own initiative or at the request of a simple majority of its members. The Chairperson shall present a provisional agenda for meetings during his or her term of office, taking into consideration the work programme of the Group. In general, the Group's discussions should not be publicly accessible, as making them open to the public could have a negative impact on building mutual trust between members, since they often address public security issues. However, after consultation with the Chairperson, the Group may decide to make public its deliberations on specific issues, and to facilitate making appropriate documentation publicly available. Requests to the Group for access to the documents relating to its activities shall be considered by the Commission in accordance with Regulation (EC) No. 1049/2001 of the European Parliament and of the Council. The Group's discussions are not public. In consultation with the Chairperson, the Group might decide to make public its deliberations on certain issues. Documents distributed to members of the Group, representatives of third parties, and experts, shall not be made available to the public unless access is granted or otherwise provided for by the Commission.

Pursuant to Article 46 of the Act, the Minister competent for computerisation shall ensure the development or maintenance of a communication and information system to support:

(1) cooperation between entities within the national cybersecurity system
(2) the generating and presenting of recommendations for actions to increase the level of cybersecurity
(3) the reporting and handling of incidents
(4) risk estimation at the national level
(5) alerts regarding cybersecurity threats.

According to the EU strategy, national NIS authorities should cooperate on and exchange information with other regulatory authorities, in particular data-protection authorities, and regularly publish on dedicated websites unclassified information on current early warnings about incidents and threats and the coordinated responses. Integrated computerisation involves a comprehensive, managerial, and organisational approach to building the state's information and communication system by public administration, which is expected to lead to developing information and communication governance in the state. The creation, development, and maintenance of a state information and communication system supports all the crucial procedures related to cybersecurity.

The establishment of the appropriate organisational areas at all levels, from independent institutions to departmental and local government activities, and building, providing, and maintaining a basic set of electronic services facilitating incident handling all require an effective combination of various public-administration activities. For administrative processes which involve different sectors, cross-sectoral projects seem essential. This is important, considering the required functionality of such a system, including aspects of information exchange, educational issues, real threats, alerting actions, and risk estimation. A communication and information system is one in which data is sent, received, stored, and processed by means of telecommunications networks. A service provided by electronic means does not include a transmission within the internal network of a given entrepreneur[7]—the intranet. Pursuant to Article 2(3) of the Act on Providing Services by Electronic Means, a communication and information system is a set of cooperating IT devices and software, ensuring processing and storage, as well as sending and receiving data through telecommunications networks by means of a terminal device appropriate for a given type of telecommunications network within the meaning of the Act of

[7]Commission Implementing Regulation (EU) 2018/151 of 30 January 2018 laying down rules for application of Directive (EU) 2016/1148 of the European Parliament and of the Council as regards further specification of the elements to be taken into account by digital service providers for managing the risks posed to the security of network and information systems and of the parameters for determining whether an incident has a substantial impact, OJ EU 2018 L 26/189.

16 July 2004—Telecommunications Law.[8] The communication between IT devices is based on the TCP/IP protocol used. The most important here is the IP protocol, which is responsible for assigning a logical IP address to each computer which is connected to the TCP/IP network.[9] The construction of the state communication and information system should be carried out in close cooperation with all the entities which are part of the national cybersecurity system. The legislators have defined the system's functionalities, which include cooperation between entities within the national cybersecurity system, the generation and transmission of recommendations for actions to increase the level of cybersecurity, incident reporting and handling, risk assessment at the national level, and warnings about cyber hazards.

The CSIRT MON, CSIRT NASK, and CSIRT GOV, sectoral cybersecurity teams, and the President of the Office of Electronic Communications may use the communication and information system under an agreement concluded with the Minister competent for computerisation.

The entities involved in the process of managing cybersecurity require enhanced security of communication systems and IT support. The Government Communications Network (GCN) was established in order to ensure the protection of information against unauthorised disclosure during telephone and video-conferencing conversations and data transmission, in particular against the loss of confidentiality, availability, and integrity.

However, the dynamic development of ICT networks, and their increasing use for data transmission, as well as for command and management, naturally made it necessary to guarantee security for the operation of the networks themselves, and for the information transmitted therein.

Therefore, the above provision ensures cooperation between the President of the Office of Electronic Communications (OEC) and other bodies—Computer Security Incident Response Teams—whose main task is to ensure the implementation and coordination of the processes of preventing, detecting, and responding to computer incidents involving communication and information systems and networks, as well as cooperation in the sphere of preventing cyber attacks. The CSIRT GOV Computer Security Incident Response Team is managed by the Head of the Internal Security Agency, and operates as a national-level CSIRT Team responsible for coordinating the process of responding to computer incidents occurring in the fields indicated in Article 26(7) of the Act of 5 July 2018 on the National Cybersecurity System. Among its fundamental tasks are recognising, preventing, and detecting threats which are detrimental to security, and important from the point of view of the continuous functioning of the state's communication and information systems of public administration authorities, and of the system of ICT networks covered by a standard list of objects, installations, devices and services categorised as critical infrastructure, as well as of the communication and information systems of owners

[8]Act of 16 July 2004—Telecommunications Law, consolidated text, Polish Journal of Laws of 2019, item 2460, as amended.

[9]Gołaczyński (2009), p. 34.

and the holders of facilities, installations, and devices of critical infrastructure referred to in Article 5b(7)(1) of the Act of 26 April 2007 on Crisis Management. CSIRT GOV and CSIRT MON, whose main task is to ensure the implementation and coordination of the processes of preventing, detecting and responding to computer incidents in the Ministry for National Defence's communication and information systems and networks, as well as CSIRT NASK, whose tasks include the monitoring of cybersecurity threats and incidents at the national level, are permitted to implement their tasks using the communication and information system operated by the Ministry for Information Technology. This usage is based on an agreement.

The legislators have decided that the basic terms and conditions for the use of communication and information systems to serve cybersecurity, and the scope of such use, will be agreed between the parties to the agreement. It should be assumed that there is also going to be an administrative agreement. The main goal of the entities concluding the agreement is the implementation of designated public tasks within the communication and information system, and the conditions and scope of this use are defined in the agreement. This form of public-administration activity is similar to civil-law contracts, which have the effect of administrative agreements primarily concerning the sphere of public law. As a rule, the mandatory provisions of this agreement have not been defined by the legislators. Nevertheless, taking into consideration the essence and purpose of the agreement on the conditions and scope of the use of the communication and information system, the agreement should specify, in particular, the parties to the agreement, its duration, whether the agreement has been concluded for a definite period of time, the subject matter of the agreement, the provisions concerning supervision over the use of the system, and the provisions concerning the form of amending or terminating the agreement.

In accordance with Article 47 of the Act on the National Cybersecurity System, the Minister competent for computerisation may perform the tasks referred to in Article 45(1) and Article 46(1) subject to the rules specified in separate provisions by means of units responsible in this respect which are subordinated to or supervised by the Minister competent for computerisation. A significant role in the implementation of tasks related to digitalisation and computerisation processes is performed by the advisory units of the Minister competent for computerisation. Such a unit is the Council for Computerisation. Pursuant to Article 17 of the UIDP the Council for Computerisation was established, whose name under the amendment of 10 January 2014[10] was changed to the Council for Computerisation. It is a consultative and advisory authority of the Minister competent for computerisation. Opinions, minutes of meetings, and other Council documents are published in a separate part of the Public Information Bulletin on the website of the Minister competent for computerisation. The Council shall present a report on its activities for each calendar year to the Minister by 30 April of the following year. The responsibilities of the Council include:

[10]Polish Journal of Laws of 2014, item 183.

(1) suggesting and providing opinions on the draft positions of the Council of Ministers on the documents of the European Commission and the European Parliament concerning computerisation, communication, and the development of the information society, at the request of the Minister competent for computerisation, including issuing opinions on the draft of the Integrated State Computerisation Programme and other government documents, including draft development strategies and draft programmes within the meaning of the Act of 6 December 2006 on the Principles of Conducting the Development Policy concerning matters of computerisation, communication or the development of the information society;
(2) issuing opinions on draft regulations published pursuant to Article 18 of the UIDP
(3) providing opinions on other draft legal Acts and other documents submitted by the Minister competent for computerisation, communication, or information society development
(4) providing opinions on reports and other studies on the computerisation of the Minister competent for computerisation

    (a) requirements and demands concerning the development of the information society
    (b) the principles of the functioning of public registers
    (c) the principles of the implementation of communication and information systems in public administration, and the status of their implementation
    (d) the current technical solutions applicable to the computerisation of administration, network development, and broadband services
    (e) Polish terminology in the fields of computer science and communications.

The Council is composed of fifteen to twenty members. Candidates for membership of the Council may be recommended by:

(1) Ministers
(2) the General Director of the State Archives
(3) the President of the Polish Committee for Standardisation
(4) the co-Chairperson of the Joint Commission of Government and Local Government
(5) scientific entities within the meaning of the Act of 30 April 2010 on the principles of science financing (Polish Journal of Laws of 2010, No. 96, item 615, as amended), which, within the framework of their statutory activities, conduct scientific research or development work in the fields of information technology and communications
(6) Chambers of Commerce representing entrepreneurs conducting business activities in the fields of the electronic economy, communications, media, the manufacturing of IT equipment, software, or providing IT services
(7) associations registered in the National Court Register whose statutory purpose is to represent the IT environment or to support the applications of IT, the electronic economy, communications, or media.

The Minister competent for computerisation appoints the members of the Council for a biennial term of office from among the candidates recommended by the entities indicated above.

The Minister competent for computerisation may appoint and dismiss the Chairperson and Deputy Chairperson of the Council from among its members. The Chairperson of the Council manages its work and represents the Council externally. In the event of the Chairperson's absence, the Deputy Chairperson shall replace him or her. The Council is supported by the office serving the Minister competent for computerisation. Other persons may be invited to meetings of the Council by the Minister competent for computerisation or the Chairperson of the Council, if it is advisable to do so in order to fulfil the tasks of the Council. The detailed procedure of the Council shall be established by its regulations, determined at the request of the Council by the Minister competent for computerisation. However, this institution has an exclusively advisory and consultative nature. The legislators have defined precisely which institutions are supervised by this authority.

Pursuant to the announcement of the Minister for Digital Affairs of 19 June 2018 on the list of organisational units subordinate to, or supervised by, the Minister for Digital Affairs, issued pursuant to Article 33(1d) of the Act on the Council of Ministers, a register of organisational units subordinate to, or supervised by, the Minister for Digital Affairs was established, constituting an appendix to the announcement. According to the announcement, the Digital Poland Projects Centre is a subordinate unit, while the following units are supervised: the Central Computer Science Centre; the Communications Institute—National Research Institute; and the Institute of Innovative Technologies EMAG and Scientific and Academic Computer Network—National Research Institute. Apparently, the scope of the delegation includes the institutions defined above.

It should be added that by Order No. 13 of the Minister for Digital Affairs of 2 May 2016 on the appointment and responsibilities of the Plenipotentiary of the Minister for Digital Affairs for International Cooperation, the Plenipotentiary of the Minister for Digital Affairs for International Cooperation was appointed, who is responsible for:

(1) representing and acting on behalf of the Minister for Digital Affairs in the international and national arenas on international issues
(2) strategic advice to the Minister for Digital Affairs on international activities
(3) developing with the Minister for Digital Affairs of a directional policy and international cooperation strategy of the Ministry
(4) monitoring the effective implementation of the Ministry's foreign policy on behalf of the Minister for Digital Affairs. Thus, the tasks of such a person include activities beyond the European Union and the regulation of the directive.

Furthermore, Order No. 30 of the Minister for Digital Affairs of 22 October 2017 on the establishment of the Operating Centre of the Minister for Digital Affairs established the Operating Centre of the Minister for Digital Affairs, which supports the implementation of the tasks of the Minister for Digital Affairs in the field of cybersecurity, as well as crisis management and defence, in particular on the security of the civil sphere of cyberspace of the Republic of Poland and the system for responding to ICT incidents and civil planning. The Centre can serve as a separate place of permanent duty and as an HNS point of contact within the meaning of Article 1(2)(1) of Order No. 19 of the Minister for Digital Affairs of 15 June 2016 on the Functioning of the HNS System in the computerisation department of government administration for the purposes of tasks resulting from the duties of the host country (The Official Gazette of the Ministry for Digital Affairs, item 21). The Centre is deployed, if necessary, by recommendation of the Minister, a member of the Management of the Ministry of Digital Affairs, or, depending on the nature of the threat or event, at the request of the Head of the organisational unit nominated in the Instruction of the Operations Centre, or by the appropriate Head of the organisational unit for exercises in the fields of cybersecurity, crisis management, and defence. The following are the main tasks of the Centre:

(1) Supporting the Minister in managing the National Cybersecurity Centre[11] operating within the National Research Institute—the Scientific and Academic Computer Network, a unit supervised by the Minister competent for responding to ICT incidents.
(2) Ensuring close cooperation with other entities involved in responding to ICT incidents, in particular with the Internal Security Agency, the Government Security Centre, and the Police.
(3) Supervising and coordinating the activities of units subordinate to, or supervised by, the Minister in a crisis situation, or in circumstances of extraordinary threats, if justified by the scale or effects of the situation.
(4) Forwarding to the appropriate organisational units of the Ministry proposals for the development of draft decisions, positions, guidelines, and recommendations concerning cybersecurity, crisis management, and defence matters, for the purposes of the Ministry's management and the Crisis Management Team of the Minister for Digital Affairs.
(5) Analysing the situation, coordinating and directing the activities of the Ministry in the event of an emergency situation causing disruptions to the functioning of IT systems, networks, or telecommunication services, or when such disruptions affect the essential (basic) services provided to the public or public-administration systems, registers, or publications.
(6) Monitoring the development of a crisis situation where justified by its extent or consequences.
(7) Ensuring permanent communication with the Office of Electronic Communications and the NCSC in the event of a disruption to the functioning of IT systems, networks or telecommunication services, or when such a disruption affects essential services provided to the public or public-administration systems, registers, or publications.

[11]National Cybersecurity Centre, "the NCSC".

(8) Ensuring the circulation of information in a crisis situation for the management of the Ministry and the Crisis Management Team of the Minister for Digital Affairs.
(9) Providing a place to perform emergency duty in the event of an alert level, or CRP alert level, for persons authorised to make decisions on the security of communication and information systems—in accordance with the Act on Anti-Terrorist Activities
(10) Ensuring the circulation of information for the purposes of tasks included in the list of the undertakings and procedures of the crisis management system
(11) Coordinating designated support arising from the obligations of the host state (HNS) in the Ministry, the Office of Electronic Communications, and entrepreneurs with special economic and defensive importance within the meaning of Article 6(1)(2) and Article 18(1) and (3) of the Act of 21 November 1967 on the Universal Duty to Defend the Republic of Poland (Polish Journal of Laws of 2017, item 430).

Units subordinate to, or supervised by, the Minister ensure that the Centre is staffed on the basis of individual contracts and agreements. While on duty, the Centre cooperates with the Ministry's Press Officer on media monitoring and information policy.

It should be emphasised that the Centre's tasks are related to situations concerning national and internal procedures instigated in a crisis situation, while the procedures defined in the National Cybersecurity Act refer to the common objective of the EU, i.e. to provide common procedures for responding to cyber threats in the area of the EU Single Market. It can be observed that the tasks of different institutions and entities in the private sector can overlap, but in both systems, the Minister competent for computerisation remains the common coordinator.

The roles entrusted to these units, including in cybersecurity, are financed in the form of an earmarked subsidy from the part of the state budget which is administered by the Minister competent for digital affairs. According to the Regulation of the Prime Minister of ^ October 2020 on the detailed scope of activity of the Minister for Digital Affairs, this Minister is the administrator of part 27 of the state budget. Article 127 of the Public Finance Act[12] delineates a list of tasks for which funds from an earmarked subsidy may be used. The detailed regulations concerning particular types of designated subsidy, the rules for their granting, and the settlement and legal consequences related to irregularities in these processes, are specified in the Act. Earmarked subsidies may be allocated for financing or subsidising statutorily defined tasks, implemented by entities other than local government units. The amount of each grant so planned, in accordance with Article 215(2) of the PFA, should be additionally described, with the appropriate type of subsidy in question as an earmarked subsidy. Such a subsidy may be used by the beneficiary in connection

[12]Act from Public Finance, Polish Journal of Laws of 2019, item 869, as amended, hereinafter "the PFA".

with a public task only after the conclusion of a subsidy agreement. From the very nature of an earmarked subsidy, it follows that it may be utilised by the subsidy beneficiary in connection with the implementation of a public task only for expenditures incurred after the conclusion of the subsidy agreement. In addition, it follows from Article 251(2) of the PFA that the use of the subsidy is made in particular through payment for the tasks for which the subsidy was awarded, or, if separate regulations provide for the method of awarding and settling the subsidy, the utilisation of the subsidy is achieved through the implementation of the objectives indicated in these regulations. Therefore, since the provision of the subsidy is made on the basis of an agreement, use of the subsidy can only be made by paying for the completed tasks resulting from the subsidy agreement, and thus performed after it has been signed (the Resolution of the College of the Regional Chamber of Auditors in Kraków of 14 August 2013. KI-411212/2013—the essence of an earmarked subsidy NZS 2013/5/10).

The Minister competent for computerisation, as the single point of contact (Articles 48–50), has the responsibility to receive and forward, at the request of the appropriate CSIRT, reports of serious or significant incidents involving two or more Member States of the European Union to ensure the representation of the Republic of Poland within the Cooperation Group, to exchange information for the benefit of the public authorities and for the competent authorities in Poland and abroad, and the CSIRT, and to meet its reporting obligations to the Cooperation Group and the European Commission. In recent years there has been a growing interest in cybersecurity, which has resulted in an increasing number of units and organisations' dealing with this issue. Nevertheless, in order to perform public tasks in this area more effectively, cooperation and exchange of information between administrative, military, and civil areas are indispensable. The Cybersecurity Strategy of the European Union proposes an open, secure and protected cyberspace,[13] and a network of national cybersecurity authorities. According to the EU strategy, national NIS authorities should cooperate and exchange information with other regulatory authorities, in particular data-protection authorities, and regularly publish, on a dedicated website, unclassified information on current early warnings about incidents and threats, as well as about coordinated responses. According to the European Commission, legal obligations should not replace or prevent informal or voluntary cooperation, including between the public and private sectors, to increase security and exchange information and best practices. An especially important and useful platform at the EU level which needs to be developed is the European Public-Private Partnership for Resilience.[14] All these tasks are not the complete catalogue of

[13]COM (2013) from 7 February 2013 JOIN(2013) 1 final.

[14]The European Public-Private Partnership for Resilience was initiated under document COM (2009) 149. The platform launched activities and increased cooperation between the public and private sectors in identifying critical resources, means, functions, and baseline requirements, for resilience, as well as the need for cooperation and mechanisms for responding to large-scale disruptions affecting electronic communications.

requirements related to the protection of national security in the digital age. This is because the process of threat emergence is ongoing; therefore, the list of needs is constantly growing. These demands must be met by an appropriate, innovative selection of regulatory instruments, and without questioning these traditional measures. Digital democracy is a form of government operation which requires public authorities and public administration authorities to counteract all tendencies which have a negative impact on national security. Government administration and local government authorities are able to provide more efficient and more effective assistance in crisis situations related to ICT infrastructure if they receive the professional support of third-sector organisations. As the Strategy emphasises, the effectiveness of governmental organisations (the Polish Armed Forces, the Police, Guards, and Inspectorates) depends largely on proper specialist support from non-governmental organisations, which can provide as much assistance in various areas of national security as government administration units. In order for such cooperation to be real, it is necessary to provide information on potential threats, incidents, and rules adopted in individual Member States. This necessity is indicated in recital 43 of the Directive, according to which, due to the global nature of the problems related to the security of network and information systems, there is a need to strengthen international cooperation in order to improve security standards and information exchange, and also to promote a common holistic approach to security issues. For the purposes of achieving the above goals, a system of so-called points of contact was designed. According to Article 8 of the Directive, each Member State shall designate a national single point of contact for the security of network and information systems (known as "the single point of contact"). Member States may designate an existing body for this purpose. In Poland, such an authority is the Minister competent for digital affairs. Should a Member State designate only one competent authority, that competent authority is also the single point of contact. Pursuant to Article 8(2) of the Directive, the single point of contact shall have a connecting function to ensure cross-border cooperation between Member States' authorities and with the appropriate authorities in other Member States, as well as with the Cooperation Group and the CSIRT network. Member States are obligated to provide the competent authorities and single points of contact with sufficient resources to enable them to accomplish their tasks effectively and efficiently with a view to achieving the objectives of the Directive. Member States shall ensure that the designated representatives in the Cooperation Group are working together effectively, efficiently, and securely. The competent authorities and the single point of contact are required to, where appropriate, and in accordance with national law, consult and cooperate with the applicable national law-enforcement authorities and national data-protection bodies. Member States are obliged to notify the European Commission, without delay, of the designation of the competent authority and the single point of contact, their tasks, and any subsequent modifications thereto, and to make public the designation of the competent authority and the single point of contact. The European Commission shall publish the list of designated single points of contact.

The main responsibilities of points of contact:

(1) Receiving from the single points of contact in other Member States of the European Union reports of a major incident, or a significant incident, involving two or more Member States of the European Union, and forwarding these reports to CSIRT MON, CSIRT NASK, CSIRT GOV, or sectoral cybersecurity teams, i.e., obtaining and communicating information about an emergency situation from other points of contact in the EU, if the situation there is more extensive, i.e. involves more than one country; it should be noted that, according to recital 32 of the Directive, the competent authorities, or computer security incident response teams, (CSIRT's), should receive incident reports. The single points of contact should not receive any incident reports directly, unless they also operate as a competent authority or a CSIRT. However, the competent authority or CSIRT should be able to instruct the single point of contact to forward incident reports to single points of contact in other Member States affected by the incident.
(2) providing to the single points of contact in other Member States of the European Union, at the request of the appropriate CSIRT MON, CSIRT NASK, or CSIRT GOV, a report of a major incident or a significant incident involving two or more Member States of the European Union—i.e. acquiring and sharing information about such an incident with the other points of contact affected by the incident.
(3) Ensuring representation of the Republic of Poland in the Cooperation Group—i.e. serving a representative function.
(4) Assuring cybersecurity cooperation with the European Commission—i.e. implementing a policy of cooperation with the EU in the sphere of cybersecurity.
(5) Coordinating cooperation between the competent authorities for cybersecurity and public authorities in the Republic of Poland and the appropriate authorities in the Member States of the European Union—i.e. coordinating state cooperation with other EU countries with regard to cybersecurity;
(6) Securing the exchange of information for the Cooperation Group and the CSIRT Network—i.e., implementing the informational aspects of cooperation.

Under recital 35 of the Preamble of the NIS Directive, the Cooperation Group should function as a tool for the exchange of best practices, for discussions on Member States' capabilities and preparedness, and, on a voluntary basis, for assisting its members in evaluating national network and information system security strategies, and capacity building. Furthermore, for the purposes of promoting advanced network and information system security, the Cooperation Group should, where appropriate, cooperate with the relevant EU institutions, authorities, offices, and agencies to exchange knowledge and best practices, and also to advise on the aspects of network and information system security which could affect their work, while respecting the existing arrangements for the exchange of proprietary information. When cooperating with law-enforcement authorities on issues concerning the security of network and information systems which could affect its work, the

Cooperation Group should take into consideration existing information channels and established networks.

In order to carry out the tasks of the Cooperation Group, the single points of contact must provide it with specific information. Information policy is fundamental to the activities related to ensuring cybersecurity.

Another essential element at this stage of civilisational advancement is the right of citizens to obtain, collect, modify, and make available critical information of a public nature. It should be noted that access to information is becoming much easier. Also relevant is the legislation which defines the scopes of available information and separates information of an undisclosed nature.[15] Nowadays, in administrative-law research, information is understood as a new and distinctive element in the tasks of the state, and a form of procedure in times of conflict.[16] Information as a value can also be protected in the context of content relevant for national security.

The Commission's rules on security regarding the protection of EU classified information, established in Commission Decisions (EU, Euratom) 2015/443 (3) and (EU, Euratom) 2015/444 (4), shall apply to any such information received or processed by or from the Cooperation Group. Information processed by the Group which is covered by the obligation of professional secrecy must be duly protected. Members of the Group, as well as representatives of third parties and experts, are bound by the confidentiality obligation referred to in this article. The Chairperson shall ensure that third-party representatives and experts are informed of their confidentiality requirements. However, the Polish legislators have decided that any data which could become information related to national security or public order may not be provided to the Cooperation Group.

The legislators did not make a direct reference to the Act on the Protection of Classified Information (PCI).[17] Its Article 5 describes the types of protected information. In their classification, the legislators referred to the effects which the disclosure of secret information could have on the Polish State. It has been indicated, among other things, that classified information will constitute a message whose disclosure could cause serious damage to the Republic of Poland by making it difficult to conduct operational or exploratory activities being undertaken to ensure state security, or for the prosecution of offenders by institutions or services authorised to do so; or will cause damage to the Republic of Poland by making it more difficult for the services or institutions responsible for the protection of the security or the fundamental interests of the Republic of Poland to perform their tasks; or will hinder the performance of tasks by the services or institutions, or the judicial authorities, responsible for the protection of public order, for the security of citizens, or for the prosecution of the perpetrators of crimes and fiscal offences,

---

[15]Gardocka (2008), p. 11.

[16]Szpor (1998), p. 24.

[17]Act of 5 August 2010 on the Protection of Classified Information, consolidated text, Polish Journal of Laws of 2019, item 742, as amended).

The aforementioned classification of confidential information has therefore been clarified by the legislators in a fairly broad manner, covering most cases which can cause damage or serious harm to the state.

Currently, classified information is governed by the following legal Acts:

(1) The Act of 5 August 2010 on the Protection of Classified Information and the secondary legislation adopted on its basis.
(2) Ratified bilateral international agreements on the mutual protection of classified information concluded with Albania, Bulgaria, Croatia, the Czech Republic, Estonia, Finland, France, Germany, Italy, Latvia, Norway, Russia, Romania, Slovakia, Spain, Sweden, Ukraine, the United Kingdom, and the United States;
(3) Agreement between the Parties to the North Atlantic Treaty for the Security of Information, done at Brussels on 6 March 1997,[18] and the Agreement Between the Parties to the North Atlantic Treaty for Cooperation Regarding Atomic Information, done at Paris on 18 June 1964.[19]

The Act on the Protection of Classified Information paved the way for the directional construction of a modern system of protection of classified information, which significantly contributed to the creation of a legal framework within which Poland's accession to the North Atlantic Alliance became possible. Over the years the Act has been in force, enormous technological progress has been accomplished, especially in the means of communication and communication and information systems, which undoubtedly has had an impact on information security, and thus on the relevance of the solutions provided in the Act and secondary legislation, especially on those issues which manifest levels far below the current technological state of the art, and are not adapted to the conditions and capabilities of modern technology. This also applies to procedures related to ensuring cybersecurity.

Regarding the information covered by the said Regulation, it can be assumed that the catalogue of information which will not be released extends beyond classified information. Meanwhile, the content of the provision does not indicate who verifies the information, and which authority makes the decision at the stage of this revision, and thus is responsible for not passing it to the Cooperation Group.

Since Member States vary widely in their level of preparedness, leading to an uneven level of consumer and business protection, and adversely affecting the overall level of security of network and information systems within the EU, it has become necessary to develop common informational procedures. Effective response to the challenges of ensuring the security of network and information systems calls for a holistic approach at the EU level, including requirements for building and planning common minimum capacities, and the exchange of information at the primary, i.e. national level. Information, which in this case is a preventive factor,

[18] Agreement between the Parties to the North Atlantic Treaty for the Security of Information, done at Brussels on 6 March 1997 Polish Journal of Laws of 2000, No. 64, item 740.

[19] Agreement Between the Parties to the North Atlantic Treaty for Cooperation Regarding Atomic Information, done at Paris on 18 June 1964 Polish Journal of Laws of 2001 No. 143, item 1594.

is a means to apply this practice. Reporting to the European Commission is essential for building a uniform, common, cybersecurity system in the EU. The Commission shall itself periodically review the functioning of this Directive and report thereon to the European Parliament and the Council. For this purpose, and with a view to further developing strategic and operational cooperation, the Commission shall take into consideration reports by the Cooperation Group and the CSIRT network on the experience gained at the strategic and operational levels. The designation by a Member State of the competent authorities, the single point of contact (their tasks and any amendments thereto, as well as information on the provisions on fines, which, in accordance with Article 21 of the Directive, should be effective, proportionate, and dissuasive) is part of a common policy to build a single cybersecurity system.

Recital 71 of the Preamble to the NIS Directive stipulates that the Commission should periodically review the Directive, in consultation with stakeholders, in particular to verify whether amendments are necessary in the light of changing social, political, technological, or market conditions. In its review, the Commission shall also assess the listings in Annexes II and III, and the consistency in the identification of the operators of essential services and the services in the sectors referred to in Annex II. The obligation to provide information contained in this provision not only arises from the need to create a coherent cybersecurity system, but is related to the provision of information by the European Commission to the European Parliament and the Council in the form of reports which assess, among other things, the consistency of the approach being taken by the Member State concerned to identify the operators of essential services. Pursuant to recital 19 of the Preamble to the Directive, in order to ensure that possible market developments are being adequately reflected, Member States should maintain under regular review a list of identified operators, and update it where necessary. Moreover, Member States should provide the Commission with the information necessary to assess to what extent this common methodology has allowed the consistent application of the definitions by Member States. The purpose of providing information concerning the tasks of CSIRT MON, CSIRT NASK, and CSIRT GOV, encompassing the main elements of incident-handling procedures, is to build a common and uniform cybersecurity system, including at the level of emergency-handling procedures, as well as the tasks of entities.

The Minister competent for digital affairs is an entity synchronising the activities of the institutions at the strategic level (at the operational level the importance of the NC Cyber and the National CSIRT should be emphasised). It is the essential element in the organisation of the cybersecurity system in Poland. It should be emphasised that the decision to appoint a special Ministry within the administration to perform cybersecurity tasks is not a permanent solution. The sphere of cybersecurity is interdisciplinary, and requires the consolidation and coordination of different elements of the state's functioning, and, within it, individual units.

References

Gardocka T (ed) (2008) Obywatelskie prawo do informacji, Warszawa
Gołaczyński J (2009) Ustawa o świadczeniu usług drogą elektroniczną, Warszawa
Szpor G (1998) Informacja w zagospodarowaniu przestrzennym, Katowice

Katarzyna Chałubińska–Jentkiewicz dr. hab. of legal sciences (University of Warsaw and the Jagiellonian University), legal advisor, associate professor, and head of the Department of Cybersecurity Law and New Technologies at the Institute of Law in the Faculty of National Security at the War Studies University in Warsaw. She is also a lecturer at the SWPS University and director of the Academic Center for Cybersecurity Policy. In the years 1996–2010, she worked as a lawyer in the National Broadcasting Council and with the public broadcaster TVP S.A. Between 2011 and 2017, she was deputy director of the National Audiovisual Institute (her competence centered on the field of digitization). As a scientist, she conducts research on cybersecurity, information security threats, the development of electronic media law, protection of intellectual property, and the impact of new technologies on the development of the state and the legal situation of the individual. Katarzyna Chałubińska–Jentkiewicz is the author of monographs and numerous articles, which include topics such as new technologies law, cyber responsibility, information security law, and audiovisual media: Regulatory conflict in the age of digitization, Audio visual media services; Regulation in the conditions of digital conversion; Information and computerization in public administration; Cultural Security Law and Reuse of public sector information. She is head of the Ministry of Science's research project "Polish cybersecurity system – a model of legal solutions."

The Duties and Legal Status of the Government Plenipotentiary for Cybersecurity and the College for Cybersecurity

Agnieszka Brzostek

Abstract The imposition of the NIS Directive results in the adoption of the NCSA. A special role in this system is played by the Government Plenipotentiary for Cybersecurity, whose primary task is to coordinate activities and implement the government's policy in the field of cybersecurity.

The Plenipotentiary supervises the risk management process of the national cybersecurity system using aggregated data and indicators developed with the participation of competent authorities for cybersecurity matters, CSIRT MON, CSIRT NASK and CSIRT GOV. The Plenipotentiary's tasks in this area also include providing opinions on government documents, including draft legal acts that affect the implementation of cybersecurity tasks.

The Government Plenipotentiary is also one of the members of the College at the Council of Ministers, which acts as an advisory and consultative body on cybersecurity.

The NCSA also indicates the scope of cooperation of the Government Plenipotentiary with the competent authorities for cybersecurity, which concerns cooperation in matters related to cybersecurity with other countries, organisations and international institutions.

1 The Legal Status of the Government Plenipotentiary for Cybersecurity

In the Polish legal system, the term "Government Plenipotentiary" appears in the Act of 8 August 1996 on the Council of Ministers. The Council of Ministers may appoint a Plenipotentiary for specific matters the assignment of which to Members of the

A. Brzostek (✉)
Instytut Prawa/Institute of Law, Akademia Sztuki Wojennej w Warszawie/War Studies University in Warsaw, Warsaw, Poland
e-mail: a.brzostek@akademia.mil.pl

K. Chałubińska-Jentkiewicz et al. (eds.), *Cybersecurity in Poland*,
https://doi.org/10.1007/978-3-030-78551-2_18

Council of Ministers is not advisable.[1] The authorisation of the Government Plenipotentiary to pursue the matters provided for in this article is restricted by Acts relating to the competences of other Ministers.[2] This general principle constitutes the basis for appointing a Government Plenipotentiary.[3]

Government Plenipotentiaries are appointed and dismissed by the Prime Minister; the Council of Ministers, by way of an ordinance, specifies the scope of the powers granted to the Plenipotentiary, the manner of supervising his or her activities, and the procedure for providing the Plenipotentiary with substantive, legal, organisational, technical, and administrative support.[4] The key point is that the Government Plenipotentiary may be either a secretary or an under-secretary of state. The Act on the Council of Ministers mentions the Government Plenipotentiary in the Chapter on Members of the Council of Ministers. At the same time, it does not refer to the Plenipotentiary as a Member of the Council of Ministers. The legal status of the Government Plenipotentiary has been of little to no interest to researchers. This post is treated briefly in the literature, and only in relation to the provisions of the Act on the Council of Ministers.[5]

In the explanatory Statement on the Act on the National Cybersecurity System,[6] the promoter did not indicate the legal nature of the Plenipotentiary, describing only his or her duties. This does not mean that the Act's promoter treated this issue differently from the way the others did. The indication that the Plenipotentiary is the secretary or under-secretary of state in the Ministry in question places the Plenipotentiary within a specific organisational structure, and at the same time ensures technical and organisational security when fulfilling duties.

Pursuant to Article 37(1) of the Act on the Council of Ministers, the Minister performs his or her duties with the assistance of the secretary and under-secretaries of state, and the Minister's political cabinet. There is no unified position within the jurisprudence or doctrine which defines the status of a secretary of state or an under-secretary of state. It is generally accepted that they serve the role of Deputy Minister. However, the Resolution adopted by the full panel of the Supreme Court indicated

> there can be no doubt that the Deputies of the Minister are neither secretaries nor under-secretaries of state who are not Members of the Council of Ministers, and that they cannot be included in government administration authorities. The professional literature describes them as an element in the political (managerial) structure of the Ministry, or, more precisely,

[1] Article 10(1) of the Act on the Council of Ministers.

[2] The Judgment of the Constitutional Tribunal of 9 May 2000, U 6/98, OTK 2000/4/108 (Statement of Grounds 6/98, Judgment of the Constitutional Tribunal 2000/4/108).

[3] As of 31 October 2019 there were 36 appointed government Government Plenipotentiaries for specific matters; see https://bip.kprm.gov.pl/kpr/bip-rady-ministrow/organy-pomocnicze/pelnomocnicy-rzadu-i-pr. Accessed on 10.05.2020

[4] Article 10(3) of the Act of 8 August 1996 on the Council of Ministers, consolidated text, Polish Journal of Laws of 2019, item 1171, as amended.

[5] E.g. Zimmermann (2016), p. 240.

[6] Explanatory statement for the Act on Court Fees in Civil-Law Matters, print 2505. https://www.sejm.gov.pl/sejm8.nsf/druk.xsp?nr=2505 (accessed on 10 May 2020).

> as Ministerial assistants, helping to run the Ministry; they are the closest associates of the Minister and the highest officials in the Ministry, but they cannot be assigned the functions of state authorities, because they perform their duties on behalf of, and under the authority of, the Minister.[7]

It should also be noted that the normative body included Article 37 of the Act on the Council of Ministers in Chapter 6 on the "Scope and principles of Ministers' activities", which defines the legal position of a Minister as the supreme entity in government administration, managing a specific department of that administration. This gave rise to the Supreme Court's conclusion that the assistance and cooperation of the secretary and under-secretaries of state are closely related only to those matters which result from managing a designated department of government administration, and thus remain in the sphere of public administration without going beyond its capacity.[8]

In a gloss to the Supreme Court's Resolution, B. Mik pointed out that the statement which placed the secretary and under-secretary of state in the role of mere assistants and associates of the Minister and top officials of the Ministry was unfounded. One can only concede that

> this particular provision, contrary to Article 37(5) of the Act on the Council of Ministers, in comparison with Article 36 of the Act on the Council of Ministers, has been unusually amiss in its wording.[9]

The indication that a literal interpretation is not sufficient to specify what it means for a Minister to perform his or her duties "with the assistance of" the Secretary, Under-Secretary, and the political cabinet, might also raise doubts. B. Mik rightly remarks that the equating of these three functions in one sentence can be misleading, because the purpose of each individual position is different. The Minister's political cabinet plays an advisory role, and has no means to influence other members of the Ministry. Similarly inappropriate is applying a functional interpretation, classifying all these positions as auxiliary roles. To that extent, the understanding of these functions would be purely service-oriented.[10] In specific regulations, the secretary of state and under-secretary of state may represent the Council of Ministers at the session of the Sejm and Senate,[11] and whether they are obliged to resign along with the resignation of the Prime Minister and the Government.[12] Thus, it is unreasonable

[7]The Resolution of the full composition of the Supreme Court of 14 November 2007 BSA (Administrative Court Office) -1410-5/07, pp. 12–13.

[8]The Resolution of the full composition ... op. cit.-1410-5/07, pp. 25–26 http://www.sn.pl/sprawy/SiteAssets/Lists/Zagadnienia_prawne/EditForm/2007.11.14.Uchwala.pelnego.skladu.SN.pdf, accessed on 14. September 2020.

[9]Mik (2008), p. 166.

[10]Mik (2008), p. 166. It is interesting that B. Mik cites an example of the interpretation of Article 115 §13 of the PC when analysing the term public official – an employee of the Government administration who performs a purely service function does not enjoy the status of a public official.

[11]Article 9(3)(1) of the Act on the Council of Ministers (the Office of the Council of Ministers).

[12]Article 38 of the Act on the Council of Ministers (the Office of the Council of Ministers). More Mik (2008), pp. 166–167.

to reduce these functions to an auxiliary role only. It is appropriate to recognise, as the legislators intended, a secretary of state or an under-secretary of state as the highest-ranking officials in a Ministry, and as a Deputy Minister, insofar as such a replacement has been appointed.[13]

A separate issue is the position of the Government Plenipotentiary within the structure of public administration. The Plenipotentiary acts as a coordinator of cybersecurity activities. The legislators, in Article 4(19) of the NCSA, while detailing a catalogue of entities covered by the national cybersecurity system, did not include the Government Plenipotentiary for Cybersecurity, but cited the position as a separate entity within the structure of the cybersecurity system. The appointment of a secretary of state or under-secretary of state as a Government Plenipotentiary does not imply that the Plenipotentiary is a public-administration authority. This is explicitly stipulated by specific laws,[14] or by the Code of Administrative Procedure.

2 The Duties of the Government Plenipotentiary for Cybersecurity

The duties which the legislators set out for the Plenipotentiary are related to the concepts of the coordination and implementation of the government's policy of ensuring cybersecurity.[15] The term coordination requires explanation here. Coordination is considered to be a legal situation, or a whole group of legal situations, which aims or aim to organise the activities of many entities, or, more precisely, to harmonise these activities.[16] According to the literature, coordination should be understood as the harmonisation of activities undertaken by organisational units of administration in order to achieve the intended goal more easily and in a uniform manner. Coordination involves actions already taken and eliminates discrepancies between them, or it can entail planned actions, and thus prevent their repetition, overlap, or competition between them.[17] It is noted that there are two sides to understanding the concept of coordination. First of all, it is about removing the contradictions which exist or can exist in the present, and this is treated as the negative side of coordination. The positive side consists of identifying and

[13]Mik (2008), pp. 166–167.

[14]The legislators defined differently e.g. the responsible bodies of the National Tax Administration—Article 11(1)(2) of the NCSA. indicated explicitly that the Head of the National Tax Administration is the authority responsible for NTA matters. Article (13) (2) indicates that the Head of NTA, who is the Secretary of State in the office supporting the Minister of Finance, is appointed by the Prime Minister at the request of the Minister competent for public finance.

[15]Article 60 of the NCSA: the Regulation of the Council of Ministers of 18 March 2018 on the appointment of a Government Plenipotentiary for Cybersecurity, Polish Journal of Laws of 2018, item 587. Act repealed.

[16]Góralczyk (2016), pp. 36–40.

[17]Zimmermann (2016), p. 230.

recommending such actions which will contribute to better performance by all entities involved in the coordinative situation in the future.[18]

Coordination mostly occurs in the decentralised model, but it can also occur in the centralised model of hierarchical subordination, because it consists of unifying and adjusting the activities of entities which might even be organisationally independent of each other. The influence of the coordinator on the behaviour of the coordinated body is indirect, and the coordinator does not assume responsibility from the coordinated body for its actions. As J. Zimmermann points out, the coordination responsibilities are not very formalised, and are fragmentarily defined in the regulations, often with the use of unclear and ambiguous phrases.[19]

Cooperation between public-administration authorities is a kind of bond akin to coordination, which can, of course, only occur in a decentralised system. The forms of cooperation are very diverse. Their basic categorisation involves distinguishing the forms resulting from constitutional law and those introduced by substantive law.[20] Such cooperation can involve taking concrete actions, as well as drawing up legal acts. The actual process of cooperation can be, for example, the exchange of information and making suggestions. Legal acts specific to this legal and administrative situation should include all bilateral (or multilateral) acts, such as agreements and settlements. They can sometimes constitute the basis for the creation of separate, permanent structures (entities) for the development of cooperation (companies, unions, and associations).[21]

Pursuant to the Regulation of the Council of Ministers of 16 March 2018 on the appointment of the Government Plenipotentiary for Cybersecurity, the secretary of state or the under-secretary of state was appointed the Plenipotentiary in the Ministry of National Defence.[22] The explanatory statement to the Act avoided specifying the status of the Plenipotentiary, but it merely announced the appointment to the position.

The duties set out in Article 62 of the Act specify in detail what the coordination activities of the Plenipotentiary should involve. These comprise the following.

- Analysing and assessing the functioning of the national cybersecurity system on the basis of aggregated data and indicators developed with the participation of public-administrative agencies, and agencies competent for cybersecurity—CSIRT (Computer Security Incident Response Team) MON (Ministry of National Defence), CSIRT NASK (Research and Academic Computer Network), and CSIRT GOV.
- Supervising the risk-management process of the national cybersecurity system with the use of aggregated data, and indicators developed with the participation of

[18] Góralczyk (2016), pp. 36–40.

[19] Zimmermann (2016), pp. 230–231.

[20] Zimmermann (2016), p. 231 et seq.

[21] Góralczyk (2016), pp. 36–40.

[22] §1 (2) of the Regulation of the Council of Ministers on the appointment of a Government Plenipotentiary for Cybersecurity.

authorities competent for cybersecurity—CSIRT MON, CSIRT NASK, and CSIRT GOV.
- Issuing opinions on government documents, including draft legal Acts affecting the implementation of cybersecurity duties.
- Popularising new solutions and initiating cybersecurity activities at the domestic level.
- Initiating national cybersecurity exercises.
- Issuing recommendations regarding the use of IT devices or software at the request of the CSIRT.

This closed catalogue has been supplemented with separate duties which the Plenipotentiary performs in consultation with the respective Ministers. These comprise the following:

- Cooperating with other countries, organisations and international institutions in matters related to cybersecurity
- Undertaking activities aimed at supporting scientific research and the development of cybersecurity technologies
- Undertaking activities aimed at increasing public awareness of threats to cybersecurity and the safe use of the Internet.[23]

The Plenipotentiary will also supervise the process of managing the risk of the national cybersecurity system with the use of aggregated data and indicators developed with the participation of authorities competent for cybersecurity—CSIRT MON, CSIRT NASK and CSIRT GOV. His or her responsibilities in this respect will also include issuing opinions on government documents, including draft legal Acts affecting the performance of cybersecurity duties.

In his or her activities, the Plenipotentiary should also popularise new solutions and instigate cybersecurity activities at the national level, initiate national exercises in cybersecurity, and issue recommendations regarding the use of IT devices and software at the request of CSIRT.[24] The Plenipotentiary prepares, and submits to the Council of Ministers, by 31 March each year, a report for the previous calendar year containing information on activities in the sphere of ensuring cybersecurity at the national level.

The Act on the national cybersecurity system also indicates the scope of cooperation of the Government Plenipotentiary with the authorities competent for cybersecurity,[25] which involves cooperation in matters related to cybersecurity with other

[23] Article 62(2) NCSA.

[24] Article 61(1) NCSA.

[25] In Article 41 the Act provided the catalogue and scope of responsibilities of the authorised entities. The entities responsible for cybersecurity are (1) for the energy sector—the Minister competent for energy; (2) for the water-transport sector—the Minister competent for the maritime economy and the Minister competent for inland navigation; (3) for the banking sector and the financial market infrastructure—the Polish Financial Supervision Authority; (4) for the health sector, with the exception of certain entities—the Minister competent for health; (5) for the

countries, organisations, and international institutions, undertaking activities aimed at supporting the scientific research and development of cybersecurity technologies, and conducting educational activities aimed at raising public awareness of cybersecurity threats and the safe use of the Internet.[26]

One of the duties of the Plenipotentiary, as indicated in the Act on the National Cybersecurity System, is cooperation with CSIRT MON, CSIRT NASK, and CSIRT GOV in order to ensure a cohesive and complete risk management system at the domestic level, the implementation of duties to counteract cross-sectoral and cross-border cybersecurity threats, and ensuring coordination to handle reported incidents.[27] In accordance with the definition of risk management adopted in the Act, this means the necessity to take coordinated actions related to cybersecurity management with regard to the estimated risk at the domestic level through the cooperation of the above-mentioned entities.[28] The Plenipotentiary may decide on the scope of authority of the CSIRTs. Each CSIRT is obliged to account for its scope of authority, as well as take an action to determine the appropriate addressee of the incident report. Where there is disagreement between the CSIRTs on the determination of their scopes of authority in the event of a critical incident, the identification of the CSIRT coordinating the incident handling should be made by the critical incident team. Responsibility for ensuring incident coordination should be acknowledged as the responsibility of the CSIRT which received the report, until possible clarification with the CSIRT expressing doubts about the chosen scope of authority. In a situation where the CSIRT does not clarify these doubts, it is possible to ask the Plenipotentiary for Cybersecurity to indicate the appropriate solution.[29]

Article 33(8) of the NCSA provides for authorisation for the Plenipotentiary to contact the authority supervising the entity which the recommendation concerned if such an entity does not follow the recommendation. In such a situation the Plenipotentiary informs the person exercising supervision about the failure to follow the recommendation. The supervisory body, within the scope of its powers, may apply supervisory measures. A letter signed by the Plenipotentiary is a sufficient form of contacting the competent authority.[30]

healthcare sector, including certain entities—the Minister of National Defence; (6) for the drinking water supply and distribution sector—the Minister competent for water management; (7) for the digital infrastructure sector—with the exception of certain entities—the Minister competent for digital affairs; (8) for the Digital infrastructure sector—Minister of National Defence; (9) for digital service providers, with the exception of certain entities, the Minister competent for digital affairs; (10) for digital service providers, including other entities—the Minister of National Defence.

[26] Article 62(2) NCSA.

[27] Article 26 NCSA

[28] Prusak-Górnicka and Silicki (2019a).

[29] Prusak-Górnicka and Silicki (2019a).

[30] Prusak-Górnicka and Silicki (2019a).

The Plenipotentiary is one of the entities[31] which, in accordance with the provisions of the Act, process personal data obtained in connection with incidents and threats to cybersecurity.[32]

3 Cooperation Between the Plenipotentiary & the College for Cybersecurity

The Plenipotentiary is also one of the Members of the College of the Council of Ministers who acts as an opinion-giving and advisory body on cybersecurity matters. The scope of responsibility of the College for Cybersecurity is defined in Article 65 of the Act, and covers, in principle, the expressing of opinions on issues related to the policies and plans for counteracting cybersecurity threats; the performance by CSIRT MON, CSIRT NASK, the Head of the Internal Security Agency performing duties under CSIRT GOV, sectoral cybersecurity teams and authorities competent for cybersecurity of duties entrusted to them in accordance with the policies and plans for counteracting cybersecurity threats; the expressing of opinions on cooperation between the authorities managing or supervising CSIRT MON, CSIRT GOV, and CSIRT NASK; cooperation between CSIRT MON, CSIRT NASK, the Head of the Internal Security Agency, and the Minister—a Member of the Council of Ministers responsible for coordinating the activities of secret services, sectoral cybersecurity teams and authorities competent for cybersecurity; the organisation of the exchange of information relevant to cybersecurity and the international position of the Republic of Poland between government administration authorities and on the proposals of the CSIRT MON, CSIRT NASK or CSIRT GOV regarding recommendations on the use of IT devices or software. Apart from the Plenipotentiary, the College comprises the Prime Minister, as the Chair, the Secretary of the College, and the Members of the College.[33]

The Act also stipulated that the Prime Minister, in order to coordinate the cybersecurity activities of the government administration, may, on the basis of the College's recommendations, issue binding directives on guaranteeing cybersecurity

[31]These bodies also include the Minister competent for digital affairs, the Director of the Government Centre for Security, and the bodies responsible for digital affairs.

[32]Article 39(4) NCSA. For more on this topic—Taczkowska-Olszewska (2019), pp. 243–256.

[33]Article 66(1) of the Act on the National Cybersecurity System stipulates that the Members of the College are the Minister competent for internal affairs, the Minister competent for digital affairs, the Minister of National Defence, the Minister competent for foreign affairs, the Head of the Chancellery of the Prime Minister, the Head of the National Security Bureau, if appointed by the President of the Republic of Poland, the Minister—a Member of the Council of Ministers responsible for the coordination of the activities of secret services or a person authorised by him or her with the rank of a secretary of state or under-secretary of state, and if the Minister—a Member of the Council of Ministers responsible for coordinating the activities of secret services has not been appointed—the Head of the Internal Security Agency.

at the domestic level and on the operation of the national cybersecurity system, and also request information and opinions in this regard from Members of the Government.[34]

The Plenipotentiary may, after securing the opinion of the College, issue, change or revoke a recommendation to use IT devices or software, in particular with regard to the impact on public security or an important interest of state security. The entity within the national cybersecurity system may raise objections to the Plenipotentiary regarding recommendations on the use of IT devices or software, if they are having a negative impact on the service provided or the public task implemented, no later than within 7 days from the date of receipt of the recommendation. It is crucial that in the justification for the objection, the entity must indicate and substantiate the negative impact of the recommendation on the service provided or the task implemented. Objections to the recommendation may be made by any of the entities in the national cybersecurity system, i.e. each of the entities listed in Article 4. The Plenipotentiary shall address the doubts immediately, but not later than within 14 days from the date of their receipt, and uphold the recommendations regarding the use of IT devices or software, or issue revised recommendations. The entity in the national cybersecurity system informs the Plenipotentiary, at his or her request, about the manner and scope of taking into account the recommendations regarding the use of IT devices or software. In the event that the recommendation regarding the use of IT devices or software is not being taken into account, this would be the basis for the Plenipotentiary to contact the authority supervising the entity to inform it about their failure to do so.[35]

IT security testing of the hardware or software used may be performed by each of the three national-level CSIRTs, i.e. CSIRT MON, CSIRT NASK, or CSIRT GOV. It is reasonable to assume that the testing may be started at the CSIRT's own initiative, or at the request of the College for Cybersecurity or the Plenipotentiary for Cybersecurity. The CSIRT is not bound by the submitted testing application, and its initiation remains at the sole discretion of the CSIRT. The purpose of the study is to identify the vulnerabilities which, when taken advantage of, might affect public security or an important interest of state security.[36]

The Plenipotentiary issues a recommendation after securing the opinion of the College for Cybersecurity on the basis of an application submitted by the appropriate CSIRT regarding the use of IT devices or software. As a consequence, when a vulnerability which may affect public safety, or an important national security interest, is detected, the CSIRT which discovered the vulnerability is obligated to request a recommendation. Therefore, it is unacceptable to issue a recommendation without the College's opinion. The Plenipotentiary also has the power to change or revoke a recommendation, but the change to or revocation of a recommendation also

---

[34]Article 67(1) NCSA.

[35]Article 33(4-8) NCSA. More on the scope of the individual activities of CSIRT Nowikowska (2019), pp. 191–210.

[36]Prusak-Górnicka and Silicki (2019a).

requires the opinion of the College. The provisions of the Code of Administrative Procedure do not apply to issuing recommendations, and the form in which they are issued is not a form of administrative decision. Therefore, no complaint may be lodged with the administrative court.[37] Such recommendations are abstract in nature. In the light of the regulations, it should be assumed that the Plenipotentiary should inform all entities in the national cybersecurity system that can be affected by the vulnerability of issuing the recommendation, using for that action the CSIRT communication channels and the authorities competent for cybersecurity.[38]

As part of his or her competences, the Plenipotentiary may submit to the Council of Ministers proposals and recommendations regarding actions which should be taken by entities within the national cybersecurity system in order to ensure cybersecurity at the domestic level, and to counteract threats in this regard.[39]

The Plenipotentiary draws up and submits to the Council of Ministers, by 31 March each year, a report on the previous calendar year containing information on activities which involve ensuring cybersecurity at the domestic level.

The College operates under the Council of Ministers, and its responsibilities are prescribed by law. These comprise the following.

(1) Policies and plans for counteracting cybersecurity threats.
(2) The performance by CSIRT MON, CSIRT NASK, and the Head of the Internal Security Agency of duties under CSIRT GOV, the sectoral cybersecurity teams, and the authorities competent for cybersecurity of duties entrusted to them in accordance with the policies and plans for counteracting cybersecurity threats.
(3) Cooperation between the managing or supervisory bodies of CSIRT MON, CSIRT GOV, and CSIRT NASK.
(4) Cooperation between CSIRT MON, CSIRT NASK entities, the Head of the Internal Security Agency, and the Minister—a Member of the Council of Ministers responsible for coordinating the activities of special services, sectoral cybersecurity teams, and the authorities competent for cybersecurity.

---

[37] Ibidem. The lack of authority to lodge a complaint to the Provincial Administrative Court is limited by Article 3 of the Law on proceedings before administrative courts, as well as by the fact that the recommendation is abstract and does not decide about rights and obligations.

[38] Prusak-Górnicka and Silicki (2019b).

[39] Article 63 NCSA. The indicated Regulation of the Council of Ministers also includes the duties of the Government Plenipotentiary for Cybersecurity. These comprise the following. (1) The analysis and assessment of cybersecurity on the basis of aggregated data and the indicators developed with the participation of the government administration authorities and computer security incident response teams operating at the Ministry of National Defence, the Internal Security Agency, and the Scientific and Academic Computer Network—the National Research Institute. (2) Developing new solutions and initiating cybersecurity activities at the domestic level. (3) Issuing opinions on draft legal acts and other government documents affecting the fulfilment of cybersecurity duties. (4) Conducting and coordinating activities carried out by government administration authorities aimed at increasing public awareness of the threats to cybersecurity and the safe use of the Internet. (5) Initiating national cybersecurity exercises. See §2 (2) of the Regulation of the Council of Ministers of 18 March 2018 on the appointment of the Government Plenipotentiary for Cybersecurity.

(5) The organisation of the exchange of information pertaining to cybersecurity and the international position of the Republic of Poland between government administration agencies.
(6) Proposals from CSIRT MON, CSIRT NASK, or CSIRT GOV regarding recommendations on the use of IT devices or software.[40]

Along with the Prime Minister as the Chair, and the Plenipotentiary for Cybersecurity, the College comprises the Secretary of the College and the Members. Under the Act the following Ministers are the Members: the Minister competent for domestic affairs, the Minister competent for digital affairs, the Minister of National Defence, and the Minister competent for foreign affairs, as well as the Minister—a Member of the Council of Ministers responsible for coordinating the activities of the secret services or a person authorised by them in the rank of secretary of state or under-secretary of state, and if the Minister—a Member of the Council of Ministers responsible for the coordination of the activities of the secret services—has not been appointed—the Head of the Internal Security Agency. The Members may also include the Head of the Chancellery of the Prime Minister and the Head of the National Security Bureau, if appointed by the President of the Republic of Poland.[41] Depending on the needs and the subject of the sessions, the meetings of the College are also attended by the Director of the Government Centre for Security, the Head of the Internal Security Agency or his or her Deputy, the Head of the Military Counterintelligence Service or his or her Deputy, the Director of the Scientific and Academic Computer Network—the National Research Institute.

The responsibilities of the College include the development of recommendations for the Council of Ministers regarding cybersecurity activities at the domestic level. On the basis of these recommendations, the Prime Minister, in order to coordinate the activities of the government administration, may issue binding guidelines on ensuring cybersecurity at the domestic level, and the operation of the national cybersecurity system, and also request information and opinions in this regard. The Prime Minister issues binding guidelines for CSIRT MON, CSIRT GOV, and CSIRT NASK related to handling critical incidents, including the designation of the CSIRT responsible for handling a specific critical incident.[42]

4 Summary

Within the scope of his or her activities, a Plenipotentiary coordinates the activities of entities and bodies with authority in cybersecurity. In a closed catalogue, the Act specifies these duties, pointing out their fairly general nature, focusing on the

[40] Article 65(1) NCSA.
[41] Article 66(1) NCSA.
[42] Article 67 NCSA.

assessment of the process of the functioning of the national cybersecurity system, and on issuing recommendations. The legislators did not provide the Plenipotentiary with the responsibilities of a public-administrative authority, thus emphasising its character as a coordinator—not a manager—of cybersecurity activities. It is also related to the legal nature of actions taken by the Plenipotentiary, which do not display the characteristics of an administrative decision, i.e. they exclude the application of the Code of Administrative Procedure. The fact that the Plenipotentiary is not designated as a public-administration authority is also related to the legal status of the Government Plenipotentiary, which, under the Act on the Council of Ministers, becomes a secretary or an under-secretary of state. The College, established as an opinion-giving and advisory body, does not raise any doubts as to its legal status. At present, it is still difficult to assess the activities of both the Plenipotentiary for Cybersecurity and the College. The creation of the cybersecurity system, and the implementation of solutions and recommendations, is ongoing, so it takes time to make a substantive assessment of the activities of the discussed entities, as well as the legal solutions.

References

Góralczyk W Jr (2016) Kierownictwo w prawie administracyjnym, Warsaw

Mik B (2008) The Gloss to the Resolution Adopted by the Full Composition of the Supreme Court of 14 November 2007, file ref. BSA (Administrative Court Office) – 4110-5/07 (regarding the right of the Minister of Justice to delegate a judge), Prokuratura i Prawo, 6

Nowikowska M (2019) Commentary on Art. 26. In: Kitler W, Taczkowska-Olszewska J, Radoniewicz F (eds) Ustawa o Krajowym Systemie Cyberbezpieczeństwa. Komentarz, Warsaw

Prusak-Górnicka K, Silicki K (2019a) Commentary on Article 26 NCSA. In: Czaplicki K, Gryszczyńska A, Szpor G (eds) Ustawa o Krajowym Systemie cyberbezpieczeństwa. Komentarz, Warsaw, LEX/el.

Prusak-Górnicka K, Silicki K (2019b) Commentary on Article 33 NCSA. In: Czaplicki K, Gryszczyńska A, Szpor G (eds) Ustawa o Krajowym Systemie cyberbezpieczeństwa. Komentarz, Warsaw, LEX/el.

Taczkowska-Olszewska J (2019) Commentary on Article 39. In: Komentarz W, Kitler J, Taczkowska-Olszewska F (eds) Ustawa o krajowym systemie cyberbezpieczeństwa. Radoniewicz, Warsaw

Zimmermann J (2016) Prawo administracyjne, Warsaw

Agnieszka Brzostek PhD, adjunct at the Institute of Law of the War Studies Academy. She is a lecturer of law and administrative procedure at studies in the field of law and administration. Scientific interests focus on administrative law and administrative procedure, as well as on the functioning of public administration, in particular on the activities of public administration bodies in the field of security and cybersecurity. Scientific interests focus on administrative law and administrative proceedings, as well as on the operation of public administration, in particular on the operation of public administration bodies in the field of security and cyber security. She is the author or co-author of numerous chapters in monographs and scientific articles.

… Legal Status of the Sovereign or Plenipotentiary for

Part III
Obligations of Other Entities Included in the National Cybersecurity System ("Participants" of the National Cybersecurity System)

Tasks of Operators of Essential Services and Digital Service Providers

Katarzyna Chałubińska-Jentkiewicz

Abstract Public tasks for cyberspace security occupy an important place in the National Security System of the Republic of Poland. The responsibility for ensuring cybersecurity lies with all network users, but public administration authorities play a significant role, with one of the basic tasks being activities to ensure public security and order. In the conditions of arrangements for the implementation of public tasks for national security, with particular emphasis on the specification of public tasks in the area of critical infrastructure protection, it is important to determine the catalogue of entities performing public tasks in the field of cyberspace security. It should be noted that these entities may be public entities performing public tasks, private entities performing public tasks based on the privatisation of public task implementation, and private entities performing their own tasks that are of significant public interest, or which were once carried out as public tasks but were subject to privatisation.

The opportunities afforded by new technologies, and the resulting necessity to adapt the administrative and legal system, are key issues concerning the development of modern public management and ensuring the security of ICT networks. Public authorities have become obligated to provide electronic services to citizens, covering both the handling of citizens' affairs and other areas of public administration functioning, not excluding the decision-making process. The computerisation processes in public administration are accompanied by changes associated with the state-citizen relationship. Furthermore, it is worth noting that in the initial period of the development of computerisation, digitalisation occurred mainly in organisational units, which based their activities on processing significant amounts of data. The first IT applications were implemented in the financial and accounting departments,

K. Chałubińska-Jentkiewicz (✉)
Akademickie Centrum Polityki Cyberbezpieczeństwa/Academic Center for Cybersecurity Policy, Akademia Sztuki Wojennej w Warszawie/War Studies University in Warsaw, Warsaw, Poland
e-mail: k.jentkiewicz@akademia.mil.pl

K. Chałubińska-Jentkiewicz et al. (eds.), *Cybersecurity in Poland*,
https://doi.org/10.1007/978-3-030-78551-2_19

where IT services for public institutions were provided.[1] Modern electronic technology facilitated data processing by means of the automation of certain work in public administration. Therefore, "information technology is becoming an essential tool for the efficiency of the administrative apparatus".[2] Thus, it can be concluded that the current development of administrative procedures in Poland is being significantly influenced by constant and advanced technical progress. The influence of new technical measures which have emerged in public administration is necessitating modifications to basic administrative-legal relations (individual-citizen), but is also significant for inter-sectoral cooperation in the implementation of public tasks. Cyberspace is a new sphere of influence of these processes. As cyberspace develops, the threats occurring in it evolve. Cyberspace is nowadays a symbol of progress, but also of freedom and privacy, and every interference in its functioning is associated with an attack on these values. For the countries involved in developing the information society, cybersecurity is considered to be one of the most serious challenges for the national security system. It involves the security of both the entire state establishment and individual citizens. Therefore, public tasks in cybersecurity occupy an important position in the Polish National Security System. The responsibility for ensuring cybersecurity rests with all network users; however, a significant role is played by public administration authorities, one of whose primary tasks is to ensure security and public order. In terms of arrangements regarding the implementation of public tasks for national security, with particular emphasis on the definition of public tasks in the sphere of critical infrastructure protection, it is important to establish a directory of entities performing public tasks in the field of cyberspace security. Furthermore, it should be noted that these entities may be public entities performing public tasks, private entities undertaking public tasks on the basis of the privatisation of public tasks, or private entities carrying out their own tasks, which are significant for the public interest, or which used to be performed as public tasks, but were subject to privatisation. Subsequently, the issue of intersectoral cooperation is becoming increasingly important in the process of creating a uniform cybersecurity system. The European Public-Private Partnership for Resilience was launched on the basis of the document COM (2009) 149. This platform has initiated activities and increased cooperation between the public and private sectors in identifying key resources, means, functions, and core requirements for resilience, as well as the need for cooperation and mechanisms to respond to large-scale disruptions to electronic communications. National network and information security authorities should cooperate and exchange information with other regulatory authorities, in particular data protection authorities. Responsible NIS authorities should also report major incidents which might be criminal in nature to law-enforcement authorities. Competent national authorities should also regularly publish, on a dedicated website, non-classified information on current early warnings of incidents and threats, and coordinated responses. Legal obligations should not replace or prevent informal or

[1] Pawłowski (2002), p. 85.

[2] Knosala et al. (1996), p. 126.

voluntary cooperation, including between the public and private sectors, aimed at increasing security and exchanging information and best practices. A particularly important and useful platform at the EU level to be developed is the European Public-Private Partnership for Resilience (EP3R15). Pursuant to recital 9 of the Preamble to the Directive, certain sectors of the economy are already regulated, or may in the future be regulated, by sector-specific Union legal acts which incorporate provisions on NIS security.

The Act of 5 July 2018 on the National Cybersecurity System under the provisions of the NIS Directive, introduced the concept of an essential service, which means a service which is crucial for maintaining critical social or economic activities, listed in the register of essential services. Additionally, the Act introduced the concept of a digital service, which means a service provided electronically within the meaning of the provisions of the Act of 18 July 2002 on Providing Services by Electronic Means,[3] listed in Annex No. 2 to the Act. The Act on the Provision of Services by Electronic Means assumes that such a service is characterised by the fact that it is provided at a distance, without the simultaneous presence of the parties (remotely), through the transmission of data, at the individual request of the recipient of the service, transmitted and received by means of devices for electronic processing, including digital compression, and the storage of data, which is entirely transmitted or received by means of a telecommunications network within the meaning of the Act of 16 July 2004—Telecommunications Law.[4]

With regard to the digital service, the Act also determines the entity providing the digital service, which is the digital service provider, i.e. a legal person, or an organisational unit without a legal personality, with its registered office or management bodies in the Republic of Poland, or a representative with an organisational unit in the Republic of Poland, providing the digital service, with the exception of micro and small businesses, as referred to in Article 7(1)(1) and (2) of the Act of 6 March 2018—The Entrepreneurs Law.[5]

The types of digital services are defined in Annex No. 2 to the Act, including **Internet trading platform**—a service which enables consumers or entrepreneurs to conclude contracts electronically with entrepreneurs on the website of the trading platform, or on the website of the entrepreneur who is using the services provided by the Internet trading platform (e.g. Allegro, ING Usługi dla Biznesu S.A.—ALEO. COM, B2B platform automicob2b.pl); **Cloud-computing service**—a service which provides access to a scalable and flexible set of computing resources for shared use by multiple users (e.g. Cloud for Business—ergonet.pl, Amazon Web Services,

[3] Act of 18 July 2002 on Providing Services by Electronic Means, consolidated text, Polish Journal of Laws of 2020, item 344, as amended.

[4] Act of 16 July 2004—Telecommunications Law, consolidated text Polish Journal of Laws of 2019, item 2460, as amended.

[5] Act of 6 March 2018—The Entrepreneurs Law, consolidated text Polish Journal of Laws of 2019, item 1292 hereinafter referred to as "EL".

Google Cloud Platform, Microsoft Azure, private and hybrid[6]); and **Internet search engine**—a service which allows users to search all websites or web pages in a given language by means of a query, by providing a key word, phrase, or other element, referring to information related to the query providing access through a link.

Commission Implementing Regulation (EU) 2018/151 of 30 January 2018 laying down rules for application of Directive (EU) 2016/1148 of the European Parliament and of the Council as regards further specification of the elements to be taken into account by digital service providers for managing the risks posed to the security of network and information systems and of the parameters for determining whether an incident has a substantial impact, specifies the procedures and determines the operating conditions for digital service providers. Pursuant to Article 4, an incident is considered to have a significant impact if at least one of the following situations has occurred: (a) the service delivered by the digital service provider has been unavailable for more than 5,000,000 user-hours, whereby the term "user-hour" refers to the number of affected users in the Union for sixty minutes; (b) the incident has led to a loss of integrity, authenticity, or confidentiality of stored, transmitted, or processed data, or related services presented or accessible via the digital service provider's network and information systems affecting more than 100,000 users in the EU; (c) the incident has created a risk to public safety or a risk of fatalities; (d) the incident has caused material damage to at least one user in the Union where the damage caused to that user exceeds EUR 1,000,000.

[6]**Colocation** is the oldest and straightforward form of service in the cloud. It involves renting a server room, with access to electricity, air conditioning, and the Internet. Other components—hardware, security (firewalls), load management, operating systems, software and applications, are paid for by the user company. Therefore, it is a fee for lending space in a server room.

IaaS—Infrastructure as a Service—a model consisting of providing the customer with an IT infrastructure, i.e. hardware, software, and maintenance. For example, the customer purchases a specific number of servers, disk space, or a specific amount of memory and computing power. Nonetheless, this does not mean that the hardware will be physically installed on the customer's premises. In this model, it happens that the customer is supplying the service provider with its own software, to be installed on the rented hardware.

PaaS—Platform as a Service—the sale of a ready-made, often customised, set of applications. There is no need to purchase hardware or install software. All the necessary programs are located on the provider's servers. The client gets access to the interface (usually in the form of a standardised working environment) through a program, e.g. a web browser. In this model, services are usually available to the user from any computer connected to the Internet.

SaaS—Software as a Service—The customer receives specific, selected software functions. They use any software they need. For this reason, they are not interested in hardware or the working environment. They only have access to specific, functional tools—not necessarily connected to each other through a uniform interface. The programs run on the provider's server. The customer is not obliged to purchase a licence for them. He or she only pays for each use of them, and access to such tools is granted on request.

CaaS—Communications as a Service—The service provider delivers a platform for a telecommunications work environment.

iPaaS—Integration Platform as a Service—A platform which provides integration between different services in the Cloud.

The tasks of a digital service provider include: (1) security of information systems and facilities; (2) incident handling; (3) business continuity management of the provider to provide a digital service; (4) monitoring, auditing, and testing; (5) the latest state of the art, including compliance with international standards as referred to in Implementing Regulation 2018/151.

1. Security of systems and facilities, as referred to in Article 16(1)(a) of the NIS Directive, means the security of network and information systems and their physical environment, and includes the following elements:

   (a) The systematic management of network and information systems—mapping information systems and establishing a set of appropriate policies for information security management, including risk analysis, human resources, operational security, security architecture, data security, system lifecycle management, and, where appropriate, encryption and management
   (b) Physical and environmental security—the availability of a set of measures to protect the security of digital service providers' networks, and information systems, against damage, using a holistic risk-based approach to threats, which takes into account, for example, system failures, human errors, malicious actions, and natural phenomena
   (c) Security of supplies—establishing and maintaining the appropriate policies to guarantee the availability, and, where appropriate, the traceability, of critical supplies used to provide services
   (d) Controls on access to network and information systems—the availability of a set of measures intended to ensure that physical access and logical access to network and information systems, including the administrative security of network and information systems, are authorised and restricted based on business and security requirements.

2. With regard to incident management, referred to in Article 16(1)(b) of the NIS Directive, measures taken by the digital service provider shall include: (a) maintaining and testing detection processes and procedures to ensure timely and appropriate intelligence on unusual events; (b) processes and policies for reporting incidents and identifying shortcomings and weaknesses in its IT systems; (c) reacting in accordance with established procedures and reporting on the results of the measures taken; (d) assessing the significance of a given incident, documenting the intelligence gained from incident analysis, and gathering relevant information which can provide evidence and support the process of continuous improvement.
3. Business continuity management, defined in Article 16(1)(c) of the NIS Directive—the ability of an organisation to maintain, or, where necessary, restore, its services at predetermined acceptable levels after a disruption, which includes:

   (a) establishing and applying contingency plans based on business impact analyses, to ensure the continuity of services delivered by digital service providers, which is assessed and tested at regular intervals, for example through practice;

(b) post-disaster recovery capabilities, which are evaluated and tested at regular intervals, for example through practice.

4. Monitoring, auditing and testing referred to in Article 16(1)(d) of the NIS Directive shall include the establishment and maintenance of policies involving:

   (a) conducting planned sequences of observations or measurements to assess whether network and information systems are operating as intended;
   (b) inspections and verifications to determine whether a standard or a set of guidelines is being applied, whether the records are accurate, and whether efficiency and effectiveness targets are being fulfilled;
   (c) a process aimed at revealing flaws in the security mechanisms of network and information systems which serve to protect data and maintain functionality as intended. This type of process includes technical processes and personnel involved in the operation flow.

5. International standards pursuant to Article 16(1)(e) of the NIS Directive—standards adopted by the international standardisation body referred to in Article 2(1)(a) of Regulation (EU) No 1025/2012 of the European Parliament and of the Council. According to Article 19 of the NIS Directive, European or recognised international standards and specifications relevant to the security of network and information systems, including existing national standards, may also be implemented.
6. Digital service providers shall ensure that the appropriate documentation is made available to the competent authority for the purposes of verifying compliance with the safeguards set out in 1, 2, 3, 4 and 5.

   In the field of its responsibilities, the digital service provider:

(1) undertakes activities which allow the detection, recording, analysis, and classification of incidents;
(2) provides, to the extent necessary, access to information for the appropriate CSIRT MON, CSIRT NASK, or CSIRT GOV about incidents classified as critical by the respective CSIRT MON, CSIRT NASK, or CSIRT GOV;
(3) qualifies the incident as significant;
(4) reports a significant incident immediately, no later than 24 hours after detection, to the appropriate CSIRT MON, CSIRT NASK, or CSIRT GOV;
(5) ensures the handling of a significant incident and critical incident in cooperation with the respective CSIRT MON, CSIRT NASK, or CSIRT GOV, furnishing the necessary information, including personal data;
(6) removes vulnerabilities;
(7) communicates to the operator of essential services which supplies the essential service through that digital service provider information about any incident affecting the continuity of the essential service of that operator.

The NIS Directive introduces a definition of the concept of "operators of essential services", according to which it is a public or private entity, belonging to one of the types referred to in Annex II of the Directive, fulfilling the criteria stipulated in Article 5(2) of the Directive, i.e.:

(a) the entity provides a service which is fundamental to maintaining critical social or economic activity
(b) the provision of this service depends on network and information systems and
(c) the incident would have a significantly disruptive effect on the provision of this service.

The concept of services is defined in Article 57 of the TFEU,[7] and means "benefits normally provided for remuneration, to the extent that they are not covered by the provisions on the free movement of goods, capital and persons". The definition of services contained in primary law is negative. Services include, in particular, (a) industrial activities; (b) commercial activities; (c) craftspersons' activities; (d) performing independent professions.

The operator of an essential service is an entity referred to in Annex No. 1 to the Act, which has an organisational unit on the territory of the Republic of Poland, in respect to which the competent authority for cybersecurity issues has issued a decision granting the status of an operator of essential services. Sectors, subsectors, and types of entity are defined in Annex No. 1 to the Act. In these circumstances, the so-called essential services have been assigned in the field relevant to cybersecurity. According to recital 19 of the Directive, Member States should be responsible for determining which entities meet the definition of an operator of essential services. To ensure a coherent approach, the definition of the operator of essential services should be applied consistently by all Member States. The NIS Directive provides for the assessment of operators in specific sectors and subsectors; the preparation of an inventory of essential services; the consideration of a common list of cross-sectoral factors to determine whether a possible incident could have a significantly disruptive effect; a consultation process involving the relevant Member States in the case of operators providing services in more than one Member State; and support from the cooperation group in the identification of operators. The operators of essential services shall guarantee an increase in the level of security of the services provided through the introduction of the effective management of the cybersecurity system, and the protection of the entities providing services in the field of cybersecurity.

The concept of service should not include services to which the Treaty's provisions on the exchange of goods, and the movement of capital and persons, do not apply. The service will therefore include all activities performed for remuneration which serve or accompany the exchange of goods and the free movement of capital and persons, including the services of so-called online intermediaries, which provide Internet-access services as well as hosting services or services by providers of platforms storing data from users and data-encryption services. The Polish regulation indicates the necessity for the service provider to have a key organisational unit

[7]The Treaty on the Functioning of the European Union of 26 October 2012, OJ EU 2012 L 326/47.

located on the territory of Poland. The Civil Code[8] indicates in Article 41, in relation to legal persons, and correspondingly in Article 33^1 in relation to organisational units without a legal personality to which the Act grants legal capacity, that the registered office is the place where their governing body is located. Each Member State shall establish a list of services, and, where an operator provides a service which is essential for maintaining critical social or economic activities, in two or more Member States, those Member States shall consult each other. This consultation occurs before the identification decision is taken (Article 5(4) of the NIS Directive).

In accordance with recital 20 of the Preamble to the Directive, in the process of identifying operators of essential services, Member States should assess, at least for each subsector referred to in this Directive, which services must be considered essential for the maintenance of critical social and economic activities, and whether entities within sectors and subsectors, and the providers of those services, meet the criteria for identifying operators. While evaluating whether an entity provides a service which is critical to maintaining vital social or economic activity, it is sufficient to examine whether the entity provides a service which is included in the list of essential services. Furthermore, it must be demonstrated that the provision of the essential service depends on network and information systems. Additionally, when assessing whether an incident could have a significantly disruptive effect on the provision of a service, Member States should take into consideration a number of cross-sectoral, and, where appropriate, sectoral factors.

Pursuant to Article 6 of the Directive, Member States shall take into account at least the following cross-sectoral factors when determining the significance of the disruptive effect: (a) the number of users dependent on the service provided by the entity; (b) the dependence of the other sectors specified in Annex II on the service provided by the entity; (c) the impact which incidents—in terms of their scale and duration—could have on economic and social activity or public security; (d) the market share of this entity; (e) the geographical coverage related to the area which could be affected by the incident; (f) the importance of the entity in maintaining a sufficient level of service, taking into account the availability of alternative means of providing this service. In order to determine whether an incident would have a significantly disruptive effect, Member States are required to take into consideration sectoral factors, where appropriate. These guidelines were taken into consideration in the secondary legislation to the Act. In accordance with the Regulation of the Council of Ministers of 31 October 2018 on serious incidents thresholds, the parameters to be taken into account to determine whether the impact of the incident is significant include the number of users affected by the disruption of the essential service; the timing of the impact of the incident on the essential service provided; the geographical coverage of the area affected by the incident, and other factors specific to the subsector; also whether the incident caused at least one of the following circumstances:

[8] The Civil Code, consolidated text of the Polish Journal of Laws of 2020, item 1740, as amended, hereinafter referred to as CC.

(a) the death of a person,
(b) serious damage to health,
(c) other than serious damage to the health of more than one person, and
(d) financial losses exceeding PLN 250,000.

For the identification of operators of essential services, holding an organisational unit in a Member State involves the need to operate efficiently and effectively through stable structures. The legal form of such structures, whether a branch or a subsidiary with legal personality, is not a determining factor in this respect (recital 21).

The process for identifying operators of essential services is specified in Article 5 of the Directive. Member States were required to identify, for each sector and subsector referred to in Annex II, by 9 November 2018 at the latest, the operators of essential services with an organisational unit on its territory.

The Polish legislators follow the definition from the NIS Directive, and therefore the operator of essential services is an entity which meets all the following conditions:

(1) will be one of the entities listed in the Annex to the Act,
(2) will provide the essential service listed in the inventory of essential services,
(3) the provision of this service will depend on information systems,
(4) the incident would have a significantly disruptive effect on its performance.

Consequently, the operator of essential services is a party to the rights and obligations under the Act, regardless of whether it has entrusted to another entity activities related to the provision of the essential service. Therefore, all issues of responsibility sharing between the various entities should be regulated internally by these bodies. An important element in the decision, as evidence of the will of the administrative authority, is the decisive resolution of the matter covered by the motion initiating the proceedings. It should be explained that a case may only be settled (within the meaning of Article 104(1) and (2) of the Code of Administrative Procedure—CAP) by a public administration authority if the facts have been duly established. For this reason, in Article 7 of CAP, the legislators assigned to the necessity of establishing the objective truth the status of the principle of administrative proceedings. Therefore, it is the duty of the authority to conduct the submission of evidence in such a way as to result in the creation of actual grounds for adopting the legal basis for the settlement. Undoubtedly, a defective establishment (or failure to establish) of facts relevant to the case prevents the authority from issuing an appropriate decision. Otherwise, an administrative decision—in accordance with Article 104 of CAP—resolves the case on its merits within the limits of the demand specified by the parties. The decision in administrative proceedings, on the other hand, consists of applying the applicable law to the established facts of an administrative case. Therefore, the public administration authority pursues the objective of the administrative procedure, which is to implement the applicable legal standard for administrative and legal relations, when these relations require such a measure. According to this objective of the administrative procedure, also the essence of the administrative decision can be distinguishing between the factual basis and the legal basis of the administrative decision. The factual basis is the findings of facts made by a public administration authority, while the legal basis is those legislative provisions which the authority has accepted as binding in a given case, and applied in its ruling.[9] Establishing the actual implementation of the conditions indicated above enables an administrative decision to be made in the context of establishing the status of the operator of essential services.

The status of the operator of essential services should be determined by means of a decision. The legislators have not specified that it is this particular form; however, it should be assumed that if the legal situation of a particular entity is determined, it is an administrative decision. An administrative decision is considered to be a declaration of will of an administrative body which has legal effects in the sphere of the administrative-legal relationship (the formation, modification or expiry of that relationship).[10] If a standard of substantive administrative law requires concretisation, the form of administrative decision is considered to be the form of such concretisation. This applies also in this case. For the operator to be recognised in its field of operation, an administrative decision must be issued. Hence, the decision is an act of authority, issued by an authorised body.[11] Article 104(2) of CAP provides that decisions shall resolve the case as to its substance in whole or in part; or otherwise the case will be closed at a given level. This interpretation of the form of operation of the public administration body derives from Article 2 of the Constitution of the Republic of Poland, which states that the Republic of Poland is a democratic legal state which follows the principles of social justice. According to the court, "From the principle of a democratic state of law, the judicial doctrine and jurisprudence derives two principles of paramount importance for the formation of the rights of the individual in relation to public administration, and thus for the interpretation of the law: the principle of the right to a trial and the principle of the right to a court. The essence of the principle of the right to a trial is to grant an individual the right to defend his or her legal interests in proceedings governed by procedural law. The principle of the right to a trial is of fundamental importance for the interpretation of the substantive law provisions on the form of settlement, towards the adoption of the principle of settling an individual's affairs in the form of an administrative decision when the substantive administrative law provision does not assume another form of settlement on an *expressis verbis* basis. The Code of Administrative Procedure does not contain a legal definition of the term "administrative decision". However, it is assumed by legal commentators and in judicial decisions that, in accordance with the provisions of Article 1(1) of the CAP, it follows that an administrative decision is a sovereign manifestation of the will of a

[9]Judgment of the Court of Appeal in Katowice of 5 April 2013. File No. III APa 55/12 LEX No. 1313277.

[10]Judgment of the Supreme Administrative Court of 25 April 2012, File No. I OSK 654/11 LEX No. 1264894.

[11]Cf. judgment of the Supreme Court of 3 April 2000, I CKN 582/98, LEX No. 50843, Borkowski (1996), p. 439.

public-administration authority, issued in proceedings pending before that authority in an individual administrative case, and constitutes its decision. Administrative decisions are the basic form of action of public administration authorities, and are therefore the primary object of appeal in administrative court proceedings. A complaint to the administrative court is available both against administrative decisions issued under the Code of Administrative Procedure and against decisions issued under another procedure regulating jurisdictional proceedings, i.e., against decisions in cases in which, pursuant to Article 3 of CAP, jurisdictional proceedings have been excluded from the scope of the Code of Administrative Procedure (exclusions of applications of the Act). The situation of the adoption of the decision in question for an administrative decision has an impact on the entity's rights to take appeal actions, which can hinder the process of determining the list of operators of essential services.

Furthermore, it shall be possible for operators in the sectors and subsectors referred to in this Directive to provide both essential and non-essential services. For the purposes of identifying operators, Member States should therefore establish a list of services which they consider to be essential (such a list is specified in Annex No. 1 to the Act).

According to Article 41 of the Act, the authorities competent for cybersecurity matters are:

(1) for the energy sector—the Minister competent for energy issues
(2) for the transport sector, excluding the water transport subsector—the Minister competent for transport
(3) for the water-transport subsector—the Minister competent for the maritime economy and the Minister competent for inland navigation
(4) for the banking sector and infrastructure of financial markets—the Polish Financial-Supervision Authority
(5) for the healthcare sector, excluding the entities mentioned in Article 26(5)—the Minister competent for health matters
(6) for the healthcare sector covering the entities mentioned in Article 26(5)—the Minister of National Defence
(7) for the drinking water supply and distribution sector—the Minister competent for water management
(8) for the digital infrastructure sector, excluding the entities referred to in Article 26(5)—the Minister competent for digital affairs.
(9) for the digital infrastructure sector including the entities referred to in Article 26 (5)—the Minister of National Defence
(10) for digital service providers, excluding the entities mentioned in Article 26 (5)—the Minister competent for digital affairs.
(11) for digital service providers including the entities mentioned in Article 26(5)—the Minister of National Defence.
(12) for entites subordinated to the Minister of National Defence or supervised by him, including those whose communication and information systems or networks are covered by a uniform list of objects, installations, devices, and

services included in the critical infrastructure referred to in Article 5b(7)(1) of the Act of 26 April 2007 on Crisis Management; and

(13) Entrepreneurs of particular economic and defensive importance, in respect of whom the Minister of National Defence is the authority organising and supervising the performance of tasks for the benefit of state defence, within the meaning of Article 5(3) of the Act of 23 August 2001 on the on the Organisation of Tasks for State Defence Performed by Enterprises.

It should be emphasised that, according to recital 45 of the preamble, the Directive applies only to those public administrations which have been identified as operators of essential services. However, Member States remain responsible for ensuring the security of the network and information systems of public administrations outside the scope of the NIS Directive.

Where an entity provides an essential service in other Member States of the European Union, the authority competent for cybersecurity matters shall, in the course of the administrative proceedings, consult with those states through the Single Points of Contact to determine whether the entity is recognised as an operator of an essential service in those states. In accordance with Article 5(4) of the Directive, where an operator provides a service referred to in 2(a) in two or more Member States, those Member States shall consult each other. Such consultation shall take place before a decision on classification is taken. This provision is equivalent to the procedure for identifying an operator of essential services as stipulated in the Directive. For the purposes of the identification process, where an entity provides an essential service in two or more Member States, these states should engage in bilateral or multilateral discussions among themselves.

In relation to an entity which no longer meets the conditions, the competent authority for cybersecurity shall issue a judgment stating that the decision to consider an operator of essential services has expired.

The content of the provision of Article 162(1) of CAP states

> a public-administration authority is obliged to determine the expiry of a decision if the following conditions are jointly met:
>
> (a) the decision became pointless,
> (b) the decision shall be declared void by a provision of law or the declaration of voidness is in the public interest or in the interests of a party.

An administrative decision which establishes the status of an operator of essential services is not indefinite. When the operator no longer meets the conditions, the authority issues a new decision, this time determining the expiry of the previous one. Similarly as the decision determining the status of an operator of essential services, the decision determining its expiry is subject to all CAP regulations. There is no doubt that in the event of a legal provision's ordering the decision to expire, a public administration authority is obliged to examine whether the conditions listed in this provision are being met. A ruling to grant the status of an essential service, or a decision to rescind such a decision, is immediately enforceable. The requirement of immediate enforceability is regulated in Article 108(1) and (2) of CAP. The essence of the immediate enforceability of administrative decisions is that the decision becomes enforceable, and constitutes an enforcement order, although it is not final. According to the above-mentioned standard, the rigour of immediate enforceability can be imposed ex-officio, or at the request of a party, only for a decision against which an appeal is being lodged, i.e. against a non-conclusive decision. The enforcement of a non-conclusive decision is exceptional; therefore the prerequisites for making the decision immediately enforceable must not be interpreted in a broadening but in a narrowing way. In the case of a regulation concerning the administrative decision determining the status of an operator of essential services, its immediate enforceability was established by law. This solution results from the special status of the regulation of services which are important for security.

Article 7 of the National Cybersecurity System Act obliges the Minister competent for digital affairs to maintain a list of operators of essential services. This list is created taking into consideration the division into sectors, subsectors, and types of entities introduced by the Act. The entry into or removal from the list is declaratory in nature, and will be a material and technical activity, implemented on the basis of administrative decisions by the competent authorities, in terms of identifying operators of essential services in the relevant sectors. This provision also defines the procedure for access to the information and the directory of entities in which the information from the list will be made available. Recital 25 of the Preamble to the Directive indicates the obligation to establish a list containing all operators of essential services, or by adopting national measures containing objective quantitative criteria, such as the end result of the operator's activities or the number of users, which make it possible to determine which entities are covered by obligations relating to network and information system security.

The public register is an institution through which a registry authority with the characteristics of a public body manages an official dataset, controls the reported information, may modify it on its own, or request specific changes, and holds the power to refuse to publish certain information with regard to its content.[12] In the traditional definition, maintaining the register and publishing the data included in it can have certain legal effects, and this occurs when the public notification and publication of the indicated data determines the effectiveness of a legal action.[13] The information contained in the register is received, recorded, and made available by means of a decision, which is an act of law, resulting in the registration.[14] Such an approach is primarily related to the nature of the register as a regulatory instrument in the sphere of organising public administration activities. The registration system is based on the state's determination of the conditions. The registration procedure involves the possibility of verifying whether the market-share requirements imposed by law on interested parties are being fulfilled.

[12]Ganczar (2009), p. 99.

[13]Ganczar (2009), p. 100.

[14]Ganczar (2009), p. 632.

The regulatory model adopted in the Act assumes that the responsibilities of sectoral institutions in the field of cybersecurity will be extended, instead of establishing a single national entity for cybersecurity at the central level. Administrative, regulatory, and control responsibilities have been assigned to the Ministers responsible for the sectors listed in the NIS Directive, namely energy, transport, banking and financial institutions, healthcare, water supply, digital infrastructure, and digital service providers (Article 41). Regarding the healthcare sector, digital infrastructure, and digital service providers, the separate entities subordinated to or supervised by the Minister of National Defence were taken into consideration. Article 42 of the Act stipulated a schedule of tasks to be performed by the competent authorities. These tasks include conducting analyses, issuing administrative decisions granting the status of an operator of essential services, rescinding the status of an operator of essential services, and monitoring the application of the Act by operators of essential services, as well as digital service providers in their respective sectors.

Data from the list of operators of essential services, to the extent necessary to implement their statutory tasks, shall be made available by the Minister competent for digital affairs, on request. The data are retained by units such as the police, the courts, prosecutor's offices, or other services for preventive purposes, for the detection of criminal activities. The following authorities are entitled to use the data under this provision: competent authorities in the field of cybersecurity, the courts, prosecutor's offices, the police, the Border Guard, the Military Police, the Military Counter-Intelligence Service, the Internal Security Agency, the Central Anti-Corruption Bureau the National Revenue Administration, the Government Security Centre and the State Protection Service. Such data should be used primarily as a source of information and evidence in criminal cases. Nonetheless, the institutions listed here have the right to use the data in the performance of their statutory tasks, also for preventive purposes. Public institutions very often benefit from such legal possibilities. Within the activities of the institutions indicated here, so-called operational and investigative activities can be distinguished.

Operational and investigative activities are non-contentious. This limits judicial control over their course—"the practice of the investigating service has been shaped as complementary or executive activities in relation to procedural activities and the tasks of preparatory proceedings".[15]

The tasks of operators of essential services include the systematic assessment and management of the risk of an incident.

Conducting systematic assessment and the management of incident risk. The first obligation of the operator of essential services concerns the creation and implementation of a security management system in the information (ICT) system, and follows from Article 14 of the Directive, according to which Member States shall ensure that operators of essential services undertake appropriate and proportionate technical and organisational measures to manage the risks to which their network and information

[15] See Szaff (1957), p. 38.

systems are exposed. Taking into consideration the state of the art, these measures must ensure a level of security of network and information systems commensurate with the existing risks. Member States shall ensure that operators of essential services adopt the appropriate measures to prevent and minimise the impact of security incidents on the network and information systems used to provide such essential services, with a view to ensuring the continuity of those services. According to Article 4(9) of the NIS Directive, 'risk' means any reasonably identifiable circumstance or event which has a potentially adverse impact on the security of network and information systems. Management is primarily involved in organising safety (defining safety requirements and the range of responsibilities, and assigning organisational functions). Information- and communication-security management is intended to ensure the security of information systems—here the information system (i.e. the information and communication system referred to in Article 3(3) of the Act of 17 February 2005 on the Computerisation of the Operations of Entities Performing Public Tasks together with the data processed in electronic form) of the data contained therein in a situation of many difficulties and adversities. Among numerous conditions which hinder this protection, it can be mentioned that communication and information systems are difficult to manage because they are highly complex, fast, and extremely diverse in terms of technology; communication and information systems and their environments are constantly changing; threats to the environment are difficult to fully identify; the management processes are highly diverse, interdisciplinary—there are often interrelationships which are not fully understood; multiple issues are difficult to identify, and, due to the human factor present here, also unpredictable. Risk assessment and the analysis of threats involves the identification of threats, the vulnerability analysis of systems, and the development and implementation of a comprehensive security plan (security policy). Therefore, in order to ensure the security of the data, and the information systems in which this information is processed, due to the complexity of these systems and processes, and their interdependence and variability over time, conscious and coordinated actions are required on the basis of the objectives set, i.e. to conduct a certain policy, referred to as the security policy in this document. Resource protection involves limiting the vulnerability of the system, and shielding it from threats by using protective measures. On the other hand, the monitoring and detection of threats involve all activities (e.g. notification) related to ensuring proper operations (including protections). The reaction to an incident is any action related to the response to the incident (security breach). Consequently, it must be assumed that the term "information system security" means a level of reasonable confidence that the potential losses resulting from the unauthorised (accidental or deliberate) disclosure, modification, destruction, or rendering inoperable the processing of information stored and transmitted through information and communication systems, will not be incurred. Information and communication security must be considered in their organisational, technical, and legal aspects. Thus, security is not a single act of introducing protections, but a continuous, dynamic, and very complex process which requires constant supervision and adaptation to fluctuating environmental conditions. Under such conditions it seems necessary to manage the information-security system. The principles of risk management in the context of telecommunications security can be discussed with reference to International Standards. The general concepts of this management are specified in ISO/IEC 27001, which was developed to support the effective implementation of a risk-management approach to security. Understanding the concepts, models, processes, and terminology outlined in ISO/IEC 27001 and ISO/IEC 27002 is crucial for understanding PN-ISO/IEC 27005:2014 Information Technology—Security Techniques—Risk Management in Information Security. The International Standard is applicable to all types of organisations (e.g., companies, governmental institutions, non-profit organisations) which intend to manage the risks which can cause information-security breaches in these organisations. Polish Standard PN-ISO/IEC 27005:2014 Information Technology—Security Techniques—Risk Management in Information Security defines the principles and methodology of risk management in security management systems within the so-called essential services—in the sphere of threats from cyberspace. Risk management should be understood as activities consisting of risk estimation, risk handling, risk acceptance, risk monitoring, and risk communication. Where ISO standards are applied, Regulation (EU) No 1025/2012 of the European Parliament and of the Council of 25 October 2012 on European standardisation, amending Council Directives 89/686/EEC and 93/15/EEC and Directives 94/9/EC, 94/25/EC, 95/16/EC, 97/23/EC, 98/34/EC, 2004/22/EC, 2007/23/EC, 2009/23/EC, and 2009/105/EC of the European Parliament and of the Council and repealing Council Decision 87/95/EEC, and Decision No 1673/2006/EC of the European Parliament and of the Council, text with EEA relevance, must be taken into consideration.[16] Risk assessment—a comprehensive process of risk identification, analysis, and assessment—is the task of a person or a team appointed by the operator of essential services. Risk analysis includes the following steps: estimating the consequences, assessing the probability of the incident, and determining the risk level. Consequence estimation consists of considering what effects on information resources or communication and information systems could be brought about by the materialisation of threats, taking into account the vulnerability of resources or systems. Incident risk assessment is to determine the frequency with which specific incidents might occur. Statistics on similar events should also be taken into consideration. This risk assessment, on the other hand, compares the designated risk levels with predefined risk-acceptance criteria, and facilitates the determination of priorities in risk management. Initial identification, i.e. risk diagnosis, is performed by the person responsible for a given resource, and who passes the identification results to the person responsible for performing the risk analysis. The whole process is coordinated by the plenipotentiary for cybersecurity of the institution. If a

[16]Regulation (EU) No 1025/2012 of the European Parliament and of the Council of 25 October 2012 on European standardisation, amending Council Directives 89/686/EEC and 93/15/EEC and Directives 94/9/EC, 94/25/EC, 95/16/EC, 97/23/EC, 98/34/EC, 2004/22/EC, 2007/23/EC, 2009/23/EC, and 2009/105/EC of the European Parliament and of the Council and repealing Council Decision 87/95/EEC, and Decision No 1673/2006/EC of the European Parliament and of the Council, text with EEA relevance, OJ EU 2012 L 316/12.

plenipotentiary is not appointed, the process is coordinated by the person designated by the operator of essential services. The list of threats and vulnerabilities may be extended as required by the operator of essential services, where the identification of risks is conducted. Such risk identification shall be carried out periodically or on an ad-hoc basis. Ad-hoc identification is performed when a threat to a system is observed, where the horizon of materialisation is shorter than the periodic identification of risks, and when a delay in identification would be significant for the system. Ad-hoc identification is also undertaken in the event of an ICT incident's resulting in a catastrophic loss of information security. Specifically, risk identification is carried out before the system is handed over for operation. Risk assessment is the process of comparing risk values with specific criteria in order to determine the significance of risk. Risk management is the coordinated management of cybersecurity in relation to the estimated risk, which includes activities leading to a change in the level of risk through applying protections, risk avoidance, risk transfer, and acceptance of risk even if its level exceeds that of residual risk. The method of risk management is to reduce the level of risk by means of a risk-control measure in the form of protections, selected commensurately with the nature of such risk. Regarding the implementation of public tasks, which is the subject of operators of essential services' activities, risk avoidance, as a rule, does not apply; neither does risk transfer. Nonetheless, the transfer of risk may be justified in the form of the insurance of the assets of the system. According to the standard, in situations in which the final risk level is less than or equal to 20% of the maximum level ($Rk \leq 9.6$) they are subject to automatic acceptance, but remain under the supervision of the risk owner for monitoring purposes. Risks for which the level is in the range of $9.6 < Rk \leq 38.4$ are subject to acceptance according to the rules established in the entity, or are re-analysed. Risks for which the level exceeds 80% of the maximum level ($Rk > 38.4$) are submitted to the entity's management for approval. Pursuant to recital 46 of the Directive, risk-management measures include actions to identify, prevent, detect, and deal with all risks of incidents and to mitigate their impact. The security of network and information systems includes the security of stored, transmitted, and processed data.

Another significant task is to implement technical and organisational measures appropriate and proportional to the estimated risk, taking into account the latest state of the art, including

(a) the maintenance and safe operation of the information system
(b) physical and environmental security, including access control
(c) the security and continuity of service delivery on which the provision of the essential service depends
(d) implementing, documenting and maintaining action plans which facilitate the continuous and uninterrupted provision of the essential service, and ensuring the confidentiality, integrity, availability, and authenticity of information
(e) covering the information system employed to provide the essential service with a continuous monitoring system.

According to recital 53 of the preamble to the Directive, in order to avoid imposing a disproportionate financial and administrative burden on the operators of essential services and digital service providers, the requirements should be proportionate to the risks associated with the network and information system concerned and should take into account the state of the art of such measures. An essential task in ensuring the protection of systems is the application of the appropriate safeguards, proportional to the needs and objectives, i.e. also non-excessive safeguards against the loss of security of the provision of essential services. These protections take the form of technical and organisational measures. The legislators have defined in general terms the actions to be taken by the operator of essential services. Ensuring the continuity of service provision is the principal duty. This is achieved by maintaining, documenting, and implementing plans to ensure the provision of the essential service, and the confidentiality, integrity, availability, and authenticity of information; the maintenance and secure operation of the information system; physical and environmental security, including access control, security and continuity of service delivery on which the provision of the essential service depends; and the inclusion of the information system used to provide the essential service under a continuous monitoring system. Consequently, the reduction of the risk level is performed in the process of dealing with the risk. The basic method of dealing with risk in the case of operators of essential services is to apply safeguards in the form of continuous monitoring, i.e. in the 24/7 system. The application of a security feature must take into account its impact on the other security attributes and may in itself be a risk factor. For example, the application of security measures to limit the risk of losing the confidentiality of information can increase the risk of loss of availability. Especially in the process of risk management, it is of particular importance to determine the category of safeguards. According to the security characteristics, the goal of a secure information and communication system is achieved through (1) covering the communication and information system with the process of risk management for the security of essential services provided in the communication and information system; (2) the limitation of reliability, consisting of treating other communication and information systems as potential sources of threats, and implementing safeguards in the communication and information system to control the exchange of services with these communication and information systems; (3) the introduction of multi-level protection of the communication and information system, consisting of the application of protections on as many different levels of organisation of the communication and information system protection as possible, in order to limit the occurrence of cases in which breaking a single protection results in a breach.[17] Another responsibility of operators of

[17]Examples of protections against threats to the communication and information system resulting from cyberspace include:

Hazard category: Malicious code penetration from WAN
Building the network topology with consideration of safe and demilitarised zones (DMZ)
Network address translation
Firewalls configured according to the principle *"everything is forbidden except what is allowed"*
AV-class software at the interconnection of WAN and LAN
IDS/IPS-class systems

essential services is to collect information about cybersecurity threats. In accordance with the methodology of cyberspace risk management in government information

---

PROXY servers (including maintaining a blacklist of URLs and IP addresses)
Spam detection and blocking
Procedures for the maintenance of the protections listed in items 3–6
Procedures for responding to detected incidents
Hazard category: Malicious code entry from LAN
AV-class software on workstations
Blocking USB ports on workstations
Supervision over unused LAN terminations
DHCP server access authorisation
Disabling software installation by users
Verifying installed software on workstations
Software upgrade procedures (patch installation)
Hazard category: DDoS or DoS attack
Network-traffic monitoring
Using content delivery networks (CDN)
Switching to static versions of the service after detecting a DDoS/DoS attack
Agreements with Internet-access providers containing clauses transferring obligations relating to actions against an attack on the provider
Blocking network traffic from specific IP addresses
Procedures in the event of detecting a DDoS/DoS attack
Hazard category: Unauthorised access to information
Procedures for granting and withdrawing privileges in the system
Procedures for reviewing authorisations in systems
Applying the need-to-know principle
Distribution of authorisation (the "eight-eyes" principle)
Hazard category: Inappropriate use of the system by the user
Initial training for new employees
Periodic training for employees currently working in the company
Implementation of applications verifying the quality of entered data
Hazard category: Breaching access security inside the system
Blocking the possibility for the user to install software
Hardening of workstations (elimination of unnecessary operating-system functions and applications)
Blocking the possibility of starting an operating system from a removable drive
Verification whether only acceptable software is available on the workstation
Periodic reviews of workstation logs by administrators
Procedures for handling detected anomalies and ways of documenting such handling
Hazard category: Data eavesdropping, data interception
Application of zoning
Application of equipment with reduced compromising emanations
Room shielding
Network cabling in closed channels, supervision of patch panels
Using fibre-optic cables instead of galvanic connections
Supervision over unused LAN terminations (disconnection of unused terminations on patch panels)
Hazard category: System of operators of essential services as a source of interference in cyberspace
Outgoing-traffic supervision
Procedures for responding to botnet detection in an entity's network
Procedures for responding to spamming attempts
Detection of illegal activities by internal users of the system

security management systems and ISO standards, the following categories of incidents in interactions between communication and information systems and cyberspace are distinguished, along with examples of vulnerabilities causing the materialisation of hazards to affect the information resource or communication and information system:[18] Incident management, on the other hand, involves incident

---

[18]Hazard category: Malicious code penetration from WAN

absence or wrong placement in the system, or lack of AV software updates
absence of or incorrect placement in network topology or incorrect firewall configuration
absence of or incorrect placement in the network topology or improper configuration of IPS/IDS software and its sensors
incorrect configuration of security mechanisms in WAN networks
absence of server load monitoring
susceptibility of users to social engineering methods in order to obtain information or enter malicious code

Hazard category: Malicious code entry from LAN

absence or wrong placement in the system, or failure to update AV software
absence of or incorrect placement in network topology or wrong firewall configuration
absence of or incorrect placement in the network topology or wrong configuration of IPS/IDS software and its sensors
incorrect configuration of security mechanisms in LANs

Hazard category: DDoS or DoS attack

absence of or incorrect placement in network topology or wrong firewall configuration
absence of or incorrect placement in the network topology or wrong configuration of IPS/IDS software and its sensors
absence of network traffic supervision (QoS)
absence of server load monitoring
software error
loss of access to WAN services (including Internet) as a result of an attack on WAN components

Hazard category: Unauthorised access to information

absence of supervision over users' rights, entitlements inadequate to tasks
too slow implementation of changes in user authorisations
absence of physical access control to system components

Hazard category: Inappropriate use of the system by the user

absence of proper user training in the use of the system
absence of quality control of data entered into the system
recovery of information from end-of-life media
users' susceptibility to social engineering methods to obtain information or enter malicious code

Hazard category: Breaching of access security inside the system

absence of supervision over user authorisations, entitlements inadequate to the tasks (e.g. possibility of installing programs, including those used to break security)
too slow implementation of changes in user authorisations
absence of supervision over users' activities in the system
absence of or wrong placement in the system, or no AV-software update
absence or incorrect placement in network topology, or wrong firewall configuration

handling, searching for links between incidents, removing the causes of incidents, and developing conclusions resulting from incident handling. Unlike risk management, incident management will cover actual situations where a security breach has occurred.

Another responsibility of operators of essential services is to collect information about cybersecurity threats. According to the methodology of cyber risk management in government information security management systems and ISO standards, the following categories of incidents: in interaction between the communication and information system and cyberspace are distinguished, as well as examples of vulnerabilities causing the materialisation of the threat to affect the information resource or communication and information system. On the other hand, monitoring and detecting hazards are any activities (e.g. notification) related to ensuring proper operations (including protections). The reaction to an incident means all actions related to the response to the incident (security breach).

Therefore, it should be assumed that the term "information and communication security" means the level of reasonable confidence that potential losses resulting from unwanted (accidental or deliberate) disclosure, modification, destruction, or disabling of the service provided through information and communication systems will not be incurred. Information and communication security must be considered in their organisational, technical, and legal aspects. Therefore, security is not a single

---

absence of or incorrect placement in the network topology or wrong configuration of IPS/IDS software and its sensors

Hazard category: Data eavesdropping, data interception

absence of network-traffic supervision (QoS)
compromising emanation
absence of encryption in WAN links
eavesdropping on information in the internal network (LAN)
retrieving information from end-of-life media

Hazard category: Breaking into a communication and information system from an external WAN (security breach)

absence of system software update
absence of or incorrect placement in network topology, or wrong firewall configuration
absence of or incorrect placement in the network topology or wrong configuration of IPS/IDS software and its sensors
absence of network traffic supervision (QoS)
absence of server load monitoring
susceptibility of users to social engineering methods in order to obtain information or enter malicious code

Hazard category: Entity (office) system as a source of interference in cyberspace

absence of network traffic supervision (QoS)
absence of or wrong placement in the system, or no AV software update
absence of or incorrect placement in network topology or wrong firewall configuration
absence of or incorrect placement in the network topology or wrong configuration of IPS/IDS software and its sensors.

act of introducing protections, but a continuous, dynamic, and at the same time highly complex process, requiring constant supervision and adaptation to changing environmental conditions.

When analysing issues of telecommunications security in the context of the security of essential services, attention should be paid to the transmission of data and information through electronic media and ICT networks. Information security law is concerned with the legal protection of telecommunications systems, which incorporates certain data enabling the provision of services, the protection of the electronic services as such, and the related content and databases, as well as the network through which such services are provided. It must therefore be assumed that information security is closely linked with the concept of telecommunications security, and more specifically to information and communication technology security, which means the protection of information processed, stored, and transmitted by means of information and communication systems against unwanted (accidental or deliberate) disclosure, modification, destruction, or prevention of its processing. Computer technology and networks (ICT—Information and Communication Technologies) have become an important part of the everyday life of people, so most of the legal regulations related to telecommunications security relate to the security of communications as such, ICT security, which represents an element of telecommunications security. The obligation of the operator of essential services, which concerns the generally defined "application of measures to prevent and mitigate the impact of incidents on the security of the information system used to provide the essential service", with particular reference to:

(a) the application of mechanisms ensuring the confidentiality, integrity, availability, and authenticity of data processed in the information system,
(b) ensuring that the software is updated,
(c) protection against unauthorised modification of the information system,
(d) immediate action when vulnerabilities or hazards of cybersecurity are identified in respect of information and communication security issues.

The term "network and information system" is defined in NIS Directive as

(a) an electronic communications network within the meaning of Article 2(a) of Directive 2002/21/EC[19];
(b) any device or group of interconnected or related devices, one or more of which, pursuant to a program, perform automatic processing of digital data; or

[19]"Electronic communications network" means transmission systems and, where applicable, switching or routing equipment and other resources which permit the conveyance of signals by wire, by radio, by optical or by other electromagnetic means, including satellite networks, fixed (circuit- and packet-switched, including Internet) and mobile terrestrial networks, electricity cable systems, to the extent that they are used for the purpose of transmitting signals, networks used for radio and television broadcasting, and cable television networks, irrespective of the type of information conveyed.

(c) digital data stored, processed, retrieved or transmitted by elements covered under points (a) and (b) for the purposes of their operation, use, protection and maintenance;

In light of the same act "security of network and information systems' means the ability of network and information systems to resist, at a given level of confidence, any action that compromises the availability, authenticity, integrity or confidentiality of stored or transmitted or processed data or the related services offered by, or accessible via, those network and information systems;

The communication and information system in the Polish legal system was defined in the Act of 17 February 2005 on the Computerisation of the Operations of Entities Performing Public Tasks,[20] and according to this definition (in Article 3 (3)) it is

> a set of cooperating IT devices and software, ensuring processing and storage, as well as sending and receiving, data through telecommunication networks by means of a terminal device appropriate for a given type of telecommunication network within the meaning of the Telecommunications Law—(the same definition is in Article 2(3) of the PSEMA).

In accordance with Article 175d of the Telecommunications Law, the Minister competent for communications may determine by way of a regulation the minimum technical and organisational measures and methods for preventing the threats referred to in Article 175a(1) and Article 175c(1), which telecommunications undertakings are obliged to apply in order to ensure the security or integrity of networks or services, taking into consideration the guidelines of the European Commission and the European Union Agency for Cybersecurity in this respect. In the Polish legal system, the issues of information and communication security in the field of electronic communication security in relation to telecommunications and ICT networks are defined in Telecommunications Law. Pursuant to Article 3(1) of this Act, the provisions of Telecommunications Law, unless ratified international agreements binding on the Republic of Poland provide otherwise, relate to the issues of network security. It should be noted that the NCSA does not apply to the telecommunications undertakings referred to in Telecommunications Law, as far as security requirements and incident reporting are concerned, as they are subject to the above-mentioned regulations on telecommunications security. Consequently, these obligations do not overlap.

With regard to ensuring the confidentiality, integrity, availability, and authenticity of data processed in the information system, several definitions should be considered. Reference is made to the definition of 'availability' in Regulation (EC) No 460/2004 of the European Parliament and of the Council of 10 March 2004 establishing the European Network and Information Security Agency. This document not only defines the concepts which constitute the definition of

[20]Consolidated text, Polish Journal of Laws of 2020, item 346, as amended.

information security, but also defines 'availability',[21] which means that data are available and services are fully operational.

While "data integrity" means the confirmation that data transmitted, received, or stored are complete and unchanged, "data confidentiality" means the protection of communications or stored data against interception and reading by unauthorised persons. It should be emphasised that the legal regulations strictly define the basic security conditions which a communication and information system should meet. First and foremost, it should ensure the confidentiality of data and information (data become information under certain conditions), but not limit its availability and integrity with other subsystems or documents.

The authenticity of data is a term indicating, above all, the importance of ensuring the reliability of data in terms of its origin and source, authorship, or possibly the ownership of databases.

Ensuring whether the integrity of systems is maintained—protection against unauthorised modification—means that the data in the system, and also the system itself will not be modified in an unauthorised manner. The application of software updates refers to the software which operates a given system, with the software being overall information in the form of a set of instructions, implemented interfaces, and integrated data designed to achieve the set objectives.

Entities providing essential services using information systems, including in the field of communication, introduce technologies and procedures for security management. However, in addition to individual solutions, systematic cross-border cooperation on ICT network security between sectors (the public-private sector), and between EU Member States, is becoming significant. Such a need arises from the fact that the problems of network security and the services it provides are of a global nature, which is determined by the features of the ICT network itself, and the ease of information transfer, especially after its digital-conversion process. Risk assessment and the analysis of threats, i.e. the identification of incidents, system-vulnerability analysis, and the development and implementation of a comprehensive security plan (security policy), are the basic responsibilities of the operator of essential services. Therefore, in order to ensure the security of the ICT services and systems in which these services are processed, due to the complexity of these systems and processes, and their interdependence and variability over time, it is required to conduct conscious and coordinated actions on the basis of the objectives set, i.e. to conduct a certain information policy, also referred to in this document as security policy. Security policy includes the obligation to communicate properly within the National Cybersecurity System.

[21]Access, within the meaning of Directive 19/2002/EC of the European Parliament and of the Council of 7 March 2002 on access to, and interconnection of, electronic communications networks and associated facilities (AD), did not mean access provided to end-users/customers, but the provision of facilities and/or services to another undertaking, under defined conditions, for the purpose of providing electronic communications services, including access to virtual network services.

The information obligations of an operator of essential services involve the identification of the person responsible for contacts with entities forming the National Cybersecurity System, i.e.:

(1) other operators of essential services;
(2) digital service providers
(3) CSIRT MON
(4) CSIRT NASK
(5) CSIRT GOV
(6) sectoral cybersecurity teams
(7) public-finance-sector entities specified in Article 9(1)-(6), (8), (9), (11) and (12) of the Act of 27 August 2009 on Public Finance
(8) research institutes
(9) National Bank of Poland
(10) Bank Gospodarstwa Krajowego
(11) Office of Technical Inspection
(12) Polish Air Navigation Services Agency
(13) Polish Centre for Accreditation
(14) National Fund for Environmental Protection and Water Management, and provincial funds for environmental protection and water management
(15) companies and partnerships performing public-utility tasks within the meaning of Article 1(2) of the Act of 20 December 1996 on Municipal Management
(16) entities providing cybersecurity services
(17) authorities providing services in the area of cybersecurity
(18) The Single Point of Contact for cybersecurity issues,[22]
(19) Government Plenipotentiary for Cybersecurity Affairs,[23]
(20) The College on Cybersecurity,[24]

The appointment of such a person is an element in security information policy, which refers to the exchange of data, and incident information in the context of a coherent and coordinated system of mutual communication. To some extent, this person acts as a spokesperson for the coordinator of cooperation with entities operating in the system.

Furthermore, providing the user of the essential service with access to the knowledge to understand cybersecurity threats, and applying effective ways of protecting against them to the extent that the essential service is provided, in particular by publishing information about them on its website, is also part of security information policy. One of the essential principles is the exchange or sharing of risk information between system stakeholders, in this case the users—recipients—of the essential service. The legislator has indicated the form of information, e.g. a message on a website. It would be good practice to prepare for the

[22]Hereinafter referred to as the "Single Point of Contact".

[23]Hereinafter referred to as the "Plenipotentiary".

[24]Hereinafter referred to as the "College".

service recipient a security policy for the essential service, and special alerts, operating on the basis of information on threats to the essential service, provided directly to the service recipient. This provision does not form a basis for such notifications to be made directly, but the openness of the directory of ways to access knowledge about cyber threats, and the application of effective means of protection against those threats to the extent of the essential service delivered, provides the opportunity to communicate such unsolicited information, which justifies the need to ensure security and act in the public interest. However, pursuant to Article 38 of the Act on the National Cybersecurity System, information processed under the Act shall not be made available if its disclosure would violate the protection of the public interest in relation to public security or order, and would adversely affect the conducting of preparatory proceedings for criminal offences, and their detection and prosecution.

It should be stressed, however, that the activities of the exchanging of information in accordance with recital 8 of the Preamble to the Directive should be without prejudice to the possibility for each Member State to take the measures necessary to ensure the protection of the essential interests of its security, to safeguard public policy and public security, and to facilitate the investigation, detection, and prosecution of criminal offences. According to Article 346 of TFEU, no Member State is required to supply information whose disclosure it considers contrary to the essential interests of its security. Therefore, Council Decision 2013/488/EU (5), and non-disclosure agreements or informal non-disclosure agreements, such as the TLP[25] confidentiality rules, apply in this context.

The operator of essential services shall also inform the authority competent for cybersecurity of the Member States of the European Union in which Member States of the European Union the entity is recognised as the operator of essential services and the date on which the provision of the essential service is terminated within 3 months of the change. The information is intended to reach the competent authority due to the nature of the service. The authorities competent for cybersecurity matters are:

(1) for the energy sector—the Minister competent for energy issues
(2) for the transport sector, excluding the water transport subsector—the Minister competent for transport issues
(3) for the water transport subsector—the Minister competent for the maritime economy and the Minister competent for inland navigation
(4) for the banking sector and the financial-market infrastructure—the Financial Supervision Authority
(5) for the healthcare sector, excluding the entities mentioned in Article 26(5)—the Minister competent for health
(6) for the healthcare sector including the entities mentioned in Article 26(5)—the Minister of National Defence

[25]TLP—Traffic Light Protocol.

(7) for the drinking water supply and distribution sector—the Minister competent for water management
(8) for the digital infrastructure sector, excluding the entities referred to in Article 26 (5)—the Minister competent for digital affairs
(9) for the digital infrastructure sector including the entities referred to in Article 26 (5)—the Minister of National Defence

The operator of essential services shall transmit to the authority competent for cybersecurity, the relevant CSIRT MON, CSIRT NASK, CSIRT GOV, and the sectoral cybersecurity team, the data on the person referred to in paragraph 1(1), including the name, surname, telephone number, and e-mail address, within 14 days from the date of their designation, as well as information on changes to these data—within 14 days from the date of their alteration. The purpose of this provision is to identify the data of the person designated to communicate with the authorities; the authority competent for cybersecurity, CSIRT MON, CSIRT NASK, CSIRT GOV, and the sectoral cybersecurity team. The 14-day deadline appears to be relatively long, given the dynamics of the processes taking place in communication and information systems, especially in crisis situations, related to incidents threatening cybersecurity, mainly due to the obligation to maintain monitoring on a continuous basis.

The notion of **Security Operations Centres (SOC)** has been introduced into the national cybersecurity system under the government bill on amending the National Cybersecurity System Act and the Public Procurement Law (published in the Public Information Bulletin on the Government Legislation Centre's website on 7 September 2020). SOCs are to replace the existing structures responsible for the cybersecurity of operators of essential services. SOCs have an established market position as structures performing all functions related to cybersecurity surveillance and management, both within the internal organisational structure, and as part of services provided to other entities. The operators of essential services will establish SOC structures within their internal organisational units, or enter into contracts with third-party providers of SOC services. SOCs will perform risk assessment, and detect and respond to incidents. The minister competent for computerisation will maintain the list of Security Operations Centres. The assessment of risk profiles of hardware or software providers will be performed by the Board at the request of its members. The entities within the national cybersecurity system, while managing risks in their information systems, will be obligated to take into account the results of risk assessment of hardware and software providers. The entities within the national cybersecurity system will not be able to put in operation any hardware, software or services which pose a substantial threat, and will have to withdraw such hardware, software and services indicated in the assessment of a given hardware or software provider no later than within 5 years of the date of the assessment notice. The Plenipotentiary will be obliged to announce risk assessment results by means of a notice published in the Official Gazette of the Government of the Republic of Poland. With a view to preventing critical incidents, and improving the effectiveness of critical incident response, it has been recommended that new articles (Article 67a-67c) be introduced to specify the new competencies of the Plenipotentiary, including the power to issue warnings and injunction orders. The bill introduces amendments to the provisions of the so called new Public Procurement Law. These amendments result from the introduction of risk assessment for hardware and software providers.

As intended by the legislators, electronic communications undertakings are due to become part of the "national cybersecurity system." They will receive support in incident response. A new category of incidents, i.e. telecommunications incidents, will be introduced. Notifications of telecommunications incidents will raise the situational awareness of national-level CSIRTs and improve the coordination of incident response. A separate CSIRT Telco is to be established to provide assistance to electronic communications undertakings, and its tasks will be analogous to those of other sector-specific CSIRTs. CSIRT Telco will be managed by the minister competent for computerisation. It should be noted that the bill is to introduce regulations concerning the obligations of telecommunications operators and trust service providers in respect of ensuring cybersecurity, which is in conflict with the provisions of Directive (EU) 2016/1148 of the European Parliament and of the Council of 6 July 2016 concerning measures for a high common level of security of network and information systems across the Union (Official Journal EU 2016 L 194/1). Under Article 1 of the Directive, the security and notification requirements shall not apply to undertakings which are subject to the requirements of Articles 13a and 13b of Directive 2002/21/EC of the European Parliament and of the Council of 7 March 2002 on a common regulatory framework for electronic communications networks and services (Official Journal EU 2002 L 108/33, hereinafter "Framework Directive"), or to trust service providers who are subject to the requirements of Article 19 of Regulation (EU) No 910/2014 of the European Parliament and of the Council of 23 July 2014 on electronic identification and trust services for electronic transactions in the internal market and repealing Directive 1999/93/EC (Official Journal EU 2014 L 257/73).

The bill sets out the obligations of electronic communications undertakings in respect of the application, following risk assessment, of appropriate and proportionate technical and organisational measures to accurately manage the risks, which implements the provisions set out in Article 40(1) of the EECC 26. The mandatory elements of the measures, arising from Recital 94 of the EECC, have been laid down. Similarly to the provisions of the Telecommunications Law currently in force, the minister competent for computerisation will have the authority to define the minimum scope of technical and organisational measures to manage the risks posed to the security of networks and services. Each undertaking will be obliged to document risk analysis and the application of the above-mentioned security measures. Article 20b defines the information obligation of an electronic communications undertaking following the detection of a security incident. Such undertaking is responsible for incident handling, and for its classification as a telecommunications incident in line with the telecommunications incident thresholds. The undertaking concerned is obliged to notify of the incident a relevant national-level CSIRT, and to cooperate with the CSIRT. This provision implements the first sentence of Article 40(2) of the EECC. In addition, such notification should be communicated to CSIRT Telco, with which the undertaking also cooperates on the handling of telecommunications and critical incidents. Article 20c sets out the principles of incident notification applicable to undertakings preparing action plans for particular threats. They will be obligated to send a security incident notification no later than within 24 hours of incident occurrence, based on the information held at the time. This information should be updated in the course of security incident handling. The thresholds of telecommunications incidents will be defined by means of a regulation of the minister competent for computerisation, and the notification obligation will be imposed on the basis of meeting the criteria for reaching the thresholds. Article 20d sets out the details concerning the contents of a telecommunications incident notification. Article 20e regulates the information obligations imposed on electronic communications undertakings operating on the retail market. In the event of a particular and significant threat of a security incident, such undertaking shall inform the users potentially affected by such a threat about any possible protective measures or remedies which can be taken by the users, including their costs, which is the implementation of the first sentence of Article 40(3) of the EECC. Furthermore, such undertaking will be obligated to inform the users of the security incident itself and its impact on the availability of the services provided, *[26 European Electronic Communication Code, EECC - Directive (EU) 2018/1972 of the European Parliament and of the Council of 11 December 2018 establishing the European Electronic Communications Code, replacing Directives 2002/19/WE, 2002/20/WE, 2002/21/WE, 2002/22/WE]*, if, in its opinion, the impact of the security incident is significant, which is the implementation of the provisions laid down in the second sentence of Article 40(3) of the EECC. Article 20f concerns the obligation of an electronic communications undertaking to block communication, and limit or interrupt the provision of electronic communications services at the network termination point from where such communication is sent. Such measures are possible if a threat to the security of networks or services is identified, and can only be taken to the extent necessary to prevent the threat, and only for as long as the cause of such a threat persists. The amendment to Article 32 will make it possible for the CSIRT Telco to inform the entities within the national cybersecurity system about any vulnerabilities and any measures for removing them, if such information was obtained from the entities within the system. Pursuant to the new wording of Article 34, CSIRT Telco and sector-specific CSIRTs may cooperate with law enforcement and judicial authorities, as well as with special forces in fulfilling their statutory tasks. The newly introduced Article 34a concerns the issue of cooperation between national-level CSIRTs and the President of the Office of Electronic Communications during telecommunications incidents. These provisions implement Article 41 (4) and (5) of the EECC. The proposed amendments to Article 39 allow the CSIRT Telco to process personal data in the course of fulfilling its statutory tasks. The amendment to Article 39(3)(2) is a technical modification which results from repealing the existing Telecommunications Law. Due to adding Article 39(4)(4), the minister competent for computerisation, the Director of the Government Centre for Security, the Plenipotentiary and competent authorities for cybersecurity will be entitled to process personal data obtained from electronic communications undertakings in the course of fulfilling their statutory duties in relation to cybersecurity threats and incidents.

The current position of telecommunications undertakings in the cybersecurity system is based on national laws, but the basic solutions in this respect are a consequence of the solutions adopted in the European Union law. Any differences concerning telecommunications undertakings refer both to counteracting and combating cybersecurity threats, and to providing information about the occurrence of such threats. Thanks to entrusting relevant tasks to the President of the Office of Electronic Communications (UKE), a possibility was provided to transfer information about incidents in the telecommunications sector to competent entities within the national cybersecurity system. The structure of sector-specific regulations in respect of cybersecurity in telecommunications corresponds to the structure of obligations imposed on operators of essential services, as provided for in general cybersecurity regulations.

The "NIS 2 Directive" aims to reform the provisions on the security of network and information systems. It is to help build a high level of cybersecurity in critical public and private sectors, such as health care and its facilities (e.g. hospitals, medical laboratories), energy networks, railways, public administration, as well as infrastructure and their services, thus significantly expanding the group of entities covered by it in relation to the so-called "NIS Directives". The general direction of regulating key sectors, in particular the telecommunications sector and the public administration sector, in the common framework of the NIS 2 Directive, will allow for the creation of a coherent cybersecurity system, both at the EU level and at the national level. Including telecommunications, or more broadly the electronic communications sector, into a uniform legal system throughout the EU is important for several key reasons: 1. Such a solution is in line with the general market development tendency resulting from the increasing use of IT technologies in telecommunications (the effect of technological convergence). Today it is telecommunications that is the provider of the Internet, which is the basis for the provision of many strategic network services, such as cloud computing. The role of software in the construction of telecommunications services and systems is also growing. Media penetration is an everyday reality. It is therefore unjustified to separate the service layer from the regulation of the telecommunications infrastructure on which these services are "embedded". The strategy of defense against cyber attacks must be comprehensive and rely on the protection of both networks and IT systems, up to end devices. The current legal status, both in the NIS Directive and in its implementation in the Polish Act on the National Cybersecurity System, caused a state of uncertainty. The NIS Directive exempted telecommunications undertakings pursuant to Article 1 para. 2 point 1 in terms of security and incident reporting requirements, and the EU legal system provided for a separate regulation for network security and integrity. This is a paradoxical situation, because in fact the NIS Directive concerned "security", and without the security of the network layer, the security of the service is in many cases impossible to implement. This impotence of precise delimitation shows that it is impossible to create a coherent cybersecurity system without the participation of the telecommunications sector and the sector of Internet access service providers.

Annex No. 1, Sectors and subsectors and types of entities, defines the areas to be regulated

Sector	Subsector (if any)	Type of entity
Energy	Mineral extraction	Entities conducting business activities in the field of natural gas extraction, on the basis of a concession referred to in Article 22(1) of the Act of 9 June 2011—Geological and Mining Law.[a]
		Entities conducting business activities in the field of crude oil mining, on the basis of a concession referred to in Article 22(1) of the Act of 9 June 2011—Geological and Mining Law.
		Entities conducting business activities in the field of lignite mining, on the basis of a concession referred to in Article 22(1) of the Act of 9 June 2011—Geological and Mining Law.
		Entities conducting business activities in the field of hard coal mining, on the basis of a concession referred to in Article 22(1) of the Act of 9 June 2011—Geological and Mining Law.
		Entities conducting business activities in the field of mining of other minerals, on the basis of a concession referred to in Article 22(1) of the Act of 9 June 2011—Geological and Mining Law.
	Electricity	An energy company mentioned in Article 3 (12) of the Act of 10 April 1997—Energy Law (Polish Journal of Laws of 2020, item 833, as amended[b]), holding a licence to conduct business activities in the field of electricity generation.
		An energy company referred to in Article 3 (24) of the Act of 10 April 1997—Energy Law, holding a concession to conduct business activities in the field of electricity transmission.
		An energy company referred to in Article 3 (25) of the Act of 10 April 1997—Energy Law, holding a concession to conduct business activities in the field of electricity distribution.
		An energy company referred to in Article 3 (12) of the Act of 10 April 1997—Energy Law, holding a concession to conduct business activities in the field of electricity trading.
		An energy company referred to in Article 3 (12) of the Act of 10 April 1997—Energy Law, conducting business activities in the field of electricity processing or storage.
		Entities conducting business activities in the field of system, quality, and energy infrastructure management services.

(continued)

Sector	Subsector (if any)	Type of entity
	Heat	An energy company referred to in Article 3 (12) of the Act of 10 April 1997—Energy Law, holding a concession to conduct business activities in the field of heat generation.
		An energy company referred to in Article 3 (12) of the Act of 10 April 1997—Energy Law, holding a concession to conduct business activities in the field of heat trading.
		An energy company referred to in Article 3 (12) of the Act of 10 April 1997—Energy Law, holding a concession to conduct business activities in the field of heat transmission.
		An energy company referred to in Article 3 (12) of the Act of 10 April 1997—Energy Law, holding a concession to perform business activities in the field of heat distribution.
	Crude oil	An energy company mentioned in Article 3 (12) of the Act of 10 April 1997—Energy Law, holding a concession for the performance of business activities in the field of the production of liquid fuels, mentioned in Article 32(1) of the Act of 10 April 1997—Energy Law.
		Entities conducting business activities in the field of crude-oil transmission.
		An energy company mentioned in Article 3 (12) of the Act of 10 April 1997—Energy Law, holding a concession for conducting business activities in the field of liquid-fuels transmission through a pipeline network, mentioned in Article 32(1) of the Act of 10 April 1997—Energy Law.
		An entity conducting business activities in the field of crude oil storage, including the tankless underground storage of crude oil, referred to in Article 22(1) of the Act of 9 June 2011—Geological and Mining Law.
		Entities engaged in the business of crude oil transhipment.
		An energy company referred to in Article 3 (12) of the Act of 10 April 1997—Energy Law, conducting business activities in the field of liquid fuels storage, referred to in Article 32 (1) of the Act of 10 April 1997—Energy Law, and an entity conducting activities in the field of the tankless underground storage of liquid fuels, referred to in Article 22(1) of the Act of 9 June 2011—Geological and Mining Law.
		An energy company mentioned in Article 3 (12) of the Act of 10 April 1997—Energy Law, performing business activities in the field of the transhipment of liquid fuels, mentioned in

(continued)

Sector	Subsector (if any)	Type of entity
		Article 32(1) of the Act of 10 April 1997—Energy Law.
		An energy company mentioned in Article 3 (12) of the Act of 10 April 1997—Energy Law, performing business activities in the field of liquid fuel trading, or in the field of liquid fuel trading with foreign countries, mentioned in Article 32(1) of the Act of 10 April 1997—Energy Law.
		Entities conducting business activities in the field of synthetic fuel production.
	Gas	An energy company referred to in Article 3 (12) of the Act of 10 April 1997—Energy Law, conducting activities in the field of gaseous fuel generation, referred to in Article 3(45) of Act of 10 April 1997—Energy Law.
		An energy company referred to in Article 3 (12) of the Act of 10 April 1997—Energy Law, holding a concession to conduct business activities in the field of gaseous fuel transmission.
		An energy company referred to in Article 3 (12) of the Act of 10 April 1997—Energy Law, holding a concession to conduct business activities in the field of natural gas trading with foreign countries, or to conduct business activities in the field of trade in gaseous fuels.
		An energy company mentioned in Article 3 (24) of the Act of 10 April 1997—Energy Law, being a gas transmission-system operator appointed by the President of the Energy Regulatory Office.
		An energy company mentioned in Article 3 (25) of the Act of 10 April 1997—Energy Law, being a gas distribution system operator appointed by the President of the Energy Regulatory Office.
		An energy company mentioned in Article 3 (26) of the Act of 10 April 1997—Energy Law, being a gaseous fuel storage system operator appointed by the President of the Energy Regulatory Office.
		An energy company, mentioned in Article 3 (27) of the Act of 10 April 1997—Energy Law, being a natural gas liquefaction system operator appointed by the President of the Energy Regulatory Office.
	Supply and services for the energy sector	Entities conducting business activities in the field of the supply of systems, machines, equipment, materials, raw materials, and services for the energy sector.

(continued)

Sector	Subsector (if any)	Type of entity
	Supervised and subordinated units	Organisational units subordinated to or supervised by the Minister competent for energy.
		Organisational units subordinated to or supervised by the Minister competent for mineral resources management.
Transportation	Air transport	An air carrier referred to in Article 3(4) of Regulation (EC) No 300/2008 of the European Parliament and of the Council of 11 March 2008 on common rules in the field of civil aviation security and repealing Regulation (EC) No 2320/2002.[c]
		An airport manager referred to in Article 2(7) of the Act of 3 July 2002—Aviation Law.[d]
		An entrepreneur referred to in Article 177(2) of the Act of 3 July 2002—Aviation Law, performing for air carriers and other aircraft users one or more categories of services referred to in Article 176 of that Act, and an entrepreneur referred to in Article 186b(1)(2) of the Act of 3 July 2002—Aviation Law, performing tasks related to security control for air carriers.
		An air navigation service provider referred to in Article 127(1) of the Act of 3 July 2002—Aviation Law.
	Rail transport	A railway-infrastructure administrator, within the meaning of Article 4(7) of the Act of 28 March 2003 on Rail Transport[e] excluding the administrators of only the inactive infrastructure referred to in Article 4(1b) of this Act, and the private infrastructure, referred to in Article 4 (1c), and the narrow-gauge railway infrastructure referred to in Article 4(1d) of this Act. A railway undertaking referred to in Article 4 (9) of the Act of 28 March 2003 on Rail Transport, whose activities are subject to licensing, and an operator of a service facility referred to in Article 4(52) of the Act of 28 March 2003 on Rail Transport, if the entrepreneur performing the function of an operator is also a railway undertaking.
	Water transport	A shipowner in the maritime transport of passengers and goods, according to the definition of maritime transport in Annex I to Regulation (EC) No 725/2004 of the European Parliament and of the Council of 31 March 2004 on enhancing ship and port facility security[f] with the exception of individual ships which these shipowners operate.

(continued)

Sector	Subsector (if any)	Type of entity
		A shipowner referred to in Article 5(1) (2) of the Act of 21 December 2000 on Inland Navigation.[g]
		An entity managing the port referred to in Article 2(6) of the Act of 20 December 1996 on Ports and Sea Harbours.[h]
		A manager of a port facility referred to in Article 2(11) of Regulation (EC) No. 725/2004 of the European Parliament, and of the Council, of 31 March 2004, on enhancing ship and port facility security.[i]
		Entities conducting activities at ports supporting maritime transport.
		The VTS (Vessel Traffic Service)—an auxiliary apparatus of the Director of the Maritime Office established in order to monitor ship traffic and transfer information, constituting a component of the National SafeSeaNet System referred to in Article 91 of the Act of 18 August 2011 on Maritime Safety.[j]
	Road transport	Authorities referred to in Article 19(2), (5) and (5a) of the Act of 21 March 1985 on Public Roads.[k]
		Entities referred to in Article 43a(1) of the Act of 21 March 1985 on Public Roads.
Banking and financial-markets infrastructure		A credit institution referred to in Article 4 (1) (17) of the Act of 29 August 1997—Banking Law.[l]
		The National Bank referred to in Article 4(1) (1) of the Act of 29 August 1997—Banking Law.
		A branch of a foreign bank referred to in Article 4(1)(20) of the Act of 29 August 1997—Banking Law.
		A branch of a credit institution referred to in Article 4(1)(18) of the Act of 29 August 1997—Banking Law.
		Cooperative savings and credit unions within the meaning of the Act of 5 November 2009 on Cooperative Savings and Credit Unions.[m]
		An entity operating the regulated market referred to in Article 14(1) of the Act of 29 July 2005 on Trading Financial Instruments.[n]
		An entity referred to in Article 3(49) of the Act of 29 July 2005 on Trading Financial Instruments

(continued)

Sector	Subsector (if any)	Type of entity
		An entity referred to in Article 48(7) of the Act of 29 July 2005 on Trading Financial Instruments.
Healthcare		A healthcare entity referred to in Article 4(1) of the Act of 15 April 2011 on Healthcare Activities (Journal of Laws of 2018, item 160, 138, 650, 1128, 1375 and 1532).
		A unit subordinated to the Minister competent for health, responsible for healthcare-information systems.
		National Health Fund.
		A healthcare entity within which the hospital pharmacy department operates, within the meaning of the Act of 6 September 2001—Pharmaceutical Law[o]
		A healthcare entity within which a hospital pharmacy operates, within the meaning of the Act of 6 September 2001—Pharmaceutical Law.
		An entrepreneur conducting the activities of a pharmaceutical wholesaler, within the meaning of the Act of 6 September 2001—Pharmaceutical Law.
		An entrepreneur or an entity conducting business activities in a Member State of the European Union or a Member State of the European Free Trade Association (EFTA)—a party to the agreement on the European Economic Area which has obtained marketing authorisation for a medicinal product.
		An importer of a medicinal product/active substance within the meaning of the Act of 6 September 2001—Pharmaceutical Law.
		A manufacturer of a medicinal product/active substance within the meaning of the Act of 6 September 2001—Pharmaceutical Law.
		A parallel importer within the meaning of the Act of 6 September 2001—Pharmaceutical Law.
		A distributor of active substances within the meaning of the Act of 6 September 2001—Pharmaceutical Law.
		An entrepreneur operating as a commercial pharmacy within the meaning of the Act of 6 September 2001—Pharmaceutical Law.
The supply and distribution of drinking water		A water supply and sewage company referred to in Article 2(4) of the Act of 7 June 2001 on Collective Water Supply and Collective Sewage Disposal[p]

(continued)

Sector	Subsector (if any)	Type of entity
Digital infrastructure		An entity which provides DNS services.
		An entity operating an Internet Exchange Point (IXP), which is a network facility which allows interconnection between more than two independent autonomous systems, mainly for the purpose of facilitating Internet traffic exchange.
		An entity managing the registration of Internet domain names within a top-level domain (TLD).

[a]Act of 9 June 2011—Geological and Mining Law, consolidated text Polish Journal of Laws of 2020, item 1064
[b]Act of 10 April 1997—Energy Law, consolidated text Polish Journal of Laws of 2020, item 833, as amended
[c]Regulation (EC) No 300/2008 of the European Parliament and of the Council of 11 March 2008 on common rules in the field of civil aviation security and repealing Regulation (EC) No 2320/2002, OJ EU 2008 L 97/72
[d]Act of 3 July 2002—Aviation Law, consolidated text Polish Journal of Laws of 2020, item 1970, as amended
[e]Act of 28 March 2003 on Rail Transport, consolidated text Polish Journal of Laws of 2020 No. 20, item 1043, as amended
[f]Regulation (EC) No 725/2004 of the European Parliament and of the Council of 31 March 2004 on enhancing ship and port facility security, OJ EU 2004 L 129/6
[g]Act of 21 December 2000 on Inland Navigation, consolidated text Polish Journal of Laws of 2020, item 1863, as amended
[h]Act of 20 December 1996 on Ports and Sea Harbours, consolidated text Polish Journal of Laws of 2020, item 998, as amended
[i]Regulation (EC) No. 725/2004 of the European Parliament and of the Council of 31 March 2004, on enhancing ship and port facility security, OJ EU 2004 L 129/6
[j]Act of 18 August 2011 on Maritime Safety, consolidated text Polish Journal of Laws of 2020, items 680, as amended
[k]Act of 21 March 1985 on Public Roads, consolidated text Polish Journal of Laws of 2020, item 470, as amended
[l]Act of 29 August 1997—Banking Law, consolidated text Polish Journal of Laws of 2020, item 1896, as amended
[m]Act of 5 November 2009 on Cooperative Savings and Credit Unions, consolidated text Polish Journal of Laws of 2020, item 1643, as amended
[n]Act of 29 July 2005 on Trading Financial Instruments, consolidated text Polish Journal of Laws of 2020, item 89, as amended
[o]Act of 6 September 2001—Pharmaceutical Law, consolidated text Polish Journal of Laws of 2020, item 944, as amended)
[p]Act of 7 June 2001 on Collective Water Supply and Collective Sewage Disposal, consolidated text Polish Journal of Laws of 2020, item 2028

References

Borkowski J (1996) In: Adamiak B, Borkowski J (eds) Kodeks postępowania administracyjnego, Komentarz. C.H. Beck, Warsaw

Ganczar M (2009) Informatyzacja administracji publicznej. Nowa jakość usług publicznych dla obywateli i przedsiębiorców, Warszawa
Knosala E Matan A Zacharko L (1996) Zarys nauki administracji. Katowice
Pawłowski A (2002) Zasoby informacyjne w administracji publicznej w Polsce. Lublin
Szaff L (1957) O niektórych problemach dotyczących zakresu postępowania przygotowawczego, Nowe Prawo 12

Katarzyna Chałubińska-Jentkiewicz dr. hab. of legal sciences (University of Warsaw and the Jagiellonian University), legal advisor, associate professor, and head of the Department of Cybersecurity Law and New Technologies at the Institute of Law in the Faculty of National Security at the War Studies University in Warsaw. She is also a lecturer at the SWPS University and director of the Academic Center for Cybersecurity Policy. In the years 1996–2010, she worked as a lawyer in the National Broadcasting Council and with the public broadcaster TVP S.A. Between 2011 and 2017, she was deputy director of the National Audiovisual Institute (her competence centered on the field of digitization). As a scientist, she conducts research on cybersecurity, information security threats, the development of electronic media law, protection of intellectual property, and the impact of new technologies on the development of the state and the legal situation of the individual. Katarzyna Chałubińska–Jentkiewicz is the author of monographs and numerous articles, which include topics such as new technologies law, cyber responsibility, information security law, and audiovisual media: Regulatory conflict in the age of digitization, Audio visual media services; Regulation in the conditions of digital conversion; Information and computerization in public administration; Cultural Security Law and Reuse of public sector information. She is head of the Ministry of Science's research project "Polish cybersecurity system—a model of legal solutions."

The Obligations of Public Entities

Krzysztof Wąsowski

Abstract The author presents the structure and principles which the Polish legislature imposes on public entities in the field of cybersecurity. The analysed regulations cover government authorities, state control authorities, law enforcement authorities, courts (both common and special), local government units and their associations (including metropolitan unions), budgetary units and Budget establishments, executive agencies, budgetary institutions, the Social Insurance Institution (ZUS) and managed funds, the Agricultural Social Insurance Fund (KRUS) and the funds managed by its President, the National Health Found, public universities, and the Polish Academy of Sciences. In addition to these public finance entities, special cybersecurity obligations have been imposed on research institutes, the National Bank of Poland, Bank Gospodarstwa Krajowego (BGK), Office of Technical Inspection (UDT), the Polish Air Navigation Services Agency (PENSA), Polish Centre for Accreditation (PCA), the National Fund for Environmental Protection and Water Management (NFEP&WM) and the provincial funds, as well as municipal companies. Despite differences in the form of activity (including possession or absence of legal personality), it is commonly agreed that the analysed regulations treat public entities as public administration authorities, at least in the functional sense, as evidenced by the indication that the obligations of public entities should be carried out within the framework of public tasks.

K. Wąsowski (✉)
Akademickie Centrum Polityki Cyberbezpieczeństwa/Academic Center for Cybersecurity Policy, Akademia Sztuki Wojennej w Warszawie/War Studies University in Warsaw, Warsaw, Poland
e-mail: k.wasowski@akademia.mil.pl

K. Chałubińska-Jentkiewicz et al. (eds.), *Cybersecurity in Poland*,
https://doi.org/10.1007/978-3-030-78551-2_20

1 Range of Public Entities Subject to Cyber Security Obligations

The National Cybersecurity System attempts to cover comprehensively and complementarily all entities which use IT tools in the spheres of both public and private activities (under private law) and are significant for state security. In addition to a number of obligations exacted on entities which are not systemically linked to the public sector (such as digital service providers and operators of essential services), the legislators also impose independent, or autonomous, obligations on public entities. It should be noted that the understanding of the term "public entity" significantly exceeds the confines of the term "public administration authority" as used by legal commentators. The legislators have outlined the range of these public institutions very broadly. The provisions contained in Chapter 5 of the National Cybersecurity System Act designate not only government administration authorities, state control authorities, and legal protection authorities, but also the courts (both common and special), local government units and their associations (including metropolitan associations), budget units and local government budget enterprises, executive agencies, budget economy institutions, the Social Insurance Institution and the funds managed by it, the Agricultural Social Insurance Fund (Kasa Rolniczego Ubezpieczenia Społecznego) and the funds managed by its President, the National Health Fund, public universities, and the Polish Academy of Sciences, as well as the organisational units created by it. Apart from these public finance sector entities, special cybersecurity obligations have been imposed on research institutes, the National Bank of Poland, Bank Gospodarstwa Krajowego, the Office of Technical Inspection, the Polish Air Navigation Services Agency, the Polish Centre for Accreditation, the National Fund for Environmental Protection and Water Management, and Voivodeship Water Management Funds. Finally, the legislators included so-called municipal companies among public entities.[1]

Despite differences in the form of activity (resulting, i.a., in having or not having legal personality), there is no doubt that the analysed regulations treat public entities as public administration authorities, at least in the functional sense,[2] by indicating that the duties of public entities should be performed while performing "public tasks".[3] The functions of public tasks may be performed by any entity to which the legislators assign relevant responsibilities in a normative Act. This is because this entity does not necessarily have to be systemically linked to the structure of public administration authorities, nor does it have to be a state legal person,[4] and it may

[1]Chałubińska-Jentkiewicz et al. (2021) passim.

[2]See more Dawidowicz (1965), pp. 5–7.

[3]Por. Biernat (1994), pp. 4–11.

[4]See more—Dybowski (1990); Szachułowicz (2000), p. 18.

operate, for example, within the structures provided for in the Code of Commercial Companies and Partnerships[5] for private commercial entities.

Government administration authorities in the political system are subject, respectively by hierarchy, to the Council of Ministers, which conducts the internal and external policies of the Republic of Poland,[6] and governs all matters of state policy not reserved for other state and local government authorities.[7] The Council of Ministers has also been given a clear mandate to lead the government administration.[8]

In addition, the Constitution of the Republic of Poland includes the following state authorities as state control and legal protection authorities: the Supreme Audit Office,[9] the Ombudsman,[10] and the National Broadcasting Council.[11] These are autonomous state authorities, with their independence from both the executive and the legislative authorities already guaranteed at system level. The cybersecurity system has also been extended to the courts and tribunals,[12] whose autonomy from other state authorities derives from the principles of tri-partition and the balance of power.[13]

Local government is an emanation of the de-centralised state system,[14] and performs all public tasks not reserved for others by the legislators.[15] Local government units also have the constitutional right to associate[16] and establish municipal associations.

Budgetary units are organisational entities in the public finance sector, with no legal personality, and whose expenditures are financed directly from the budget, while they transfer the collected revenues to the account of the state budget revenue, or the budget of a local government unit, respectively.[17] A local government budget entity, in turn, is a separate, autonomous, unit within the structure of a specific territorial government unit, and within its activities in the field of broadly understood municipal management, performing tasks of a public-utility type.[18] The cyber

[5]The Commercial Companies Code of 15 September 2000, consolidated text of 2019, item 505, as amended.

[6]See Article 146 (1) of the Constitution of the Republic of Poland.

[7]See Article 146 (2) of the Constitution of the Republic of Poland.

[8]See Article 146 (3) of the Constitution of the Republic of Poland.

[9]See Articles 202–207 of the Constitution of the Republic of Poland.

[10]See Articles 208–212 of the Constitution of the Republic of Poland.

[11]See Articles 214–215 of the Constitution of the Republic of Poland.

[12]See Articles 173–201 See Article 10 of the Constitution of the Republic of Poland.

[13]See Article 10 of the Constitution of the Republic of Poland.

[14]See Article 15 (1) of the Constitution of the Republic of Poland.

[15]See Article 10 of the Constitution of the Republic of Poland.

[16]See Article 172 (1) of the Constitution of the Republic of Poland.

[17]According to the requirements of Article 11 (1) of the Act on Public Finances of 27 August 2009, consolidated text Polish Journal of Laws of 2019, item 869, as amended.

[18]See more—Banasiński and Jaroszyński (2017), p. 28.

security system also includes executive agencies, which are referred to as new public management institutions,[19] the aim of which is to implement the transition from the bureaucratic model of public management to the so-called managerial model.[20] Cybersecurity obligations are also imposed on budgetary-economy institutions, i.e. the public finance sector units created in order to perform public tasks, with their typical features including the implementation of the public tasks entrusted to them for remuneration, and covering their operational costs and liabilities from the revenues obtained.[21]

The Social Insurance Institution (Zakład Ubezpieczeń Społecznych—ZUS) is a state organisational unit with legal personality. The scope, tasks, and responsibilities of ZUS are defined by law.[22] ZUS is managed by its President, who performs his or her functions with the help of the management board—a collegial authority. The control function is performed by the Supervisory Board, appointed by the Prime Minister, with the reservation that individual members of the Board should be appointed by the appropriate public administration authorities and organisations of employers, employees and pensioners.[23] The legislators have differentiated the Head Office from the field organisational units within the structure of ZUS. The main task of this public undertaking is to implement the social security regulations.[24] As part of its public tasks, ZUS is also obligated to maintain a contact point for the exchange of data within the System for Electronic Exchange of Social Security Information.[25]

The Agricultural Social Insurance Fund (Kasa Rolniczego Ubezpieczenia Społecznego—KRUS) is a state organisational unit, with a status not clearly defined by law. The legislators have given KRUS the basic task of administering social insurance for farmers.[26] The fund is managed by its President, who has the status of a central government administration authority, and reports to the Minister competent for rural development.[27]

[19] See Zieliński (2014).

[20] See Marchewka-Bartkowiak (2011).

[21] See Article 23 (1) of the Act on Public Finances of 27 August 2009.

[22] See Chapter 7 of the Social Insurance System Act of 13 October 1998, consolidated text, Polish Journal of Laws of 2019, item 300, as amended.

[23] See Article 75 of the Social Insurance System Act.

[24] See Article 68 (1) (1) of the Social Insurance System Act.

[25] See Article 68a(1) of the Social Security System Act, in conjunction with Regulation (EC) No 987/2009 of the European Parliament and of the Council of 16 September 2009 laying down the procedure for implementing Regulation (EC) No. 883/2004 on the coordination of social security systems (OJ EU 2009 L 284/1, as amended).

[26] See Article 2 (1) of the Agricultural Social Insurance Fund of 20 December 1990, consolidated text, Polish Journal of Laws of 2019, item 299, as amended.

[27] See Article 2 (2) of the Agricultural Social Insurance Fund.

The National Health Fund (Narodowy Fundusz Zdrowia—NFZ) is a state organisational unit with legal personality.[28] A National Contact Point for cross-border healthcare has also been established at the Headquarters of the Fund.[29]

Public universities which were established by a state authority are also covered by the regulations in respect of the cybersecurity system.[30] Research institutes have also been included in this system. They are defined in the Act as state development units, independent in legal, organisational, economic, and financial terms, which conduct research and development work aimed at the implementation and practical application of its results.[31] The Polish Academy of Sciences (Polska Akademia Nauk—PAN), in turn, is a "state scientific institution",[32] with legal personality.[33]

The National Bank of Poland (NBP) is the central bank of the country, which has the exclusive right to issue money, and to establish and implement monetary policy.[34] This entity has legal personality.[35] In contrast, Bank Gospodarstwa Krajowego is the state bank,[36] which means that it is not a state enterprise, nor is it a state organisational unit or a public finance sector entity, nor is it subject to registration in the National Court Register. The basic objective of BGK is to support the economic policy of the Council of Ministers, governmental social and economic programmes, including guarantee and suretyship programmes, and local government and regional development programmes.[37]

The Office of Technical Inspection (Urząd Dozoru Technicznego—UDT) is a state entity with legal personality, which is not responsible for the liabilities of the Treasury, and the Treasury is not responsible for the obligations of UDT. The Polish Air Navigation Services Agency is a state entity with legal personality,[38] and its statutory tasks include ensuring safe, continuous, smooth-running, and effective air

[28]See Article 96(1) of the Act on Health Care Services Financed from Public Funds of 27 August 2004, consolidated text, Polish Journal of Laws of 2019, item 1373, as amended.

[29]See Article 97a of the Act on Public Health Care Services.

[30]See Article 14 of the Higher Education and Science Law of 20 July 2018, Polish Journal of Laws of 2018, item 1668, as amended.

[31]See Article 1 (1) of the Act on Research Institutes of 30 April 2010, consolidated text, Polish Journal of Laws of 2019, item 1350, as amended.

[32]See Article 1(1) of the Act on the Polish Academy of Sciences of 30 April 2010, consolidated text, Polish Journal of Laws of 2019, item 1183, as amended.

[33]See Article 3 (1) of the Act on the Polish Academy of Sciences.

[34]See Article 227 (1) of the Constitution of the Republic of Poland.

[35]See Article 2 (2) of the Act on the National Bank of Poland of 29 August 1997, consolidated text, Polish Journal of Laws of 2019, item 1810, as amended.

[36]Within the meaning of Article 14 et seq. of Banking Law of 29 August 1997, consolidated text, Polish Journal of Laws of 2018, item 2187, as amended.

[37]See Article 4 of the Bank Gospodarstwa Krajowego Act of 14 March 2003, consolidated text, Polish Journal of Laws of 2018, item 1543, as amended.

[38]See Article 1 (2) of the Act on the Polish Air Navigation Services Agency of 8 December 2006, consolidated text, Polish Journal of Laws of 2017, item 1967, as amended.

navigation in Polish airspace.[39] The Polish Accreditation Centre is a national accreditation authority which is a state legal entity.[40] The National Fund for Environmental Protection and Water Management, and the provincial funds for environmental protection and water management, are environmental protection institutions.[41] The National Fund is a state institution with legal personality,[42] while voivodeship funds have the status of local government units with legal personalities,[43] but they are not local government organisational units.[44]

This general review of the legal status of individual entities charged with taking certain actions within the framework of the functioning of the cybersecurity system shows that their systemic nature is quite diverse. The principle of the functional approach to public entities is clearly apparent, and is closely related to the public tasks implemented by these entities.

2 Obligation to Report and Handle an Incident in a Public Entity

An obligation placed on a public entity becomes enforceable only when the task imposed on that entity is carried out using an information system. The concept of an information system has been legally defined by reference to the concept of an information and communication system,[45] supplemented by the fact that it also involves processing data in an electronic form in that system. If a certain public entity does not perform public tasks at all, it will not be subject to this obligation. Such a situation is difficult to imagine in the current legal regime, and would require the intervention of the legislators, who would prohibit a public entity indicated in this provision from the fulfilment of public tasks in general, or would order such an entity not to fulfil its tasks using the information system, which nowadays seems unlikely.[46] Ensuring "incident management" includes, at the same time, an obligation to ensure access to know-how, and a procedure to inform certain entities of the

[39]See Article 3 (1) of the Act on the Polish Air Navigation Services Agency.

[40]See Article 38 (2) of the Act on Conformity Assessment and Market Supervision of 13 April 2016, Polish Journal of Laws of 2019, item 544, as amended.

[41]See Article 386 (3) of the Environmental Protection Law of 27 April 2001, consolidated text of 2019, item 1396, as amended.

[42]See Article 400 (1) of the Environmental Protection Law.

[43]See Article 400 (2) of the Environmental Protection Law.

[44]See Article 400 (3) of the Environmental Protection Law.

[45]Within the meaning of Article 3 point 3 of the Act on the Computerisation of the Activities of Entities Performing Public Tasks of 17 February 2005, consolidated text, Polish Journal of Laws of 2019, item 700, as amended.

[46]Por. Wąsowski (2019), pp. 188–189.

designation of the responsible person. It is worth pointing out that the catalogue of these duties is of closed nature (*numerus clausus*).

Incident management as a term is understood by the legislators not only as "dealing with" such incidents, but also detecting links between them, removing their causes, and developing the appropriate proposals addressed at, inter alia, detecting them more effectively, and taking action to prevent such events in the future. An obligation characterised in this way provides a legal basis for any action, both managerial and organisational-technical, which it should carry out, not only within its "own" capacities, but also with "external" assistance—of a public entity in this respect.

Notwithstanding the obligation to undertake incident management, a public entity must immediately report a detected "in-house" incident to the competent Computer Security Incident Response Team (CSIRT). The determination of competence is reduced to the scope of subject-matter competence based on a catalogue of incident types (also in terms of the sector in which the incident has been detected). In this case, the legislators did not specify any exact rules for the observance of competence ex-officio by the applicable CSIRT. The rules for the assessment and observance of competence as laid down in the Code of Administrative Procedure do not apply. A notification to the competent CSIRT should be made without undue (culpable) delay, no later than 24 hours after the detection of such an incident. It is worth noting that the legislators have not specified in detail the technology of such an electronic form. It will be reasonable to assume that the notification should be made by e-mail, while the public authority is obliged to provide the e-mail address of the competent CSIRT.[47] Where it is not possible to communicate the information by electronic means, any other way of passing on the notification is acceptable. However, it is worth assuming that in each of the possible ways chosen by the informant there should be a guarantee that the information (notification) reaches the addressee. Only then will it be possible to consider the act of notification as having been carried out.

The handling of an incident and a critical occurrence in a public entity has been entrusted to a public entity cooperating with the competent CSIRT. The entity obliged to provide a service has been indicated as a public entity, and the cooperating entity as the competent CSIRT, which should support the public entity in carrying out such an obligation. The legislators have also included an obligation imposed on a public entity, carried out during incident handling, to provide essential data, including personal details. All data (other than personal) which might be (even indirectly) related to the detection and response to incidents should be treated as essential.

Public entities are also responsible for the implementation of the material and technical task of providing the beneficiaries of public tasks with access to know-how and useful information on cybersecurity. This obligation is manifestly described in more detail when the necessary information on cybersecurity is published. Similarly

[47]See Article 22 (5) of the National Cybersecurity System Act of 5 July 2018, Polish Journal of Laws of 2018, item 1560, as amended.

to other cybersecurity tasks imposed on public entities, the legislators have not provided for direct legal sanctions.[48]

3 Formal Requirements for Reporting an Incident in a Public Entity

The reporting of incidents is conditional on numerous formal and informational requirements. The informational obligations involve the transfer of data of a subjective nature (data on the public entity, the reporting person, and the person authorised to provide explanations) and of an objective nature (containing information on what caused the incident, its essential features, the effects it had or might have had, and about the preventive actions taken or planned).

The obligation to include data on the public entity in the notification is defined at the basic level (name, number in the relevant register, registered office, and address). It is worth pointing out that in situations in which a public entity is not subject to the obligation of registration (e.g. public administration authorities), it will not be able to indicate the register number.

The person submitting the notification should, in principle, be the responsible person designated by the public entity. However, the legislators do not grant such a person specific exclusivity to undertake such duties. When reporting an incident, the time and speed with which the competent CSIRT is informed of such an event is of crucial importance. Therefore, the obligation to make a report in emergency situations may be fulfilled by persons other than the one responsible. Also, the informant should indicate his or her name, telephone number, and e-mail address.

A person entitled to submit explanations is another party whose data should be disclosed in the notification. The scope of the disclosure of the information about such a person is the same as that of the person submitting the notification. The mere mention of such a person in the notification means that he or she has given a specific authorisation to clarify the submitted information. No additional document is required to confirm such an authorisation. Nor is there any formal limitation on the person who reports to be shown as entitled to submit explanations at the same time.

Details of the public task should be included in the description of the incident, which should be linked to an indication of the legal basis for carrying out such a task. The estimate of the number of people affected by the incident need not be clearly defined. In a situation in which it would be impossible to determine a precise figure, an estimate of the number of people who were affected by such an incident should be given. Correct timing is important and should be presented in the most precise way possible. In a virtual reality, the requirement to define the geographical area affected might concern the entire region, although, where possible, a precisely defined area

---

[48] Wąsowski (2019), pp. 190–192.

should be identified. The most important element in the description, by general consent, is the identification of the causes of the incident, its course, and the effects of its impact on the information systems of the public entity. This description should indicate all the relevant facts which had a direct and indirect impact on the occurrence, course, and consequences of the incident. The cause and source of the incident are important, so the standard-setter acknowledges such an obligation, both as part of the description of the impact of the incident on the public task being carried out and as a stand-alone criterion in the incident report.

It is also important to describe any preventive measures which were taken after the incident had occurred, in order to prevent the recurrence of such an event. The description of such activities should be disclosed in the most transparent way possible. The notification shall also include a listing and description of all corrective actions taken after the incident occurred. Notwithstanding the required factual information, the notification shall include any information which might contribute to the identification of the incident, its assessment, and the taking of corrective and preventive action. The legislators have also introduced an obligation to supplement the information in the notification as an ongoing and permanent duty. The addendum shall be communicated without delay, at the same time, and in the same way, as the original notification.

Any restrictions on the transmission of information contained in the notification would involve information classified as legally protected secrets. In particular, a company secret has the status of such a clause. It is worth mentioning at this point that in addition to company secrets, current legislation regulates almost 70 types of legally protected secrets.[49] Such limitations may only be ignored if the disclosure is necessary to carry out the tasks of the competent CRSIT MON, CSIRT NASK, or CSIRT GOV, and, in addition, if the scope of the information disclosed is incomplete or limited to what is essential. Such legally protected information may also be disclosed at the request of the competent CSIRT, and its disclosure shall be subject to the same restrictions as if it had been transmitted by a public entity on its own initiative. In the notification, the protected legal information disclosed shall be classified, and shall be separated and secured in such a way that it cannot be disclosed to unauthorised persons.

4 Obligation to Designate a Person Responsible for Contacts with National Cyber Security System Operators

The general norm requires the public entities listed in the Act to appoint a person responsible for maintaining contact with the entities in the national cyber security system. The concept of "responsible person" has not been clarified by the legislators.

[49]For more information on this subject, see Polok (2006), pp. 23–25.

It can be speculated on—particularly in the light of what is known as a logical-linguistic interpretation—that this could be both a natural person and a legal person. However, it is more difficult to indicate at this level of interpretation that the term "responsible person" may also be used to describe an organisational unit without legal personality. In the light of a systemic interpretation, it appears that the legislators aimed at referring to a specific natural person, since it distinguishes the concept of a "person" from that of an "entity" (or "entities"), which has a much broader scope of meaning.[50]

An obligation imposed on the indicated public entity should be implemented by way of "appointing" a responsible person. Legal commentators in administrative law tend to avoid defining "appointing" as a legal form of administration. It is more often determined as a result of the application of some legal form of administrative authority (e.g. an administrative act or an internal management act). It can therefore be assumed that the concept of "appointing" a specific responsible person is intended to signify an effect achieved by a public entity through the use of an indeterminate form of administrative action. On the other hand, the legal form of such appointment, although not explicitly indicated in the Act, should first relate to internal forms of administrative activity, due to the context of the provision suggesting the designation of a person who is organisationally related to a public entity, and, second, take the form of a specific declaration of will by the entity. The question remains of how to express this will. At first glance, it seems that the appointment should be made unilaterally, either in an individualised form, resembling a type of official order, or in a normative form, assigning the duties of the appointed person to a function, which may be carried out in the form of regulations, guidelines, or internal orders. It seems, however, that this "appointment" may also be done in a bilateral, even contractual, format—especially if the allocated person is not an employee of a public entity. The term "person" itself, and not, e.g., "employee", shows that the legislators do not limit the circle of appointed persons to those who are organisationally related to the public entity.

The "appointed person" of the entity will, in turn, be required to "maintain contact with the entities in the national cybersecurity system." The legislators are not setting out here the framework for such an obligation. The appointed person will have to be disclosed to the competent CSIRT MON, CSIRT NASK, or CSIRT GOV in the manner specified therein, without regulating the procedure for the other entities forming the national cybersecurity system, as a kind of "contact point" for those entities.[51] With this wording it is difficult to prove any "exclusivity" for such an appointed person to maintain these contacts. In the practice of a public entity, other persons (formally "non-appointed") performing specific tasks within the entity may also maintain contact with entities in the national cybersecurity system. Regardless of the formula for "appointing" a contact person, it is worthwhile setting out in such an "appointment act", or in a kind of "appointment agreement", the rules (even

[50] Zob. Wąsowski (2019), pp. 185–192.

[51] See Article 22(1)(5) of the NCSA.

procedures) for implementing the obligation of the designated person to maintain contact with the entities in the national cybersecurity system.

Nor do the legislators specify what the responsibilities of the designated person will be. The issue of a possible transfer of responsibility from a public authority to the designated person has also not been resolved. In this respect, the lack of a clear directive by the legislators should be taken as an indication that the designation of the person responsible by a public entity does not in any way supersede the responsibility of the public entity in question for efficiently maintaining contact with all the "elements" in the national cybersecurity system. It is puzzling that there are no sanctions (in particular of a criminal-administrative nature) for failure to comply with a public entity's obligation by not appointing an appropriate contact person with the entities in the national cybersecurity system, while for operators of essential services for failure to comply with a similar duty[52] there *are* imposed specific sanctions of an administrative nature.[53]

The use of wording referring to appointing the "competent person" (using the singular instead of the plural) suggests that a public entity has the right to appoint only one person, instead of, for example, a team of responsible persons. Such a literal interpretation does not seem to be conclusive, however, as the legislators clearly limit the "circle" of designated responsible persons to "one". Thus, it should be recognised that more than one individual can be a "responsible person". Even if a strictly literal interpretation is considered binding, it should be pointed out that the provisions of this regulation do not restrict public entities to indicating a specific sequence in the assuming of the obligation to maintain contacts by the deputies (in the event of an even temporary inability to perform their duties) of the designated responsible person.

As public entities, public administration authorities are treated specially in terms of appointing the responsible person. First, they may only appoint "one" responsible person. Second, that person will be required to cooperate ("maintain contact") with the entities in the national cyber-security system to a specific extent, namely with regard to "*public tasks dependent on information systems*". In today's complexity of individual public tasks (understood as tasks imposed by the standards of the universally applicable law, aimed at the realisation of the common good), it is difficult to imagine a total separation between the operation of a public administration authority and the use of even the least-complicated information systems. It is clear, therefore, that it should be recognised that, within the practice of public administration authorities, all public tasks performed by these authorities will be related to the use of information systems and, in this sense, will depend on their use.

It appears that the specificity of a "single responsible person" does not involve the performance of public tasks dependent on information systems, but the appointment of a common responsible person for a given public administration authority and the units subordinate to or supervised by it. At the same time it could be assumed that the

[52]See Article 73 (1) of the NCSA.

[53]See Article 9 (1) of the NCSA.

wording presented by the legislators was not so much about one (in the literal sense—the only) person for the public administration authority and its related entities, but about the possibility of appointing even several persons (similarly to other public entities), with these persons, within the scope of their responsibilities, also having entities related by ties of subordination or supervision to the given public administration authority. The relations of supremacy—subordination and supervision—have been described quite extensively in the literature on the subject.[54] The essence of superiority lies in the competence of a public administration authority vis-à-vis a subordinate entity which authorises the superior to have a binding influence on the activities undertaken by the subordinate entity, and on the personnel of such an entity. Speaking in simple terms, supervision means the authority (resulting from the provisions of generally applicable law) which allows the supervisor to control the supervised entity, and, in the modes specified by law, to influence the decisions of the supervised entity.

A similar system of appointing "one" person, as in the case of public administration authorities, has been applied to local government units. Local government units currently include communes, districts, and self-government voivodships. These units have been given legal personality by the legislators, which is certainly different from the situation with public administration authorities, which in principle do not have such a personality. The problem is that acting on behalf of local government units are their bodies (both constituting and executive), which also perform the function of public administration authorities (this group, sometimes also referred to as "state" authorities, is divided into government administration authorities, and, i.a., local government administration authorities, including local government authorities). In this context, the introduction of the differentiation of responsibilities in the analysed provision between public administration authorities (paragraph 2) and local government units (paragraph 3) loses its significance.

Within the framework of the cooperation of public entities with the competent CSIRT, the legislators have also introduced a specific informational procedure for transferring the data of the responsible person appointed on the basis of the National Cybersecurity System Act. Formal requirements shall include the name of the responsible person, his or her telephone number, and e-mail address. Failure to indicate one of the three formal elements results in failure to comply with this requirement. The legislators do not, however, attribute clear consequences in the form of statutory sanctions for such deficiencies. The obligation to provide the basic data of the responsible person shall be fulfilled within 14 days of the appointment of that person. The same applies to the time limit for the passing on of information on changes to such data. With today's technological progress and the need to quickly (in principle immediately) respond to incidents, such an extensive time frame seems to be too wide.

[54] See more—Cieślak (2014), pp. 75–85.

5 Obligation to Provide Information to the Competent CSIRT

This provision sets the legal basis for allowing public entities carrying out public tasks, which depend on information systems, to communicate to the competent CSIRT information about other incidents, cyber-security threats relating to risk assessment, vulnerabilities, and the technologies used. This possibility has also been attributed to the operators of essential services. This task is complementary to the informational obligations imposed on public entities in the field of cybersecurity; it aims at the broadest possible prevention involving early detection and analysis of any phenomena which might affect the functioning of the cybersecurity system.

The information procedure has not been formalised in principle. It is sufficient for such information to be provided in an electronic form (in the simplest way, by e-mail). In the event that the electronic transmission of such information is impossible or excessively difficult, the communication of information (as is the case with the notification) should take place by any available means. Written (paper) correspondence may therefore be delivered by conventional means. The legislators have also not stipulated any time limits—unlike in the case of the notification—on the information to be provided under a kind of early warning system. However, the essence of the National Cybersecurity System is that this information should also be provided immediately. The Act provides for the possibility of obtaining the status of an operator of essential services by a public entity under general principles after obtaining an appropriate administrative decision. There are no special restrictions or privileges for public entities in the procedure for becoming operators of essential services.

The legislators have limited the performance of related obligations by a public entity with the status of an operator of essential services to specific essential services which relate to the exercising of the function of an operator of that service. In activities not directly related to the essential service, the public entity is not obliged to fulfil any obligations imposed by law on the operator of essential services.[55]

6 Summary

Within the framework of the regulation contained in the National Cybersecurity System Act, the inclusion of such a large number of public entities under the regime of this regulation results from the desire to build a comprehensive and systemic approach to the national cybersecurity system,[56] rather than the implementation of

[55] See Wąsowski (2019), pp. 192–193.

[56] See Czaplicki (2019).

the NIS Directive itself.[57] The directive applies to operators of essential services and digital service providers, and the National Cybersecurity System Act goes beyond the implementation of the NIS Directive, and also defines other elements which influence national cybersecurity policy. Some public entities may be recognised as operators of essential services, and will then have obligations similar to other such entities. The NIS Directive allows each Member State to take the necessary measures to ensure the protection of the essential interests of its security, public order, and public safety. Such a directive certainly includes a broad (and not closed) definition of the circle of public entities, and assigning them legal obligations of an informational nature. It is also an attempt at a procedural and organisational response to the dangers of cyberspace.

References

Banasiński C, Jaroszyński K (2017) Ustawa o gospodarce komunalnej. Komentarz, Warsaw

Biernat S (1994) Prywatyzacja zadań publicznych, Warsaw – Cracow

Chałubińska-Jentkiewicz K, Karpiuk M, Kostrubiec J (2021) The legal status of public entities in the field of cybersecurity in Poland. Lex Localis Press, Maribor

Cieślak Z (ed) (2014) Nauka administracji, Warsaw

Czaplicki K (2019) In: Czaplicki K, Gryszczyńska A, Szpor G (eds) Ustawa o krajowym systemie cyberbezpieczeństwa. Komentarz, Warsaw

Dawidowicz W (1965) Nauka prawa administracyjnego. Zarys wykładu. Tom I, Zagadnienia podstawowe, Warsaw

Dybowski T (1990) Własność Skarbu Państwa i państwowych osób prawnych w świetle art. 128 KC, Państwo i Prawo 4

Marchewka-Bartkowiak K (2011) Agencje wykonawcze, Biuro Analiz Sejmowych (18.08.2011)

Polok M (2006) Ochrona tajemnicy państwowej i tajemnicy służbowej w polskim systemie prawnym, Warsaw

Szachułowicz J (2000) Własność publiczna, Warsaw

Wąsowski K (2019) In: Kitler W, Radoniewicz F, Taczkowska-Olszewska J (eds) Ustawa o krajowym systemie cyberbezpieczeństwa. Komentarz, Warsaw

Zieliński M (2014) Agencje wykonawcze UE. Europejski Przegląd Sądowy 6

Krzysztof Wąsowski PhD, advocate. Graduated from the Faculty of Law and Administration at the University of Warsaw, Poland and ARGO Top Public Management at the IESE Business School in Barcelona, Spain. Adjunct at the Department of Cybersecurity and New Technologies and an expert at the Academic Center for Cybersecurity Policy at the War Studies University in Warsaw. Partner of the law firm "WLP Legal" in Warsaw, Poland.

[57]Directive 2016/1148 of the European Parliament and of the Council of 6 July 2016 on measures for a high common level of security of networks and information systems within the Union, OJ EU 2016 L 194/1.

The System of Control and Supervision of Operators of Essential Services, Digital Service Providers and Entities Providing Cybersecurity Services

Monika Nowikowska

Abstract Cyberspace has become a new security environment. Technological progress added a new type of threat to the so-called "physical" threats—"ICT threats". This entails the need to make numerous changes, both in legal and organisational terms. The considerations undertaken at work are aimed at defining the control and supervision system in the cyberspace environment. The issue of the system of control and supervision of operators of essential services, digital service providers and entities providing services in the field of cybersecurity is an important research issue. The Polish legislators have introduced the principle of supervision over the functioning of the national cybersecurity system, which is exercised by the minister competent for computerisation and competent authorities for cybersecurity. The article discusses the principles of supervision and control adopted in the Act of 5 July 2018 on the National Cybersecurity System in Poland.

The issue of the system of control and supervision of operators of essential services, digital service providers, and entities providing cybersecurity services, is a current and important research problem. The Polish legislators regulated the issue of supervision and control in the National Cybersecurity System Act of 5 July 2018 (the NCSA). The provisions of Article 53 of the NCSA introduce the principle of supervision over the functioning of the national cybersecurity system which is exercised by the Minister competent for computerisation and the authorities accountable for matters of cybersecurity.

It should be stressed that the National Cybersecurity System Act regulates both control and supervision. It is worth noting that in the Polish legal system, the terms "control" (*kontrola*) and "supervision" (*nadzór*) are often perceived as synonymous and applied interchangeably. Therefore, it seems appropriate to attempt to define the notion and essence of "control" within the present theoretical framework, and in compliance with the requirements of the existing practice, and to analyse the term

M. Nowikowska (✉)
Instytut Prawa/Institute of Law, Akademia Sztuki Wojennej w Warszawie/War Studies University in Warsaw, Warsaw, Poland
e-mail: m.nowikowska@akademia.mil.pl

K. Chałubińska-Jentkiewicz et al. (eds.), *Cybersecurity in Poland*,
https://doi.org/10.1007/978-3-030-78551-2_21

"control" as opposed to "supervision". The deliberations presented below are an attempt to clarify the meaning of these coexisting terms. Finding, confronting, and commenting on the analogies and differences between them might be helpful in the context of legal terminology. Accuracy in nomenclature is as vital in the domain of control as in any other field. The proper interpretation of the increasingly complex reality would be difficult without a correct hierarchy and classification, and it would be even more difficult to modify it in the desired direction.

The term "*kontrola*" has been in use for a long time, and the scope of the discussed notion has evolved over the centuries as the volume of sample material has increased. The dispute over the origin of the word in the Polish language still continues. French and British origins are considered. While the French etymology of the word "*le contrôle*" suggests an association with documenting taxes collected from taxpayers,[1] and indirectly emphasises the function of document authentication,[2] the Anglo-Saxon etymology of "*control*" points to the concept of power, i.e. the analogy between control and exercising public authority.[3] In this case, "control" means "exercising political authority" (administration).[4]

In the Polish language, "*kontrola*" combines both traditions. It generally means verifying, assessing something, reviewing an activity. On the other hand, the term also expresses the essence of having an impact, influence on someone. The phrase "someone controls something" is associated with power, having an influence on something.

Two different approaches to the definition of control are distinguished in the literature:[5] (a) general (control in the managerial sense) and (b) specific (control in the functional sense).

In the case of the general approach, control is defined as an approved management system (procedures, instructions, principles, mechanisms) for obtaining the rational certainty that the objectives of management will be achieved; the process by which specific actions are managed.

The specific approach, concerning "the functional dimension of control", emphasises the process of verification and assessment. Academic textbooks and scientific studies provide definitions referring to a sequence of actions identified in this manner.[6]

J. Płoskonka stresses that control in the functional aspect relates to observations and review (of a case or result), assessment (based on a specific pattern), diagnosis

[1]Filipek (2001), p. 215.

[2]Kiczka (2018), p. 37.

[3]Jagielski (2012), p. 14; Jagielski (2004), pp. 13–30.

[4]Kałużny (2008), pp. 16 and 20.

[5]For more information, see Jagielski (2012), pp. 13–22; Płoskonka (2006), p. 8; Nitkowski (2013), p. 19; Bogacz-Miętka (2018), p. 18; Celarek (2015), p. 33.

[6]K. Nitkowski notes that institutional control "is a component of a complex control system applied in an organisation." This approach enables the institutional control to be properly placed within the system. See Nitkowski (2013), p. 19.

formulated if any irregularities are found, and reaching conclusions.[7] The process of comparing the existing and desired state of affairs encompasses the sequence of consecutive actions: review—identification—assessment—diagnosis—conclusions.

Clearly, control is one of the functions of management defined as a comparison between what has been implemented and what is desired, as the identification of discrepancies and explanations for their reasons.[8] The definition formulated by J. Jagielski, describing control as a function encompassing four phases, is worth distinguishing from among the definitions provided by legal commentators. The first phase involves the monitoring and reviewing of activities; the second relates to the assessment of such activities by confronting the actual picture with the respective initial assumptions. The purpose of the assessment is to determine regularities or irregularities in specific actions. The diagnosis concerning the potential reasons for irregularities is enumerated by the author as the third phase, and conclusions on the future of such actions are mentioned as the fourth phase. "The discussed aspects of control show that control is not limited only to a single action, but rather that it assumes a certain process.[9]" Accordingly, E. Chojna-Duch points out that "control is interpreted as a process (activity) involving a comparison between the regulated condition (postulated, defined) and the factual one (implemented, real). Therefore, to control is to ensure coherence between the required and the actual condition.[10]" In the opinion of B. R. Kuc, "control is a phase (an intrinsic component), a cycle, of an organised action. In general, conclusions drawn from it are the starting point for the next action."[11] K. Winiarska presents the opinion that "control is about continuously ensuring that the result of an action is consistent with its objectives, and that all activities and measures applied in the process of control are effective.[12]"

In defining control, J. Gnoiński[13] and M. Zembaty emphasise its correlation with human activities. "Control is integral in organising and directing human activities. Its function is to compare the specific and actual condition with the objectives, and to identify any potential irregularities in the actual condition as compared to the assumed framework of reference.[14]" No activities may be carried out in an organised and reliable manner without proper control. W. Kieżun additionally emphasises that, as a rule, "man is not keen on working, so he must be forced to work and permanently controlled". Therefore, control is also an element of pressure generating a sense of threat, and thus, motivating a human being to work.[15]

---

[7]Płoskonka (2006), p. 8.

[8]Winiarska (2003), p. 157; Owczarek (1990), p. 1; Jemioła (1987), p. 48.

[9]Jagielski (2012), p. 157.

[10]Chojna-Duch (2003), p. 13.

[11]Kuc (1983), p. 14.

[12]Winiarska (2003), p. 163.

[13]Gnoiński (1972b), p. 24; Gnoiński (1972a), p. 40; Gnoiński (1974), p. 5.

[14]Zembaty (1988), p. 58.

[15]Kieżun (1972), p. 34.

S. Kałużny states that the following actions are the components of the notion of control: determining the existing condition (the objectives); determining the actual condition (the performance); comparing the performance and objectives in order to identify regularities or irregularities within them; and explaining the reasons for the regularities or irregularities found in the performance and objectives. The author points out that the two basic elements of human activities—objectives and performance—are the starting point for defining the notion of "control".[16] Special attention should be paid to the problem of setting objectives. It should be noted that the setting of objectives is not part of control activities, and that it goes beyond the notion of control. However, control may be used for analysing and identifying the objectives which are not adjusted to the actual reality, and hamper or obstruct the achievement of the defined objectives.[17] As K. Wierzbicki rightly notes, control assessments may not be based on the imagination and intuition of the controller, i.e. on subjective premises. Control does not exist if it is not accompanied by the specific objectives accepted as the basis of comparison.

J. Płoskonka presents a new approach to the notion of control by contrasting the "contemporary" and "traditional" approaches. According to the author, the traditional method focuses on inspection, responding to the violation of the applicable law. Control actions interpreted in this way are of horizontal and corrective nature. The contemporary method concentrates on the assessment of the achieved results, where compliance with the law is the necessary, but incomplete, condition.[18]

The deliberations presented above suggest that the term "control" can be interpreted in different ways: as functional (specific); as an extensive process of reviewing and assessing (a sequence of the consecutive actions: identification—assessment—diagnosis—conclusions); and managerial (general) as a management support system applied in an organisation. Therefore, the notion of control has a broad meaning. A specific definition should be applied for the purpose of deliberations on the control exercised over the operators of essential services, digital service providers, and entities providing cybersecurity services. In this sense, control serves as a tool for comparing the actual condition with the postulated one.

In Article 53 of the NCSA, the term "control" is accompanied by the term "supervision" ("*nadzór*"). These notions are closely interrelated, but markedly different despite their many common features. In the Polish language, "nadzór" is a concept broader than "kontrola". It encompasses not only the verification, but also the components, of management. In the case of supervision, there is primacy (domination and subordination), i.e. the attributes missing in the notion of control. It means that, as well as controlling an entity's activities, a supervisory authority may also issue binding instructions to such an entity. Supervision is not limited to monitoring, but it is linked with management through directives.[19] In this case,

---

[16] Kałużny (2008), p. 21.

[17] Gnoiński (1974), pp. 7–8.

[18] Płoskonka (2006), p. 7; Płoskonka (2005), pp. 138–165.

[19] Kałużny (2008), p. 25.

control activities are carried out by a permanent control department at the request of the supervising authority. If the control is carried out by the control department, binding decisions are issued by the supervisory authority, not by the control department. J. Starościak notes "where there is the right to give and observe instructions, there is supervision.[20]" Accordingly, supervision is not limited to monitoring, but it is linked with an aspect of management.[21] Control does not provide the right to issue follow-up recommendations based on the results of control and aimed at regulating specific matters. The powers of control are limited only to the issuance of recommendations and conclusions. These powers encompass only the right to recommend the observance of something which was regulated but remains neglected. Such recommendations, however, do not relate to administration or management, which are associated with supervision.

J. Gnoiński defines supervision as "the permanent, active monitoring of the activities of a given entity, and, consequently, associated with acts of intervention (the issuance of decisions). Therefore, it is a combination of control activities and management.[22]"

There is one more significant difference between control and supervision, i.e. supervisors are responsible for the substantive activities of the supervised entities, whereas the control authorities monitor the proper course of control.

Additionally, J. Jagielski suggests that, in general, supervision is a legal category not defined by the norms, which appears in various domains of legal regulations.[23]

Supervision has a meaning broader than control. Supervision always encompasses control with the option of giving imperative instructions. To be more precise, supervision is permanent and concurrent control over the activities of dependent or subordinated entities, exercised by the authorities or organisational units having the right to issue the relevant decisions aimed to improve, order, guide or advance the activities of the above category of authorities or organisational units.[24]

Supervision can take three forms: preventive, successive, and repressive. In the case of the preventive form of supervision, a lower executive is obliged to consult on his or her decision with a supervisor before such a decision is made, or to submit the draft decision to the higher executive for approval. Supervision in the successive form consists of entrusting the higher executive with the right to annul the decision which is made at any stage. When supervision takes the repressive form, the supervisory authority has the right to impose disciplinary sanctions on the supervised personnel. These aspects are absent in the process of control.

The above analysis shows the basic differences between the notions of control and supervision. It seems that supervision is similar to overseeing, the essence of which is based on the simple protection of the matters exercised directly by the

[20]Starościak (1971), p. 356; Starościak (1975), p. 346.

[21]See Longchamps de Berier (1964), p. 4; Lang (1963), p. 40.

[22]Gnoiński (1972a), p. 43; Gnoiński (1974), p. 10.

[23]Jagielski (2012), p. 30.

[24]Antoniak (2012), p. 16.

overseeing authority. The organisational, hierarchical, relations between the supervisor and the supervised entity are key components of supervision. As O. Bogacz-Miętka rightly notes, supervision is broader than control, "as it consists of not only control powers, but also the authority to issue guidelines and recommendations to the supervised entity.[25]" On the other hand, individuals exercising control who are not superiors (supervisors) might give their instructions only with regard to the matters concerning control. Other authorisations than the issuance of binding instructions are missing in the case of control. Control only entails a reliable observer obliged to present the so-called "control snapshot". However, he or she is not involved in management, and is not responsible for the circumstances existing in the controlled entity, but only for the reliability of the control as such.[26]

The Polish legislators have appointed the Minister competent for computerisation as the supervisory authority. The Minister verifies whether the internal structures or entities providing cybersecurity services, appointed by the operator of an essential service, are observing

(1) the requirement to satisfy the organisational and technical conditions ensuring the cybersecurity of the supported operator of an essential service
(2) the requirement to have the premises facilitating the provision of the services with regard to incident-handling, protected against physical and environmental risks
(3) the requirement to apply protections aimed at ensuring the confidentiality, integrity, availability, and authenticity of the processed information involved, including the safety of people, operations, and system architecture.

Therefore, the authorities in charge of cybersecurity matters verify whether the operators of essential services are fulfilling the obligations arising from the Act concerning counteracting cybersecurity risks, and reporting major incidents, and whether digital service providers are satisfying the requirements concerning the safety of the digital services provided by them, defined in Implementing Regulation 2018/151, and whether they are meeting the obligations arising from the Act concerning the reporting of major incidents.

The Polish legislators have rightly noted that supervision is limited to control and the authority to impose fines on the operators of essential services and digital service providers. It means that control is one of the mechanisms of supervision.

The provisions of the NCSA define the material and subjective scopes of control. The material scope encompasses the activities of internal structures appointed by the operators of essential services, or the entities providing cybersecurity services. On the other hand, the subjective scope relates to the requirement to satisfy the organisational and technical conditions ensuring the cybersecurity of the supported operator of an essential service; the requirement to have the premises facilitating the provision of services in the field of incident-handling protected against physical and

[25]Bogacz-Miętka (2018), p. 18; also: Nitkowski (2013), p. 20.
[26]Popławski (1965), p. 7.

environmental risks; and the requirement to apply protections aimed at ensuring the confidentiality, integrity, availability, and authenticity of the processed information, including the safety of people, operations, and system architecture. The NCSA also defines the additional components of the control procedure, especially the resulting powers and obligations of the supervisory authority and the controlled entity. In this ambit, the discussed regulation leads to a large number of various legal solutions with regard to control procedures.

The provisions of Chapter 5 of the Entrepreneurs Law should be applied to the control proceedings instigated by the Minister competent for computerisation, aimed at verifying whether the statutory requirements are satisfied by the internal structures or entities providing services in the field of cybersecurity, which were appointed by the operator of an essential service.[27] In general, control needs to be exercised under the rules defined in the Act on Entrepreneurs, and the provisions of the specific Acts should be applied to control which exceeds the scope regulated under the above-mentioned law. Control authorities have an absolute obligation to apply the provisions of Chapter 5, which defines specific control standards, and then the provisions of the specific Acts. The latter may be applied in a scope not regulated by the provisions of the Entrepreneurs Law.

The control exercised under the Entrepreneurs Law needs to be carried out in accordance with the following principles: the principle of legality, proportionality, and the selection of a legal measure applicable to a specific situation; the principle of minimising the burden of the control procedure; the principle of balancing the public interest and the legitimate interests of the controlled entities; the principle of objectivity; and the principle of the right of the controlled entrepreneur to information concerning the control procedure.[28]

It should be noted that where the authorities responsible for matters of cybersecurity are carrying out controls to verify whether the operators of essential services are fulfilling the obligations arising from the Act involving counteracting the threats to cybersecurity and reporting major incidents, and whether digital service providers, being entrepreneurs, are satisfying the requirements of the security of the services provided by them specified in Implementing Regulation No. 2018/151; and whether they are implementing the obligations arising from the Act concerning the reporting of major incidents, such authorities should apply the provisions of Chapter 5 of the Act of Entrepreneurs. The provisions of the Act of 15 July 2011 on Control in State Administration should also be applied to the above-mentioned entities which are not entrepreneurs.[29]

In Article 55 of the NCSA, the legislators defined the rights of individuals controlling entities who are entrepreneurs. This provision introduces an extensive

[27] Act of 6 March 2018 on Entrepreneurs, consolidated text Polish Journal of Laws of 2019, item 1292, as amended.

[28] Blicharz (2013), pp. 103–108.

[29] Act of 15 July 2011 on Control in State Administration, consolidated text Polish Journal of Laws of 2020, item 224, as amended.

catalogue of powers entrusted to the controller, the implementation of which is intended to ensure an efficient control process. This control cannot be carried out without free access to the documents and materials encompassed by the scope of control. The right to review documents, file applications for the preparation of copies, duplicates, or extracts from the documents and estimates needed to exercise control, is also important. An employee requested by the controller to prepare such documents, or to make them available, may not reject this request. According to Article 55 of the NCSA, controllers have the right of free access and movement around the controlled entity without a pass. However, the controller is obliged to observe the principles of conduct concerning the access-control systems implemented in the controlled entity. The controller should observe the control procedures implemented in certain controlled entities, e.g. concerning luggage control.[30]

Special attention should be paid to Article 55(4) on the processing of personal data in the scope needed to achieve the purpose of the control. The Head of the controlled entity may not refuse the controller access to personal data solely on the basis of the lack of the relevant authorisation to process personal data issued by the controlled entity, or the failure to show such authorisation issued by the controlling entity.[31] The controller needs to process this personal data for the purpose of the control, and to exercise the powers and obligations entrusted to the controlling entity under the NCSA.

Under Article 55(5) and (6), the legislators established the principle under which evidence assessment may be freely applied. The controller may request the submission of oral or written explanations on the matters concerning the scope of control, and visually inspect the informational equipment, carriers, and systems. The principle of the free assessment of evidence is the main basis of evidentiary proceedings. The acceptance of the concept that the evidentiary proceedings should be based on the principle of the free assessment of evidence is justified by the fact that an authority establishing the facts on the basis of the evidence should not be restricted by any provisions as far as the value of individual types of evidence is concerned, and it should be able to freely establish the state of facts in a given case, based on the assessment of the result of the evidentiary proceedings (preliminary investigation), i.e. according to its sole discretion. The free assessment of evidence needs to be made in accordance with the standards of procedural law and the observance of the specific rules on assessment. These rules are as follows: relying on evidence collected by such an authority, making assessments on the basis of all the evidence, establishing the importance and value of the evidence, and reasoning in accordance with the rules of logic.

The provisions of Article 55 of the NCSA are consistent with the provisions concerning the obligations of the controlled entities who are entrepreneurs as defined in Article 56 of the Act. The controlled entity is obliged to ensure the conditions

[30] Bolek and Dobruk (2018), pp. 140–141.

[31] Ninard (2017), p. 105.

needed to carry out the control in a reliable manner. The obligation of reliable cooperation with controllers, especially in the form of the submission of documentation and written and oral explanations in line with the best knowledge, is imposed on the employees of the controlled entity. This provision expresses the principle of the efficiency of the procedure. The legislators have imposed on the Head of the controlled entity specific obligations to provide controllers with the genuine facility to carry out the control in accordance with the directives arising from the principle of minimising the burden of control activities. The controlled entity is obliged to afford the controllers conditions allowing the reliable course of control, by

(1) immediately submitting the requested documents
(2) providing timely oral and written explanations on the controlled matters
(3) making available the necessary technical means
(4) preparing, at its own cost, duplicates or printouts of documents and information stored on information carriers, equipment, and systems.

It should be noted that the Polish legislators have imposed on the controlled entrepreneur the obligation to ensure reliable cooperation with the controllers. The regulation provided in Article 56 of the NCSA confirms the reliable and correct course of the control procedure. The obligations imposed on the controlled entity under the Act do not supersede the solutions commonly applied within this scope, and concerning other control procedures. The appointment of an employee responsible for cooperation with controllers on behalf of the entrepreneur, and for the implementation of the obligations imposed on the controlled entity under the Act, is the solution often applied in the practice of control.

The main obligation of the controlled entity is to ensure the immediate submission of the requested documents. The term "document" is not uniformly interpreted in the field of control. This notion is used with regard to the so-called "carrier of information" which can be meaningful in the control procedure, i.e. the source of evidence in a written form. Under the NCSA, a broad interpretation of a document may be applied. The following are the important components of a document serving as evidence in the control procedure: the written form i.e., its graphical aspect, the content of a document, i.e., the information contained therein, and the author of the document, i.e. the entity expressing an opinion in the document.[32] To be considered as a document, an item needs to be prepared in writing. It should be produced with the use of graphic characters—writing (handwriting, print, typewriting). It seems that plans, sketches, and designs may also be considered documents, because they are graphical representations expressing particular content, replacing verbal description, or placed next to it. Second, the document should express human thought in the form of a statement of will or knowledge, so it should encompass a certain intellectual content. Due to the content's being information for the controlling authority, a document becomes the source of evidence for a particular control fact. The issue of the authorship of a document is associated with the person who prepared it. A

[32]Nowikowska and Walczuk (2018), p. 96.

document provides evidence in the form of intellectual content, i.e. the thought content. Then, evidence from a document is collected by rewriting its content in the control report.

The controlled entity is obliged to certify that the submitted documents are consistent with their originals. If confirmation of consistency with the originals is refused, the documents should be authenticated by the person carrying out the control activities, and the fact of such authentication should be mentioned in the control report. The controlled entity is also obliged to provide written and oral explanations on the controlled matters on time. Information on the established facts may be provided to the controller by a present or former employee.

Pursuant to Article 57 of the NCSA, the person carrying out control activities with respect of entities who are entrepreneurs establishes the facts on the basis of evidence collected in the course of the control, especially documents, items, and visual controls, as well as oral or written explanations and statements. That Article reflects one of the basic principles of the control procedure—the principle of objective truth. According to this principle, control findings should illustrate the true picture of the controlled activities. The principle of the objective truth applied in the control takes the form of the objective and honest establishment or presentation of the control findings, based on reliably collected evidence.

Evidentiary proceedings are one of the most important stages in the control procedure. Under the control procedure, the controller establishes the actual state and the control facts based on the collected evidence. The actual state must correspond to the reality, i.e. it needs to be proved. The interpretation of the provision set out in Article 57 allows us to state that the issue of the selection of evidence is entrusted to the controller. In an attempt to establish the actual state of the facts, the controller selects evidence at his or her sole discretion.[33] It should be noted that the Polish legislators have pointed out that evidence encompasses, in particular, documents, items, visual controls, and oral or written explanations or statements. The provisions of the NCSA do not provide a hierarchy of evidence. Each piece of evidence with an impact on the establishment of the actual state needs to be considered.[34]

In the context of Article 57 of the NCSA, an analysis of the notion of evidence leads to the conclusion that treating a document, statement, or item as evidence is only a mental shortcut. A clear distinction among the following notions—evidence, element of proof, and source of evidence—is particularly important for the proper understanding of the discussed issue. A control fact, which is provided to the controller in the course of the control procedure by, e.g., the content of the document, is the subject of reasoning. The content of the document does not form the evidence, but it is rather an element of proof used by the controller to establish the

[33]Cz (1968), p. 62.

[34]See Judgment of the Provincial Administrative Court in Kraków of 09.05.2017, III S.A./Kr 384/16, Lex No. 2286959; Judgment of the Supreme Administrative Court of 29.03.2017, II OSK 1936/15, Lex No. 2283181.

control fact. On the other hand, the document itself is the source of evidence. The evidence source contains potential evidence which is only revealed to the controller.[35] An analysis of Article 57 of the NCSA shows that, while defining the control evidence, the legislators used the three meanings of evidence—as a source of evidence: a document or an item; an element of proof: oral explanations or statements; and also as a method of collecting evidence—inspection. It seems that the discussed structure forms a kind of mental shortcut.

The NCSA enumerates the following types of evidence: (1) documents, (2) objects, (3) visual inspection, (4) oral or written explanations or statements. The enumerated evidence does not form a complete catalogue. The phrase "in particular" used by the legislators suggests that this catalogue is open, and it means that the controller may accept other evidence not enumerated in the Act, but should also define the manner of the evidence-taking by the proper application of the provisions concerning the pieces of evidence defined in the Act. As a result, these are unnamed pieces of evidence. In the Judgment of 20 July 2017, the Court of Appeal in Poznań noted that, in addition to documents, expert opinions and visual inspections, photographs found on the Internet, may also be considered evidence.[36]

In control practice, physical evidence is not used as often as documentary evidence. However, physical evidence is worth considering due to the quality of the provided information. As far as physical evidence is concerned, the pieces of evidence obtained from it are not easily distorted in terms of the manner in which they are perceived, remembered, and restored. In particular, any object with features which can provide the controller with information may form physical evidence. When the items are examined, the controller establishes the findings by analysing the external features of such objects. Visual inspection is the method of accepting physical evidence.[37]

Visual inspections of objects are made in order to establish their external or internal properties. Their perceived features need to be confirmed in the visual inspection report. The purpose of visual inspection is to establish the state of the objects and their properties. The need for deriving evidence from the items is each time decided by the controller. The control practice shows that the most common mistakes made in formulating findings from visual inspections are (a) the provision of data which cannot be established under visual inspection, but which arise from other documents, (b) subjective opinions and assessments, and (c) explanations and statements given by individuals participating in the visual inspection.

Explanations and statements are yet another type of evidence providing the controller with information from personal sources.

---

[35] Warchoł (2013), p. 565; Ponikowski (2012), p. 266.

[36] See Judgment of the Administrative Court in Poznań of 20.07.2017, IV SA/Po 167/17, Lex No. 2341989; Judgment of the Provincial Administrative Court in Kraków of 19.12.2017, II SA/Kr 1203/17, Lex No. 2425316; Judgment of the Provincial Administrative Court in Kraków of 15.12.2017, I SA/Kr 233/17, Lex No. 2442272.

[37] Jarkiewicz (1972), p. 21.

Each employee, including the head of the controlled entity, may be requested to provide explanations. In general, the circumstances accompanying disclosed irregularities are usually the subject of provided explanations. The procedure for documenting explanations can take two forms: written—when the person giving explanations prepares the explanations individually and submits them to the controller, and oral—when the controller writes down the explanations in the form of a report and signs it along with the person giving the explanations.

While taking evidence in the form of explanations, the controller is obliged to make sure that the explanations are comprehensive. The controller has the right to request explanations, and may exercise this right at his or her sole discretion. In practical terms, it is necessary to obtain explanations from persons named as being responsible for the disclosed irregularities. Irregularities in control findings presented in follow-up opinions and obtained explanations are inadmissible. If this happens, the disclosed irregularities need to be justified by the collected evidence defining the part of the explanations incompatible with the truth, and providing the reasoning behind such irregularities.

As far as statements are concerned, a current or former employee of the controlled entity, as well as any other person providing the controller with information covered by the control, may be a source of evidence. Therefore, the subjective catalogue is broader, and it can also include persons from outside the controlled entity. The source of the initiative is the basic difference between evidence from explanations and statements. In the case of explanations, the controller is always the originator, and in the second case, it is the person giving the statement.[38] It should be stressed that if statements are taken, the controller's conduct depends on the type of information given in the statement. If the information lies within the scope of the control, and its value is significant, it may be used in the control process as evidence. If it deviates from the subject of the control, it may be used as a starting point for further actions, such as broadening the control subject or disregarding it without consideration.

In Article 58 of the NCSA, the legislators assumed the principle according to which a report of the controlled activities carried out with reference to entities who are entrepreneurs needs to be drawn up. According to the implemented solutions, the findings made in the course of the control should be documented in the control format to which the appeal procedure may be applied. This format encompasses the mandatory elements defined under the Act, including the trade name or the name and surname and address of the controlled entity; the name and surname of the person representing the controlled entity; the name of the authority representing the entity; the name, surname, function, and authorisation number of the controller; the start and completion dates of the control activities; the identification of the subject and scope of the control; a description of the actual state established in the course of the control; and other information of significant importance for the carried-out control, including the scope of, reasons for, and results of the disclosed irregularities, and a

[38] Kowalski (1971), p. 27.

list of appendices. The legislators do not impose any limitations concerning the volume of the document, but it should be remembered that conciseness is one of the features of a properly prepared follow-up document.

The report includes the trade name or the name and surname and address of the controlled entity. Generally, there should be no doubt about the interpretation of this provision. Sometimes, however, the fact that the entity is based in various locations, or its address changes during the course of the control, can raise some difficulties. The report includes the name, surname, and official position and authorisation number of the controller. All persons carrying out the control need to be named, whether the control is carried out by a single person or a group of controllers.

In Article 58(2)(4) of the NCSA, the legislators stated that the report should include the date of the start and completion of the control activities. This is technical information. Generally, the date of the start of a control is the same as the date given in the authorisation. On the other hand, the date when the controller or a control team finishes their work in the controlled entity is assumed as the date of the completion of the control activities. It should be stressed that all breaks taken in the course of the control may be recorded in the control report.

The schedule also includes the subject and scope of the control. The subject of the control relates to the issues which need to be verified, and the scope relates to the timeline when these issues will be verified.

The control report should also include a description of the actual state established in the course of the control, and other information of significant importance for the control being carried out, including the scope of, reasons for, and results of any irregularities. This is the most important element in the follow-up document—the essence of the control procedure. The ability to establish the actual state of facts should be the basic feature of the controller's skills. It should be stressed that the purpose of a control carried out in accordance with the provisions of the NCSA is to establish the actual situation, and any potential irregularities. These are the basics of the controller's work, because a control consists of an examination or review, the purpose of which is to establish the actual state of the facts, to compare it with the desired state of the facts, and to make an assessment of them. Here it should be noted that in the findings the controller should discuss any irregularities, and also the examined elements which should be considered as positive.

If any irregularities are found, their scope, reasons, and results should be discussed. These elements form the so-called control facts. The concept of the control facts on which the description of the actual state of facts is based, encompasses the following components: the applicable legal standard, any action or neglect departing from the rule, the reasons for and results of any derogation from the rule, and the identification of responsible persons.[39] The control fact may not be merely an allegation—it has to correspond to reality, i.e. it needs to be proved. The scope of, reasons for, and results of irregularities have to arise directly from the evidence collected under the control procedure. The basic tasks of the controller include

[39]Wiechowski (1969), p. 58.

establishing the scope of the irregularities (what happened), the reasons (why it happened) and the effects of the disclosed irregularities (what the results were).

The control report is handed over to the person representing the controlled entity. It needs to be signed by the controller—the person carrying out the control activities—and the person representing the controlled entity. The controller is responsible for the document as its author. The controller's signature on the document means that its content has been accepted by the controller. If the control is carried out by a group of controllers, the document needs to be signed by all the persons carrying out the control activities. The signing of the control report by the expert delivering the opinion on the control subject does not seem to be appropriate. The expert is not the controller.

The analysis of Article 58 of the NCSA shows that the control report does not include any instructions addressed to the person representing the controlled entity concerning the right to submit a statement of objections to the report. The controlled entity may submit the statement of objections before the report is signed, 7 days from the date when it is presented to the controlled entity for signing. The person representing the controlled entity has the right to report any objections before the document is signed. The person needs to do so within 7 days from the day when the report is submitted for signing. This is a relatively short period of time. The objections should be expressed in writing, and reasoned, i.e. their justification should be presented. The objections should point out the part of the document prompting the objections, what is being questioned by the objecting party, and why. Moreover, the objections should include supporting evidence, and, potentially, the suggested new content of the document.

The procedure assumed by the legislators in this situation ensures the observance of the adversarial principle for the benefit of the controlled entity, and it also provides an opportunity for collecting the complete evidence which is the basis for the actual state of the facts. Apart from the adversarial principle, the discussed provisions relate to the principle of using the written form. The objections expressed by the controlled entity should be submitted in writing. The submitted objections should indicate the new facts, and present specific information or documents. If possible, any additional documents should be attached to the objections in the form of appendices. If objections are reported, the person carrying out the control activities analyses them, and, as necessary, carries out additional control activities, and if the objections are found to be justified, the person modifies or complements the relevant part of the document in the form of an annex to the report. Article 58(4) and (6) may be interpreted as a certain whole. They define the right to file objections, the manner and procedure concerning the consideration of objections to the control report and any potential modification to the content of the document if the submitted objections are found justified. Article 58 of the NCSA combines several methods relating to the consideration of the submitted objections, and not only by the persons carrying out the control activities. Article 58(4) refers to the rights of the person representing the controlled entity, (5) facilitates carrying out additional control activities, and (6) refers to the method in which objections should be handled. The person carrying out the control activities modifies or complements the relevant part of the document in the form of an annex to the report, if this person considers the objections justified. If the objections are not considered in full or in part, the person carrying out the control activities informs the controlled entity about it in writing. These provisions form a logical and integral whole.

The procedure involving the consideration of objections to the control report needs to be performed by the person carrying out the control activities. This person should decide on the manner of considering the objections. The objections are analysed in formal and substantive terms. According to Article 58(5) and (6), the controller has, *de facto,* four options. The first one is the dismissal of the submitted objections. This is the case when the objections are filed after the expiry of the 7-day period. Consequently, written information on the above sent to the objecting party is sufficient. If possible, the controllers should be flexible in handling the formal aspects concerning the submitted objections. Any potential doubts about the formal aspects of filing an objection should be considered for the benefit of the controlled entity to enable the substantive consideration of the objections. The second option relates to the positive consideration of objections—the assessment of their validity. This is the case when the controllers consider the objections as substantially justified. The third and fourth options concern the dismissal of the objections in full or in part. This is the case when the person carrying out the control activities does not consider the arguments arising from the objections as convincing. It should be noted that passing on information only if the objections are dismissed in full or in part forms a statutory requirement. Therefore, there is no requirement to inform about objections. The controlled entity will obtain such information while reading the control report. The delivered opinion should satisfy specific criteria: it should be signed by the person carrying out the control activities, and should provide justification of how individual objections will be handled. The arguments given in justifications to the individual objections should be addressed, and own arguments should be presented.

According to the provisions of Article 58(6) of the NCSA, the person carrying out the control activities reviews the objections and informs the controlled entity about the decision in writing. The Act does not provide any further appeal procedure, e.g. a complaint lodged with an administrative court. This phase of the control procedure is thus completed. The legislators have provided the opportunity for refusing to sign the report by the person representing the controlled entity. In such a case, the person carrying out the control activities records this in the report with the date. The schedule in paper form is produced in two counterparts, one of which should be handed over to the controlled entity and the other to the controller.

If the controlled entity confirms in the document the probability of a violation of the provisions of the NCSA, according to Article 59 the authority responsible for matters of cybersecurity or the Minister competent for computerisation hands over the follow-up recommendations concerning the removal of the irregularity. Recommendations are the essential feature of the control procedure. The recommendations should be formulated objectively, and should be based on the findings made in the course of the control, supported with evidence. The recommendations need to be based on facts, and not on opinions or experiences (impartiality). Bias is defined as a non-objective approach to problem solving, in the form of an attempt to confirm the individual assumptions to the detriment of the main control objectives. Distortion of information under the control procedure, bias in the presented opinions, and disclosing only the negative aspects of the activities carried out by the controlled entity, are examples of the violation of impartiality in the control procedure.

The NCSA includes definitions of follow-up recommendations. An analysis of Article 59(1) shows that the recommendations should involve the elimination of irregularities. There is no appeal procedure concerning follow-up recommendations, which means that they are binding.[40] It should be assumed that this phase of the control is completed, and the document will not be analysed by any administrative court.[41] It means that the follow-up recommendations may not be compared with an administrative decision, i.e. a unilateral, superior act issued by an administrative authority solving an individual case of a specific addressee.[42] In Article 59(3), the legislators provided the opportunity for obtaining information if the controlled entity implements the follow-up recommendations. It should be noted that this is the purpose of handing over to the controlled entity the results of the control, including the established state of the facts and recommendations to the controlled entity. Based on this knowledge, the controlled entity should take the proper managerial measures to remedy the disclosed irregularities. Only in the results of these activities is a given area really changed, because these actions form the actual meeting of the expectations of the authority competent for cybersecurity matters or the Minister competent for computerisation. Moreover, the solution provided under the Act facilitates assessments concerning the accuracy of the findings. The controlled entity is obliged to state how the irregularities should be removed within the prescribed period. The legislators do not make a precise reference to the period in which the appropriate authority should be informed. According to the legislators, this period may be freely defined. On each occasion, the period will be dependent on the circumstances accompanying the given control procedure and the nature of the disclosed irregularities.

The deliberations presented in this paper relate also to the presentation of the issue of the functionality of control and supervision of the operators of essential services, digital service providers, and entities providing cybersecurity services, based on the NCSA. It is the institutional system having a broad subjective spectrum and a precisely defined objective range of impact. In the subjective and objective scopes, the system is complete, which means that it features no significant gaps.

To sum up the presented discussion, it may be stated that the control objectives should be defined from the perspective of the functioning of the entire cybersecurity system. An effective control system should promote the proper course of the implementation processes and the achievement of the best possible results in any type of activity. The efficiency of controls comprises two main elements. The proper

---

[40] Nowikowska and Cieślak (2015), p. 187.

[41] Judgment of the Provincial Administrative Court in Warsaw of 22.11.2010, V S.A./Wa 2517/10, Lex No. 781401.

[42] Jarzęcka-Siwik and Skwarka (2013), p. 29 *et al.*

selection of the control subject is the first one. So-called control proficiency is the second. It should be understood as the proper training of controllers in substantive and ethical terms. It should be noted that the good aspects are promoted only by the hard work of controllers, their achievements, and tradition, as well as constant improvements in the control procedure.

References

Antoniak M (2012) Kontrola rządowa w administracji publicznej. Poradnik dla kontrolujących i kontrolowanych, Warsaw
Blicharz R (2013) In: Blicharz R (ed) Kontrola przedsiębiorcy, Warsaw
Bogacz-Miętka O (2018) Kompendium wiedzy o nadzorze i kontroli nad przedsiębiorstwem, Warsaw
Bolek T, Dobruk M (2018) Ustawa o kontroli w administracji rządowej. Komentarz z wzorami dokumentów, Warsaw
Celarek K (2015) Prawne i praktyczne aspekty kontroli i nadzoru nad działalnością samorządu terytorialnego, Warsaw
Chojna-Duch E (2003) Kontrola finansowa i audyt – ustawowe implikacje. In: Kontrola i audyt w administracji publicznej, Stan i perspektywy, 1st Conference, Warsaw
Cz B (1968) Dowód z dokumentu w postępowaniu kontrolnym, Kontrola Państwowa 2
Filipek J (2001) Prawo administracyjne. Instytucje ogólne, part II, Kraków
Gnoiński J (1972a) Formy działania kontrolnego i odpowiadająca im terminologia, Kontrola Państwowa 3
Gnoiński J (1972b) Próba określenia pojęcia i istoty kontroli, Kontrola Państwowa 2
Gnoiński J (1974) Niektóre zagadnienia teorii działania kontrolnego, Kontrola Państwowa 7
Jagielski J (2004) Współczesna funkcja kontroli administracji publicznej (kilka refleksji teoretycznych). Kontrola Państwowa 1
Jagielski J (2012) Kontrola administracji publicznej, Warsaw
Jarkiewicz Z (1972) Rola oględzin w procesie kontrolnym, Kontrola Państwowa 1
Jarzęcka-Siwik E, Skwarka B (2013) Dopuszczalność zaskarżania wyników kontroli – możliwość weryfikacji ustaleń pokontrolnych, Kontrola Państwowa 4
Jemioła S (1987) O zaktywizowanie i wzmocnienie kontroli wewnętrznej, Kontrola Państwowa 1
Kałużny S (2008) Kontrola wewnętrzna. Teoria i praktyka, Warsaw
Kiczka K (2018) Pozycja kontroli w publicznym prawie gospodarczym. In: Kocicińska K (ed) Kontrola działań administracji publicznej w sferze gospodarki, Poznań
Kieżun W (1972) Problemy kontroli w systemach zarządzania, Kontrola Państwowa 3
Kowalski A (1971) Wyjaśnienia i oświadczenia jako środki dowodowe w procesie kontroli, Kontrola Państwowa 4
Kuc BR (1983) Kontrola w systemie zarządzania, Warsaw
Lang W (1963) Struktura kontroli prawnej organów państwowych Polskiej, Kraków
Longchamps de Berier F (1964) Rzut oka na system kontroli nad administracją, Kontrola Państwowa 3
Ninard G (2017) Udzielenie upoważnienia do przetwarzania danych osobowych a udostępnienie akt podmiotowi kontrolującemu, Nowe Zeszyty Samorządowe 6
Nitkowski K (2013) Kontrola wewnętrzna instytucjonalna w systemie kontroli w przedsiębiorstwie, Warsaw
Nowikowska M, Cieślak J (2015) O potrzebie zmian w ustawie o kontroli w administracji rządowej – uwagi de lege ferenda, Kontrola Państwowa 4
Nowikowska M, Walczuk K (2018) Dowody w postępowaniu kontrolnym (w trybie ustawy o kontroli w administracji rządowej) i możliwość ich wykorzystania w postępowaniu karnym. In:

Paszkowski M, Daniluk D, Rzewuska M (eds) Teoretyczne i praktyczne aspekty postępowania dowodowego, KPP Monographs, Olsztyn
Owczarek T (1990) Kontrola – integralna funkcja zarządzania, Kontrola Państwowa 1
Płoskonka J (2005) Zmiany w stosowanych przez polską administrację publiczną metodach i narzędziach. Kontrola Państwowa 1
Płoskonka J (2006) Pojęcie kontroli w ujęciu zarządczym. Kontrola Państwowa 2
Ponikowski R (2012) Dowody – zagadnienia podstawowe i systemowe. In: Skorupka J (ed) Postępowanie karne. Część ogólna, Warsaw
Popławski H (1965) Obowiązki kierownika przedsiębiorstwa w zakresie kontroli i nadzoru. Kontrola Państwowa 2
Starościak J (1971) Zarys nauki administracji, Warsaw
Starościak J (1975) Prawo administracyjne, Warsaw
Warchoł M (2013) Dowody. In: Hofmański P (ed) System Prawa Karnego Procesowego v. II, Proces karny. Rozwiązania modelowe w ujęciu prawno porównawczym, Warsaw
Wiechowski Z (1969) Fakt kontrolny – teoria a praktyka, Kontrola Państwowa 6
Winiarska K (2003) Definicja i klasyfikacja kontroli. In: Kontrola i audyt w administracji publicznej, Stan i perspektywy, 1st Conference, Warsaw 2003
Zembaty M (1988) Z rozważań nad teorią kontroli, Kontrola Państwowa 4

Monika Nowikowska PhD, adjunct at the Department of Cybersecurity Law and New Technologies of the Institute of Law of the War Studies University. Author of several dozen scientific publications in the field of intellectual property law and the media. He also specializes in issues related to security, such as audit, protection of classified information and personal data. Internal auditor, legal advisor.

Monetary Penalties in the National Cybersecurity System Act

Filip Radoniewicz

Abstract This chapter presents the provisions of Chapter 14 ("Provisions regarding monetary penalties") of NCSA containing provisions directed at implementing the provisions of Art. 21 of the NIS which obliging Member States to lay down sanctions applicable to infringements of the national provisions adopted pursuant to the NIS Directive and to take all necessary measures to ensure their implementation.

Pursuant to the above provision of the NIS Directive, the Polish legislator adopted an appropriate provisions providing for administrative liability for three groups of entities: operators of essential services, digital service providers and (additionally) managers of operators of essential services.

To the penalties imposed on the basis of the NCSA, the provisions of the Code of Administrative Procedure apply, which results directly from the content of art. 189a Code of Administrative Procedure.

In this case, provisions of NCSA are 'lex specialis' and take precedence over codex regulations. On the other hand, however, it is difficult to consider the statutory regulation as complete (in Chapter 14, in principle, only provisions regulating the types of violations and the amount of administrative penalties are provided), hence the need to apply the provisions of the Code of Administrative Procedure.

1 Introductory Remarks

The provisions of Chapter 14 of the NCSA ("Provisions regarding monetary penalties") reflect the provisions of Article 21 of the NIS Directive, under which Member States are obligated to penalise infringements of the national provisions adopted

F. Radoniewicz (✉)
Akademickie Centrum Polityki Cyberbezpieczeństwa/Academic Center for Cybersecurity Policy, Akademia Sztuki Wojennej w Warszawie/War Studies University in Warsaw, Warsaw, Poland
e-mail: filip.radoniewicz@radoniewicz.eu

K. Chałubińska-Jentkiewicz et al. (eds.), *Cybersecurity in Poland*,
https://doi.org/10.1007/978-3-030-78551-2_22

pursuant to this Directive, and to take all measures necessary to ensure that they are implemented.

In line with the said NIS Directive provision, the Polish legislator adopted an appropriate regulation to govern the administrative liability of three groups of entities:

(1) operators of essential services, entities whose organisational units are located within the territory of the Republic of Poland, which have been recognised by the authority competent for cybersecurity as operators of essential services (operators of services, which are essential for the maintenance of critical societal and economic activities included in the list of essential services). These include banks, energy-sector companies and healthcare entities. It is reasonable to assume that in addition to legal persons and organizational units not being legal persons which have been granted the legal capacity by virtue of statutory law (such as commercial partnerships); such operators might also be natural-person entrepreneurs;[1]
(2) digital-service providers, legal persons or organizational units not being legal persons which have been granted the legal capacity by virtue of statutory law (art, 33^1 of the CC) which have their head office or management office within the territory of Poland, or whose representative has an organisational unit in Poland, which provides digital services, i.e. services provided by electronic means as defined by the Act on the Provision of Services by Electronic Means (PSEMA), listed in Annex 2 to the NCSA, an online marketplace, cloud computing or online search services;
    and more:
(3) managers of operators of essential services.

Article 21 of the NIS Directive requires Member States to impose effective, proportionate and dissuasive penalties for infringements of national provisions adopted pursuant to this Directive, and to take all measures necessary to ensure that they are implemented.

By using the word "penalties", the EU legislator refrained from specifying their nature, thus, they may include criminal, civil, as well as administrative sanctions, as in the case of Poland. Effective penalties should be understood as sanctions designed to enforce an objective enshrined in EU laws, which has not been met due to the infringement of the national provisions. Hence, the underlying purpose of administrative penalties is to enforce compliance with the law. Penalties should be proportionate to the type, nature and circumstances of the infringement. In other words, they should be strictly necessary (essential) for the achievement of the objectives enshrined in law. In this sense the principle of proportionality safeguards the rights of individuals. Dissuasive penalties are sanctions, which deter infringement and enforce future compliance.[2]

[1]Radoniewicz (2019), p. 343.
[2]Cf. Fajgielski (2018); Łacny (2011), pp. 477–489.

Notably, administrative liability is not based upon the principle of guilt. Instead, it has an objective nature. Accordingly, administrative penalties are adjudged regardless of the possible fault, since the very fact of infringement provides a basis for their imposition. This is confirmed by the rulings of the Polish Constitutional Tribunal. For example, in its rationale to the judgement of the 25th of March 2010 in case P 9/08 (Legalis) the Tribunal found that monetary penalties represent measures to mobilise entities to comply with their obligations towards the State in a timely and appropriate manner, and that they are used automatically, and legally, and serve preventive functions. By warning against the negative consequences of the infringement of the obligations set forth in law or administrative decision, they encourage statutory compliance. However, it is the objective infringement of the law, which alone provides the basis for imposing a monetary penalty. Not surprisingly, the same stance may be found in the rulings of the Supreme Administrative Court (SAC).[3]

Indeed, the monetary penalties imposed under the are governed by the provisions of the Code of Administrative Procedure[4] (CAP), as explicitly stipulated by Article 189a of the CAP, which requires the provisions of Section IVa of the CAP to be applied in cases involving the imposition or determination of administrative monetary penalties, or the granting of relief in their enforcement, subject to § 2 and § 3, which provide for partial or full derogations from the application of the provisions of this section. The first derogation applies to cases, in which a particular Act governs specific subject matters (preconditions for the determination of administrative monetary penalties, abstaining from the imposition of such penalties, prescription periods for their imposition or enforcement, interest on overdue administrative monetary penalties, and granting relief from their enforcement), thus constituting a *lex specialis*. The other derogation explicitly excludes the application of the CAP in cases involving the imposition or determination of penalties by public administration authorities based on the provisions governing petty offences, disciplinary liability and employees' liability for maintenance of order, and liability for public-finance discipline.

Here, NCSA provisions represent a *lex specialis* and take precedence over CAP regulations. On the other hand, it is difficult to consider the statutory regulation as complete (Chapter 14 essentially governs only the types of infringements and the amounts of administrative penalties). Hence the need to apply CAP provisions (not only those mentioned in Section IVa).

In accordance with Article 189b CAP, an administrative monetary penalty is a statutorily defined financial penalty imposed through an administrative decision issued by a public administration authority for an infringement of the law involving non-compliance or infringement by a natural person, legal person or organizational units not being legal persons which have been granted the legal capacity by virtue of statutory law.

[3]See e.g. SAC Judgement of 27 January 2016, II GSK, 694/14, Legalis.

[4]Act of 14 June 1960—the Code of Administrative Procedure, consolidated text, Polish Journal of Laws of 2020, item 256, as amended.

The straightforward expressions used by the legislator in the provisions of Article 73 (1) ("a monetary penalty shall be imposed on operators of essential services") and Article 73 (2) ("a monetary penalty shall be imposed on digital-service providers") of the NCSA make it clear that the penalties provided for operators of essential services and digital-service providers (in contrast to natural persons, managers of operators of essential services, on whom "may be imposed a monetary penalty" by the authorities competent for cybersecurity, see below) are mandatory in nature, resulting in the competent authority being obliged to determine a financial penalty where it has found an infringement of the said provision (unless Article 189f CAP applies). However, the authority has the freedom to decide on the amount of the penalty, as such, the penalty is relative. In one instance the legislator provided for an absolute penalty, the infringement defined in Article 73 (1) (10) of the NCSA, which involves the neglect of a duty, as referred to in Article 14 (1) of the NCSA (i.e. failure to establish internal structures responsible for cybersecurity, or, alternatively, to enter into an appropriate agreement with a provider of cybersecurity services), is subject to a fixed monetary penalty of 100,000 PLN. As a side note, it is worth pointing out that the legislator was "careless" in setting the fixed amount of the penalty while also stipulating that such an amount may not be lower than 15,000 PLN (Article 73 (4) (3) of the NCSA).

2 Administrative Penalties Provided for in the NCSA

In addition to serving the retributive function (as particularly shown by the regulations of Article 73 (5) of the NCSA), administrative monetary penalties are intended primarily as preventive and admonitory measures, both generally (especially with regard to the negative aspect, by dissuading the addressees of the Act from infringing its provisions) and specifically (acting as a deterrent for the penalised operator). Moreover, they are usually designed to force the penalised operator to comply with the obligation set forth in the provisions of the said Act.[5] As mentioned above, almost all monetary penalties defined in the Act are relative. The Act sets the upper limit of the amount of the penalty, which may be determined for an infringement, as well as, for operators of essential services, its lower limit. The legislator has not defined the lower limit of the penalties imposed on digital-service providers. This might pose problems with their determination. In the existing situation this limit should be 1PLN.[6]

In its comments on the draft of NCSA, the Polish Entrepreneurs' Association noted that financial penalties would be imposed on institutions and not on the natural persons who serve managerial functions at them, postulating the introduction of

[5]Cf. Banasiński and Nowak (2018), pp. 170–171.

[6]Radoniewicz (2019), p. 346.

criminal penalties "which would provide the motivation to comply with the Act". In their opinion the PEA proposed the following types of prohibited acts:

(1) failing to ensure adequate data security, especially by operators of essential services, or putting data processed in information systems at risk of being disclosed or lost;
(2) intentionally (on purpose or through gross negligence) disclosing data processed in information systems.

The Council of Digital Affairs issued an opinion proposing that criminal liability be introduced, applicable only to managers of local government units, with the possible penalty being limited to 100,000 PLN per infringement. However, the legislator did not go so far as to introduce criminal liability for members of governing bodies at entities, which commit infringements, instead providing only for the possibility of imposing monetary penalties on managers of operators of essential services (Article 75 of the NCSA).

Ultimately, the legislator provided only for financial penalties in relation to operators of essential services and digital-service providers (the Polish Bank Association criticised this in its opinion), and they have increased them compared to the ones provided in the draft Act, although not going beyond setting the rates. I believe that the comments to the draft NCSA were right to note the need to introduce rates with the amount determined as a percentage of the revenue of the infringing entity. It seems worth considering other measures, which are equally harsh or even harsher than financial penalties, the same as those provided in the Act on the liability of collective entities[7] (LCEA), under which the catalogue of available penalties against collective entities (i.e. legal persons or organizational units not being legal persons which have been granted the legal capacity by virtue of statutory law (excluding the State Treasury, local government units and their associations), commercial companies with a State Treasury holding, local government units or their associations, companies under formation, entities in liquidation, entrepreneurs, who are not natural persons, foreign organisational units (Article 2 (1) and (2) of the LCEA) includes such measures as the prohibition of promotion and advertising, using grants, subsidies or other forms of public financial support, and the prohibition of entering public procurement procedures).

3 Catalogue of Penalties

Almost all infringements penalised under the NCSA involve non-performance or improper performance (failure to notify the appropriate CSIRT MON, CSIRT NASK or CSIRT GOV about a serious incident within twenty four hours from its

[7]The Act of 28 October 2002 on Liability of Collective Entities for Prohibited Acts Punishable by Sanction, consolidated text, Polish Journal of Laws of 2020 item 358, as amended.

identification; hence, an untimely notification might represent an infringement) by operators of essential services of their obligations imposed under the NCSA. The other two instances relate to infringements of procedural rules provided for in the NCSA and involve obstructing inspection and failure to comply with post-inspection recommendations.[8] Provided below are infringements defined in Article 73 (1) the NCSA, including the penalties to which, operators of essential services are subject for such infringements:

(1) failure to perform incident risk assessment on a regular basis or to manage incident risk (negligence of the duty defined in Article 8 (1) of the NCSA) is subject to a monetary penalty of up to 150,000 PLN, but not less than 5000 PLN;
(2) monetary penalties of up to 100,000 PLN (but not less than 5000 PLN) may be imposed for failure to implement technical and organisational measures, which are appropriate for, and proportionate to, the assessed risk, taking into account the requirements referred to in Article 8 (2) (a–e), such as in particular:
    (a) the maintenance and safe operation of the information system;
    (b) physical and environmental security, including access control;
    (c) the security and continuity of services essential for the provision of critical services;
    (d) implementing, documenting, and maintaining action plans to enable the continued and uninterrupted provision of critical services, and to ensure the confidentiality, integrity, availability and authenticity of information;
    (e) establishing a system for the continuous monitoring of the information system used to provide an essential service;
(3) monetary penalties of up to 50,000 PLN (but not less than 5000 PLN) may be imposed for failing to implement the measures referred to in Article 8 (5) (a–d) of the NCSA, i.e. measures to prevent and mitigate the impact of incidents on the security of the information system used to provide an essential service, including the following measures:
    (a) using mechanisms to ensure the confidentiality, integrity, availability and authenticity of data processed in the information system;
    (b) keeping software up-to-date
    (c) providing protection against unauthorised modifications in the information system;
    (d) responding promptly to any identified cybersecurity vulnerabilities or threats;
(4) failure to appoint a contact person to communicate with entities within the national cybersecurity system (Article 9 (1) (1) of the NCSA) is subject to a monetary penalty of up to 15,000 PLN, but not less than 1000 PLN;
(5) failure to perform the duties referred to in Article 10 (1) of the NCSA, i.e. failure to draft documentation on the cybersecurity of the information

[8] Banasiński and Nowak (2018), pp. 170–171.

system used to provide an essential service, or failing to apply or update such documentation despite its being in place is subject to a monetary penalty of 50,000 PLN;

(6) failure to perform the duty referred to in Article 11 (1) (1) of the NCSA, i.e. failure to handle an incident, is subject to a monetary penalty of up to 15,000 PLN (but not less than 5000 PLN) for each identified negligence of such a duty;

(7) failure to perform the duty referred to in Article 11 (1) (4) of the NCSA, i.e. failure to notify the appropriate CSIRT MON, CSIRT NASK or CSIRT GOV about a serious incident within twenty four hours from its identification (under this provision the monetary penalty is also imposed when the operator of essential services reported the incident after twenty four hours from its identification; this should be taken into account when determining the amount of the monetary penalty) is subject to a monetary penalty of 20,000 PLN (but not less than 5000 PLN) for each identified failure to notify an incident;

(8) failure to perform the duty referred to in Article 11 (1) (5) of the NCSA, i.e. failure to provide CSIRT MON, CSIRT NASK or CSIRT GOV with the data necessary to handle a serious incident, or personal data, is subject to a monetary penalty of 5000 PLN to 20,000 PLN;

(9) a monetary penalty of up to 20,000 PLN (but not less than 5000 PLN) is imposed for failure to resolve in a timely manner the vulnerabilities referred to in Article 32 (2) of the NCSA, i.e. ones, which have caused or could cause a serious, significant or critical incident, and the resolution of which has been demanded by the competent authority at the request of CSIRT MON, CSIRT NASK or CSIRT GOV, which coordinate the handling of such an incident;

(10) negligence of the duty referred to in Article 14 (1) of the NCSA, which involves establishing internal structures responsible for cybersecurity, or, alternatively, entering into an agreement with a provider of cybersecurity services, is subject to a monetary penalty of PLN 100,000 (but not less than PLN 15,000);

(11) failure to have an audit is subject to a monetary penalty of PLN 200,000 (but not less than PLN 15,000);

(12) monetary penalties of up to PLN 50,000 (but not less than PLN 5000) are imposed for obstructing inspections by the authority competent for cybersecurity or the minister competent for computerization, as defined in Article 53 (2) (1) of the NCSA, i.e.

   (a) for the minister competent for computerization, inspections on compliance by the internal structures responsible for cybersecurity and the cybersecurity service providers referred to in Article 14 (2) of the NCSA with the requirements referred to in Article 14 (2) of the NCSA, i.e.:

      – meeting the organisational and technical requirements to ensure cybersecurity for the operator of essential services;
      – the availability of incident-response rooms protected against physical and environmental threats; having safeguards in place to ensure the

confidentiality, integrity, availability and authenticity of processed information, taking into account personal safety and the operation and architecture of the systems;

(b) for the authority competent for cybersecurity:

- the fulfilment by operators of essential services of their statutory obligations related to counteracting cybersecurity threats and reporting serious incidents;
- the fulfilment by digital-service providers of the safety requirements related to the digital services provided by them, as laid down by Implementing Regulation 2018/151, and their statutory obligations related to reporting significant incidents;

(13) failure to comply with post-inspection recommendations on resolving irregularities, as referred to in Article 59 (1) of the NCSA (i.e. possible irregularities found by the authority competent for cybersecurity or the minister competent for computerisation based on the information contained in the inspection report) is subject to a monetary penalty of up to 200,000 PLN, but not lower than 15,000 PLN.

As emphasised in the rationale to the draft Act, in accordance with the NIS Directive digital-service providers may be subject to sanctions in the form of monetary penalties only when such providers have infringed the national provisions, which implement the NIS Directive. It is not an option to impose monetary penalties for the infringement of the provisions of the EU legislation, which supplements the NIS Directive (including provisions governing the protection of the information systems designed to provide digital services, as defined in Implementing Regulation 2018/151).

Of course, the catalogue of infringements for which digital-service providers are subject to monetary penalties is much smaller than that applicable to operators of essential services, since they have fewer duties under the Act. Accordingly, monetary penalties apply only to matters associated with the reporting and handling of significant incidents, resolving vulnerabilities, which have or could have led to significant incidents, or which have or could have harmed national defence and state security, public order or the safety, health and lives of people. Digital-service providers are liable for failure to promptly (i.e. within twenty hours from identification) notify a significant incident to the appropriate CSIRT MON, CSIRT NASK or CSIRT GOV (the obligation referred to in Article 18 (1) (4) of the NCSA). Such providers are subject to monetary penalties of up to 20,000 PLN for each failure to report such an incident. Digital-service providers, who fail to provide the appropriate CSIRT MON, CSIRT NASK or CSIRT GOV with the necessary data, including personal data, when handling a significant or critical incident, are subject to a monetary penalty of up to 20,000 PLN. Providers who have failed to resolve the vulnerabilities referred to in Article 32 (2) of the NCSA (i.e. vulnerabilities that have or could have caused a serious, significant or critical incident) despite being ordered to do so by the authority competent for cybersecurity at the request of CSIRT MON,

CSIRT NASK or CSIRT GOV, depending on which one is handling the given incident, may be imposed a monetary penalty of up to 20,000 PLN by such an authority.

4 Penalty Increase

Article 73 (5) of the NCSA provides the authority competent for cybersecurity with the option of imposing an increased monetary penalty of up to 1,000,000 PLN (as already mentioned, the amount was 200,000 PLN in the initial version of the draft), should an inspection find that the operator of essential services or digital-service provider repeatedly infringes the NCSA, causing the consequences listed in the said provision, i.e.:

(1) a direct and serious cybersecurity threat to national defence and state security, public order and the safety, health and lives of people;
(2) the threat of serious damage to property, or serious essential-service disruptions.

Marked by many ambiguous expressions, this provision affords considerable freedom to the authority competent for cybersecurity. In order for the penalty to be imposed, two objective preconditions must be met, the provisions of the Act have been infringed ("repeatedly" suggests that there must be more than one infringement) and such infringements have caused a threat (as stipulated in Article 73 (5) (1) or (2) of the NCSA). However, it is at the discretion of the authority competent for cybersecurity to decide whether the infringements have been committed repeatedly, and also whether their consequences meet the preconditions specified in the said provision (i.e. whether the cybersecurity threat for national defence, state security, public order and the safety, health and lives of people caused by such infringements has been "direct and serious", or whether the potential property damage as a result of such infringements may be described as serious, or whether essential-service disruptions caused by such infringements were serious in nature), and whether to impose a monetary penalty, accordingly.

The administrative penalties referred to in Article 73 of the NCSA are imposed by the authority competent for cybersecurity (i.e. respective ministers, depending on the sector in which the given operator of essential services or digital-service provider operates, as defined in Annex I to the NCSA to ministers competent for energy, transport, maritime economy, inland navigation, health, national defence, computerisation and the Financial Supervision Authority, see Article 41 (4)) by an administrative decision.

Since the administrative penalties set forth in the said provision are subject to administrative discretion (being obligatory but falling within a specified bracket of amounts), and since the legislator has not defined the factors, which should guide the authority's determination of the penalty, the decisions in this regard are governed by the degree-of-penalty directives ("general requirements for the determination of administrative penalties) defined in Article 189d CAP, namely:

(1) the gravity and circumstances of the infringement, including in particular with regard to the protection of life or health, the protection of assets of substantial value, or the safeguarding of an important public interest, or a particularly important interest of a party, and the duration of such an infringement;
(2) past recurring events of non-compliance or infringements of the same type as that which is subject to the penalty;
(3) a record of penalties imposed for the same behaviour, offence, fiscal offence, petty offence and fiscal petty offence;
(4) the degree to which the party to be penalised has contributed to the infringement of the law;
(5) the actions taken voluntarily by the party to be penalised to avoid the consequences of the infringement of the law;
(6) the size of the benefit gained, or the loss avoided, by the party to be penalised; this will be taken into consideration only when the determination alone of the infringement is contingent upon whether the party to be penalised has gained a benefit or avoided a loss through that infringement;
(7) in the case of a natural person, the personal circumstances of the party to be penalised.

In the case of digital-service providers, as legal persons and organizational units not being legal persons which have been granted the legal capacity by virtue of statutory law, it is clear that the last precondition mentioned in the said provision shall not apply, as opposed to operators of essential services, who (at least theoretically) may be natural persons, and their managers. An analogous situation applies to the precondition described in item 4 (it is difficult to accuse a legal person or organisational unit of "contributing" to an infringement of the law).

Since the competent authorities are either supreme authorities (ministers) or central authorities (the Financial Supervision Authority), administrative procedures concerning the imposition of monetary penalties pursuant to provisions of the NCSA are single-instance procedures (i.e. the decisions may not be appealed against). Accordingly, under Article 127 § 3 of the CAP the penalised entity may (in the case of a decision issued by the Financial Supervision Authority, under Article 127 § 3 of the CAP in conjunction with Article 11 (5) of the Financial-Market Supervision Act) lodge a motion for reconsideration. This motion may, however, be relinquished in accordance with Article 127a § 1 of the CAP, resulting in the decision becoming final and irrevocable as of the date on which the public administration authority is served the declaration on the relinquishment of the right to appeal made by the last party to the proceedings.

Since, as already mentioned, under Article 127 § 3 of the CAP motions for reconsideration are governed by the provisions on appeals, under Article 128 CAP there is no requirement to substantiate such motions. It is sufficient that the motion expresses the party's discontent with the decision; unless specific provisions lay down other requirements as to the contents of such motions (no such provisions exist in this case). The time limit for lodging the motion is fourteen days from the service of the decision, and if the decision has been announced orally, from the date of such an announcement. The decision may not be enforced before this time limit has lapsed, and the lodging of the motion suspends the enforcement of the decision, unless an order of immediate enforceability has been issued by a court (Article 108 of the CAP), or the decision is immediately enforceable by statute (Article 130 § 1, 2 and 3 of the CAP). If the decision satisfies the demands of all the parties, or if all the parties have relinquished their right to appeal (Article 130 § 4 of the CAP), the decision becomes enforceable before the said time limit expires.

A complaint may be filed with the appropriate administrative court against the decision issued after the examination of the motion for reconsideration, in which case general rules for such complaints apply (Article 3 § 2 (1) of the Law on proceedings before administrative courts[9] [LPACA]).

Due to the nature of the operations conducted by operators of essential services and digital-service providers, involving personal-data processing and cross-border ICT networks, a considerable role is played by Article 189f § 1 of the CAP, which provides public administration authorities with the option to refrain, through a decision, from imposing a monetary penalty, and instead only issue a warning. This is the case where the gravity of the infringement is negligible and the party has remedied such an infringement, or where an administrative penalty has been previously imposed by an appropriate public administration authority under a final and irrevocable decision for the same infringement, or where the party has been penalised under a final and irrevocable decision for a petty offence or fiscal petty offence, or where the party has been sentenced under a final and irrevocable judgement for a fiscal offence and the previous penalty serves the purpose underlying the possible administrative penalty. This provision makes it possible to avoid a double penalty for the same infringement as a result of the concurrence of legal rules prescribed in the NCSA, such as with GDPR or cybersecurity regulations applicable in other EU Member States, as might be the case with cross-border incidents.

Article 189f § 2 and 3 of the CAP provides for the possibility of waiving the penalty in cases other than those described in Article 189f § 1 of the CAP, should this serve the purposes of the possible administrative penalty. In this situation a public administration authority may issue a decision to set a time limit for the party to furnish evidence that the infringement of the law has been remedied, or that the appropriate entities have been notified of the infringement, prescribing the time limit for, and manner of, such a notification (Article 189f §2 of the CAP). Where the entity has furnished evidence that the requirements of the decision have been met, the public administration authority shall refrain from imposing an administrative penalty and instead only issues a warning to that entity. Adjudication with regard to refraining from imposing an administrative penalty, as a determination of the merits of the case (i.e. a subject-matter determination), should take the form of an administrative decision.[10]

[9]Act of 30 August 2002—the Law on proceedings before administrative courts, consolidated text, Polish Journal of Laws of 2019, item 2325, as amended.

[10]Stankiewicz (2020).

Article 76 of the NCSA ("the penalty referred to in Article 73 may also be imposed where the entity has remedied the infringement or the damage caused by such an infringement, provided that the authority competent for cybersecurity finds that this is justified due to the duration, scope and consequences of the infringement") seems to suggest *a contrario* that the administrative penalty prescribed in Article 73 may not be imposed where the entity concerned has remedied the infringement or damage caused by such an infringement, unless the authority competent for cybersecurity finds that this is justified due to the duration, scope or consequences of the infringement.[11] However, it seems that in reality this provision is somewhat amiss, modifying the general regulation applicable to refraining from a penalty, as stipulated by Article 189f § 2 and 3 of the CAP. Indeed, it enables the competent authority to impose a monetary penalty even in the circumstances described in Article 189f § 3 of the CAP (Article 189f § 3 of the CAP do not provide for options other than refraining from the penalty). Notably, the legislator has afforded the authority competent for cybersecurity considerable freedom in its decision-making. Hence, the exercise of the right to impose a monetary penalty is contingent here on the authority's finding that such a monetary penalty is justified by the vaguely described statutory preconditions, i.e. the duration, scope or consequences of the infringement.

The original version of the draft of NCSA (discussed as part of public consultations held before it being submitted for further Parliamentary processing) expected that before instigating penalty proceedings the authority competent for cybersecurity could request the operator of essential services (the original draft did not provide for digital-service provider's liability) to remedy the infringement within a specified time limit, provided that this is justified due to the nature of the infringement (Article 58 (2) of the original bill). This provision, however, was eventually removed from the final version of the Act. Possibly, it was considered redundant, since similar solutions are provided by the above-discussed provisions of Article 189f § 2 and 3 of the CAP. I believe this supports the above-presented interpretation.

An adjudication made pursuant to Article 76 of the NCSA should take the form of an administrative decision.

Since the NCSA does not address the prescription period for the ruling and the enforcement of the penalty, CAP provisions apply, stipulating that an administrative penalty may not be imposed once five years have lapsed after the infringement date or the date on which the consequences of the infringement occurred, unless separate laws prescribe a time limit after which administrative-penalty or infringement proceedings, involving a potential monetary penalty, may not be instigated. Such a penalty may not be enforced once five years have lapsed from the date on which the penalty should have been enforced. The prescription period for, as well as the enforcement of, the administrative penalty cease upon the declaration of bankruptcy by the party concerned (Article 189h and 189j CAP).

[11]Banasiński and Nowak (2018), pp. 170–171.

In accordance with Article 189 of the CAP, where justified due to an important public interest or an important interest of the party concerned, the public administration authority, which has imposed an administrative penalty at the request of the party may grant relief in the enforcement of the administrative penalty by:

(1) postponing the date by which the administrative penalty is to be enforced, or dividing the monetary penalty into instalments;
(2) postponing the date by which the outstanding administrative penalty is to be enforced, or dividing the monetary penalty into instalments;
(3) forgiving the administrative penalty in full or in part (where an outstanding administrative penalty is forgiven, this also includes late-payment interest in full or in part, to the extent that such an outstanding administrative penalty has been forgiven);
(4) forgiving, fully or partly, late-payment interest.

In proceedings concerning relief in an administrative-penalty enforcement a party to which is a business entity, the authority has the obligation to determine whether such a relief represents state aid as defined by EU law. No such relief may be granted where it represents *de minimis* aid or *de minimis* aid in agriculture or fisheries. Where the relief is found to be state aid other than *de minimis* aid, it may be granted, provided that:

(1) its purpose would be to redress/remedy any damages caused by natural disasters or other force majeure;
(2) it would help to address serious economic disturbances;
(3) it would be compatible with the internal EU market rules, and that it has been considered admissible by the appropriate EU authorities for purposes other than those mentioned in items (a) and (b) above.[12]

Pursuant to Article 189e CAP where the infringement was due to force majeure, operators of essential services and their managers, and digital-service providers are not subject to penalty (Article 189e of the CAP). A force majeure is an external event beyond the control of the affected entity, which has no influence on the occurrence and consequences of that event. Three categories of force majeure are distinguished: natural disasters, legislative and executive acts, and serious public disorders.[13] As noted by A. Wróbel, Article 189e of the CAP applies to situations where the affected entity failed to meet its obligation (through an infringement or non-compliance) as a result of a force majeure.[14]

The exclusion of penalty is a construct derived from criminal law. The Penal Code (PC) provides for such a solution where the perpetrator abandons the prohibited act or prevented its consequence (Article 15 § 1 of the PC), or where the co-perpetrator voluntarily prevents the prohibited act (Article 23 of the PC), or in

[12]For more on the subject, see Wróbel (2019a).

[13]Warkałło (1949), pp. 100–102.

[14]Wróbel (2019b).

the event that the limits of necessary defence have been exceeded due to fright or emotional distress, as justified by the circumstances of the attack.[15] It is a prerequisite for criminal proceedings, as defined in Article 17 § 4 of the CAP, representing a circumstance on which the admissibility of criminal proceedings is contingent (i.e. a circumstance which, if found to exist, result in the refusal to instigate proceedings or to discontinue pending proceedings), and which is substantive (meaning that it derives from, and causes consequences in, the substantive-law sphere), absolute (irresolvable), common (applicable always, regardless of the procedure) and negative (meaning that its occurrence shall preclude the instigation of the proceedings).[16] In the context of administrative proceedings, this means that an infringement of the law due to force majeure shall not result in the instigation of proceedings to impose a monetary penalty, and if the circumstance was found to exist in the course of the proceedings, such proceedings are discontinued.[17]

5 The Liability of Managers of Operators of Essential Services

The Act uses the term "managers of operators of essential services" (no liability is provided for "managers of digital-service providers") without providing any definition (e.g., in the "glossary" in Article 2) of what it means. Clearly, no such position exists in the organisational structures of organisational units, which operate, for instance, under the Code of Commercial Partnerships and Companies, and since operators of essential services (as well as digital-service providers) are usually entrepreneurs (see Annex 1 to the NCSA) within the meaning of Article 4 (1) and (2) in conjunction with Article 3 of the Entrepreneurs Law Act[18] (LEA) (i.e. natural persons, legal persons or organizational units not being legal persons which have been granted the legal capacity by virtue of statutory law which conduct business activities, i.e. organised for-profit activities carried out continuously and in their own name, and also partners in civil-law partnerships to the extent of their business activities), in legal transactions they usually operate as commercial entities, i.e. partnerships and, above all, companies. A similar problem is encountered in the Act on the protection of classified information[19] (PCIA), in which the term "manager" is used in relation to the so-called industrial-security proceedings (i.e. proceedings conducted by the Internal Security Agency or the Military

[15]Cf. Wróbel (2019b).

[16]Grzegorczyk (2014), pp. 108–109.

[17]Cf. Krawczyk (2018).

[18]Act of 6 March 2018—the Entrepreneurs Law, consolidated text, Polish Journal of Laws of 2019 item 1292, as amended.

[19]Act of 5 August 2010 on the Protection of Classified Information, consolidated text, Polish Journal of Laws of 2019, item 742, as amended.

Counterintelligence Service to establish whether an entrepreneur seeking, or planning to seek, to enter contracts associated with access to classified information, or an entrepreneur already bound by such contracts, or fulfilling statutory responsibilities associated with access to classified information provides the conditions required to protect classified information). However, the PCIA defines the term "entrepreneur's manager" as the sole Management Board member, or the member of a different single-member governing body, and if the governing body comprises multiple members, the entire body or the member or members of such a body appointed at least under a Management Board resolution to serve in the capacity of entrepreneur's manager, excluding any proxies appointed by such a body or unit; in the case of general partnerships and civil-law partnerships, entrepreneur's managers are the partners in charge of the partnership's affairs, and in the case of professional partnerships, the partners in charge of the partnership's affairs or the Management Board, and in relation to limited partnerships and limited joint-stock companies, the general partners in charge of the partnership's or company's affairs; in the case of natural-person entrepreneurs the entrepreneur's manager is the natural person concerned; liquidators, trustees in bankruptcy and receivers are also considered to be entrepreneur's managers; an entrepreneur's manager is an organisational-unit manager within the meaning of the Act (Article 2 (14) of the PCIA). The term manager, or unit manager, more specifically, is also used in the Accounting Act. For the purposes of this Act, Article 3 (1) (6) thereof stipulates that an organisational-unit manager is a member of the Management Board or other governing body, and if that body comprises multiple members, the members of that body, excluding any proxies appointed by the unit. In the case of general partnerships and civil-law partnerships, the role of unit manager is ascribed to the partners in charge of the partnership's affairs, and in the case of professional partnerships, the partners in charge of the partnership's affairs or the Management Board, and in relation to limited partnerships and limited joint-stock companies, the general partners in charge of the partnership's or company's affairs. In the case of natural-person entrepreneurs, unit managers are the natural persons concerned; and the same provision applies to individuals practising liberal professions, accordingly. Unit managers are also liquidators, trustees in bankruptcy and receivers appointed in reorganisation proceedings, as well as succession administrators, as referred to in the Act on succession administration (ASA), or the individuals referred to in Article 14 of the said Act, who performed the filing referred to in Article 12 (1c) of the Act on the registration and identification of taxpayers and taxable persons. The Accounting Act also provides the definition of the term "governing-body member" as a natural person serving in the capacity of member of the Management Board or other governing body, member of the Supervisory Board or other supervisory body, as well as member of other administrative body of the unit, appointed in accordance with the Articles of Association, Partnership Agreement or other laws applicable to the unit (Article 3 (1) (5a) of the Accounting Act). It seems that the definition provided in the Accounting Act is more appropriate for the purposes of interpreting the term "manager of an operator of essential services".

The liability of managers of operators of essential services is limited to cases involving failure by such managers to exercise due care to fulfil the obligations laid down in the said provision, i.e. to perform incident risk assessment on a regular basis and to manage incident risk (Article 8 (1) of the NCSA), appoint a contact person to communicate with entities within the national cybersecurity system (Article 9 (1) (1) of the NCSA), and to have, at least every two years, a security audit of the information system used to provide the essential service (Article 15 (1) of the NCSA). Monetary penalties on managers of operators of essential services are optional (as opposed to operators of essential services and digital-service operators, where such monetary penalties are mandatory).

As already mentioned, during the public consultations on the NCSA a suggestion was put forward (in the comments made by the Polish Entrepreneurs' Association with regard to the draft of NCSA) to introduce criminal liability for individuals in managerial positions, the rationale being that ensuring cybersecurity was of considerable significance. However, the legislator chose not to implement this solution.

References

Banasiński C, Nowak W (2018) Europejski i krajowy system cyberbezpieczeństwa. In: Cyberbezpieczeństwo. Zarys wykładu, Warsaw

Fajgielski P (2018) In: Ogólne rozporzadzenie o ochronie danych, Commentary on Article 83 GDPR, section 8. LEX/el

Grzegorczyk T (2014) Kodeks postępowania karnego, Warsaw

Krawczyk A (2018) In: Chroscielewski W, Kmieciak Z (eds) Kodeks postepowania administracyjnego. Komentarz, Commentary on article. 189e CAP, Warsaw LEX/el

Łacny J (2011) Skuteczna, proporcjonalna i odstraszająca sankcja za naruszenie prawa UE. In: Wróbel A (ed) Zapewnienie efektywności orzeczeń sądów międzynarodowych w polskim porządku prawnym, Warsaw

Radoniewicz F (2019) In: Kitler W, Taczkowska-Olszewska J, Radoniewicz F (eds) Ustawa o krajowym systemie cyberbezpieczeństwa. Komentarz, Warsaw

Stankiewicz R (2020) In: Hauser R, Wierzbowski M (eds) Kodeks postępowania administracyjnego. Komentarz, Commentary on Article 189f CAP, Warsaw LEX/el

Warkałło W (1949) Siła wyższa jako zasada nieodpowiedzialności i domniemanie przypadkowości szkody, Państwo i Prawo 9–10

Wróbel A (2019a) Komentarz do art. 189e KPA. In: Jaśkowska M, Wilbrandt-Gotowicz M, Wróbel A (eds) Komentarz zaktualizowany do Kodeksu postępowania administracyjnego. Warsaw, LEX/el

Wróbel A (2019b) Komentarz do art. 189k KPA. In: Jaśkowska M, Wilbrandt-Gotowicz M, Wróbel A (eds) Komentarz zaktualizowany do Kodeksu postępowania administracyjnego. Warsaw, LEX/el

Filip Radoniewicz PhD; legal advisor; adjunct in the Department of Cybersecurity Law and New Technologies at the Institute of Law, War Studies University, Warsaw; expert at the Academic Centre for Cybersecurity Policy (War Studies University) and in the Ministry of Justice; he worked as an assistant judge (in the Fourth Criminal and Sixth Penitentiary Department of the Regional Court in Lublin); graduate of post-graduate studies: "European Union Law" at the Jagiellonian University, "Human Rights and Freedoms", co-organized by the Institute of Legal Sciences of the Polish Academy of Sciences and the Helsinki Foundation for Human Rights, and "Computer Network Administration" at the Lublin University of Technology; author or co-author of approximately fifty publications, mainly in the field of broadly understood criminal law, new technology law and human rights. Selected publications: F. Radoniewicz (2016) Odpowiedzialność karna za hacking i inne przestępstwa przeciwko danym komputerowym i systemom informatycznym / Criminal liability for hacking and other offences against computer data and information systems/, Wolters Kluwer, Warszawa; Ustawa o krajowym systemie cyberbezpieczeństwa. Komentarz /Act on the National Cybersecurity System. Commentary/ (2019) ed. W. Kitler, J. Taczkowska-Olszewska, F. Radoniewicz, CH. Beck, Warszawa.

[illegible]

The Liability of Entities Providing Services by Electronic Means for Digital Content

Paweł Zając

Abstract As a result of computerisation, digitisation and informatisation of human activities, cyber responsibility became a key and indispensable issue related to human functioning in cyberspace. One of its aspects is the liability of service providers for digital content shared in network and information systems. This issue is increasingly important as the Internet has become a medium of exchange for ideas, views and content, and thus, a potential place of abuse, both from service providers and end users.

This article aims to show the legal regulations regarding the scope of liability of entities providing electronic services for digital content provided under Polish legislation, with particular emphasis on the obligations incumbent on service providers and indication of limitations of liability in the case of mere conduit, caching and hosting services, upon fulfilling certain regulatory requirements. This article also deals with the issue of protecting the copyrights to works unlawfully made available on the web by users and the scope of responsibility of service providers for the above activities.

1 General Remarks

The overall picture of our society has been transformed as a result of technological and technical progress. New forms of communication and new social habits have become engrained in society's DNA. We have become an information society for which creating, collecting and sharing information are crucial, and computers, the Internet, and digital technologies in general, are becoming some of the most important aspects of life.[1] Thanks to the web, every user has become a potential author of content, and information has become a commodity. That is why the digital

[1]Golka (2005), p. 254. Chałubińska-Jentkiewicz and Karpiuk (2015), Part I, Chapter 2, point 3.

P. Zając (✉)
Instytut Prawa/Institute of Law, Akademia Sztuki Wojennej w Warszawie/War Studies University in Warsaw, Warsaw, Poland
e-mail: p.zajac@akademia.mil.pl

K. Chałubińska-Jentkiewicz et al. (eds.), *Cybersecurity in Poland*,
https://doi.org/10.1007/978-3-030-78551-2_23

revolution has had an impact on law. The creation of legal regulations on the economic use of the Internet is of key importance in the information society in harmonising activities related to e-services. One aspect of the regulations is the definition of legal responsibility for content posted on the Internet, and, more specifically, of who is responsible, and under what conditions, for the infringement of third-party rights caused by posting content on the Internet. Until the adoption of the Directive on electronic commerce[2] by the European Union, the issue of business activities on the Internet, and, consequently, the liability of entities providing services by electronic means, had remained the prerogative of individual states, which did not know exactly how they should classify legal infringements on the Internet. The situations described below should serve as clear examples.

On 6 May 1996, the Paris police arrived on the premises of World-NET and FranceNet, two French companies providing Internet services in France, with a search warrant for all their premises and equipment.[3] As a result, the head of World-NET and the CEO of FranceNet were charged under Articles 227-23 of the French penal code[4] for the dissemination, recording, and transmission of child pornography. The reason for the arrest and detention was that companies provided access to Internet groups and forums on which paedophilic content was posted and exchanged. During the court hearing, the adjudicating authority concluded that the service provider could not be held liable, because it did not have the authority to filter the content posted on the Internet by other users, as this was contrary to French constitutional law.[5] The case for paedophilia was dropped.

In 1998, an action for disseminating a naked image of a model on the Internet was brought against Valentin Lacambre, one of the French owners of a server—a device on which websites are stored in the computer's memory and which provides access to the network.[6] The photo had previously appeared in a French magazine, and was then uploaded onto the server by one of the network users who used the hosting service of the server's owner. In the first instance, the referring judge, Jean-Jacques Gomez, stated "It is necessary to specify that the hosting provider is obliged to guarantee the moral standing of those it hosts and that these parties respect the statutory rights of third parties". The judge adjudicated against Valentin Lacambre, imposing a penalty of 100,000 Francs, and prohibited any dissemination of the image of the model in the photo.[7] An appeal was lodged against this ruling. Judge

[2]Directive 2000/31/EC of the European Parliament and of the Council of 8 June 2000 on certain legal aspects of information society services, in particular electronic commerce, in the Internal Market, OJ EC 2000 L 178/1 [hereinafter the e-Commerce Directive].

[3]*Une contre-histoire de l'Internet*, realisation S. Bergere, France 2013.

[4]*Code penale*, https://www.legifrance.gouv.fr/affichCode.do?cidTexte=LEGITEXT000006070719 [Accessed 10 April 2020].

[5]See *World-Net and FranceNet blanchis par la justice*, https://www.itespresso.fr/world-net-et-francenet-blanchis-par-la-justice-3594.html [Accessed on 20 December 2020].

[6]*Une contre-histoire de l'Internet*, realisation S. Bergere, France 2013.

[7]*Responsabilités des fournisseurs d'accès et d'hébergements: une première*, https://www.legalis.net/actualite/responsabilites-des-fournisseurs-dacces-et-dhebergements-une-premiere/ [accessed on

Marais, hearing the case in the second instance, ruled that, in so far as the defendant allowed Internet users to express themselves online, he "has clearly exceeded the role of a mere conduit of information" and must therefore be responsible for the content of the sites he hosted. The defendant was ordered to pay 300,000 Francs compensation and 100,000 Francs penalty per day.[8]

What do these two cases have in common? They are both related to the activities of entities providing services by electronic means, and involve data produced and delivered in digital form, and also raise the issue of liability for such activities. Furthermore, they initiated a public debate on the obligations and powers of Internet service providers, and specifically whether electronic-service providers are responsible for the content posted by network users.

The issue of defining the scope of responsibility of entities providing services by electronic means also become a subject of public debate in Poland. It resulted in the enactment of the Act on Providing Services by Electronic Means by the Sejm of the Republic of Poland on 18 July 2002.[9] This Act contained regulations implementing the Directive on electronic commerce, despite the fact that Poland was not yet formally a Member of the European Union.

2 What Is Digital Content?

Under Polish law, for the first time, the definition of "digital content" was included by the legislators in Article 2 of the Act on Consumer Rights of 30 May 2014,[10] according to which digital content should be understood as data produced and supplied in digital form. This definition, taken from Article 2(11) of Directive 2011/83/EU of the European Parliament and of the Council of 25 October 2011 on consumer rights[11] (and subsequently repeated in the Digital Content Directive[12]),

20 December 2020]. The same logical argument was used in other judgments. See Tribunal de Grande Instance de Nanterre 08 décembre 1999 – Affaire Lynda L. c/ Sté Multimania, Sté France Cybermédia, Sté SPPI, Sté Esterel.

[8]La décision: Cour d'appel de Paris, 14ème chambre, 10 février 1999E. Hallyday contre V. Lacambre, https://www.alain-bensoussan.com/wp-content/uploads/5446189.pdf. Accessed on 20.12.2020.

[9]Act of 18 July 2002 on Providing Services by Electronic Means, consolidated text Polish Journal of Laws of 2020, item 344, as amended (PSEMA).

[10]Act of 30 May 2014 on Consumer Rights, consolidated text Polish Journal of Laws of 2020, item 287, as amended.

[11]Directive 2011/83/EU of the European Parliament and of the Council of 25 October 2011 on consumer rights, amending Council Directive 93/13/EEC and Directive 1999/44/EC of the European Parliament and of the Council and repealing Council Directive 85/577/EEC and Directive 97/7/EC of the European Parliament and of the Council Text with EEA relevance, OJ EU 2011 L 304/64.

[12]Directive 2019/770 of the European Parliament and of the Council of 20 May 2019 on certain aspects concerning contracts for the provision of digital content and digital services, OJ EU 2019 L

is very vague, and, therefore, includes a broad and open catalogue of the possible scope of digital content. Recital 19 of the abovementioned Directive, which specifies "Digital content means data produced and supplied in digital form, such as computer programs, applications, games, music, videos or texts, irrespective of whether they are accessed through downloading or streaming, from a tangible medium or through any other means", is helpful in interpreting this provision.[13]

It appears that the meaning of digital content as suggested by the legislators is justified. The digital revolution is characterised by rapid technological and technical development, and, thanks to such a universal, general, and technologically neutral approach to the definition of digital content, this definition does not become outdated.[14]

The definition covers data produced and supplied in digital form "irrespective of whether they are accessed through downloading or streaming, from a tangible medium or through any other means". Therefore, the category of digital content will also include data in other forms, which will then be digitised and delivered in digital form.[15]

Seemingly, the Polish legislators approached the issue of digital content in a slightly different way in Article 2(29a) of the Act on Payment Services of 19 August 2011,[16] stipulating that this term should be understood as "goods or services produced and supplied or rendered in digital form, which may be used or enjoyed exclusively by means of a technical device, excluding the use and consumption of physical goods or services". The legislators have thus explicitly described the scope of digital content as including goods and services. However, the discrepancies in terminology which arise from the interpretation of the concept of digital content

136/1. The proposal for the directive originally contained a different definition, according to which digital content was considered to be: "(a) data produced and supplied in digital form (e.g. video, audio, application, digital games, other software; (b) a service allowing the creation, processing or storage in digital form of data provided by the consumer; (c) a service allowing the sharing of data and interaction with data in digital form, if those data are provided by other users of the service", COM(2015) 634 final.

[13]A slightly different definition of digital content is formulated in the Proposal for a Regulation of the European Parliament and of the Council on a Common European Sales Law. "Digital content means data which are produced and supplied in digital form, whether or not according to the buyer's specifications, including video, audio, picture or written digital content, digital games, software and digital content which makes it possible to personalise existing hardware or software; it excludes: (i) financial services, including online banking services; (ii) legal or financial advice provided in electronic form; (iii) electronic healthcare services; (iv) electronic communications services and networks, and associated facilities and services; (v) gambling; (vi) the creation of new digital content and the amendment of existing digital content by consumers or any other interaction with the creations of other users;", COM (2011) 635: Proposal for a Regulation of the European Parliament and of the Council on a *Common European Sales Law*, https://eur-lex.europa.eu/procedure/PL/2011_284. Accessed 12 December 2020.

[14]See Kaczmarek-Templin (2015), p. 96.

[15]Macierzyńska-Franaszczyk (2018), p. 133.

[16]Act of 19 August 2011 on Payment Services, consolidated text, Polish Journal of Laws of 2020, item 794, as amended. There is no obligation to filter content... or is there?

contained in the Act on Consumer Rights and the Act on Payment Services do not concern the very essence of digital content, but affect the nature of a contract the subject of which is digital content.[17]

Digital content is data produced and delivered in digital form. The term "data" usually means everything which is or can be processed, either mentally or by a computer, and is transmitted to the recipient's consciousness in the form of a message.[18] We use specific means to obtain information from data. In the case of digital content, information is obtained through the use of appropriate hardware and software, examples of which include material in the form of music files, photographs, videos, e-books, or apps.[19] In general, data must meet two conditions in order to be referred to as digital content—it must be produced and delivered in digital form, but the production does not have to mean original production—and the original form may be analog which has been digitised.[20] As far as supply is concerned, the term should be understood as "transmission by electronic means – either wired or wireless, and reception by means of devices facilitating their processing, storage, and reproduction".[21]

On the basis of recital 19 of the E-Commerce Directive, two types of digital content can be distinguished, i.e. data received on a tangible medium, or received through any other means. This distinction is pertinent for determining the legal nature of contracts for the supply of digital content, since, according to recital 12 of the Digital Content Directive, "This Directive should also not determine the legal nature of contracts for the supply of digital content or a digital service, and the question of whether such contracts constitute, for instance, a sales, service, rental or sui generis contract, should be left to national law". More importantly, however, the provisions of the Digital Content Directive will apply, notwithstanding the medium used to transmit or make available a digital content or service. This means that where digital content is received on a tangible medium used exclusively for the supply of digital content, the provisions of the Directive apply to both the medium, provided that it functions only for the supply of digital content, and the content recorded on it (Article 3(3). Digital content contained in goods or interconnected with them is excluded from the scope of the Directive. Here, the EU legislators have introduced a category of "goods with digital elements", such as smart phones, which contain pre-installed applications, and included them in the ambit of Directive 2019/771.[22]

The legal definition of a tangible medium is contained in Article 2(4) of the Act on Consumer Rights. On the basis of Article 2(4) of the Act on Consumer Rights,

---

[17]For more details see Macierzyńska-Franaszczyk (2018), pp. 133–134.

[18]See Grabowski and Zając (2009), p. 111.

[19]Chałubińska-Jentkiewicz (2019), p. 148.

[20]Dziomdziora (2014), p. 33.

[21]Dziomdziora (2014), p. 33.

[22]Directive 2019/771 of the European Parliament and of the Council of 20 May 2019 concerning contracts for the sale of goods, amending Regulation (EU) 2017/2394 and Directive 2009/22/EC, and repealing Directive 1999/44/EC, OJ EU 2019 L 136/28.

> Any material or tool which enables a consumer or trader to store information addressed personally to him or her in a way which allows future access to the information for a period of time adequate for the purposes for which the information is intended, and which allows the unchanged reproduction of the information stored, should be regarded as a tangible medium.

A similar definition exists under the Digital Content Directive, except that instead of "material or tool", the EU legislators have used the term "instrument". (Article 2 (13)). However, in the Digital Content Directive itself, the EU legislators introduced yet another term, namely "durable medium", which causes some conceptual confusion. The question therefore arises whether "durable medium" and "tangible medium" are identical expressions. When interpreting recital 20 of the Digital Content Directive[23]and recital 23 of the Consumer Rights Directive,[24] it becomes clear that both concepts describe similar categories of media. However, as K. Chałubińska-Jentkiewicz points out, "A tangible medium does not include information stored in broadly defined electronic mail or in cloud tools".[25] Therefore, we cannot consider these concepts to be identical.[26]

Receiving digital content through any other means can include, inter alia, downloading from the network, streaming in the form of access to digital content stored in the cloud, and accessing social media.

When considering matters relating to digital content, the issue described in recital 42 of the Digital Content Directive also requires considering. It stipulates that digital content should be characterised by security, functionality, compatibility, and interoperability. We can find an explanation of the different qualities of digital content in the directive itself, which states in recital 43

> The notion of functionality should be understood to refer to the ways in which digital content or a digital service can be used. For instance, the absence or presence of any technical restrictions such as protection via Digital Rights Management or region coding could have an impact on the ability of the digital content or digital service to perform all its functions having regard to its purpose. The notion of interoperability relates to whether and to what extent digital content or a digital service is able to function with hardware or software that is different from those with which digital content or digital services of the same type are normally used. Successful functioning could include, for instance, the ability of the digital content or digital service to exchange information with such other software or hardware and to use the information exchanged.

In addition, Article 2(10) includes a definition of compatibility, which should be understood to mean the ability to interact with devices and software with which digital content is normally used, without having to be transformed.

---

[23]"... on a tangible medium such as DVDs, CDs, USB flash drives, and memory cards..."

[24]"Such media should include, in particular, paper, USB sticks, CD-ROMs, DVDs, memory cards, or computer hard disks, as well as electronic mail".

[25]Chałubińska-Jentkiewicz (2019), p. 157.

[26]For more details see Kaczmarek-Templin (2014).

3 Entities Providing Services by Electronic Means

In order to decode the notion of an entity providing services by electronical means, the two statutory concepts contained in Article 2(4) and (6), of the PSEMA should be interpreted—electronically supplied services, and the service provider. Such a process will make it possible to identify the subject and the issue in question.

According to the legislators' intent, providing services by electronic means involves the performance of services which must meet all the following conditions: the service must be performed without the parties' being present at the same time, i.e. remotely; the service must be performed by transmitting data at the individual request of the service recipient; the data must be sent and received by means of electronic-processing devices, including digital compression and data storage; and the data must be transmitted, received, or transmitted by means of a telecommunications network within the meaning of the Telecommunications Law of 16 July 2004. It follows from the above that the legislators did not introduce a definition of a service provided by electronic means, but defined it by indicating the elements of the method of its provision.[27]

The lack of the simultaneous presence of both parties means that there is no physical or direct contact between the provider and the recipient in the same location in the performance of the service, which is sent and received by means of electronic devices designed to store or process the data transmitted. As emphasised by legal commentators,

> It is significant that the moment of performance of the service decides, and not the moment of ordering the service (the conclusion of the contract), as in the case of distance contracts within the meaning of Article 6 of the Act on the Protection of Certain Consumer Rights and Liability for Damage Caused by a Dangerous Product of 2 March 2000.[28,29]

An individual request means the provision of a service "at the request" of the recipient, namely at a place and at a time individually chosen by the recipient.[30] Examples include VOD (video-on-demand) services, web browsing, and sending text and image messages. However, this category does not include services consisting of the transmission of data received by an unlimited number of people, such as radio and television broadcasts, because the recipient of the service does not have the possibility to choose the time of providing the service—he or she can only join it.[31]

The legislators did not include a definition of a "device for the electronic processing and storage of data", which can give rise to some interpretation problems

---

[27]Świerczyński (2009a).

[28]*Act of 2 March 2000 on the Protection of Certain Consumer Rights and Liability for Damage Caused by a Dangerous Product,* Polish Journal of Laws No. 22, item 271, as amended. No longer in force.

[29]Lubasz and Chomiczewski (2011).

[30]Konarski (2004), p. 69.

[31]Świerczyński (2009a).

in practice. In the literature, we might encounter opinions that this term should be understood as

> part of a communication and information system in the form of a telecommunications terminal device within the meaning of the Telecommunications Law. Sending, receiving, processing, and storing data, from a technical point of view, will be effected by means of such a device. This premise is connected with an important feature of a service provided by electronic means, i.e. the absence of a material substrate.[32]

According to Article 2(46) in conjunction with (48) of the Telecommunications Law,[33] telecommunications equipment is any electric or electronic device intended to provide telecommunications, i.e. to transmit signals on a telecommunications network. However, not every use of such equipment will be equivalent to the provision of electronic services, such as ATMs, motorway toll collecting devices, or medical consultations by telephone.[34]

The final requirement is the transmission, receiving, or transmitting data over a telecommunications network, meaning "transmission systems, and switching or routing equipment and other resources, including network elements which are not active, which permit the transmission, reception, or transmission of signals by wire, by radio, by optical or other means using electromagnetic energy, regardless of their type". (Article 2(36) of the Telecommunications Law).

Bearing in mind that the provisions of the PSEMA are a transposition of the regulations contained in the *E-Commerce Directive*, it is worthwhile at this point to refer to the solutions adopted by the European Union. The EU legislators do not use the term included in the Polish legal order. Instead, they introduce the concept of "Information Society services", which, in accordance with Directive 98/34/EC,[35] should be understood to mean any service normally provided for remuneration, at a distance, by electronic means, and at the individual request of a recipient of services. It can be noted that the PSEMA does not refer to the gainful nature of services, which is present in the case of "Information Society services". However, this does not mean that the PSEMA applies to a category of services wider than Directive 2000/31/EC. This gap is filled by Article 2(6) of the PSEMA, which provides a legal definition of a service provider. According to this definition, a service provider may be a natural person, a legal person, or an organisational entity without a legal personality, which provides services electronically, even if it is performing as an incidental, gainful, or professional activity. Legal commentators therefore assume that the term

---

[32]Lubasz and Chomiczewski (2011).

[33]Act of 16 July 2004 Telecommunications Law, consolidated text, Polish Journal of Laws of 2019, item 2460, as amended.

[34]Kot (2001), pp. 47–49.

[35]Directive 98/48/EC of the European Parliament and of the Council of 20 July 1998 amending Directive 98/34/EC laying down a procedure for the provision of information in the field of technical standards and regulations, OJ EC 1998 L 217/8.

"Information Society services" is synonymous with "services provided by electronic means".[36]

An entity does not have to provide a service in an organised and continuous manner to be recognised as a service provider, as described in Article 3 of the Entrepreneurs' Law. Such a solution is supported by the use of the phrase "even if only incidentally", which also makes it possible to classify as a service provider those entities which only incidentally provide services by electronic means.[37]

As M. Świerczewski rightly points out,

> The provision of Article 2(6) of the PSEMA is modelled on Article 2(b) of Directive 2000/31/EC. The term 'usługodawca' is equivalent to the term service provider used in the Directive. In Directive 2000/31/EC, in addition to the concept of service provider, there is also the concept of 'ustanowiony usługodawca' (established provider). The introduction of this category of service providers is important mainly depending on the country-of-origin principle.[38]

Legal commentators distinguish between providers of electronic services. J. Barta and R. Markiewicz differentiate the following categories of entities: administrators/operators of a telecommunications network—telecommunications companies; access providers—entities providing a service to facilitate access to a network without any influence on the content transmitted in the network; original-content providers in the network; content providers—entities whose activities consist of introducing "own" content into the network, which allows downstream users to use this material; and service providers.[39] M. Zieliński distinguishes three categories of service providers: access providers, network providers and intermediary service providers, who transmit, store and make information available on the Internet. It also identifies content providers.[40] The introduction of the categorisation of entities is of great importance in the issue of determining liability for a breach of law in the network, because liability is determined on the basis of the type of activity of entities providing services by electronic means. Furthermore, in some cases there is a convergence of services provided by the same entity, which makes it difficult to assert the rights of third parties.

When interpreting the individual provisions contained in the PSEMA, we can notice that the Polish legislators have also introduced a categorisation of entities which should be understood as entities providing services by electronic means. This list has been included in Articles 12–14 of the PSEMA, on the basis of which we can point to mere conduit service providers; hosting service administrators (host providers), and entities providing caching services. It should be remembered, however, that this is not an exhaustive list, and these are not all the entities which fall under the

---

[36] Konarski (2004), p. 65; Zieliński (2013).

[37] Świerczyński (2009a).

[38] Świerczyński (2009a).

[39] Barta and Markiewicz (1998), pp. 213–215. See more.: Gęsicka (2014), pp. 40–49.

[40] Zieliński (2013), p. 38. A similar distinction is made by P. Litwiński, see Litwiński (2004), pp. 176–178.

definition. The criterion used by the legislators to distinguish the above categories is the possibility to exclude liability in connection with the provision of specific electronic services.

4 The Liability of the Providers of Services by Electronic Means

The type and extent of the liability borne by the providers of services by electronic means is diverse. In the Polish legal system, content providers are fully and directly liable for the infringement of third-party rights on general terms.[41] This is due to the fact that they are the "authors" of the content they post, which will ensure that "in terms of liability, their legal situation does not differ in any way from the status of other legal entities responsible for their own actions".[42] Thus, depending on the nature of the infringement they commit, they will be held criminally, civilly, or administratively liable under the rules of a particular domain of law.

In contrast, the issue of liability has been regulated with regard to so-called intermediary service providers, with which we can include services of: mere conduit, data storage for accelerating data transmission (*catching*) and data storage for sharing (*hosting*). In these cases, the liability of the intermediary for the transmitted digital content may be waived if the statutory requirements of the PSEMA are met. The drawing up of the exclusions has been implemented from *the E-Commerce Directive*, where it is of a horizontal nature, thus eliminating any liability for a breach of law—whether on criminal, civil, or administrative grounds.

5 Mere Conduit

An entity providing services by electronic means, including the transmission in a telecommunications network of data transferred to the recipient of the service, or the provision of access to a telecommunications network, having fulfilled the conditions of Article 12(1) of the PSEMA, is not liable for the digital content transmitted in this manner, or the activities related to it.[43] The transmission in question is a service involving mere conduit of information, i.e. passive participation in data transmission (without involvement in its content, structure, or circle of addressees).

To benefit from the exemption, the provider of a mere conduit service may not initiate the transfer, may not select the recipient of the data, and may not delete or

[41]Chałubińska-Jentkiewicz (2019), pp. 176–178.
[42]Zieliński (2013), p. 38.
[43]Frań-Adamek (2002).

modify the data subject to the transfer.[44] These conditions must be cumulative. Such a construct is modelled on the exclusion of the courier's responsibility for the content of the letters and parcels he or she delivers. In addition, the Polish legislators, in Article 12(2) of the PSEMA, have also extended the exclusion of liability to the automatic and short-term indirect storage of transmitted data, if this action is exclusively aimed at carrying out the transmission, and the data are not stored longer than it is normally necessary to carry out the transmission.

A mere conduit service should be neutral, consisting of a purely technical delivery (with no knowledge of the information being transmitted or stored) and a lack of cooperation with the recipient which would have involved transmitting illegal content.[45]

The Polish legislators have not implemented the solution resulting from Article 12(3) of *the E-Commerce Directive*, which allows for the possibility of imposing an obligation on the provider of mere conduit services, by courts or administrative authorities, to stop or prevent an infringement. However, literature sources state that the absence of an appropriate provision does not eliminate the exclusion of prohibitive claims against service providers.[46]

As a result of technological progress, the providers of mere conduit services have begun to use *deep packet inspection* technology, which provides greater security for data transmission. It also gives the opportunity to monitor data traffic, as well as to personalise advertisements and profile consumers. Polański notes

> The use of DPI technology for marketing purposes by providers of a simple message service may be the basis for waiving the exclusion of liability under Article 12 (...) For in order to be able to attach advertising messages to the content downloaded by the recipient of the service, intermediaries must temporarily change the direction of data transmission, i.e. the recipient of data.[47]

Furthermore, service providers using DPI modify the information contained in the message by attaching an advertising message, which affects its integrity. Therefore, it is not possible to justify such an action with a technical service process in order to improve the effectiveness of the message.

Under copyright law, there is a particular form of evasion of liability for infringing digital content by mere conduit service providers. Article 23^1 of the Copyright Law[48] provides the author's consent is not required for a temporary reproduction, transient or incidental in nature, that has no independent economic significance and

---

[44]Recital 47 of the E-Commerce Directive allows for the possibility of modifying the content which is the subject of a simple communication service, where the modification involves "manipulations of a technical nature which take place in the course of the transmission as they do not alter the integrity of the information contained in the transmission."

[45]See Polański (2020), p. 25.

[46]Lubasz (2013).

[47]Polański (2020), p. 28. See also: Litwiński (2002), p. 12.

[48]Act of 4 February 1994 on Copyright and Related Rights, consolidated text Polish Journal of Laws of 2019, item 1231, as amended.

is an integral and essential part of a technological process whose sole purpose is to facilitate: 1) the transmission of a work in an information and communication system between third parties by an intermediary, or 2) the lawful use of the work.

This provision has been transposed from Directive 2001/29/EC. Accordingly, the possibility of transmitting content infringing copyright and related rights under the mere conduit service is permitted if all the following conditions are met: the act is temporary; it is transient or incidental; it is not economically significant; it is an integral and essential part of a technological process; the purpose of the process is to transmit content through an intermediary between third parties or to allow the lawful use of the work. Legal commentators assume that Article 23^1 of the Copyright Law is a special provision of Article 12 of the PSEMA, and is therefore the only basis for evading liability.[49]

6 Caching

The essence of caching is to "automatically and briefly store on an intermediary server someone else's data, by creating a copy of them, in order for the end user to download it more quickly in the future" (buffering), which reduces the intensity of packet traffic transmitted within the network, which in turn increases network efficiency.[50]

A distinction must be made here between a mere conduit service and a caching service. Mere conduit, like the caching service, is the automatic and short-term indirect storage of transmitted data. It would therefore appear that we are dealing with the same service. The difference is, however, apparent in the purpose of storing data. In the case of caching, it will be to accelerate access to data. In the case of mere conduit, however, the aim is to facilitate data transmission. The difference is also the duration of data storage, which will be shorter in the mere conduit service. The question arises, therefore, as to the temporal scope of the data storage in the caching service. Legal commentators take the position that "no strictly defined storage period for caching data should be introduced and defined by the caching function. In other words, as long as the storage of the data is to facilitate their faster downloading in the future, it must be regarded as caching".[51] The specification of the time of data storage has a significant impact, because a service aimed at storing information for a longer period of time, e.g. a *mirror-caching* service (storing the content of entire websites for a longer period of time), will not be exempted from liability.[52]

[49]Polański (2020), p. 34.

[50]Chomiczewski (2013), Accessed: 18.12.2020.

[51]Ibid. See also Konarski (2004), p. 135; Chomiczewski (2011).

[52]Świerczyński (2009b); cf. Julia-Barcelo (2000), p. 14.

In Article 13(1) of the PSEMA, the legislators state

> No entity transmitting data and providing automatic and short-term indirect storage of such data in order to expedite their retrieval at the request of another party shall be liable for the data stored if 1) it does not modify the data; 2) it uses recognised and customary information technology for the technical parameters for accessing and updating the data, and 3) it does not interfere with the use of recognised and customary information technology for the collection of information on the use of the collected data.

In addition, (2) lays down an obligation for the service provider to delete the data, or to prevent access to the stored data, without delay, when it becomes aware that the data have been deleted from the initial source of transmission, or access to the data has been prevented, or when a court or other competent authority has ordered for the data to be deleted or access to them prevented. The fulfilment of these conditions cumulatively allows the service provider to avoid liability.

The caching service provider should not modify the stored data, as this can affect their integrity.[53] In practice this means that a copy of the data stored on the servers should be consistent with the content of the data on the input server.[54] The legislators also require the service provider to use recognised and customary information technology for this type of activity, specifying the technical parameters for accessing the data. As legal commentators indicate, "The purpose of this provision is to ensure that a website copied and stored on a proxy server is accessible to users on the same terms and to the same extent as the same website on the input server".[55]

An important reason for excluding liability is to remove or prevent access to content where the service provider becomes aware that it has been blocked or removed from the input server. or where an order has been received from a court or administrative authority. The question arises as to what is to be understood by the notion of obtaining information. and whether the service provider is obliged to keep track of the original content which is subject to the caching service. From the content of the provision it seems that any information which reaches the service provider is a message. Furthermore, the interpretation used by the legislators leads to the assumption that an entity providing a caching service has an active obligation to monitor the content which is subject to its service.[56]

7 Hosting

Hosting is one of the most popular services provided in the network. Its essence consists of making the resources of an information and communication system (the virtual memory on the server) available by the service provider to another entity in

[53] Konarski (2004), p. 135.
[54] Chomiczewski (2011).
[55] Chomiczewski (2011).
[56] See Monarcha-Matlak (2008).

order to keep the data stored by it in those resources.[57] Legal commentators distinguish between classic and virtual hosting. The former relates to the storage of websites on a remote server of the service provider in order to make them available to network users. Virtual hosting, on the other hand, consists of making available to the users of a given service the disk space of the provider of a classic hosting service.[58]

In accordance with Article 14(1) of the PSEMA,

> Anyone who, while making available the resources of an information and communication system for the storage of data by a recipient of a service, is not aware of the unlawful nature of the data, or of any activity relating to them, shall not be liable for the data stored, and shall immediately prevent access to the data if he or she receives official notification, or if he or she obtains reliable information on the unlawful nature of the data, or of any activity relating to them.

The legislators have thus limited the liability of the hosting provider to a situation in which the provider had no knowledge of the unlawfulness of the content stored, or of the activities related to it; in other words, as long as it is not aware that users are publishing illegal content through the provider, it cannot be held liable for possible legal liability (civil, criminal, or administrative). This provision corresponds to the general principle contained in Article 15 of the PSEMA, according to which the service provider is not obliged to filter the data transmitted, stored, or made available by it. However, where it acquires knowledge as a result of an official notice or actual knowledge of the illegality of digital content stored on its servers, this disclaimer of liability shall be removed unless it blocks access to it. Official notification is to be understood here as information provided by an authorised official (court, public prosecutor's office, police, public administration authority), in an appropriate (official) form, and with due process. It seems problematic to obtain knowledge about the illegality of data from a source such as "actual knowledge". Legal commentators assume that such information can be obtained by the service provider from third parties or by itself, but in this case it has to check its veracity.[59] To this end, appropriate notification procedures should be developed, in particular as regards the indication of the minimum data necessary for the verification of the notification, not specified in the PSEMA, with the obligation to create them being passed on to the service providers themselves.[60] In its judgment of 18 April 2017 the Court of Appeal in Warsaw ruled

[57]Błaszyk (2018), p. 291.

[58]Polański (2020), pp. 53–54.

[59]See Siwicki (2011). According to the judgment of the Court of Appeal in Warsaw (Case No. VI ACa 1910/16) "Knowledge of the hosting service provider about the illegal nature of Internet users' entries does not necessarily have to come from the persons affected by the incriminated comments. The source of reliable information is legally neutral here, to the extent that such information can also be the result of the own observations of employees or representatives of the web-portal administrator, and the technical means used by him or her".

[60]Gienas (2008), pkt. 2.3.

> The purposive interpretation of Article 14 of the Act on Providing Services by Electronic Means of 2002 indicates that a host provider is not obliged to conduct a detailed investigation to verify whether the information about the unlawful nature of data or activities related to them is reliable. Therefore, a person requesting the prevention of access to the data should supply the host provider with such information on the basis of which the unlawful nature of the data or activities related to it becomes apparent, and leads it to conclude that it has knowledge of the unlawful nature of the data within the meaning of Article 14(1) of the PSEMA.[61]

Such an interpretation was also confirmed by the Court of Appeal in Lublin in the judgment of 18 January 2011, which stated

> The service provider is not obliged to monitor the network; furthermore, it is not obliged to take steps to implement monitoring software. The only situation which undoubtedly leads to the liability of the service provider is its being aware of the infringement, or of the unlawful nature of the infringement.[62]

The notification procedure indicated in Article 14(1) of the PSEMA could be included in the procedure for blocking content referred to as Notice-and-Takedown, adopted in US legislation, where the service provider, on becoming aware of the illegality of the content, must immediately block access to it,[63] but only in respect of the case in which the service provider has become aware of the illegality of the content on the basis of an official notification, as provided for in Article 14(2) of the PSEMA. In addition, in such a situation, the service provider shall not be liable for any failure to perform or for the inadequate performance of an obligation between it and the content provider.[64] However, the Polish legislators have gone beyond the American model by introducing, in a parallel manner, the Stay-and-Stay procedure, the essence of which is contained in Article 14(3) of the PSEMA, according to which the service provider is obliged to immediately notify the recipient of the service of its intention to prevent access to illegal content posted by it.[65] Fulfilling this obligation removes its liability towards the recipient of the service for damage resulting from preventing access to the data.

The exclusions of liability in Article 14(1) to (3) of the PSEMA do not apply if the provider has taken control of the recipient of the service, that is to say, if the provider of the illegal content acts under the authorisation or supervision of the provider.

When an entity providing services by electronic means cannot invoke the exclusions set out in the PSEMA, the general principles of liability contained in particular domains of law shall apply to it. In the case of civil law, as noted by M. Zieliński, "The liability of intermediary service providers is possible on the basis of many tort regulations, based on both the fault and the risk principles". In view of the subsidiary nature of ISP activity, however, with regard to the storage or transmission of

---

[61]Case file No. I ACa 55/16, LEX No. 2317742.

[62]Case file No. I ACa 544/10, LEX No. 736495.

[63]See *Digital Milllennium Copyright Act*, section 512 (C).

[64]Janowski (2008).

[65]Cf. Polański (2020), p. 81.

information on behalf of users of their services, their liability as direct perpetrators should always be excluded, on the basis of Article 415 of the Civil Code. Particular importance in this context should be attached to the interpretation of the liability for aiding within the meaning of Article 422 of the Civil Code.[66] In the case of the infringement of personal rights by statements by anonymous internet users placed on Internet portals, the liability of the administrator (service provider) should be considered on the basis of Article 24 § 1 of the Civil Code. Pursuant to the judgment of the Court of Appeal in Warsaw of 29 November 2018,

> The provision of Article 24 § 1 of the Civil Code does not limit its application to direct infringers of personal rights, but covers all the actions of a specific entity which in any way cause or contribute to the infringement of the injured party's personal rights, or to the aggravation of the infringement of those rights, previously committed by other entities.[67]

As far as the liability of service providers under copyright law is concerned, the Court of Appeal in Kraków ruled on this on 18 September 2017. In accordance with the operative part of the judgment,

> An entity participating in the implementation of transfers infringing property copyrights is a co-perpetrator, and co-infringer of other persons' rights to the works. Thus, the position stating that the manner in which the entity operates makes it unable to be treated as an entity subject to Article 14 of the Act on Providing Services by Electronic Means, but it is simply an entity which also illegally distributes works protected by copyright, is fully justified. If so, the entity cannot invoke Articles 14 and 15 of the Act on Providing Services by Electronic Means, and Article 79 of the Act on Providing Services by Electronic Means should be applied to accept its responsibility.[68,69]

8 There Is No Obligation to Filter Content... Or Is There?

The legislators, in Article 15 of the PSEMA, did not impose a general obligation on the providers of mere conduit, caching or hosting services to check the data transmitted, stored, or made available by them. As the Court of Appeal in Warsaw emphasised in one of its rulings,

> This excludes the possibility of imposing general data monitoring obligations on these service providers. The assessment that the standard of behaviour and professionalism requires the controller to filter and remove any statements which violate the law, or which might violate the law in an objective manner, without prior notice, cannot be accepted.[70]

Thus, the Polish Act lacks the full implementation of the provision contained in Article 15(1) of the E-Commerce Directive, which additionally provides for the lack of a general obligation to actively seek the facts and circumstances indicating an

[66]Zieliński (2013).

[67]Case file No. I ACa 974/17, LEX No. 2691182.

[68]Case file No. I ACa 1494/15, LEX No. 2354397.

[69]Copyright and Related Rights Act.

[70]Case file No. I ACa 1247/15, LEX No. 2138249.

illegal activity. However, the literature stresses that, despite the lack of the above obligation, the understanding of the provision of Article 15 of the PSEMA should be read in the spirit of the Directive.[71]

However, this does not mean a total ban on filtering content, as recital 47 of the directive provides for the possibility of making it compulsory for service providers to filter certain types of content. The possibility of doing so is left to individual Member States to consider. The Polish legislators did not provide for such a possibility in the PSEMA.

In spite of the fact that the E-Commerce Directive, and thus the PSEMA, did not impose a general obligation on service providers to check content, the European Union tried to push through the filtering obligation in the Directive of the European Parliament and of the Council on copyright in the digital single market.[72] Article 13 of the Directive provided for this.

> Information society service providers that store and provide to the public access to large amounts of works or other subject-matter uploaded by their users shall, in cooperation with rightholders, take measures to ensure the functioning of agreements concluded with rightholders for the use of their works or other subject-matter or to prevent the availability on their services of works or other subject-matter identified by rightholders through the cooperation with the service providers. Those measures, such as the use of effective content recognition technologies, shall be appropriate and proportionate. The service providers shall provide rightholders with adequate information on the functioning and the deployment of the measures, as well as, when relevant, adequate reporting on the recognition and use of the works and other subject-matter.

As a result of protests by electronic-service providers and the public, the European Parliament did not adopt the Directive as proposed. However, this did not mean that work on the regulation of a general obligation to filter content in terms of copyright was stopped. Such an obligation was adopted indirectly in Article 17 of the Directive on copyright and related rights in the digital single market.[73] Service providers who produce a large number of works protected by copyright available for profit have been obliged to conclude licence agreements with copyright holders. Under the provisions of the Directive, they are legally liable if they make available content published by users for which they have not paid the authors, unless they show that they have made every effort to obtain authorisation; that they have made efforts to block access to unlawful content; and that they have acted promptly on receipt of the notification. Here, the legislators have introduced an economic criterion for service providers and restrictions on their liability. New providers of online content services whose services have been available to the public in the Union for less than three years. and whose annual turnover does not exceed EUR 10 million,

---

[71]Gęsicka (2014).

[72]Proposal for a directive of the European Parliament and of the Council on copyright in the Digital Single Market, COM(2016) 593 final 2016/0280 (COD).

[73]Directive 2019/790 of the European Parliament and of the Council of 17 April 2019 on copyright and related rights in the Digital Single Market and amending Directives 96/9/EC and 2001/29/EC OJ EU 2019 L 130/92.

may waive their liability if they have made every effort to obtain authorisation and have acted promptly after receiving a relevant reasoned objection in order to block access to the protected works and subject matter covered by the objection, or to remove those works and subject matter from their websites (Article 17(6)).

The EU legislators also imposed an obligation on Member States to enact legislation stipulating

> online content-sharing service providers put in place an effective and expeditious complaint and redress mechanism that is available to users of their services in the event of disputes over the disabling of access to, or the removal of, works or other subject matter uploaded by them.

As legal commentators emphasise,

> Although the Directive as such does not impose a general obligation of supervision on the owner of the platform in question, it is currently still difficult to determine how they will be able to discharge their responsibility without implementing such a control-and-supervision system, based on intelligent technology for identifying and recognising content.[74]

The directive also provides for exemptions from the service provider's liability for user-generated content in online content services. The restrictions concern quotations, criticism, review, and the use of illegal content for the purposes of caricature, parody, or pastiche (Article 17(7)).

Poland has not yet implemented the Directive's provisions in its national legal system.[75]

References

Barta J, Markiewicz R (1998) Internet a prawo. Cracow

Błaszyk C (2018) Prowadzenie działalności gospodarczej w cyberprzestrzeni. In: Banasiński C (ed) Cyberbezpieczeństwo. Zarys wykładu, Warsaw

Bzózka P (2019) Prawo autorskie na jednolitym rynku cyfrowym. Największe wątpliwości po wejściu w życie unijnej dyrektywy. 'Dziennik Gazeta Prawna' https://serwisy.gazetaprawna.pl/prawo-autorskie/artykuly/1418336,dyrektywa-o-prawach-autorskich-watpliwosci.html. Accessed 10 Oct 2020

Chałubińska-Jentkiewicz K (2019) Cyberodpowiedzialność. Toruń

Chałubińska-Jentkiewicz K, Karpiuk M (2015) Prawo nowych technologii. Wybrane zagadnienia. LEX/el

Chomiczewski W (2011) Artykuł 13 ustawy o świadczeniu usług drogą elektroniczną. In: Chomiczewski W, Klafkowska-Waśniowska K, Lubasz D et al (eds) Świadczenie usług drogą elektroniczną oraz dostęp warunkowy. Komentarz do ustaw. Wydawnictwo Prawnicze LexisNexis

---

[74] Bzózka (2019).

[75] Poland has lodged a complaint with the Court of Justice of the European Union concerning the directive, justifying its complaint with controversy over Article 17, which may threaten freedom of expression on the Internet and is contrary to EU values.

Chomiczewski W (2013) Pojęcie caching providera i zasady jego odpowiedzialności za przechowywane dane. https://portalprawait.com/entry/pojecie-caching-providera-i-zasady-jego-odpowiedzialnosci-za-przechowywane-dane/. Accessed 10 Oct 2020

Dziomdziora WZ (2014) Umowy dotyczące treści cyfrowych niezapisanych na nośniku materialnym w świetle ustawy o prawach konsumenta. Internetowy Kwartalnik Antymonopolowy i Regulacyjny 8

Frań-Adamek A (2002) Article 12. [in] Świadczenie usług drogą elektroniczną. Komentarz. Sopot, LEX/el

Gęsicka DK (2014) Wyłączenie odpowiedzialności cywilnoprawnej dostawców usług sieciowych za treści użytkowników. LEX/el

Gienas K (2008) Odpowiedzialność podmiotów świadczących usługi w internecie w prawie polskim. In: Systemy Digital Rights Management w świetle prawa autorskiego. Cracow

Golka M (2005) Czym jest społeczeństwo informacyjne. Ruch prawniczy, ekonomiczny i socjologiczny 4(67)

Grabowski M, Zając A (2009) Dane, informacja, wiedza-próba definicji. Zeszyty Naukowe Uniwersytetu Ekonomicznego w Krakowie 798

Janowski J (2008) Kontrakty elektroniczne w obrocie prawnym. Warszawa, LEX/el

Julia-Barcelo R (2000) On-line intermediary liability issues: comparing EU and U.S. legal frameworks. Electronic Commerce Legal Issues Platform

Kaczmarek-Templin B (2014) Komentarz do art. 2. In: Kaczmarek-Templin B, Stec P, Szostek D (eds) Ustawa o prawach konsumenta. Kodeks cywilny (wyciąg). Komentarz, Warsaw

Kaczmarek-Templin B (2015) Specyfika umów o dostarczanie treści cyfrowych w świetle ustawy o prawach konsumenta. In: Karczewska D, Namysłowska M, Skoczny T (eds) Ustawa o prawach konsumenta, Warsaw

Konarski X (2004) Komentarz do ustawy o świadczeniu usług drogą elektroniczną. Warsaw

Kot D (2001) Dyrektywa Unii Europejskiej o handlu elektronicznym i jej implikacje dla prawa cywilnego. Kwartalnik Prawa Prywatnego 1

Litwiński P (2002) Zasady odpowiedzialności pośredników w dostarczaniu informacji w Internecie (Intermediary Service Providers - ISP). Gospodarka elektroniczna - dodatek do MoP 24

Litwiński P (2004) Podobnego rozróżnienia dokonuje P. Litwiński, see. P. Litwiński, Świadczenie usług drogą elektroniczną. In: Podrecki P (ed) Prawo Internetu, Warsaw

Lubasz D (2013) Handel elektroniczny. Bariery prawne. Wydawnictwo Prawnicze. LexisNexis, LEX/el

Lubasz D, Chomiczewski W(2011) Artykuł 2 ustawy o świadczeniu usług drogą elektroniczną. In: Chomiczewski W, Klafkowska-Waśniowska K, Lubasz D et al (eds) Świadczenie usług drogąelektroniczną oraz dostęp warunkowy. Komentarz do ustaw. Wydawnictwo Prawnicze LexisNexis, LEX/el

Macierzyńska-Franaszczyk E (2018) Digital content – a definition in EU and national legal regulations. Internet Antitrust and Regulatory Quarterly 6

Monarcha-Matlak A (2008) Obowiązki administracji w komunikacji elektronicznej. Oficyna, LEX/el

Polański P (2020) Odpowiedzialność prawna za treści rozpowszechniane w Internecie. Warsaw: Centrum Europejskie Natolin

Siwicki M (2011) Nielegalna i szkodliwa treść w Internecie. Aspekty prawnokarne. Warsaw, LEX/el

Świerczyński M (2009a) In: Gołaczyński J, Kowalik-Bańczyk K, Majchrowska A, Świerczyński M, Ustawa o świadczeniu usług drogą elektroniczną. Komentarz. Oficyna, LEX/el

Świerczyński M (2009b) Article 13. In: Gołaczyński J (ed) Ustawa o świadczeniu usług drogą elektroniczną. Komentarz. Oficyna, LEX/el

Zieliński M (2013) Odpowiedzialność deliktowa pośredniczących dostawców internetowych. Analiza prawno porównawcza, Warsaw

Paweł Zając PhD, doctor of law sciences; adjunct at the Law History and Theory Department at the War Studies University. He gained his professional experience working as a coordinator of the Cybersecurity Studies Center, Legal Analyzes and Expertise Center "de Virion", and an expert at a law firm. He participated in the drafting and giving opinions on normative acts. In his research work, he dealt with issues related to i-voting in relation to respecting the principle of secret elections. Currently, he conducts research in the field of broadly understood military law in the medical and ethical aspect. Author of publications in the field of new technologies law, state security in the context of constitutional value and medical law.

Part IV
Combating Cybercrime as a Special Task in the Area of Cybersecurity

Cybercrime and Cyberterrorism in Polish Law

Filip Radoniewicz

Abstract The aim of the paper is to analyze the provisions criminalizing the phenomenon of "computer crimes" ("cybercrimes") in the strict sense, i.e. acts in which a computer or network is the target of a crime ("a victim"). The paper consists of two parts—the main part in which analysis of articles 267-269c of the Penal Code of 1997 (Chapter XXXIII, entitled "Offenses against the protection of information")—in which the Polish legislator defined these offenses—is carried out. The second part refers to the "cyberterrorist offense" which is an "ordinary" computer crime carried out with a "terrorist purpose".

1 Computer Crimes in the Penal Code of 1997

The Polish regulation of prohibited acts set out in Directive 2013/40 is included in Chapter XXXIII of the Penal Code titled "Crimes Against the Protection of Information", in the provisions of Articles 267-269c. It owes its present form to three amendments: the first one, introduced by way of the Act of the 18th of March 2004 Amending the following Acts: the Penal Code, the Criminal Procedure Code, and the Code of Minor Offences,[1] intended to adapt Polish regulations to the provisions of the aforesaid Convention on Cybercrime;[2] the second one, introduced by way of the Act of the 24th of October 2008 Amending the Penal Code and Certain Other

[1]Act of 18 March 2004 on amending the Penal Code, the Code of Criminal Proceedings and the Code of Offences, Polish Journal of Laws No. 69, item 626.

[2]Convention on Cybercrime of the Council of Europe of 23 November 2001. Polish Journal of Laws of 2015, item 728.

F. Radoniewicz (✉)
Akademickie Centrum Polityki Cyberbezpieczeństwa/Academic Center for Cybersecurity Policy, Akademia Sztuki Wojennej w Warszawie/War Studies University in Warsaw, Warsaw, Poland
e-mail: filip.radoniewicz@radoniewicz.eu

K. Chałubińska-Jentkiewicz et al. (eds.), *Cybersecurity in Poland*,
https://doi.org/10.1007/978-3-030-78551-2_24

Acts,[3] intended to implement Framework Decision 2005/222/JHA on attacks against information systems;[4] and the third one, introduced by way of the Act of the 23rd of March 2017 Amending the Penal Code and Certain Other Acts,[5] the main purpose of which was to implement Directive 2014/42/EU of the 3rd of April 2014 on the freezing and confiscation of instruments and proceeds of crime in the European Union[6] and, "partially" (as formulated in the Act), Directive 2013/40 on attacks against information systems and replacing Council Framework Decision 2005/222/JHA.[7]

Article 267(1) of the PC provides for penal responsibility of the offender for gaining unauthorised access to information[8] not intended for him/her. It penalises three acts, which constitute attacks on the security of information systems and the data processed in those systems.

First, connecting to a telecommunications network[9] or, in other words, the offender's obtaining physical access to that network, e.g. by connecting to the server

[3] Act of 24 October 2008 Amending the Penal Code and Certain Other Acts Polish Journal of Laws No. 214, item. 1344.

[4] Council Framework Decision 2005/222/JHA of 24 February 2005 on attacks against information systems, OJ EU 2005 L 69/67.

[5] Act of 23 March 2017 Amending the Penal Code and Certain Other Acts Polish Journal of Laws of 2017, item 768.

[6] Directive 2014/42/EU of the European Parliament and of the Council of 3 April 2014 on the freezing and confiscation of instrumentalities and proceeds of crime in the European Union, OJ EU 2014 L 127/39.

[7] Directive 2013/40/EU of the European Parliament and of the Council of 12 August 2013 on attacks against information systems and replacing Council Framework Dec22/222/JHA, OJ EU 2013 L 218/8.

[8] From the very beginning, it is necessary to take note of the fact that the instruments of international and EU law concerned with the security of computer networks, in order to specify the object of protection, use the term "computer data", and not "information". The Polish legislator, in principle, identifies the concept of information with the concept of data despite the obvious differences between these two. In the light of Article 2(b) of Directive 2014/30, "computer data" is to be understood as "a representation of facts, information or concepts in a form suitable for processing in an information system, including a programme suitable for causing an information system to perform a function". The Convention on Cybercrime adopted a similar definition. With regard to the above, computer data is a carrier (medium) of information, facts and concepts, which, only after they are converted to the form of computer data, are readable by a computer (or information) system. Computer programs fall within the scope of that concept as well. The distinction between "computer data" and "information" is important from a legal standpoint, for one may take possession of computer data; however, he/she may not be able to make of use of the information contained in it, not knowing the algorithm used to encode it, for example. The destruction of data does not always mean the destruction of information and, conversely, the seizure of data does not have to mean theft of information. Cf. Adamski (2000), p. 37 et seq.

[9] According to the definition formulated in Article 2(35) of the Act of Telecommunications Law a telecommunications network means "transmission systems, and commutation or redirecting devices, as well as other resources, such as inactive network elements, enabling the sending, reception or transmission of signals through wires, radio waves, optical waves or other means using electromagnetic energy, regardless of their kind". These are, for instance, satellite networks,

via the network and obtaining access to the data stored in that server (actions including the interception of data during transmission are penalised by Article 267 (3) of the PC).

Second, obtaining access to information by breaking electronic, magnetic, computer or any other special protection. It follows that only the information, which is stored in computer systems, and which has been protected against unauthorised access by its holder, is protected. Electronic, magnetic or computer protection is to be understood as "any forms of hindering access to information, the breaking of which requires expert knowledge or a special device or code",[10] whereas "other special protection" is a complementary category, which includes means that cannot be classified with any of the kinds provided for in the applicable regulation, and the removal of which causes difficulties for the offender no lesser than the breaking of electronic, magnetic or computer protection.[11] Computer data can be protected either directly, e.g. by encoding or securing access with a password, or indirectly, as part of the overall protection of a computer system itself, by means of firewalls, break detection systems or authentication procedures. "Security breach" is the direct interference of the offender with the protection mechanism, which leads to the loss of its protective function and does not have to involve its removal.[12] In the doctrine, it is indicated that it must be actual and active at the time of committing the act. Otherwise, the statutory criteria of a crime are not met.[13]

Third, omitting the above-mentioned protection and gaining access to information due to that omission. One should bear in mind that the breaching of protection is merely one of the many techniques (and not the most popular one) used by hackers to penetrate computer systems. The other techniques are omitting protection, and they consist of misleading people (the so-called social engineering, which are, for instance, wheedling passwords out of people), misleading a system (e.g. the so-called IP spoofing, i.e. the creation of false addresses, directed at manipulating the source from which the data comes), or taking advantage of gaps (errors) in, or

permanent networks relying on the commutation of connections (circuit switching, in other words, commutation of channels or circuits, consists in establishing, on demand, a "permanent" dedicated connection between two or more network points for their exclusive use for the duration of the communication session) and the commutation of packets (packet switching—a method of data transmission which consists in grouping data into packets, each of which may reach its destination via a different route; the process of transferring packets is called routing and takes place between several network nodes—routers), cable television networks or power networks which enable the transmission of signals. Commutation devices are devices used for circuit switching (e.g. switchboards), whereas redirecting devices are devices used for packet switching (mainly routers). Commutation or redirection devices are not always required for signal transmission. There are networks that do not contain them. Cf. Krasuski (2015), Commentary on Art. 2(35); Piątek (2019), Commentary on Art. 2(35); Radoniewicz (2016), pp. 278–282.

[10]Wróbel and Zając (2017) Commentary on Art. 267 PC.

[11]Kardas (2000), p. 71.

[12]Kardas (2000), pp. 71–72; Kozłowska-Kalisz (2020) Commentary on Art. 267 PC; Wróbel and Zając (2017) Commentary on Art. 267 PC.

[13]Cf. Bukowski (2006), pp. 142–143; Kardas (2000), p. 64.

vulnerabilities of, operating systems, applications or protocols (sets of rules, which specify the communication processes responsible for identifying computers in a network, among other things), using programmes called exploits.[14]

In Article 267(2) of the PC, the legislator penalises unauthorised access to the whole or part of an information system.[15] The authors of the 2008 amendment, which introduced the provision, pointed out rightly, in the justification, that the purpose of obtaining unauthorised access to a system may be not only obtaining access to information contained in such computer data, but may also serve, to some extent, as a first step to other activities such as, using the example taken from the justification, installing on a computer a programme enabling one to take control over the computer, in order to create a botnet[16] by means of which the offender intends to launch a dDoS attack.[17] That provision is applied when the offender's purpose, as he

---

[14]See more Radoniewicz (2021).

[15]The interpretation of the concept, basically from the very moment it appeared in the Penal Code, created problems (cf. Radoniewicz 2016, pp. 275–278; Siwicki 2013), which intensified after Poland ratified the Convention on Cybercrime. Since Article 267(2) of the PC was added by way of the 2008 amendment, connected with the implementation of Framework Decision 2005/222, it would be advisable to construe the term according to the definition set out in the Act and in Directive 2013/40, which replaces it, namely, both as a single device that processes computer data and a set of such devices, in other words, a network (see earlier observations). A lot of errors were made in the translation of the Convention on Cybercrime. One of them was translating the term *"computer system"* as "system informatyczny" [information system]. As mentioned earlier, the substantive scope of the concept of a computer system, as defined in the Convention, is narrower than the one of an "information system" as applied in Directive 2013/40. That calls into question the scope of the concept of the information system in view of the Penal Code. It is important to stress that, although the Convention on Cybercrime, upon its ratification, became part of the legal order, the definition of an "information system" (computer system) may not be applied directly, owing to the problems discussed. The existing confusion is intensified by the fact that, in the translation of the definition of computer data in Article 2(b) of the Convention (*computer data* translated as "dane informatyczne" [information data]), the translator used the concept of a computer system ("computer data means a representation of facts, information or concepts in a form suitable for processing in a computer system, including a programme suitable for causing an information system to perform a function"). In addition, the term "computer system" was used in the translation of the Additional Protocol to the Convention on Cybercrime, concerning the criminalisation of acts of a racist and xenophobic nature committed through computer systems of 28 January 2003 (Polish Journal of Laws of 2015, item 2015, item 730). Cf. Radoniewicz (2019a), pp. 42–47; Radoniewicz (2016), pp. 244–249, 275–285.

[16]Botnets, which are networks of computers on which the offender (without the users' knowledge) installed special programmes—the so-called zombies (hence the infected computers are called "zombie computers"), which are booted up under remote direction at a certain moment, e.g. in order to launch a dDoS attack. Since it is possible to use a tremendous number of computers (even several thousand, spread all over the world), the actual source of the attack remains unknown. At present, in the Internet, one may obtain both programmes designed to launch DoS attacks and "ready-to-use" botnets to launch dDoS attacks. In addition, botnets can be used, among other things, to send spam (unwanted e-mail messages). Cf. Adamski (2013), pp. 68–69.

[17]DoS attacks (denial-of-service attacks) usually aim at impairing the operation of a network (and blocking the network). In principle, one can assume that they consist in generating huge network traffic leading to the hung-up of a server, or to an overload of a router or network devices. They may

has gained unauthorised access, is to commit a "common" crime (the offender's conduct may involve, for instance, accessing another user's account on an Internet auction site in order to commit fraud) or when he/she was guided by some other motives such as verifying his/her own skills or earning respect in the "hacker circles". Therefore, the objective, which the offender was to achieve or the motive by which he/she was guided are irrelevant to the essence of the crime defined in Article 267(2) of the PC.[18]

Access to the whole or part of an information system should be understood as having an opportunity to use its resources, which basically means the data processed by it. This, however, is not tantamount to access to information since the data may be, for instance, either encoded or entirely incomprehensible to the offender.

Within the meaning of this provision, unauthorised access should be understood as access without an authorisation or access, which exceeds the limits of such an authorisation.

The solution adopted by the legislator in Article 267(2) of the PC received justified criticism for three basic reasons. First of all, it was a word-for-word copy of Article 2 of Framework Decision 2005/222 ("Each Member State shall take the necessary measures to ensure that the intentional access without right to the whole or any part of an information system is punishable as a criminal offence, at least for cases which are not minor"). It should be stressed that framework decisions were aimed to harmonise legal provisions of Member States. They set out objectives to be achieved, whereas Member States were free to choose the forms and methods to achieve them. Therefore, the provisions formulated in the objectives are very general. The framework decisions, which harmonise substantive criminal law, are not suitable for literal transposition. Second, Article 267(2) of the PC is extremely laden with content. The statutory criteria of the act defined in the article are met by the offender who "obtains unlawful access" to data because that is what obtaining access to a system in principle means, and in order to be held criminally responsible, he/she does not have to breach protection. The sole condition is access that is unauthorised. It should be assumed that the provision set out in Article 267(2) of the PC is applicable to cases, in which the main element of the offender's act was gaining access to an information system, and not obtaining access to information. This is the case, for instance, when one breaks into a computer in order to insert a bot. Because of the broad subjective scope of Article 267(2) of the PC, also some of the acts penalised by Article 267(3) of the PC, defined as computer eavesdropping, may be potentially qualified also under Article 267(2) of the PC. Obtaining unauthorised access to a network is tantamount to gaining access to the data that is transferred over that network; the offender, therefore, meets the statutory criteria of a prohibited act under Article 267(3) of the PC.

---

be also targeted at specific computers, disabling their communication with the server. Their "enhanced" versions are dDoS attacks (distributed denial-of-service attacks), which make use of botnets.

[18]See more Radoniewicz (2021).

Third, the only condition to be met in order to press charges against the offender for breaching Article 267(2) of the PC is the offender's gaining access without an authorisation. The issue of access rights to the resources of an information system is, in most cases, regulated by "soft law", the internal rules and regulations of a network. The granting of access rights for users and the scope of such rights are within the discretion of the system administrator. Such reference to non-legal norms is dangerous and difficult to reconcile with the principle of the specificity of a crime.[19]

The last amendment added provision 269c, pursuant to which one is not subject to punishment for the crime set out Article 267(2) or Article 269a, for acting exclusively for the purpose of protecting an information system, an ICT system or an ICT network, or for developing a method for such protection, and has immediately informed the holder of that system or network of the revealed threats, and his/her actions did not violate public or private interests, or did not do any damage.

The tool for combating the so-called computer eavesdropping[20] is the already mentioned Article 267(3) of the PC, which penalises the installation or use of, in order to obtain information,[21] a listening, visual or other device or software.

It should be stressed that it penalises only the interception of computer data during its transmission. If the offender obtains data stored, for instance, on a server or private computer, this act should be qualified under Article 267(1) or Article 267 (2) of the PC. The unlawfulness of the offender's conduct is obviously derogated if the conduct that meets the statutory criteria of a crime is connected with lawful operations of law enforcement authorities (i.e. it follows from the relevant legal provisions[22]).[23]

Article 268(2) of the PC penalises any unauthorised interference with computer data that consists in destroying, damaging, deleting or altering significant

---

[19]Cf. Adamski (2007), pp. 7–8; Radoniewicz (2016), pp. 301–303.

[20]Computer eavesdropping is a colloquial term for the surveillance of information systems. It is often called, not entirely correctly, *sniffing* which is only one of its techniques. There are two types of computer eavesdropping: the passive one, when the offender only reads the information being accessed, and the active one, when the offender modifies the data that is transmitted, e.g. by redirecting the transmission to somewhere else in the network.

[21]It is worth noting that Directive 2013/40 does not stipulate that the offender committing an act of illegal interception of data must satisfy any other premises in order for penal responsibility to be imposed—e.g. "dishonest" intent or acting for a specific purpose ("Member States shall take the necessary measures to ensure that intercepting, by technical means, non-public transmissions of computer data to, from or within an information system, including electromagnetic emissions from an information system carrying such computer data, intentionally and without right, is punishable as a criminal offence, at least for cases which are not minor"—Article 6 of Directive 2013/40).

[22]First of all, one should indicate the provisions of the Criminal Procedure Code, the Act of 6 April 1990 on the Police Service (Consolidated text, Polish Journal of Laws of 2020 item 360, as amended), the Act of 24 May 2002 on the Internal Security Agency and the Foreign Intelligence Agency (Consolidated text, Polish Journal of Laws of 2020 item 27, as amended).

[23]See more Radoniewicz (2017a), pp. 181–196.

information on a computer data carrier,[24] and in limiting its accessibility for an authorised person[25] by foiling or hindering, in any other manner, the familiarisation with such information recorded on such a computer data carrier.

The information that is the object of the offender's act must be "significant", especially in the objective sense (because of its content, weight and significance[26]), taking into consideration the interests of an authorised person to familiarise him or herself with that information[27] for the purpose that was intended or supposed to have been intended.[28]

As the protection concerns "information recorded on an electronic data carrier", Article 268(2) of the PC is not applicable to any cases where the familiarisation with such information is hindered by disturbances in the network functioning (in this case, the offender's conduct should be qualified under Article 268a (1) or (2), or Article 269a of the PC).

In this case, the aggravated crime corresponds to the act described in Article 268 (2) of the PC, with substantial property damage caused by the offender being considered an element of that offence.

The first part of Article 268a (1) of the PC penalises acts such as destruction, modification of data, and hindering access to it. The second part, in turn, penalises acts such as disturbing (in other words, hindering the operation of an information system) or preventing the processing, storing or transferring of computer data. The statement refers to any acts which impinge on these processes, and which lead to any irregularities in, or slowdown of, these processes, as well as the distortion or modification of the computer data that is processed, transferred or stored.[29]

In this case, the aggravated crime corresponds to the act described in Article 268a (2) of the PC, with the substantial property damage caused by the offender being considered an element of that offence.

The essence of the so-called computer sabotage defined in Article 269 (1) of the PC is the impairment, damaging or alteration of computer data of special significance to the State's defence, communications security, the operation of the public administration, other public authorities or institutions, or a local government body, or disrupting or hindering the automatic processing, storage or transfer of such data. Pursuant to Article 269 (2) of the PC, computer sabotage may also include damaging

[24]In the light of Article 3(1) of the Act on the Computerisation of the Operations of Entities Performing Public Tasks, hereinafter: the Act on Computerisation, it is a "material or device designed to save, store and read data in digital form", which encompasses all data carriers such as: floppy disks, which are rare at present, hard drives (magnetic data carriers), CDs and DVDs (optical carriers), semiconductor memory (RAM—*Random Access Memory*, ROM—*Read Only Memory*, in-built memory e.g. in printers, to name a few), *flash* memory etc.

[25]Cf. Adamski (2000), pp. 64–65.

[26]Kardas (2000), p. 88.

[27]Ibid. Cf. Kozłowska-Kalisz (2020), Commentary on Art. 268 PC; Wróbel and Zając (2017), Commentary on Art. 268 PC.

[28]Górniok (2005), pp. 363–364; Kalitowski (2012), p. 1209.

[29]Wróbel and Zając (2017) Commentary on Art. 268a PC. See more Radoniewicz (2020), pp. 241–250.

or replacing a data carrier, or damaging or impairing a device designed to automatically process, store or transfer protected computer data. It is punishable by imprisonment from six months to eight years, which is a heavy sentence.[30]

In view of the much greater significance of the information protected under Article 269 (1) of the PC, in comparison with the information subject to protection under Article 268 (2) of the PC, and the identicality of the remaining statutory criteria of prohibited acts penalised under those provisions, the crime described in 269 (1) of the PC is considered an aggravated crime in relation to the crime defined in Article 268 (2) of the PC.[31] For these reasons, such a statement appears justified also in the case of the relationship between the crimes defined in Article 268a of the PC, or 269a and 269 (1) of the PC.

Article 269a of the PC provides for penal responsibility of the person who, without an authorisation, to a large extent disrupts the operation of an information system, an ICT system[32] or an ICT network,[33] through actions of a logical character such as the transmission, destruction, impairment or alteration of computer data. The protection applies to the secure operation of a computer system and, in consequence, to accessibility of the computer data processed in that system.

An attack on the operation of an information system, an ICT system and an ICT network is a logical, rather than a physical attack. Disruption is to be caused by the transmission, destruction, impairment or alteration of computer data. These will include, for instance, DoS attacks.

As pointed out by Andrzej Adamski[34] and Włodzimierz Wróbel and Dominik Zając,[35] the provisions set out in Articles 268a and 269a of the PC overlap. The definitions "to a large extent disrupts or hinders the automatic processing, storing or transferring of data" and "to a large extent disrupts the operation of an information

[30]See more Radoniewicz (2019b), pp. 199–209.

[31]Kardas (2000), p. 96. Cf. Adamski (2000), p. 77; Kalitowski (2012), p. 1211.

[32]Pursuant to Article 2(3) of the Act on Computerisation, this corresponds to a set of compatible hardware and software which together ensure the processing and storage, as well as sending and receiving data via telecommunication networks, by means of the appropriate end-point device, within the meaning of the Telecommunication Law; the same definition can be found in the Act of 18 July 2002 on Providing Services by Electronic Means (Consolidated text, Polish Journal of Laws of 2017, item 1030 as amended). It is assumed that an information system serves the purpose of processing data, while a telecommunication system is used for sending such data. Hence, the ICT system is an information system (in which computer data is processed) connected to a telecommunications network, via which it can send and receive data. Cf. Konarski (2004), pp. 62–64; Radoniewicz (2016), pp. 282–284.

[33]At present, the concept is not defined in any legal instrument. An ICT network is a set of ICT systems, in other words, information systems in which data is processed, interconnected telecommunications networks by means of which data is transferred between those systems. It is an extensive structure, created as a result of the convergence of information technology and telecommunications. Cf. Konarski (2004), pp. 62–64; Radoniewicz (2016), p. 284; Świerczyński (2009), p. 39; Urbanek (1999), pp. 4–5.

[34]Adamski (2005), pp. 58–59.

[35]Wróbel and Zając (2017), Commentary on Art. 269a PC.

system, an ICT system and an ICT network" are essentially identical. The operation of the said systems and the ICT network consists in the processing, storing and transferring of data. As further proposed by Andrzej Adamski, Article 268a of the PC could be treated as a tool to prosecute the offenders, whose conduct does not meet the criteria of the perpetrator defined in Article 269a of the PC,[36] while Włodzimierz Wróbel and Dominik Zając claimed that the said article should be applied when the operation of an information system or an ICT network has been disturbed.[37] The offence under Article 269(1) of the PC should be considered as aggravated type to the offence described in Article 269a of the PC.[38]

As in the case of the act described in Article 267 (2) of the PC, the provision of Article 269c of the PC may apply here.

Article 269b of the PC penalises prohibited acts committed with the use of "hacking tools". Article 269b (1) of the PC, which is the equivalent of Article 7 of Directive 2013/40, penalises the creation, acquisition, sales or making available: 1) hardware or software adapted to committing the crime defined in Article 165 (1) (4) of the PC (causing danger to the life or health of many people, or resulting in large-scale damage to property), and in Article 267 (3), Article 268a (1) or 268a (2), in connection with 268a (1), art. 269 (1) or 269 (2), or Article 269a of the PC; 2) computer passwords, access codes or other data which enable unauthorised access to the information stored in an information system, an ICT system or an ICT network.

The solutions adopted in Article 269b (1) of the PC, from the moment of its inclusion in the Penal Code by way of the 2004 amendment, were widely criticised. For the most part, the critics pointed out that there was no provision excluding the penal responsibility of administrators and persons in charge of the security of information systems, who use such software in the process of developing and testing protection for systems, or authors of antivirus software.[39] In order to eliminate the shortcomings, section 1a was added to Article 269b, reading as follows: "Anyone who acts solely with the purpose of securing an information system, an ICT system or an ICT network against the crimes listed herein, or with the purpose of developing such a security method, shall not be considered as committing the crime referred to in section 1". The primary aim of the amendment was, however, to increase the upper limit of the statutory penalty for the crime to five years of imprisonment, which was justified solely by indicating the necessity to make it possible for one to subject the offender to the so-called extended forfeit, as provided for in Article

[36]Adamski (2005), p. 58.

[37]Wróbel and Zając (2017), Commentary on Art. 269a PC.

[38]Radoniewicz (2020), pp. 252–255.

[39]Gienas (2005), p. 82; Radoniewicz (2016), p. 336. Cf. Wróbel and Zając (2017), Commentary on Art. 269b PC.

45 (2) of the PC.[40] This also met with fair criticism.[41] No matter what the intentions of the authors of the amendment were, one should take note of the fact that, essentially from the moment of the inclusion of Article 269b (1) to the Penal Code (by way of the 2004 amendment), emphasis was on the sanctions (the power to impose a penalty of up to three years of imprisonment). The provision actually penalises the acts or actions performed by a criminal offender in order to prepare to commit the crimes set out in the provision, some of which are punishable by the same or lesser sanctions.[42] As for other "shortcomings" of the provision, one should give attention, in the first place, to the fact that Article 269b of the PC does not include hacking, whether in the form of unauthorised access to information under Article 267 (1) of the PC or unauthorised access to an information system under Article 267 (2) of the PC, in the list of crimes (for the commission of which the creation, acquisition, sales and sharing of hardware and software are penalised).[43]

As far as other shortcomings of Article 269b (1) of the PC are concerned, the provision mainly refers to software "adapted" to commit the crimes specified therein. A problem, therefore, arises in connection with qualifying the actions of creators of software serving several functions (the so-called dual-nature software),[44] which is then used by third parties for criminal purposes, contrary to the creator' intent.[45] With the aim of complying with the *ratio legis* of that provision and avoiding excessive criminalisation, Włodzimierz Wróbel proposed that it be interpreted in line with the definition of punishable preparatory activities under Article 16 (1) of the PC, which requires that the offender creating or acquiring the tools listed therein acts with direct intent (or, as regards selling and providing access, with indirect intent).[46] As it seems, however, most representatives of the doctrine (except for Włodzimierz Wróbel and Dominik Zając, Joanna Piórkowska-Flieger, Barbara Kunicka-Michalska[47] and Andrzej Marek[48] are of the opinion that, in order

[40]The justification to the government's bill amending the Penal Code and Certain Other Acts, form No. 1186, section 4.6.

[41]On (the lack of) penal responsibility for identifying gaps in information systems and networks—a legal opinion of the Foundation of Frank Bold and the Cracow Institute of Criminal Law, http://blog.frankbold.pl/bug-bounty/. Accessed on 1.12.2020.

[42]As regards problems that arise from this fact, cf. Radoniewicz (2016), pp. 347–349.

[43]The fact that the crime under Article 268(2) of the PC is not included in the list appears less problematic—the same programmes will serve one to commit the crime set out therein as in the case of acts under Article 268a(1) and 268a(2) of the PC and Article 165(1)(4) of the PC (viruses).

[44]By way of example, network monitors, also referred to as protocol analysers, which allow administrators to analyse network traffic, may be used by hackers as *sniffers*.

[45]Cf. Adamski (2005), p. 60.

[46]Wróbel and Zając (2017) Commentary to Article 269b. Cf. Piórkowska-Flieger (2012), p. 713.

[47]B. Kunicka-Michalska thinks that it is difficult to imagine creation, acquisition or selling without the offender's direct intent; see Kunicka-Michalska (2010), p. 748.

[48]According to A. Marek, the causative acts listed in Article 269b (1) of the PC may be committed with direct intent only, while indirect intent may apply solely to the intended purpose of devices, programmes, passwords, access codes and other data; see Marek (2010), p. 576. J. W. Giezek, by critically referring to the viewpoint that creation and acquisition can only be done with direct intent, stresses that it seems more probable that the crime is committed with indirect intent, when the

for guilt to be attributed to the offender, it suffices that he/she has acted with indirect intent.[49]

The Polish legislation on computer crimes undoubtedly needs change. First of all, the conceptual framework should be standardised. At present, in the light of the ratification of the Convention on Cybercrime, it is not necessary to define the concept of information (computer) data as the definition offered by it has the character of a self-executing norm and may be applied directly. In view of the broadly discussed doubts about the scope of the concepts of an "information system", those should be defined. The same applies to the term "ICT network".

I believe that limiting the scope of criminalisation under Article 267(1) of the PC to the cases of violation of the secrecy of correspondence should be considered, along with assigning the principal role in combating hacking (i.e. obtaining unauthorised access to an information system) to Article 267(2) of the PC, by adding the requirement that the offender mitigates or omits the magnetic, electronic, computer or other security feature (which would also conform to the content of Article 3 of Directive 2013/40 recommending such a solution[50]).

It is also necessary to modify the Polish regulation of computer eavesdropping. Article 267(3) of the PC requires the direct intent of the offender, while no such premise is contained in Article 6 of Directive 2013/40. One should possibly consider leaving that provision as it is (or mostly as it is), and at the same time adding a provision (in conformity with Article 6 of Directive 2013/40) determining the act in relation to which the offence defined in the current Article 267 (3) of the PC would constitute the aggravated offence.[51]

Amendments to Article 269b (1) of the PC are also warranted. It appears necessary to limit the penal responsibility to direct intent, and to specify that it concerns the hardware and software "most of all" or "primarily" (as was used in the English-language version of Directive 2013/40) serving the purpose of committing crimes. Moreover, the list of crimes for which they could be utilised should be extended at least by the remaining acts under discussion. It would be also advisable to ease the sanctions.

---

offender only agrees that his/her conduct meets the statutory criteria of the crime, since the situation usually look as if he/she did not want to create, acquire, sell or share certain hardware or software but, with some probability only, assumed that they might turn out to be adapted to committing one of the crimes set out in the Article, agreeing that it would be just so. The author plainly suggests that the "uncertainty of diagnosis", e.g. as regards the adjustment of hardware or software, allows one to assume that, in such a case, we are actually dealing with indirect intent only, Giezek (2014), pp. 1007–1008.

[49]See Adamski (2005), p. 61; Gienas (2005), pp. 81–82; Górniok (2006), pp. 369–370; Kalitowski (2012), p. 1214; Kozłowska-Kalisz (2020), Commentary to Article 269b.

[50]"Member States shall take the necessary measures to ensure that, when committed intentionally, the access without right, to the whole or to any part of an information system, is punishable as a criminal offence where committed by infringing a security measure, at least for cases which are not minor." See also: Radoniewicz (2016), p. 459.

[51]See more Radoniewicz (2017b), pp. 303–317.

2 Cyberterrorism: "Cybercrimes of a Terrorist Nature"

Framework Decision 2002/475[52] was transposed into Polish legislation by way of the Act of the 16th of April 2004 Amending the Penal Code and Certain Other Acts.[53] As mentioned earlier, its provisions are similar to those set out in the Directive 2017/541/EU,[54] and the definition of a "terrorist" offence (in PC—offence of a terrorist nature) has a similar shape.[55] The Polish legislator, however, did not decide on its literal transposition, instead creating a more synthetic one (Article 115 (20) of the PC), whereby emphasis was placed on the criterion of the offender's purpose. Similar to Article 1 (1) of Framework Decision 2002/475 and Article 3 (2) of Directive 2017/541, the following were listed alternatively as the offender's purposes:

(1) severely intimidating many people,
(2) forcing a state authority of the Republic of Poland or other state, or a body of an international organisation, to undertake or relinquish certain actions,
(3) causing serious disruptions in the political system or economy of the Republic of Poland, another state or an international organisation.

The second element of the definition in Article 115 (20) of the PC was formulated differently from the original definition in Framework Decision 2002/475 (and is, in consequence, different from that in Directive 2017/541). The list of crimes which, when committed for any of the purposes listed in the definition, are viewed as corresponding to terrorist acts was replaced with a formal criterion, a requirement that the offence was punishable by a maximum term of imprisonment of at least five years.. Therefore, this provision does not result in *delictum sui generis* but it makes any offence (a crime and a more serious act punishable by deprivation of liberty for a maximum term of imprisonment of at least five years), committed for any of the purposes listed in the definition, be considered an offence of a terrorist nature. Pursuant to the provisions set out in Framework Decision 2002/475 (and Directive 2017/541), an offence of a terrorist nature also includes threat to commit such a crime (Article 115(20) in fine).[56]

In the light of the above definition, cybercrimes of a terrorist nature may be the following prohibited acts: Article 165 (1)(4) of the PC (causing danger to the life or health of many people, or resulting in large-scale damage to property), Article 268

[52]Council Framework Decision 2002/475/JHA of 13 June 2002 on combating terrorism. OJ EC 2002 L 164/3.

[53]Act of 16 April 2004 Amending the Penal Code and Certain Other Acts Polish Journal of Laws of 2004, No. 93, item 889.

[54]Directive 2017/541/EU of the European Parliament and of the Council, of 15 March 2017 on combating terrorism and replacing Council Framework Decision 2002/475/JHA and amending Council Decision 2005/671/JHA, OJ EU 2017 L 88/6.

[55]Radoniewicz (2019c), pp. 193–205.

[56]Giezek (2012), p. 738. Cf. Radoniewicz (2015), pp. 192–196.

(3) of the PC (preventing one from accessing information, which results in gross material damage), Article 268a(2) of the PC (an attack on computer data or the processing of such data which results in gross material damage), Article 269 of the PC (an attack on computer data of special significance), Article 269a of the PC (disturbing the operation of an information system, an ICT system or an ICT network) and—paradoxically (see earlier remarks)—Article 269b(1) of the PC (offences connected with "hacker tools").

References

Adamski A 2000) Prawo karne komputerowe, Warsaw

Adamski A (2005) Cyberprzestępczość – aspekty prawne i kryminologiczne, Studia Prawnicze 4

Adamski A (2007) Nowe ujęcie cyberprzestępstw w kodeksie karnym – ale czy lepsze?, Prawo Teleinformatyczne 3

Adamski A (2013) Botnety jako zagadnienie prawno-kryminologiczna na tle doświadczeń amerykańskich, Prokuratura i Prawo 1

Bukowski S (2006) Przestępstwo hackingu, Przegląd Sądowy 4

Gienas P (2005) Uwagi do przestępstwa stypizowanego w art. 269b Kodeksu karnego, Prokurator 1

Giezek J (2012) In: Giezek JW (ed) Kodeks karny. Część ogólna. Komentarz, Warsaw

Giezek JW (2014) In: Giezek JW (ed) Kodeks karny. Część szczególna. Komentarz, Warsaw

Górniok O (2005) In: Górniok O et al (eds) Kodeks karny. Komentarz, vol 2, Gdańsk

Górniok O (2006) In: Górniok O et al (eds) Kodeks karny. Komentarz, Warszawa

Kalitowski M (2012) In: Filar M (ed) Kodeks karny. Komentarz, Warsaw

Kardas P (2000) Prawnokarna ochrona informacji w polskim prawie karnym z perspektywy przestępstw komputerowych. Analiza dogmatyczna i strukturalna w świetle aktualnie obowiązującego stanu prawnego, Czasopismo Prawa Karnego i Nauk Penalnych 1

Konarski X (2004) Komentarz do ustawy o świadczeniu usług drogą elektroniczną. Warszawa

Kozłowska-Kalisz P (2020) In: Mozgawa M (ed) Kodeks karny. Praktyczny komentarz, Lex/el

Krasuski A (2015) Prawo telekomunikacyjne. Komentarz, Lex/el

Kunicka-Michalska B (2010) In: Wąsek A, Zawłocki R (eds) Kodeks karny. Część szczególna. Komentarz. Komentarz do artykułów 222-316, vol II, Warsaw

Marek A (2010) Kodeks karny. Komentarz, Warsaw

Piątek S (2019) Prawo telekomunikacyjne. Komentarz, LEX/el

Piórkowska-Flieger J (2012) In: Bojarski T (ed) Kodeks karny. Komentarz, Warsaw

Radoniewicz F (2015) Techniki implementacji do polskiego porządku prawnego postanowień decyzji ramowych Rady Unii Europejskiej dotyczących prawa karnego materialnego, Przegląd Prawa Konstytucyjnego 3

Radoniewicz F (2016) Odpowiedziaość karna za hacking i inne przestępstwa przeciwko komputerowym i systemom informatycznym, Warsaw

Radoniewicz F (2017a) Podsłuch komputerowy. In: Chałubińska-Jentkiewicz K, Kakareko K, Sobczak J (eds) Prawo prywatności jako reguła społeczeństwa informacyjnego. C.H. Beck, Warszawa

Radoniewicz F (2017b) Ujęcie przestępstw przeciwko ochronie informacji w Kodeksie karnym a postanowienia dyrektywy 2013/40/UE dotyczącej ataków na systemy informatyczne – aspekty wybrane. In: Kitler W, Taczkowska-Olszewska J (eds) Bezpieczeństwo informacyjne. Aspekty prawno-administracyjne, Warsaw

Radoniewicz F (2019a) In: Kitler W, Taczkowska-Olszewska J, Radoniewicz F (eds) Ustawa o krajowym systemie cyberbezpieczeństwa. Komentarz, Warsaw

Radoniewicz F (2019b) Przestępstwo "sabotażu informatycznego" (art. 269 k.k.). In: Badźmirowska-Masłowska K (ed) System bezpieczeństwa w cyberprzestrzeni RP. Warsaw

Radoniewicz F (2019c) Zwalczanie cybeterroryzmu w prawie UE – aspekty karnomaterialne. Cybersecurity and Law 2

Radoniewicz F (2020) Przestępstwo zakłócenia sieci teleinformatycznej – wybrane aspekty karnomaterialne oraz techniczne. In: Przestępczość teleinformatyczna 2019, "Rocznik Bezpieczeństwa Morskiego"

Radoniewicz F (2021) Przestępstwo hackingu – wybrane aspekty techniczne oraz karnomaterialne. In: Przestępczość teleinformatyczna 2020, "Rocznik Bezpieczeństwa Morskiego" – in press

Siwicki M (2013) Cyberprzestępczość, Legalis

Świerczyński M (2009) In: Gołaczyński J, Kowalik-Bańczyk K, Majchrowska A, Świerczyński M, Ustawa o świadczeniu usług drogą elektroniczną. Komentarz. Oficyna, LEX/el

Urbanek A (1999) In: Chustecki J et al Vademecum teleinformatyka, Warsaw

Wróbel W, Zając D (2017) In: Wróbel W, Zoll A (eds) Kodeks karny. Komentarz. Część szczególna, t. II, cz. II, Komentarz do artykułów 117-277d k.k., Warsaw, LEX/el

Filip Radoniewicz PhD; legal advisor; adjunct in the Department of Cybersecurity Law and New Technologies at the Institute of Law, War Studies University, Warsaw; expert at the Academic Centre for Cybersecurity Policy (War Studies University) and in the Ministry of Justice; he worked as an assistant judge (in the Fourth Criminal and Sixth Penitentiary Department of the Regional Court in Lublin); graduate of post-graduate studies: "European Union Law" at the Jagiellonian University, "Human Rights and Freedoms", co-organized by the Institute of Legal Sciences of the Polish Academy of Sciences and the Helsinki Foundation for Human Rights, and "Computer Network Administration" at the Lublin University of Technology; author or co-author of approximately fifty publications, mainly in the field of broadly understood criminal law, new technology law and human rights. Selected publications: F. Radoniewicz (2016) Odpowiedzialność karna za hacking i inne przestępstwa przeciwko danym komputerowym i systemom informatycznym / Criminal liability for hacking and other offences against computer data and information systems/, Wolters Kluwer, Warszawa; Ustawa o krajowym systemie cyberbezpieczeństwa. Komentarz /Act on the National Cybersecurity System. Commentary/ (2019) ed. W. Kitler, J. Taczkowska-Olszewska, F. Radoniewicz, CH. Beck, Warszawa.

Cybercrime in Selected European Countries

Filip Radoniewicz

Abstract This study does not claim to exhaust all the abundant comparative legal issues. Therefore, it has been limited to discussing the penal provisions of eight European countries, without going into detailed considerations on issues related to e.g. form of offences committed or the liability of legal persons. The overarching intention was to present as diverse regulations as possible.

All countries whose regulations were discussed have signed and ratified the Convention on Cybercrime and are members (except United Kingdom) of the European Union, which resulted in their obligation to implement Framework Decision 2005/222 on attacks against information systems, and the need to adapt their regulations to the provisions of Directive 2013/40, which has replaced this decision.

1 Introduction

Firstly, it should be emphasised that the present study does not claim to exhaust the whole of the complex comparative-law issue, particularly as only one of over twenty Chapters has been devoted to it. Therefore, it has been narrowed down to discussing the substantive penal-law regulations of several European countries, without entering into detailed deliberations on the issues related to, for example, the stages of a crime, and forms of accessory liability for a crime, or the liability of legal persons, while the overriding intention was to present as diverse regulations as possible.[1]

All the states, whose regulations have been discussed here, signed and ratified the Convention on Cybercrime, and they are, or were (the United Kingdom), Member States of the European Union, which is why their regulations are based on Council

[1]For more information about cybercrime law in other European countries see Radoniewicz (2016), pp. 359–421.

F. Radoniewicz (✉)
Akademickie Centrum Polityki Cyberbezpieczeństwa/Academic Center for Cybersecurity Policy, Akademia Sztuki Wojennej w Warszawie/War Studies University in Warsaw, Warsaw, Poland
e-mail: filip.radoniewicz@radoniewicz.eu

K. Chałubińska-Jentkiewicz et al. (eds.), *Cybersecurity in Poland*,
https://doi.org/10.1007/978-3-030-78551-2_25

Framework Decision 2005/222/JHA of the 24th of February 2005 concerning attacks against information systems and Directive 2013/40/EU of the European Parliament and of the Council of the 12th of August 2013 on attacks against information systems and replacing Council Framework Decision 2005/222/JHA (OJ EU L 218, 14.08.2013, p. 8.). Consequently, similar solutions have been adopted in these countries.

As regards an offence involving illegal access, most legislators make the offender's penal liability conditional on the elimination of safeguards designed to protect against unauthorised access to the data or system. Such a requirement was introduced in Czech, Estonian, French and German regulations.

Regarding the remaining offences, which are the subject of this study (assaults on the integrity of computer data and computer systems and networks, computer eavesdropping and the production, possession and distribution of hacking tools), the regulations in question demonstrate certain similarities, differing mainly in the level of detail and types of aggravated crimes and, with regard to offences against the integrity of data and computer systems, in the introduction of the requirement for the offender to cause a consequence (Spain), the significant importance of the data to the victim (Germany), and action with the intent to cause harm (Spain).

Unique solutions are found in the laws developed on the basis of English Law (Computer Misuse Act of 1990). Several countries followed suit, including Malta, whose regulations are discussed in this chapter, and some non-European countries, such as Singapore.[2]

The texts of the penal laws under discussion, in addition to respective Government websites, are available, for example, via the Council of Europe's Legislationline service[3] and on the website of the World Intellectual Property Organisation.[4]

2 The Czech Republic

The Czech Penal Code[5] is the most recent of the discussed laws. It was adopted on the 8th of January 2009,[6] and entered into force after a *vacatio legis* period of almost one year, on the 1st of January 2010. The Czech legislator included computer-related

[2]The Act No. 19/1993 of 30 August 1993—Computer Misuse and Cybersecurity Act, as amended by the Act of 31 July 2007 (Chapter 50A), http://statutes.agc.gov.sg, accessed on 15.12.2020.

[3]www.legislationline.org, accessed on 15.12.2020.

[4]http://www.wipo.int/wipolex, accessed on 15.12.2020.

[5]The Penal Code of the Czech Republic of 8 January 2009 (Zákon trestní zákoník; Trestni zákoník), Zakon č. 40/2009 Sb., http://aplikace.mvcr.cz/sbirka-zakonu, accessed on 15.12.2020.

[6]This happened after the Czech Republic signed the Convention on Cybercrime, which took place on 9 February 2005, but before its ratification, which took place on 22 August 2013 (for the Czech Republic, the Convention entered into force on 1 December 2013).

crimes, being the subject of this study, in two chapters of the Code. The vast majority of them, namely the offences of unauthorised access, unauthorised alteration of data, disruption of networks and the development and distribution of "hacking tools", have been classified as offences against property (Division V of the Code). Computer eavesdropping has been rightly considered to be an attack on the right to privacy, and therefore it is laid down in Chapter 2 "Offences against personal interests and the secrecy of private life and correspondence" of Division II of the Code, entitled "Offences against freedom, personal interests and privacy of private life and correspondence." The discussion regarding the Czech regulation should begin with this issue.

Computer eavesdropping is categorised in Section 182(1) (b), and Subsection (c) of that Section defines the basic type of such an offence. According to these provisions, imprisonment of up to two years or a prohibition of an activity (*zákaz činnosti*) may be imposed on an offender who committed an intentional breach of the confidentiality of communication (data, text, images, sounds), which may be attributed to a particular participant in the data exchange process or user to whom the data are transferred via electronic communication networks or via private transmission of computer data to, from or within a computer system, including by analysing electromagnetic emissions generated by the computer system in connection with the data transfer. The same sanction shall be imposed on anyone who, with the intention of causing damage to a third party or of gaining an illegal advantage for himself or a third party, discloses information (constituting a secret) not intended for him or her, which he or she obtained from a letter, telegram, telephone conversation or transmission via electronic communication network, or who uses such information (Section 182(2)). The Czech Penal Code is quite strict and prescriptive.[7] There are numerous types of aggravated crimes, and computer eavesdropping may serve as a good example here. When identifying its aggravated type under Section 182(3), the legislator indicated as aggravating circumstances the commission of the acts referred to in Section 182(1) or 182 (2) within an organised group, acting with a malicious intent or with the aim of causing significant damage,[8] or with the intention of obtaining a substantial benefit for the offender or for a third party. Such an offence is punishable by imprisonment for a period of six months to three years or a prohibition of an activity. Whereas, if the perpetrator of the act described in Section 182(1) or 182(2) is a public officer, or causes large-scale damage or, while committing the act, intends to obtain a considerable benefit for himself\herself or for a third party, he/she shall be liable under Section 182(4), which provides for a term of imprisonment of between one and five years or a fine. Pursuant to Section 182(5), a similar sanction (i.e. imprisonment of between one and five years, a fine and, moreover, a prohibition of an activity) is imposed on a person, who being an

[7]More on the Czech Penal Code in W. Radecki, Nowy czeski kodeks karny, Prok. i Pr. 2009, No. 7-8, p. 185 et seq.

[8]A significant damage—as defined in Article 138(1) of the Czech Penal Code—is a damage of at least CZK 500,000, and a large-scale damage is damage of at least CZK 5,000,000.

employee of a postal or telecommunications service provider, computer system operator or anyone engaged in rendering communication services:

(1) commits an act referred to in Section 182(1) or 182 (2), or
(2) intentionally facilitates the commission of the said acts by a third party, or
(3) alters or loses a document sent by post or courier service or a message sent privately as computer data, by telegraph, telephone or other similar means.

The above offence has an aggravated type, representing a (particularly) serious crime.[9] In accordance with Section 182 (6), the perpetrator, whose conduct meets the criteria of an offence under Section 182 (5), and causes large-scale damage or who acts with the intention of obtaining substantial benefits for himself/herself or a third party, shall be subject to the penalty of imprisonment for a period of three to ten years.

The group of computer crimes listed in Division V of the Code includes the unauthorised access to the computer system or its part (Section 230). Infringement of security measures constitutes a condition for the perpetrator to be indicted for such offence. The offence is subject to imprisonment for a period of up to two years, a prohibition of an activity or the forfeiture of movable property.

The second offence mentioned in this Section is the act of obtaining access by the perpetrator to a computer system or information medium (there is no requirement that such access be unauthorised) and:

(1) the unlawful use of data stored in that computer system or on that information medium, or
(2) the unlawful erasure or other destruction or damage, alteration, deletion of data or rendering the data stored on that computer system or on that information medium unusable, or
(3) falsification or alteration of data stored in a computer system or information medium in order to make it appear to be accurate, or make the system or medium treat it as if it were accurate, whether or not such data are directly legible and understandable, or
(4) unlawful input of data into a computer system or onto an information medium or otherwise affects computer software or hardware or other technical device for data processing.

The perpetrator of this offence shall be liable to a term of imprisonment of up to three years, a prohibition of activity or the forfeiture of property.

The offences discussed above, as well as computer eavesdropping, have a wide range of aggravated types. They are defined, first and foremost, in Section 230(3), under which it is stipulated that the penalty of imprisonment for a period of six

[9]Pursuant to Section 14(2) of the Czech Penal Code, misdemeanours include all unintentional acts and those intentional acts for which the penal law provides for a prison sentence with an upper limit of up to five years. Serious crimes include all those offences that are not misdemeanours. On the other hand, particularly serious crimes are all those which are punishable by imprisonment, the upper limit of which is at least ten years (Section 14(3)).

months to four years shall be imposed on a person who commits the act referred to in Section 230(1) or 230(2) with the intention of causing damage to a third party, or other harm, or of obtaining a substantial benefit for himself/herself or a third party, or with the intention of limiting the operation of a computer system or other technical device used for data processing. Secondly, pursuant to Section 230(4), the offence referred to in Section 230(1) or 230(2) shall be punishable by a term of imprisonment of one year to five years or by a fine, if the offender:

(1) acted as a member of an organised group,
(2) caused significant damage,
(3) caused by his conduct a serious disruption in the activities of a State administration body, local government body, court or other public authority,
(4) obtained a significant benefit for himself or for a third party,
(5) caused a serious disruption of the activities of a legal person or natural person acting as an entrepreneur.

On the other hand, pursuant to Section 230(5), the offender who, as a result of the committed offence, has caused large-scale damage or thus obtained for himself/herself or a third party significant benefits, shall be subject to a penalty of imprisonment for a period of three to eight years. As already indicated above, due to the level of the sanction, this offence is classified as a serious crime.

Section 231 of the Czech Penal Code criminalises acts related to the development of, and trade in, hacking tools. Under this provision, the penalty of imprisonment for a period of up to two years, prohibition of activity or forfeiture of property shall be imposed on anyone who, with the intention of violating the secrecy of correspondence, an offence under Section 182(1)(b) and 182(1)(c) or of obtaining access to a computer system or information medium, an offence under Section 230(1) and 230 (2), produces, markets, imports, exports, transports, offers, arranges, disposes of, or otherwise makes available to himself/herself or a third party, distributes or stores:

(1) any device or component, tool or other means, including a computer program designed or adapted to gain unauthorised access to an electronic communication network, computer system or parts thereof, or
(2) a computer password, access code or other similar means by which it is possible to access a computer system or parts thereof.

The Czech legislator provided for two types of aggravated offences. The first, referred to in Section 231(2), is punishable by imprisonment of up to three years, a prohibition of activity or the forfeiture of property, and the aggravating features include the offender's commitment of the act within an organised group or the obtaining of a significant benefit by the offender for himself/herself or for a third party. The second type, provided for in Section 231(3), is punishable by imprisonment for a term of between six months and five years, and the aggravating feature includes the offender's obtaining for himself/herself or for a third party a benefit of considerable value.

According to Section 232 of the Czech Penal Code, the offence of damage to a computer system and information medium and interference with a computer device due to negligence (unintentionally) is an offence, which is not covered by any other legislation. It is applicable to a person who violates, with gross negligence, his or her obligations arising from his or her employment, profession, position or function, whether by law or by contract, and:

(1) destroys, damages, alters or otherwise renders unusable data stored in a computer system or on an information medium, or
(2) interferes with software or hardware on a computer or other technical data processing device,

resulting in a significant damage to the property of a third party.

This offence is subject to a maximum of six months' imprisonment, prohibition of activity and/or forfeiture of property. Section 232(2) provides for its aggravated type depending on the value of the damage caused, in the case of causing large-scale damage, the offender may be sentenced to imprisonment of up to two years (and a prohibition of activity or forfeiture of property).

3 Estonia

Estonian Penal Code (Karistusseadustik)[10] was adopted on the 6th of June 2001 and became valid into force on the 1st of September 2002. The Republic of Estonia is one of the earliest countries to ratify the Convention on Cybercrime, it did so on the 12th of May 2003 (the Convention on Cybercrime entered into force on the 1st of July 2004). The offences covered by this study are listed in Chapter 13 "Offences against property", Division 1 "Offences against ownership", Subdivision 2 "Damage to property" (Sections 206 and 207 of the Estonian Penal Code) and in Division 2 ("Offences against all types of property"), Subdivision 3 "Unlawful use" (Sections 216^1, 217).

Furthermore, Section 206 defines the offence of impacting computer data by illegally altering, deleting, or damaging computer data in a computer system, or rendering such data inaccessible. This act is punishable by a fine or imprisonment of up to three years. Nevertheless, where the offence in question is:

(1) directed against the data processed in a significant number of computer systems or programs or devices specified in Section 216^1 (hacking tools) were used to commit thereof;
(2) an act committed within a group;

[10] The Penal Code of the Republic of Estonia (RT I 2001, 61, 364). The text is available on the website of the official journal, Riigi Teataja (https://www.riigiteataja.ee). Since 1 June 2010, Riigi Teataja has been published exclusively on the Internet. English translations of some legislation, including the Penal Code, are available on this website (and updated relatively frequently).

(3) targeted against data processed in a computer system of strategic significance for the State;
(4) it has caused significant damage;

the perpetrator shall be subject to a fine or up to five years' imprisonment (Section 206(2)).

Illegal interference with a computer system or disruption of its operation, consisting of downloading data from it, sending data to it, deleting, damaging or altering the data processed therein or rendering such data inaccessible, constitutes an offence under Section 207(1). It is subject to a financial penalty or imprisonment of up to three years. The aggravated type is provided for in Section 207(2). The aggravating features are similar to those of the act under Section 206(2):

(1) the offence was directed against a significant number of computer systems or was committed using the programs or devices or as defined in Section 216^1;
(2) the offence was committed within a group;
(3) the impact of the act includes an influence on, or interference with, a computer system of strategic or public service significance;
(4) the offence caused substantial damage.

However, the sanction is identical to that provided for in the case of the offence under Section 206(2), it is a financial penalty or a penalty of imprisonment of up to five years.

Division 2, which refers to offences against all types of property, includes the provision laid down in Section 217 (Subsdivision 3 "Unlawful use") under which unlawful access to a computer system by eliminating or circumventing security measures is punishable as a criminal offence. The sanction for this offence is a fine or imprisonment of up to three years. However, if the perpetrator has caused significant damage, gained access to a computer system processing information constituting State secrets (or other qualified types thereof) or the computer system, to which he gained access is of strategic significance, he or she shall be sentenced to imprisonment for a period of up to five years.

Furthermore, Section 216^1 criminalises conducts, which are preparatory activities to the commission of computer crimes, consisting of supplying, preparing, possessing, distributing or disclosing in any other way, in order to be used to commit an offence indicated in this provision (i.e. defined in Section 206, 207, 213[11] or 217), or with the intention of facilitating its perpetration by a third party, a device or a computer program created or adapted specifically for committing the offences referred to in this provision or the means of gaining access to a computer system. The perpetrator of such an act shall be subject to a financial penalty or to

[11]This provision defines the offence of computer fraud, consisting in causing financial loss as a result of gaining unauthorised access to a computer program or data or altering, deleting, destroying or blocking access to a computer program or data or otherwise interfering unlawfully with the processing of data in order to obtain a financial benefits.

imprisonment of up to two years. The forfeiture of property directly derived from the committed crime, as defined in Section 83, may be ordered against the offender.

On the other hand, among the offences against fundamental freedoms (Part 2 in Chapter 10 "Offences against civil and political rights"); Section 156(1) stipulates the offence of violating the secrecy of correspondence "by letter or via other means of communication". The perpetrators of this act are only subject to a fine. It appears that the term "other means of communication" can be understood as electronic means of communication. As regards the aggravated type (Section 156 (2)), this offence is punishable by a fine or a penalty of up to one year's imprisonment and the aggravating feature is the perpetrator's exercising his or her powers.[12]

4 France

The current French Penal Code of 1992[13] (Code Pénal) replaced the Napoleonic Code Pénal (so-called Ancien Code Pénal) of 1810. Computer-related crimes were already included in its original version, and are defined in Chapter III ("Offences against automated data processing systems"), Title II ("Other offences against property") of Book III ("Crimes and misdemeanours against property"), in the provisions of Articles 323-1 to 323-8, which derive their current wording from the amendments to the Code Pénal made under Acts 2004-575 of the 21st of June 2004, 2009-526 of the 12th of May 2009, 2012-410 of the 27th of March 2012, 2013-1168 of the 18th of December 2013, 2014-1353 of the 13th of November 2014 and 2015-912 of the 24th of July 2015.

Article 323-1 defines the offence of fraudulent obtaining (*frauduleusement*)[14] of an access to all or part of an automated data-processing system or to maintain access to such a system. The latter characteristic refers to the perpetrator's behaviour consisting in obtaining authorised access (i.e. on the basis of his or her powers) and then gaining access to parts of the system to which he or she is not authorised to enter. The offence under Article 323-1 is punishable by two years' imprisonment and a fine of 60,000 EUR. When the behaviour of the offender causes destruction or

[12]Furthermore, in this chapter, the following acts have been criminalised: unlawful disclosure of personal data under Article 157, under Article 157[1]—disclosure of sensitive personal data, and under Article 157[2]—identity theft understood as using the identity of a third party in order to gain access to data or cause harm to another person or conceal the offence.

[13]The Penal Code of the French Republic was adopted in sections. The first four books (as Acts No: 92-683; 92-684; 92-685 and 92-686) were published in Official Journal No. 169 of 23.07.1992. Book V was adopted under Act No. 92-1336 and published in Official Journal No. 296 of 23 December 1992 [cf. Rogacka-Rzewnicka (2004), pp. 456–457]. The text of the Code is available in the official Legifrance database: http://www.legifrance.gouv.fr (accessed on 15.11.2020).

[14]For the occurrence of this offence, it is not required that the offender breaks the security measures, provided that the fraudulent (deceptive) nature of his or her act is proven, which may be evidenced by circumventing the security features by e.g. using spyware or a Trojan horse and thus entering into possession of a password or access code to the system. Cf. Féral-Schuhl (2010), pp. 915–916.

alteration of the data stored in this system or any disruption (deterioration) in the functioning of the system, the offender shall be liable to a penalty of three years' imprisonment and a fine of up to 100,000 EUR (Article 323-1(2)).

Article 323-1(3) provides for an aggravated type of both of the above mentioned offences. The aggravating features include the type of system and the nature of the data processed therein. In the event of the State system where personal data are processed, the offenders are liable to a five-year imprisonment sentence and a fine of 150,000 EUR.

Another offence against automated data processing systems is to hinder or interfere with the operation of such a system, as specified in Article 323-2. The perpetrator is punishable by imprisonment for a period of five years and a fine of 150,000 EUR. As in the case of the offence involving fraudulent access, considering the type of the system attacked and the nature of the data processed in it (the State system processing personal data), the legislator provided for an aggravated type of such an offence, punishable by imprisonment for a period of seven years and a fine of 300,000 EUR.

Article 323-3 criminalises the act of maliciously entering data into an automated data-processing system or of fraudulently downloading, retaining, copying, transmitting, deleting or altering data within that system. The perpetrator of such an act is punishable by five years' imprisonment and a fine of 150,000 EUR. Likewise, as in the aforementioned offences, the constituent feature of the aggravated type of the offence is the nature of the object affected by the commission of the offence, in the case of a State system that automatically processes personal data. This act is punishable by imprisonment for a period of seven years and a fine of 300,000 EUR (Art. 323-3(2)).

By means of an amendment under Act No. 2004-575, following the adoption of the Convention on Cybercrime,[15] the provision in Art. 323-3-1 relating to "hacking tools" was added. On this basis, a given conduct is punishable if it is performed without a legal basis (i.e. unauthorised), which may in particular include conducting research or ensuring information security, involving the import, possession, sale, transmission or making available (including via the Internet) of any device, tool, computer program (or data of any kind) designed or specially adapted to commit one or more of the offences referred to in Articles 323-1 to 323-3. As regards the penalty envisaged, an unusual solution was applied. The perpetrators are subject to a punishment for the offence for which a "hacking tool" can be used. If it can be applied in several offences, such a perpetrator is subject to the most severe penalty. Therefore, he or she is treated virtually as an accomplice in committing an offence (somewhat equivalent to aiding in the commission of a crime in the Polish legal code), with the significant difference, however, that his or her liability is not of an accessory nature, i.e. it does not matter whether the "hacking tool" was used to commit the offence, or in the case of committing such an offence, whether the perpetrator's guilt was proven.

[15]Representatives of France participated in the work on the Convention on Cybercrime. It was signed by them on 23 November 2001, ratified on 10 January 2006 and entered into force for France on 1 May 2006.

Attempting to commit any of the above mentioned offences is punishable by law. The offender shall be liable, as it is the case in Polish law, within the limits provided for the offence actually committed (Article 323-7).

Article 323-4 criminalises membership in a criminal group or arrangement formed in order to prepare one or more of the offences referred to in Articles 323-1 to 323-3-1. Participation in such a group is punishable on the grounds of its undertaking at least one act demonstrating such an objective for its establishment, subject to the penalty provided for the act, which the members of the group or association intended to commit. In the event that the preparatory measures the group has taken could lead to acts bearing the features of several offences, and it is therefore necessary to choose the specific legal basis for the penalty, the provision stipulating that the most severe penalty shall apply. Under the Act 2014-1353 of the 13th of November 2014, Article 323-4-1 was added, specifying an aggravated type of offences as defined in Articles 323-1 to 323-3-1. The aggravating feature includes the fact that an offence has been committed against a public data processing system within an organised group, which is punishable by ten years' imprisonment and a fine of 300,000 EUR.

In Code Pénal, there are other offences against data or data processing systems. First and foremost, emphasis should be placed on Chapter VI ("Offences against personal rights"), Title II ("Offences against persons"), Book II ("Serious crimes and offences against persons"). In Section IV ("Violation of secrecy"), in par. 2 ("Violation of secrecy of correspondence"), in Article 226-15(2), the offence of computer eavesdropping is defined as an intentionally malicious act of interception, diversion, use or disclosure of correspondence sent, transmitted or received via an electronic communications network or the installation of devices intended for that purpose. The punishments for this offence include one year of imprisonment and a fine of 45,000 EUR. But when it is committed by the spouse or cohabiting partner of the victim or the partner linked to the victim by a civil solidarity pact, this act is punishable by two years' imprisonment and a fine of 60,000 EUR. . Section V ("Violations of personal rights resulting from the processing of computer files") consolidates the provisions criminalising unlawful processing of personal data (in particular, acts performed in breach of Act No. 78-17 of the 6th of January 1978 concerning information technology, computer files and freedoms).

5 Germany

In the Penal Code of 1871 in force in Germany (Strafgesetzbuch—StGB)[16] the offences in question have been defined in Chapter XV, which contains offences against private secrecy (computer espionage, Section 202a, interception of data,

[16]German Penal Code of 15 May 1871 (Strafgesetzbuch—StGB) as published on 13 November 1998 (BGBl. I S. 3322). Its contents (also in English, but not fully updated) can be accessed on the Internet via Gesetze im Internet (http://www.gesetze-im-internet.de).

Section 202b, offences related to hacking tools, Section 202 c) and in Chapter XXVII among offences involving damage to property (data alteration, Section 303a, and computer sabotage, Section 303 b).

The offence of computer espionage as defined in Section 202a (*Ausspähen von Daten*) entails unauthorised access by the perpetrator, for himself/herself or for a third party, to data not intended for them, provided that his or her actions are accompanied by the infringement of the specific security measures protecting against unauthorised access. In Subsection 2 of the aforementioned Section, it is clarified that only data, which are stored or transmitted electronically or magnetically or in any other imperceivable (*nicht unmittelbar wahrnehmbar*—not perceivable by the senses) manner shall be considered as data. Computer espionage is punishable by imprisonment for a period of up to three years or a fine.

The next offence listed in Chapter XV, interception of data (*Abfamgen von Daten*) as defined in Section 202b of the StGB, shall be committed by anyone who intercepts data, for himself/herself or a third party (within the meaning of Section 202a (2) of the StGB), which is not intended for them during their non-public transmission or electromagnetic emissions generated by a data processing system during such transmission, without authorisation. The perpetrator of such an offence shall be subject to imprisonment of up to two years or a fine, unless a more severe penalty is provided for in specific legislation.

In accordance with Section 202c of the StGB, the development and distribution of hacking tools is punishable as a criminal offence. Under this provision, it is prohibited to undertake preparatory activities leading to the commission of the offences referred to in Section 202a and Section 202b, consisting of the development or procurement (for oneself or for a third party), selling or transferring to a third party, disseminating, or making available in any other way, passwords or other security codes enabling access to data within the meaning of Section 202a (2), or computer programs designed to commit a criminal offence. This offence is punishable by imprisonment of up to one year or a fine. Pursuant to Section 202b (2), the provisions of Section 149(2) and (3) apply accordingly to this offence.[17] In other words, the perpetrator is not punished if the following two conditions are met jointly. First, the offender will resign from committing the planned offence and, at the same time, will prevent the threat of a third party's continuing preparations for, or perpetrating, the offence, or prevents the completion of the offence. Secondly, at the same time (also on a voluntary basis) the offender shall destroy or render unusable the instruments intended to commit the offence (if they still exist and are suitable for such use), or notify the State authorities of their existence or deliver such tools to the responsible authorities. On the other hand, in a situation when the danger of preparing for, or committing, an offence has been prevented without the intervention of the perpetrator, or its commission has been made impossible, and thus the perpetrator is unable to fulfil the first condition for avoiding punishment specified in Section 202c, such condition is nonetheless deemed satisfied if the perpetrator

[17]Section 149 of the StGB criminalises preparatory actions for the crime of money counterfeiting.

demonstrates with his or her conduct that he or she voluntarily and zealously sought to achieve this.

As mentioned, subsequent offences against data and computer systems have been classified by the German legislator as property destruction offences (Chapter XXVII). In Section 303a, the offence of data modification as unlawful deletion, blocking, alteration or rendering useless has been identified. The perpetrator of this offence is subject to a penalty of imprisonment of up to two years or a fine. In accordance with Subsection 2, attempting to commit this act is punishable and, in accordance with Subsection 3, Section 202c shall apply accordingly to preparation for committing such offence.

The offence of computer sabotage referred to in section 303b is an act committed by a person who significantly (materially) interferes with the processing of data, which are essential to a third party through:

(1) committing the act referred to in Section 303a (1), or
(2) entering or transmitting data with the intention of causing harm to a third party, or
(3) destroying, damaging, rendering useless, supressing or modifying an electronic data-processing system or data carrier.

The perpetrator is subject to imprisonment of up to three years or a fine. Attempting is punishable (Section 303b(3)). However, on the basis of Subsection. 5, Section 202c may apply accordingly in the case of preparation for committing such offence.

Section 303b (2) and (4) provides for aggravated types of computer sabotage. In the first case, the aggravating feature is the weight of the data processed in it. If the undisturbed functioning of the system is of significant importance to someone else's economic activities, another person's company or a State office, the perpetrator shall be subject to a penalty of imprisonment of up to five years or a fine. In the second case (which is in fact of the aggravated type of act under Subsection. 2), the aggravating feature involves particularly serious circumstances of the offence under Subsection 2. Their occurrence results in the possibility of sentences ranging from six months' to ten years' imprisonment. The legislator decided that such particularly serious incidents usually occur in a situation where the perpetrator:

(1) causes substantial financial loss, or
(2) has made proceeds from criminal activities a stable source of income or is a member of a criminal organisation, which has been formed to commit the offence of computer sabotage on a continuous basis, or
(3) through crime, he or she disrupts the provision of vital goods or services to the population, or impairs the security of the State.

To conclude the discussion on *Strafgesetzbuch*, it is worth mentioning Section 269. It may be applied (in some cases in conjunction with Section 303a) to aggravate the liability for IP-spoofing. In its basic type (Section 269 (1)), it is an offence punishable by imprisonment of up to five years or a fine,[18] imposed on a person who, for the purpose of fraudulent legal transactions, collects or modifies evidentiary data by falsifying or altering a document, which could be made in the course of the transaction or which uses such data.[19]

6 The United Kingdom

The main objective of the Computer Misuse Act 1990 (CMA)[20] was primarily to combat the offence of gaining unauthorised access to computer data and programs. Very soon it became obvious that it needed to be amended, it was emphasised, above all, the powerlessness of the law enforcement authorities in their fight against the perpetrators of DoS attacks, which could not be brought to justice on the basis of the CMA. Given these opinions and the fact that the United Kingdom signed the Convention on Cybercrime[21] and the necessity to implement the provisions of Framework Decision 2005/222, which has been made by means of adopting the Police and Justice Act 2006,[22] a number of substantial changes were introduced. For instance, the provision of Section 3 criminalising the disruption of computer operations was thoroughly modified (inter alia, enabling the prosecution of perpetrators of DoS attacks on its basis), and the provision of Section 3A, criminalising the development and distribution of hacking tools, was introduced. Furthermore, sanctions have been reinforced.[23] Under the most recent amendment (Serious Crime Act 2015[24]) the offence of causing, or threatening to cause, considerable damage has been added.

Currently, the Computer Misuse Act contains provisions criminalising four categories of infringement:

(1) acts related to obtaining unauthorised access (unauthorised access to a computer program or data in electronic form—Section 1; unauthorised access with intent to commit further offences—Section 2);

[18]For aggravated types of the offence, the penalty can be even up to ten years' imprisonment (see section 269(3) of StGB).

[19]Cf. Hoeren (2012), pp. 492–493.

[20]An Act to make provision for securing computer material against unauthorised access or modification; and for connected purposes (c. 18); the discussed legal acts are available on the official website http://www.legislation.gov.uk, accessed on 15.05.2020. CMA applies throughout the UK.

[21]The United Kingdom signed the Convention on Cybercrime on 23 November 2001, but ratified it until 25 May 2011, followed by its entry into force on 1 September 2011.

[22]Police and Justice Act 2006 (c. 48).

[23]Smith (2007), pp. 1019–1020; Murray (2010), pp. 338–340, 346–348; Walden (2007), pp. 174–175.

[24]Serious Crime Act 2015 (c. 9).

(2) unauthorised acts with intent to impair, or with recklessness as to impairing, operation of computer, network etc.—Section 3;
(3) unauthorised acts causing, or creating risk of, serious damage—section 3ZA;
(4) making, supplying or obtaining "hacking tools"—Section 3A.

The offence of unauthorised access, as defined in Section 1 (1), consists of causing a computer to perform any activity with the intent to secure access to any program or to data stored in any computer. This offence may be committed only intentionally. Section 1(1) (c) indicates that the offender must be aware, at the time of the action, that he is not entitled to access the data or the program. Simultaneously, it is stipulated that the intent of the perpetrator does not need to be to secure unauthorised access to a specific program or data (or even to a specific type of program or data), or to data or software held in any particular computer [Section 1 (2)]. In other words, it is not necessary to prove that the perpetrator of the act in question intended to obtain specific information or acted for specific reasons in order to bring charges against him or her. The intent of the offence is not a decisive factor in determining whether an offence has been committed or not, it could be, for example, to break the safeguards to test one's skills or simply to make a "joke". Moreover, it is also not necessary to prove that the perpetrator has actually gained access in order to attribute criminal liability to a given act. It is sufficient for him or her to initiate the appropriate measures resulting in operations that may enable him or her to do so.

The amount of the penalty that may be imposed depends on the type of proceedings under which this is to take place. In the case of summary proceedings (this is a procedure without a jury, currently conducted by a single professional judge), the offence is punishable by imprisonment of not more than twelve months or a fine, or both. In general, these are the highest penalties that may be imposed under this procedure. However, if the judge considers it necessary to impose a more severe sanction, the case may be referred to the Crown Court, which may impose a sentence of up to two years' imprisonment or a fine (without limiting its amount), or both at the same time.

Section 2 of the Computer Misuse Act criminalises the practice of obtaining unauthorised access with the intent to commit or facilitate the commission of further offences. It is committed by the offender whose conduct has the attributes of an offence referred to in Section 1, which constitutes a kind of activity preceding the commission of another offence, as referred to in that Section, or activity facilitating the commission of such an offence (whether by himself or herself or a third party).

It is irrelevant to the existence of the offence in question whether a "further offence" was committed at the time of unauthorised access or whether it happened later. The perpetrator of this offence is also liable if this further offence has not been committed, or even if it was impossible.[25] The perpetrator is liable to a more severe penalty than the one provided for unauthorised access only. It is punishable by

[25]Cf. Clough (2013), p. 51.

imprisonment of up to five years or a fine (or both). However, where summary procedure is applied, the situation is analogous to that of the case of an unlawful act referred to in Section 1.

The second group of offences provided for in the Computer Misuse Act includes conduct consisting of the perpetrator's intentional or reckless unauthorised act in relation to a computer, which is intended or likely to disrupt the operation of a computer, network, etc. This category includes two types of offences, which differ in the *mens rea* component. The first one is committed with intentional fault, the perpetrator commits an unauthorised act with the intention of causing the consequences indicated in Section 3 (2), i.e., to impair the operation of any computer, to prevent or hinder access to any program or data held on any computer, to impair the operation of any such program or the reliability of any such data. The second type of crime in question may be committed out of recklessness. Under Section 3 (3), the perpetrator, when undertaking unauthorised acts as referred to in Section 3 (1) is reckless as to whether the consequences indicated in Section 3 (2) occur (i.e. program or data impairment etc.). For both categories of the criminal act in question, the offender's conduct must be accompanied by the awareness that the act is unauthorised. It is not mandatory to prove that such conduct has led to any impairment in the operation of a computer [(or to any other consequence laid down in Section 3 (2)].[26] Furthermore, as in the case of the offence of unauthorised access, it is irrelevant from the perspective of the offence in question whether the offender's action was directed against a particular computer, program or specific data, or a computer, program or data of any specific type (cf. comments to Section 1). Consequently, the impairment, prevention or hindering of access is also punishable if it is transitory in nature. Under proceedings held before the Crown Court, a prison sentence of up to ten years or a fine may be imposed. Under the summary proceedings—as in the case of the offences discussed earlier—it is possible to impose the highest penalties provided for by this type of procedure.

Section 3ZA defines the offence of unauthorised causing, or creating risk of, serious damage. This is an unauthorised act in relation to a computer (as defined in Section 3). The condition for liability is that the perpetrator, at the time of committing the act, is aware that he or she is not authorised to perform the actions that he or she is attempting. This offence may be committed both intentionally and with recklessness. The concept of serious damage of a material kind is understood broadly. According to Section 3ZA (2), it is damage to human welfare or to the environment, in any place it occurs (or may occur), or damage to the economy or national security of any country. Whereas, pursuant to Section 3 ZA (3), damage to human welfare is understood as:

(1) loss to human life,
(2) human illness or injury,
(3) disruption of money, food, water, energy or fuel supplies,

[26]Cf. Smith (2007), pp. 1020–1023.

(4) disruption of the communication system (understood as the transmission of information),
(5) disruption of facilities for transport,
(6) disruption of the services related to health.

Section 3ZA (4) stipulates that it is immaterial whether the perpetrator's behaviour was the sole or principal cause of the damage, as well as whether it was a direct or indirect consequence of his or her act.

Due to the seriousness of the crime, the proceedings for the aforementioned offence are exclusively held before the Crown Court, which may impose a sentence of up to fourteen years' imprisonment, a fine, or both. However, where the act of the perpetrator has resulted in the death of a human being or damage to health or substantial harm to national security (or has brought about a threat thereof), the perpetrator shall be liable to imprisonment for life or to a fine, or to both.

Provisions criminalizing the conduct of producing, supplying or obtaining "hacking tools" are contained in Section 3A of the CMA. Three prohibited acts are defined. The first one includes making, adapting, supplying and offering to supply any "article" (this term should be understood as any programs and data held in electronic form)[27] with the intention that it should be used to commit (or to assist in the commission of) any of the offences referred to in Sections 1, 3 or 3ZA. It is immaterial to the liability of the offender whether the tool created (provided) was used to commit the offence, or even whether it was suitable for that purpose. The offender's intention to enable a third party to commit a crime is crucial. The act may therefore be committed only intentionally, in contrast to the second offence, which is described in Section 3A, which may also be committed out of recklessness. It consists in supplying or offering to supply any "article" believing that it is likely to be used to commit (or assist in the commission of) any of the offences specified in Sections 1, 3 or 3ZA of the CMA. The third offence identified in Section 3A is the obtaining of any "article" with the intention of using it to commit (or assist in the commission of) any of the offences under Sections 1, 3 or 3ZA or of its being supplied to a third party with the intention of using it to commit (or assist in the commission of) any of the offences under Sections 1, 3 or 3ZA.

In summary proceedings, as in the case of other offences, the maximum penalties provided for under such procedure may be imposed, while in the case of conviction on indictment before the Crown Court, the offender may be sentenced to imprisonment of up to two years, to a fine, or both.

[27] In order to hold the perpetrator liable under this provision, it is sufficient that the object of his or her action is a single "article".

7 Spain

The applicable Penal Code of the Kingdom of Spain[28] (Código Penal) was adopted on the 23rd of November 1995, replacing the Code of 1870, which had been subject to multiple amendments.

Spain signed the Convention on CyberCrime on the 23rd of November 2001 and ratified it on the 3rd of June 2010. The offences in question are defined in Articles 197, 197 bis, 197 ter, 197 quater and 198 (Title X "Offences against privacy, the right to personal image and the inviolability of housing", Chapter I "Discovery and disclosure of secrets") and Articles 264, 264 bis, 264 ter (Title XIII "Offences against property and social and economic order", Chapter VIII "Damage") of Código Penal. The Spanish regulation in its present form is the result of a comprehensive amendment introduced under the Act of the 31st of March 2015[29] (which became valid on the 1st of July 2015), harmonising the Code regulations with EU laws.

According to Article 197(1), an imprisonment sentence of one to four years and a fine, or a sentence of twelve to twenty four months is imposed upon the perpetrator who, in order to discover (uncover) the secrets or to breach privacy of another person, without his or her consent, acquires any letters, e-mails or any other personal documents or belongings, intercepts telecommunications of that nature or uses technical means to eavesdrop on the transmission, recording or reproduction of sound or image or other manifestations of interpersonal communication. Pursuant to Paragraph 2, the same penalty may be imposed on an offender who, without being authorised to do so, intercepts, uses or alters proprietary[30] data of a personal or family nature stored as files on a computer, on information or electronic media, or in any similar data filing system, whether public or private, to the detriment of a third party (i.e. both the person directly harmed by the actions of the perpetrator, the data holder, i.e. usually the data subject, and any other third party who is affected by the act for any reason). The same penalty shall be imposed on anyone who, without being authorised to do so, accesses such data by any means, and alters or uses such data to the detriment of the owner or third party.

Furthermore, a sentence of between two and five years' imprisonment is provided for a person who disseminates, discloses or transfers to third parties data or facts coming to his or her knowledge as a result of committing the acts referred to in Article 197(1) and (2) or images obtained in this way (Subparagraph 1 of Article 197 (3)). A person who is aware of the illegal origin of the data or images (i.e. the fact

[28]Organic Law No. 10/1995 of 23 November 1995 (BOE No. 281 of 24 November 1995). The text is available on the Iberlex website (http://www.boe.es, accessed on 15.12.2020).

[29]Organic Law No. 1/2015 of 30 March 2015 (BOE No. 77 of 31 March 2015).

[30]According to the views of legal commentators and the views expressed in the case law of the Spanish Supreme Court, this concept is broader than sensitive data. It contains all the private data that is usually not disclosed to a wide circle of people, meaning persons other than closest relatives and friends. Cf. Letai, p. 246.

that they were obtained by means of one of the offences referred to in Article 197(1)-(2)), if he or she did not participate in obtaining the data or images, but performs the aforementioned activities, shall be liable to a fine and a sentence of between twelve and twenty four months or to imprisonment of between one and three years (Article 197(3), Subpara. 2).

Further Código Penal provisions in Art. 197 provide for a number of types of aggravated crimes under Article 197(1-2). Pursuant to Paragraph 4, the perpetrator of these offences shall be subject to more severe sanctions (imprisonment of three to five years) if he or she was the person responsible for the files, storage medium, electronic archive or register in which the data were processed or which were under his or her custody, or if the data, which were the subject of the offence were personal data and the perpetrator was not authorised to use them. Whereas, where private data classified as proprietary data (as referred to in Para. 2) are disseminated, transmitted or disclosed to a third party, the offender shall be subject to a penalty within the upper half of the range provided by law (Article 197(4), Subpara. 2). The nature of data being the object of offence constitutes a factor aggravating criminal liability pursuant to Article 197(5), in which it is stipulated that where the object of the offences referred to in the previous provisions includes data concerning religion, religious denomination, health, ethnic origin, race, sexual orientation (i.e. sensitive data), or where the victim is a minor or a person with disability in need of special care, the penalty imposed should fall within the upper half of the range provided by law.

In accordance with Article 197(6), if the offence referred to in the preceding paragraphs is committed for the purpose of making a profit, the offender shall be sentenced to a penalty, which falls within the upper half of the penalty range provided by law. However, if the offence affected data referred to in Para. 6 (sensitive data), the offender is liable to even more severe sentences, ranging from to seven years' imprisonment.

The first Subparagraph of Para. 7 of the discussed Article provides for a type of criminal act, which does not constitute a typical computer crime, but which may be committed using information technology. According to this provision, a person who, without the consent of the person concerned, distributes, discloses or transmits to third parties photographs or audio-visual recordings, which he or she has obtained with his or her consent in his or her place of residence or in other circumstances, which demonstrate their private nature and the intention not to disclose them to others shall be liable to imprisonment for a term of between three months and one year, or a fine and a sentence of between six and twelve months ("domicilio o en cualquier otro lugar fuera del alcance de la mirada de terceros") if disclosure is likely to infringe the privacy of that person.

The perpetrator can face a more severe penalty (imposed at the upper half of the penalty range) if he or she is or has been the spouse of the victim or has been in a similar relationship with him or her (but not necessarily cohabitation), or if the victim was a minor or a person with disability in need of special care, or if the offence was committed for the purpose of financial gain (Article 197(7) Subpara. 2).

The subsequent articles (197 bis, 197 ter, 197 quater), added under the amendment of the 31st of March 2015, are intended to implement the provisions of Directive 2013/40. Article 197 bis (1) provides for a penalty of six months to two years' imprisonment for obtaining or facilitating unauthorised access to the whole or any part of an information system by any means or method and after infringing security measures, or for remaining in the information system despite the opposition of the person, who has the right to prohibit it, (thus exceeding the limits of the powers conferred on the user). The second Subparagraph of that provision criminalises the unauthorised interception, by technical means, of non-public transmissions of computer data from, or within, an information system, including electromagnetic emissions. The said act is punishable by imprisonment for a period of three months to two years or a fine and a sentence of between three and twelve months.

The issue of the interrelation between the provisions of Art. 197 bis (1) and (2), and those of Art. 197 are particularly interesting. Unfortunately, the framework of this study does not allow this issue to be analysed.

The criminalisation of acts relating to hacking tools is provided for in Art. 197 ter. It prohibits, on pain of imprisonment for a term of between six months and two years or a fine of between three and eighteen months, unauthorised production, procurement for use, import or making available in any way to third parties, with the intention of facilitating the commission of any of the offences referred to in Article 197 (1) and (2) or Article 197 bis: a computer program designed or adapted primarily to commit such offences, or a computer password, access code or similar data enabling access to all or part of an information system.

Art. 197 quater provides for the aggravation of criminal liability where the acts referred to in this Chapter of the Code have been committed within the framework of a criminal organisation or group, a higher level of punishment than is provided in the Code may be imposed.

Article 198 defines the aggravated type for all offences referred to in Article 197. The aggravating feature is related to the *mens rea* component of the offence. This provision refers to persons who, acting as public officers and taking advantage of their function, commit an offence, which fulfils the characteristics of any of the prohibited acts specified in Article 197. Such offender shall be subject to a penalty appropriate to the offence in its upper half range. In addition, he or she is liable to an "absolute prohibition" (*la inhabilitación absoluta*) ordered for a period from six to twelve years.

The offences against the integrity of computer data and systems have been identified in Article 264 of the Código Penal, which has been thoroughly modified by the aforementioned amendment, and in the subsequent articles added as a result of the amendment. Under Article 264(1), a penalty of six months to three years' imprisonment shall be imposed on a person who, by any means whatsoever, without right, erases, damages, deteriorates, alters, deletes or renders inaccessible data, computer programs or electronic documents belonging to third parties, provided that the consequences of the act are serious. The aggravated type of this offence is provided for in the next Paragraph. According to its contents, the perpetrator is subject to increased liability if the action:

(1) has been committed within an organised criminal group, or
(2) has caused serious disruption, or has been directed against a significant number of information systems, or
(3) has jeopardised the provision of essential public services or the essential needs of the population, or
(4) has affected a critical infrastructure information system or created a serious threat to the security of a Member State, the EU or an EU Member State, or
(5) has been committed using the measures specified in Article 264 ter (i.e. "hacking tools").

The penalty provided for includes imprisonment for a term of between two and five years and a fine, which may be imposed of up to ten times the equivalent of the damage caused. However, if the offence has had particularly serious consequences, an imprisonment sentence higher by one level may be imposed (Article 264(3)). Nevertheless, pursuant to Article 264 (4), penalties for the acts referred to in that Article are imposed applying the upper half range if, in committing them, the offender concerned has used the identity of a third party in order to gain access to an information system or to win the trust of a third party.

The next Article (Article 264 bis) criminalises attacks involving the unauthorised, substantial disruption or interruption of the operation of an information system belonging to a third party through the performance of acts described in the preceding provisions, the input or transmission of data, destruction, damage, deactivation, removal or replacement of an information system or mass storage. This offence is punishable by imprisonment for a term of six months to three years. Nonetheless, if it has had a significant impact on the activities of the enterprise or on the functioning of the public administration, the penalty shall be applied within upper half range, and may be increased by one level.

Article 264 bis (2) stipulates that where the act referred to in Para. 1 has been committed in the circumstances described in Article 264(2), the perpetrators are liable to a term of imprisonment of between three and eight years, and to a fine of between three and ten times the value of the damage caused. Similarly to the offences under Article 264, penalties for the acts, referred to in the said Article, are imposed in their upper half range if, in committing them, the offender has used the identity of a third party in order to gain access to an information system or to win the trust of a third party (Article 264 bis (3)).

Article 264 ter criminalises acts relating to hacking tools used to commit the offences referred to in the aforementioned provisions. It has the same wording as Article 197 ter, as discussed above, so it is not necessary to cite it again.

References

Clough J (2013) Principles of cybercrime. New York
Féral-Schuhl Ch (2010) Cyberdroit: le droit à l'épreuve de l'Internet. Paris
Hoeren T (2012) Internet- und Kommunikationsrecht: Praxis-Lehrbuch. Cologne
Letai P, Spain Part VII. Computer related crime. In: Blanpain R (ed) International encyclopaedia of laws. Vol 3. Cyber law (ed. J. Dumortier). Kluwer Law International
Murray A (2010) Information technology law. The Law and Society, Oxford–New York
Radoniewicz F (2016) Odpowiedzialność karna za hacking i inne przestępstwa przeciwko danym komputerowym i systemom informatycznym. Warsaw
Rogacka-Rzewnicka M (2004) In: Machowska A, Wojtyczek K (eds) Prawo Francuskie, vol I. Cracow
Smith GJH (ed) (2007) Internet law and regulation. London
Walden I (2007) Computer crimes and digital investigations. Oxford

Filip Radoniewicz PhD; legal advisor; adjunct in the Department of Cybersecurity Law and New Technologies at the Institute of Law, War Studies University, Warsaw; expert at the Academic Centre for Cybersecurity Policy (War Studies University) and in the Ministry of Justice; he worked as an assistant judge (in the Fourth Criminal and Sixth Penitentiary Department of the Regional Court in Lublin); graduate of post-graduate studies: "European Union Law" at the Jagiellonian University, "Human Rights and Freedoms", co-organized by the Institute of Legal Sciences of the Polish Academy of Sciences and the Helsinki Foundation for Human Rights, and "Computer Network Administration" at the Lublin University of Technology; author or co-author of approximately fifty publications, mainly in the field of broadly understood criminal law, new technology law and human rights. Selected publications: F. Radoniewicz (2016) Odpowiedzialność karna za hacking i inne przestępstwa przeciwko danym komputerowym i systemom informatycznym / Criminal liability for hacking and other offences against computer data and information systems/, Wolters Kluwer, Warszawa; Ustawa o krajowym systemie cyberbezpieczeństwa. Komentarz /Act on the National Cybersecurity System. Commentary/ (2019) ed. W. Kitler, J. Taczkowska-Olszewska, F. Radoniewicz, CH. Beck, Warszawa.

The Entities and Institutions in Charge of Combating Cybercrime in Poland

Jerzy Kosiński

Abstract This chapter presents the relationship between cybersecurity and national and internal security and identifies the effects of cybercrime and the need to combat it. The author, pointing to selected main state institutions and authorities, describes their activities in ensuring cybersecurity and combating cybercrime.

1 Introduction

Cybersecurity is most often understood as the security of globally connected information systems (e.g. the Internet infrastructure), telecommunications networks, computer systems, and industrial control systems. Cybersecurity breaches can serve the purpose of numerous criminal acts which cause substantial financial and non-financial losses for organisations, businesses, and individuals. It is hardly questionable that this problem is also significant in the context of internal security, and, hence, national security.

In 2003, Dan Verton wrote that the uninterrupted functioning of cyberspace[1] in highly developed countries was fundamental, not only for the proper functioning of the economy, but also for national security.[2] This statement, concerning both external and internal security, has become even more pertinent with the development of information and communication technologies.

[1]The emergence of cyberspace is connected with the establishing of the political concept of "the information superhighway" during Bill Clinton's presidential campaign in 1992, defined as all types of information containing text, sounds, and images, which could be transferred over large distances, in a quick and uninhibited manner. However, it is to Vice President Al Gore to whom greater credit in this field should be attributed, as he continued to promote the development of the information superhighway later during Clinton's presidency. It is worth noting that the technical and functional concepts of the information superhighway derive from the Infostrada concept proposed in the early 1970s by Prof. Andrzej Targowski.

[2]Verton (2004), p. 76.

J. Kosiński (✉)
Akademia Marynarki Wojennej w Gdyni/Polish Naval Academy in Gdynia, Gdynia, Poland
e-mail: j.kosinski@amw.gdynia.pl

K. Chałubińska-Jentkiewicz et al. (eds.), *Cybersecurity in Poland*,
https://doi.org/10.1007/978-3-030-78551-2_26

The rapid technological advancement observed in recent years, and in particular the development of telecommunication technologies and the progressing computerisation in virtually every sphere of human life, have made information the most precious resource. Information is the key to success in politics and business, and in the planning and conducting of military operations. It is no less significant to note that the uninterrupted flow of, and access to, information is indispensable for the proper functioning of the economy, administration, and specialised forces of every country.[3]

No elements in national power are free from, or independent of, information. The Army, the Police, the financial system, the economy, transportation, energy, healthcare, and the media—all these rely on the functioning of communication and information systems. Information contained and processed in such systems should be protected, as is done with every material good. Information has become the object of conflicts, the tools for which include any means adjusted to its collection, disruption, and protection. Information warfare is aimed at obtaining and using the kind of information resources which contain classified, confidential, and inaccessible information. While it is frequently conducted with a view to gaining access to personal data, it sometimes involves competing businesses and corporations. Information warfare also takes place at the national and regional levels.[4]

The information warfare concept can be approached by analysing its major elements, i.e. information resources and antagonists, as well as offensive and defensive operations.[5] One of the domains of information warfare includes crimes[6] which are usually perpetrated, together with Open Source Intelligence (OSINT), and competitive intelligence, for the purpose of offensive operations, while combating cybercrime is among the major duties of governments as regards defensive operations.

What is specific to the threats emerging from the use of ICTs is the absence of physical contact with the perpetrator. The fact that there is no clearly defined adversary makes the threats seem blurred, and less real, which triggers an imminent need to develop and maintain an appropriate security system. The lack of universal social understanding in this field is also a threat in itself, as it hinders reasonable efforts leading to the shaping of cybersecurity space in a multidimensional, concurrent and substantively consistent manner.[7]

It is worth noting that constructing an absolutely secure communication and information system is practically impossible from the technical point of view. Threats to communication and information systems can involve both technological and human factors. On the one hand, threats posed by technology, such as hard drive

[3] *The White Book on the National Security of the Republic of Poland*, National Security Bureau (BBN), Warsaw 2013, p. 63.

[4] Cf. Ciborowski (2001), p. 9.

[5] More information in Denning (2002), pp. 23–48.

[6] Denning (2002), p. 59.

[7] Ciborowski (2001), pp. 178–179.

failure, are usually foreseeable, and can be properly mitigated (e.g. by doubling the critical system elements), or a desirable level of security can be ensured through risk analysis (e.g. by incremental backups). Threats induced by humans, on the other hand, are much harder to foresee. An attacker might be an outsider in breach of security, or an insider, i.e. a person from within the organisation whose conduct gives rise to a threat. Although the media are much more inclined to publicise information on outsider attacks, various research and analyses have indicated that insider attacks (i.e. perpetrated by current or former employees, contractors, or other business partners) are in fact more dangerous and cause more severe losses.[8]

The Council of the European Union, in its conclusions of 2013 on setting the EU priorities for the fight against serious and organised crime between 2014 and 2017,[9] recognised as one of its priorities combating cybercrime committed by organised criminal groups and generating large criminal profits, such as online and payment card fraud, cybercrimes which cause serious harm to their victims, such as online child sexual exploitation, and cyber attacks which affect critical infrastructure and information systems in the EU. In 2017, the Council decided to continue the series of EU policy on serious and organised international crime in 2018–2021.[10] Also, it should be borne in mind that the previously adopted Cybersecurity Strategy of the European Union[11] emphasised the need to increase the operational capability for combating cybercrime and increasing IT infrastructure's resilience. Based on the same document, a comprehensive approach to the cybersecurity problem should combine three pillars—network and information security, law enforcement, and defence—which are also governed by various legal frameworks.

The scale of cybercrime also appears alarming, with 378 million victims per year, which corresponds to 12 people falling victim to cybercriminals every second. In 2017, cybercriminals stole $172 billion from 978 million victims in 20 countries. Although the average direct loss dropped to USD 142/victim, cybercrime consequences took on average nearly 24 h (which equals 3 full working days) to be removed. In the United States alone, 143 million consumers have fallen victim to cybercrime, which accounts for over 50% of the adult U.S. population present online.[12]

---

[8]Increase in Insider Threat Cases Highlight Significant Risks to Business Networks and Proprietary Information, http://www.ic3.gov/media/2014/140923.aspx, Survey: More Attacks Coming From Outsiders, Insider Attacks More Costly, http://www.securityweek.com/survey-more-attacks-coming-outsiders-insider-attacks-more-costly and Lynch (2006). Accessed on 1 December 2020.

[9]Council conclusions on setting the EU's priorities for the fight against serious and organised crime between 2014 and 2017. Doc 137401/13.

[10]https://www.consilium.europa.eu/pl/policies/eu-fight-against-organised-crime-2018-2021/. Accessed on 1 December 2020.

[11]Communication to the European Parliament, the Council, the Economic and Social Committee, and the Committee of the Regions, of 7 February 2013 *Cybersecurity Strategy of the European Union: An Open, Safe and Secure Cyberspace,* doc. JOIN (2013)1.

[12]https://us.norton.com/cyber-security-insights-2017. Accessed on 1 December 2020.

In testifying before the U.S. Congress on 20 March 2009, Edward Amoroso, CSO of AT&T, estimated that the annual profits made by cybercriminals exceeded $1 trillion ($10^{12}$), i.e. more than the revenue generated by the entire IT industry, and corresponding to approximately 7% of the U.S. GDP.[13] This value, however, might have been overestimated, as it was quoted in connection with applying for financial aid.

Based on the survey conducted by the British Department for Business, Innovation & Skills, in collaboration with PwC, the level of costs incurred by British entrepreneurs due to cybersecurity breaches has reached billions of pounds per year, and these costs have tripled since 2012.[14] The same survey revealed that 87% of small enterprises and 93% of large organisations recorded at least one security breach in 2012. The most severe breaches of cybersecurity cost small enterprises an average of £50,000, and large enterprises (with more than 250 employees) approximately £650,000. To get the bigger picture, these costs should be added to the expenditures on cybersecurity, accounting for approximately 10% of the total IT costs in enterprises. In 2013, for the above reasons, the British Government launched a special CISP[15] platform, comprising officers of the GCHQ,[16] the NCA,[17] MI5, UK CERT, and representatives of business circles (at first from critical infrastructure sectors—defence, energy, finance, pharmaceuticals, and telecommunications), to defend companies against the growing threat of cyber attacks from China, Russia, and Iran.

Although most cyber attacks were outsider violations performed by criminals, hackers, or competitors, internal threats were also reported. 36% of the most severe security breach cases were caused by unintentional human behaviour, and another 10% resulted from systems' being deliberately abused by employees.

Khoo Boon Hui, President of Interpol, at the 41st European Regional Conference,[18] quoted an academic study by the London Metropolitan University, which found "80 per cent of crime committed online is now connected with organised gangs operating across borders." He also remarked that "the cost of cybercrime is larger than the combined cost of cocaine, marijuana, and heroin trafficking. In Europe, the cost of cybercrime has apparently reached 750 billion Euros a year,

[13]National Research Council. Proceedings of a Workshop on Deterring Cyberattacks: Informing Strategies and Developing Options for U.S. Policy. Washington, DC: The National Academies Press, 2010, p. 8, http://www.nap.edu/download.php?record_id=12997. Accessed on 1 December 2020.

[14]http://www.ft.com/intl/cms/s/0/bb3fcc90-ab4a-11e2-ac71-00144feabdc0.html#axzz2ROfLvggZ. Accessed on 1 December 2020.

[15]The Cyber Security Information Sharing Partnership, https://www.gov.uk/government/news/government-launches-information-sharing-partnership-on-cyber-security. Accessed on 1 December 2020.

[16]Government Communications Headquarters.

[17]The National Crime Agency.

[18]http://www.interpol.int/content/download/14086/99246/version/1/file/41ER-Khoo-Open-ing-Speech.pdf. Accessed on 1 December 2020.

[…] with US banks purportedly losing $900 million to bank robbers but $12 billion to cyber criminals [in 2011]." Perhaps, this was not a landmark finding, considering that Valerie McNevin, an advisor to the U.S. Treasury International Technical Assistance Office, estimated earlier (in 2005) that the global revenue from e-crime had exceeded USD 105 billion in 2004. The proceeds from illegal drug trafficking in the corresponding period had been lower,[19] though better documented. In 2012, the Federal Bureau of Investigation (FBI) recorded a decrease in "physical crime", including bank robbery, which was in contrast to cybercrime, which had been growing at an alarming rate.[20]

General Keith Alexander, Director of the U.S. National Security Agency supervising the U.S. Cyber Command, warned in July 2012 that illicit cyberspace activities essentially amounted to "the greatest transfer of wealth in history[21]". The UNODC report of 2010 revealed that the annual revenue of criminals from identity theft (being the most profitable cybercrime) amounted to $ 1 billion, and from child pornography to $ 250 million.[22] In the 2012 survey by McAfee, it was estimated that the global cost of cybersecurity amounted to $ 1 trillion.[23] Obviously, any such findings, especially when they concern phenomena which are hard to measure, such as the cost of cybercrime, should be approached with caution.[24] However, even if its level were 50% lower, it would still be a huge sum. In the 2014 report, McAfee analysts stated that the Internet generated $2–3 trillion in revenue in the global economy per year (with a steady upward trend), but that value was, in fact, reduced by 15–20% due to cybercrime.[25]

More and more frequently, cybercrime can be treated as a sort of type of "service" rendered by criminals. In simple terms, there are four categories of "services" rendered by the Internet's criminal underworld:

---

[19]http://news.techworld.com/security/4881/cybercrime-more-profitable-than-drugs. This finding has been questioned several times, e.g. http://www.informationweek.com/experts-debate-whether-cybercrime-profits-surpass-drug-trafficking/d/d-id/1038656?. Accessed on 1 December 2020.

[20]http://www.wmbfnews.com/story/20972727/robberies-decrease-as-cyber-crime-increases-fbi-says. Accessed on 1 December 2020.

[21]http://www.ibtimes.com/americas-top-cyberwarrior-says-cyberattacks-cost-250-billion-year-722559. Accessed on 1 December 2020.

[22]The TOCTA 2010 Report, UNODC, pp. 205, 211, https://www.unodc.org/documents/data-and-analysis/tocta/10.Cybercrime.pdf. Accessed on 1 December 2020.

[23]http://truth-out.org/news/item/10700-does-cybercrime-really-cost-1-trillion. This value, however, is often questioned. Further details on the calculation method can be found in a report entitled *The Economic Impact of Cybercrime and Cyber Espionage*, McAfee 2013, http://www.mcafee.com/sg/resources/reports/rp-economic-impact-cybercrime.pdf. Accessed on 1 December 2020.

[24]The cybercrime cost estimation method can be found in D. Florencio, C. Herley, Sex, Lies, and Cyber-crime Surveys, MSR-TR-2011-75, June 2011, http://research.microsoft.com/pubs/149886/sexliesandcybercrimesu-rveys.pdf. Accessed on 1 December 2020.

[25]Net Losses: Estimating the Global Cost of Cybercrime Economic impact of cybercrime II, McAfee 2014. http://csis.org/files/attachments/140609_rp_economic_impact_cybercrime_report.pdf. Accessed on 1 December 2020.

(1) *Research-as-a-Service*—some criminal groups specialise in facilitating the sales of vulnerabilities on the black market, before modifications to mitigate such vulnerabilities are published by their producers (*zero-day vulnerabilities*). There are also people who act as intermediaries in the sales of this specific kind of intellectual property. Contrary to the other three categories, research as a Service does not necessarily come from illegal sources.
(2) *Crimeware-as-a-Service*—this category features the "service" of creating and developing malicious software which is aimed at exploiting programming errors, and then using them for specific criminal acts, as well as developing auxiliary software to foster an attack (downloaders, keyloggers, bots, etc.), tools to disguise malicious software with some security mechanisms (keypads, obfuscators, polymorphic malware, etc.), and spam tools. In addition, it can also include creating hardware to be used for data acquisition (e.g. magnetic card skimmers) or security breaking devices (e.g. antennae, eavesdropping devices);
(3) *Cybercrime Infrastructure-as-a-Service*—this involves the situation in which other cybercriminals can use a set of tools, once developed, against their victims. An example is renting a computer network for perpetrating an attack, as well as providing access to an online platform for the purpose of independently configuring cybercrime tools, or maintaining a platform facilitating the acquisition or exchange of tools enabling criminal activity.
(4) *Hacking-as-a-Service*—this involves the complete outsourcing of an attack. In this case, the person ordering the service does not need to have any technical expertise. However, this service can cost more than purchasing tools and conducting an attack independently. This category also covers such services as providing information to be used for identity theft, and acquiring credit card data and website login details.[26]

Another problem arises from the fact that politicians, law enforcement authorities, and the judiciary underestimate the scale of computer-crime threats, and its associations with business. The social costs of cybercrime are frequently neglected, as the focus is only on the financial impact. In addition, the real extent of cybercrime is hard to determine, which largely stems from the fact that such crimes are often revealed accidentally, mainly due to errors made by the perpetrators themselves. Police statistics usually include only those crimes which have been identified. While the Police authorities tend to proudly publicise the numbers of detected crimes, they are reluctant to mention that approximately 70% of these are crimes whose perpetrators were already known at the time of the crime's detection[27] (e.g. they had been identified by the victim or the victim's services).

[26]Cf. a report entitled *Cybercrime Exposed. Cybercrime-as-a-Service*, McAfee 2013, p. 3, http://www.mcafee.com/uk/resources/white-papers/wp-cybercrime-exposed.pdf. Accessed on 1 December 2020.

[27]This is the author's own study of computer fraud in Poland (Adamski and Kosiński 2007, pp. 131–149), but the results in other countries are similar.

The Republic of Poland has a centralised cyberspace-protection system. The responsibilities regarding cybersecurity are shared, *inter alia*, by the Ministry of Digital Affairs, the Ministry of Interior and Administration, the Ministry of National Defence, the Ministry of Justice, the Government Centre for Security, the Office of Electronic Communications, the Inspector General for Personal Data Protection, the Ministry of Economic Development, the Ministry of Foreign Affairs, the Internal Security Agency, the Police, the Intelligence Service, the Military Counterintelligence Service, and the National Bank of Poland, as well as CERT POLSKA, forming part of the Research and Academic Computer Network (NASK).

This study, rather than providing a detailed description of the responsibilities assigned to all these entities, focuses on combating cybercrime, and on briefly outlining the responsibilities of those entities with whom law enforcement a engage in close cooperation.

2 The Ministry Competent for Computerisation

Let us begin by outlining and presenting the responsibilities of the ministry competent for computerisation, as it is a single central public institution, responsible for both cybersecurity policy and cybersecurity itself. The ministry competent for computerisation is in charge of the political and strategic coordination of cyberspace to guarantee Poland's security. Duties in this field include establishing the minimum ICT-security requirements in public administration, and defining the minimum requirements for public records and electronic information exchange, as well as the minimum requirements for communication and information systems (based on the Act of 2005 on the Computerisation of the Operations of the Entities Performing Public Tasks, and the Regulation of the Council of Ministers of 2012 on National Interoperability Frameworks). In addition, the ministry of competent for computerisation has also been entrusted with supervising the Office of Electronic Communication, to which telecommunications operators report major incidents regarding telecommunication networks (in compliance with the Act of 2004—Telecommunications Law). The Ministry also supervises the activities pursued by the Research and Academic Computer Network, as a research institute, and as a data-transmission network operator, and the National Cybersecurity Centre (NC Cyber NASK), established in July 2016 as a major centre in charge of the cybersecurity of the Republic of Poland. NC Cyber NASK has been separated, in organisational terms, from the Research and Academic Computer Network's structure. Some of its duties have been delegated to other sections of that research institute. Dyżurnet.pl is one of the NC Cyber NASK divisions, which acts as a point of contact responding to reports received from Internet users about potentially illegal material (mainly related to the sexual abuse of children, and child pornography, but also to acts of aggression for racist, ethnic, religious, and other motives). Another major duty of NC Cyber NASK is to conduct the ongoing monitoring of network threats such as botnets, and of the working methods of their owners.

3 The Internal Security Agency

The Internal Security Agency (ISA) is another public administration authority dealing with cybersecurity as well as cybercrime. The ISA's activities relating to cyber threats focus on coordinating responses to incidents threatening the security of communication and information systems and networks used by state authorities (the duty of CERT.GOV.PL), as well as on developing the capabilities of public administration for protecting ICT resources, and on supervising the early warning system of threats to public administration networks (ARAKIS-GOV). Another of the ISA's activities is to combat cyberterrorism (illegal attacks or threats of attacks on computers, networks, or information systems, resulting from the activities of terrorist groups or foreign intelligence services).

The ISA is mainly in charge of recognising, preventing, and combating threats to the country's internal security and its constitutional order, and in particular to the sovereignty and international standing, independence, and integrity of its territory, and defence. The ISA may collect any personal data (including classified information), and also so-called sensitive data, where justified by the character of the implemented tasks. The ISA has the right to use both such data and information obtained through investigative operations undertaken by authorised bodies, services, and public institutions, and to process such data and information, in compliance with the Act on Personal Data Protection, without the knowledge and consent of the data subjects. If any information or materials obtained through the activities of the bodies, services, or institutions authorised to perform investigative operations indicate that the case constituting the subject matter of such activities falls within the scope of the ISA's duties, these bodies, services, or institutions shall obligatorily transfer the obtained information and materials to the Agency. If, however, any information and materials obtained through the ISA's activities indicate that the case constituting their subject matter falls within the scope of duties of other authorities, services, or institutions, the ISA's Head shall transfer the obtained information and materials to the authorised body, service or institution.

On 1 February 2008, the Governmental Computer Security Incident Response Team (CERT.GOV.PL) was established within the ISA's structure, to ensure and develop the capabilities of public administration units regarding protection from cyber threats, and in particular from attacks on infrastructures comprising information systems and networks, the destruction or disruption of which can severely threaten the lives and health of the country's population, national heritage, or environment, or can lead to substantial financial losses, or obstruct the functioning of public sector entities. In compliance with the CERT.GOV.PL policy, it essentially acts as a computer security incident response team in the domain of government administration. The principal duty of CERT.GOV.PL is to carry out operations related to the security of the information systems of state bodies. This involves ensuring and developing the capabilities of public administration authorities to protect themselves from cyber threats, and in particular from attacks on ICT infrastructure. CERT.GOV.PL mainly deals with cyber incidents in the public sector, and its duties include coordinating the response to incidents, and handling and analysing incidents, as well as coordinating the response to security breaches. In the case of incidents with a wide spectrum of impacts, CERT.GOV.PL coordinates the measures taken in connection with a given incident and responds to it, and also exchanges information with the entities directly affected by the cyber attack. It also uses the experience gathered from previous incidents, prepares warnings containing technical information and recommendations for further measures, and supplies them to government administration units. This process is aimed at preventing similar attacks on other institutions, or at reducing the likelihood of their occurrence.

4 The Police

Preparatory proceedings in cybercrime cases are conducted by the Police, and are governed by the Act on the Police.

In October 2014, the Department for Fighting Cybercrime was established within the Criminal Office of the National Police Headquarters. Its activities were supported by the Departments for Fighting Cybercrime operating within individual Provincial Police Headquarters. Similar departments were also established in the Capital Police Headquarters in Warsaw, and in the Central Bureau of Investigation. In December 2016, the Department for Fighting Cybercrime operating within the National Police Headquarters was transformed into the Office for Fighting Cybercrime.

The OFC is primarily in charge of implementing activities related to creating the conditions for the effective detection of crimes perpetrated with the use of advanced communication and information technologies. Its duties include, in particular, supervising, coordinating, and supporting activities undertaken by the Departments for Fighting Cybercrime operating within individual Provincial Police Headquarters, and performing investigative operations. These duties are implemented in cooperation with government administration authorities, the courts, public prosecutor's offices, public institutions dealing with cybersecurity, and private entities operating in that field. The following units operate within the Office: the Operations Department, the Investigative Department (including the 24/7 Service Division), the Investigation and Analysis Department, the Support and Research Department, and the General Affairs Department.[28]

Notably, the fact that the Office's activities were limited to investigative operations was a drawback of the described structure. While undoubtedly these activities are extremely important in the fight against cybercrime, this rather narrow formulation of the Office's responsibilities has some serious implications.

[28] http://bip.kgp.policja.gov.pl/kgp/struktura-organizacyjn/22759,STRUKTURA-ORGANIZACYJNA-KOMENDY-GLOWNEJ-POLICJI.html. Accessed on 1 December 2020.

Ultimately, the Office's activities frequently result in drawing up a notification of a crime, which, together with the gathered intelligence, is lodged with the police unit or public prosecutor's office with appropriate territorial jurisdiction, with a view to instituting the relevant preparatory proceedings. At the Police, it is often assigned to an officer who has a limited knowledge of cybercrime. This significantly affects the course of the preparatory proceedings at the initial stage, which is when there should be the collection and securing of evidentiary material, which is then handed over to the public prosecutor, and, eventually, to the court. The fact that no Police officers from the criminal investigation division were from the outset expressly delegated to conducting preparatory proceedings related to cybercrime had a negative impact on the quality of the handling of cases in this field. Fortunately, this approach was modified in 2018, and, since then, both the Office and the Departments for Fighting Cybercrime have conducted (inquiry and investigation) proceedings.

It is worth mentioning that in June 2017 the State Public Prosecutor's Office, jointly with the Research and Academic Computer Network, conducted training aimed at identifying the potential systemic, organisational, and legislative barriers which were negatively influencing the pace of proceedings in the event of incidents (cybercrime), thus making it difficult to hold the perpetrators of such acts accountable. The training was attended by representatives of the State Public Prosecutor's Office, the Provincial Public Prosecutor's Office in Warsaw, the Office for Fighting Cybercrime operating within the National Police Headquarters, NC Cyber NASK, and the Research and Academic Computer Network.

As brought to light by the training, the major identified problem which inhibited incident handling, and thus affected the further course of the preparatory proceedings, was the need to precisely determine the appropriate unit or organisational section of the Police to be in charge of conducting procedural activities related to the identified incident. A major finding was also that the officers of the Regional, District and Municipal Police Headquarters, i.e. those units to which cases are handed over once proceedings begin, did not have specialised knowledge of cybercrime, and, in particular, knowledge of the methods and techniques for securing evidence in this field. Those officers also usually lacked the specialised IT tools which would let them effectively, and in particular quickly, conduct activities at the preliminary stage of the preparatory proceedings. Notably, the above-mentioned police units were also overloaded with other criminal cases which they were handling at any given time. Finally, it should be borne in mind that the Police collaborate directly with EUROPOL and INTERPOL, and in cybercrime cases such cooperation is an absolute necessity.

5 The Public Prosecutor's Office

It seems that the Prosecutor's Office is the most important element in combating cybercrime, as the preparatory proceedings in cybercrime cases are either conducted or supervised by Public Prosecutors. However, the common organisational units of the Prosecution Service generally lack a uniform structure dedicated to fighting against this type of crime.

The former General Public Prosecutor's Office, which had operated until June 2016, and was then changed into the State Public Prosecutor's Office, by way of the Act of 28 January 2016 on the Law on Public Prosecutor's Offices,[29] had no organisational structure whatsoever dedicated to fighting cybercrime. Within the framework of the General Public Prosecutor's Office, three prosecutors were appointed to deal with this issue, and in particular with handling international issues related to this type of crime.

It was only in the Regulation of the Minister of Justice of 7 April 2016—the internal rules of the common organisational units of the Prosecution Service,[30] that the function of the Prosecution Service to combat cybercrime was expressly mentioned. In §21(1)(a) of the Regulation, concerning the role of the Economic Crime Department, the following statement was included: "Supervising and coordinating preparatory proceedings in cases involving serious crimes perpetrated via the Internet, advanced technologies, and computer systems (cybercrime), conducted by regional, provincial and district Public Prosecutor's offices.[31]" This provision should be interpreted as a sign of a change in the Prosecution Service authorities' approach to the issues of cybercrime.

In the same paragraph, and more specifically in Point 4, the need to engage in international cooperation in the field of combating cybercrime, and to prosecute its perpetrators, were recognised, along with the requirement to cooperate with the Polish representation in EUROJUST, as regards the Prosecution Service's activities, and with other international and supranational organisations acting under international agreements, ratified by the Republic of Poland, on combating cybercrime.[32]

Moreover, in § 20(1)(b) of the Regulation, the responsibilities of the Organised Crime and Corruption Department were formulated, i.e. "supervising and coordinating preparatory proceedings in cases involving crimes perpetrated via the Internet, advanced technologies, and computer systems, with a national or international reach (organised cybercrime)[33]".

In the same paragraph, and more specifically in Point 6, the necessity to engage in international cooperation in the field of combating organised cybercrime and to prosecute its perpetrators was also recognised, along with the requirement to cooperate with the Polish representation in EUROJUST, as regards the Prosecution Service's activities, and with other international and supranational organisations

[29]Act of 28 January 2016 of the Law on Public Prosecutor's Offices Consolidated text, Polish Journal of Laws of 2019, item 740, as amended.

[30]Regulation of the Minister of Justice of 7 April 2016—the internal rules of the common organisational units of the Prosecution Service Consolidated text, Polish Journal of Laws of 2017, item 1206.

[31]The Regulation: The internal rules of the common organisational units of the Prosecution Service.

[32]The Regulation: The internal rules of the common organisational units of the Prosecution Service.

[33]The Regulation: The internal rules of the common organisational units of the Prosecution Service.

acting under international agreements, ratified by the Republic of Poland, on combating organised cybercrime.

In consequence of formulating the above-mentioned brief of the Economic Crime Department and the Organised Crime and Corruption Department, Chapter 3 of the Internal rules—"The organisational structure and tasks implemented by regional, provincial and district Public Prosecutor's offices"—envisaged the possibility of establishing new organisational units. In § 27 on regional Public Prosecutor's offices, and in § 29 on provincial Public Prosecutor's offices, the possibility of establishing organisational units to deal with conducting and supervising cases involving crimes perpetrated via the Internet, advanced technologies, and computer systems (cybercrime) was anticipated. As regards regional Public Prosecutor's offices, a condition was made that these should be multi-person cases involving serious crimes.[34]

Last but not least, the justice system, or the judiciary, should be discussed. Within the courts, there is no organisational structure dedicated to considering cybercrime cases. Nor are there any reliable data on the number of judges with cybercrime expertise, as the Ministry of Justice does not maintain any statistics regarding this matter.

Although the National School of Judiciary and Public Prosecution has for several years organised courses in this field, addressed to judges and judicial assistants, there are no data which would allow us to determine the number of such professionals' being trained in cybercrime issues. Data on the courts in which the judges train in, and, with expertise on cybercrime issues, currently preside, are also non-existent. These circumstances, in combination with the fact that cases are randomly delegated to various judges' sections, lead to the conclusion that both the indictments from, and findings of, incidental preparatory proceedings, as well as the requests for temporary detention as regards cybercrime cases, are assigned to individual judges in a random manner.

While the situation in the judiciary is as such, the Ministry of Justice, as an entity supervising the courts in administrative terms, has already become aware of how serious the problem of cybercrime is. Notably, the Ministry of Justice features central information systems of great significance, not only for the judiciary, such as the National Criminal Register, but also for economic transactions, such as the National Court Register, the Electronic Land and Mortgage Register, and the National Registered Pledge Information Retrieval System. The Ministry of Justice also acts as the administrator of the information systems used in the courts' work.

Previously, the responsibilities related to cybercrime prevention and cybersecurity had been implemented by the Computerisation and Court Registers Department, but in June 2017 they were delegated to the newly established Digital Security and Protection Office. Along with the underlying duties related to ensuring the protection of classified information, running the Secret Office, and guaranteeing security, the Office also undertakes activities aimed at supervising the functioning of the

[34]The Regulation: The internal rules of the common organisational units of the Prosecution Service.

cybersecurity protection system at the Ministry of Justice, and its subsidiary units, which includes detecting and preventing threats to cybersecurity, as well as monitoring and analysing the information security status in the Ministry of Justice cyberspace.[35]

6 The Ministry of Defence

The Computer Incident Response System (CIRS) of the Ministry of Defence implements tasks in the field of coordinating the processes of preventing, detecting, and responding to computer incidents in the communication and information systems and networks of that Ministry.

The CIRS features a three-level structure which is compliant with NATO's recommendations (the CIRS Coordination Centre, the CIRS Support Centre, which implements tasks consistent with the scope of the responsibilities assigned to CERTs, and the administrators of the communication and information systems of the organisational units and some sections of the Ministry).

The principal activities of the CIRS include coordinating responses to computer incidents, handling and analysing events and incidents, and implementing measures aimed at increasing awareness regarding communication and information security. As part of its activities, the CIRS collaborates with the organisational units and sections of the Ministry of Defence, and with organisations from outside the Ministry, both domestic and international.

In May 2019, following the merger of the National Cryptologic Centre and the Information Technology Inspectorate, the establishment of the Cyberspace Defence Troops was announced. On 1 July 2019, the National Cybersecurity Centre was set up through the consolidation of scattered units of the Ministry of Defence, in charge of cybersecurity, cryptography and ICT. The Cyberspace Defence Troops concept assumes establishing, by 2022, the Polish Command of the Cyberspace Defence Troops, and their achieving of operational readiness by 2024.

7 Summary

The above review of the bodies and institutions in charge of combating cybercrime in Poland demonstrates that certain measures to secure cyberspace and to combat cybercrime are indeed being implemented. Unfortunately, most of these are not planned and systemic measures, and they rarely display the requisite coordination.

---

[35] https://bip.ms.gov.pl/pl/ministerstwo/struktura-organizacyjna/biuro-ochrony-i-bezpieczenstwa-cyfrowego/. Accessed on 1 of December 2020.

They are often limited-range and stop-gap measures forced by necessary modifications arising from Poland's international obligations.

References

Adamski A, Kosiński J (2007) Oszustwa internetowe w ocenie polskich I amerykańskich policjantów. Archiwum kryminologii. Vol. XXVIII

Ciborowski L (2001) Walka informacyjna. Toruń

Denning DE (2002) Wojna informacyjna i bezpieczeństwo informacji. Warsaw, Chapter 2. Teoria wojny informacyjnej

Lynch DM (2006) Securing against insider attacks. Information Security and Risk Management 11

Verton D (2004) Black Ice: niewidzialna groźba cyberterroryzmu. Warsaw

Jerzy Kosiński dr hab. Eng., the associate professor of the Department of Security Systems at the Polish Naval Academy in Gdynia. Until 2018 he served in the Police, dealing with cybercrime, digital evidence, internet OSInt and infringements of intellectual property on the Internet. The organizer of cyclical international conferences "Technical aspects of ICT crime" (20 editions), which next changed their name to "ICT crime XXI" (2 editions). Author of many publications and speeches at conferences in the field of his scientific specialty. He is a witness expert in the field of computer crime and payment cards from the list of the District Court in Olsztyn. He also conducted trainings in the field of cybercrime for the services of other countries (including Armenia, China, Moldova).

Operational Activities in the Field of Cybersecurity

Justyna Kurek

Abstract The increase in cybercrime and the importance of cyberspace for the preparatory stage of crimes led to the redefinition of operational and exploratory activities. It has become desirable to move away from the concept of targeted surveillance and towards prevention systems used on a massive scale. This trend is manifested in using technological achievements like hacking software for legal purposes. The goal of this article is to define the concept of state-run on-line remote search of information systems, including the use of breakthrough security software like spyware, in the context of procedural- and pre-trial guarantees, the presumption of innocence and protection of privacy. The article attempts to verify the following research hypothesis: that the creation of new appropriate guarantees (institutional, substantive and procedural) for the digital environment is required since the existing safeguards appropriate to the actions in the real world cannot be applied by analogy in the digital environment without influencing the effectiveness of the measures. The legal framework for operational activities in the digital world must take into account the requirement of subsidiarity and necessity of maintaining a balance between effective criminal law and respect for privacy.

1 Foreword

The twenty-first century is described as the information age.[1] The transformation from machinery-based production to an information-based economy, in which the intellectual factor[2] plays a crucial part, has resulted in the development of the

[1]The concept of the *Information Age* was put forward by M. Castells in the thesis entitled "End of Millennium. The Information Age. Economy, Society, and Culture", Castells (1998). M. Castells's trilogy was also published in the Polish language—Castells (2010).

[2]Wang (2010), p. 4.

J. Kurek (✉)
Faculty of National Defence, Akademia Sztuki Wojennej w Warszawie/War Studies University in Warsaw, Warsaw, Poland
e-mail: j.kurek@akademia.mil.pl

K. Chałubińska-Jentkiewicz et al. (eds.), *Cybersecurity in Poland*,
https://doi.org/10.1007/978-3-030-78551-2_27

information society. The efficiency of the new economy is driven by knowledge. These processes are accompanied by the continued reduction in the costs related to the aggregation of knowledge and the services related to the latest technology.[3,4] On entering the information age, some cultural changes have been closely related to the evolution and development of communications. A transformation has been evident from the traditional mass media like TV and radio, predominant in the twentieth century,[5] to horizontal communication networks based on the Internet and wireless communication.[6] Computer networks, *open-source* software (including Internet protocols), the rapid development of digital connections, and data transmission with telecommunications networks resulted, at the beginning of the 1990s, in the expansion of the Internet and its use for private purposes. At the same time, a revolution started involving communications and the dynamic development of wireless communication.[7] The Internet and Internet-based technologies also contributed to a revolution in the understanding of traditional legal terms and institutions. T. Hoeren defined these changes as law deconstruction, depersonalisation, distortion, and de-territorialisation.[8]

All these technological developments, and the related social changes, resulted in the establishment of the information society,[9] based on permanent access to information, which is essential for both businesses and private lives.[10] The establishing of the new social structure was connected with, and resulted from, the massive success of the Internet, and its growing influence, in particular its non-commercial resources. It facilitated the conceptualisation of real phenomena in the digital world.[11]

2 The Information Society and the Challenges Related to Security

Digitisation processes resulted not only in changes to the economy and private lives, but also to the functioning of criminal groups and types of crime. The increase in cyber threats has had an impact on public expectations regarding the security measures provided by the state and the authorities. Concerns caused by external threats (*inter alia*, terrorism, the spread of organised crime, and cybercrime) have resulted in rising expectations towards the state regarding security, which also

[3]Picot and Neuburger (2004), p. 6.

[4]Wang (2010), p. 6 et seq.

[5]Broad analyses of mass media—cf. Kocot (2004), p. 13 et seq.; Polański (2007); Polański (2006), p. 241 et seq.; Kuliński (2010); Janowski (2008); Konieczny (2005).

[6]Castells (2010), p. 9.

[7]Castells (2010), p. 16.

[8]Hoeren (2008), p. 2615.

[9]Mickel and Bergmann (2005).

[10]Picot and Neuburger (2004), p. 1; Yukins (2004), p. 667 et seq.

[11]Mik (1999), p. 63.

include, in addition to traditional military actions and non-military activities, protection against crime and violence.[12] With reference to changes taking place in the information society, redefining the objects regarding the protection of public security in the context of individuals' rights appears crucial. As rightly noted by K. Chałubińska-Jentkiewicz and M. Nowikowska, "constitutional rights provide grounds for any restrictions, as well as for activities performed by public administration authorities, and for the use of certain tools by public authorities[13]". Expectations towards the state as a guarantor of security have also led to social acceptance of the infringement of individuals' fundamental rights if such actions serve the purpose of achieving the objective, which is protecting the security of the public.[14]

The growth in cybercrime, and the increased significance of cyberspace's providing a preparatory stage for criminal activities, has enforced the redefinition of the operational activities and practices performed by the police and the special services, including in the field of broader prevention.[15] Consequently, departures from targeted surveillance were accepted, and replaced with prevention measures used on a massive scale.[16] This trend is being demonstrated with the use of the latest technological developments by the police and the special services, including spyware. Seizing and securing data carriers or computing equipment is not sufficient for the purpose of the efficient collection and securing of evidence in cyberspace. Law-enforcement authorities taking action in an overt manner would thwart the effects of these operational activities. Moreover, the transferred content is usually encrypted, and the supply of services in the cloud results in the transfer of informational resources outside the physical devices of suspected or accused persons. Efficient operational activities require covert performance, obtaining access, or extracting data remotely, as well as security breaches and hacking to obtain access to encrypted data. To cope with a variety of tasks related to combating crime, the state must employ hackers, and engage in some justifiable activities in terms of legal defence, avoiding the illegality of acts meeting the criteria for hacking. Possible inevitable side-effects of such operational activities, in particular preventive measures taken on a massive scale, often involve interference with the private lives of third parties not engaged in criminal activities. Securing evidence and operational activities can also result in the disclosure of legally protected data and information—providing the foundation for a fair trial—*inter alia,* interfering with the professional secrecy of defence counsels.

Actually, it is difficult to imagine activities in cyberspace, in particular those involving crime combating and prevention, without close cooperation with the

---

[12]Zalewski (2013), p. 6.

[13]Chałubińska-Jentkiewicz and Nowikowska (2020).

[14]Kurek (2016), p. 163.

[15]Adamski (2015), p. 2.

[16]Working Document 1 on the US and EU Surveillance programmes and their impact on EU citizens fundamental rights. European Parliament, Committee on Civil Liberties, Justice and Home Affairs, Rapporteur: Claude Moraes, 11.12.2013 (DT/2012434Pl.doc), p. 2.

private sector, and the use of its infrastructure. It was perfectly expressed by a German philosopher E.-W. Böckenförde, who commented that "a pillar of a democratic and secular state includes values which the state by itself is not able to guarantee. This is a risky undertaking which the state performs in the name of freedom".[17] Therefore, the system which efficiently provides cybersecurity must include not only state bodies responsible for crime prevention and combating through cybersecurity, but also the network of private businesses supplying services related to the monitoring and identification of potentially dangerous incidents.[18] Numerous regulations impose certain obligations regarding the reporting of incidents, *inter alia*, the Polish law on the national cybersecurity system. Cooperation with the private sector will ensure the supply of information regarding vulnerabilities and incidents. The digital environment provided and controlled by telecommunications operators and Internet-service providers collects transmission data and digital footprints, which are indispensable for the performance of operational activities.

3 Technological Aspects of Covert Operations

The transparent and widely available methods for the collection and acquisition of information from the private sector are not enough. Accordingly, to face challenges related to cybersecurity, the state and its local authorities must also develop certain covert tools which facilitate the gathering of data without the active engagement of the private sector. However, the operational scope of such tools must not be random, and their use should only be justified in view of existential threats. The development of related software can present a significant challenge. It is certain that it cannot be standard software widely available on the market. Moreover, it is necessary to answer some questions regarding the scope of the cooperation established between the law-enforcement authorities and the private sector during the development of such tools. Can the state use ready-made commercial solutions? Or is the development of customised solutions designed for public entities absolutely necessary?

Notably, even in the case of solutions dedicated for law enforcement authorities, their use poses a risk of unauthorised access to the software and difficulties regarding the protection of source codes. Probably, the development of such tools by a specialised department of law-enforcement authorities would provide a safe, but also costly, solution.[19] When analysing these issues, can the key question be answered regarding codes for this software, i.e. can they be handled by the private sector? Can such source codes be made available to the private sector by public

---

[17] *Der freiheitliche, säkularisierte Staat lebt von Voraussetzungen, die er selbst nicht garantieren kann. Das ist das große Wagnis, das er, um der Freiheit willen, eingegangen ist* W: Buchholtz (2016), s. 910 after Böckenförde (1976), p. 60.

[18] Cf. Kurek (2019), p. 152.

[19] Kurek (2016), p. 161.

entities for the purpose of setup and upgrade or further development in the context of security?

4 Redefining State Activities—New Tools for Crime Prevention—Spyware in the Service of Security

Due to encryption and cryptographic protection, actions taken by law-enforcement authorities are not limited to acquiring data from telecommunications operators and Internet service providers. Data can be acquired unilaterally, with bypass mechanisms and security breaches using malware, e.g. spyware, trojans, sniffers and keyloggers, i.e. applications which record keystrokes.[20] Such software is installed remotely, without the user's consent, to provide information on his or her computer system.[21] This raises the question not of the deployment of such investigation methods, but of the required logistics and IT-related protection for such operations.

During covert operations, the relevant body should act with due diligence to minimise immissions and safeguard the use of information in forms essential for operational activities. Any information obtained from the system not directly connected with the object of the investigation should be immediately deleted. Moreover, the performance of such activities exposes some gaps and vulnerabilities in the system. The infected system can be more vulnerable to external attacks due to the operation of spyware. In this case, certain solutions adopted by Germany should be considered which oblige the body performing operational activities to provide additional protection for the resources under surveillance. On the completion of operational activities, any security gaps and vulnerabilities should be remedied.[22]

The performance of covert operations raises additional questions regarding the right to information in the case of operations performed by the investigating authorities which do not result in the detection of crimes. Should the user of resources be advised accordingly about this surveillance, and his or her security system's being hacked, when there are no charges brought? Considering the analysis regarding potential threats to information resources, the key is the precise documentation of spyware software operation by the body performing the operational activities. For example, the German BKAG law introduced an obligation to log activities. The report must include information regarding the types of technical measures and the times of use thereof; data enabling the identification of the system and any implemented changes; and data enabling the identification of the acquired information.

Another crucial issue is securing the right to privacy. For example, German regulations, in line with recommendations by the BVerfG

[20]Kurek (2016), p. 161.

[21]Cf. Kurek (2013), p. 66 et seq., and references included therein.

[22]A detailed analysis of German solutions in Kurek (2020), s. 225–240.

(Bundesverfassungsgericht—the highest German Court), established the principle of a two-level privacy-protection test.[23] First, the employment of any remote-intrusion solution is forbidden when it would only ensure access to information on private lives. Second, the authority responsible for the performance of operational activities should provide conclusive verification that the acquired data do not only relate to private lives, and if they do, any such data should be deleted immediately.[24] These solutions are in line with recommendations laid down in European Community strategy and European case law. For example, the European Data Protection Supervisors, on the grounds of case law in the European Court of Justice and the European Court of Human Rights, defined four essential guarantees which should be implemented within national legal systems to minimise interference with private lives to the degree required, and in the scope accepted, in a democratic society, in cases of employed intrusive means of supervision—i.e. (1) processing must be based on transparent, clear, and precise rules; (2) necessity and proportionality must be substantiated with regard to legitimate purposes; (3) an independent supervisory mechanism should be provided; and (4) effective remedies should be available.[25]

5 Conflicts of Interest Regarding Data Protected by Law

As highlighted by the BVerfG, "State security is essential for public order and peace, and the concomitant respect for human dignity and self-esteem must be guaranteed to ensure public security, as provided by the Constitution's provisions, and are treated equally with other constitutional rights[26]". The protection of public order and national security also contribute to the protection of the rights and freedoms of other people.[27] Security should therefore be perceived as a provision contributing to freedom.[28] The deployment of spyware in the course of performing operational activities can include not only the surveillance of current and potential criminals, but also of innocent persons.[29] Due to the high intrusiveness of such tools and interference with fundamental rights, including the protection of privacy, and the confidentiality of information and trade secrets, legal and public acceptance for such

[23]Kutscha (2012), p. 392.

[24]Roggan (2009), p. 262.

[25]Working Document 1/2016 of 13.04.2016 (16/EN/WP/237) on the justification of interferences with the fundamental rights to privacy and data protection through surveillance measures when transferring personal data—EuropeanEssentialGuarantees.

[26]Point 100 of BVerfG ruling in cases No. BVR 966/09 and 1 BvR 1140/09.

[27]Point 53—ECJ ruling of 15 February 2016 in case No. C-601/15.

[28]Buchholtz (2016), p. 909.

[29]Also in Adamski (2015), p. 2.

activities requires the establishing of institutional, substantive, and procedural rules.[30]

An axiological basis for legal regulations concerning covert operations performed by investigating authorities using spyware is provided, *inter alia*, by case law in German courts. The ruling of BVerfG of 20 April 2016 regarding cases No. 1 BvR 966/09 and 1 BvR 1140/09[31] indicated that the special services' rights whose scope interferes with private lives shall be limited to security matters and the enhancement of essential legitimate interests, i.e. it should be exercised exclusively in cases of serious crimes, and for the protection of life, health, freedom, and national security. The criterion fulfilling this unique condition is the safeguarding of values fundamental to the common interest.[32] So, the BVerfG sustained the previous case-law line, for example, in the ruling of 27 February 2008 regarding case No. 1 BvR 370/07, when, examining the right to use online surveillance, it cited the relevance and proportionality rules, and stated that the deployment of surveillance measures highly interfering with private lives might follow only if the method in question was one which could prevent a hazard posed to legally protected rights. Therefore, online surveillance must relate to unique means whose use shall be justified in cases of utmost importance. The German Supreme Court also alluded to the proportionality rule. The BGH's ruling of 31 January 2007 regarding case No. StB 18/06[33] indicated clearly that these means could be employed only if a serious crime is suspected, and thus their use should be subjected to very restricted formal procedures.

The ruling of 20 April 2016 regarding cases No. 1 BvR 966/09 and 1 BvR 1140/09 BVerfG also highlighted the protection of the private lives of persons who, by accident, were within the range of operational measures. The Court cited the issue of third parties not being targeted by the special services, but who are accompanying a suspect (a targeted person). Such persons may be closest persons, family members, friends in close relationships with the suspect, or criminal, whose correspondence, due to its nature (e.g. defence counsels, lawyers) shall be under protection.

6 Summary

In the light of the changes in society, redefining the law enforcement authorities' activities involving the prevention and combating of serious crime seems to be inevitable. Ensuring adequate protection is now impossible without engaging the

---

[30]Cf. Kurek (2018).

[31]BVerfG ruling of 20 April 2016 in case No. 1 BvR 966/09 i 1 BvR 1140/09, <https://www.bundesverfassungsgericht.de/SharedDocs/Entscheidungen/DE/2016/04/rs20160420_1bvr096609.html>, accessed 1.10.2020 r.

[32]Rössel (2016), p. 149.

[33]BGH ruling of 31 January 2007 in case No. StB 18/06, <http://juris.bundesgerichtshof.de/cgibin/rechtsprechung/document.py?Gericht=bgh&Art=pm&Datum=2007&Sort=3&nr=38779&linked=bes&Blank=1&file=dokument.pdf, accessed on 1.10.2020.

private sector or interfering with business and human rights. The functioning of the state under such conditions, and the activities conducted by its authorities to combat crime, require the employment of technology related to surveillance and technological advancements, also including the use of operational measures enabling surveillance on a large-scale. The efficient prevention and combating of crime in the digital environment includes the use of *spyware* tools. This should be based on the assumption that protection cannot be ensured at an adequate level without monitoring private computer resources, and includes the surveillance of current and potential criminals, as well as innocent people.[34] Due to the high intrusiveness of such tools and interference with the fundamental rights, including the protection of privacy, the confidentiality of information and trade secrets, the legal and public acceptance of such activities requires the establishing of institutional, substantive, and procedural rules.[35]

References

Adamski A (2015) Dane telekomunikacyjne jako środek inwigilacji masowej w demokratycznym państwie prawa. In: Majewski J (ed) Przeciwdziałanie przestępczości. Jawność i jej ograniczenia, vol X

Böckenförde E-W (1976) Staat, Gesellschaft, Freiheit, Frankfurt

Buchholtz G (2016) Kein Sonderopfer für die Siecherheits BVerfG erklärt BKAG für verfassungswidrig, NVwZ

Castells M (1998) End of millennium. The information age. Economy, society, and culture, Oxford

Castells M (2010) Wiek Informacji. Ekonomia, społeczeństwo i kultura, Warsaw

Chałubińska-Jentkiewicz K, Nowikowska M (2020) Bezpieczeństwo, prywatność, tożsamość – aspekty prawne, Warsaw

Hoeren T (2008) Das Pherd frisst keinen Gurkensalat – Uberlegungen zur Internet Governance, NJW, No. 36

Janowski J (2008) Elektroniczny obrót prawny, Warsaw

Kocot W (2004) Wpływ Internetu na prawo umów, Warsaw

Konieczny P (2005) Komunikacja od mowy do internetu. http://histmag.org/?id=744. Accessed 1 Oct 2020

Kuliński M (2010) Regulacje komunikacji elektronicznej w rozwoju społeczeństwa informacyjnego Unii Europejskiej, Warsaw

Kurek J (2013) Ochrona przed niezamówioną korespondencją w komunikacji elektronicznej, Warsaw

Kurek J (2016) Wykorzystanie szpiegowskiego oprogramowania w działalności operacyjnej organów ścigania. Gwarancje konstytucyjne i procesowe z perspektywy doświadczeń niemieckich, Przegląd Policyjny 1

Kurek J (2018) Online search. Postulaty de lege ferenda. In: Kitler W, Chałubińska-Jentkiewicz K, Badźmirowska-Masłowska K (eds) System Bezpieczeństwa w Cyberprzestrzeni, Warsaw

Kurek J (2019) Cyberprzestrzeń jako sfera aktywności normatywnej państwa - analiza w kontekście przeciwdziałania przestępczości. In: Taczkowska-Olszewska J, Oręziak B, Wielec M (eds) Zarządzanie ludźmi w organizacji, Warsaw

[34]Also in Adamski (2015), p. 2.

[35]Cf. Kurek (2018).

Kurek J (2020) Prawne bezpieczeństwo rozwiązań w zakresie przeszukań on-line. Nowe ramy regulacyjne w Niemczech BKA - Gesetz 2017. In: Kosiński J, Krasnodębski G (eds) Przestępczość teleinformatyczna 2019 / - Gdynia

Kutscha M (2012) Das Computer-Grundrecht — eine Erfolgsgeschichte, Datenschutz und Datensicherheit 6

Mickel WW, Bergmann J (2005) Handlexikon der Europäischen Union, Warsaw

Mik C (1999) Media masowe w europejskim prawie wspólnotowym, Toruń

Picot A, Neuburger R (2004) In: Hoeren T, Sieber U (eds) Handbuch Multimedia-Recht München

Polański P (2006) Usługi społeczeństwa informacyjnego na tle reformy usług w Unii Europejskiej. Quo Vadis Europo, Warsaw

Polański P (2007) Customary law of the internet, in the search for a supranational cyberspace law, Hague

Roggan F (2009) Das neue BKA-Gesetz — Zur weiteren Zentralisierung der deutschen Sicherheitsarchitektur, Neue Juristische Wochenschrift 5

Rössel M (2016) Teilweise Verfassungswidrigkeit des BKAG. ITRB

Wang FF (2010) Internet jurisdiction and choice of law. Legal practices in EU, US and China, Cambridge

Yukins ChR (2004) Making federal information technology accessible: a case study in social policy and procurement, Public Contract Law Journal 33

Zalewski S (2013) Bezpieczeństwo Polityczne. Zarys Problematyki, Siedlce

Justyna Kurek PhD, an attorney at law and adjunct at the National Security Faculty of the War Studies University in Warsaw. Justyna Kurek is a lecturer in the field of international crime fighting, the law of new technologies, security of electronic communication, protection of classified information, and protection of personal data. Dr Kurek was a long-term employee of central public administration bodies—the Office of Competition and Consumer Protection and the Office of Electronic Communications. She is the author of the scientific monograph "Protection against spam in electronic communication" (2013), over 20 chapters in other scientific monographs, and over 30 scientific articles.

Operational Activities and the Right to Privacy

Katarzyna Chałubińska-Jentkiewicz

Abstract The confidentiality of the services and the lack of external control may lead to excessive autonomy or subjectification of the very purpose of operational activity and failure to exercise due restraint in encroaching on civil rights and liberties. Sometimes, such a situation may result from excessive ideological or political considerations in the operations of the executive authorities. In other words, the secrecy of operational control may lead to abuse. An additional aspect is the development of electronic communication facilities and the related cybercrime. The development of cyberspace requires control activities to be undertaken also in this area. The experience of modern democratic states indicates that the executive power responsible for public security and order, including its subordinate entities conducting operational and reconnaissance activities, has at its disposal resources which, in the name of defending public order, may lead to the destruction of democratic institutions and reduction of civil rights, including privacy rights.

The confidentiality of the services and the lack of external control may lead to excessive autonomy or subjectification of the very purpose of operational activity and failure to exercise due restraint in encroaching on civil rights and freedoms. Sometimes, such a situation may result from excessive ideological or political considerations in the operations of the executive authorities. In other words, the secrecy of operational control may lead to abuse. An additional aspect is the development of electronic communication facilities and the related cybercrime. The development of cyberspace requires control activities to be undertaken also in this area. Public security, considered as a fundamental in principle justifying the limitation of civil rights by the legislator, requires respecting the proportionality of acceptable encroachment in the name of safeguarding the safety and smooth functioning of the control system, while maintaining this proportionality in practice.

K. Chałubińska-Jentkiewicz (✉)
Akademickie Centrum Polityki Cyberbezpieczeństwa/Academic Center for Cybersecurity Policy, Akademia Sztuki Wojennej w Warszawie/War Studies University in Warsaw, Warsaw, Poland
e-mail: k.jentkiewicz@akademia.mil.pl

K. Chałubińska-Jentkiewicz et al. (eds.), *Cybersecurity in Poland*,
https://doi.org/10.1007/978-3-030-78551-2_28

Otherwise, the safety protection measures in the form of legally acceptable operational activities might in themselves present a risk to rights and liberties. Such will be the situation if, first, the introduced limitations prove arbitrary and disproportionate to the potential threats and, second, if they are removed (legally or effectively) from the control of democratic institutions. The conflict over the limits on applying operational and technical activities is familiar in any democratic country respecting the rule of law or, in practice, in international bodies in which, under Article 8 of the Convention on the Protection of Human Rights and Fundamental Freedoms,[1] universal standards have been developed. These standards are to benefit the assessment of proportions between public authorities' interference and individual rights in this domain. The experience of modern democratic countries shows that executive authorities responsible for public order and safety, including their subsidiary bodies responsible for operational and exploratory activities, deploy measures whose utilisation—in the name of public safety protection—can lead to the deterioration of democratic institutions and a reduction in civil liberties, including the right to privacy.

The Polish Constitutional Tribunal, in its judgment of 19 February 2002,[2] expressed its opinion on the nature of the right to privacy. The Tribunal claimed that a vital component of the right to privacy is the so-called informational autonomy of the individual, which implies the autonomous right to disclose one's personal information, as well as the right to exercising control over such information which is held by other entities. The right to privacy is guaranteed by Article 47 of the Constitution of the Republic of Poland and the informational autonomy of the individual is guaranteed primarily by Article 51. Under Article 51(1), no one may be compelled, except when based on an Act, to disclose information concerning himself or herself. Article 51(4) of the Constitution of the Republic of Poland establishes that everyone is entitled to have such information which is incorrect, incomplete, and collected in a way which is contrary to the law, to be corrected or removed. Furthermore, it is required for the principles and procedures of collecting and accessing information to be specified by an Act (Article 51(4) of the Constitution of the Republic of Poland). In the Court's view, *lege non distinguente,* this last provision shall also be applied to the collecting and sharing of information by private entities. This line was also followed by P. Winczorek, "The right to privacy declared in the provision is protected, not only in relations between individuals and the public authorities, but also with other individuals and public and private institutions (vertical and horizontal application of law)".[3]

However, in view of the growing number of terrorist attacks, particularly with the use of new technologies, the boundaries of interference with the right of privacy are

[1] The European Convention for the Protection of Human Rights and Fundamental Freedoms signed in Rome on 4 November 1950, hereinafter referred to as the Convention.

[2] The judgment of the Polish Constitutional Tribunal of 19 February 2002, file No. 3/01, Polish Journal of Laws of 2002, No. 19, item 197.

[3] Winczorek (2010), p. 114.

greatly widening. In the Court's view, as expressed in the judgment of the European Court of Human Rights of 12 January 2016, No. 37138/14 (The right to privacy, home, and correspondence), exercising covert control by bodies with executive power is a natural consequence of the forms terrorism takes. The government's use of the latest technologies with the purpose of staying ahead of such attacks, including the mass monitoring of communications which could contain clues concerning pending incidents, might constitute the only reasonable solution. The techniques used in such monitoring operations have seen significant progress in recent years. These techniques have reached a degree of sophistication hardly imaginable to the average citizen, especially taking into consideration the technological facilitation and prevalence of automated and system-based data collection. Due to this progress, the Court had to examine the question of whether the development of control methods resulting in the immensity of collected data is paralleled by a simultaneous development in the legal provisions protecting the observance of citizens' rights as envisaged in the Convention. These data often contain further information on the conditions in which essential components intercepted by public authorities have emerged, involving components such as the time and place, as well as the equipment used to produce computer files, digital photographs, electronic and text messages, and the like. Indeed, the aim of the government's efforts, whose target is to limit terrorism and thereby to restore citizens' confidence in the government's ability to maintain public safety, would be undermined if a terrorist threat was paradoxically replaced by a visible threat triggered by the unhindered authority of executive power to intervene in the sphere of the private lives of citizens using uncontrollable, and at the same time far-reaching, control techniques and prerogatives. Potential interference with electronic correspondence, including mobile phone and Internet services, as well as covert mass control, attract the Convention-based protection of private life to an even larger extent. Such interference might be justified only under Article 8(2) of the Convention, if it is in accordance with the law, pursues one or more legally justified goals as indicated in Article 8(2), and is crucial in a democratic society to achieve any of these goals. The provision, as it allows an exception to the right provided by the Convention, must be interpreted narrowly. Powers to covertly control citizens, which are a feature of a Police State, are tolerated exclusively under the Convention only to the extent that they are strictly necessary for the protection of democratic institutions. The Court has concluded that the aim of the said interference is the protection of public safety, and/or the safeguarding of order and crime prevention, in line with Article 8(2) of the Convention.

In accordance with the view of the European Court of Human Rights regarding the privacy of the individual protected under Article 8 of the Convention, it is potentially permissible for the authority (legislative, executive, judicial) to interfere in this privacy as long as it meets certain criteria. Any such encroachment must, nonetheless, pass the three-tier evaluation test. This means that it is not permissible to implement restrictions (on privacy) with legal provisions of ranks other than an Act.[4]

In the cases against France (cases Kruslin v France, 11801/85 and Huvig v France, 11105/84 of 24 April 1990), it was pointed out that the Convention required from the national legislature that an applicable act define the category of persons for which such operational control could be used on the basis of a court order; the type of crime such an order could be issued against; the maximum control period; the reporting procedure concerning the content of recorded conversations (the case was about telephone tapping); measures providing the transfer of intact recordings and enabling their full control by the judge and the defence; and defining the cases in which the recordings may or must be destroyed, especially when the investigation was discontinued or the convicted person was acquitted by the judge. French legislation was declared as not meeting the criteria, similarly to the national legislation in the case of Malone v the United Kingdom (8691/79) in the judgment of 2 August 1984 (the cases concerned the collection of information and telephone tapping). It was recognised that the local acts were too vague and non-specific, which led to a situation in which, although the activities were statutory, they were also not in line with the Convention. It is not sufficient to refer to the factor of purposefulness. It appears vital to prove the necessity, strictly, of the specific (concerning the range and manner) limitation established by an ordinary Act. Therefore, collecting information in the course of operational control must be dealt with in legislation and, additionally, in the Police practice, as a subsidiary procedure in the intervention aim (as a safeguard to the public interest), mentioned in Article 8 of the Convention, including national security, public safety, the economic welfare of the country, crime prevention and the protection of order; the safeguarding of health and morality; and the freedom of other individuals. A similar provision was introduced into the Constitution of the Republic of Poland. Article 31(3) of the Constitution specifies that the restrictions on the exercise of fundamental constitutional freedoms and rights may be imposed only by law, and only when necessary in a democratic state for the protection of its security or public order, or for the protection of the natural environment, health, or public morals, or the freedom or rights of other persons. These limitations, however, cannot violate the essence of freedoms and rights.

In each case, it is necessary to demonstrate a plausible need for taking such limitation measures, and solely in the name of protecting the very rules of democratic order. A situation in which, by "incidentally" collecting operationally useful data, operational control gathers private data, which go beyond the aim of the control, means that the authority is operating beyond the scope of permissible intervention in the private domain.

[4]Even made as a provision, it is still too general, blanket and vague in character, taking into consideration the fact that it is an eligibility law which serves as a source of the application of objectives to measures—in such a case, the premise of a sufficient statutory basis is not met.

The European Court of Human Rights has acknowledged, however, that the covert control of individuals is "necessary in today's reality in a democratic society for national security and in order to safeguard order and prevent crime", whereby it recognised that the fact of "the failure to inform about observation" does not violate the Convention (see the reasoning of the judgment of 6 September 1978 in the case of Klass and others v Germany (5029/71)), as well as D. Gajdus, B. Gronowska, Stosowanie podsłuchu telefonicznego w ocenie Europejskiej Komisji i Europejskiego Trybunału Praw Człowieka (Refleksje na tle rozwiązań polskich), "Palestra" No. 11/1994, pp. 115 and 116). Although the judgment in the case of Klass and others v Germany was in favour of the German legislature, the law was amended after the judgment had been passed in Strasbourg. As a result of the amendment, there was an increase in the protection standards by imposing an obligation to inform ex-post the person against whom such operational activities were being conducted, under Article G-10, that such a control was being carried out against him or her (Article 5(5)).[5]

In its judgment of 4 May 2000 (Rotaru v Romania, 28341/95) the European Court of Human Rights established that systems of covert invigilation must contain legislative (procedural) guarantees applicable to the control of actions by the appropriate departments. According to that Court, the investigative procedures must correspond to the values of a democratic society as closely as possible, and must in particular correspond to the rule of law. According to the ruling, the interference of an executive authority with the rights of individuals should be subject to effective control. The control should be carried out by external bodies in respect of the appropriate authorities carrying out operational actions. It is highly desirable that—in normal circumstances—it be done by judicial bodies. A judicial review guarantees independence, impartiality, and the application of the correct procedures. The Court considers that non-judicial control, exercised by other external bodies against the controlled person, with a properly representative composition, does not prejudice the standards of the Convention. An alternative to subjecting operational and exploratory activities to judicial control might be subjecting activities to the control of a special body whose location and composition ensure independence from the executive authority. Only then will the objectivity of the results of the control be guaranteed. It should be noted that, in the justification of the judgment by the European Court of Human Rights in the aforementioned case of Klass and others v Germany, it was deemed appropriate to exclude judicial control in cases in which telephone tapping was used. The ruling was delivered against a different regulation in which the function of control over tapping was entrusted to an official "with

[5]It should be pointed out that, for instance, the German anti-terrorist legislation of 1968 (Act of 13 August 1968 limiting the secrecy of correspondence and telephone conversations, commonly referred to as Act G-10) successfully passed the test of correctness and conformity with "the objective necessary in a democratic society" (the case was about wiretapping in connection with a suspicion of terrorism, which were to remain a secret for the interested parties), as well as the proportionality of the used limitation and the provision of adequate appeal and control measures (albeit these were not judicial measures, but control by a specially created representative body).

qualifications for a judicial office" with the concurrent guarantee of stable parliamentary control, exercised by a three-member commission, as well as a five-member Board of the Union Parliament. In the judgment of 27 April 2004, in the case of Doerga v the Netherlands (50210/99), the European Court of Human Rights stressed that any intervention in subjective rights guaranteed by the Convention must be in accordance with the rule of law. This, in turn, requires the foremost compliance of operational activity with the requirements of the national law. According to the Court's case law, intervention in private life and correspondence include not only the individual means of covert control aimed at particular entities but also the strategic monitoring of connections and obtaining the personal data of communicating entities. The question was considered in the case of Weber and Saravia v Germany, in which German provisions regulating the strategic monitoring of telecommunication connections, whose aim was to record the telephone conversations of an unspecified number of callers, and then identify, using key-word information included in the conversations, which could potentially identify the offenders or their criminal plans, were challenged (the case of Weber and Saravia, Application No. 54934/00). Collecting and storing data connected with an entity by the state services, irrespective of the means by which they were collected (the citied case of Rotaru v Romania, Application No. 28341/95), also constitute an encroachment into the private sphere of an entity. In order to assume that there was an intervention in the law guaranteed by Article 8 of the Convention, it is enough to determine whether there was a collection of data on entities, regardless of how it would be used in the future. Nevertheless, the possibility of covertly obtaining information about persons by public authorities was not ruled out. The Court pointed to their indispensability as a tool enabling effective security guarantees, as well as the protection of a democratic state's institutions against sophisticated forms of threats, notably espionage and terrorism.

The standards of collecting and processing data by competent authorities are defined by judgments in the cases of Zakharov v Russia, Application No. 47413/06, and Szabó and Vissy v Hungary, Application No. 37138/14. The applicant, Roman Zakharov, used the services of several mobile network operators, and on 23 December 2003 filed a lawsuit against three phone operators, claiming that they had committed an infringement of his rights to the privacy of telephone communication. He further claimed that, according to Regulation No. 70 of the Ministry of Communication, the mobile network operators had installed a device which enabled the Federal Security Service to intercept phone calls without the prior authorisation of a judicial authority. Regulation No. 70, which has never been published, excessively limited his right to privacy. Roman Zakharov requested the Court to issue a warrant under Regulation No. 70, ordering the installed device to be removed, and to make telephone communication available only to authorised persons. The provisions of Russian law regulating the interception of communication transmission do not take into consideration any adequate and effective guarantees against the risk of such malpractice, which is integral to every system of invigilation, and which is particularly high in a system in which secret services and the Police have direct access, via technical means, to all telephone communication. In particular, the circumstances in which public authorities are authorised to use secret surveillance measures are not expressed in sufficiently precise terms. The provisions regulating the discontinuation of using secret surveillance measures do not provide sufficient safeguards against arbitrary interferences. National laws allow the automatic interception of suspect data; in addition, it is not clearly specified in which cases the intercepted material should be stored or destroyed at the end of the test.

The procedures for authorisation cannot guarantee that secret surveillance measures will be used only in situations in which they are "necessary in a democratic society". Nowadays, control over intercepted communication does not fulfil the requirements of independence, nor that which pertains to the entrusted authority and power which would be sufficient for effective and constant control. The effectiveness of appeal mechanisms is weakened because the person whose communication is being intercepted is not informed of the fact, and, furthermore, because of the lack of effective access to the documentation pertaining to the interception. Providing executive authorities with unlimited decision-making powers in the matters of national security would be contrary to the rule of law. The law must mark with sufficient clarity the limits of every decision-making freedom conferred on any competent authority, as well as the means by which it is exercised, keeping in mind the legal aim of the measures, so as to provide the entities with adequate protection against arbitrary interference. What is required is prior judicial authorisation, providing an essential safeguard against arbitrariness.

Similarly, the European Court of Human Rights concluded that the Hungarian Act on the Police infringed the right to privacy. Following the amendments introduced in 2011, the Act now enables special anti-terrorist units to carry out covert house searches, to tap phones, to open packages and letters, and to perform the uncontrolled viewing and recording of electronic mail. The Court consistently holds that the rules on the special powers of the secret services should provide for strong control of their actions, and for informing citizens of the fact that they are under surveillance. In the case of Szabo and Vissy v Hungary, the Court ruled that the contested regulations could apply to any person staying on the territory of the country and to any property located there, and people have no way of verifying whether they are being surveilled or not. The introduction of special powers for the services to fight terrorism is, according to the Court, justified; however, Hungary should, at the same time, guarantee sufficient protection of its citizens' rights. The legal provisions should indicate that tapping and intercepting communication is allowed only in the case of persons for whom there is a reason to suppose that they are participating in terrorist activities. The undertaken measures should be subject to external, preferably judicial, control, also that conducted ex-post. The Court has also been critical towards the fact that the Hungarian regulations do not take into consideration the deletion of stored personal data which have proven useless, or any clear indication of whether it is possible to extend several times the use of privacy-infringing control measures. This should be achieved by external control, and by providing the people with an effective tool enabling them to assert their rights. The first step, though insufficient, is stating whether a person is being subjected to a special inspection.

It should be stressed that nations are equipped with what has been referred by the Court as the margin of appreciation; in other words, a degree of freedom to balance the rights of individuals against national security (vide 5 Leander v Sweden, 9248/81, § 59, 26 March 1987). As early as in the 1970's, the Court observed that legislation allowing the covert monitoring of the mail and telecommunication in a democratic country was necessary in exceptional circumstances, in the interests of national security, and/or in order to prevent hostile actions or crime. More recently, the Court has found that the invigilation of terrorist suspects using GPS does not infringe their right to privacy as guaranteed by Article 8 of the Convention (Lass and others v Germany, 5029/71, 6 September 1978, Series A, No. 28, § 48, as well as Uzun v Germany, 35623/05, § 80, the European Court of Human Rights, 2010 (fragments)). The Court ruled that sufficient safeguards had been used in providing protection against the arbitrary use of such methods. On the other hand, the powers conferred on the Police by special anti-terrorist legislation, to detain and search any person on no sufficiently defined basis for suspicion of violation, are deemed as infringing the applicant's rights to the respect of his or her private life.[6]

So far, there has been no single Act in Poland which would thoroughly regulate the question of the detection, prevention, and elimination of terrorist threats, or the issue of removing the effects of such attacks. Basic regulations to this effect have been included in the following Acts:

(1) The Act of 6 June 1997—Penal Code, which, *inter alia*, contains a definition of a terrorist crime (Article 115 § 20), and penalises the founding and leadership of, and involvement in, an organised group or association whose aim is to commit a terrorist crime (Article 258 § 2 and 4), the financing of a terrorist crime (Article 165a), as well as distributing or publicly presenting content which can facilitate the perpetration of a terrorist crime (Article 255a);
(2) The Act of 26 April 2007 on Crisis Management, which determines the authorities responsible for cases of crisis management, as well as their tasks, and the principles of action in the field, as well as defines, *inter alia*, the concept of a terrorist incident;
(3) The Act of 1 March 2018 on Preventing Money Laundering and the Financing of Terrorism,[7] which determines the principles and manner of preventing the financing of terrorism.

The basic aim of the new regulations is to raise the effectiveness of the Polish anti-terrorist system, thus increasing the safety of all Polish citizens through facilitating effective actions in cases of suspected terrorist crimes, including setting up preliminary procedures. The issue of responding to terrorist threats has also been recognised in regulations concerning emergencies. In addition, the issues related to

[6]Gillan and Quinton v the United Kingdom, 4158/05, § 87, the European Court of Human Rights, 2010 (fragments).

[7]Act of 1 March 2018 on Preventing Money Laundering and the Financing of Terrorism, consolidated text, consolidated text Polish Journal of Laws of 2020, item 971.

the tasks and authorisations of services and institutions with regard to terrorist threats are contained in competence acts regulating their action (e.g. the Act of 6 April 1990 on the Police, the Act of 12 October 1990 on Border Guards,[8] and the Act of 24 May 2002 on the Internal Security Agency and on the Intelligence Service[9]), as well as other legal acts covering selected aspects pertaining to a particular type of threat (such as the Act of 4 September 2008 on the Protection of Maritime Traffic and Sea Ports, and the Act of 12 October 1990 on the Protection of the State Border). In order to strengthen the state's preparations to the emergency of terrorist threats, it is crucial to integrate activities implemented by particular members of the multi-party anti-terrorist system in Poland. Of key importance in the effective functioning of an anti-terrorist system in Poland is providing the optimal coordination of actions and mechanisms of cooperation on the strategic, operational, and tactical levels. For this purpose, the Act of 10 June 2016 on Anti-Terrorism was adopted. According to the definition contained in this Act, these are activities of public administration authorities whose aim is to prevent terrorist actions, to prepare for taking control of them through planned actions, to react in the event of such actions, and to remove their effects, including by restoring the resources targeted at reacting to them (Article 2(1)). Article 25 of the Act provides for a special mode of preliminary proceedings in case there is a suspicion of an attempt at committing a crime or making preparations for a terrorist crime, with the aim of detecting or detaining, or compulsory appearance of, any person suspected, and also in order to find items which could constitute evidence in the case, or which could be confiscated in the criminal proceedings. This mode refers, *inter alia*, to the possibility that the prosecutor issues a provision to search any premises identified in the provision, or to detain a suspect, should there be justified reasons to assume that the suspect or the listed items might be present in the area. In order to find objects which can be considered evidence in a case, or be subject to seizure in criminal proceedings, the Article also provides for the possibility to search persons present on the premises, their clothing and objects they have on them. The above-mentioned actions may be carried out at any time of day or night.

The European Court of Human Rights, in its judgment on Sher and others v the United Kingdom (No. 5201/11), ruled that, in the case of proceedings relating to terrorist crimes, there is justification for allowing such a search or detention to be performed based on conditions considered more broadly than in other cases. In particular, as pointed out by the Court, there is no violation of the European Convention of Human Rights and Fundamental Freedoms if the search is performed on the conditions indicated above, and in a situation in which there is a right of appeal against the above-mentioned activities. Under Article 23 of the Act on Anti-Terrorist Activities, and amendments to other Acts, with regard to the scope not regulated herein, Article 236 of the Act of 6 June 1997 of the Code of Criminal

---

[8] Act of 12 October 1990 on Border Guards, consolidated text, Polish Journal of Laws of 2020, item 305, as amended.

[9] Act of 24 May 2002 on the Internal Security Agency and on the Intelligence Service, consolidated text Polish Journal of Laws of 2020, item 27, as amended.

Proceedings[10] shall apply, in accordance with which any persons whose rights have been violated are entitled to lodge a complaint. Furthermore, it has been pointed out in Article 26 of the Anti-Terrorist Act, relating to the situation in which there is a suspicion of committing a terrorist crime, that if it is in the best interests of preparatory proceedings, an order for the bringing of charges may be drawn up on the basis of information obtained as a result of operational and exploratory activities, including the activities referred to in Article 9 of the Act, i.e. laid down by the Head of the Internal Security Agency against a non-citizen of Poland, in whose case there exists a justified suspicion of terrorist activities, for a period not exceeding 3 months, and covert operational and exploratory activities. In order to detect, prevent or fight crime, the Head of the Internal Security Agency may order against a non-Polish citizen in whose case there exists a justified suspicion of terrorist activities, for a period not exceeding 3 months, covert activities including:

(1) obtaining and recording the content of conversations using technical means, including telecommunication networks
(2) obtaining and recording the images and sounds of persons from rooms, public transport, or places other than public places
(3) obtaining and recording correspondence content, including correspondence via means of electronic communication
(4) obtaining and recording data recorded on digital-data media, communications terminal equipment, information, and information and communication systems
(5) obtaining access to and control of the content of consignments.

Moreover, in this case, the Court, at the request of the Prosecutor, may order a provisional detention for a period not exceeding 14 days. An autonomous indication for the implementation of a provisional detention is the likelihood of committing, or preparations to commit, a terrorist crime. Under Article 6 of the Act, the Head of the Internal Security Agency, complying with the requirements concerning classified-information protection, keeps an updated list containing information on persons undertaking activities intended for the purpose of terrorist organisations or organisations connected with terrorist activities, or members of such organisations; wanted persons conducting terrorist activities or persons suspected of committing terrorist crimes, against whom in Poland there is an order of arrest or search, or against whom there is an arrest warrant, as well as those wanted on the basis of a European arrest warrant; persons against whom there is a justified suspicion that they might carry out actions whose aim is to commit a terrorist crime, including persons posing a threat to the safety of Polish civil aviation; or persons taking part in terrorist training, or travelling with the aim of committing a terrorist crime. Additionally, under Article 10 of the Act, within the framework of the entitlement to collect palmprint image data, to copy facial images, and to collect DNA material, the officers of the Internal Security Agency, the Police and the Border Guard are entitled to collect palmprint

[10] Act of 6 June 1997 of the Code of Criminal Proceedings, consolidated text, Polish Journal of Laws of 2020, item 30, as amended hereinafter referred to as the CCP.

images, to capture facial images and to collect biological material in a non-intrusive way in order to determine the DNA profile of a non-Polish citizen, in cases where: (1) there is a justified doubt concerning the person's identity, or (2) there is a justified suspicion that the person has illegally crossed the border of Poland, or doubt about the declared purpose of that person's stay on Polish territory, or (3) there is a suspicion concerning the intention of that person's unlawful presence on Polish territory, or (4) there is a justified suspicion that the person might be in some way involved in terrorist activity, or (5) the person might have taken part in terrorist training. Under Article 26 of the Anti-Terrorist Act, should there arise a suspicion of a terrorist crime, for the sake of preparatory proceedings, the decision to present charges may be drawn up on the basis of information obtained in the course of operational and exploratory activities. It is worth adding that, in accordance with Article 60 of the Act which establishes a registration obligation in the case of pre-paid services, the subscribers to pre-paid services who signed a contract prior to the date of the entry of the regulation into force, have been duly summoned to supply the pre-paid services provider with the data specified in the Act of 16 July 2004—Telecommunications Law (Article 60b—the obligation to supply personal data by the subscriber). In accordance with the Act, subscribers (excluding those who use publicly available phone services provided using public phones, or by dialling the network access number to the service provider's network, or pre-paid services subscribers whose aim is to broadcast or distribute TV programmes through ground, cable or satellite), should supply the provider with the following data:

(1) for subscribers who are natural persons:
   (a) name and surname
   (b) personal identification number (PESEL), if assigned, the series and number of a document confirming the person's identity, and, in the case of a foreigner not being a citizen of a Member State or the Swiss Confederation—the passport number or residence permit;
(2) for subscribers who are not natural persons:
   (a) name
   (b) the business registry number (REGON) or the tax identification number (NIP), or the National Court Register (KRS) number, or the Business Register Number, or a number affixed in any other register.

The service provider begins to provide telecommunication services:

(1) not earlier than the conformity of the data provided by the subscriber is confirmed against the data included in the document stating the subscriber's identity as a natural person, included in a specific register, or after the subscriber provides his or her personal data, and these are confirmed electronically using electronic identification means serving to authenticate, in the IT system of the national bank, the data verified using a qualified certificate of an electronic signature, or electronic identification means serving authentication purposes in the IT system of the telecommunication service provider, if the subscriber's

personal data have already been verified in connection with a different contract, and electronic identification means serving authentication purposes in the IT system which meets the requirements specified in the regulations issued on the basis of Article 20a(3) of the Act of 17 February 2005 on the Computerisation of the Operations of Entities Performing Public Tasks.

Confirmation may also be made by the service provider through a third party operating on behalf of that service provider. A pre-paid service provider of a public telecommunication network shall immediately cease to provide such services to subscribers who fail to deliver such data, or whose data have not been confirmed. Similar solutions regarding interference in the right to privacy have been introduced in Article 180a of the Telecommunications Law, which regulates the issue of data retention. Both the public telecommunication network operator and the publicly available telecommunications service provider are obliged, at their own cost, to:

retain and store data relating to the network termination point, telecommunications terminal equipment, the end user: initiating the connection, and to whom the connection is addressed; as well as determining:

(a) the date and time of the connection, and its duration
(b) the type of the connection
(c) the location of the telecommunications terminal equipment generated in the telecommunications network, or processed by them within the Polish territory, for the period of 12 months counting from the day of the connection or the failed connection, and to destroy the data after the end of this period, with the exception of information which has been saved in accordance with separate provisions, and to share data concerning the entity initiating the connection, as well as the one to whom the connection is addressed with the competent authorities, the Court, and the Prosecutor, on the terms and conditions, and in the mode, as specified in separate provisions. These authorities include the Police. Under Article 20c of the Act on the Police [Obtaining and processing telecommunication, postal and Internet data], in order to detect or prevent crime, including fiscal crimes, or in order to save human life or health, or to support search-and-rescue actions, the Police may obtain data which do not constitute a telecommunications transmission, a transported postal item, or an electronic service ("telecommunications, postal or Internet data"), and may process the same without the persons concerned being informed and/or having given their consent to it.

The Chief Police Commander, the Head of the Central Bureau of Investigation, the Head of the Police Internal Affairs Office, and the Regional Police Commander maintain registers of telecommunications, postal or Internet data requests. These requests contain information identifying the Police unit and the Police officer obtaining such data, their type, the purpose for which they are being obtained, and the time at which they are being obtained. These registers are electronic, without prejudice to the rules of protecting classified information. The data are also collected from, and shared with, law-enforcement authorities of the European Union, and other countries, European Union agencies engaged in crime prevention and combat, and the International Crime Police Organisation—Interpol, on their due request, if this is aimed at detecting crime and prosecuting perpetrators, protecting human lives and health, or searching for missing persons. Under Article 20a, control over telecommunication, postal or Internet data collection by the Police is exercised by the Regional Court appropriate for the Police unit to which the data are made available. The Police authority, with the provision on the protection of classified information, submits to the Regional Court, on a half-yearly basis, a report covering

(1) the number of cases in which telecommunications, postal or Internet data were obtained in a given reporting period, as well as the type of requested data;
(2) the legal classification of the actions with regard to which there were requests for obtaining telecommunications, postal or Internet data, or information concerning such acquisition of data in order to save human life or health, or in order to support search and rescue operations.

As part of the control, the Regional Court might need to view the materials which justify sharing such telecommunications, postal or Internet data with the Police. The Regional Court then informs the Police authorities of the outcome of the control within 30 days of its completion. As a consequence, the ex-post system of operational and exploratory control allows the establishing of whether such an intervention in private life was purposeful, proportionate, and necessary.

Social changes which are the result of civilisational developments stimulate the democratic processes and constitute a space in which various business, economic, organisational, and socially desirable aims can be achieved, but they also tend to be the reason for regressive actions. This applies to virtually every sphere of human activity, and it applies to human rights and basic freedoms in particular. The risk of such dangers for an individual grows in proportion to the process of weakening the country as a structure and an institution. As a consequence, an individual citizen loses his or her sense of security. This feeling is related to the new situations in which an individual, a citizen, exists. Globalisation, the crisis of the institution of the state as a regulator, doubts connected with the territory, information exchange, the intermingling of cultures, the identity crisis, the world economic crisis, and terrorism with its new sources, all create a new space in which rights and basic freedoms require special public attention, and the redefinition of aims for choosing the proper protection measures. An additional aspect of these changes is the question of safeguarding public safety which, also for the above-mentioned reasons, requires redefinition. The protection of public safety is one of the most crucial aims of the state's actions and, consequently, those of public authorities and the entire public administration. Thus, it is worth stressing that public security is composed of various elements, such as personal and individual safety.

While wielding its attributes of power, the state uses various legal instruments and institutions whose aim is to protect the public interest, morals, and national security. A situation in which the state is weakened, like no other, poses a direct risk to public security and, as a consequence, to individual safety. For this reason, it has become vital to determine the status of the individual against the state, within the framework of public authority directed at the protection of the individual by ensuring public safety. Undoubtedly, operational and exploratory control is such a measure. If one analyses the status of such a control guarantee, it becomes vital to supplement its scope with an assessment of the citizens' responsibilities and limitations connected with public safety, including such spheres of individual functioning as are related to a citizen's privacy and identity—though always in accordance with the principle of Christian Wolff, the continuator of Pufendorf's thinking that *homo persona moralis est quaternus spectatur tanquam subiectum certarum obligationum atque iurium certarum.*[11]

References

Conrad H (2006) Individuum und Gemeinschaft in der Privatrechtsordnung des 18 und beginnenden 19 Jahrdundderts, Karlsruhe

Sójka-Zielińska K. Jednostka a państwo w dziejach europejskiej kultury politycznej. In: Wyrzykowski M (ed) Prawa stają się prawem. Status jednostki a tendencje rozwojowe, Liber Warszawa

Winczorek P (2010) Komentarz do Konstytucji Rzeczypospolitej Polskiej, Warsaw

Katarzyna Chałubińska-Jentkiewicz dr. hab. of legal sciences (University of Warsaw and the Jagiellonian University), legal advisor, associate professor, and head of the Department of Cyber-security Law and New Technologies at the Institute of Law in the Faculty of National Security at the War Studies University in Warsaw. She is also a lecturer at the SWPS University and director of the Academic Center for Cybersecurity Policy. In the years 1996–2010, she worked as a lawyer in the National Broadcasting Council and with the public broadcaster TVP S.A. Between 2011 and 2017, she was deputy director of the National Audiovisual Institute (her competence centered on the field of digitization). As a scientist, she conducts research on cybersecurity, information security threats, the development of electronic media law, protection of intellectual property, and the impact of new technologies on the development of the state and the legal situation of the individual. Katarzyna Chałubińska-Jentkiewicz is the author of monographs and numerous articles, which include topics such as new technologies law, cyber responsibility, information security law, and audiovisual media: Regulatory conflict in the age of digitization, Audio visual media services; Regulation in the conditions of digital conversion; Information and computerization in public administration; Cultural Security Law and Reuse of public sector information. She is head of the Ministry of Science's research project "Polish cybersecurity system – a model of legal solutions."

[11]Conrad (2006), p. 16, source: Sójka-Zielińska, p. 170.

Summary

Katarzyna Chałubińska-Jentkiewicz

An area that has been partially regulated by law, and one that has special prominence in law systems, is cybersecurity. Cybersecurity needs to be considered as an interdisciplinary concept that draws on multiple fields, including various domains of law. But in order to distinguish it from the legal and administrative system as a whole (in relation to the latter especially in organisational and objective terms), and to categorise it and identify regulatory areas, it is necessary to define the scope of activity that this sphere involves (in subjective, objective, functional and organisational terms). Only then will it be possible to systematise the issue of the legal protection of cyberspace.

When addressing issues related to cybersecurity, in addition to the analysis of systemic solutions, it is important to consider the following questions: What is cyberspace, generally speaking, and how are we responsible for any actions within it? and What legal regulations have so far been adopted within national and international law? How are these enforced and is it correct for these to be based on the regulations concerning reality? What is cybercrime? What are the powers of the organisations responsible for fighting cyber crime?, and, by extension, What are the rights and responsibilities of actors operating in cyberspace, and also Are network users responsible for their online actions? Are they responsible jointly and severally with service providers? And also, How should we balance individual interests, including the right to privacy, and the public interest, which involves actions related to defining responsibility for online actions. The backdrop for these problems are such issues as current strategic and regulatory policies for cyberspace, and the related security challenges and legal regulations to ensure a secure cyberspace.

Ensuring cybersecurity in the EU requires a new policy for prosecuting and penalising individuals and organisations found guilty of breaching communication

K. Chałubińska-Jentkiewicz (✉)
Akademickie Centrum Polityki Cyberbezpieczeństwa/Academic Center for Cybersecurity Policy, Akademia Sztuki Wojennej w Warszawie/War Studies University in Warsaw, Warsaw, Poland
e-mail: k.jentkiewicz@akademia.mil.pl

K. Chałubińska-Jentkiewicz et al. (eds.), *Cybersecurity in Poland*,
https://doi.org/10.1007/978-3-030-78551-2_29

and information systems. The introduction of new, more effective, solutions, including a review of Directive 2013/40/EU of 12 August 2013 on attacks against information systems and replacing Council Framework Decision 2005/222/JHA, and also the provisions of the EU's new Cybersecurity Strategy, should be accompanied by a serious discussion on how to strengthen law enforcement authorities at the EU and national levels.

Relevant data shows the need to take action. In 2018, the CERT Polska team received 19,439 security reports and recorded 3739 security incidents, which corresponds to an increase in incident number by 17.5% compared to 2017. In 2019 CERT Polska (CSIRT NASK) recorded 6484 such incidents. This means a massive increase in incidents—by 73% compared to 2018. In the first half of 2020 CSIRT NASK received as many as 16,689 reports, of which 5205 were considered incidents, so the number of incidents in 2020 could be twice as that in 2019. The data presented in CSIRT ABW reports are also alarming. In 2018 CSIRT ABW received 31,865 reports, of which 6236 were considered incidents, and in 2019 there were 226,914 reports, of which 12,405 were considered incidents.

The proposal for the new directive, known as NIS 2, is the product of a review of the currently applicable NIS Directive and is to be part of a broader package including also separate regulations for financial institutions (Regulation on Digital Operational Resilience for the financial Sector, or DORA) and the Resilience of Critical Entities Directive.

It seems that the legislation currently in force is producing certain divergences between individual Member States in relation to the regulated matter. And one of the by-products of this is the lack of restriction instruments to enforce this law against the regulated entities, which significantly undermines cybersecurity. The decision to adopt the new directive seems to be the right thing to do. The new directive will be a minimum harmonisation one, which allows Member States to take further steps to introduce solutions for a higher level of cybersecurity (see Article 3). The proposal provides for the establishment of a Cooperation Group (Article 12) and CSIRTs network (Article 13), and the European Cyber Crises Liaison Organisation Network (EU – CyCLONe) to support the management of large-scale cyberincidents and crises (Article 14). This is crucial due to the extra-territorial nature of these. In the context of 5G network construction, but not only, it is important to introduce provisions on coordinated supply chain risk assessments (Article 19 and Section 47 of the Preamble) and certification schemes (Article 21). Important elements of the directive are also standardisation (Article 22) and information-sharing (Article 26). Without a doubt these areas will affect market activities. While the Commission will decide which categories of key entities (and this status can be held by public entities and private entities which perform public tasks or their own tasks) will be required to obtain certification, the new obligations under NIS 2 will require the involvement of various entities in areas that have not been covered by such regulations. However, certification should apply to device manufacturers rather than entities providing services based on such devices. Political considerations concerning the provenance of the entities selling such devices on the market should not affect the operations of electronic communication services providers. If the certification obligation is imposed on manufacturers, service providers and network operators will not have to recall the equipment, which can be costly, and manufacturers will need to ensure appropriate manufacturing conditions. With the digitisation and computerisation of the economy, cybersecurity is becoming crucial for more and more fields. And this generates new responsibilities for a new group of entities—important entities. Not everyone will be happy about this, but these regulations are not about market-oriented reforms. The public interest does not always go hand in hand with individual or economic interests.

Whatever their size, businesses providing electronic communication services will need to comply with NIS2 regulations. The directive also provides for heavy fines for entities that fail to appropriately meet their obligations. Maximum fines are to be up to EUR 10,000,000 or 2% of the business' total annual global revenue, whichever is higher. These fines can be particularly painful for smaller businesses which are only entering the cybersecurity system. Perhaps some graduation of fines would be useful here. In order to answer the question about whether this new directive meets market requirements, it is necessary to remember what was the primary goal behind these provisions. And this goal was extensive cooperation between different sectors to ensure cybersecurity. Cybersecurity-oriented actions of Member States and their public authorities, taken within the common and uniform telecommunications market, need to be supported by all its actors. This is also required from telecommunications businesses and all other entities whose operations could or do affect cybersecurity. Without such cooperation and coordination there can be no safe and secure cyberspace.

What is problematic about these solutions for the telecommunications market is that the amended Directive can possibly create collisions with the provisions of other regulations, such as Directive (EU) 2018/1972 of the European Parliament and of the Council of 11 December 2018 establishing the European Electronic Communications Code, which also addresses the security of electronic communications networks and services, and, in practice, those requirements have been in place for many years. However, it is also important to note that requirements imposed by telecom regulations are one thing, and requirements related to the establishment of a uniform cybersecurity system with the national administration system are another. But it is worth emphasising that new cybersecurity objectives can cause an increase in business costs among the relevant entities, which can be a valid reason to increase the prices for end users.

Irrespective of the above-mentioned concerns, the new directive can contribute to increased resilience to cyberattacks, provided that it is successfully implemented by Member States. Nevertheless, the key factors to ensure security in cyberspace are risk awareness and education. Man is at the centre of cybersecurity.

Personnel training and acquiring the necessary cybersecurity skills are long-term processes, and this needs to be taken into consideration when designing and implementing any cybersecurity mechanisms and requirements. Member States need to become actively involved, also by allocating sufficient funds for this purpose in their budgets, in building professional education about, and training in, cybersecurity, while closely cooperating with businesses to ensure that the system provides a sufficient number of job candidates with in-demand skills.

Despite all disappointments, failures and tragic mistakes, people will build a better world. If they were not to act with that thought, we would lose all faith in humanity and its potential, in which case it would be better not to live at all my friends.

Stanisław Lem, Dialogues[1]

Katarzyna Chałubińska-Jentkiewicz dr. hab. of legal sciences (University of Warsaw and the Jagiellonian University), legal advisor, associate professor, and head of the Department of Cybersecurity Law and New Technologies at the Institute of Law in the Faculty of National Security at the War Studies University in Warsaw. She is also a lecturer at the SWPS University and director of the Academic Center for Cybersecurity Policy. In the years 1996–2010, she worked as a lawyer in the National Broadcasting Council and with the public broadcaster TVP S.A. Between 2011 and 2017, she was deputy director of the National Audiovisual Institute (her competence centered on the field of digitization). As a scientist, she conducts research on cybersecurity, information security threats, the development of electronic media law, protection of intellectual property, and the impact of new technologies on the development of the state and the legal situation of the individual. Katarzyna Chałubińska-Jentkiewicz is the author of monographs and numerous articles, which include topics such as new technologies law, cyber responsibility, information security law, and audiovisual media: Regulatory conflict in the age of digitization, Audio visual media services; Regulation in the conditions of digital conversion; Information and computerization in public administration; Cultural Security Law and Reuse of public sector information. She is head of the Ministry of Science's research project "Polish cybersecurity system – a model of legal solutions."

[1]Dialogi Wydawnictwo Literackie, Kraków – Wrocław 1984, p. 287.

References

Literature

Adamiak B (1996) Komentarz do Kodeksu postępowania administracyjnego. Warsaw

Adamiak B (1998) Właściwość organów. In: Adamiak B, Borkowski J (eds) Kodeks postępowania administracyjnego. Komentarz. Warsaw

Adamski A (2000) Prawo karne komputerowe. Warsaw

Adamski A (2001) Przestępczość w cyberprzestrzeni. Prawne środki przeciwdziałania zjawisku w Polsce na tle projektu konwencji Rady Europy. Toruń

Adamski A (2005) Cyberprzestępczość – aspekty prawne i kryminologiczne. Studia Prawnicze 4

Adamski A (2007) Nowe ujęcie cyberprzestępstw w kodeksie karnym – ale czy lepsze? Prawo Teleinformatyczne 3

Adamski A (2011) Cyberprzestępczość – rozwój regulacji prawnej w Europie. Doświadczenia krajowe na tle implementacji prawnych instrumentów zwalczania cyberprzestępczości (London, 11-12 November 2010). Prokuratura i Prawo 6

Adamski A (2013) Botnety jako zagadnienie prawno-kryminologiczna na tle doświadczeń amerykańskich. Prokuratura i Prawo 1

Adamski A (2015) Dane telekomunikacyjne jako środek inwigilacji masowej w demokratycznym państwie prawa. In: Majewski J (ed) Przeciwdziałanie przestępczości. Jawność i jej ograniczenia Vol. X, Warsaw

Adamski A, Kosiński J (2007) Oszustwa internetowe w ocenie polskich I amerykańskich policjantów. Archiwum kryminologii. Vol. XXVIII

Aleksandrowicz TR (2011) Bezpieczeństwo w Unii Europejskiej, Warsaw

Aleksandrowicz TR (2014) Świat w sieci. Państwa, społeczeństwa, ludzie w poszukiwaniu nowego paradygmatu bezpieczeństwa narodowego, Warsaw

Aleksandrowicz TR, Liedel T (2014) Społeczeństwo informacyjne – sieć, cyberprzestrzeń. Nowe zagrożenia. In: Aleksandrowicz TR, Liedel K, Piasecka P (eds) Sieciocentryczne bezpieczeństwo. Wojna, pokój i terroryzm w epoce informacji, Warsaw

Antoniak M (2012) Kontrola rządowa w administracji publicznej. Poradnik dla kontrolujących i kontrolowanych, Warsaw

Bączek P (2006) Zagrożenia informacyjne a bezpieczeństwo państwa polskiego, Toruń

Bałut D, Budek K. Cyberbezpieczeństwo dla przedsiębiorców: Nowa era zagrożeń, https://marketingibiznes.pl/it/cyberbezpieczenstwo/. Accessed 10 Oct 2020

Banasik M, Rogozińska A (2019) W aspekcie niemilitarnych instrumentów oddziaływania Federacji Rosyjskiej, Warsaw

K. Chałubińska-Jentkiewicz et al. (eds.), *Cybersecurity in Poland*,
https://doi.org/10.1007/978-3-030-78551-2

Banasiński C (2018) Podstawowe pojęcia i podstawy prawne bezpieczeństwa w cyberprzestrzeni. In: Banasiński C (ed) Cyberbezpieczeństwo. Zarys wykładu, Warsaw
Banasiński C, Jaroszyński K (2017) Ustawa o gospodarce komunalnej. Komentarz, Warsaw
Banasiński C, Nowak W (2018) Europejski i krajowy system cyberbezpieczeństwa. In: Cyberbezpieczeństwo. Zarys wykładu, Warsaw
Barta J, Markiewicz R (1998) Internet a prawo, Kraków
Beaufre A (1988) Wstęp do strategii. Odstraszanie
Berkowitz M, Bock PG (1965) American National Security. A Reader in Theory on Policy. The Free Press, New York
Bień-Kacała A, Jirásek J, Ciulka L, Drinóczi T (2016) Kategoria bezpieczeństwa w regulacjach konstytucyjnych i praktyce ustrojowej państw Grupy Wyszehradzkiej, Toruń
Biernat S (1994) Prywatyzacja zadań publicznych, Warsaw – Cracow
Błaszyk B (2018) Prowadzenie działalności gospodarczej w cyberprzestrzeni. In: Banasiński C (ed) Cyberbezpieczeństwo. Zarys wykładu, Warsaw
Blicharz R (2013) In: Blicharz R (ed) Kontrola przedsiębiorcy, Warsaw
Boć J (2003) Administracja publiczna, Wrocław
Böckenförde E-W (1976) Staat, Gesellschaft, Freiheit, Frankfurt
Bogacz-Miętka O (2018) Kompendium wiedzy o nadzorze i kontroli nad przedsiębiorstwem, Warsaw
Bolek TD (2018) M. Ustawa o kontroli w administracji rządowej. Komentarz z wzorami dokumentów, Warsaw
Borkowski J (1980) Zakres przedmiotowy kodeksu postępowania administracyjnego w świetle nowelizacji. Państwo i Prawo 5
Borkowski J (1996) In: Adamiak B, Borkowski J (eds) Kodeks postępowania administracyjnego, Komentarz. C.H. Beck, Warsaw
Borkowski M (2013) Cyberprzestrzeń a bezpieczeństwo jednostki, Warsaw
Borkowski P. Polska wobec zjawiska cyberterroryzmu, http://www.psz.pl/Piotr-Borkowski-Polska-wobeczjawiska-cyberterroryzmu. Accessed 22 May 2020
Brodie B (1973) War and Politics, New York
Brzostek A (2019) Polityka ochrony cyberprzestrzeni administracji publicznej na przykładzie organów administracji rządowej wskazanych w ustawie o Krajowym Systemie Cyberbezpieczeń. In: Kitler W, Chałubińska-Jentkiewicz K, Badźmirowska-Masłowska K (eds) System bezpieczeństwa w Cyberprzestrzeni RP, Warszawa
Brzozowski W (2006) Konstytucyjna zasada dobra wspólnego. Państwo i Prawo 61(11)
Buchholtz G (2016) Kein Sonderopfer für die Siecherheits BVerfG erklärt BKAG für verfassungswidrig. NVwZ 2016
Bukowski S (2006) Przestępstwo hackingu. Przegląd Sądowy 4
Bzózka P (2019) Prawo autorskie na jednolitym rynku cyfrowym. Największe wątpliwości po wejściu w życie unijnej dyrektywy. Dziennik Gazeta Prawna. https://serwisy.gazetaprawna.pl/prawo-autorskie/artykuly/1418336,dyrektywa-o-prawach-autorskich-watpliwosci.html. Accessed 10 Oct 2020
Campen S (ed) (1996) The First Information. AFCEA, Washington
Castells M (1998) End of Millennium. The Information Age. Economy, Society, and Culture, Oxford
Castells M (2010) Wiek Informacji. Ekonomia, społeczeństwo i kultura, Warsaw
Celarek K (2015) Prawne i praktyczne aspekty kontroli i nadzoru nad działalnością samorządu terytorialnego, Warsaw
Chałubińska-Jentkiewicz K (2014) Bezpieczeństwo cyberprzestrzeni jako zadanie publiczne w systemie bezpieczeństwa narodowego RP. Zeszyty Naukowe AON 3(2)
Chałubińska-Jentkiewicz K (2019a) Cyberbezpieczeństwo – zagadnienia definicyjne. Cybersecurity and Law 2
Chałubińska-Jentkiewicz K (2019b) Cyberodpowiedzialność, Toruń
Chałubińska-Jentkiewicz K, Karpiuk M (2015) Prawo nowych technologii. Wybrane zagadnienia. LEX/el

Chałubińska-Jentkiewicz K, Nowikowska M (2020) Bezpieczeństwo, prywatność, tożsamość – aspekty prawne, Warszawa
Chmielewski A (2009) Bezpieczeństwo energetyczne państwa. Geopolityczne uwarunkowania, Warsaw
Chojna-Duch E (2003) Kontrola finansowa i audyt – ustawowe implikacje. In: Kontrola i audyt w administracji publicznej, Stan i perspektywy, 1st Conference, Warsaw
Chojnowski L (2018) Bezpieczeństwo człowieka i społeczeństw w procesie dziejowym, Słupsk
Chomiczewski W (2011) Artykuł 13 ustawy o świadczeniu usług drogą elektroniczną. In: Chomiczewski W, Klafkowska-Waśniowska K, Lubasz D et al (eds) Świadczenie usług drogą elektroniczną oraz dostęp warunkowy. Komentarz do ustaw. Wydawnictwo Prawnicze LexisNexis, LEX/el
Chomiczewski W (2013) Pojęcie caching providera i zasady jego odpowiedzialności za przechowywane dane, https://portalprawait.com/entry/pojecie-caching-providera-i-zasady-jego-odpowiedzialnosci-za-przechowywane-dane/. Accessed 10 Oct 2020
Chróścielewski W (2015) Postępowanie administracyjne – Komisja Nadzoru Finansowego – wyłączenie od udziału w sprawie. Glosa to the Judgment of the Polish Supreme Administrative Court (NSA) of 29 April 2014 r., II GSK 320/13 – a partly critical gloss
Chrzczonowicz P (2007) Francja. In: Adamski A, Bojarski J, Chrzczonowicz P, Filar M, Girdwoyń P (eds) Prawo karne i wymiar sprawiedliwości państw Unii Europejskiej. Wybrane zagadnienia, Toruń
Ciborowski L (2001) Walka informacyjna, Toruń
Cichy A, Szyjko CT (2015) Wybrane zagadnienia bezpieczeństwa społecznego w Unii Europejskiej, Warsaw
Ciekanowski Z, Wojciechowska-Filipek S (2016) Bezpieczeństwo funkcjonowania w cyberprzestrzeni Jednostki – Organizacji – Państwa, Warsaw
Cieślak Z (1992) Zbiory zachowań w administracji państwowej. Zagadnienia podstawowe, Warsaw
Cieślak Z (2013) Podstawowe instytucje prawa administracyjnego. In: Niewiadomski Z (ed) Prawo administracyjne, Warsaw
Cieślak Z (ed) (2014) Nauka administracji, Warsaw
Cilak M (2020) Komentarz do art. 9. In: Ofiarski Z (ed) Ustawa o finansach publicznych. Komentarz. LEX/el.
Clough J (2013) Principles of Cybercrime, New York
Complak K (2007) Normy I Rozdziału Konstytucji RP, Acta Universitatis Wratislaviensis (Prawo CCCI) 2956
Conrad H (2006) Individuum und Gemeinschaft in der Privatrechtsordnung des 18 und beginnenden 19 Jahrdundderts. Karlsruhe
Crapko M (2012) CMMI, Doskonalenie procesów w organizacji
Crowther Alexander G (2018) National Defense and the Cyber Domain, https://www.heritage.org/sites/default/files/2017-09/2018_IndexOfUSMilitaryStrength_CROWTHER.pdf. Accessed 3 Oct 2020
Cyberbezpieczeństwo w Polsce: ochrona urządzeń końcowych przed cyberatakami. Analiza sytuacji i rekomendacje działań, A report prepared by Cyfrowa Polska, Warsaw 2019
Cybersecurity Strategy of the Republic of Poland for 2017 – 2022 (Strategia Cyberbezpieczeństwa Rzeczypospolitej Polskiej na lata 2017-2022) Warsaw 2017., https://mc.gov.pl/aktualnosci/strategia-cyberbezpieczenstwa-rzeczypospolitej-polskiej-na-lata-2017-2022. Accessed 24 May 2020
Cyberspace Protection Policy of the Republic of Poland, a document adopted by the Ministry of Administration and Digitisation and the Internal Security Agency (2013), Warsaw
Cyberspace Protection Policy of the Republic of Poland (departmental comments by ISSA Poland) in: http://mac.gov.pl/wp-content/uploads/2012/09/polityka-CBR-stan-na-18-09-2012-konsultacje-resortowe-.pdf. Accessed 10 Oct 2020
Cz B (1968) Dowód z dokumentu w postępowaniu kontrolnym, Kontrola Państwowa 2

Czachór ZD (2016) Sprawiedliwość oraz bezpieczeństwo wewnętrzne Unii Europejskiej i jej obywateli. Wybrane pola badawcze w ujęciu instytucjonalno – prawnym. In: Chabasińska A, Czapur Z (eds) Bezpieczeństwo narodowe Polski. Zagrożenia i determinanty zmian, Warsaw

Czaplicki K (2019) In: Czaplicki K, Gryszczyńska A, Szpor G (eds) Ustawa o krajowym systemie cyberbezpieczeństwa. Komentarz, Warsaw

Czaputowicz J (2013) Kryteria bezpieczeństwa międzynarodowego państwa – aspekty teoretyczne. In: Dębski S, Górka-Winter B (eds) Kryteria bezpieczeństwa międzynarodowego państwa, Warsaw

Czaputowicz J (2018) Suwerenność, Warsaw

Czarny P (2019) In: Tuleja P (ed) Komentarz do art. 149 Konstytucji RP, in Konstytucja Rzeczypospolitej Polskiej. Komentarz. Wolters Kluwer, Warsaw, LEX/el.

Czechowski R, Sienkiewicz P (1993) Przestępcze oblicza komputerów, Warsaw

Dawidowicz W (1965) Nauka prawa administracyjnego. Zarys wykładu. Tom I, Zagadnienia podstawowe, Warsaw

Dawidowicz W (1974) Wstęp do nauk prawno-administracyjnych, Warsaw

Dawidowicz W (1989) Zarys procesu administracyjnego, Warsaw

Dawidziak P, Łęcki B, Stolarski M (2009) Sieć Internet – znaczenie dla nowoczesnego państwa oraz problemy bezpieczeństwa. In: Madej M, Terlikowski M (eds) Bezpieczeństwo teleinformatyczne państwa, Warsaw

Denning DE (2002) Wojna informacyjna i bezpieczeństwo informacji, Warsaw, Chapter 2. Teoria wojny informacyjnej, Warsaw

Department of Defence Dictionary of Military and Associated Terms (2010) (Joint Publication 1-02), https://fas.org/irp/doddir/dod/jp1_02.pdf. Accessed 10 Oct 2020

Dobkowski J (2004) Struktura interesu publicznego a zasady rozdzielenia odpowiedzialności publicznoprawnej w Administracji, in: Jednostka – państwo – Administracja. Nowy wymiar, Rzeszów

Dubiel AJ (2018) System Bezpieczeństwa Narodowego, https://mil.link/en/wp-content/uploads/2018/01/SBN.pdf. Accessed 10 Oct 2020

Dudka K (1998) Kontrola korespondencji i podsłuch w polskim procesie karnym, Lublin

Dybowski T. (1990) Własność Skarbu Państwa i państwowych osób prawnych w świetle art. 128 KC, Państwo i Prawo 4

Dziomdziora WZ (2014) Umowy dotyczące treści cyfrowych niezapisanych na nośniku materialnym w świetle ustawy o prawach konsumenta. Internetowy Kwartalnik Antymonopolowy i Regulacyjny 8

Eggert D (2005) Transatlantycka wspólnota bezpieczeństwa, Żurawia Papers 5

Ejdys J (2018) Zaufanie do technologii w e-administracji, Białystok

Fajgielski P (2018) Ogólne rozporządzenie o ochronie danych, a commentary to Article 83 GDPR, section 8. LEX/el.

Féral-Schuhl C (2010) Cyberdroit: le droit à l'épreuve de l'Internet, Paris

Filipek J (1974) Rola prawa w działalności administracji państwowej. Warsaw-Kraków

Filipek J (2001) Prawo administracyjne. Instytucje ogólne, part II, Kraków

Fischer B (2000) Przestępstwa komputerowe i ochrona informacji, Kraków

Florencio D, Herley C (2011) Sex, Lies, and Cyber-crime Surveys, MSR-TR-2011-75, June 2011, http://research.microsoft.com/pubs/149886/sexliesandcybercrimesu-rveys.pdf. Accessed 10 Oct 2020

Frań-Adamek A (2002) Article 12. [in] Świadczenie usług drogą elektroniczną. Komentarz. Sopot, LEX/el

Ganczar M (2009) Informatyzacja administracji publicznej. Nowa jakość usług publicznych dla obywateli i przedsiębiorców, Warszawa

Ganczar M (2017) Umowne partnerstwo publiczno-prywatne w kontekście bezpieczeństwa sieci i informacji administracji publicznej. In: Szpor G, Gryszczyńska A (eds) Internet. Strategie bezpieczeństwa, Warsaw

Gardocka T (ed) (2008) Obywatelskie prawo do informacji, Warszawa

Garlicki L (2010) Aksjologiczne podstawy reinterpretacji Konstytucji. In: Zubik M (ed) Dwadzieścia lat transformacji ustrojowej w Polsce. Ogólnopolski Zjazd Katedr i Zakładów Prawa Konstytucyjnego, 19-21 czerwca 2009, Warsaw
Gawłowski S, Listowska-Gawłowska R, Piecuch T (2010) Bezpieczeństwo energetyczne kraju, Koszalin
Gercke M (2011) Understanding Cybercrime: A Guide for Developing Countries, https://www.itu.int/ITU-D/cyb/cybersecurity/docs/ITU_Guide_A5_12072011.pdf. Accessed 10 Oct 2020
Gęsicka DK (2014) Wyłączenie odpowiedzialności cywilnoprawnej dostawców usług sieciowych za treści użytkowników. LEX/el
Gibson W (2009) Neuromancer. Katowice
Gienas P (2005) Uwagi do przestępstwa stypizowanego w art. 269b kodeksu karnego. Prokurator 1
Gienas K (2008) Odpowiedzialność podmiotów świadczących usługi w internecie w prawie polskim. In: Systemy Digital Rights Management w świetle prawa autorskiego, Kraków
Giezek JW (2012) In: Giezek J (ed) Kodeks karny. Część ogólna. Komentarz, Warsaw
Giezek JW (2014) In: Giezek JW (ed) Kodeks karny. Część szczególna. Komentarz, Warsaw
Gillies, A. (2011) Improving the quality of information security management systems with ISO27000, The TQM Journal: the international review of organizational improvement 23(4)
Glińska E, Kowalewska A (2011) Identyfikacja współczesnych zagrożeń bezpieczeństwa obywateli w świetle badań własnych z 2008 r. In: Guzik-Makaruk EM (ed) Poczucie bezpieczeństwa obywateli w Polsce. Identyfikacja i przeciwdziałanie współczesnym zagrożeniom, Warsaw
Gnoiński J (1972a) Formy działania kontrolnego i odpowiadająca im terminologia. Kontrola Państwowa 3
Gnoiński J (1972b) Próba określenia pojęcia i istoty kontroli. Kontrola Państwowa 2
Gnoiński J (1974) Niektóre zagadnienia teorii działania kontrolnego. Kontrola Państwowa 7
Gołaczyński J (2009) Ustawa o świadczeniu usług drogą elektroniczną, Warszawa
Gołda-Sobczak M (2016) Krym jako przedmiot sporu ukraińsko-rosyjskiego, Poznań
Gołda-Sobczak M (2017) Bezpieczeństwo kulturowe w sieci. In: Wojtaszek A (ed) Europa wobec problemów bezpieczeństwa w XXI wieku, Szczecin
Gołębiowska A (2015) Local Government in the Constitution of the Republic of Poland of 1997. Ius Novum 2(29)
Golka M (2005) Czym jest społeczeństwo informacyjne. Ruch prawniczy, ekonomiczny i socjologiczny 4(67)
Góral L (2012) Komentarz do art. 3 in: Ustawa o nadzorze nad rynkiem finansowym. Komentarz, LEX/el
Góralczyk W Jr (2016) Kierownictwo w prawie administracyjnym, Warsaw
Górniok O (2005) In: Górniok O et al (eds) Kodeks karny. Komentarz, vol 2, Gdańsk
Górniok O (2006) In: Górniok O et al (eds) Kodeks karny. Komentarz, Warszawa
Grab L (2018) Dyplomacja obronna w procesie kształtowania bezpieczeństwa RP, Warsaw
Grabosky P (2006) Electronic Crime, New Jersey
Grabowski M, Zając A (2009) Dane, informacja, wiedza-próba definicji, Zeszyty Naukowe Uniwersytetu Ekonomicznego w Krakowie 798
Granat M (2002) Opinia na temat konieczności kontrasygnaty aktu Prezydenta o wyznaczeniu Marszałka Seniora. Ekspertyzy i opinie prawne. Biuletyn Ekspertyz i Opinii Prawnych
Grosset R (2011) Tożsamość bezpieczeństwa wewnętrznego – miejsce, rola i funkcje, Warsaw
Grzegorczyk T (2014) Kodeks postępowania karnego, Warsaw
Grzelak M, Lidel K (2012) Bezpieczeństwo w cyberprzestrzeni. Zagrożenia i wyzwania dla Polski – zarys problemu. Bezpieczeństwo Narodowe 22
Grzelak M, Liedel K, Bezpieczeństwo w cyberprzestrzeni. Zagrożenia i wyzwania dla Polski – zarys problemu. https://www.bbn.gov.pl/download/1/11469/str125-139MichalGrzelakKrzysztofLiedel.pdf. Accessed 10 Oct 2020
Gzicki W (2013) Państwo wobec cyberterroryzmu in: Podraza, P. Potakowski, P. Wiak, K. Cyberterroryzm zagrożeniem XXI wieku. Perspektywa politologiczna i prawna, Warsaw
Hausner J (2005) Administracja publiczna, Warsaw

Hoeren T (2008) Das Pherd frisst keinen Gurkensalat – Uberlegungen zur Internet Governance. NJW (36)

Hoeren T (2012) Internet- und Kommunikationsrecht: Praxis-Lehrbuch, Cologne

Hołyst B (2009) Internet jako miejsce popełnienia przestępstwa, Prokuratura i Prawo 4

Hubbard AM, Schjølberg S. Harmonizing national legal approaches on cybercrime. http://www.itu.int/osg/spu/cybersecurity//docs/Background_Paper_Harmonizing_National_and_Legal_Approaches_on_Cybercrime.pdf. Accessed 10 Oct 2020

Humphreys E (2007) Implementing the ISO/IEC 27001 Information Security Management System Standard. Artech House, Norwood

Ile waży praca? (2017). https://www.forbes.pl/technologie/jak-wiele-danych-produkujemy-kazdego-dnia/4mn4w69. Accessed 10 Oct 2020

Izdebski H, Kulesza M (2004) Administracja publiczna – zagadnienia ogólne, Warsaw

Jagielski J (2004) Współczesna funkcja kontroli administracji publicznej (kilka refleksji teoretycznych). Kontrola Państwowa 1

Jagielski J (2012) Kontrola administracji publicznej, Warsaw

Jagusiak B (2015) Bezpieczeństwo socjalne współczesnego państwa, Warsaw

Jancz J (2015) Relacjonowanie wydarzeń w czasie rzeczywistym przez środki masowego przekazu, a bezpieczeństwo i proces podejmowania decyzji. In: Skarżyński M, Andruszkiewicz I (eds) Media w systemie bezpieczeństwa narodowego, Poznań

Janowski J (2008a) Elektroniczny obrót prawny, Warsaw

Janowski J (2008b) Kontrakty elektroniczne w obrocie prawnym, Warsaw, LEX/el

Jarkiewicz Z (1972) Rola oględzin w procesie kontrolnym. Kontrola Państwowa 1

Jarzęcka-Siwik E, Skwarka B (2013) Dopuszczalność zaskarżania wyników kontroli – możliwość weryfikacji ustaleń pokontrolnych. Kontrola Państwowa 4

Jaśkiewicz J (2014) Ustawa o zasadach prowadzenia polityki rozwoju. Komentarz, LEX/el

Jaxa Dębicka A (2008) Sprawne państwo, Warszawa, LEX/el

Jemioła S. (1987) O zaktywizowanie i wzmocnienie kontroli wewnętrznej, Kontrola Państwowa 1

Kaczmarek-Templin B (2014) Komentarz do art. 2. In: Kaczmarek-Templin B, Stec P, Szostek D (eds) Ustawa o prawach konsumenta. Kodeks cywilny (wyciąg). Komentarz, Warsaw

Kaczmarek-Templin B (2015) Specyfika umów o dostarczanie treści cyfrowych w świetle ustawy o prawach konsumenta. In: Karczewska D, Namysłowska M, Skoczny T (eds) Ustawa o prawach konsumenta, Warsaw

Kaczmarski M (2010) Bezpieczeństwo energetyczne Unii Europejskiej, Warsaw

Kalitowski M (2012) In: Filar M (ed) Kodeks karny. Komentarz, Warsaw

Kałużny S (2008) Kontrola wewnętrzna. Teoria i praktyka, Warsaw

Kamiński MA (2019a) Military Law in the Republic of Poland. Safety & Defence 5

Kamiński MA (2019b) Prawo bezpieczeństwa narodowego. Wiedza Obronna 3(268)

Kardas P (2000) Prawnokarna ochrona informacji w polskim prawie karnym z perspektywy przestępstw komputerowych. Analiza dogmatyczna i strukturalna w świetle aktualnie obowiązującego stanu prawnego. Czasopismo Prawa Karnego i Nauk Penalnych 1

Kasprzyk R, Maj M, Tarapata Z (2015) Przestępstwa w cyberprzestrzeni. Aspekty technologiczne i prawne. In: Przestępczość w XXI wieku. Zapobieganie i zwalczanie. Problemy technologiczno-informatyczne, Warsaw

Kiczka K (2018) Pozycja kontroli w publicznym prawie gospodarczym. In: Kocińska K (ed) Kontrola działań administracji publicznej w sferze gospodarki, Poznań

Kieżun W (1972) Problemy kontroli w systemach zarządzania. Kontrola Państwowa 3

Kitler W (2011) Bezpieczeństwo narodowe RP. Podstawowe kategorie. Uwarunkowania. System, Warsaw

Kmieciak, Z. (2008) Wniosek o ponowne rozpatrzenie sprawy w KPA (Odwołanie czy remonstracja?) Państwo i Prawo 3

Knosala E, Matan A, Zacharko L (1996) Zarys nauki administracji, Katowice

Kocot W (2004) Wpływ Internetu na prawo umów, Warsaw

Konarski X (2004) Komentarz do ustawy o świadczeniu usług drogą elektroniczną, Warsaw

Konieczny P (2005) Komunikacja od mowy do internet. http://histmag.org/?id=744. Accessed 1 Oct 2020
Korzeniowski P (2012) Bezpieczeństwo ekologiczne jako instytucja prawna ochrony środowiska, Łódź
Kosiński J (2013) Cyberprzestępczość. In: Jasiński W, Mądrzejowski W, Wiciak K (eds) Przestępczość zorganizowana. Fenomen. Współczesne zagrożenia. Zwalczanie. Ujęcie praktyczne, Szczytno
Kosiński J (2015) Paradygmaty cyberprzestępczości, Warsaw
Kot D (2001) Dyrektywa Unii Europejskiej o handlu elektronicznym i jej implikacje dla prawa cywilnego. Kwartalnik Prawa Prywatnego 1
Kowalewski M (2015) Aspekty bezpieczeństwa narodowego Rzeczypospolitej Polskiej, Warsaw
Kowalski A (1971) Wyjaśnienia i oświadczenia jako środki dowodowe w procesie kontroli. Kontrola Państwowa 4
Koziej S (1998a) Szkic do dyskusji o przyszłej strategii poszerzonego NATO (spojrzenie z polskiej perspektywy), Warsaw-Toruń
Koziej S (1998b) Tezy i komentarze do prac nad Strategią Bezpieczeństwa i Obronności Rzeczypospolitej Polskiej, Warsaw-Toruń
Koziej S, Brzozowski A (2014) 25 lat polskiej strategii bezpieczeństwa. Bezpieczeństwo Narodowe 2
Koziej S, Brzozowski A (2015) Strategie Bezpieczeństwa RP 1990-2014. Refleksje na ćwierćwiecze. In: Kupiecki R (ed) Strategia Bezpieczeństwa Narodowego Rzeczypospolitej Polskiej. Pierwsze 25 lat, Wojskowe Centrum Edukacji Obywatelskiej im. płk. dypl. Mariana Porwita, Warsaw
Koziński M (2010) Bezpieczeństwo kryzysowe, Gdańsk 2010
Kozłowska-Kalisz P (2020) In: Mozgawa M (ed) Kodeks karny. Praktyczny komentarz, LEX/el
Kozłowski K (2016) In: Safjan M, Bosek L (eds) Konstytucja RP, vol II, Komentarz, Warsaw
Krasuski A (2015) Prawo telekomunikacyjne. Komentarz, Warsaw
Krawczyk, A Kodeks postepowania administracyjnego. Komentarz, W. Chroscielewski, Z. Kmieciak, commentary to article. 189e
Księżopolski KM (2009) Problemy bezpieczeństwa wewnętrznego i bezpieczeństwa międzynarodowego, Warsaw
Kubicka J (2007) International organizations – The United Nations Organization – its activity and reforms, Dąbrowa Górnicza
Kuc BR (1983) Kontrola w systemie zarządzania, Warsaw
Kuciński R (2008) Nauka o państwie i prawie, Warsaw
Kuliński M (2010) Regulacje komunikacji elektronicznej w rozwoju społeczeństwa informacyjnego Unii Europejskiej, Warsaw
Kunicka-Michalska B (2010) In: Wąsek A, Zawłocki R (eds) Kodeks karny. Część szczególna. Komentarz. Komentarz do artykułów 222-316, vol II, Warsaw
Kupiecki R (2015) Strategia Bezpieczeństwa Narodowego RP 2014 jako instrument polityki państwa. Uwarunkowania zewnętrzne i aspekty procesowe. Bezpieczeństwo Narodowe 1
Kurek J (2013) Ochrona przed niezamówioną korespondencją w komunikacji elektronicznej, Warsaw
Kurek J (2016) Wykorzystanie szpiegowskiego oprogramowania w działalności operacyjnej organów ścigania. Gwarancje konstytucyjne i procesowe z perspektywy doświadczeń niemieckich. Przegląd Policyjny 1
Kurek J (2018) J. Online search. Postulaty de lege ferenda. In: Kitler W, Chałubińska K, Jentkiewicz, Badźmirowska-Masłowska K (eds) System Bezpieczeństwa w Cyberprzestrzeni, Warsaw
Kurek J (2019) Cyberprzestrzeń jako sfera aktywności normatywnej państwa – analiza w kontekście przeciwdziałania przestępczości. In: Taczkowska-Olszewska J, Oręziak B, Wielec M (eds) Zarządzanie ludźmi w organizacji, Warsaw

Kurek J (2020, 2020) In: Kosiński J, Krasnodębski G (eds) Prawne bezpieczeństwo rozwiązań w zakresie przeszukań on-line. Nowe ramy regulacyjne w Niemczech BKA – Gesetz 2017, Przestępczość teleinformatyczna 2019, Gdynia
Kutscha M (2012) Das Computer-Grundrecht — eine Erfolgsgeschichte. Datenschutz und Datensicherheit 6
Kuźniar R (2004) Strategia państwowa. Zeszyty Akademii Dyplomatycznej 15
Łacny J (2011) Skuteczna, proporcjonalna i odstraszająca sankcja za naruszenie prawa UE. In: Wróbel A (ed) Zapewnienie efektywności orzeczeń sadów międzynarodowych w polskim porządku prawnym, Warsaw
Lakomy M (2015) Cyberprzestrzeń jako nowy wymiar rywalizacji i współpracy państw, Katowice
Lang W (1963) Struktura kontroli prawnej organów państwowych Polskiej, Warsaw
Lang L (1997) Zagadnienia wstępne. In: Wierzbowski M (ed) Prawo administracyjne, Warsaw
Letai, P. Spain Part VII. Computer Related Crime R. Blanpain (ed.), International Encyclopaedia of Laws. Vol. 3. Cyber Law (J. Dumortier), Kluwer Law International
Liderman K (2002) Bezpieczeństwo teleinformatyczne, Wyższa Szkoła Informatyki Stosowanej i Zarządzania, Warsaw
Liderman K (2017) Bezpieczeństwo informacyjne, Warszawa
Lipiec-Warzecha L (2011) Ustawa o finansach publicznych. Komentarz, Warsaw
Lisiak-Felicka D, Szmit M (2016) Cyberbezpieczeństwo administracji publicznej w Polsce. Wybrane zagadnienia, Kraków
Litwiński P (2002) Zasady odpowiedzialności pośredników w dostarczaniu informacji w Internecie (Intermediary Service Providers - ISP). Gospodarka elektroniczna - dodatek do MoP 24
Litwiński P (2004) Świadczenie usług drogą elektroniczną in: Prawo Internetu, ed. P. Podrecki, Warsaw
Longchamps de Berier F (1964) Rzut oka na system kontroli nad administracją, Kontrola Państwowa 3
Łoś-Nowak T (ed) (2009) Organizacje w stosunkach międzynarodowych. Istota – Mechanizmy działania – Zasięg, Warsaw
Lubasz D (2013) Handel elektroniczny. Bariery prawne. Wydawnictwo Prawnicze. LexisNexis, LEX/el
Lubasz D, Chomiczewski W (2011) Artykuł 2 ustawy o świadczeniu usług drogą elektroniczną. In: Chomiczewski W, Klafkowska-Waśniowska K, Lubasz D et al (eds) Świadczenie usług drogą elektroniczną oraz dostęp warunkowy. Komentarz do ustaw. Wydawnictwo Prawnicze LexisNexis, LEX/el
Lulkiewicz E (2013) E. E-administracja Korzyści i zagrożenia. In: Stanisławski T, Przywora B, Jurek Ł (eds) E-administracja. Szanse i zagrożenia, Lublin
Lynch DM (2006) Securing Against Insider Attacks, Information Security And Risk Management 11
Macierzyńska-Franaszczyk E (2018) Digital Content – a definition in EU and national legal regulations. Internet Antitrust and Regulatory Quarterly 6
Macioszek M (2003) Dyplomacja prewencyjna Unii Europejskiej w pozimnowojennej Europie, Toruń
Maj E, Mazurek K, Sokół W, Szwed-Walczak A (eds) (2016) Bezpieczeństwo Europy, bezpieczeństwo Polski, Lublin
Marchewka-Bartkowiak K (2011) Agencje wykonawcze, Biuro Analiz Sejmowych (18.08.2011)
Marczak J (2008) Założenia polityki i strategii bezpieczeństwa narodowego. In: Jakubczak R, Skrabacz A, Gąsiorek K (eds) Obrona narodowa w tworzeniu bezpieczeństwa Polski w XXI wieku, Warsaw
Marczak J (2011) Bezpieczeństwo narodowe In: R. Jakubczak J. Marczak, Bezpieczeństwo narodowe Polski w XXI wieku, Warsaw
Marczuk KP (2012) Bezpieczeństwo wewnętrzne państw członkowskich Unii Europejskiej. Od bezpieczeństwa państwa do bezpieczeństwa ludzi, Warsaw
Marczuk KP (2014) Bezpieczeństwo funkcjonalne państw regionu Europy Północnej, Warsaw

Marek A (2010) Kodeks karny. Komentarz, Warsaw
Martysz CZ, Szpor G, Wojsyk K (eds) (2015) Ustawa o informatyzacji działalności podmiotów realizujących zadania publiczne. Komentarz. LEX/el
Mickel WW, Bergmann J (2005) Handlexikon der Europäischen Union, Warsaw
Mickiewicz P (2018) System bezpieczeństwa narodowego w rozwiązaniach systemowych wybranych państw, Warsaw
Mickiewicz P, Sokołowska P (2010) Bezpieczeństwo energetyczne Europy Środkowej, Toruń
Mik C (1999) Media masowe w europejskim prawie wspólnotowym, Toruń
Mik C (2008) the Gloss to the Resolution Adopted by the Full Composition of the Supreme Court of 14 November 2007, file ref. BSA (Administrative Court Office) – 4110-5/07 (regarding the right of the Minister of Justice to delegate a judge). Prokuratura i Prawo 6
Mituś A (2013) E-administracja: korzyści i zagrożenia in: Wpływ przemian cywilizacyjnych na prawo administracyjne i administrację publiczną, Suwaj JP, Zimmerman J ed., LEX/el
Monarcha-Matlak A (2008) Obowiązki administracji publicznej w komunikacji elektronicznej, Warsaw
Moranta S (2018) Security in Outer Space: Perspectives on Transatlantic Relations, 12th ESPI Autumn Conference Vienna, September 27th 2018
Murdoch A (2003) Komunikowanie w kryzysie. Jak ratować wizerunek firmy, Warsaw
Murray A (2010) Information Technology Law. The Law and Society, Oxford
Ninard G (2017) Udzielenie upoważnienia do przetwarzania danych osobowych a udostępnienie akt podmiotowi kontrolującemu. Nowe Zeszyty Samorządowe 6
Nitkowski J (2013) Kontrola wewnętrzna instytucjonalna w systemie kontroli w przedsiębiorstwie, Warsaw
Nowacki M (2010) Prawne aspekty bezpieczeństwa energetycznego w UE, Warsaw
Nowak E, Nowak M (2011) Zarys teorii bezpieczeństwa narodowego, Warsaw
Nowakowski Z (2008) Bezpieczeństwo narodowe. Ewolucja pojęcia i zakresu. In: Jemioło T, Rajchel K (eds) Bezpieczeństwo narodowe i zarządzanie kryzysowe w Polsce w XXI wieku. Wyzwania i dylematy, Warsaw
Nowakowski Z, Rajchel J, Szafran H, Szafran R (2014) Strategia bezpieczeństwa narodowego Polski na tle strategii bezpieczeństwa wybranych państw, Warsaw
Nowikowska M (2018) Ochrona danych osobowych w dokumentach kontrolnych. In: Taczkowska-Olszewska J, Nowikowska M, Brzostek A (eds) Reforma ochrony danych osobowych. Cel, narzędzia, skutki, Poznań
Nowikowska M (2019a) Zasady udostępniania informacji i przetwarzania danych osobowych. In: Taczkowska-Olszewska J, Chałubińska-Jentkiewicz K, Nowikowska M (eds) Retencja, migracja i przepływ danych w cyberprzestrzeni. Ochrona danych osobowych w systemie bezpieczeństwa państwa, Warsaw
Nowikowska M (2019b) Komentarz do art. 26 ustawy o KSC. In: Kitler W, Taczkowska-Olszewska J, Radoniewicz F (eds) Ustawa o Krajowym Systemie Cyberbezpieczeństwa. Komentarz, Warsaw
Nowikowska M, Cieślak J (2015) O potrzebie zmian w ustawie o kontroli w administracji rządowej – uwagi de lege ferenda. Kontrola Państwowa 4
Nowikowska M, Walczuk K (2018) Dowody w postępowaniu kontrolnym (w trybie ustawy o kontroli w administracji rządowej) i możliwość ich wykorzystania w postępowaniu karnym. In: Paszkowski M, Daniluk D, Rzewuska M (eds) Teoretyczne i praktyczne aspekty postępowania dowodowego. KPP Monographs, Olsztyn
Ochendowski E (ed) (2002) Prawo administracyjne – część ogólna, Toruń, p 18
Olechnicki M, Załęcki P (1997) Słownik socjologiczny, Toruń
Oleksiewicz I, Krztoń W (2017) Bezpieczeństwo współczesnego społeczeństwa informacyjnego w cyberprzestrzeni, Warsaw
Oleksiewicz I, Michalski K, Sienkiewicz E (2017) Bezpieczeństwo w społeczeństwie informacyjnym. Zagadnienia w wymiarze online i offline, Warsaw

Opaliński W (2013) Prawnoustrojowe uwarunkowania struktury Rady Ministrów. Przegląd Legislacyjny 1

Otis R., Lorents P, Cyberspace: Definition and Implications, the Cooperative Cyber Defence Centre of Excellence, Tallinn. http://dumitrudumbrava.files.wordpress.com/2012/01/cyberspace-definition-and-impications.pdf. Accessed 1 Oct 2020

Owczarek T (1990) Kontrola – integralna funkcja zarządzania. Kontrola Państwowa 1

Pawłowski A (2002) Zasoby informacyjne w administracji publicznej w Polsce, Lublin

Piasecka P (2011) Zagrożenia ładu i bezpieczeństwa międzynarodowego we współczesnym świecie. In: Liedel K (ed) Transsektorowe obszary bezpieczeństwa narodowego, Warsaw

Piątek S (2019) Prawo telekomunikacyjne. Komentarz, LEX/el

Picot A, Neuburger R (2004) In: Hoeren T, Sieber U (eds) Handbuch Multimedia-Recht München

Piechowiak M (2013) Aksjologiczne podstawy polskiego prawa. In: Guz T, Głuchowski J, Pałupska M (eds) Synteza prawa polskiego od 1989 roku, Warsaw

Piechowiak M (2020) Preambuła Konstytucji Rzeczpospolitej Polskiej z 1997 r. Aksjologiczne podstawy prawa, Warsaw

Piórkowska-Flieger J (2012) In: Bojarski T (ed) Kodeks karny. Komentarz, Warsaw

Piszczek K, Piszczek P (2008) Wniosek o ponowne rozpatrzenie sprawy – kontrowersje wokół jego istoty. Prokuratura i Prawo 11

Płoskonka J (2005) Zmiany w stosowanych przez polską administrację publiczną metodach i narzędziach. Kontrola Państwowa 1

Płoskonka J (2006) Pojęcie kontroli w ujęciu zarządczym. Kontrola Państwowa 2

Pływaczewski E (2017) Bezpieczeństwo obywateli. Prawa człowieka. Zrównoważony rozwój, Białystok

Polański P (2006) Usługi społeczeństwa informacyjnego na tle reformy usług w Unii Europejskiej. Quo Vadis Europo, Warsaw

Polański P (2007) Customary Law of the Internet, In the Search for a Supranational Cyberspace Law, Hague

Polański P (2020) Odpowiedzialność prawna za treści rozpowszechniane w Internecie. Centrum Europejskie Natolin, Warsaw

Polkowska M (2016) Polish Space Agency pursues task of developing country's space expertise, Room. The Space Journal 2(8)

Polkowska M (2019) European challenges in SSA. Poland example, presentation at the Space Situational Awareness Workshop: Perspectives on the Future, Directions for Korea, Seoul 24-25 January 2019

Polkowska M, Ryzenko J (2016) Aktywność Polski w przestrzeni kosmicznej- nauka, polityka i prawo. Stan obecny. Gdańskie Studia Prawnicze XXXVI

Polok M (2006) Ochrona tajemnicy państwowej i tajemnicy służbowej w polskim systemie prawnym, Warsaw

Polok M (2008) Bezpieczeństwo danych osobowych, Warsaw

Ponikowski R (2012) In: Skorupka J (ed) Dowody – zagadnienia podstawowe i systemowe, in: Postępowanie karne. Część ogólna, Warsaw

Popławski H (1965) Obowiązki kierownika przedsiębiorstwa w zakresie kontroli i nadzoru. Kontrola Państwowa 2

Portelli, C. (2017) EU SST Consortium governance, initial operation and current status Nov 21th 2017., Roma

Potejko P (2015) In: Chałubińska-Jentkiewicz K, Karpiuk M (eds) Bezpieczeństwo informacyjne [in:] Prawo nowych technologii - wybrane zagadnienia, Warsaw

Potrzeszcz J (2013) Bezpieczeństwo prawne z perspektywy filozofii prawa, Lublin

Pronińska KM (2012) Bezpieczeństwo energetyczne w stosunkach UE – Rosja. Geopolityka i ekonomia surowców energetycznych, Warsaw

Prusak-Górniak K, Silicki K (2019) Commentary on NCSA. In: Czaplicki K, Gryszczyńska A, Szpor G (eds) Ustawa o Krajowym Systemie cyberbezpieczeństwa. Komentarz, Warsaw, LEX/el

Przybysz P (2019) Komentarz do art. 127 KPA. In: Przybysz P (ed) Komentarz do kodeksu postępowania administracyjnego, Komentarz aktualizowany, LEX/el
Radecki W (2009) Nowy czeski kodeks karny. Prokuratura i Prawo 7–8
Radoniewicz F (2015) Techniki implementacji do polskiego porządku prawnego postanowień decyzji ramowych Rady Unii Europejskiej dotyczących prawa karnego materialnego. Przegląd Prawa Konstytucyjnego 3
Radoniewicz F (2016) Odpowiedzialność karna za hacking i inne przestępstwa przeciwko danym komputerowym i systemom informatycznym, Warsaw
Radoniewicz F (2017a) Podsłuch komputerowy. In: Chałubińska-Jentkiewicz K, Kakareko K, Sobczak J (eds) Prawo prywatności jako reguła społeczeństwa informacyjnego. C.H. Beck, Warszawa
Radoniewicz F (2017b) Ujęcie przestępstw przeciwko ochronie informacji w Kodeksie karnym a postanowienia dyrektywy 2013/40/UE dotyczącej ataków na systemy informatyczne – aspekty wybrane. In: Kitler W, Taczkowska-Olszewska J (eds) Bezpieczeństwo informacyjne. Aspekty prawno-administracyjne, Warsaw
Radoniewicz F (2018) Identity Theft in the Polish Criminal Code. In: Brzostek A, Nowikowska M, Taczkowska-Olszewska J (eds) Reform Of Protection Of Personal Data System - Purpose, Tools, Poznań
Radoniewicz F (2019a) In: Kitler W, Taczkowska-Olszewska J, Radoniewicz F (eds) Ustawa o krajowym systemie cyberbezpieczeństwa. Komentarz. Warsaw
Radoniewicz F (2019b) Przestępstwo "sabotażu informatycznego" (art. 269 k.k.). In: Badźmirowska-Masłowska K (ed) System bezpieczeństwa w cyberprzestrzeni RP, Warsaw
Radoniewicz F (2019c) Zwalczanie cybeterroryzmu w prawie UE – aspekty karnomaterialne. Cybersecurity and Law 2
Radoniewicz F (2020) Przestępstwo zakłócenia sieci teleinformatycznej – wybrane aspekty karnomaterialne oraz techniczne. In: Przestępczość teleinformatyczna 2019, "Rocznik Bezpieczeństwa Morskiego"
Radoniewicz F (2021) Przestępstwo hackingu – wybrane aspekty techniczne oraz karnomaterialne. In: Przestępczość teleinformatyczna 2020, "Rocznik Bezpieczeństwa Morskiego" – in press
Rattray GT (2004) Wojna strategiczna w cyberprzestrzeni [T.N. – original title: Strategic Warfare in Cyberspace], Warsaw
Rechlewicz W (2012) Elementy filozofii bezpieczeństwa. Bezpieczeństwo z perspektywy historii filozofii i filozofii polityki, Warsaw
Robertson D (2009) Słownik polityki, Warsaw
Rogacka-Rzewnicka M (2004) In: Machowska A, Wojtyczek K (eds) Prawo Francuskie, vol I, Kraków
Roggan F (2009) Das neue BKA-Gesetz — Zur weiteren Zentralisierung der deutschen Sicherheitsarchitektur. Neue Juristische Wochenschrift 5
Rössel M (2016) Teilweise Verfassungswidrigkeit des BKAG. ITRB
Rudkowski D (2006) Interwencja humanitarna w prawie międzynarodowym, Warsaw
Rzucidło J, Węgrzyn J (2015) Stany nadzwyczajne w sytuacji szczególnego zagrożenia państwa w cyberprzestrzeni. Przegląd Prawa Konstytucyjnego 5(27)
Sadlok M (2011) Cyberterroryzm, cyberprzestępczość – wirtualne czy realne zagrożenie? http://www.racjonalista.pl/kk.php/s,846. Accessed 22 May 2020
Safjan M (1999) Ochrona danych osobowych – granice autonomii i informacji. In: Wyrzykowski M (ed) Ochrona danych osobowych, Warsaw
Sarnecki P (2000) Prezydent Rzeczypospolitej Polskiej. Komentarz do przepisów, Kraków
Savin A (2017) EU Internet Law, Cheltenham–Northamnton
Schjølberg S. History of Global Harmonization on Cybercrime Legislation – The Road to Geneva, http://www.cybercrimelaw.net. Accessed 10 Oct 2020
Ściborek Z, Wiśniewski B, Kuc R, Dawidczyk A (2015) Bezpieczeństwo wewnętrzne. Podręcznik akademicki, Toruń

Serafin, T. Parszowki, S. (2011) Bezpieczeństwo społeczności lokalnych. Programy prewencyjne w systemie bezpieczeństwa, Warszawa

Shinder DL, Tittel E (2004) Cyberprzestępczość. Jak walczyć z łamaniem prawa w sieci [Original title: Scene of the Cybercrime. Computer Forensics Handbook]. Polish Version, Gliwice

Sieber U (1998) Legal Aspects of Computer-Related Crime in the Information Society – Comcrime-Study, Würzburg

Sieńczyło-Chlabicz J, Zawadzka Z, Nowikowska M (2019) Prawo prasowe, Warsaw

Sienkiewicz P (2009) Terroryzm w cyberprzestrzeni. In: Jamioło T, Kisielnicki J, Rajchel K (eds) Cyberterroryzm – nowe wyzwania XXI wieku, Warsaw

Sienkiewicz P (2012) In: Sienkiewicz P (ed) Bezpieczeństwo cyberprzestrzeni [in:] Metodologia badań bezpieczeństwa narodowego, vol 3, Warsaw

Sienkiewicz P. (2015), Ontologia cyberprzestrzeni. Zaszyty Naukowe Warszawskiej Wyższej Szkoły Informatyki 13(9)

Siupiński A (2013) Wspólna polityka bezpieczeństwa i obrony Unii Europejskiej. Geneza. Rozwój. Funkcjonowanie, Warsaw

Siwicki M (2011) Nielegalna i szkodliwa treść w Internecie. Aspekty prawnokarne. Wolters Kluwer, LEX/el, Warsaw

Siwicki M (2012) Definicje i podział cyberprzestępstw. Prokuratura i Prawo 7–8

Siwicki M (2013) Cyberprzestępczość, Legalis 2013

Skarżyński M (2015) Media w systemie bezpieczeństwa narodowego, Poznań

Skrzypczak J (2015) Obowiązki mediów w sytuacjach nadzwyczajnych. In: Skarżyński M, Andruszkiewicz I (eds) Media w systemie bezpieczeństwa narodowego, Poznań

Śledziewska K, Levai A, Zięba D (2016) Use of e-Government in Poland in comparison to other European Union Member States. Information Systems in Management 1(5)

Słomczyńska J (2007) Europejska polityka bezpieczeństwa i obrony. Uwarunkowania, struktury, funkcjonowanie. In: Zięba LR (ed) Bezpieczeństwo międzynarodowe w XXI wieku, Warsaw

Słota-Bohosiewicz A (2015) Zarzadzanie bezpieczeństwem w cyberprzestrzeni obywatela. In: Wybrane aspekty bezpieczeństwa cybernetycznego sił zbrojnych Rzeczypospolitej Polskiej. vol. 2, Warsaw

Słownik terminów zakresu bezpieczeństwa narodowego, Warsaw 2002

Smarzewski M (2014) Cyberprzestępczość a zmiany w polskim prawie karnym. In: Sepioło-Jankowska I (ed) Reforma prawa karnego. Księga po Zjeździe Młodych Karnistów, Warsaw

Smith GJH (ed) (2007) Internet law and regulation, London

Sobczak J (2012) Aksjologiczne Podstawy Konstytucji RP. In: Miluska J (ed) Wartości w świecie polityki, Poznań

Sobczak J (2013) Wymiar sprawiedliwości w systemie bezpieczeństwa państwa. In: Wojciechowski S, Wejkszner A (eds) Kluczowe determinanty bezpieczeństwa Polski na początku XX wieku, Warsaw

Sobczak J, Kakareko K (2017) Prawo do ochrony kultury w systemie prawnym w Unii Europejskiej. In: Babiusz H, Kapustka P, Michalska J (eds) Aktualne problemy Konstytucji. Księga Jubileuszowa z okazji 40-lecia pracy naukowej Profesora Bogusława Banaszaka, Legnica

Sobczak J, Sobczak W (2017) Aksjologia regionalnych aktów normatywnych stojących na straży praw człowieka. In: Jaskiernia J, Stryszak K (eds) Ochrona praw człowieka w wymiarze uniwersalnym. Aksjologia – instytucje – nowe wyzwania praktyka, Toruń

Sójka-Zielińska K Jednostka a państwo w dziejach europejskiej kultury politycznej. In: Wyrzykowski M (ed) Prawa stają się prawem. Status jednostki a tendencje rozwojowe. Liber, Warszawa

Sowa M (2001) Ogólna charakterystyka przestępczości internetowej, Palestra 5–6

Stańczyk J (1996) Współczesne pojmowanie bezpieczeństwa, Warsaw

Stankiewicz R (2020) In: Hauser R, Wierzbowski M (eds)., a commentary to Article 189f Kodeks postępowania administracyjnego. Komentarz, Warsaw LEX/el

Starościak J (1971) Zarys nauki administracji, Warsaw

Starościak J (1975) Prawo administracyjne, Warsaw
Stępniewska P (2018) Współczesne bezpieczeństwo ekologiczne. Bezpieczeństwo. Teoria i Praktyka 30(1)
Stolarczyk M (2004) Wzrost kontrowersji w stosunkach transatlantyckich i ich implikacje dla bezpieczeństwa europejskiego. In: Stolarczyk M (ed) Bezpieczeństwo Polski i bezpieczeństwo europejskie na początku XXI wieku. Wybrane aspekty, Katowice
Suchorzewska A (2010) Ochrona prawna systemów informatycznych wobec zagrożenia cyberterroryzmem, Warsaw
Surma J (2017) In: Wydawnictwo Naukowe PWN (ed) Cyfryzacja życia w erze Big Data, Warsaw
Sweny G (2019) Cyber Lead for Defence & Space, 1 April 2019, Space for Cyber Security..in Space? https://pwc.blogs.com/cyber_security_updates/2019/04/space-for-cyber-security-in-space.html. Accessed 10 Oct 2020
Świątkiewicz B (2005) Przestępstwa internetowe w praktyce policyjnej, Studia Prawnicze 4
Świerczyński M (2009) In: Gołaczyński J, Kowalik-Bańczyk K, Majchrowska A, Świerczyński M, Ustawa o świadczeniu usług drogą elektroniczną. Komentarz. Oficyna, LEX/el
Szachułowicz J (2000) Własność publiczna, Warsaw
Szaff L (1957) O niektórych problemach dotyczących zakresu postępowania przygotowawczego, Nowe Prawo 12
Szczepaniuk E (2016) Bezpieczeństwo struktur administracyjnych w warunkach zagrożeń cyberprzestrzeni państwa, Warsaw
Szostek I (2017) Prawo do informacji publicznej a ochrona danych osobowych w polskim systemie prawnym. In: Kitler W, Taczkowska-Olszewska J (eds) Bezpieczeństwo informacyjne. Aspekty prawno-administracyjne, Warsaw
Szpor G (1998) Informacja w zagospodarowaniu przestrzennym, Katowice
Szuniewicz M (2016) Ochrona bezpieczeństwa państwa jako przesłanka ograniczenia praw i wolności jednostki w świetle Europejskiej Konwencji Praw Człowieka, Warszawa
Szymczak M (1989) Słownik języka polskiego, vol III, Warsaw
Taczkowska-Olszewska J (2019) Dane osobowe w cyberprzestrzeni. In: Taczkowska-Olszewska J, Chałubińska-Jentkiewicz K, Nowikowska M (eds) Retencja, migracja i przepływ danych w cyberprzestrzeni. Ochrona danych osobowych w systemie bezpieczeństwa państwa, Warsaw
Taczkowska-Olszewska J Commentary on Article 39. In: Kitler W, Taczkowska-Olszewska J, Radoniewicz F (eds) Ustawa o krajowym systemie cyberbezpieczeństwa. Komentarz, Warsaw
Taczkowska-Olszewska J, Nowikowska M (2019) Prawo do informacji publicznej, Informacje niejawne. Ochrona danych osobowych, Warsaw
Tadeusiewicz R (2010) Zagrożenia w cyberprzestrzeni. Nauka 4
Tarnogórski R (2009) Konwencja o cyberprzestępczości – międzynarodowa odpowiedź na przestępczość ery informacyjnej. In: Madej M, Terlikowski M (eds) Bezpieczeństwo teleinformatyczne państwa, Warsaw
Tenet GJ (1998) Information Security Risks, Opportunities, and the Bottom Line. https://www.cia.gov/news-information/speeches-testimony/1998/dci_speech_040698.html. Accessed 3 Oct 2020
The statement from the G8 Summit held in Heiligendamm on 8 June 2007 on combating terrorism, http://www.g8.utoronto.ca/summit/2007heiligendamm/g8-2007-ct.html. Accessed 10 Oct 2020
Trąbiński P (2018) Podział kompetencji w zapewnianiu cyberbezpieczeństwa. In: Szpor G, Gryszczyńska A (eds) Internet. Strategie bezpieczeństwa, Warsaw
Trejnis P, Trejnis Z (2017) Polityka ochrony cyberprzestrzeni w państwie współczesnym. Studia Bobolanum 28(3)
Urbanek A (1999) In: Chustecki J et al Vademecum teleinformatyka, Warsaw
Uwe Schrögl K (2018) Security in Outer Space: Rising Stakes for Civilian Space Programmes, ESPI Conference September 27th 2018
Verton D (2004a) Black Ice. Niewidzialna groźba cyberterroryzmu [Original title: Black Ice: The Invisible Threat of Cyber-Terrorism], Polish edition: Gliwice
Verton D (2004b) Black Ice: niewidzialna groźba cyberterroryzmu, Warsaw

Wajda P (2009) Pozycja prawnoustrojowa i skład Komisji Nadzoru Finansowego – kilka uwag krytycznych, Przegląd Prawa Publicznego, 7–8
Walczuk K (2019a) Komentarz do art. 43 ustawy o KSC. In: Kitler W, Taczkowska-Olszewska J, Radoniewicz F (eds) Ustawa o krajowym systemie cyberbezpieczeństwa. Komentarz
Walczuk K (2019b) Komentarz do art. 44 ustawy o KSC. In: Kitler W, Taczkowska-Olszewska J, Radoniewicz F (eds) Ustawa o krajowym systemie cyberbezpieczeństwa. Komentarz, Warsaw
Walden I (2007) Computer crimes and digital investigations, Oxford
Wall D (2013) Cybercrime. The Transformation of Crime in the Information Age, Malden
Wang FF (2010) Internet jurisdiction and choice of law. Legal practices in EU, US and China, Cambridge
Warchoł M (2013) Dowody. In: Hofmański P (ed) System Prawa Karnego Procesowego v. II, Proces karny. Rozwiązania modelowe w ujęciu prawno porównawczym, Warsaw
Warden JA (1995) The Enemy as a System. Airpower Journal 9(1)
Warkałło W (1949) Siła wyższa jako zasada nieodpowiedzialności i domniemanie przypadkowości szkody, Państwo i Prawo 9–10
Wasilewski J (2013) Zarys definicyjny cyberprzestrzeni. Przegląd Bezpieczeństwa Wewnętrznego 9
Wasiuta O, Klepka R, Kopeć R (2018) Vademecum bezpieczeństwa, Kraków
Wąsowski K (2019) In: Kitler W, Radoniewicz F, Taczkowska-Olszewska J (eds) Ustawa o krajowym systemie cyberbezpieczeństwa. Komentarz, Warsaw
Wawrzyk P (2009) Bezpieczeństwo wewnętrzne Unii Europejskiej, Warsaw
Wedel-Domaradzka A (2013) Wolność zgromadzeń a obowiązki zapewnienia bezpieczeństwa przez państwo. In: Jastrzębski M, Kuczur, Jastrzębski T (eds) Bezpieczeństwo państwa a wolność jednostki. Wybrane aspekty prawne i polityczne, Toruń
Węglowski MG (2018) Działania antyterrorystyczne. Komentarz, Warsaw
Werner J (2014) Zagrożenia bezpieczeństwa w cyberprzestrzeni, Warsaw
Wiechowski Z (1969) Fakt kontrolny – teoria a praktyka. Kontrola Państwowa 6
Winczorek P (1996) Nowa Konstytucja Rzeczypospolitej Polskiej. Problem aksjologii. Przegląd Sejmowy 4
Winczorek P (2010) Komentarz do Konstytucji Rzeczypospolitej Polskiej, Warsaw
Winiarska K (2003) Definicja i klasyfikacja kontroli, in: Kontrola i audyt w administracji publicznej, Stan i perspektywy, 1st Conference, Warsaw
Wiśniewski P (2012) Radiofonia i telewizja jako elementy społeczeństwa informacyjnego w Polsce. Aspekt prawny. Zagadnienia wybrane. In: Misztal-Konecka J, Tylec G (eds) Wizja europejskiego społeczeństwa informacyjnego i jej realizacja w prawie polskim, Lublin
Wojciechowska-Filipek S (2016) In: Ciekanowski Z (ed) Bezpieczeństwo funkcjonowania w cyberprzestrzeni jednostki – organizacji – państwa, Warszawa
Wójcik JW (1999) Przestępstwa komputerowe. Część I. Fenomen cywilizacji, Warsaw
Worona J (2020) Cyberprzestrzeń a prawo międzynarodowe. In: On the function of the media in security protection, Warsaw
Wróbel A (2019a) Komentarz do art. 189e KPA. In: Jaśkowska M, Wilbrandt-Gotowicz M, Wróbel A (eds) Komentarz zaktualizowany do Kodeksu postępowania administracyjnego. Warsaw, LEX/el
Wróbel A (2019b) Komentarz do art. 189k KPA. In: Jaśkowska M, Wilbrandt-Gotowicz M, Wróbel A (eds)) Komentarz zaktualizowany do Kodeksu postępowania administracyjnego. Warsaw, LEX/el
Wróbel A (2020a). Komentarz do art. 20 KPA. In: Jaśkowska M, Wilbrandt-Gotowicz M,Wróbel A (eds) Komentarz zaktualizowany do Kodeksu postępowania administracyjnego, Warsaw, LEX/el
Wróbel A (2020b). Komentarz do art. 127 KPA. In: Jaśkowska M, Wilbrandt-Gotowicz M,Wróbel A (eds) Komentarz zaktualizowany do Kodeksu postępowania administracyjnego, Warsaw, LEX/el
Wróbel W, Zając D (2017) In: Wróbel W, Zoll A (eds) Kodeks karny. Komentarz. Część szczególna, t. II, cz. II, Komentarz do artykułów 117-277d k.k., Warsaw, LEX/el

Wróblewski D (2015) Zarządzanie ryzykiem – przegląd wybranych metodyk, Józefów
Wrona J (2015) Jurysdykcja państw a zwalczanie cyberprzestępczości. In: Pływaczewski EW, Filipkowski W, Rau Z (eds) Przestępczość w XXI wieku. Zapobieganie i zwalczanie. Problemy prawno-kryminologiczne, Warsaw
Yukins CHR (2004) Making federal information technology accessible: a case study in social policy and procurement. Public Contract Law Journal 33
Zając J, Zięba R (2011) Budowa zintegrowanego systemu bezpieczeństwa narodowego Polski. Ekspertyza na potrzeby realizacji średniozakresowej strategii rozwoju RP na lata 2014-2020, Warsaw
Zajadło J (2005) Dylematy humanitarnej interwencji, Gdańsk
Zalewski S (2013) Bezpieczeństwo Polityczne. Zarys Problematyki, Siedlce
Żebrowski A (2009) Instrumenty Rady Ministrów w realizacji polityki bezpieczeństwa państwa. In: Księżopolski KM (ed) Problemy bezpieczeństwa wewnętrznego i bezpieczeństwa międzynarodowego, Warsaw
Zembaty M (1988) Z rozważań nad teorią kontroli. Kontrola Państwowa 4
Zięba R (1997) In: Bobrow DB, Haliżak E, Zięba R (eds) Bezpieczeństwo narodowe i międzynarodowe u schyłku XX wieku, Warsaw
Zieliński M (2013) Odpowiedzialność deliktowa pośredniczących dostawców internetowych. Analiza prawno porównawcza, Warsaw
Zieliński M (2014) Agencje wykonawcze UE. Europejski Przegląd Sądowy 6
Zimmermann J (2016) *Prawo administracyjne*, Warsaw
Żurawski vel Grajewski P (2003) Militarny wymiar strategii bezpieczeństwa narodowego Polski 2007 i program profesjonalizacji sił zbrojnych z 2008 roku a NATO. In: Czulda R, Łoś R, Reginia-Zacharski J (eds) NATO wobec wyzwań współczesnego świata, Warsaw.-Łódź

Judgments

Judgment of the European Court of Human Rights of 6 September 1978, case Klass and others v Germany (5029/71)
Judgment of the European Court of Human Rights of 2 August 1984, case Malone v the United Kingdom (8691/79)
Judgment of the European Court of Human Rights of 24 April 1990, case Kruslin and Huvig v France, joined cases (11801/85, 11105/84)
Judgment of the European Court of Human Rights of 26 March 1987, case Leander v Sweden (9248/81)
Judgment of the European Court of Human Rights of 4 May 2000, case Rotaru v Romania (28341/95)
Judgment of the European Court of Human Rights of 27 April 2004, case Doerga v the Netherlands (50210/99)
Judgment of the European Court of Human Rights of 29 June 2006, case Weber and Saravia (54934/00)
Judgment of the European Court of Human Rights 12 January 2010, case Gillan and Quinton v the United Kingdom, (4158/05),
Judgment of the European Court of Human Rights of 29 September 2010, case Uzun v Germany (35623/05)
Judgment of the European Court of Human Rights of 4 December 2015 Zakharov v Russia, (47143/06),
Judgment of the European Court of Human Rights of 12 January 2016, case Szabó and Vissy v Hungary (37138/14)

Judgment of the European Court of Justice of 8 April 2014, joined cases C-293/12 and C-594/12, Digital Rights Ireland Ltd vs. the Minister for Communications et al., ECLI:EU:C:2014:238
Judgment of Polish Constitutional Tribunal of 9 May 2000, U 6/98, OTK 2000/4/108 (Statement of Grounds 6/98, Judgment of the Constitutional Tribunal 2000/4/108)
Judgment of the Polish Constitutional Tribunal of 15 June 2001, K 2/09, OTK-A 2011/5/42
Judgment of Polish Constitutional Tribunal of 19 February 2002, file No. 3/01, Polish Journal of Laws of 2002, No. 19, item 197.
Judgment of the German Constitutional BVerfG ruling in cases No. BVR 966/09 and 1 BvR 1140/09 ECJ ruling of 15 February 2016 in case No. C-601/15
Judgment of the German Constitutional Court BVerfG ruling of 20 April 2016 in case No. 1 BvR 966/09 i 1 BvR 1140/09., https://www.bundesverfassungsgericht.de/SharedDocs/Entscheidungen/DE/2016/04/rs20160420_1bvr096609.html. Accessed 10 Oct 2020
Tribunal de Grande Instance de Nanterre 08 décembre 1999 – Affaire Lynda L. c/ Sté Multimania, Sté France Cybermédia, Sté SPPI, Sté Esterel.
Judgment of the Polish Supreme Court of 3 April 2000, I CKN 582/98, LEX No. 50843
Judgment of the German High Court (BGH) of 31 January 2007 in case No. StB 18/06., http://juris.bundesgerichtshof.de/cgibin/rechtsprechung/document.py?Gericht=bgh&Art=pm&Datum=2007&Sort=3&nr=38779&linked=bes&Blank=1&file=dokument.pdf. Accessed 10 Oct 2020
Judgment of Polish Supreme Administrative Court of 21 February 2012, II GSK 67/11, No. 3891604
Judgment of the Polish Supreme Administrative Court of 25 April 2012, I OSK 654/11 LEX No. 1264894
Judgment of the Polish Supreme Administrative Court of 29 March 2017, II OSK 1936/15, Lex No. 2283181
La décision Cour d'appel de Paris, 14ème chambre,10 février 1999E. Hallyday contre V. Lacambre, https://www.alain-bensoussan.com/wp-content/uploads/5446189.pdf. Accessed 20 Dec 2020
Judgment of the Polish Court of Appeal in Katowice of 5 April 2013. File No. III APa 55/12 LEX No. 1313277
Judgment of the Polish Court of Appeal in Warsaw, Case No. VI ACa 1910/16)
Judgment of the Polish Provincial Administrative Court in Warsaw of 22.11.2010, V S.A./Wa 2517/10, Lex No. 781401.
Judgement of Polish Provincial Administrative Court of 27 January 2016, II GSK, 694/14, Legalis
Judgment of the Polish Provincial Administrative Court in Kraków of 09.05.2017, III S.A./Kr 384/16, Lex No. 2286959
Judgment of the Polish Provincial Administrative Court in Kraków of 15.12.2017, I SA/Kr 233/17, Lex No. 2442272
Judgment of the Polish Provincial Administrative Court in Poznań of 20.07.2017, IV SA/Po 167/17, Lex No. 2341989
Judgment of the Polish Provincial Administrative Court in Kraków of 19.12.2017, II SA/Kr 1203/17, Lex No. 2425316;

Legal Acts

National Law

Act of 14 June 1960 – the Code of Administrative Procedure, consolidated text, Polish Journal of Laws of 2020, item 256, as amended

Act of 23 April 1964 – the Civil Code, consolidated text, Polish Journal of Laws of 2020, item 1740, as amended
Act of 21 November 1967 on the Universal Duty to Defend the Republic of Poland, consolidated text, Polish Journal of Laws of 2019, item 1541, as amended
Act of 21 March 1985 on Public Roads, consolidated text, Polish Journal of Laws of 2020 item 470, as amended
Act of 29 May 1989 on Transferring the Powers Previously Held by the Council of State to the President of the Polish People's Republic and Other State bodies, consolidated text, Polish Journal of Laws of 1989, No. 34, item 178, 19 July 1989
Act of 12 October 1990 on Border Guards, consolidated text, Polish Journal of Laws of 2020, item 305, as amended
Agricultural Social Insurance Fund of 20 December 1990, consolidated text, Polish Journal of Laws of 2019, item 299, as amended
Act of 7 September 1991 on the Education System, consolidated text, Polish Journal of Laws of 2020, item 1327, as amended
Act on the Universal Duty to Defend the Republic of Poland through the Act of 25 October 1991, amending the Act on the Universal Duty to Defend the Polish People's Republic and Certain Other Acts (Polish Journal of Laws of 1991, No. 113, item 491)
Act of 4 February 1994 on Copyright and Related Rights, consolidated text, Polish Journal of Laws of 209, item 1231, as amended
Act of 8 August 1996 on the Council of Ministers, consolidated text, Polish Journal of Laws of 2019, item 1171, as amended
Act of 20 December 1996 on Municipal Services, consolidated text, Polish Journal of Laws of 2019, item 712, as amended.
Act of 20 December 1996 on Ports and Sea Harbours, consolidated text, Polish Journal of Laws of 2020, item 998, as amended
Act of 10 April 1997 – Energy Law, consolidated text, Polish Journal of Laws of 2020, item 833 as amended
Act of 6 June 1997 – the Penal Code, consolidated text, Polish Journal of Laws of 2020, item 1444, as amended
Act of 6 June 1997 of the Code of Criminal Proceedings, consolidated text, Polish Journal of Laws of 2020, item 30, as amended
Act of 29 August 1997 – Banking Law, consolidated text, Polish Journal of Laws of 2020, Item 1896, as amended
Act of 4 September 1997 on Branches of Government Administration, consolidated text, Polish Journal of Laws of 2020, item 1220, as amended
Act of 4 September 1997 on Government Administration Departments, consolidated text, Polish Journal of Laws of 2020, item 1220, as amended
Act of 2 March 2000 on the Protection of Certain Consumer Rights and Liability for Damage Caused by a Dangerous Product, consolidated text, Polish Journal of Laws No. 22, item 271, as amended
Act of 21 December 2000 on Inland Navigation, consolidated text, Polish Journal of Laws of 220, item 1863, as amended
Act of 7 June 2001 on Collective Water Supply and Collective Sewage Disposal, consolidated text, Journal of Laws of 2020, item 2028, as amended
Act of 23 August 2001 on the Organisation of Tasks for State Defence Performed by Enterprises, consolidated text, Polish Journal of Laws of 2020 item 1669
Act of 6 September 2001 – Pharmaceutical Law, consolidated text, Polish Journal of Laws of 2020, item 944, as amended
Act of 6 September 2001 on Access to Public Information, consolidated text, Polish Journal of Laws of 2019, item 1429, as amended
Act of 6 September 2001 on Road Transport, consolidated text, Polish Journal of Laws of 2017, item 2200, as amended.

Act of 18 April 2002 on Natural Disasters, consolidated text, Polish Journal of Laws of 2017, item 1897, as amended
Act of 21 June 2002 of the State of Emergency Act, consolidated text, Polish Journal of Laws of 2016, item 886, as amended
Act of 18 July 2002 on Providing Services by Electronic Means, consolidated text, Polish Journal of Law of 2020 item 344, as amended
Act of 24 May 2002 on the Agency of National Security and the Intelligence Service, consolidated text, Polish Journal of Laws of 2020, item 27, as amended
Act of 24 May 2002 on the Internal Security Agency and on the Intelligence Service, consolidated text, Polish Journal of Laws of 2020, item 27, as amended
Act of 3 July 2002 – Aviation Law, consolidated text, Polish Journal of Laws of 2020, item 1970, as amended
Act of 29 August 2002 on Martial Law and the Competences of the Commander-in-Chief of the Army and the Rules of the Commander-in-Chief's Subordination to the Constitutional Authorities of the Republic of Poland, consolidated text, Polish Journal of Laws of 2016, item 851, as amended
Act of 30 August 2002 – the Law on proceedings before administrative courts, consolidated text, Polish Journal of Laws of 2019, item 2325, as amended
Act of 28 October 2002 on Liability of Collective Entities for Prohibited Acts Punishable by Sanction, consolidated text, Polish Journal of Laws of 2020 item 358, as amended
Act of 28 March 2003 on Rail Transport, consolidated text, Polish Journal of Laws 0f 2020 No. 20 item 1043, as amended
Act of 29 January 2004 – Public Procurement Law, consolidated text, Polish Journal of Laws of 2019, item 1843, as amended
Act of 16 April 2004 amending the Penal Code and Certain Other Acts, consolidated text, Polish Journal of Laws of 2004, No. 93, item 889
Act of 16 July 2004 – Telecommunications Law, consolidated text, Polish Journal of Laws of 2019, item 2460, as amended
Act of 17 February 2005 on the Computerisation of the Operations of Entities Performing Public Tasks consolidated text, Polish Journal of Laws of 2020, item 346, as amended
Act of 29 July 2005 on Trading Financial Instruments, consolidated text, Polish Journal of Laws of 2020, item 89, as amended
Act of 29 July 2005 on Capital Market Supervision, consolidated text, Polish Journal of Laws of 2020, item 1400, as amended
Act of 9 June 2006 on the Military Counterintelligence Service and the Military Intelligence Service, consolidated text, Polish Journal of Laws of 2019, item 687, as amended
Act of 6 December 2006 on the Principles of Conducting the Development Policy, consolidated text, Polish Journal of Laws of 2009 No. 84, item 712, as amended
Act of 26 April 2007 on Crisis Management, consolidated text, Polish Journal of Laws of 2020, item 1856, as amended
Act of 24 October 2008 Amending the Penal Code and Certain Other Acts, consolidated text, Polish Journal of Laws No. 214, item. 1344
Act of 27 August 2009 Public Finance, consolidated text, Polish Journal of Law of 2019 item 869, as amended
Act of 5 November 2009 on Cooperative Savings and Credit Unions, consolidated text, Polish Journal of Laws of 2020, item 1643, as amended
Act of 30 April 2010 on Research Institutes, consolidated text, Polish Journal of Laws of 2020, item 1383, as amended
Act of 5 August 2010 on the Protection of Classified Information, consolidated text, Polish Journal of Laws of 2019, item 742, as amended
Act of 9 June 2011 – Geological and Mining Law, consolidated text, Polish Journal of Laws of 2020 item 1064, as amended

Act of 15 July 2011 on Control in State Administration, consolidated text, Polish Journal of Laws of 2020 item 224, as amended
Act of 18 August 2011 on Maritime Safety, consolidated text, (Polish Journal of Laws of 2020, items 680, as amended
Act of 19 August 2011 on Payment Services, consolidated text, Polish Journal of Laws of 2020 item 794, as amended
Act of 30 May 2014 on Consumer Rights, consolidated text, Polish Journal of Laws of 2020 item 287, as amended
Act of 26 September 2014 on the Polish Space Agency, consolidated text, Polish Journal of Laws of 2020 item 1927, as amended
Act of 31 March 2015 Organic Law No. 1/2015 of 30 March 2015 (BOE No. 77 of 31 March 2015) (http://www.boe.es)
Act of 28 January 2016 – the Law on Public Prosecutor's Offices, consolidated text, Polish Journal of Laws of 2019 item 740, as amended
Act of 10 June 2016 on Anti-Terrorism, consolidated text, Polish Journal of Laws of 2019, items 796, as amended
Act of 23 March 2017 amending the Penal Code and Certain Other Acts, consolidated text, Polish Journal of Laws of 2017, item 768
Act of 1 March 2018 on Preventing Money Laundering and the Financing of Terrorism, consolidated text, Polish Journal of Laws of 2020, item 971
Act of 6 March 2018 – the Entrepreneurs Law, consolidated text, Polish Journal of Laws of 2019 item 1292, as amended
Act of 10 May 2018 on Personal-Data Protection, consolidated text, Polish Journal of Laws of 2019, item 1781, as amended
Act of 5 July 2018 on the National Cybersecurity System, consolidated text, Polish Journal of Laws of 2020, item 1369, as amended
Computer Misuse Act 1990 (CMA) (c. 18 http://www.legislation.gov.uk)
Criminal Justice Act 1982. (c. 48), http://www.legislation.gov.uk)
Criminal Proceedings etc. (Reform) (Scotland) Act 2007 (2007 asp 6)
Czech Penal Code of 8 January 2009 (Zakon č. 40/2009 Sb., http://aplikace.mvcr.cz/sbirka-zakonu)
French Penal Code of 1992 (Acts No: 92-683; 92-684; 92-685 and 92-686 were published in Official Journal No. 169 of 23.07.1992. Act No. 92-1336 and published in Official Journal No. 296 of 23 December 1992)
German Penal Code of 15 May 1871 as published on 13 November 1998 (BGBl. I S. 3322). Gesetze im Internet (http://www.gesetze-im-internet.de)
Penal Code of the Kingdom of Spain – Organic Law No. 10/1995 of 23 November 1995 (BOE No. 281 of 24 November 1995). http://www.boe.es
Penal Code of the Republic of Estonia (RT I 2001, 61, 364 https://www.riigiteataja.ee
Police and Justice Act 2006 (c. 48). http://www.legislation.gov.uk
Serious Crime Act 2015 (c. 9). http://www.legislation.gov.uk
Regulation of the Council of Ministers of 18 March 2003 on the establishing of the Ministry of Science and Computerisation, and the abolition of the office of the Scientific Research Committee Polish Journal of Laws of 2003 No. 51, item 443
Regulation of the Prime Minister of 31 October 2005 on the detailed scope of activities of the Minister for Internal Affairs and Administration
Regulation of the Council of Ministers of 12 April 2012 on the National Interoperability Framework (KRI), the minimum requirements for public records and the exchange of information in electronic form, and the minimum requirements for communication and information systems, Consolidated text: Polish Journal of Laws of 2017 item 2247 as amended
Regulation of the Prime Minister of 22 September 2014 on the detailed scope of activities of the Minister for Administration and Digital Affairs, Polish Journal of Laws of 2014, item 1254

Regulation of the Minister of Justice of 7 April 2016 – the internal rules of the common organisational units of the Prosecution Service Consolidated text: Polish Journal of Laws of 2017 item 1206

Regulation of the Council of Ministers of 13 December 2017 on the detailed scope of activities of the Minister of Digital Affairs, Polish Journal of Laws of 2017 item 2327

Regulation of the Minister for Digital Affairs of 10 September 2018 on the organisational and technical conditions for entities providing cybersecurity services, and internal structures responsible for cybersecurity Polish Journal of Laws of 2018, item 1780

Regulation of the Council of Ministers of 11 September 2018, a list of essential services and significance thresholds of the consequences of incidents disrupting the provision of essential services Polish Journal of Laws of 2018 r., item. 1806

Regulation of the Minister for Digital Affairs of 12 October 2018 on the list of certificates authorising the performance of audits, Polish Journal of Laws of 2018, item 1999

Regulation of the Council of Ministers of 16 October 2018 on documents regarding cybersecurity of the information system used for the provision of essential services, Polish Journal of Laws of 2018, item 2080

Regulation of the Council of Ministers of 2 October 2018 on the scope of activities and the working procedure of the College for Cybersecurity, Polish Journal of Laws of 2018, item 1952

Regulation of the Council of Ministers of 31 October 2018 on serious incidents thresholds Polish Journal of Laws of 2018, item 2180

Regulation of the Minister for Digital Affairs of 4 December 2019 on the organisational and technical conditions for entities providing cybersecurity services, and internal organisational structures of operators of essential services responsible for cybersecurity, Polish Journal of Laws of 2019, item 2479

Regulation of the Council of Ministers of 6 October 2020 on the detailed scope of activities of the Minister of Digital Affairs, Polish Journal of Laws of 2020 item 1716

Order No. 43 of the Prime Minister of 15 July 2014 on granting a charter to the Ministry of Administration and Digital Affairs Official Gazette of the Government of the Republic of Poland of 2014, item 582

Resolution No. 104 of the Council of Ministers of 18 June 2013 on adopting the Strategy for Human Capital Development 2020a, Official Gazette of the Government of the Republic of Poland of 2013, item 640

Resolution No. 102 of the Council of Ministers of 17 September 2019 on adopting the National Regional Development Strategy 2030, Official Gazette of the Government of the Republic of Poland of 2019a, item 1060

Resolution by the Council of Ministers. On 22 October 2019, the Council of Ministers adopted a Resolution on the Cybersecurity Strategy of the Republic of Poland for 2017-2022 (Official Gazette of the Government of the Republic of Poland of 2019, item 1037)

Resolution No. 105 of the Council of Ministers of 24 September 2019b on adopting the Strategy for Sustainable Transport Development 2030, Official Gazette of the Government of the Republic of Poland of 2019, item 1054

Resolution No. 111/2013 of the Council of Ministers of 25 June 2013a on the Cyberspace Protection Policy of the Republic of Poland, KPRM, RM-111-103-13

Resolution No. 114 of the Council of Ministers of 1 October 2019c on adopting the Strategy for Capital Market Development, Official Gazette of the Government of the Republic of Poland of 2019, item 1027

Resolution No. 121 of the Council of Ministers of 11 July 2013 on adopting the updated Socio-Economic Development Strategy for Eastern Poland by 2020b, Official Gazette of the Government of the Republic of Poland of 2013, item 641

Resolution No. 123 of the Council of Ministers of 15 October 2019 on adopting the Strategy for Sustainable Rural Development, Agriculture, and Fisheries 2030, Official Gazette of the Government of the Republic of Poland of 2019, item 1150

Resolution No. 125 of the Council of Ministers of 22 October 2019 on the Cybersecurity Strategy of the Republic of Poland for 2019-2024 (Official Gazette of the Government of the Republic of Poland of 30 October 2019, item 1037)
Resolution No. 17 of the Council of Ministers of 12 February 2013 on adopting the Efficient State Strategy 2020, Official Gazette of the Government of the Republic of Poland of 2013, item 136.
Resolution No. 3 of the Council of Ministers of 8 January 2014 on adopting the Development Strategy for Southern Poland by 2020, Official Gazette of the Government of the Republic of Poland of 2014, item 152
Resolution No. 52/2017 of the Council of Ministers of 27 April 2017 on the National Framework of Cybersecurity Policy of the Republic of Poland for 2017–2022 (KPRM), RM-111-52-17
Resolution No. 58 of the Council of Ministers of 15 April 2014 on adopting the Strategy for Energy Security and Environment – a perspective by 2020, Official Gazette of the Government of the Republic of Poland of 2014, item 469, as amended
Resolution No. 6 of the Council of Ministers of 26 January 2017 on adopting the Polish Space Strategy, Official Gazette of the Government of the Republic of Poland of 2017, item 203
Resolution No. 60 of the Council of Ministers of 30 April 2014 on adopting the Development Strategy for Western Poland by 2020c, Official Gazette of the Government of the Republic of Poland of 2014, item 452
Resolution No. 61 of the Council of Ministers of 26 March 2013 on adopting the Social Capital Strategy 2020, Official Gazette of the Government of the Republic of Poland of 2013b, item 378
Resolution No. 7 of the Council of Ministers of 15 January 2013 on the Innovation Strategy for Economic Efficiency – Dynamic Poland 2020" 2020, Official Gazette of the Government of the Republic of Poland of 2013, item 73
Resolution of Parliament of 19 May 2002 Calling for Legislative Measures Against High-Tech Crime, Unpublished
Resolution of the Constitutional Tribunal of 27 October 1994, case file No. W 10/93 OTK 1994, No. 2, item 46
Resolution of the Council of Ministers of 29 October 2013 Internal Working Regulations of the Council of Ministers. Official Gazette of the Government of the Republic of Poland of 2016, item 1006, as amended
Resolution No. 125 of the Council of Ministers of 22 October 2019 on the Cybersecurity Strategy of the Republic of Poland for 2019-2024 (Official Gazette of the Government of the Republic of Poland of 2019d, item 1037)
Resolution of the full composition of the Supreme Court of 14 November 2007 BSA (Administrative Court Office) -1410-5/07, p. 12–13
The Strategy of the Development of the National Security System of the Republic of Poland 2022 (2013), adopted by way of Resolution No. 67 of the Council of Ministers of 9 April 2013, Polish Journal Monitor Polski 2013, item 377

Others

The Cybersecurity Strategy of the Republic of Poland for 2017-2022, Annex to Resolution No. 125 of the Council of Ministers of 22 October 2019 Official Gazette of the Government of the Republic of Poland of 2019, item 1037
The Communication of the Minister for Digital Affairs of 19 September 2019 on the agreement between CSIRT GOV and CSIRT NASK regarding the delegation of duties Official Journal of the Ministry of Digital Affairs of 2019, item 26
Decision of the President of the Republic of Poland of 12 May 2020 on the approval of the National Security Strategy of the Republic of Poland, Official Gazette of the Government of the Republic of Poland of. 2020, item 413

Notice of the Minister of National Defence of 16 January 2019, Official Gazette of the Government of the Republic of Poland of 2019 of 2019 item 48
Communication No. 1 of the Head of the Internal Security Agency of 29 August 2019 regarding the conclusion of an agreement on the delegation of duties related to incidents reported by the Polish Air Navigation Services Agency Official Journal of the Internal Security Agency of 2019, item 15
Communication No. 2 of the Head of the Internal Security Agency of 28 November 2019 regarding the conclusion of an agreement on the delegation of duties related to incidents reported by the Research and Academic Computer Network – National Research Institute Official Journal of the Internal Security Agency of 2019, item 22
Communication No. 3 of the Head of the Internal Security Agency of 28 November 2019 regarding the conclusion of an agreement on the delegation of duties related to incidents reported by companies being members of the Capital Group of PGE Polska Grupa Energetyczna S.A Official Journal of the Internal Security Agency of 2019, item 23
The Memorandum of Understanding no. 17/2018 of the meeting of the Council of Ministers on April 26, 2018 (RM-000-17-18) – https://legislacja.rcl.gov.pl/docs//2/12304650/12466740/12466745/dokument341423.pdf
Biała Księga Bezpieczeństwa Narodowego [White Book of National Security of the Republic of Poland]. file:///Users/admin/Downloads/WhiteBook_NationalSecurity_PL_2013.pdf
Cybersecurity Doctrine of the Republic of Poland (2015). https://www.bbn.gov.pl/ftp/dok/01/DCB.pdf
Government Cyberspace Protection Programme of the Republic of Poland for the years 2011–2016.
Justification to the government's bill amending the Penal Code and Certain Other Acts., form No. 1186, section 4.6

International Law

United Nations

General Assembly Resolution 53/70 of 3 December 1998, 54/49 of 1 December 1999, Developments in the Field of Information and Telecommunications in the Context of International Security
General Assembly Resolution 54/49 of 1 December 1999, Developments in the Field of Information and Telecommunications in the Context of International Security
General Assembly Resolution 55/28 of 20 November 2000, Developments in the Field of Information and Telecommunications in the Context of International Security
General Assembly Resolution 55/63 of 4 December 2000, Combating the Criminal Misuse of Information Technology
General Assembly Resolution 56/19 of 29 November 2001, Developments in the Field of Information and Telecommunications in the Context of International Security
General Assembly Resolution 56/121 of 19 December 2001a, Combating the Criminal Misuse of Information Technology
General Assembly Resolution 56/183 of 21 December 2001, the World Summit on the Information Society (WSIS)
General Assembly Resolution 56/121 of 19 December 2001b, Combating the Criminal Misuse of Information Technology
General Assembly Resolution 57/53 of 22 November 2002, Developments in the Field of Information and Telecommunications in the Context of International Security

General Assembly Resolution 57/239 of 20 December 2002, Creation of a Global Culture of Cybersecurity
General Assembly Resolution 58/32 of 18 December 2003, Developments in the Field of Information and Telecommunications in the Context of International Security
General Assembly Resolution 58/199 of 23 December 2003, Creation of a Global Culture of Cybersecurity and the Protection of Critical Information Infrastructures
General Assembly Resolution 59/61 of 3 December 2004, Developments in the Field of Information and Telecommunications in the Context of International Security
General Assembly Resolution 60/45 of 8 December 2005, Developments in the Field of Information and Telecommunications in the Context of International Security
General Assembly Resolution 61/54 of 6 December 2006, Developments in the Field of Information and Telecommunications in the Context of International Security
General Assembly Resolution 62/17 of 5 December 2007, Developments in the Field of Information and Telecommunications in the Context of International Security
General Assembly Resolution 63/37 of 2 December 2008, Developments in the Field of Information and Telecommunications in the Context of International Security
General Assembly Resolution 64/25 of 2 December 2009, Developments in the Field of Information and Telecommunications in the Context of International Security
General Assembly Resolution 64/211 64/211 of 21 December 2009, Creation of a Global Culture of Cybersecurity and taking stock of national efforts to protect Critical Information Infrastructures)
General Assembly Resolution 65/41 of 8 December 2010, Developments in the Field of Information and Telecommunications in the Context of International Security
General Assembly Resolution 66/24 of 2 December 2011, Developments in the Field of Information and Telecommunications in the Context of International Security
General Assembly Resolution 67/27 of 3 December 2012, Developments in the Field of Information and Telecommunications in the Context of International Security
General Assembly Resolution 68/243 of 27 December 2013, Developments in the Field of Information and Telecommunications in the Context of International Security
General Assembly Resolution 69/28 of 2 December 2014, Developments in the Field of Information and Telecommunications in the Context of International Security
General Assembly Resolution 70/237 of 23 December 2015, Developments in the Field of Information and Telecommunications in the Context of International Security
General Assembly Resolution 71/28 of 5 December 2016, Developments in the Field of Information and Telecommunications in the Context of International Security
General Assembly Resolution 73/27 of 5 December 2018a, Developments in the Field of Information and Telecommunications in the Context of International Security
General Assembly Resolution 73/266 of 22 December 2018b, Developments in the Field of Information and Telecommunications in the Context of International Security
General Assembly Resolution 74/28 of 12 December 2019a, Developments in the Field of Information and Telecommunications in the Context of International Security
General Assembly Resolution 74/29 of 12 December 2019b, Developments in the Field of Information and Telecommunications in the Context of International Security
Havana Declaration adopted on Eighth United Nations Congress on the Prevention of Crime and the Treatment of Offenders (27 August 1990 – 7 September 1990), annex to General Assembly Resolution nr 45/121of 15 December 1990
"Vienna Declaration on Crime and Justice: Meeting the Challenges of the Twenty-first century" adopted by the Tenth United Nations Congress on the Prevention of Crime and the Treatment of Offenders in Vienna (10–17 April 2000 r.) annex to General Assembly Resolution nr 45/121of 4 December 2000
Bangkok Declaration on Synergies and Responses: Strategic Alliances in Crime Prevention and Criminal Justice adopted by Eleventh United Nations Congress on Crime Prevention and Criminal Justice in Bangkok (18–25 April 2005) annex to General Assembly Resolution

60/177 of 16 December 2005 r. Follow-up to the Eleventh United Nations Congress on Crime Prevention and Criminal Justice

Salvador Declaration on Comprehensive Strategies for Global Challenges: Crime Prevention and Criminal Justice Systems and Their Development in a Changing World adopted by Twelfth United Nations Congress on Crime Prevention and Criminal Justice in Salvador (12–19 April 2010,) annex to General Assembly Resolution 65/230 of 21 December 2010

Doha Declaration on integrating crime prevention and criminal justice into the wider United Nations agenda to address social and economic challenges and to promote the rule of law at the national and international levels, and public participation adopted by Thirteenth United Nations Congress on Crime Prevention and Criminal Justice in Doha (11–19 April 2015)

Plan of action for the implementation of the Vienna Declaration on Crime and Justice: Meeting the Challenges of the Twenty-first century (annex to General Assembly Resolution 56/261 of 31 January 2002)

The Information Economy Report, UN Conference on Trade and Development, http://www.unctad.org/en/docs/sdteecb20051ch6_en.pdf

The Information Economy Report, UN Conference on Trade and Development, http://www.unctad.org/en/docs/sdteecb20051ch6_en.pdf

The TOCTA 2010 Report, UNODC, pp. 205, 211, https://www.unodc.org/documents/data-and-analysis/tocta/10.Cybercrime.pdf

Council of Europe

The European Convention for the Protection of Human Rights and Fundamental Freedoms signed in Rome on 4 November 1950

Convention No. 108 for the Protection of Individuals with regard to Automatic Processing of Personal Data, done at Strasbourg on 28 January 1981, https://www.coe.int/en/web/data-protection/convention108-and-protocol. Accessed 1 Dec 2020

Convention on Cybercrime of the Council of Europe of 23 November 2001, Polish Journal of Laws of 2015, item 728, https://www.coe.int/en/web/conventions/full-list/-/conventions/treaty/185. Accessed 1 Sept 2020

Additional Protocol to the Convention on Cybercrime, concerning the criminalisation of acts of a racist and xenophobic nature committed through computer systems of 28 January 2003, https://rm.coe.int/CoERMPublicCommonSearchServices/DisplayDCTMContent?documentId=090000168008160f?? Accessed 1 Dec 2020

Convention No. 201 on the Protection of Children against Sexual Exploitation and Sexual Abuse, done at Lanzarote on 25 October 2007, https://rm.coe.int/1680084822. Accessed 1 Dec 2020

Recommendation No. R(89)9 on Computer-Related Crime

Recommendation CM/R(2009)1 electronic democracy (e-democracy) of 18 February 2009

Recommendation CM/R(99)5 on the protection of privacy on the Internet of 23 February 1999

OSCE. – Organization for Security and Co-operation in Europe

Decision No. 5/16 of 9 December 2016 on enhancing OSCE efforts to reduce the risks of conflict stemming from the use of information and communication technologies

Decision No. 5/17 of 8 December 2016 on enhancing OSCE efforts to reduce the risks of conflict stemming from the use of information and communication technologies

Ministerial Council OSCE Decision of 7 December 2004 No. 3/04 on combating the use of the Internet for terrorist purposes

Ministerial Council OSCE Decision of 7 December 2006 No. 7/06 on combating the use of the Internet for terrorist purposes

OECD. – Organization for Economic Co-operation and Development

Recommendation of the Council concerning Guidelines Governing the Protection of Privacy and Transborder Flows of Personal Data of 23 September 1980 (C(80)58(final)
Recommendation of the Council concerning Guidelines for the Security of Information Systems of 26 November 1992 (C(92)188/FINAL)
Recommendation of the Council Concerning Guidelines for the Security of Information Systems and Networks – Towards a Culture of Security of 25 July 2002, (C(2002)131)
Recommendation of the Council on Cross-Border Co-operation in the Enforcement of Laws against Spam of 13 April 2006 (C(2006) 57)
Recommendation of the Council on Cross-border Co-operation in the Enforcement of Laws Protecting Privacy of 12 December 2007 (C (2007) 67 (final)
Recommendation of the Council on Protection of Critical Information Infrastructures of 30 April 2008 (C(2008)35)
Recommendation of the Council on Digital Risk Management for Economic and Social Prosperity of 17 September 2015 (C(2015)115)

G7/G8 Group

G8 Muskoka Declaration: Recovery and New Beginnings, http://www.g7.utoronto.ca/summit/2010muskoka/communique.html#peace
G7 Ise-Shima Leaders' Declaration, http://www.g8.utoronto.ca/summit/2016shima/ise-shima-declaration-en.html
G7 Biarritz Leaders' Declaration; http://www.g8.utoronto.ca/summit/2019biarritz/declaration-of-leaders.html
Taormina Leaders' Communiqué; http://www.g8.utoronto.ca/summit/2017taormina/communique.html
The Charlevoix G7 Summit Communiqué. http://www.g8.utoronto.ca/summit/2018charlevoix/index.html
Statement by G8's Justice and Home Affairs Ministries of 11 May 2004, the Summit of G8's Justice and Home Affairs Ministries held in Washington on 10–11 May 2004., http://www.g8.utoronto.ca/justice/justice040511_comm.htm
Communiqué of the Ministerial Conference of the G8 Countries on Combating Transnational Organized Crime
General objectives adopted at the Summit of G8's Justice and Home Affairs Ministries on 16–17 June 2005., http://www.g8.utoronto.ca/justice/justice_uk2005.htm
NATO. – North Atlantic Treaty Organization
Agreement Between the Parties to the North Atlantic Treaty for Cooperation Regarding Atomic Information, done at Paris on 18 June 1964 Polish Journal of Laws of 2001 No. 143, item 1594
Agreement between the Parties to the North Atlantic Treaty for the Security of Information, done at Brussels on 6 March 1997 Polish Journal of Laws of 2000, No. 64, item 740
NATO Glossary of Terms and Definitions AAP-06 Edition 2018. https://nso.nato.int/nso/ZPUBLIC/_BRANCHINFO/TERMINOLOGY_PUBLIC/NON-CLASSIFIED%20NATO%20GLOSSARIES/AAP-6.PDF

European Union

The Treaty on the Functioning of the European Union of 26 October 2012, OJ EU 2012 L 326/47

Regulation (EC) No 460/2004 of the European Parliament and of the Council of 10 March 2004 establishing the European Network and Information Security Agency (Text with EEA relevance), OJ EU 2004 L 77/1

Regulation (EC) No. 725/2004 of the European Parliament, and of the Council, of 31 March 2004, on Enhancing Ship and Port-Facility Security, OJ EU 2004 L 129/6

Regulation (EC) No 300/2008 of the European Parliament and of the Council of 11 March 2008 on Common Rules in the Field of Civil Aviation Security and repealing Regulation (EC) No 2320/2002, OJ EU 2008 L 97/72

Regulation (EC) No 1007/2008 of the European Parliament and of the Council of 24 September 2008 amending Regulation (EC) No 460/2004 establishing the European Network and Information Security Agency as regards its duration (Text with EEA relevance), OJ EU 2008 L 293/1

Regulation (EU) No 580/2011 of the European Parliament and of the Council of 8 June 2011 amending Regulation (EC) No 460/2004 establishing the European Network and Information Security Agency as regards its duration Text with EEA relevance, OJ EU 2011 L 165/3

Regulation (EU) No 1025/2012 of the European Parliament and of the Council of 25 October 2012 on European Standardisation, amending Council Directives 89/686/EEC and 93/15/EEC and Directives 94/9/EC, 94/25/EC, 95/16/EC, 97/23/EC, 98/34/EC, 2004/22/EC, 2007/23/EC, 2009/23/EC, and 2009/105/EC of the European Parliament and of the Council and repealing Council Decision 87/95/EEC, and Decision No 1673/2006/EC of the European Parliament and of the Council, text with EEA relevance, OJ EU 2012 L 316/12

Regulation (EU) No 526/2013 of the European Parliament and of the Council of 21 May 2013 concerning the European Union Agency for Network and Information Security (ENISA) and repealing Regulation (EC) No 460/2004 Text with EEA relevance, OJ EU 2013 L 165/4

Regulation (EU) No 910/2014 of the European Parliament and of the Council of 23 July 2014 on electronic identification and trust services for electronic transactions in the internal market and repealing Directive 1999/93/EC, OJ EU 2014 L 257/73

Regulation (EU) 2016/679 of the European Parliament and of the Council of 27 April 2016 on the protection of natural persons with regard to the processing of personal data and on the free movement of such data, and repealing Directive 95/46/EC (The General Data Protection Regulation), OJ EU 2016 L 119/1, as amended

Regulation (EU) 2019/881 of the European Parliament and of the Council of 17 April 2019 on ENISA (the European Union Agency for Cybersecurity) and on information and communications technology cybersecurity certification and repealing Regulation (EU) No 526/2013 (Cybersecurity Act) (Text with EEA relevance), OJ EU 2019 L 151/15

Proposal for a Regulation of the European Parliament and of the Council on a Common European Sales Law, https://eur-lex.europa.eu/procedure/PL/2011_284 COM (2011) 635

Council Directive 2008/114/EC of 8 December 2008 on the identification and designation of European critical infrastructures and the assessment of the need to improve their protection (Text with EEA relevance), OJ EU 2008 L 345/7

Directive 98/48/EC of the European Parliament and of the Council of 20 July 1998 amending Directive 98/34/EC laying down a procedure for the provision of information in the field of technical standards and regulations, OJ EC 1998 L 217/8

Directive 2000/31/EC of the European Parliament and of the Council of 8 June 2000 on certain legal aspects of information society services, in particular electronic commerce, in the Internal Market, OJ EC 2000 L 178/1

Directive 2002/19/EC of the European Parliament and of the Council of 7 March 2002 on the access to and the interconnection of electronic communications networks and associated facilities (Access Directive), OJ EC 2002 L 108/7

Directive 2002/20/EC of the European Parliament and of the Council of 7 March 2002 on the authorisation of electronic communications networks and services (Authorisation Directive), OJ EC 2002 L 108/21

Directive 2002/21/EC of the European Parliament and of the Council of 7 March 2002 on a common regulatory framework for electronic communications networks and services (Framework Directive), OJ EC 2002 L 108/33

Directive 2002/22/EC iigof the European Parliament and of the Council of 7 March 2002 on universal service and users' rights relating to electronic communications networks and services (Universal Service Directive), OJ EC 2002 L 108/51

Directive 2006/24/EC of the European Parliament and of the Council of 15 March 2006 on the retention of data generated or processed in connection with the provision of publicly available electronic communications services or of public communications networks and amending Directive 2002/58/EC, OJ EU 2006 L 105/54

Directive 2011/83/EU of the European Parliament and of the Council of 25 October 2011 on consumer rights, amending Council Directive 93/13/EEC and Directive 1999/44/EC of the European Parliament and of the Council and repealing Council Directive 85/577/EEC and Directive 97/7/EC of the European Parliament and of the Council Text with EEA relevance, OJ EU 2011 L 304/64

Directive 2011/93/EU of the European Parliament and of the Council of 13 December 2011 on combating the sexual abuse and sexual exploitation of children and child pornography, and replacing Council Framework Decision 2004/68/JHA, OJ EU 2011 L 335/1

Directive 2013/40/EU of the European Parliament and of the Council of 12 August 2013 on attacks against information systems and replacing Council Framework Decision 2005/222/JHA, OJ EU 2013 L 218/8

Directive 2014/42/EU of the European Parliament and of the Council of 3 April 2014 on the freezing and confiscation of instrumentalities and proceeds of crime in the European Union, OJ EU 2014 L 127/39

Directive 2016/1148 of the European Parliament, and of the Council (EU), of 6 July 2016, concerning measures for a high common level of security of network and information systems across the Union, OJ EU 2016 L 194/1

Directive 2017/541/EU of the European Parliament and of the Council, of 15 March 2017 on combating terrorism and replacing Council Framework Decision 2002/475/JHA and amending Council Decision 2005/671/JHA, OJ EU 2017 L 88/6

Directive (EU) 2018/1972 of the European Parliament and of the Council of 11 December 2018 establishing the European Electronic Communications Code (Recast) Text with EEA relevance. PE/52/2018/REV/1, OJ EU 2018 L 321/36

Directive 2019/770 of the European Parliament and of the Council of 20 May 2019 on certain aspects of contracts for the provision of digital content and services, OJ EU 2019 L 136/1

Directive 2019/771 of the European Parliament and of the Council of 20 May 2019 concerning contracts for the sale of goods, amending Regulation (EU) 2017/2394 and Directive 2009/22/EC, and repealing Directive 1999/44/EC, OJ EU 2019 136/28

Directive 2019/790 of the European Parliament and of the Council of 17 April 2019 on copyright and related rights in the digital single market and amending Directives 96/9/EC and 2001/29/EC, OJ EU 2019 L 130/92

Proposal for a Directive of the European Parliament and of the Council on certain aspects concerning contracts for the supply of digital content COM(2015) 634 final

Proposal for a Directive of the European Parliament and of the Council on copyright in the digital single market, COM (2016) 593 final 2016/0280 (COD)

Council Framework Decision 2002/475/JHA of 13 June 2002 on combating terrorism. OJ EC 2002 L 164/3

Council Framework Decision 2005/222/JHA of 24 February 2005 on attacks against information systems, OJ EU 2005 L 69/67

Council Framework Decision 2008/841/JHA of 24 October 2008 on the fight against organised crime, OJ EU 2008 L 300/42
Council Decision 92/242/EEC of 31 March 1992 in the Field of Security of Information Systems, OJ EU L 123/19
Council Decision of 23 September 2013 on the Security Rules for Protecting EU Classified Information (2013/488/EU), OJ EU 2012 L 27/1
Decision 243/2012/UE of the European Parliament and of the Council of 14 March 2012 establishing a multi-annual radio spectrum policy programme. Text with EEA relevance, OJ EU 2012 L 81/7
Proposal for a Council Framework Decision on attacks against information systems, COM (2002) 0173
Commission Implementing Decision (EU) 2017/179 of 1 February 2017 laying down procedural arrangements necessary for the functioning of the Cooperation Group pursuant to Article 11 (5) of the Directive (EU) 2016/1148 of the European Parliament and of the Council concerning measures for a high common level of security of network and information systems across the Union, OJ EU 2017 L 28/7
Commission Implementing Regulation (EU) 2018/151 of 30 January 2018 laying down rules for application of Directive (EU) 2016/1148 of the European Parliament and of the Council as regards further specification of the elements to be taken into account by digital service providers for managing the risks posed to the security of network and information systems and of the parameters for determining whether an incident has a substantial impact, OJ EU 2018 L 26/48
The Council Resolution of 28 January 2002 on a Common Approach and Specific Actions in the Field of Network and Information Security, OJ EC 2002 C 43/2
Commission Communication: eEurope – An Information Society for All, COM (1999) 687
Communication from the Commission to the Council and the European Parliament Tackling
Communication from the Commission to the Council, the European Parliament, the Economic and Social Committee and the Committee of the Regions COM (2000)890 on Creating a Safer Information Society by Improving the Security of Information Infrastructures and Combating Computer-related Crime of 26 January 2001
Crime in our Digital Age: Establishing a European Cybercrime Centre COM/2012/0140 final
A Digital Single Market Strategy Communication COM (2015)192 from the Commission to the European Parliament, the Council, the Economic and Social Committee, and the Committee of the Regions
Communication from the Commission to the European Parliament and the Council: Making the most of NIS – towards the effective implementation of Directive (EU) 2016/1148 concerning measures for a high common level of security of network and information systems across the Union COM (2017) 476 final 2
Joint communication to the European Parliament, The Council, The European Economic and Social Committee and the Committee of the Regions Cybersecurity Strategy of the European union: An Open, Safe and Secure Cyberspace COM (2013) from 7 February 2013 JOIN(2013) 1 final
Joint Communication to the European Parliament and the Council – Resilience, Deterrence, and Defence: Building strong cybersecurity for the EU JOIN(2017) 450 final
Council Recommendation 95/144/EC of 7 April 1995 on Common Information Technology Security Evaluation Criteria, OJ EC 1995 C 93/27
Council Recommendation of 25 June 2001 on Contact Points Maintaining a 24-hour Service for Combating High-Tech Crime, OJ EC 2001 C 187/5
Commission Recommendation (EU) 2017/1584 of 13 September 2017 on coordinated response to large-scale cybersecurity incidents and crises, OJ EU 2017 L 239/36

Council conclusions on setting the EU's priorities for the fight against serious and organised crime between 2014 and 2017. Doc 137401/13

Working Document 1 on the US and EU Surveillance programmes and their impact on EU citizens fundamental rights. European Parliament, Committee on Civil Liberties, Justice and Home Affairs, Rapporteur: Claude Moraes, 11.12.2013 (DT/2012434Pl.doc)

Working Document 1/2016 of 13.04.2016 (16/EN/WP/237) on the justification of interferences with the fundamental rights to privacy and data protection through surveillance measures when transferring personal data – EuropeanEssentialGuarantee

Commission Staff Working Document – Assessment of the EU 2013 Cybersecurity Strategy SWD (2017) 295 final of 13.9.2017

Standards

ISO/IEC 27000:2014 Information technology – Security techniques – Information security management systems – Overview and vocabulary. https://www.iso.org/standard/63411.html. Accessed 10 Oct 2020

PN-ISO/IEC 31000:2012 – Zarządzanie ryzykiem – Zasady i wytyczne. http://pbsg.pl/polski-komitet-normalizacyjny-pbsg-polrisk-i-zakonczyly-z-sukcesem-prace-nad-opracowaniem-pierw/. Accessed 22 May 2021